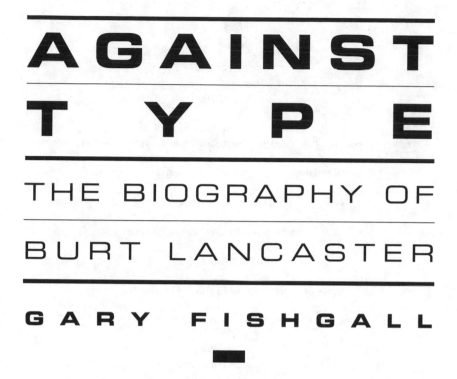

AGAINST TYPE

THE BIOGRAPHY OF BURT LANCASTER

GARY FISHGALL

A LISA DREW BOOK

SCRIBNER

New York   London   Toronto   Sydney   Tokyo   Singapore

SCRIBNER
1230 Avenue of the Americas
New York, NY 10020

SCRIBNER and design are trademarks of Simon & Schuster Inc.

Designed by Janet Tingey

Manufactured in the United States of America

1 3 5 7 9 10 8 6 4 2

Library of Congress Cataloging-in-Publication Data
Fishgall, Gary.
Against type: the biography of Burt Lancaster/Gary Fishgall.
p. cm.
"A Lisa Drew Book."
Includes bibliographical references and index.
1. Lancaster, Burt, 1913– .
2. Motion picture actors and actresses—United States—Biography. I. Title.
PN2287.L246F57   1995
791.43'028'092—dc20
[B]
95–11923
CIP

ISBN 0-684-80705-X

Contents

Acknowledgments

Weaving together the strands of a person's life is a daunting task—even when that life is as public as Burt Lancaster's. I can assure you no biographer does it alone. In my case, I had the help of hundreds of people, and I would be terribly remiss if I did not recognize their contributions here.

For starters, more than 160 of Lancaster's colleagues recalled for me the nature of their professional association with Burt. Some of these conversations took several hours, and quite a few resulted in follow-up inquiries, all of which were kindly indulged. Thanks, then, to: Julia (Julie) Adams, Michael Anderson, Edward Anhalt, Kirk Axtell, Earl Bellamy, Leonardo Bercovicci, Bernardo Bertolucci, Whit Bissell, Bob Blumofe, Phil Bowles, Hilyard Brown, Paul Brown, Duke Callaghan, Claudia Cardinale, Matthew Carlisle, Barbara Carrera, Liliana Cavani, Jo Champa, Marvin Chomsky, Susan Clark, Ronald Cohen, Ben Cooper, Jeff Corey, George Cosmatos, Richard Crenna, Hume Cronyn, Jon Cypher, John Dales Jr., Suso Cecchi D'Amico, Charles Dance, Ossie Davis, Bruce Davison, Ruby Dee, Bruce Dern, Walter Doniger, Robert Douglas, Charles Durning, Robert Duvall, Alan Edmiston, Jack Elam, Julius Epstein, Gerald Fisher, Rhonda Fleming, Penelope Foster, Gene Fowler Jr., Marjorie Fowler, Brian Frankish, John Gay, Anita Gillette, Grant Gilmore, John Glover, Don Guest, Lynn Guthrie, Scott Guthrie, Barbara Hale, Guy Hamilton, Katharine Hepburn, Michael Herzberg, Charlton Heston, Earl Holliman, Ross Hunter, Richard Jaeckel, Lamont Johnson, Stan Jolley, Shirley Jones, Peter Jurasik, Jeff Kanew, Robert Katz, Elia Kazan, Deborah Kerr, Richard Kiley, Alexandra King, Phyllis King, Werner Klemperer, Stanley Kramer, Shirley Lantz, John Phillip Law, Christopher Lee, Ernest Lehman, Idalah Luria, Alexander Mackendrick, Karl Malden, Louis Malle, Mike Mamakos, Abby Mann, Delbert Mann, Albert Marre, Walter Matthau, Virginia Mayo, Doug McClure, Richard McWhorter, Dina Merrill, Ed Milkovich, J. P. Miller, Martin Milner, Michael Mindlin, Giuliano Montaldo, Terry Moore, Tom Moore, Harry Morgan, Diana Muldaur, Don Murray, N. Richard Nash, Alberto Negrin, Salvatore Nocita, Kathleen Nolan, Sheree North, Hugh O'Brian, Peter O'Toole, Patty Page, Robert Parrish, Morgan Paull, Frank Perry, Daniel Petrie, Lee Phillips, Amos Poe, Hal Polaire, Ted Post, Danny Quinn, Martin Ransohoff, David Rayfiel, Don Rickles, Peter Riegert, Donald Roberts, Gilbert Roland, Cesar Romero, Bernard Sabath, John Savage, John Saxon, Maximilian Schell, Charles Scott, Lizabeth Scott, Walter Seltzer, Alan Sharp, Tom Shaw, Willard Sheldon, Ed Sherin, Jean Simmons, Marc Singer, Robert Steadman, Rod Steiger, George Stevens Jr., Don Taylor, Phyllis Thaxter, Tommy Thompson, Ingrid Thulin, Pamela Tiffin, Julian Ullman, Leon Uris, Mike Wallace, Jack Warden, Craig Wasson, Robert Whitehead, Elizabeth Wilson, Paul Winfield, Henry Winkler, Michael Winner, Burt Young, Max Youngstein, Harris Yulin, Fred Zinnemann, and Tim Zinnemann. I also want to acknowledge these individuals' agents and/or managers for taking the time from their busy schedules to arrange interviews with their clients—and in some cases persuade their clients to chat.

Special thanks must go to Jackie Bone and Bob Quarry, who knew Burt particularly well, and to those who wish to remain anonymous. Others in the Los Angeles area who helped me include Leith Adams, corporate archivist, Warner Bros.; Guido Corso and Fabiana Pregellio, RAI Corporation; Clinta Dayton, Screen Actors Guild; Greg Downes, American Cinemateque; Harry Flynn; Jane Marquet, Producers Guild of America; Harry Medved, Screen Actors Guild; Janice Metz, Century City Chamber of Commerce; Judith and Stefan Rudnicki; and Carmen Snyder, American Society of Cinematographers. In New York, thanks are due Anita Alleyne, supervisor, Personnel Records, CBS, Inc.; Dr. Lilia Antonucci, Italian Cultural Institute; Bob Cozenza, the Kobal Collection; Rena Donlon and Alyssa Schwartz, *Donahue;* Kent Jones; Victor S. Navasky; and Gaia Striano. In Germany, Peter Rehnke of the Bavaria Film Studio sought information on *Sins of the Fathers.* And, from Washington, D.C., Linda Burstyn shared her insights into Lancaster's work with the American Civil Liberties Union.

In addition, I must pay tribute to several performing-arts libraries and their staffs. In Los Angeles: Sam Gill and his associates at the Margaret Herrick Library, Academy of Motion Picture Arts and Sciences; Alan Braun, Louis B. Mayer Library, American Film Institute, and the AFI's associate director, Rod Merl; Bergitta Kiueppers, Arts Special Collections, University Research Library, University of California, Los Angeles;

Ned Comstock, Cinema-Television Library, Doheny Library, University of Southern California; Stuart Ng, the Warners Archive, School of Cinema-Television, University of Southern California; and the library of the Television Academy of Motion Picture Arts and Sciences. In New York: the staff of the Billy Rose Theatre Collection, Lincoln Center Library for the Performing Arts; and Charles Silver, supervisor, Study Center, Department of Film, the Museum of Modern Art. And, in Madison, Wisconsin: Ben Brewster, assistant director, Wisconsin Center for Film and Theater Research. Beyond their extensive clippings files and useful collections of books, several of these institutions are the repositories of the private papers of film studios, producers, directors, and others associated with the motion picture industry. These primary materials are absolutely invaluable; more than any other single source, they help the researcher understand what transpired at a given time and place. Anyone reading this who may be thinking of donating his or her papers to such an institution is strongly encouraged to do so.

Fleshing out Lancaster's thirty-plus years before stardom was especially challenging. For their memories of East Harlem, thanks to George Calvert, Danny Grandone, Pete Pascale, Sal Sala, Jean A. Smith, Sal Thomasetti, and Tootsie and Jeanette V. Tully; and to Kathy Benson, Education Department, Museum of the City of New York; Pamela J. Carnes, supervisory personnel assistant, United States Office of Personnel Management, St. Louis, Missouri; Ken Cobb, Municipal Archives, New York City Department of Records and Information Services; Tracy Flaum, assistant to legal counsel, Hunter College; Annette Lopes, assistant registrar, Columbia University; and Claire McCurdy and David Ment, Special Collections, Milbank Memorial Library, Teachers College, Columbia University. With regard specifically to the Union Settlement House, I must thank the current executive director, Gene Sklar; one of his predecessors, William Kirk; and a drama teacher who directed Lancaster in a play there, Pauline Swanson. At DeWitt Clinton High School, I had the help of Barbara Chafetz, librarian, and Terry Hlubik, then a member of the English Department, plus the following alumni: Marvin Hirsch, Joseph Kertman, Elmer A. Kirsch, Vincent O'Connor, Abe Platt, Harold Posner, John H. Prentiss, Mortimer J. Propp, Clement Segal, Frank Shain, and David Schwartz. At New York University, I must thank Nancy Cricco, university archivist; Dan Quilty, athletic director; Scott Page, Registrar's Office; Pat Reardon and Claire Rich, Alumni Relations; Larry Siegel, Office for University Development; and the following alumni: George Ourgourlian, Vincent B. Starace, Robert J. Tierney, and Josephine Turner.

A number of those who knew Burt as a circus performer shared their memories. These individuals include Ernestine Baer, Mary Burdick, Bill Ketrow, and Bill Powell. Thanks must also go to Fay Alexander; Harold Barnes; Joseph T. Bradbury; Fred Dahlinger Jr., director, and Tim Spindler, archivist, Robert L. Parkinson Library and Research Center, Circus World Museum, Baraboo, Wisconsin; Steve Gossard, curator of Circus Collections, Milner Library Special Collections, Illinois State University, Normal, Illinois; and Ruth Kerns, then librarian/archivist, George Mason University, Fairfax, Virginia.

For an understanding of Lancaster's years of military service, I am indebted to Louise A. Arnold-Friend, reference historian, U.S. Army Military History Institute, Department of the Army, Carlisle, Pennsylvania; Mary B. Dennis, deputy clerk of court, United States Army Judiciary, Department of the Army, Falls Church, Virginia; Russell Gilmore, museum director and historian, Fort Hamilton, Brooklyn, New York; Maria T. Hanna, Suitland Reference Branch, Textual Reference Division, National Archives, Washingon, D.C.; William McKale, museum specialist, Museum Division, DPTM, Fort Riley, Kansas; Richard W. Peuser, Military Reference Branch, National Archives, Washington, D.C.; and Eric V. Voelz, archivist, Military Operations Branch, National Personnel Records Center, St. Louis, Missouri. For background information on Norma Lancaster and the Anderson family, I am grateful to Joan Erickson, secretary, Webster Area Catholic Churches; Cora Graham; and Gary King of the *Intercounty Leader,* Webster, Wisconsin; and to Dr. John Fitzpatrick, who helped me gain some understanding of alcoholism, especially as it was perceived in earlier decades.

Finally, for their suggestions and advice, I thank fellow biographers Larry Grobel, Charles Higham, Larry Swindel, Evan Thomas, and Selden West, and journalist Leonard Maltin.

In closing, I must extend my deepest appreciation to my editor, Lisa Drew, who brought enthusiasm, support, and understanding to the project; to her always helpful, always cheerful assistant, Katherine Boyle Ekrem; to Kate's replacement, Marysue Rucci, and to my agent, Alexander Hoyt, who had faith in me and who was with me every step of the way.

AGAINST TYPE

CHAPTER ONE

East Harlem

The four-story walk-up at 209 E. 106th Street was dark, shabby, and un-inviting. It had been home to the Roberts family for decades, but when Elizabeth Roberts Lancaster inherited the property from her dad, she, her husband, James, and their children occupied the top floor only; they rented out the lower floors for badly needed income.

Elizabeth had been born in South Norwalk, Connecticut, on May 13, 1877, to James Roberts and Jennie Smith Roberts, both from Ireland. The family claimed kinship to Lord Roberts, the supreme commander of the British forces in South Africa during the Boer War.

Not to be outdone, her husband's family maintained that they were descended from the House of Lancaster, which had placed three kings on the throne of England in the fifteenth century. The first of the line to come to America was British-born James Lancaster, and his wife, the former Susanna Murray of Ireland. Their only surviving child, the fellow whom Elizabeth would marry, was born in New York City on December 6, 1876. "I'm told that as a young man my dad was the most handsome man on the East Side," their son Burt would recall, "and my mother, even in her forties, was so beautiful and sexy that guys whistled at her when she walked down the street."

The Lancasters lived in an area known as East Harlem. In the decades after the Civil War, it had been home to Irish laborers, but since then, émigrés from Naples, Palermo, and other Italian towns had come to dominate the sector of the community that ran from 104th to 115th Streets and between Third Avenue and the East River.[1]

James and Elizabeth differed from their neighbors in that they were native-born Americans and spoke unaccented English. Moreover, Eliza-

---

1. Italian East Harlem would extend to 125th Street by the 1920s.

beth owned property and James would, in time, become a civil servant. These distinctions placed them a rung or two higher on the community social ladder, and although they were not snobs, a hint of noblesse oblige can be seen in their dealings with those around them. Burt, for example, recalled that his mother "used to talk broken English to the neighbors because *they* talked broken English," a kind gesture but one tinged with condescension. This may partly explain the air of self-confidence that he developed early and maintained throughout his life.

In this closely knit, tightly packed community, everyone knew everyone else's business. Thus, when the neighbors heard that Elizabeth was about to give birth one cold, damp November morning, they gathered outside the Lancaster home. Finally, the expectant father, age thirty-six, announced the arrival of the new child—a boy. Unlike most of those in the crowd, who relied upon midwives for childbirths, the Lancasters had arranged for a physician, Dr. Burton Thom, to deliver the infant, whom they named in his honor—Burton Stephen. The assembled neighbors cheered the news. The date was November 2, 1913, and Burt Lancaster had already satisfied his first audience.

Burt had been preceded by three siblings: four-year-old Jennie Dorothea, called Jane; three-year-old James Roberts; and one-and-a-half-year-old William Henry. They and their parents shared a railroad flat, a monotonous series of rooms laid out in succession; the toilet was in the hallway and was used by everyone on the floor. For warmth, they had to rely on coal stoves.[2]

Around the time of Burton's birth, his father, who had been a stone-cutter, got a job with the post office. Eventually, he rose to the rank of supervisor, earning a then-respectable $48 a week. But, even with the extra income from the family's rental properties, the money did not go far. "Though I came from what you'd call an underprivileged family," Burt said many years later, "I never felt underprivileged. We ate well and had a happy home." His clothes were handed down to him from Jim and Willie, but that did not concern him. Many years later, the wealthy, famous movie star was still perfectly content with a $2 western shirt.

As Burton grew a bit older, he and his brothers held down typical boys' jobs to help bolster the Lancaster coffers. In the winter, they "used to stand in the snow all night," he remembered, "with our feet

2. The tenement at 209 E. 106th Street was torn down in 1961 to make room for the Benjamin Franklin Housing Development.

wrapped in burlap waiting for a chance to shovel snow for fifty cents, but somehow we felt a part of the family, a real economic part." The enterprising youngster also sold newspapers and shined shoes. Once, he decided to set up his shoeshine operation outside Macy's Department Store, way downtown on Thirty-fourth Street and Broadway. "It's the most profitable spot in town," he told his dad. "That's where the shoe salesmen go in and come out. They have to have a shine twice a day, and I catch 'em coming and going."

"I didn't have much time to devote to the children," James Lancaster would later recall, "with my post-office job in the daytime and in the evening repair work on a couple of small houses I owned and rented. I was a Sunday father—'a fun father,' Burt puts it."

James *was* fun—"a gentle, kind, warm sort of man," the future star would call him. When James was young, he had been something of a performer himself. His song-and-dance routine, called "The Broadway Swell and the Bowery Bum," captured a number of prizes at the local theaters' amateur nights. He had a pleasing voice and could play a variety of instruments, including the accordion and the harmonica.

Where James was easygoing, Elizabeth was, in her son's words, "a strong-willed, formidable character—a woman who insisted on honesty, truth, and loyalty." She was also a stern disciplinarian. "Mother beat hell out of us," Burt recalled. "She'd have wild outbursts, then cuddle us and overcompensate for the lickings." The actor would display that mode of behavior himself. "When he lost his temper, he lost control of himself," said cinematographer Duke Callaghan. "It was just part of Burt's nature: to get mad and say whatever came to his mind and then forget it."

When Elizabeth was angry, it was best to let her speak her piece. According to her husband, young Burton once tried to argue with her at such a time and was rewarded with a spanking that left him unable to sit down for a week. On most occasions, however, he got around Elizabeth with charm. "He'd see his mother coming after him with fire in her eye and a switch in her hand," his dad remembered, "and he'd start singing 'When Irish Eyes Are Smiling' in his good Irish tenor. It usually worked. Or he'd throw his arms around his mother's neck, smile that beautiful smile of his, and say, with more schmaltz than you'd hear in a Viennese waltz, 'Mother dear, you don't love me anymore.' Mrs. Lancaster, I regret to say, would melt, while Willie and Jim, no charm boys, looked on in utter disgust."

It was Elizabeth who taught Burt to be honest. As an adult, he vividly recounted the time she gave him a quarter, asked him to go the store to buy a quart of milk, and then whipped him when he got home for failing to notice the extra nickel that the grocer had given him in change. After the spanking, she sent him back to the store to return the money. A few years later, at the age of thirteen, he discovered a $20-bill stuck on a fire hydrant outside a bank. "Why, I'd never even had a whole dollar I could call my own," he recalled. Stifling the impulse to dash off with his find, he stayed for nearly half an hour to see if anyone would come to claim it. Finally, to his great dismay, a frantic elderly woman appeared. "It broke my heart, but Mom's lesson stuck with me," Burt said. "I handed it over."

Elizabeth was as generous as she was honest. "Bums were forever knocking at our door for handouts," Burt recalled. "First my mother would bawl them out. Then she'd feed them." And she lacked prejudice, instilling in her son a lifelong tolerance for people from different races and faiths. "I saw the way she treated black people who lived in the neighborhood," he said. "She would invite them in for tea and coffee and talk to them, the way she related to the Jewish people there. Now, we as children, my two brothers, my sister, and myself, we saw all this. It was expected that we would do these kind of things. This was our Bible of our upbringing."

In 1916, when Burt was three, the formidable Mrs. Lancaster, then thirty-nine, gave birth once more—to a girl whom the family named Florence. Sadly, the child contracted diphtheria and died on April 28, 1918, a month before her second birthday.

About eight months thereafter, Burt made his acting debut in the Christmas pageant at the Church of the Son of Man. This small nondenominational Protestant chapel on E. 104th Street was operated by the Union Settlement House, and the Lancasters were part of its largely Irish and German congregation. During the performance, in which Burt played an angel, he discovered that a piece of gum had stuck to the bottom of his shoe, and his efforts to remove the offending confection brought down the house. His budding career was not ruined, however; for years, he and his brothers played the Three Wise Men in the church's Nativity observance.

In February of 1920, young Lancaster entered P.S. 121, located on E. 102nd Street between Second and Third Avenues. An intelligent child, he quickly demonstrated his aptitude for reading and writing, even skipping over the second semester of the third grade in June of 1922 to enter the fourth grade. But the jump proved precipitous, and he had to repeat the term the following September, concurrently with the second semester of the fourth grade.

The Galileo, as P.S. 121 was called, housed only the lower elementary-school grades, so in the fall of 1923, Burton transferred to the Galvani, P.S. 83, at 110th Street, east of Third Avenue. He remained there through junior high school.

"Mentally, Burt was way ahead in school," recalled his friend Nick Cravat. "He can't bear to not know how and why things add up. We all looked up to him, and when we doubted his knowledge on any subject, we'd check at the library and what he'd told us was right." Burt had a sharp mind, but he was also cocky and easily bored. He got by on his wits—which stood him better in courses like English and history than in math. "He wasn't much good at arithmetic problems in school," his father recalled. In addition, he was always tardy.

Outside the classroom, Burt was often late too—because he was always getting lost. His father remembered that, at the annual Coney Island picnic for postal employees and their families, the lad would invariably disappear, and his older brother Willie would be forced to spend the rest of the day looking for him. "Burt's wanderings," wrote his father, "were mostly due to his great curiosity. As a kid he was interested in everything . . . I guess I've heard him say a million times, 'But I want to know *why.*' "

Burton's hunger for information—and adventure—made him an avid reader. "I read the whole library on 110th Street by the time I was fourteen—everything from Lang's fairy tales to Shakespeare," he recalled. His love of books would stay with him for the rest of his life. "When he wasn't working, he was always reading," said actor Earl Holliman, and actress Barbara Carrera concurred: "He read constantly. Anything that had letters on it captured his attention."

When Burt was not losing himself in books, he was escaping at the movies. His hero was the king of the swashbucklers, Douglas Fairbanks. "When the *Mark of Zorro* played the Atlas Theatre in our neighborhood [in 1920], Burt was there when the doors opened at eleven," his father remembered. "He was still there at eleven that night, forgetting all about lunch and dinner." Once again poor Willie had to fetch him home. For days, thereafter, the seven-year-old bounded around the living-room furniture, imitating Fairbanks' feats of derring-do.

Despite such antics, Burton had no interest in becoming an actor. In fact, he wanted to be an opera singer. Until he was fifteen, he sang soprano in the choir at the Church of the Son of Man. Then he entered puberty, his voice changed, and his dreams of a singing career came to an end. Concert pianist was also out; he took piano lessons, but he never developed an aptitude for the instrument.

Still, music remained his passion. He relished the records of Irish standards—"Kathleen Mavoureen," "Mother Machree"—which he played on his mother's old Victrola. And he loved symphonic music. His father would often come home late at night to find him lost in a symphony, his ear pressed close to the family's radio console with the volume low so that his mother, sister, and brothers could sleep. But the youngster's favorite was opera, to which he was introduced by his friend Nick Cravat. Nick's mother had a collection of Caruso records, which the boys played over and over again. When they could scrape up the cash, they would take a subway to the old Metropolitan Opera House, purchase standing-room tickets for $1.10 apiece, and thrill to the likes of Rosa Ponselle. As with reading, Burt's love of opera would endure for the rest of his life. When he was on location, his records and a player invariably traveled with him.

Such intellectual pursuits as literature and grand opera are hardly in keeping with the robust athlete that Lancaster personified on film. But he was short and pudgy as a child, and as is often the case with such youngsters, he lived in his imagination. He frequently became a target for bullies as well, but he fought back. "Out in the streets, fighting at an early age made me tough and it made me want to win," he recalled. Sometimes, he would not have to look far to find a battle. His father remembered the time that Burt and his brother Jim got into an argument over a baseball game. To make his point, the youngest Lancaster rapped his sibling on the head with a bat.

At about the age of thirteen, Burton began to shoot up and to lose his baby fat. After that, "Dutch" Lancaster, as his Italian friends called him, took to the streets. "We boys had the run of New York," he recalled, "and all of it was exciting." Stickball, ring-a-levio, stoopball—urban kids were creatures of the street. Apartments were too small to contain their restless energy, and in the 1920s there was not much traffic to worry about—although Lancaster managed to get hit by cars eight times. Eventually, he learned that he could have just as much fun in nearby Central Park. Sundays often meant outings there with Dad Lancaster, wonderful afternoons of ball, snacks, and visits to the zoo. For swimming, there were the piers along the East River.

"The life of the streets had warmth in my childhood," Burt recalled. Indeed, Italian East Harlem was alive with the cries of pushcart vendors, women gossiping out of tenement windows, young men congregating on street corners, and senior citizens sipping espresso at little coffee-houses that resembled the cafés back home.

In warm weather, the stoop was the gathering place—for adults as well as youngsters. Burt remembered that his father would take his guitar out on the steps and croon the old Irish melodies to the delight of the Italian neighbors. "One night I joined in the singing," Burt said. "He dropped out, just playing the accompaniment. That way I rated the applause. . . . I thoroughly enjoyed it."

Although the neighbors were supportive, East Harlem was a dangerous place. For confirmation, Burton had to look no farther than his own backyard, where a child was murdered one night—the accidental victim of a war between rival mobs of gangsters. Youngsters, as well as adults, banded together for protection. "You'd take your life in your hands, Billy," the actor would later tell his son, "if you walked east of Second Avenue, except if you were challenging their block to a game and you went over with a gang." But street fighting had not yet progressed beyond the use of bare skin.

What saved Lancaster from the city's mean streets—aside from his family—was the Union Settlement House.

The settlement movement, which began in Great Britain in 1884, sought to improve the conditions of lower-class communities through a combination of activities and social action and to help menial laborers advance through training and education.

Sponsored by the Union Theological Seminary, a nondenominational Protestant institution, the Union Settlement House began modestly in a tenement on E. 96th Street in May of 1895 but soon moved to larger quarters on E. 104th Street, between Second and Third Avenues. By 1915, when Burt was two years old, it boasted about thirty resident workers, and its facilities included an assembly hall and a gym, and a boys camp on Lake Stahahie in Palisades International Park. Its program included the first kindergarten in East Harlem, the first public bathhouses, and the first playground for small children. Indeed, youngsters were a particular focus. For them, the Settlement House was a treasure trove of fun and exciting things to learn—arts and crafts, foreign languages, dramatics, sports, woodworking.

One of the workers who exerted a particular influence on Burton and his brother Jim was Ben Puleo, who coached basketball. Like the Lancaster boys, Puleo was from the neighborhood, but when Burt knew him, he was a student at CCNY, where he earned nine varsity letters.

Puleo once said, "Burt showed lots of promise as an athlete. . . . He could have been a really good basketball player if he had stuck with the game."

Burt partook of just about everything that Union Settlement had to offer. But his favorite part was camp. "For a kid from East Harlem in the early 1920s to go to camp was really something," he said. "You looked forward to it all year."

In order to attend, one had to earn a requisite number of credits by participating in Settlement House activities. Burt picked up points by appearing in plays. When he was about eleven, he was cast as an invalid, dying of leukemia, in *Three Pills in a Bottle* by Booth Tarkington. Richard Boleslavsky, the celebrated director of the American Laboratory Theatre, caught his performance and was so impressed that he met with Mrs. Lancaster to see about sending the boy to drama school. But Burton was not interested. "Aw, no, that's sissy stuff," he told his mother.

It was at camp, at the age of nine, that Burt met the fellow who would know him longer than anyone except his family and would come to know him even better than they—Nick Cravat. Born in 1912, the feisty young Italian, whose real name was Cuccio, lived a few blocks from the Lancasters. His mother was a coat maker who, to quote Burt, "spent her life lighting candles for his soul." Little wonder. Diminutive Nick Cuccio—who would only reach five foot three inches in his maturity—was like a Chihuahua: just about anything could set him to yapping and snapping. "He was the toughest kid on the block," recalled Sal Thomasetti, an acquaintance from the neighborhood. "He wouldn't take nothing from nobody. Everybody was afraid of him. That was a scrappy guy." Those who knew Burt as an adult maintained that he did not form friendships easily, but once he let a person get close to him, that individual remained a pal for as long as he wished. No one exemplified that better than Nick. Despite nearly constant fights and reconciliations, the bond between Lancaster and Cravat endured until Nick's death at the age of eighty-two in January of 1994.

Burt graduated from P.S. 83 on June 30, 1926, managing, despite the jump-ahead-fall-back mishap in the fourth grade, to cram eight years of schooling into just six. In September, he entered high school.

Then, as now, New Yorkers could choose the high school they wanted to attend. There were three types of study: (1) academic or general, which was for those who wished to go on to college; (2) commercial, which offered preparation for business careers; and (3) trade or technical, which helped students become semiskilled laborers.

Although brother Jim was enrolled at Stuyvesant, it was decided that Burt would go to DeWitt Clinton and pursue an academic course of study. By then, his sister Jane was already a sophomore at Hunter, the women's branch of CCNY, majoring in history and social science.

DeWitt Clinton High School was located on Fifty-ninth Street near Tenth Avenue in what was known as Hell's Kitchen. "There were plenty of things going on in the area," recalled one of Burt's classmates, Abe Platt, "but we weren't subjected to it." The school building, which opened in 1906, was elaborately ornamental, in keeping with the architectural tastes of the day. "But there was not a bit of grass about it," said Clement Segal, another of Burt's classmates. "It was a building from one corner to the other corner."

Clinton was one of the largest and best high schools in the city, with an enrollment in 1926 of six thousand—all boys. Burt was a decent student who maintained a respectable average, but he was not exceptional. Still, Clement Segal remembered him as an extrovert who was "ready to give opinions fairly quickly . . . a standout" among the fellows, and Abe Platt recalled, "People liked Burt. He wasn't standoffish. He was a regular guy." Nevertheless, the Union Settlement House and the old neighborhood remained the centers of his social life. "Downtown nobody hung around," said Platt. "When you got through with school, you went home."

That changed in Burt's senior year, when Clinton moved to Mosholu Parkway in the Bronx. "Now you went to a school that was constructed somewhat like a college," explained Clement Segal. "The buildings were low, there was nothing more than three stories. There was a sort of a campus around it, nice walkways, grass, very pleasant-looking. There was a good deal of pride in going to a school that was state-of-the-art." The official dedication took place in the new auditorium on October 29, 1929. But, for Burt, the occasion was marred by his mother's illness: that week she had contracted chronic intestinal nephritis. On November 29, she died.

The impact of this loss on sixteen-year-old Burt is incalculable. "He adored his mother and admired her and loved her," said Jackie Bone, his longtime companion. "When she died, he was devastated, I believe."

Still, the relationship between Burt and Elizabeth was not simple. With her strong opinions and violent temper, she was a domineering, sometimes frightening, woman. "Mom was like a little dictator with us kids, and lots of times she was wrong," Burt once said.

Perhaps because of Elizabeth, Burt was not terribly comfortable with members of the opposite sex. "He's uneasy with women," observed screenwriter Alan Sharp. Shirley Jones, Burt's *Elmer Gantry* costar, agreed: "I've watched him in several of his other films, and I think he's least comfortable in a love scene. I've never asked him that, and I don't know whether he'd say yes to that or not, but I've always felt that he's much more comfortable in action scenes and scenes with men than scenes with women."

In his public remarks, Burt only mentioned one youthful relationship with a girl, saying, "At fourteen, I learned my first respect for stern Jewish morality because I had fallen in love with a Jewish girl." That he had few other adolescent relationships was confirmed by his father, who wrote, "When he was in his teens, he never seemed to bother much about girls, but I suspect he made up for lost time later, after he'd left home." Of course, Burt had little money for dating, and as a student of all-boy schools, he had minimal opportunities to meet members of the opposite sex. As an adult, he would often display uncommon courtesy toward women—he was frequently described by friends and colleagues as a real gentleman—and at other times he maintained a cavalier nonchalance reflected in a string of one-night stands and short-term affairs. It is likely that this blend of the reverential and the licentious had its roots in a largely sexless adolescence—abetted perhaps by the ambivalence toward women that his mother fostered.

Regardless of the impact that Elizabeth may have had upon her son's sexual and emotional development, she left him with many of the fundamental values that he would carry through life. As he once remarked, "[S]he instilled concepts as strong as an orthodox religion. However poor you were, you never lied, you never stole, and you always stuck by a promise. I've always remembered her rules because she made sure I would. If I didn't honor them, I could expect—and got—a cuff."

Although his mother's passing cast a pall over Burt's senior year, he managed to participate in the major noncurricular activity of his high school career—he was a forward on the Clinton varsity basketball team. Becoming a Red and Black Courtman was no mean feat: Coach William A. Spiegel selected only ten students out of the two hundred who tried out. With just one veteran from the previous year, the team had not been expected to distinguish itself, but with Burt's help, they emerged as the champions of the Bronx.

Burt graduated from DeWitt Clinton on June 26, 1930. Principal A. Mortimer Clark marked the occasion by exhorting his charges to remember the values that Clinton had sought to instill in them: "We hope that you have learned that if a job is to be done at all, it is to be done thoroughly. Life has no place for slipshod work. Give your best to everything you do. Finish what you start." Burton Stephen Lancaster took the admonition to heart.

CHAPTER TWO

From First-of-May Guy to Entertainment Specialist

An athletic scholarship from the Union Settlement House enabled Burt to enter New York University on September 21, 1931, some fourteen months after he graduated high school. Although his brother Jim was a sophomore in the School of Commerce, Burt chose to enroll in the School of Education as a physical education major—with the idea of becoming a gym teacher.

Contrary to what one might expect, the curriculum was hardly a breeze. The required courses included a mixture of English, public speaking, psychology, and a heavy load of sciences: chemistry, biology, anatomy, and physiology. Young Burton, however, was uninspired. "One of the educational problems of the time was that the classes were so large," he recalled. "One hundred and fifty to two hundred in a class, and the teacher would get up and address us over a loudspeaker system. We just sat there and made notes. If you got up to ask questions, they said, 'Sorry, we've got no time for questions—just copy the notes on the lecture.' And I'd be sitting there with the boys all around me reading papers or snoozing. So I lost my enthusiasm for school."

Meanwhile, brother Jim was thriving, having made the varsity basketball squad during Burt's freshman year; he would go on to lead NYU to its undefeated 1933/34 season. "I was an adoring younger brother," Burt recalled, but he had found his own niche—as a gymnast. Classmate George Ourgourlian remembered that "when he used to get on the apparatus—like on the rings or the parallels—we all used to stand around and watch him, he was so good."

It is little wonder that Lancaster impressed his classmates, for, during his freshman year, he had started training with a "stick man"—a professional acrobat by the name of Curley Brent. They had met by chance one afternoon at the gym of the Union Settlement House, where Burt worked part-time as a condition of his scholarship.

"Gee, that's wonderful," Burt had said hesitantly when the well-built Australian completed a series of swings and flips on the horizontal bar. Then, the youngster confessed, "You know, I'm a physical education major. I'm good at things where I move around—I'm fast and shifty, I play basketball—but when it comes to standing on my head on bars, I'm terrible." Brent offered to help, and Burt gladly accepted. Shortly thereafter, they were joined by Nick, who, by then, had found the perfect outlet for his natural aggression—he had become a professional boxer.

What began as a simple avocation soon turned serious—for Nick as well as Burt. Inspiration came, at least in part, from their nearly concurrent exposure to the world of the big top. They could not afford tickets to the Ringling Brothers Circus, but they managed to sneak into Madison Square Garden, the troupe's New York home, to watch a dress rehearsal in the spring of 1930. They returned to see the show the following year and, again, the year after that.

Why not become circus performers themselves? they reasoned. First, however, they needed plenty of training. Helen Harris, then the Settlement's headworker,[1] kindly allowed them to punch holes in the gym floor, so that they could secure their apparatus, and carved out time for them to practice. Occasionally, some of the younger kids would sneak in to watch. "I was amazed, the things they did on those things," said Sal Sala, about ten years their junior.

Although Harris later described Burt as "one of the most difficult youngsters that we ever had at the Settlement," the headworker did the young man an enormous service. But he nearly did not survive to reap the benefits of her generosity, for, one evening during his freshman year at NYU, he was working as the locker-room boy on the sixth-floor Settlement gym when he got into a scuffle with two rough fifteen-year-olds. They had arrived before the start of the evening's program, so one of the resident workers asked them to deliver a message to Burt. "They ran up the stairs and into the gym," Harris recalled, "and Burt said righteously, 'Get outta here! You can't come in here!' " Instead of explaining their purpose, they turned defiant, a fight ensued, and one of the boys stabbed Lancaster in the thigh with a knife. According to Harris, the wound led to "streptococcus infections," causing Burt four months of hospitalization.

1. Executive director.

• • •

Contrary to the star's later assertions, he did not complete two years of college; he withdrew from NYU early in his sophomore year. "I was pretty exasperated when he left college and went off with Nick to join a circus," James Lancaster later wrote. "If his mother had been alive at the time . . . I don't think he would have made this break." It was a bold step, but "Burt never knew fear," Jane Lancaster Sternberger recalled. "He did what he wanted."

The boys waited until spring, when circuses commence operations, to pile their meager belongings into an old jalopy and hook up with the Kay Brothers, a relatively small outfit about which Burt had read in *Billboard,* the industry trade publication. According to Bob Ketrow, one of the sons of the circus' owner, the outfit was setting up "in Plainfield, New Jersey . . . [when] a broken-down Model T Ford pulled onto the lot with two young men about eighteen years of age."[2]

"Kay Brothers Circus," recalled Bob Ketrow's friend Harold Barnes, "was a small, family-owned motorized circus commonly referred to as a 'mud show,' " from the days when "the wagons were pulled across country by horses and the elephants walked from town to town." The troupe primarily toured the East Coast, concentrating particularly on the Mid-Atlantic states and Virginia.

After watching the outfit set up, Burt and Nick asked the owner, William Ketrow, for jobs, only to be told that the troupe had a full complement of performers. Undaunted, the young men sauntered into the main tent where Bob was installing the horizontal bars for the act that he performed with two other fellows. "The horizontal bar is similar to the high bar in Olympic competition," explained Harold Barnes, "but three are placed approximately eight feet apart and the bars are made of hickory instead of steel." Performers swing from one bar to another, performing twists, flyovers, somersaults, and other tricks along the way. "It is said that the triple-bar performance is the most rigorous of all circus performances," asserted Frank Robie, the president of Circus Fans of America. "It takes the most muscle and the most expertise."

Although Burt and Nick had worked out on a single bar not a triple, they asked Bob Ketrow if they could demonstrate their proficiency. When he acquiesced, they donned their boxing tights and swung up on the bars. "On my first jump-up I didn't get enough swing to carry me across," Burt recalled. "I hit my knees and fell down. Of course, I was

2. Lancaster maintained in 1948 that he and Nick joined Kay Brothers at the troupe's winter headquarters in Petersburg, Virginia, while Nick asserted that they found the circus in West Virginia.

nervous. And then I tried it again. My timing was still off, and I missed the bar and tore my tights."

Despite the lackluster exhibition, Ketrow pleaded their case with his father since, in his words, "two extra men would strengthen the bar act, and it would be one of the highlights of the performance." William Ketrow relented. According to Nick, they did not even know what their salaries would be until they received their first pay envelopes. "When Burt nervously opened his first," Nick later wrote, "we discovered we were earning three $1 bills each, per week. We were ashamed to go home, admitting that, so we stayed." Poorly paid as they were, they had fulfilled their dream. They were "first-of-May guys"—the name given to newcomers because, as Burt later explained, "that's when you are the greenest and when the circus first gets on the road."

Kay Brothers was, in Burt's words, "a little circus," a one-ring affair, in which each act was presented in succession under a large tent. When not performing, he and Nick worked as roustabouts, helping to raise and tear down the big top as the troupe moved from venue to venue. Green though they were, they eventually got a raise—to $5 a week.

The work was rigorous, but they still found time to practice. What they ultimately developed was a comic horizontal-bar act, mixing pratfalls, contortions, and funny faces with giant swings, somersaults, and other feats of skill. Nick did the comedy and Burt was the straight man. Tightrope walker Bill Powell, who shared the bill with Burt a few years later, called Lancaster "a very fine bar performer. And his size made him look even better, because he was a big boy and that's a small guy's act." But, as Burt's onetime sister-in-law Mary Ernst Burdick, herself an acrobat, put it, "He wasn't a polished performer because he hadn't had enough experience at that time."

The members of the Kay Brothers troupe readily took to Lancaster, and the feeling was mutual. "We were a family group, just as real as any I have ever known," Burt recalled. "When one guy was out of dough, there was always a friend to help out. When the box office was low, salaries had to be skipped, but we always knew that no one else was doing much better. Food was not fancy but plenty." Cravat was not as popular. He was, to quote Ketrow, "sullen, and he didn't hit it off with the rest of the performers."

Late in the season, Nick missed a trick and fell to the ground—on his nose. The injury required hospitalization, so he returned to New York. Meanwhile, Burt carried on with the troupe, fully expecting Nick to rejoin him later. When he learned that Ketrow would not take Nick back, he quit.

Even in the best of times, circus performers faced the off-season, when another means of earning a living had to be found. That dreary prospect confronted Burt and Nick back in New York during the winter of 1933. After two months of hanging around the Union Settlement House, "achieving nothing," to quote Nick, they found an agent and tried vaudeville. Because Burt thought his last name was too long for a theater marquee, they billed themselves as Lang and Cravat.[3]

From 1881, when Tony Pastor's jewel-like Fourteenth Street Theatre in lower Manhattan began offering "entertainment clean as a hound's tooth," until the mid-1920s, vaudeville was a lively, colorful, quintessentially American, and extraordinarily popular form of entertainment. In an age without movies, radio, or television, whole families could enjoy— for a relatively low fee—a pastiche of diversions lasting several hours.

But, by the 1930s, when Burt and Nick came on the scene, vaudeville's heyday had long since passed. Most theaters were no longer even offering live entertainment, except as an adjunct to movies—and double features were starting to cut into bookings even on that basis. Moreover, Burt and Nick's act was not really attractive to theater operators: few wanted holes drilled in the floors of their showplaces so that the horizontal bars could be securely bolted down.

Consequently, in the spring of 1934, Burt signed on as a technician with the Russell Brothers Circus. Like Kay Brothers, Russell Brothers was a motorized outfit, but it was considerably larger. Burt's job was boss property man. As such, he was responsible for the setup of the acts' riggings and insuring that such items as balls and batons were placed properly and in good working order before each performance. According to aerialist Ernestine Clark Baer, who would share the bill with Lancaster the following year, he would have earned more money as the boss property man than he did as a Kay Brothers acrobat—perhaps double the amount. In addition, he was making connections with people who could further his career as a performer.

● ● ●

3. The 1940 Blue Book for the Barnes-Carruthers Fair Booking Association, Inc., spells Burt's pseudonym as *Lange,* but in most references to the actor's vaudeville career, the *e* does not appear.

The Russell Brothers stayed on the road until October 27, covering Ohio, Pennsylvania, New York, portions of New England, and several states in the South. It was shortly after his return to New York that Burt encountered a major influence in his life. Her name was Ora Ernst.

Born in 1893 in Denver, Colorado, Ora Noreen Blush had formed a horizontal-bar act with her twin sister, Bertha Pauline, called Polly. In 1914, the Loretta Twins, as they were billed, joined the fabled Barnum & Bailey Circus and gained widespread acclaim.[4] According to circus historian Pierre Couderc, "Nowhere in all the world has there ever been another female bar act that could compare with the Loretta Twins!"

Later, Ora married George Ernst, a trapeze artist and circus entrepreneur, and gave birth to three children: June, born in Australia in 1916, Mary, and John George, better known as J.G. Then, in 1926, George died, the result of a fall during a performance.

Burt had been given Ora's mid-Manhattan address by a veteran "stick man," Ed Jenkins. Paying a call one evening, he was charmed by the lady acrobat, whom Frank Robie described as "a gentle, quiet-spoken little woman with a great deal of grit and determination." The Ernsts were taken with the enthusiastic novice as well. "He was just like he was in *Elmer Gantry*," said Mary, "flaying his arms and singing and a big, broad grin."

Thus, when Burt purchased a camper late that year or in early 1935, he invited Ora and the kids to go with him and Nick to Florida; they wound up in a campgrounds in Tampa. "We didn't do much of anything, just lazed around and had fun," Mary recalled. But they needed to earn some money. So Ora arranged a few bookings at fairs in Tarpon Springs and Jacksonville. "Well, the boys didn't do so good with their act," said Mary. "They didn't know how to take care of their hands in the damp weather; they'd fall off the bars. They were canceled, but they kept our act, which we kids all filled in with trapeze and acrobatics. Then we went back to New York City."

As Burt got better acquainted with the Ernsts, a particularly warm relationship blossomed between him and Ora's oldest daughter, June, who, when not in school, performed with members of her family.

"June was little and slender and pretty," recalled Ernestine Clark Baer. Mary compared her with Audrey Hepburn. Like Burt, she loved to read and listen to classical music. "When I was around them," said Mary, "they just seemed compatible and fun-loving. My sister giggled a lot, and he was flamboyant and outgoing."

4. The Barnum & Bailey and Ringling Brothers circuses did not merge until 1919.

In early 1935, after dating for several months, Burt and June eloped to the Hudson River valley.[5] He was twenty-one, and she was eighteen. Although Ora thought June too young to marry, she accepted the union. She even held a dinner reception for the newlyweds when they returned to the city. She also probably arranged for Burt and Nick to join the Gorman Brothers Circus—a troupe founded in 1934 by motion-picture and vaudeville producer Tom Gorman—on which she was already booked for the 1935 season.

This time, instead of using the name Lang, Burt billed the act as the Lancasters—there was no marquee to worry about with a tent show. In addition to Nick, he included Ora's son, J.G., and—according to Ernestine Clark Baer—June.

The Gorman show opened in Hackensack, New Jersey, on April 20, but Ora left the troupe—for reasons unknown—on May 17. Her children and son-in-law stayed until mid-June. Then, when the circus reached Waterbury, Connecticut, Burt, June, and Nick departed—and ended up working at New York's Luna Park for several months.

"If you were engaged for the season, it had to be something really unusual for an act to leave," explained Ernestine Clark Baer. "Particularly a little show like that, when every act counted." Still, she said, folks were not surprised by the Lancasters' departure; Burt had clearly been unhappy. Other acts left the outfit as well, forcing an abrupt end to the tour on August 7.

In 1937, the Lancasters signed on with the New York unit of the WPA's Federal Theatre Circus. June took a job in the wardrobe department while Burt and Nick performed their two-man comic horizontal-bar routine.

Although it may be best remembered for daring adaptations of Shakespeare's tragedies by Orson Welles and John Houseman and for the premiere of Marc Blitzstein's "opera of labor" *The Cradle Will Rock*, the Federal Theatre Program, founded in 1935, also offered the Living Newspaper, a Gilbert and Sullivan company, a vaudeville unit, marionette troupes, and even a minstrel show. Its circus division maintained several troupes around the country, the largest of which was in the New York area.

The New York circus was a traditional three-ring affair with an enormous company—375 people in its inaugural season. The 1937 edition, with Lancaster and Cravat in the ninth spot, opened in Sunnyside,

5. An exact date cannot be determined, but Burt and June had to have gotten married before April 20, 1935, the kickoff date for the Gorman Brothers season, for which they were both engaged.

Queens, during the week of May 17 and then toured the metropolitan area for a total of twenty-one weeks, playing before more than 225,000 people.

Shortly thereafter, the Lancasters' marriage fell apart. "We never had any fights," Burt said in 1948. "We just got tired of each other." According to Frank Robie, Lancaster wanted children, and June did not. But the major rift stemmed from their career goals. "June wanted to be a dancer," said her sister, Mary, with Burt as her partner. But her husband preferred the world of the circus. "It was a great life," he said many years later.

With no children, no appreciable assets, and no concerns about middle-class propriety, Burt and June simply went their separate ways, not bothering to divorce—according to Mary and Frank Robie—until the 1940s. In future years, the actor said little in public about his first wife, but when the subject arose, he spoke of her warmly. In 1988, for example, he described her as a "wonderful girl" and their relationship as "a very nice marriage, if you can call a marriage that lasts three years nice."[6]

In 1938, Lancaster also separated—albeit temporarily—from Cravat. While Nick worked the Ringling Brothers as a part of Walter Guice's bar act and later rejoined the Federal Theatre Circus, Burt signed on with the Newton Brothers. Once again, the booking probably came through Ora, who was also on the tour. J.G. took Nick's place, accompanied by Mary, who also performed with her mother.

While on tour, Burt struck up a friendship with tightrope walker Bill Powell. "He was always kidding," Powell recalled, likening Burt to the robust, foolish Italian truck driver that he would later play in *The Rose Tattoo:* "That was his character—acting silly and carrying on." Apparently, the town girls were not impressed. "We used to have to get dates for him," said Powell.

Once, when they played the New York area, Lancaster took his friend to the Metropolitan Opera. "We got some cheap seats in the balcony," said the tightrope walker, "and he sat up there and sang with the singers." In the sticks, they settled for more mundane pursuits. One evening they were playing penny-ante poker in Burt's trailer during a rainstorm. The rickety old camper had holes everywhere, forcing them to hold newspapers over their heads to ward off the elements. Burt

6. June was never able to fulfill her dream of becoming a professional dancer. In time, she remarried, to a jewelry salesman in Denver, Colorado, her mother's hometown, and died in the 1960s.

alone was untroubled. His camper may have leaked, but at least he had one, which was a mark of distinction among circus performers. Those without slept in tents.

Right from the March 30 opening, the Newton Brothers Circus was plagued by dismal weather. Moreover, the troupe faced serious competition from a handful of other circuses playing the same area at the same time. Finally, in early August, they were in Willoughby, Ohio, when a brutal storm blew out the big top—bringing an end to the season.

The Newton Brothers' misfortunes were echoed throughout the circus world. "In 1938, the business really reached its nadir with several circuses closing prematurely," said Fred Dahlinger Jr. of the Circus World Museum. "This included the Ringling Brothers–Barnum & Bailey Circus, Cole Brothers, and the Miller Brothers 101 Ranch."

The situation did not get any better. By the end of the thirties, the number of American circuses had declined precipitously—from forty-two in 1930 to roughly half that number. Consequently, Burt and Nick, always on the fringe of the circus world, had to scramble ever more nimbly to earn a living. They continued to pursue bookings in vaudeville, working for a while on New England's Poli circuit, but that was small-time, paying only about $15 a date.

Because the horizontal bars remained an impediment for bookings, they developed an act on a new apparatus—the perch pole. As Fay Alexander, who did much of the stunt work in Lancaster's 1956 film *Trapeze,* described it, "Nick Cravat held a long pole on his shoulder and Burt would climb up that pole—it would be maybe twenty to twenty-five feet high—and do tricks up there, handstands and so forth." That five-foot-three-inch Nick was the one holding the pole that supported six-foot-two-inch Burt made a good sight gag and, at the same time, said much about Nick's upper-body strength.[7] Occasionally, however, the proscenium was so low that Burt ended up performing above the sight lines of the audience. In time, the partners were joined by a third stick man, Jack McCarthy, who became the anchor while Burt and Nick simultaneously rendered acrobatic feats.

It was a difficult life, trouping around. Once, the boys' tights were stolen, and they had to perform in their street clothes until they could

7. In Burt's 1950 picture *The Flame and the Arrow,* the actor and Cravat re-created a bit of their perch-pole act. Thus, this small but intriguing facet of Lancaster's pre-Hollywood career has been preserved.

afford new ones. They also had to drive from booking to booking, which meant long hours on the road, often in treacherous weather. On one occasion, they damaged their equipment—which they lacked the funds to replace, until bandleader Ozzie Nelson, who was on the bill with them, loaned them the requisite $1,000. For years thereafter, Ozzie and his wife, Harriet, would arrive at bookings to find envelopes with $10, $20, or occasionally even $50, as partial repayments from Burt Lancaster until, finally, the debt was satisfied.

Once in a while, however, Burt and Nick managed a good booking. At the end of 1939, for example, they were on the bill at Shea's Buffalo in New York State, with comedian Red Skelton and the Harry James orchestra featuring vocalist Frank Sinatra. Lang and Cravat also played the prestigious Orpheum in Los Angeles. While there, for a lark, Burt sought a screen test at Warner Bros. But the studio was not interested.

By the late 1930s, a new venue for entertainment was catching fire— the nightclub. Swanky spots like the Rainbow Room, which opened in Manhattan's Rockefeller Center in 1934, invigorated a host of acts—not only singers, dancers, and comedians, but also specialty and novelty acts. Burt and Nick played where they could, but horizontal-bar and perch-pole routines were no more suited to nightclubs than they were to theaters—and for the exact same reasons. The dimensions of these rooms were not conducive to watching a performance twenty feet in the air, and the owners of the Brown Derby and the El Morocco were about as eager to have holes put in their stage floors as the managers of the Palace and the Keith.

Of all the outlets for Burt and Nick's skills, fairgrounds and carnivals were the most inviting—outside of circuses, of course. Although carnivals and circuses toured and could offer up to six months' employment, fairs were mounted by individual sponsors and were of short duration. The idea was to try to put together a string of such bookings. To assist them in doing so, Burt and Nick signed up with Chicago's Barnes-Carruthers Fair Booking Association. Along with Jack McCarthy, they billed themselves as the Three Toppers, offering exhibitors a choice of either the perch-pole act or the horizontal-bar act.

But nothing really helped. "We worked one week and laid off five," Burt recalled. Worse perhaps was the sense that their big breakthrough was always just around the corner. Nick remembered a time when they were playing a fair in Hammond, Indiana: "We went over big and sat around gassing about how we would play New York's Rainbow Room and live the fat life." Three weeks later, they were appearing in a Kansas City burlesque house.

It was in 1940, while they were performing at the opposite end of Missouri—in St. Louis—that Burt was sidelined with a serious injury to his right hand. During the layoff, he took stock of his situation, and he did not like what he saw. "We're not getting anywhere," he told Nick. Consequently, he decided to quit.

Nick tried to convince him otherwise, but Burt could not be swayed. Cravat eventually teamed up with a dancer for a magic act, and in time they married. Meanwhile, Burt, with one suit and $20 to his name, headed for Chicago to stay with circus friends Vic and Ethel Smith while he tried to figure out what to do with the rest of his life.

He started by getting a job as a floorwalker at Marshall Field. "They were like service managers," explained the store's present personnel director, Bob Atkinson. "They would literally walk the floors and be available to sign documents requiring authorization—checks, returns—and help if lines at the cash registers got long." Burt was assigned to women's lingerie. "A more violent man would have learned to hate women," he said years later, "but I managed to keep a clear head, learn how to deal with dames on the prowl for bargain panties and nighties—then escaped to men's haberdashery."

Selling men's furnishings required a different sort of adjustment. As Burt put it, the department was "fast-moving and ultracompetitive. My counter companions knew the routine backwards, and the few potential buyers I managed to get started with were usually pirated in midsale. On a commission job I was starving."

One day, out of frustration or boredom, he performed a handstand on a countertop and then cartwheeled down the aisle. "Understandably, a flip-flopping salesman created something of a stir," he recalled. "But I had succeeded in distinguishing myself from the wallpaper for the first time since arriving on the job. The acrobatics also served as some sort of release for me. My attitude on the job soon became satisfactorily outgoing, and my salary satisfactorily incoming." From this experience Lancaster drew a lesson that would later serve him well as a pitchman for his own production company: "Sell yourself first if you want to sell anything."

Thereafter, he warmed to the challenge of selling. "I owe my ex-customers a lot," he said. "I learned more about human psychology from that time of my life than from any other jobs I've had." Specifically, he harvested another lesson for the future: "'Don't look down at your customers or your audience—give them credit for intelligence."

After leaving Marshall Field, Burt worked for the Fulton Market Refrigeration Company, which operated seventy freezers at various packing plants around town. Burt's job was to insure that each unit maintained the appropriate temperature. According to a studio biography, he also worked during this period as a highway construction laborer and a fireman. Finally, someone from Marshall Field told him about an available job selling concert packages for Columbia Concerts, a division of CBS. In mid-1942, after impressing the bureau's local representatives, he was sent to New York to meet with the division's directors.

Then he was drafted. While a permanent new job no longer made sense, he spent the interval before his induction—the last half of 1942—as a singing waiter in Union City, New Jersey. The Torch Club paid $75 a week plus tips, and Burt only had to work on Fridays, Saturdays, and Sundays. In addition to rendering standards like "Old Man River," he served as the straight man for the master of ceremonies. He had been performing in front of people since 1933, but this was the first time that he had spoken in front of an audience since his days at the Union Settlement House.

On December 26, 1942, more than a year after the bombing of Pearl Harbor, twenty-nine-year-old Burton S. Lancaster, serial number 32694076, became a member of the United States Army. He was ordered to report to Fort Riley, Kansas, the day after New Year's, January 2, 1943.

Although he had hoped that his experience as a circus rigger would lead to an assignment with the Engineering Corps, he was posted to Special Services. Not as prestigious as the Engineers, Special Services nevertheless had a significant role to play in the drama of World War II: its mission was to entertain the fighting men and to provide them with off-hour amenities. Given the largely civilian makeup of the Army, the Pentagon placed a high priority on such morale-boosting endeavors.

The 21st Special Service Unit, to which Lancaster was assigned, had been activated on December 20, 1942, just six days before his induction. In fact, Burt was part of the wave of draftees who brought the outfit up to strength; it had 102 enlisted men as of January 11, 1943.

Initially, Burt was an athletic instructor, helping to organize teams, referee boxing matches, run calisthenics programs, and maintain athletic equipment. But the Army's way never quite became his way. When, for example, a lieutenant tried to give him some pointers about his job, Private Lancaster said, "Climb the hell out of my hair and leave me alone." Still, he was sufficiently adept at his duties to earn promotion to Tech 5 (equivalent to a corporal) on March 1, 1943, and to Tech 4 (equivalent to a sergeant) exactly one month later. Shortly thereafter, he and the 21st were forwarded to Camp Sibert, Alabama.

In November of 1942, the Allies had launched Operation Torch, the invasion of North Africa. Seven months later, when the campaign ended in victory, 750,000 Allied servicemen were stationed along the southern banks of the Mediterranean, eager for a bit of entertainment. The 21st, attached to the newly formed Fifth Army under Lt. Gen. Mark Clark, was sent to meet the need.[8]

They began at Camp Don B in Casablanca, with a revue called *Let's Go*, which had debuted back in Alabama. Then, on September 18, they were posted to Bizerte, a port city in Tunisia. Here, they kicked off a new revue called *Stars and Gripes*—with Burt involved as a skit writer, director, and performer. His participation would indicate that he had switched from athletic instructor to what the Army called an entertainment specialist somewhere around the time of the company's overseas posting.[9]

Burt's association with the revue brought him two lifelong friends. One was Irving Burns, a vaudeville comic two years his junior. Ted Post, who was with the 235th Engineer Combat Battalion and much later directed Lancaster in *Go Tell the Spartans*, recalled that a highlight of *Stars and Gripes* was the Lancaster-Burns rendition of "Sonny Boy," with the tall Lancaster playing the child.

Like Burns, Thom Conroy was a New Yorker. Tall and bony, with a mustache and an ever-present cigarette, he had been an actor, stage manager, and director before the war. He too performed with Burt in *Stars and Gripes*. "We did a vaudeville turn together, patter stuff," Conroy recalled. "It took a lot of goading to get Burt to talk up when he finally got his chance to speak before an audience." Behind the scenes was another matter. "[H]e seemed to know all there was to know about putting on shows," said Conroy.

---

8. By an odd coincidence, Lancaster would play a character named Mark Cork in 1981's *La Pelle*. Cork was obviously intended to be Clark.

9. *Entertainment specialist* is military jargon for anyone who is involved with the organization or creation of, performs in, or provides technical assistance for theatrical or musical presentations.

Finally, in mid-December, when the outfit was in Algiers, Burt's inso-lence got the better of him. After refusing to clean up the office of M. Sgt. James C. Dages as ordered, he was brought up on charges. Conroy later maintained that Burt's refusal to obey the order stemmed from "what he considered unjust treatment of two other men." These fellows were, according to Burt, "fine pianists with fine hands. And they were forced to scrub floors. It was asinine." Nevertheless, on December 17, a summary court-martial found him guilty of insubordination. He was fined $25 (he was then earning $93.60 a month) and busted back to private.

Stars and Gripes was a huge success. Such was the demand for enter-tainment that the soldiers gave ninety-five performances between Sep-tember and Thanksgiving, playing to a total of seventy-five thousand combat-weary GIs. As they performed, they worked their way up the Italian peninsula, Clark and the Fifth Army having reached Naples on October 1. Although Italy had surrendered in September, the occupying Germans still had to be defeated, and several performances of *Stars and Gripes* were interrupted by gunfire. In later years, Lancaster made light of such hazards: "We often went up on the lines and did perfor-mances during breaks in the firing, but, to be frank, we were never in any real danger."

As the drive north continued, *Stars and Gripes* became the first live show to play Anzio, which had been besieged for four months by the German Army after its Allied capture on January 22. And it was the first American show to appear in Rome, which fell to Clark's forces on June 5. Finally, in the latter part of 1944, the 21st took up residence in Mon-tecatini, a small but lively city northwest of Florence. A spa for cen-turies, it was well suited to serve as a rest center for the men of the Fifth Army. With six theaters, one library (later two), and a sports cen-ter at its command, the 21st was accommodating some twenty thousand GIs a day. The unit also hosted the myriad USO-Camp Shows that came to the spa. Given the prevalence of these entertainments, it is likely that Montecatini was the site of Burt's encounter with Norma Anderson, the woman who would become his second wife—although various accounts over the years have placed their meeting at Pisa and Caserta.

Norma Mari Anderson was born on June 30, 1917, in Webster, Wiscon-sin, a tiny hamlet close to the Minnesota border. Her father, Charles, born in Sweden in 1877, took up farming in the area in 1896. Her mother, Mary Elizabeth (Mae) Carrol, hailed from Minnesota and became a teacher.

Charles and Mae Anderson had six children. Beside Norma, there were two girls, Margaret and Dorothy, and three boys, Karl, William, and Norma's twin, James. They "were a close-knit, hardworking, fun-loving family," maintained Cora Everson Graham, who knew Norma as a child.

In time, Mae's asthma prompted the family to move to Opa-Locka, Florida, just north of Miami. But, after graduating from Miami Edison High School in 1933, the lively Norma—nicknamed Hot-cha—headed for New York City, where she took a job with a radio producer. She married, but her husband, an Army flier, was killed during the war. Then, she began working as a secretary for the United Service Organization. When a chorine in one of the dance troupes took sick, she volunteered as a replacement.

It was on Norma's sole junket with the USO that she met the second man she would marry. According to one of his first studio biographies, issued by Universal in 1947, Norma caught sight of Burt "shuffling along a dirt road [in Italy] and asked a surprised colonel to get her a date with him." But, in 1962, the actor said that Norma first noticed him during a performance of *Stars and Gripes* and sought him out afterward. "At first I wasn't in the mood and didn't feel like meeting her," he recalled. "So all we said was hello. We didn't get acquainted until later, at a dance."

However they met, the tall, handsome soldier and the USO entertainer, four years his junior, fell in love. According to that Universal press release, Norma's troupe was dispatched south, to Caserta, shortly thereafter, and Burt went AWOL to visit her there. After a very brief reunion, he was hauled back to Montecatini by the military police. She then went "AWOL" to join him at his post, and the two of them escaped to Pisa, where they were married. After a three-day honeymoon, the MPs again caught up with them, and Norma was shipped back to New York.

It is probable that much, if not all, of this story was fabricated. For an American serviceman to marry another American in a foreign country during wartime would have required the completion of certain U.S. Army forms and permission from the GI's commanding officer. No such documents can be found in Lancaster's military dossier, nor is there any indication on his record of his having gone AWOL. Whatever may or may not have transpired between Burt and Norma during her tour of Italy, what is clear is they fell in love, and that they parted with the hope of seeing one another again at war's end.

∎ ∎ ∎

V-E Day found Burt—promoted to private first class a week earlier—in Modena, about eighty-five miles north of Montecatini, where *Stars and Gripes* was enjoying a two-week stand. He remained in Italy until mid-June, when the 21st was transferred to the Pacific theater by way of the United States. But the day after the unit docked in Hampton Roads, Virginia, the Japanese government surrendered aboard the USS *Missouri* in Tokyo Bay.

During the first chaotic days of peace, as the future of the 21st was being sorted out, Burt, who had been promoted to Tech 5 on August 1, was given what amounted to an extended leave. At the end of this period—first thirty days and then forty-five—he was expected to report back to Camp Lee, Virginia. But, as things happened, his tour of duty with the U.S. Army had come to an end.

CHAPTER THREE

"He'll Be a Star"

Burt decided to spend his liberty in New York, visiting his family and looking for a job. After two years and nine months in the Army, he faced the same concerns about future and stability that had dogged him since giving up acrobatics.

But, while he figured out what to do, he was without an income—until Nick Cravat came to his rescue. The ex-partners had not seen each other for several years, Nick having been with the USO during the war. Nevertheless, the diminutive ex-acrobat loaned Lancaster funds until he could get a job. It was a gesture of friendship that Burt would never forget.

Then a chance encounter changed his life forever.

One day, Burt decided to visit Norma Anderson, then working as a secretary for Ray Knight, the supervisor of Ed Wynn's new ABC radio program. Still in uniform, Lancaster entered the lobby elevator of the RCA Building where Knight's offices were located.[1] As he made his ascent, a swarthy, somewhat seedy fellow passenger asked if he was an actor. Burt answered that he was a "dumb actor," the industry designation for anyone—a juggler, a clown, or, as in Burt's case, an acrobat—who performs without using words. When the elevator reached Burt's destination, he got out while the stranger continued on to another floor. A few minutes later, however, the man telephoned Knight's offices, identified himself as Jack Mahlor, and invited Burt to audition for a Broadway play called *A Sound of Hunting.*

1. In several versions of the story that Lancaster told over the years, he alternately designated the RCA Building and the Royalton Hotel as the site of this encounter. As the offices of the ABC radio network, formerly the Blue Network of NBC, were housed in the RCA Building in September 1945, it seems likely that this was where the chance meeting took place, assuming, of course, that he was, as he stated, on his way to visit Norma Anderson at the time.

• • •

Jack Mahlor was not an agent, a producer, or a casting director. He trafficked in information. "He was the kind of a guy who found out things," recalled Leonardo Bercovicci, a Broadway playwright and director who later wrote Lancaster's film *Kiss the Blood off My Hands.* "Then he'd go to a producer and say, 'I heard this.' " The producer that Mahlor went to about Burt was Irving A. Jacobs.

If Mahlor was the ultimate Broadway insider, Irving Jacobs, the young owner of a Denver sports arena, was an outlander: *A Sound of Hunting* was his first Broadway play.

It was also the first play for its author, Harry Brown, best known for his "Pfc. Greengrace" columns in *Yank.* Like Brown's recent, critically acclaimed novel, *A Walk in the Sun, A Sound of Hunting* was about World War II. Specifically, the play, set in Cassino, Italy, in January 1944, focused on a platoon of grimy, battle-weary GIs, one of whom, a screwup by the name of Small, is cut off from the unit by a virtually impregnable German machine-gun nest. It then falls to the rest of the fellows to try to save him without getting themselves killed.

Lancaster was asked to read for the role of S/Sgt. Joseph Mooney, the tough but good-natured ramrod of the outfit. Despite Burt's lack of experience, he understood the character. Less than five months earlier, he had been where Mooney was, in the Italian theater of war. His reading met with silence, but he was asked to come back a day or two later to audition for the playwright. Again, when he finished, his acting failed to spark a response.

"Look, I'm wasting your time," he said. "And you're wasting my time. You don't seem to like this."

"No, no, we love it," they responded.

"Then why don't you say so?" he asked. Even at this, the outset of his acting career, he was unafraid to speak his mind.

The part was his, but technically he was still in the Army. To take advantage of this incredible opportunity, he had to travel to Fort Dix, New Jersey, to plead for his discharge—which he finally won on October 10, 1945. Eleven days later, his casting was announced in *The New York Times.* It was his first public notice, and his name was spelled wrong—"Bert."

To play the lead in the drama, a lazy, wiseass private from Brooklyn, Jacobs cast Sam Levene, the veteran of such hit Broadway comedies as *Room Service* and *Three Men on a Horse.* And to direct, he chose Anthony Brown (no relation to the playwright), whose *Tobacco Road* was among the biggest hits in Broadway history. But the rest of the company was largely composed of newcomers. Of the other billed actors—Frank Lovejoy, Carl Frank, Bruce Evans, and George Tyne—only Evans had extensive New York stage credits.

Still, all of them had more experience than Burt. As he later quipped, his entire working vocabulary as an acrobat had consisted of two words, "Allez-oop!" Further, as he put it, "I never took a lesson in my life" nor had he seriously considered a career in acting. As he later conceded, "I never dreamed I was capable of doing something like that," a rather telling remark.

But Lancaster had no time to worry about his lack of seasoning as he prepared for his Broadway debut. "We rehearsed twenty-four hours a day," he recalled. A scant three weeks later, on November 6, the play opened for two weeks of tryouts in Philadelphia. Given the raves of the local critics, the company had every reason to expect success when *A Sound of Hunting* opened in New York's Lyceum Theater on November 20, 1945.

But the reviews were only lukewarm. Howard Barnes of the *Herald Tribune* called the play "an extended sketch, full of promise but lean on the theatrical compulsion," and Ward Morehouse of the *Sun* deemed it "too slow, too static, too talky, too fragmentary." Both critics singled out Lancaster for special mention, but Burt's best review came from Robert Garland of the *Journal-American,* who wrote, "Burton Lancaster as S/Sgt. Mooney is the noncom every private prays for." Indeed, the budding actor was ideally suited for his role, a somewhat cruder, less proficient version of the character he would play in *From Here to Eternity* eight years later.

Within days of the opening, Jacobs announced that *A Sound of Hunting* would close after a three-week run.

Among those who caught it before it closed was screenwriter-director Abby Mann, who would write two of Lancaster's films in the 1960s. He found Burt in his professional debut "kind of unformed, but damned good. . . . He was an authentic personality." The actor was less effusive in a later estimate of his own work, saying, "I yelled each and every one of my lines at the top of my voice. I succeeded in making everybody—including the audience—completely miserable."

Nevertheless, he drew considerable attention during the show's brief run, notably from talent agents and film-studio scouts, who were drawn to the play by its numerous unknowns. "They were offering me all these promises," he recalled. "One wanted me to star in a play opposite Margaret Sullavan. I'd been around show business for years—and I figured how did they know what Margaret Sullavan would do the following season. Nobody was kidding me."

This response was typical Burt. In an industry accustomed to gushing, grateful newcomers, he brought a disconcerting skepticism and self-command to the opportunities that confronted him in the burgeoning stages of his career. But what many took for arrogance was, in fact, caution. And fear. "I was scared," he later admitted. "Scared stiff. And I did a lot of things and said a lot of things [in those early years] that rubbed people the wrong way. I guess I was compensating for my insecurity."

The star of the play and its most experienced hand, Sam Levene, generously offered to help the newcomer maximize his opportunity. The first thing he needed, Levene realized, was an agent. Among those in the bidding was the Famous Artists Agency, the prestigious firm of agent-producer Charles K. Feldman. "They promised to make me a star," Lancaster recalled after he was one, but the entreaty failed to have its desired effect. He was more impressed with another agent whom he met through Levene. That encounter would prove to be one of the most important of his life.

Once described as "a rather short, entirely unimposing gent," Harold Hecht was, like Lancaster, an Army vet trying to readjust to civilian life. He was only six years older than Burt, but he had been part of the theater and film community for more than twenty years, having started as an assistant to Richard Boleslavsky of the American Laboratory Theatre at the age of sixteen. He had also been a dancer with the Martha Graham Company, a movie choreographer, and the head of the literary department at the Nat Goldstone Agency. It was after the war that he formed his own agency with Lou Rantz and began representing actors, directors, and writers.

After Levene introduced them, Lancaster and Hecht met several times. Instead of offering grand visions of stardom, the agent appealed to the actor by saying, "I know everybody, but I have few clients. If you sign with me, you'd be important to me. I'd work harder for you because I want to eat and I'd have to keep you working."

Burt liked that. But Hecht's pitch included one fanciful idea, something that genuinely stirred the actor's imagination: the notion that he and Burt could produce movies of their own. "If you turn out to be the star I think you'll be," the agent asserted, "we should be making them within five years." For a moment, Burt was awestruck. Then he and Hecht started to laugh. "Here we were, a couple of bums without a quarter between us," he recalled, "discussing producing our own pictures."

Ironically, after he signed with Hecht, Lancaster received a concrete offer from the Feldman office, which was perhaps more capable of making him a star than he realized. It was the role of John Wayne's adopted son in *Red River.* The role in the Howard Hawks Western subsequently went to another newcomer, Montgomery Clift.

Now that he had an agent, Lancaster had to sift through the myriad offers he had received. The Margaret Sullavan play aside, he and Hecht seem to have decided early on that his future lay in movies rather than on the stage. The money was certainly better.

Most of the major studios wanted to sign Lancaster to a seven-year contract. Although such agreements were the industry norm, he was reluctant to yield complete control over his career to anyone for such a long period. However, one offer was different. Hal Wallis, who had left Warner Bros. the previous year to form his own independent company at Paramount, proposed a contract that would cover the standard seven-year period but would require Burt's services for no more than two films per year. The actor would otherwise be free to accept any job opportunities he wished.

Walter Seltzer, then Wallis' director of publicity, explained that such a contract was a matter of sound business logic: "His own program wasn't large enough to accommodate multipicture deals. And also, by that time, actors were getting a taste of freedom, and they didn't want to sign [standard seven-year contracts]. The next best thing was to get as many pictures as you could with the right to loan out, and Wallis pursued that very, very successfully."

In Burt's case, the logic worked, and a contract between Hal Wallis Productions, Inc., and Burton Lancaster was issued on January 8, 1946, one month to the day after the curtain fell on the twenty-third and final Broadway performance of *A Sound of Hunting.*

Shortly after Hecht completed his contract negotiations with Wallis, Lancaster took the train to California. His earnings from *A Sound of Hunting* virtually gone, he sported $30 in cash and a borrowed pair of shoes. Although he was not normally clothes-minded (even after he became a star, he usually had only two suits), he decided to have his garments cleaned during a stopover in Chicago. Then, unable to retrieve his laundry, he arrived in Los Angeles with, to quote Hecht, "one suit to his name—really a cardigan jacket, pants, and a cherry red tie." Hecht added, "For two months he wore that tie!"

Burt had a contract, but that did not guarantee him a movie; he still had to pass a screen test. The first step was to see Hal Wallis.

Hal Wallis "was a brilliant producer," maintained Charlton Heston, who joined the organization four years after Lancaster. Walter Seltzer said, "He knew every aspect of the business. He could have been an editor. He could have been a director. He could been a story-department executive. He knew advertising. He knew publicity. He had complete control of his craft."

Born in Chicago in 1898, Harold Brent Wallis had joined Warner Bros. in 1923 as the assistant to the studio's publicity director. A decade later, he was charge of production. Then, in February 1942, he stepped down as studio chief to become an independent producer on the Warners lot, with a commitment for four films a year, two of which were *Yankee Doodle Dandy* and *Casablanca.*

It was in 1944 that Wallis formed his own unit at Paramount. As he noted in his autobiography, "profit participation, a producer's fee, and complete autonomy in making our films" made this arrangement "the first truly independent setup in the business, setting a pattern for all future independent film production," including Lancaster's own foray into the field in 1947.

By the time Burt drove through Paramount's arched marble gates, the producer's roster included Lizabeth Scott, Kirk Douglas, and Wendell Corey, newcomers all. Lancaster would make the fourth, assuming he passed his screen test. As was customary, Wallis would pay him $100 a week for the four weeks that it would take to produce the test and render the verdict on Burt's screen presence.

To direct the test, Wallis turned to Byron Haskin, the former head of the Warners special-effects department, who had come to Paramount as part of the producer's team. Eschewing the customary sport coat and slacks, Burt arrived for his first meeting with Haskin dressed in corduroy pants and a sweatshirt. According to one account, he proceeded to deliver a long harangue on the poor state of Hollywood movies, adding his theories about acting and directing along the way. The forty-seven-year-old former cameraman, a veteran of the motion picture industry since 1919, was stunned.

Haskin then asked Lancaster to read something. Choosing a scene from *A Sound of Hunting,* the newcomer began rearranging the office furniture to simulate the set. Then he started to act. As Hedda Hopper recounted, "Stenographers, office boys, writers, and producers scurried down from the ends of the halls to find out what all the excitement was about. Before Burt finished, he was playing to a full room."

The test was shot on January 29, 1946. Appearing with Lancaster in a scene from what was to become *Desert Fury* was Lizabeth Scott. "We rehearsed the scene a number of times before we even got on the set, and it worked out beautifully," she recalled.

It didn't take the discerning eye of a Hal Wallis to appreciate Lancaster's presence on film. Sometimes what the camera manages to catch is inexplicable to the viewer on the spot, but not so with Burt. He was six feet two, weighed 180 pounds, and sported a forty-two-inch chest and a thirty-one-inch waist, and, although he was thirty-two, he looked ten years younger. Wallis lost little time in signing his contract. The date was February 7, 1946.

For his screen debut, Lancaster was assigned a costarring role in *Desert Fury.* His starting salary was to be $1,250 a week with an eight-week guarantee. His earnings would then jump to $1,500 a week for a second film in 1946, should Wallis choose to put him in one (he did). More substantial increases would follow in each succeeding year. In addition, he was entitled to 25 percent of any monies in excess of his regular salary received by the company from loan-outs for his services. And he was given the right to accept at least one outside job offer per year (two in 1948, 1950, and 1952), although he had to notify his employer of any such opportunities and give Wallis five days to preempt his services if he wished.

Because *Desert Fury* was not scheduled to go before the cameras until August, Lancaster had all but decided to return to New York for the interim. Then he heard about an available role in a Mark Hellinger production and decided to stay in town.

Like Wallis, Mark Hellinger had learned his trade at Warner Bros, and he too was a hands-on producer. But the similarities ended there. Where Wallis was stubborn, cold, and intimidating, Hellinger was expansive and gregarious. One could respect Wallis. One could respect—and love—Hellinger.

Born in New York in 1903, Hellinger had been a well-known journalist and Broadway producer before he entered the motion picture industry at the age of thirty-four. Starting as a writer, he graduated to producer, overseeing—under Wallis' supervision—a number of hard-edged crime dramas, including *They Drive by Night* and *High Sierra.* But the war—and a stint as a correspondent—had left him restless. In August of

1945, he formed his own independent production company with Universal-International on terms akin to those between Wallis and Paramount.

For his premiere project, Hellinger chose "The Killers," a short story by Ernest Hemingway, first published in *Scribner's* magazine in 1927.

As written, two hoods come to a small town to kill an ex-boxer, Ole Andreson, who passively accepts his fate. The tale, only eight pages long in print, would take a mere fifteen minutes of screen time, but Hellinger's idea was to open with the author's original story and then flash back to the events that lead to the Swede's demise.

Screenwriter Anthony Veiller and his unbilled collaborator, director-screenwriter John Huston (who was still in the Army and technically unable to take film assignments), effectively turned "The Killers" into the basis for a film noir classic. As they envisioned it, the Swede's downfall was due to a woman, Kitty Collins, who convinces him to double-cross the gang with whom he pulls off a major robbery. Then, she, in turn, double-crosses him. The story would be told in episodic fashion à la *Citizen Kane,* as insurance investigator Jim Riordan conducts an unrelenting inquiry into the Swede's death.

In March, Hellinger was ready to start casting. He borrowed Edmond O'Brien from Universal and Ava Gardner from MGM for Riordan and Kitty respectively. The twenty-four-year-old Gardner had made her film debut in 1942 but had yet to catch fire with the public; *The Killers* would change that. To direct, Hellinger chose Robert Siodmak, a refugee from Nazi persecution who had scored with several dark thrillers including 1944's *The Phantom Lady* and *The Spiral Staircase* earlier in 1946.[2]

Mark's only problem lay in casting the all-important role of Swede. He had initially considered Wayne Morris and Sonny Tufts, but the latter lacked the requisite screen presence, and Warners wanted too much to loan out the former. "I tested potential 'Swedes' until I thought I was going slightly daffy," he wrote later. "If somebody had suggested Garbo, I would have tested her too."

Then, one afternoon, he was having lunch with Marty Juroc, who had worked for him at Warners and was now an assistant to Hal Wallis. Juroc told him about the new kid that Wallis had just signed up. Intrigued, Hellinger arranged to view Lancaster's screen test and then asked to meet the actor.

"I was returning from lunch the following afternoon," the producer recalled, "when I saw a character standing on the steps of Walter Wanger's bungalow, reading a letter. When I say character, that's pre-

2. The son of a Leipzig banker and an American mother, Siodmak was actually born in Memphis, Tennessee, but raised from early childhood in Germany.

cisely what I mean. This guy was big. Really big. His hair was tousled. He needed a shave. No tie. And his suit looked as though it hadn't been pressed since C. Aubrey Smith wore short pants."[3]

As they talked in Hellinger's bungalow, the producer could not help noticing that the actor was somewhat awkward and clumsy; in this, he was perfect for the Swede. Several years later, he said, "You know what I think? I think that all the time I was talking to him, that smart guy was playing the Swede for me," which, of course, was so. A former acrobat, Lancaster was anything but ungainly. Looking back on the same encounter, the actor proudly noted that he had even managed to spill some coffee during his chat with Hellinger, just to add to the effect.

Lancaster and the producer then turned their discussion toward *The Killers.* According to Hellinger, he gave Lancaster a copy of the script to read.

"I read it," Burt told him. "My agent had a copy."

Taken aback, the producer asked how he liked it.

"Fair," Lancaster replied. "My part's fair too."

"Only fair?"

Lancaster shrugged. "Well, it may be better than I think. Or it may be worse. You see, it's the first movie script I ever read!"

Hellinger was quite taken with the young actor, whom he asked to test for the role. Lancaster was not eager to do so. He knew that the producer had seen the Wallis footage and believed that this offered sufficient evidence of his screen presence. But Hellinger insisted, and Hecht convinced Lancaster to relent. Reading with him in the test was a newcomer by the name of Connie Dowling, whose sister, Doris Dowling, was an established actress.

Hellinger was not completely certain about Lancaster after viewing the new footage, so he screened it for his wife, Gladys, a former Ziegfeld Follies girl. She told her husband, "Well, he isn't handsome, Mark, but the women will go for him. He has muscle, and he looks manly."

That decided it. On April 29, Hellinger placed the actor under contract—he was not about to make Lancaster a star just so Hal Wallis could reap all the benefits. While recognizing the primacy of Lancaster's prior agreement, Burt's new contract called for him to do one picture a year for Mark Hellinger Productions for up to five years. He was to be paid $2,500 a week for *The Killers,* which was double the sum he was to receive for his first Wallis film. His specified earnings for subsequent Hellinger outings—$4,500 and $6,500 in 1947 and 1948 respectively—continued to outpace his equivalent earnings with Wallis.

3. C. Aubrey Smith was a British character actor who had been born in 1863 and was, at the age of eighty-three, still making films in 1946. He died in 1948.

All that remained was the selection of Burt's professional name. Originally, Wallis had decided to call him Stuart Chase, but changed his mind when he learned that there was a well-known economist by that name. Now that Burt was under contract to Hellinger, Mark also became engrossed in the search. Finally, Hellinger's secretary had an idea, and tongue in cheek, he phoned it in to Wallis. "Hal," he said excitedly, "Myrtle suggests something that nobody thought of. What about using his real name—Burt Lancaster?" Wallis agreed, and as Hellinger said later, that is how "Burt Lancaster became Burt Lancaster. Isn't it remarkable what we Hollywood masterminds can accomplish if only we try?"

The buildup began immediately. On March 28, a month before the actual consummation of Hellinger's contract with Lancaster, Universal Studios released its official biography of the actor, starting with a summary of the events that had led to his casting in *The Killers:* "A glass slipper served Cinderella as her ticket to the blissful life, but in the case of Burt Lancaster it was his Broadway debut as a blustering sergeant in Harry Browne's [sic] *A Sound of Hunting* that overnight brought him a deal for Hollywood and almost certain stardom." On April 27, columnist John Todd weighed in with, "Today's best bet for top movie stardom goes to work in his first picture Monday. His name is Burt Lancaster. . . . His only other appearances before the cameras were tests—one with Lizabeth Scott for Hal Wallis, who originally signed him, and one with Constance Dowling for Hellinger, who now owns half his contract. Your reporter saw both tests. Lancaster is terrific." A photo of Burt with Mark and Gladys Hellinger in *Modern Screen* offered what the magazine claimed was the "first glimpse of the lad."

As Todd had reported, *The Killers* went before the cameras on April 29, 1946, but Lancaster's first day on the set was not until May 1, when shooting began on the Swede's final professional bout.

Lancaster "had a great deal of humility" during the making of his first film, recalled Paul Brown, who was cast as Nick Adams, Hemingway's alter ego. "He recognized that he was in a new field, and he had an intense curiosity, an eager, seeking mind, and he wanted to learn." Humble, he may have been, but not downright submissive. As Hellinger saw it, "He likes to analyze everything. . . . He wants to know why about everything. He argues every point, and he gives in only when he's convinced he's wrong."

Guiding Lancaster was Siodmak, whom Jeff Corey, cast as a member of the gang, described as "a slight man, wonderful bug eyes, curious about the world, great wit, never pouty, never angry, always accepting, always playful." Lancaster was also assisted by Sam Levene, his mentor from *A Sound of Hunting,* who had landed—in what would seem to be pure coincidence—a major supporting role in *The Killers,* that of the Swede's boyhood friend Lt. Sam Lubinsky. "It was lucky he was on the set with Burt," maintained Corey, "because Burt didn't feel too comfortable in his first film. Sam would frequently get on his ass. 'C'mon, c'mon. Do the goddamn thing. You pick up the piece of jewelry. Can't you do that and say the fucking line?' Burt was never offended. He appreciated it, because he loved Sam. Everyone did."

The work was hard, but it was exciting. "Siodmak and Hellinger gave us a feeling of being part of something important and a sense of what we could do with a scene that gave us extraordinary confidence," O'Brien remembered. And the atmosphere on the set was upbeat. "One thing I especially liked about filming *The Killers,*" Gardner recalled, "was that Burt and Eddie and the rest of us were in the early stages of our careers, fresh kids enjoying life."

Lancaster's first scene with Ava came on May 10. Later, he confessed that he considered her "easily one of the most beautiful women that ever lived. And when I had to kiss her, I found myself deeply stirred. It took a form of some embarrassment." His and Gardner's mutual admiration society was not lost on Corey: "I have reason to believe that they enjoyed kissing each other a great deal. They both had mentioned that to me."

Hellinger was thrilled with Burt's work. So much so that when he watched the rushes of the newcomer's first scene, he yelled, "So help me, may all my actors be acrobats." Lancaster's own response to seeing himself on the screen was more muted: "I didn't recognize my voice, and my hair looked like a bird's nest going all over the place."

Shortly before the release of *The Killers,* Hellinger wrote Abel Green of *Variety:* "I have never told you before that I made a great motion picture. *The Killers* is a great motion picture." Hemingway shared the producer's enthusiasm.

The picture's effectiveness was due in no small measure to Lancaster's presence. Fortunately for him, the Swede was an elemental, uncomplicated character, a role that placed minimal demands on his as yet unrefined talent. "I could be very simple in the part," he explained later, "there was no need to be highly ostentatious or theatrical. For a new actor this is much easier than something histrionic. There's no question about the good fortune of being ushered into films in that kind of role."

"He knocked them dead with his looks," future costar Virginia Mayo recalled. "He didn't have much to say in the picture, but he just had a great persona. There was nobody like him. That's what makes a star." His looks were certainly a major factor in his initial impact. He was rugged, but under the film's deeply shadowed lighting and its stark black-and-white photography, he radiated something akin to beauty, the planes of his face sharp and clean. Moreover, he evidenced an almost childlike vulnerability, enhanced by his surprisingly soft and gentle voice. And there was something else. As Corey put it, "There was something street-smart about Burt. He was for real."

In short, the combination of the tender and the tough, the handsome and the rugged, the larger than life and the average guy from the street defined a new and potent screen persona. Although in time Burt's skill as an actor would develop far beyond the proficiency he commanded at the outset of his career, and he would embrace roles of infinitely greater subtlety than the Swede, he would continue to evoke over the next forty-four years elements of the screen image that he introduced in *The Killers*.

Shortly after the film wrapped on June 26, Lancaster drove east, where a telegram from Hellinger reached him—in Ventnor, New Jersey. Jubilant over the response to the film's previews, the producer crowed, "I'm afraid you're destined to be a big star, you poor guy."

Lancaster had a compelling reason for returning home that summer. On June 30, Norma had given birth to his child. It was a boy, whom they named James, after his father and her twin brother. But the new parents would not wed until the end of the year. It is unclear why they did not marry in New York while they had the chance, but it may have been that Burt and his first wife, June Ernst, had yet to divorce. Indeed, June's sister, Mary, and family friend Frank Robie maintained that Burt and June did not formalize their estrangement until Burt's involvement with Norma.

Despite his domestic situation, Burt joined Mark and Gladys Hellinger and Edmond O'Brien during the first week of August for a brisk tour of twenty key cities to promote *The Killers* prior to its release. In Pittsburgh, Lancaster asked Hellinger if he could bring some friends to the local press party. Permission granted, he arrived with, in the producer's words, "four old, beat-up acrobats. He paid little attention to the press that day; just sat around and gabbed with his former pals." Hellinger was impressed. Lancaster might have been on the verge of major stardom, but he had not forgotten his roots.

On August 29, *The Killers* premiered at the Winter Garden in New

York. With enormous poster art decorating the theater and ads that proclaimed, "Every kiss carved his name on another bullet," and, "Some guys never find out . . . WOMEN can be KILLERS too!" audiences were primed for what *Variety* called "a hard-hitting example of forthright melodrama in the best Hemingway style." Initially Hellinger planned on billing Burt last among the featured players with the tag "Introducing Burt Lancaster as Swede," but he changed his mind. In the print ads and in the film's title cards, Lancaster was given first billing.

The opening day in New York set a new house record, confirming Burt's and Mark's hopes: *The Killers* was an enormous box-office and critical hit. Bosley Crowther of *The New York Times* called it a "taut and absorbing explanation" of Hemingway's story, and Otis L. Guernsey Jr. of the New York *Herald Tribune* said it was "a polished and tantalizing chase melodrama . . . a deft combination of acting and mystery." Guernsey also dubbed Lancaster "a likable fall guy in a most promising screen debut."

Among those who saw an early screening was Byron Haskin, the man who had directed Lancaster's test for Wallis. In a note of congratulations to Hellinger, Haskin called the picture "sensational," adding: "It also justifies the faith I had in 'Boit' Lancaster—he'll be a star."

CHAPTER FOUR

Playing the Tough Guy

"I woke up one day a star," Lancaster said in 1950. "It was terrifying."

Burt may have been intimidated by instant celebrity, but Hal Wallis was thrilled. "He very much enjoyed the fact that he sent an unknown over to Hellinger, and the guy came back a star," recalled Walter Seltzer. Wallis even expanded Lancaster's role in *Desert Fury* once his success became apparent.

The film, based on a 1945 novel, *Desert Town* by Ramona Stewart, centered on young, beautiful, headstrong Paula Heller, who falls in love with a big-time racketeer, Eddie Bendix (called Benedict in the book). Burt was the "nice guy" alternative, Tom Hanson, an affable but ruggedly independent deputy sheriff who manages to win her in the end.

Lancaster's role was an amalgam of two of the novel's characters: the embittered, sadistic deputy sheriff, Tom Hansen, and a likable highway patrolman named Luke Sheridan. Neither character was romantically linked to Paula; that was screenwriter Robert Rossen's contribution. Rossen also changed the affect of the property—from a desert *Peyton Place* (although the novel was published ten years before Grace Metalious' book) to the tempestuous tale of a headstrong, rebellious girl in love with the wrong man.

To play Paula, Wallis turned to the only leading lady he had under contract, Lizabeth Scott. Like Burt, the twenty-four-year-old beauty with honey-blond hair and a throaty voice was a newcomer to films, having appeared in two of the producer's previous independent pictures, *You Came Along* and *The Strange Love of Martha Ivers*. For

Bendix, Wallis chose the handsome John Hodiak, whose screen debut had come with *A Stranger in Town* in 1943.

Principal photography began on August 16, about two weeks before the release of *The Killers*. Although most of the scenes were shot on the Paramount lot, Burt traveled with the company to Sedona, Arizona, to capture some of the rich desert atmosphere for the Technicolor production. As he remembered it, "We'd go into town—there was only one place to buy liquor—and some of us would purposely get drunk, it was so hot at night, so we could sleep."

Lizabeth Scott admired her costar. "He was very exciting to look at," she recalled. "He was virile, he was handsome, he was enthusiastic. He had an aura about him." And, on the whole, she enjoyed working with him, although she noticed that "he dissected every scene of the film intellectually," which she sometimes found annoying.

Their director was Lewis Allen, a forty-one-year-old Briton who had a way with romances, period pieces, and comedies. But *Desert Fury* demanded a harder edge than he could comfortably render. Although Burt considered the director "sweet," he got into a fierce argument with him one day on the set. "He wanted me to do something," Lancaster recalled, "and I said, 'No, that's not right, I'm not going to do it.' I turned around and walked to the dressing room." Richard McWhorter, who was the assistant director on *Desert Fury* as well as most of Lancaster's other pictures for Wallis (he also worked for Lancaster's production company in the fifties), warned him that such behavior at this early stage in his career could ruin him. "Oh, fuck the career," Burt answered. "I'm not going to do it, that's all." It was an attitude that never changed.

"Burt has had some real problems with directors," McWhorter maintained, "because if he didn't think something was right, he would get mad. Then, afterward, he would apologize." The actor's fury invariably stemmed from his intense involvement with the work. "He wasn't like many other stars who were terribly demanding about personal things," asserted assistant director Hal Polaire, who made two films with Burt in the 1960s. From Lancaster's perspective, he had a right—even an obligation—to make his views known. "I don't want to run the show," he once said. "But if I feel that a scene is going wrong, I want to do everything in my power to correct it, even if it means an argument with the director."

What made Lancaster enormously intimidating at such times was the *way* he expressed himself. His voice rose, his face turned red, and his arms flailed about in large, pointed gestures. He was a big man, and when he got angry, he was frightening. Actor Marc Singer said with a chuckle, "I think Burt—like all powerful personalities—had a tendency to not quite realize the impact of his opinions and how he expressed them."

If quality control was Lancaster's principal concern, he had begun to realize even by this, his second, film, that the ultimate power to influence the character of a motion picture did not rest with the star. Thus, he set his sights on directing.

The filming of *Desert Fury* came to an end on November 9, 1946, virtually four weeks after the original stop date. Lancaster was able to enjoy a month's rest before he had to report for work on his second Wallis picture of the year, *I Walk Alone.* He spent some of the time in conference with Mark Hellinger on their follow-up to *The Killers,* a prison movie called *Brute Force.*

Having wanted to make a picture about convicts for almost ten years, Hellinger developed his own story idea, then engaged Robert Patterson, a reporter for the *San Francisco Examiner,* to fashion it into a scenario. What they devised was a seething, violent indictment of the penal system, which pitted a group of hardened cons against a sadistic captain of the guards. The script was written by Richard Brooks, author of *Swell Guy,* Hellinger's lone film between *The Killers* and *Brute Force.*

From the outset, the producer had wanted to inject a little romance into the story in order to appeal to the female audience—not an easy thing to do with a prison picture. Thus he, Patterson, and Brooks created a series of flashbacks in which four of the convicts recall the women who purposely or not—caused their downfalls. Initially, one actress was to play all four roles.

It may have been this casting idea that fostered a meeting between Hellinger, Lancaster, and Universal's sultry twenty-four-year-old contract player Yvonne De Carlo in late 1946. At the conference, De Carlo could not concentrate on anything but Lancaster. "I had no doubts that Burt knew exactly what he wanted, and at the moment it was me," she wrote in her autobiography. "He had tremendous intensity and was the kind of macho man who says nothing but takes the girl by the hand and leads her off to his lair."

Lancaster invited De Carlo to a cocktail party and dinner, and she quickly accepted. Later, they returned to her home and made love in her backyard—on her mink coat. As she recalled the moment, "It was so spontaneous and so explosive, I thought I was playing a scene from a blazing romantic novel. Talk about being swept away!" The following week, Lancaster left for a visit to New York, marking the end of what she called "a mutual fling, brief but memorable."

Eventually, the idea of having one actress play all four women in *Brute Force* was abandoned. De Carlo would still be in the cast, but opposite Howard Duff, while Burt was paired with Ann Blyth.

On December 9, 1946, Lancaster checked in at Paramount to start work on *I Walk Alone.* He was again teamed with Lizabeth Scott, whom he had to share this time with Wallis' other rugged contract player, Kirk Douglas.

Douglas was five years younger than Lancaster but had more experience, having studied at the Academy of Dramatic Arts in New York and honed his craft on Broadway. He had also started in films first, playing Barbara Stanwyck's drunken husband in *The Strange Love of Martha Ivers* the year before *The Killers.* But it would take his eighth film, *Champion,* in 1949 to give him the kind of visibility that Lancaster had already achieved. Testament to their relative statures on *I Walk Alone* was the placement of Lancaster's name first and before the title; Douglas was billed fourth and after the title.

Because of their numerous screen pairings over the years, the public came to see Burt and Kirk as a rugged Tweedledum and Tweedledee. In some ways they were alike. Both grew up in poverty in New York State. Both were physical actors and sexy without being classically handsome. And both were considered difficult, because each took an active creative role in the making of his pictures. But there were marked differences as well. Burt tended to be more cerebral, as a person and as an actor; Kirk more emotional. Actor Charles Durning, who worked with them both, drew another distinction: "Kirk is very stiff in his approach to people [at work], and Lancaster is just the opposite."

At the outset of their first picture together, Lancaster and Douglas were just two newcomers under contract to the same producer. And they did not become pals during filming. There was, to quote Walter Seltzer, "a friendly rivalry between them and a mutual dislike of what they were doing. Both of them hated the picture."

Their disdain was not without foundation. Even by 1946, a plot about two gangsters—former pals—who become rivals in business and love was hardly new.

Deadlock, as the film was originally called, began as a play entitled

The Beggars Are Coming to Town by Theodore Reeves, which had opened on Broadway on October 27, 1945. Starring Paul Kelly and Luther Adler, it centered on two former bootleggers, Frankie Madison and Noll Turner, who struggle for control over an elegant nightclub. It was not a hit.

The film's screenplay by Charles Schnee essentially followed the plot of the play to its climax, in which Frankie (Lancaster) discovers the convoluted corporate structure that protects Noll's (Douglas') enterprise. It then continued with a series of action sequences. Punctuating the gangsters' warfare was a lame romance between Frankie's and Noll's girlfriend, torch singer Kay Lawrence (Scott).

I Walk Alone reunited Burt with Byron Haskin, who had not directed a feature since 1928. "I got the assignment because all the cast were newcomers—they didn't know enough to have any objections to me," the director joked years later. Haskin's extensive experience as a cameraman on such notable Warner pictures as *The Roaring Twenties, The Sea Hawk,* and *High Sierra* prepared him well to orchestrate and compose a scene, but he was, by his own admission, less experienced at working with actors. Lancaster, then still learning his craft, could have benefited from a surer hand. As Haskin later confessed, "Burt was so full of energy, he was a difficult man to harness."

About a week into the shooting, Lancaster and Scott took a couple of days away from *I Walk Alone* to film a joint cameo appearance in Paramount's *Variety Girl,* a throwback to the studio's *Big Broadcast* pictures of the 1930s. Dedicated to the Variety Clubs of America, *Variety Girl* was a whimsical backstage extravaganza, with guest spots for just about everyone on the Paramount lot, including Bob Hope, Bing Crosby, Gary Cooper, Barbara Stanwyck, and Paulette Goddard. Lancaster and Scott gave a humorous exhibition of marksmanship, with Burt as the not-so-expert sharpshooter and Scott as his unfortunate assistant.

On Saturday, December 28, Burt took another hiatus—to marry Norma Anderson in Yuma, Arizona. His best man was Army buddy Irving Burns, whom Lancaster, with typical loyalty, had made his dresser. Yuma was chosen as the site of the wedding because, unlike California, Arizona did not impose a three-day waiting period. The border town sported several wedding chapels, and the courthouse issued marriage licenses twenty-four hours a day. "A lot of movie stars came in," explained Carol Brooks, curator of the Arizona Historical Society–Yuma, because "they were guaranteed that they could arrive and get married, and there would be no publicity."

Because of the death of Burt's brother William on November 23, the affair was low-key. Willie, who had become a social worker with the New York City Department of Welfare, had moved to Los Angeles to help Burt manage his business affairs. Only thirty-four, he suffered from endocarditis—inflammation of the heart—the result of rheumatic fever contracted in childhood. Burt and he had been particularly close, and the actor was devastated by the loss.

Quickly returning to Los Angeles, Burt settled his new bride and son in the home he had rented in Malibu, a beach community about an hour's drive from Paramount. Then he went back to work on *I Walk Alone*.

Despite his disdain for the material, he labored faithfully on the picture. So did Douglas. As Lizabeth Scott recalled, "Kirk wanted to excel, and Burt wanted to excel. Therefore, I had the best of it, because I had two leading men that I played off of." She reserved particularly warm words for Lancaster: "He was tender, he was sweet, he was kind. There was a humanity about him from the very beginning, and as he developed, those qualities, I think, grew stronger."

On February 21, Lancaster started shooting *Brute Force*. He liked playing Joe Collins, the tough, determined convict who instigates a breakout at fictitious Westgate Prison. The character was not all that different from *I Walk Alone*'s Frankie Madison, but the Hellinger film had a leaner, more literate script, and the presence of a director, Jules Dassin, more adept than Byron Haskin. Dassin, who had started as an actor, had half a dozen MGM features to his credit by the time he commenced work on *Brute Force*.[1]

Principal photography began with the flashback sequences, involving the wives and girlfriends (Blyth, De Carlo, Ella Raines, and Anita Colby) of Collins and three of his cellmates (Lancaster, Whit Bissell, Howard Duff, and John Hoyt). Then, in mid-March, the company moved outdoors, to shoot the sequences in the convicts' work station, an enormous drainpipe that served as the staging area for their breakout. For ten grueling days, water, released from overhead faucets, dripped down Burt's neck, smearing his clothes and face with mud and caking dirt in his ears and hair. Hellinger called him "the human mud pie." He and the

1. Today Dassin is best known for the European films that he made after being blacklisted in Hollywood in 1950, notably 1960's *Never on Sunday* starring his wife, Melina Mercouri.

other members of the work detail were so filthy that they were, in Burt's words, "embarrassed eating with clean people. The other players claim we're getting their costumes dirty in the café, so we all go in to eat in a bunch—for moral support."

At one luncheon, they were joined by columnist Shcilah Graham, who was eager to interview the new star. As she began, Burt, in her words, "decided to have some fun with me. I'd ask a straight question, he'd pick it up and announce it to the others, and his reply was intended to and did embarrass me. I didn't know why he was doing it, but pretty soon I felt a choking sensation, a mixture of rage and tears, and made an excuse and left." From that time on, Graham, who had been an early Lancaster booster, became an ardent enemy.

The star's inexplicable treatment of a powerful Hollywood columnist was indicative of his general impertinence on the set. "Burt really kind of wanted to take over [the picture]," observed Jeff Corey, a colleague from *The Killers* who played one of Burt's cellmates. "I was amazed; he suddenly had this confidence that he knew what was right." Even Hellinger, who liked Lancaster enormously, was put off by his attitude. "This kid," he said during filming, "has made one picture out here [*sic*] and already he knows more than anyone on the lot. . . . He's a frustrated Freudian, a body in search of a brain. Mr. Know-It-All from the Big Town."

Why did Burt behave so badly? In part because, as we have already seen, he refused to limit his creative involvement on a project to the mere interpretation of his role. On this point, he would never change. "If you're just going to show up for a part, you might as well be a robot," he remarked as late as 1988. "If you can't contribute by suggesting things to a director, then what's the use? What's the fun?" In the Hollywood of the 1940s, such an attitude was not welcome. The paternalism of the studio system held that actors were children whose careers were best directed by the heads of the studios to which they were under contract. Contract players were expected to go along, not make waves, not ask questions.

But something more was at work during Burt's first heady days of stardom—his ego was out of control. As he later put it, "I was so sure of myself. I argued with directors, fought with them. . . . What I needed was a plunge into cold water." Everyone on the lot was fair game, but he drove himself hardest of all. Indeed, he was mortified one day, during the shooting of *Brute Force,* when he arrived twenty minutes past his call. Dassin mildly rebuked him, and he replied furiously, "I know I'm late, and everybody on the set knows I'm late. Isn't that punishment enough?"

Only two years older than Lancaster, Dassin was well equipped to deal with Burt's temperament. He was, to quote Hume Cronyn, who played the sadistic captain of the guards, Munsey, "a very good director. Very passionate." Even Lancaster conceded that Dassin "could excite new ideas in terms of how you wanted to play the part." Moreover, the director was not unsympathetic with Burt's need for creative involvement. Corey observed that Lancaster and "Julie did not lock horns; they collaborated."

Brute Force wrapped on April 21. Thereafter, Hellinger rushed to complete the editing in anticipation of an early-summer opening—despite a prolonged battle over the film's contents with Joseph Breen, the administrator of the Production Code of the Motion Picture Producers and Distributors of America, the industry's powerful censorship bureau.[2] Thus, the film—Lancaster's fourth—became his second to hit the nation's screens.

With ads screaming, "They knew but one law, the law of BRUTE FORCE," the picture premiered on June 30, 1947. Despite the love scenes, Hellinger soon realized that its grosses would fall short of *The Killers; Brute Force* was fundamentally a man's picture. In retrospect, Lancaster maintained that the flashbacks worked to the film's detriment, and he was right. "But this was all part of Hollywood then," he said in 1973. "The emphasis was always with the love story. . . . They believed that what was known to work well at the box office should not be tampered with."

Still, the critics gave *Brute Force* high marks, although several found it a lesser film than *The Killers*. They also acknowledged Lancaster's contribution, which Otis Guernsey Jr. of the New York *Herald Tribune* called a "brooding, effective performance." Indeed, Burt was more economical and cleaner in his delivery than he was playing a similar tough guy in *I Walk Alone*. The actor himself was pleased with the film. "It was very potent," he acknowledged years later. "The characters were all very strong, and very romantically written."

During the summer of 1947, while Lancaster was in New York promoting *Brute Force*, he took the time to meet with Irene Mayer Selznick, the former wife of film producer David O. Selznick, in order to discuss a

2. Subsequently called the Motion Picture Association of America.

drama that she planned to bring to Broadway the following season. It was *A Streetcar Named Desire* by Tennessee Williams.

Selznick had initially sought John Garfield for the male lead—Stanley Kowalski, the common, brutal brother-in-law of a fading Southern belle—but after Garfield rejected the part, she pursued Lancaster. Burt was intrigued, but he reluctantly had to turn her down. He was to start work on the film version of *All My Sons* in September and would be shooting while *Streetcar* was in rehearsal. "Years later Burt told me how he had yearned to do the part," Selznick recalled in her autobiography.

Competing for Lancaster's attention during the making of *Brute Force*—and perhaps contributing to his rudeness on the set—was his fierce contract dispute with Hal Wallis.

The conflict was sparked by the producer's intent to loan Lancaster and Lizabeth Scott to RKO for a picture entitled *White Swamp,* which Burt did not want to do. Nevertheless, the actor's attempt to break free of Hal Wallis Productions had less to do with one film than the belief—doubtlessly accurate—that he could earn more on his own than as a contract player. Moreover, Burt and Hecht had decided that the time had come to launch their own independent production company, and the Wallis contract was an unwelcome hindrance to their plans. Finally, Burt did not like Wallis and did not want to work for him. His antipathy dated back to their initial meetings in New York during the run of *A Sound of Hunting.* One day, for example, while the two men were walking along Broadway, Wallis pointed to a theater marquee, saying, "I produced that picture," and Lancaster replied, "I saw it in Italy. It stinks."

That Burt did not like Wallis hardly distinguished him; the producer was not a popular man in Hollywood. Screenwriter Walter Doniger spoke for many of Hal's associates when he said, "Wallis was very stubborn. He didn't want to make adjustments to make people happy." But, unlike other detractors, Burt would not even acknowledge Wallis' skill as a producer, deeming him unworthy of credit for such enduring films as *Casablanca,* which he had produced at Warners. "He had nothing to do with the pictures," Lancaster asserted years later, "nothing to speak of, nothing creative." Moreover, Burt thought Wallis was cheap. Said the actor, "His ploy would be to wait till nobody wanted a Tennessee Williams play because they didn't think it was viable for the screen, and he'd sneak in and buy it for a song. He did the same thing with *Come Back, Little Sheba.*" Not so. Wallis paid $100,000 for *Sheba,* which was a hefty sum at the time, and additionally gave the playwright, William Inge, a percentage of the picture. He also paid handsomely for Williams' *The Rose Tattoo,* which costarred Lancaster in 1955.

It *is* fair to say that, during the early life of Wallis' production company, the producer was less adventuresome in his choice of material than he had been at Warners. "Very consciously, I made a series of melodramatic films with strong characters and situations, films that proved to be extremely popular," he wrote in his autobiography. *Desert Fury* and *I Walk Alone*—cases in point—were not up to the quality of the films that Burt did with Hellinger, but they performed far better at the box office. Moreover, the same conservative approach could be said of Lancaster during the initial phase of *his* production company—which speaks no less for Burt than it did for Wallis. Both men were simply being prudent, letting their ventures gain strength before risking creative challenges.

The basis for Lancaster's action against Wallis lay in their original agreement, which specified one picture *(Desert Fury)*. Anything that transpired between the producer and the actor thereafter was relegated to a series of options. Technically, therefore, the contract could have been viewed as a one-picture agreement. As such, it did not conform to the provisions for freelance players set forth in the Basic Agreement of 1945 between the Screen Actors Guild and the signatory producers, including Wallis. It was on that technicality that Burt and Harold pinned their hopes. Wallis' attorneys, by contrast, maintained that the agreement was not a freelance contract, but "a one-picture deal plus options" that "contemplates and establishes a continuing relationship" between the actor and the producer.

On April 13, John Dales Jr. of the Guild informed Hal that he agreed with Lancaster and Hecht's assessment—it *was* a freelance agreement and it was improperly drawn—and he requested a meeting with the contesting parties to arbitrate the matter. On April 22 and 23, the conference took place, with Hecht and attorney Leon Kaplan representing Burt, and Wallis' assistant Paul Nathan and attorneys Sidney Justin and Berman Schwartz representing the producer.

Nothing was decided. At the end of the second day, Nathan informed Wallis that Lancaster had a good case and that the actor was very determined. "Harold has assured me that Burt wants his freedom," Nathan wrote, "and is not interested in any more money, or anything else, other than to be free of his Wallis contract."

But, as the negotiations continued, Hecht backed down. He surely must have realized that, Dale's assessment notwithstanding, Burt's contract clearly reflected the intent to establish a long-term relationship between the actor and the producer. Thereafter, both parties brought a series of proposals and counterproposals to the table and, at last, reached an agreement on July 23. According to the new contract, which was ultimately dated September 27, 1947, and scheduled to take effect in January of 1948, Lancaster agreed to appear in two films for Wallis between May 2, 1949, and May 1, 1950 (the first option period), at a salary of $5,000 per week with an eight-week guarantee per film. Over the five ensuing option periods, which called for typical salary escalators at each stage, Wallis could have Lancaster for one film a year, except for the third year, in which he could have him twice. During the life of the contract, Lancaster was given the right to accept eight outside projects, two in the second, fourth, and fifth years and one in the others. Additionally, Burt could buy his way out of the sixth year by paying Wallis a fee of $75,000.

The war was over, but the friction between the two men remained. It was not overt, but, as Walter Seltzer observed, "They were abrasive with each other."

In addition to a new contract, September of 1947 brought another change: Burt and Norma leased a home in Westwood, a middle-class community on the fringes of Beverly Hills and the site of UCLA. Although they had two months remaining on the rental of the Malibu house, Westwood offered the advantage of being considerably closer to the studios. But the primary reason for the move was their proximity to St. John's Hospital in Santa Monica. The Lancasters were expecting a baby in November.

September also saw the premiere of *Desert Fury* on the twenty-fourth, almost nine months after the production wrapped.

The picture was not a critical success. Archer Winsten of the *New York Post* spoke for many of his colleagues when he called it "a magnificently decorated package inside which somebody has forgotten to place the gift. The desert, the color, the music, the motion, and the conflicts are all there on the screen. And every bit of it is a complete waste of time."

It was in the critical pairing between Lizabeth Scott and John Hodiak that *Desert Fury* was particularly wanting. Scott, though visibly inexperienced, radiated an appealing vulnerability, but Hodiak, who became a leading man during World War II when competition was in short supply, lacked the charisma to spark the Bogart-Bacall-style romance.

Lancaster—billed third before the film's title—acquitted himself well in the essentially thankless "other man" role. Still, if *Desert Fury* had marked his screen debut as originally planned, it is unlikely that he would have achieved stardom quite so quickly. Not only did the film lack the stylish impact of *The Killers*, but so did the actor. Without the smoldering intensity of the Swede and his first picture's moody black-and-white photography, he appeared to be more of a regular fellow, and guy-next-door types rarely become overnight sensations.

All My Sons was a well-crafted morality play about war profiteering and its impact on one particular family, the fictitious Kellers. The drama opened on Broadway on January 29, 1947, thereby introducing theater-goers to Arthur Miller, one of the foremost American playwrights of the postwar era. It went on to win the New York Drama Critics' Circle Award for the Best Play of 1946/47; shortly thereafter, Universal producer–writer Chester Erskine announced that he would bring the drama to the screen.

Although Erskine was a director, he engaged Irving Reis to direct *All My Sons*. The "dark, intense young man," as one reporter described him, had served with George Stevens' photographic unit during World War II. He had directed two features since his return, including *The Bachelor and the Bobby-Soxer,* a comedy with Cary Grant, Myrna Loy, and Shirley Temple.

The leading character in *All My Sons,* originated by Ed Begley on Broadway, was Joe Keller, a manufacturer who knowingly ships defective airplane parts during World War II in order to meet his deadline, then lets his partner go to jail for his crime. The diminutive tough guy of the thirties' gangster pictures, Edward G. Robinson, won the demanding role for the film.

There was also an extremely good supporting part, that of Keller's son, Chris, played onstage by Arthur Kennedy. Lancaster wanted the role badly. "Why, it's a little like casting Boris Karloff as a baby-sitter," quipped Erskine initially. But Burt was undaunted. So far his film career had consisted of characters who had either been in jail, were just out of jail, or enjoyed putting people in jail. Chris—idealistic, in love, and independent, but a dutiful son—was his chance to show a completely different side of his persona. Wallis considered Burt unsuited for the role, but, as the actor said, "I was so eager to get the part that I pleaded lengthily and expensively . . . by transatlantic telephone to get his permission." In the end, money was the deciding factor. Universal agreed to pay $100,000 for Burt's services, with the lion's share of the income going to Hal Wallis Productions. Burt did win a major concession for himself, however. U-I agreed to finance his first independent project, *Kiss the Blood off My Hands.*

To play opposite Burt, Erskine chose Louisa Horton, whom he had caught in her Broadway debut, *The Voice of the Turtle,* and whom he tested for the role (with Burt) a mere week before *All My Sons* went before the cameras. *All My Sons* would be Horton's first film.

"The theme of the picture is the clash of moralities—the morality of the younger generation pitted against that of the older," said Reis at the start of filming. "Our problem is to present this theme without exaggeration—in terms of a simple, average American family in a typical American town." To represent this quintessential community, he chose Santa Rosa, California, about fifty miles north of San Francisco. It was there that shooting began on October 1, 1947.

The picture was shot in only forty-three days—an extremely tight schedule—eight of which were on location. Like the other principals, Burt put in long hours while in Santa Rosa. Still, he managed to find time to address the drama class at the local public high school.

On their sixth day in town, Burt and Louisa shot the sequence in which Chris tells Ann that he loves her. Tender, slightly awkward, and loving, Lancaster showed a genuine and endearing quality in the scene; it represented one of his best and most natural moments on film to date.

On October 9, the company wrapped in Santa Rosa and commenced shooting on the Universal lot the following day. Burt and the rest of the cast were invigorated by the material, and filming proceeded relatively smoothly. Nevertheless, an atmosphere of tension pervaded the set, stemming from events that were transpiring on the other end of the continent.

On September 27, the House Un-American Activities Committee, chaired by J. Parnell Thomas, subpoenaed thirty-four members of the Hollywood community to appear at hearings in Washington in October. Under investigation was the extent to which the motion picture industry had been infiltrated by communists and communist sympathizers. Edward G. Robinson was not summoned, but numerous publications had cited him as a member of communist front organizations, and he had every reason for concern. Most of the other leading members of the

All My Sons company, including Burt, were either at risk or outraged by the committee's actions, which was not surprising: *All My Sons* was a project with anticapitalist overtones, although Erskine's screenplay had considerably muted the leftist sentiments in Arthur Miller's play.

As the filming of *All My Sons* continued, directors William Wyler and John Huston and screenwriter Philip Dunne formed an organization called the Committee for the First Amendment, to oppose the HUAC hearings. When supportive members of the Hollywood community gathered at the home of Ira Gershwin to formulate a plan of action, Burt and Robinson were there, as were Judy Garland, Humphrey Bogart, Lauren Bacall, Gene Kelly, Danny Kaye, Billy Wilder, and, of course, Huston, Wyler, and Dunne.

On October 20, the HUAC hearings began, with several Hollywood luminaries present to register their opposition (the shooting of *All My Sons* precluded Lancaster's and Robinson's attendance). In the end, eleven subpoenaed witnesses were cited for contempt of Congress after they refused to divulge their political affiliations. One of them, German playwright Bertolt Brecht, left the country; the others became known as the Hollywood Ten.[3] A dark era, marked by blacklists and creative artists testifying against their associates, had begun. Lancaster, as we shall see, did not escape entirely unscathed. Moreover, his involvement with the Committee for the First Amendment marked the start of his long public commitment to liberal causes.

As the filming of *All My Sons* wound down, Norma neared the end of her pregnancy. Finally, on November 17, she gave birth to a boy at St. John's Hospital in Santa Monica. He weighed six pounds ten ounces and was named William, for Burt's deceased brother. On November 20, Lancaster took time off from shooting to bring his wife and son home from the hospital. The following day, he returned to the studio, and on November 24, five days behind schedule, *All My Sons* wrapped.

Less than a month later, on December 21, Mark Hellinger died. The producer was only forty-four years old, but he had lived precariously, driving himself relentlessly at the studio during the day, and, at night, drinking prodigious amounts of cognac, hanging out with friends, and getting by with minimal sleep.

3. The Hollywood Ten were Alvah Bessie, Herbert Biberman, Lester Cole, Edward Dmytryk, Ring Lardner Jr., John Howard Lawson, Albert Maltz, Samuel Ornitz, Adrian Scott, and Dalton Trumbo.

"He was quite a guy," Lancaster said years later. One can see Mark's influence on the actor. First, Hellinger had become an independent producer because he wanted to make movies his own way and be answerable only to himself. So did Burt. Hellinger was among the first to give directors, writers, and actors percentages of his pictures as incentives. Burt would employ that practice himself. Hellinger believed, as Lancaster did, that movies could carry messages, that they could inspire change, and he shared the actor's view of the industry's conservative nature in that regard. "Hollywood is gutless," Hellinger asserted just four days before his death. "You can't make an honest, forceful picture here. Hollywood is the whipping boy, the natural target for all kinds of pressure groups, and the industry does not stand up to them." That could have been Burt talking.

CHAPTER FIVE

"Just About the Most Wanted Guy in Hollywood"

On January 22, 1948, *I Walk Alone* premiered. In general, Kirk Douglas garnered positive notices, but Lancaster did not. *Newsweek* asserted that Burt was "tougher than he is convincing," and Bosley Crowther wrote, "Burt Lancaster plays the would-be 'muscler' with the blank-faced aplomb of Tarzan."

That Lancaster was still learning his craft was obvious. Most of the time, he simply had to smolder and seethe, but when the role—his largest on-screen to date—made the occasional emotional demand, as in the scene when he angrily tells Lizabeth Scott that he is an ex-con, he lacked the requisite subtlety and honesty. He was more effective in the quiet love scenes, and those with Wendell Corey as an old pal, moments that enabled him to tap into the vulnerable, gentle side that he had displayed so effectively as the Swede.

By the time *I Walk Alone* opened, Burt was immersed in his next project, Hal Wallis' *Sorry, Wrong Number,* which began filming on January 12.

Many moviegoers were already familiar with *Sorry, Wrong Number,* which had begun as a one-woman radio drama. In its original incarnation, writer Lucille Fletcher cleverly told a suspenseful story—about an invalid who increasingly fears that her husband is going to murder her—solely through telephone conversations. Agnes Moorehead had won glowing reviews in the role.

Anatole Litvak, who directed and coproduced the film version with Wallis, conceived of bringing the radio drama to the screen. Tola, as his friends called him, was a Russian émigré who had directed *Tovarich,*

Confessions of a Nazi Spy, and a string of other movies at Warners. He would earn an Oscar nomination for *The Snake Pit* the same year as *Sorry, Wrong Number.*

Litvak hired Fletcher to expand her own drama and worked closely with her on the transfer from the airwaves to the screen. After considering Jennifer Jones and Claudette Colbert for the spoiled, neurotic hypochondriac, Leona Stevenson, Tola and Wallis cast Barbara Stanwyck. It was a terrific opportunity, for the role allowed the actress to run the gamut from arrogance to abject terror. The husband, Henry Stevenson, a businessman corrupted by his wife's wealth, was far less skillfully drawn. Because the character was a moral weakling, Wallis had not considered Lancaster. But Burt, recognizing an opportunity to depart once again from his tough-guy image, campaigned aggressively for the role. He pointed out the value of starting with, as he put it, "a strong-looking boy on the threshold of life [who] allows a woman to buy him and then suffers for it [until] all of his character has been drained out of him." It was a convincing argument. With Burt on board, the role of the husband was expanded and flashbacks added to highlight his character's station and outlook before the marriage.

Short and stocky with brilliant blue eyes, Litvak eschewed extensive planning for each scene. "I let them [the actors] rehearse it and play the scene the way they want," he explained. For the longer, more difficult, or more important sequences, he then went home, considered what the actors had done, devised a shooting plan, and came back the following day to commit the work to film.

Litvak's methodology suited Lancaster. Before they started their collaboration, the director was aware of Burt's reputation for being difficult, but Litvak maintained that "there was no trouble with him at all" during the making of *Sorry, Wrong Number.* Richard McWhorter attributed the lack of fireworks to the energy Burt was diverting toward his own production, *Kiss the Blood off My Hands,* which was to go before the cameras when *Sorry, Wrong Number* wrapped. Another contributing factor may have been the actor's regard for his costar. "There was a great mutual admiration between Stanwyck and Burt," Walter Seltzer remembered. "They both liked each other and admired each other very much." But, ultimately, there was little in *Sorry, Wrong Number* for Burt to fret over. His role was relatively straightforward, and he did it well. Otherwise, it was really Stanwyck's picture. For twelve entire days of shooting, she was, in fact, the only actor on the set.

●　●　●

In mid-February, while *Sorry, Wrong Number* was in production,[1] Lancaster had to confront the unpleasant repercussions of Mark Hellinger's death.

Since May of 1946, when Hellinger acquired the film rights to *Criss Cross*, a 1934 potboiler by Don Tracy, the producer had been developing the property for Lancaster. He had engaged Anthony Veiller, who had coauthored *The Killers*, to write the screenplay with the idea of turning the story into the anatomy of a big heist. According to Burt, "He had an exciting *Rififi* approach to the whole thing."[2]

The property was still in development when Hellinger died. On February 19, 1948, the board of directors of his company, then called Mark Productions, Inc., voted to sell *Criss Cross* to Universal, along with two other properties, as a means of resolving its indebtedness to the studio. Its option for Lancaster's services for the picture was transferred to U-I as well. Concurrently, Burt was given the opportunity to buy his way out of the rest of his contract with Mark Productions for $25,000. He ultimately used his earnings from *Kiss the Blood off My Hands* to make the payment, indemnifying the Hellinger company in the meantime by taking out a life insurance policy for the equivalent amount and naming Mark Productions as the beneficiary.

The only problem was that Lancaster did not want to do *Criss Cross*. Without Mark's guiding hand, it had degenerated, he felt, into a routine gangster picture—and he was right. At first, the outraged directors of Hellinger's company informed him that he had to appear in the film and that a refusal would be considered a breach of contract. A day later, he was given several alternatives. He could accept a loan-out to MGM for a film called *Act of Violence*, if the Hellinger people were able to finalize the negotiations (they were not).[3] Or he could attempt to arrange another loan-out. If these efforts failed to produce a concrete offer by March 7, however, he would have to do *Criss Cross*.

Lancaster and Hecht came close to striking a deal with Fox for a film called *Down to the Sea in Ships*. They even got Wallis to adjust the timetable for his next Lancaster film, *Rope of Sand*, in order to accommodate the shooting schedule. But, at the last moment, the deal fell through.[4]

● ● ●

1. It wrapped on March 2, 1948.
2. Directed by Jules Dassin, *Rififi* was a gripping 1954 picture about a robbery, which critic–film historian Leonard Maltin has called the "granddaddy of all caper/heist movies."
3. Robert Ryan ended up playing the role in *Act of Violence*.
4. Lancaster's role in *Down to the Sea in Ships* went to Richard Widmark.

A week later, on March 15, 1948, Lancaster went to work on *Kiss the Blood off My Hands,* the premier project of his new company with Harold called Hecht-Norma Productions.

Independent productions were not new. In fact, they accounted for 20 percent of the most commercially successful films from the silent era to the late 1940s. Until the end of World War II, the field had been dominated by men like Wallis and Hellinger, capable producers who simply preferred to finance and nurture their own projects rather than work under contract for a major studio.

But the postwar years saw the emergence of a group that *Variety* called "semi-independents." Unlike the Selznicks, Goldwyns, Stanley Kramers, and Walter Wangers, these new producers did not underwrite their ventures themselves. Instead, they went to the major studios for financing. In return, the underwriter took a percentage of the film and a distribution fee. Moreover, most of the semi-independents were not career producers; they were actors, directors, and other creative artists.

Hecht-Norma was among the first of the semi-independents, along with the companies founded by James Cagney and Humphrey Bogart. By the end of the 1950s, thanks in part to the conspicuous success of Lancaster's company, which far outpaced those of either Cagney or Bogart, independents were everywhere. In 1959 alone, Columbia had contracts with twenty-eight such units, MGM had eleven, as did Paramount, and Fox had eight.

Many of those who opted for semi-independent status were attracted by the tax savings that such a corporate structure offered; instead of paying 75 or 80 percent of their earnings to the government, artists with their own production companies could remit a mere 25 percent or so by turning ordinary income into long-term capital gains. But others found that, even with the studio chiefs overseeing their efforts, they could exercise more creative control over their work than they were able to do otherwise. That relative freedom, not the tax savings, was the main attraction for Lancaster.

Kiss the Blood off My Hands came to Burt and Harold by way of Richard Vernon, a British producer who had acquired the novel of the same name by Gerald Butler. Formerly with the Rank Organization, Vernon served as the producer of *Kiss the Blood,* his first American venture.

Burt was cast as Bill Saunders, a Canadian merchant sailor whose incarceration in a Nazi prison camp during World War II left him with shattered nerves and a violent temper. After accidentally killing a man in a London pub, he takes refuge in the apartment of a nurse, Jane Wharton, with whom he eventually falls in love. To play the caring, lonely woman, Burt and Hecht selected Joan Fontaine, a stylish, sophisticated actress who had leaped to stardom in Alfred Hitchcock's first American film, *Rebecca*, in 1940 and won an Oscar a year later for the director's *Suspicion*. The third principal role, that of the villainous black marketeer Harry Carter, went to Robert Newton, who had recently played Bill Sykes in David Lean's *Oliver Twist*. To direct, the producers chose Norman Foster, once described as "a bouncy little guy who likes to think that Hollywood is not the hub of the universe." Foster had directed several of the Mr. Moto and Charlie Chan programmers of the 1930s and early 1940s.

Foster could have used several weeks of location shooting to do justice to the film's British setting, but in the late 1940s, such excursions were quite rare. Instead, a sizable percentage of *Kiss the Blood*'s $1.1 million budget went toward re-creating postwar London on Universal's sound stages. The center of activity was Stage 12, where 98 percent of the picture's interiors were shot. For some of the exteriors, the company journeyed to sites around Los Angeles, including the Griffith Park Zoo, but the street scenes were filmed on sets created by Nathan Juran. His clever design consisted of portable units that could be assembled and reassembled in different combinations to appear as a variety of locales.

Kiss the Blood went before the cameras without a completed script. It had been written by Ben Maddow and Walter Bernstein, but, according to screenwriter Leonardo Bercovicci, "it was more of a skeleton than it was a screenplay." The weekend before filming began, Bercovicci, who had known Hecht as an agent, agreed to do a rewrite. "So on Saturday and Sunday, I wrote two or three scenes," he recalled, which is what Foster filmed when production commenced. Thereafter, Bercovicci fed the company material until he completed the screenplay a few weeks later.

Bercovicci worked solely from the original screenplay; he never read the novel. There were striking differences between the two. Paramount among them was the treatment of Lancaster's character. In the book, Bill was an amoral thief and con artist. By turning him into a former prisoner of war with shattered nerves, the screenplay made him more sympathetic—and also gave the drama a touch of social relevance. Moreover, in Butler's version, Bill and Fontaine's character managed to flee the country after she commits a murder. The sensibilities of the film industry in the 1940s demanded that the lovers turn themselves in to face retribution for their crimes.

• • •

In addition to the script difficulties, several other problems hampered the shooting. The first had to do with Robert Newton. "He was hopelessly drunk," recalled Bercovicci. "Sometimes you had to wait it out. Sometimes he came very late. And sometimes he had to leave early." But the actor's prodigious talent was such that his alcoholism did not detract from his performance.

Then shortly before the start of production Fontaine discovered that she was pregnant, causing her to miss seven days of shooting during the first three weeks and to endure frequent bouts of morning sickness. Finally, about midway through the production, her condition stabilized. But, by then, Foster had to shoot her remaining scenes back-to-back in order to free her for her next assignment.

Burt established a professional, if not a warm, relationship with his costar, who was understandably distracted. According to Bercovicci, "there was no hostility [between them], but there wasn't any great camaraderie."

As a new producer, Lancaster had distractions of his own. "Instead of thinking only of how my performance was going," he said during filming, "as the cameras turned, I also thought of how the other actors were getting across. Then, between scenes, I worried about costly production delays.[5] Finally I came to the conclusion which other actor-producers have no doubt reached in time. I decided to let director Norman Foster and his staff do the worrying—and I would concentrate on performing. Otherwise, I'd have gone batty."

Lancaster drew on several older hands to help him find the persona of the moody, unbalanced former POW, the most complicated character that he had attempted so far. In addition to Foster, he had Thom Conroy, whom he engaged as the film's dialogue director, the first of many such assignments that he would arrange over the years for his old Army friend. Bercovicci helped as well. "I spent an enormous amount of time with Burt in the back room, rehearsing his part," the screenwriter recalled. "Burt at that point in his career needed help in projecting character. Dialogue wasn't easy for him in those days. His ear was far from perfect." But he was a hard worker. Diligence, in fact, was why so many of Lancaster's coworkers over the years found him aloof. "He's distant," said Bercovicci, "because when he has a job to do, he concentrates on it. And that's it."

Kiss the Blood wrapped on May 8.

• • •

---

5. Lancaster had good reason to worry. *Kiss the Blood* finished nine days behind schedule.

On March 27, while *Kiss the Blood* was in production, *All My Sons* premiered, earning Lancaster some of his best notices to date. Even *The New York Times'* Bosley Crowther, who had criticized a number of the actor's previous performances, asserted, "Burt Lancaster is surprisingly good."

And he was right. With Irving Reis' help, Burt worked in a simpler and cleaner fashion in *All My Sons* than ever before, building on the uncluttered style that he had found in *Brute Force* to project a decent, affable, ordinary guy. If anything, he underplayed some of the film's most dramatic moments, as in the prison scene when his father's partner tells him how the defective parts came to be shipped.

The picture as a whole drew mixed reviews. Edwin Schallert of the *Los Angeles Times* found it "more direct and compact [than the play] and gains on that account. The characters are also more vividly etched." But the New York *Herald Tribune's* Howard Barnes asserted that "Miller wrote a scattered play, in which stern truths were badly mixed up with plot contrivances. Chester Erskine has not improved matters a whit in his adaptation." Audiences were not drawn to the depressing drama, which became the first box-office failure of Lancaster's career. Burt did not regret the assignment, however. "I believed in the picture," he said later. "I've never been sorry. I'd still be the same punk kid I used to be back home in the Depression if I was afraid to take a chance."

On June 13, after more than a month to himself, Burt started work on *Criss Cross*—which reunited him with the director of *The Killers*, Robert Siodmak. In the intervening years, the German refugee had directed three films, *Time Out of Mind, Dark Mirror,* and *Cry of the City,* none of which measured up to *The Killers* or *The Spiral Staircase.* Nor would *Criss Cross,* where the idea of a decent guy (Lancaster) falling in with a group of crooks to pull off a big heist out of love for the wrong woman seemed all too familiar to anyone who had seen the earlier Siodmak-Lancaster collaboration.

The role of Anna, the femme fatale, went to Yvonne De Carlo. She was under contract to Universal, as were Siodmak and the other principal members of the company—Dan Duryea, Stephen McNally, and Richard Long. Another studio player, a newcomer, made his debut in the film. He had only one scene, in which he danced with De Carlo, but he made an impression. His name was Tony Curtis.

Lancaster developed a fondness for the kid who, like him, grew up poor on Manhattan's mean streets under the purview of a domineering mother. "We became really fast friends," Curtis recalled. Perhaps the best evidence of this was the way Lancaster made Tony the butt of his practical jokes. Once, Burt sent him off to find a left-handed can of film. On another occasion, he and some other fellows soaked Curtis' towel with eucalyptus oil, and as they were sweating it out in the steam room and talking about a cheap whore they'd set Tony up with, the heat from the towel on Curtis' sexual organ convinced him that the lady had given him the clap. But the best joke came when Burt and Howard Duff sneaked into Curtis' apartment one day while Tony was at the studio. They took all of his belongings out of the room and then changed the locks on the door. Curtis got home and could not figure out what had happened. "I was going crazy until I went to the studio and saw Burt laughing," he wrote in his autobiography.

Criss Cross was shot in a brisk thirty-nine days (on a thirty-four-day schedule). Six days were devoted to filming in various locales around the older, unglamorous sections of Los Angeles, the transplanted locale from the novel's Baltimore. But most of the work took place at the studio, where Universal employed the same approach that had proved so efficient with *Kiss the Blood.* In the case of *Criss Cross,* about 85 percent of the interiors were contained within a single soundstage, and as with the previous picture, quick setups and easy scheduling changes resulted from the proximity of the various sets.

Although the production wrapped on July 28, five days later than scheduled, *Criss Cross* appears to have been a very smooth shoot. On many days, Siodmak was able to film three or four pages, which was quite good, and his working relationship with Burt proceeded without major incident. "He's just the same—except a better actor," asserted the director, recalling their previous work on *The Killers.* "He still fights me when he doesn't want to do a scene as I outline it. But he did that before too, when he knew nothing about pictures. You have to give him a reason for everything. Once you do, he's easy to direct."

After *Criss Cross,* Lancaster would have five and a half months—until January 17, 1949—to pursue a variety of personal and professional endeavors.

The first of these took place while *Criss Cross* was still in production. On July 14, Burt moved his family from the rented house in Westwood to a home of his own in Bel-Air. He was thirty-four, and it was the first house he had ever owned.

Located north of Westwood, just past Sunset Boulevard, Bel-Air, with its steep slopes and plunging valleys, offered the twin benefits of seclusion and rusticity and attracted many members of the film industry. It was a far cry from the crowded urban streets of Lancaster's youth.

Burt's new home was a large, two-story, $150,000 American colonial of wood and stone, set atop a hill at 830 Linda Flora Drive. It was only modestly furnished when the Lancasters moved in; Norma wanted to wait until *Criss Cross* wrapped to start decorating, so that her husband could participate.

In 1948, the household included the two boys, Jimmy and Billy (Norma would become pregnant with the Lancasters' third child in November), as well as Burt's father, who had moved to California the previous year to live with his son. Sister-in-law Julia, William's widow, lived there too. She handled Burt's fan mail.

Over the next decade, Burt would add to the home and the grounds, installing at various times a swimming pool, a tennis court, a guest bungalow, a film-projection room, a gym, a kennel, and a baseball diamond for the kids. He also began collecting art, mostly modern French masters. By August of 1961, the house had twelve rooms, and the property was valued at $300,000.

According to Julian Ullman, a Warners projectionist who ran films for the family, the kitchen was the main gathering place. This was also the domain of the maids: Alberta, who had accompanied the Lancasters from Westwood, and Adele, who joined the family in mid-1951, after the arrival of the Lancasters' fourth child, Joanna.

But Burt spent much of the summer of 1948 at Universal, shepherding *Kiss the Blood off My Hands* through postproduction. A major focus of attention was the film's title, which had been rejected by the Motion Picture Association of America before filming began. Lancaster, Hecht, and U-I had fought to retain the name in order to tie the film to the success of the novel. They won, but then, inexplicably, they tried other, less graphic alternatives—*Blood on My Hands* and *Blood on the Moon*—before settling on *The Unafraid.* It was with this essentially meaningless title that the movie previewed on August 11 in Inglewood and the twelfth in Studio City. Complaints from several members of the audience fostered a return to the original title on the thirteenth.

Two weeks later, on September 1, *Sorry, Wrong Number* opened. Although Howard Barnes of the New York *Herald Tribune* found it "a surprisingly effective film," a number of his colleagues felt that the impact of the original radio drama had been dissipated by the feature-length extension. There was no argument about Stanwyck's performance, however; it earned her an Oscar nomination.

Billed alongside Stanwyck, Lancaster enjoyed every bit as much screen time as his costar, but to less dramatic effect. If his role lacked equivalent emotive power, he nonetheless endowed it with the same simple conviction that had marked his work in *Brute Force* and *All My Sons.* Overall, he created not so much a man who is weak as one who is trapped—between his obligation toward his sick wife, whom he may even love on some level, and her father's ability to keep him ensconced in a meaningless job. After praising his work in *All My Sons, The New York Times'* Bosley Crowther considered Lancaster's latest performance "painfully obtuse," but on the whole, Burt earned high critical marks. Moreover, the picture became an unqualified hit, ending up as the year's twenty-fifth-highest box-office draw.

At the end of September, Burt, Norma, and the Hechts took the train to New York to promote *Kiss the Blood,* which opened on October 30— less than two months after the release of *Sorry, Wrong Number.* The ads blazed with "A Hunted Man! A Love-Haunted Woman! Caught! With Every Kiss More Reckless, More Dangerous Than the Last," but the critics perceptively noted that the film was really, to quote *Cue,* "a somber, penetrating study of two lost souls in the confusion of the postwar era." Indeed, it was the unusual attention to character development that elevated it above the typical B-movie crime melodrama. Virtually all of the reviews commented on the title, which *Time* called "dismal," but generally the picture, director Norman Foster, and the three stars drew considerable praise.

Burt relied on his usual tough-guy manner to convey Bill Saunders' animalistic side, while trusting his innate vulnerability and underlying sweetness to redeem the character. Fontaine's poise and polish contrasted nicely with his rough edges, her light color and grace counterbalancing his dark heaviness, and the chemistry between them made the romance work.

In retrospect, however, it was the film's exciting opening sequence that truly distinguished Lancaster's performance. Chased by a bobby through Juran's elaborate re-creation of London, he ran through alleyways, scaled walls, and even performed a bit of gymnastics on some construction scaffolding, thereby hinting at the athleticism that would become a much greater part of his 1950s persona.

● ● ●

"Burt is never a quick friend," said director-screenwriter Richard Brooks. "But he is a lasting one." In the late fall of 1948, the actor's thoughts turned toward his old circus partner. "I want to do something for Nick," he said in September. "I owe him plenty."

Thus, on November 18, Lancaster and Cravat revived their old vaudeville act at the Oriental Theater in Chicago—at $10,000 a week, an impressive sum reflecting Burt's stardom after less than two years in the movies. The routine lasted about twenty minutes. Also on the bill were two singers, Julie Wilson and Charlene Harris, and Bob Hall, a "comic rhymester." The act moved on to the Riverside Theater in Milwaukee and finally opened at the Capitol in New York on December 23.

While Burt was in Manhattan, Wallis notified Hecht that the actor was expected to report for rehearsals and wardrobe fittings for *Rope of Sand* on January 3. This created a minor crisis, as Burt and Nick were booked in New York until mid-January. Wallis, having already accommodated the schedules of *Kiss the Blood* and the aborted *Down to the Sea in Ships,* once again adjusted his plans to suit his star, postponing the start of production until January 17.

"I read an item about a town in southwest Africa where you can't get in or out without permission," said Walter Doniger. "It's the center of the diamond-mining area, where diamonds are found on the ground. I thought it would make a wonderful picture, so I wrote a script about it."

The screenwriter imagined *Rope of Sand* as a reunion vehicle for Humphrey Bogart and Ingrid Bergman. Instead, he got their *Casablanca* costars Paul Henreid, Claude Rains, and Peter Lorre. But, in the leads, Hal Wallis, who had acquired the property, cast Lancaster and Corinne Calvet.

Sometimes it seemed that Lancaster and Wallis took turns talking each other into projects. For every *I Walk Alone* that the producer convinced Burt to do, there was an *All My Sons* for which the actor had to fight. With *Rope of Sand,* it was Wallis' turn. "When I think of my least favorite [picture]," Burt said in 1984, "I think of . . . *Rope of Sand.* . . . I did that thing under great duress. I hated it." He was unhappy, at least in part, because he had gotten Wallis to agree to involve him in the developmental stages of their projects, but the producer did not consult him as Doniger and another screenwriter, John Paxton, labored away at their separate rewrites.[6]

6. Paxton, the author of such hard-hitting screenplays as *Farewell, My Lovely, Crack-Up,* and *Crossfire,* ended up getting credit for additional dialogue. The screenplay was attributed solely to Doniger.

Burt was to play Mike Davis, a hunter who has discovered a hidden cache of diamonds in the mining area controlled by the charming but ruthless Fred Martingale (Rains) and his sadistic underling, district commandant Paul Vogel (Henreid). Martingale hires a beautiful French con artist, Suzanne Renault, to find out where the gems are located, but of course she falls in love with Mike. According to Doniger, Wallis cast Calvet as Suzanne because he "thought he could make a star out of her, and he could get her a lot cheaper than Bergman."

The stunning Parisian actress, touted as the new Rita Hayworth, had been brought to America in 1947 for a film at Paramount, but when her English proved inadequate, she was replaced. After studying the language for two years, she was ready to make her American debut in *Rope of Sand.*

Nervous and eager to do well, she had a hard time communicating with the film's director, William Dieterle, whom she likened to Hitler. Others thought more highly of him. "William Dieterle was to me the most talented director that Wallis ever had," maintained assistant director Richard McWhorter. Henreid too held Dieterle in high regard, describing him as "not only a great director, but a respected one" with "considerable clout." Indeed, the fifty-five-year-old German émigré had such acclaimed Warners biopics as *The Life of Emile Zola, The Story of Louis Pasteur, Juarez,* and *Dr. Ehrlich's Magic Bullet* to his credit.

But Dieterle was as eccentric as he was talented. He always wore white gloves, and because he was a devout believer in astrology, he arranged his shooting schedules to suit the alignment of the stars. He also had a thick accent, which Calvet found impossible to understand. Although she considered Burt "reserved" and found it "hard to talk to him between scenes," she reached out to him. "Would you be kind enough to direct me?" she asked. He did. "The success that came to me in that picture can be attributed to Burt Lancaster's guidance," Calvet later asserted. "He gave me confidence."

One day, however, she was beyond help. She and Burt were shooting a love scene when, as she put it, "I began to perspire. I felt nauseous. Suddenly the food I had eaten that day started to churn in my stomach." She got through one take. "But," she confessed, "to my everlasting humiliation, in the middle of the second take, my stomach turned and I threw up, all over Burt Lancaster." She apologized and quickly left the set, not to return for the rest of the day. "No one ever mentioned the incident again," she wrote. "When we got around to shooting the scene that had embarrassed me, Burt Lancaster was very kind to me, and it was in earnest that I put my cheek on his skin and willed love and devotion to appear on my face."

• • •

When Lancaster was not coaching Calvet, he was busy arguing with Doniger. "Burt and I used to fight over the script all the time," the screenwriter recalled. "He would want to change lines and I would say, 'No,' and Wallis would side with me." On one such occasion, Doniger told Lancaster, "Don't you talk to me about the script. I saw *Kiss the Blood off My Hands.*" The screenwriter laughed. "I was a cocky kid. He liked me because I was defiant."

For the desert scenes, the company traveled to Yuma, Arizona. "The sand dunes were so wide, tall, and virginal that it was easy to imagine that we were indeed in Africa," wrote Calvet. Bad weather caused near-disastrous production delays, but McWhorter credited Dieterle's efficiency and vision with enabling the company to get the required footage in the requisite time. The climax of the picture, the fight between Burt and Henreid, was fought in a raging sandstorm. "It was ghastly work," wrote Henreid in his autobiography. "Our eyes and mouths would fill with sand, and they had to stop shooting constantly to let us clean them out. They even flew in a doctor from Los Angeles to wash out our eyes for us. But after all these heroics they got back to the studio and discovered that the sandstorm didn't photograph properly. The winds were too fast for the camera, and the sand too fine to register. To solve this, they trucked a mess of sand into the studio and reshot all the close-up scenes there, using a wind machine!"

On March 12, four days before *Rope of Sand* wrapped, *Criss Cross* premiered.

It would be unfair to say that Burt walked through his role, but clearly playing the nice, not too bright armored-car guard made no demand on his talent. As James S. Barstow of the New York *Herald Tribune* wrote, "Lancaster is almost forced into a parody of his previous dumb-brute portrayals in the Daniel Fuchs script."

One can see why he did not want to do the film. Although the location work produced some wonderfully atmospheric glimpses of late-1940s Los Angeles—nicely photographed in black and white by Franz Planer—the screenplay was, to quote Thomas M. Pryor of *The New York Times,* "verbose, redundant, and imitative."

The casting was not much better. Third-billed Dan Duryea lacked menace—or even much interest—as the villain, but worse, there was something wanting in the Lancaster–De Carlo matchup. Despite—or perhaps because of—what had once transpired between the costars in real life, there was an absence of magic between them on the screen.

• • •

After finishing *Rope of Sand,* Lancaster went to New York, where he found theatergoers buzzing about the success of *South Pacific,* the brand-new Rodgers and Hammerstein musical. Despite the clamor for tickets, he was able to secure two good seats for the second night's performance. Norma, six months pregnant, was back in Los Angeles, so, when he ran into Shelley Winters at their hotel, the Gotham, he asked her to join him. Although she had her own ticket for *South Pacific* that night, she accepted. "As I got into his limousine," she wrote in her 1980 autobiography, "I reminded myself this beautiful man was very married, but I quickly brushed the thought from my mind. After all, I was only going to the theatre with a fellow actor from U-I."

After the show, Burt and Shelley drove through Central Park and then dined at Le Pavillon. Clearly, they were strongly attracted to one another. Later, Burt invited her to his room to listen to opera records. "I don't know quite how it happened," she wrote, "but all I remember is being on a blue and white bedspread on a thick white rug on the living-room floor and Burt didn't have any clothes on and he was gorgeous and I didn't have any clothes on and I felt gorgeous and now Gigli was singing 'O Paradiso' on the phonograph."

The next morning they breakfasted together while Burt talked about his marital difficulties, which he blamed on his involvement with his career. Winters was certain that he was not about to leave his wife and family, but "on that lovely spring morning," she recalled, "I put all voices and doubts behind me and gloried in the fact that my Mr. Right had arrived."

Shortly thereafter, "Mr. Right" left for Louisville, Kentucky, and an engagement with the Cole Brothers Circus, for which he and Nick were earning $11,000 a week—"one of the highest sums ever paid a circus performer," proclaimed *Variety.* Cole Brothers was the second-largest circus in the country; it moved from engagement to engagement by train. Lancaster was given his own private railroad car, which, in his words, was "all fixed up with sixty-five thousand dollars' worth of furnishings; woodwork carvings, staterooms, [and] colored chef." He used it for three days, then borrowed the manager's car and drove from one venue to another. "Instead of being shuttled around on sidings half the night," he recalled, "I had a nice comfortable hotel room, time to eat dinner and take a walk or see a picture if I wanted to."

At each performance, Burt entered the tented arena in a convertible, circled the playing area so that everyone could get a good look at him, and then made a few remarks from the center ring. He concluded by asking if the audience would like to see him perform, and following the inevitable affirmative reply, he and Nick went into their horizontal-bar routine, which lasted about eight minutes.

After the opening in Louisville, Lancaster and Cravat toured with the circus through Illinois, Indiana, Ohio, and Pennsylvania.

When the tour ended, Lancaster returned home and resumed his affair with Winters. At the time, she was living with her parents, which put a crimp in the relationship, especially since her folks disapproved of the affair. In time, Burt found her a penthouse apartment, but in the meantime, they made do with Winters' dressing room at U-I, and Burt's at Paramount.

Reading *Shelley, Also Known as Shirley,* one is left with little doubt about Winters' love for Lancaster. But how did he feel about her? It is widely held among Burt's associates that he frequently indulged in extramarital affairs during his marriage to Norma, most of which were of little consequence and of short duration. He loved his wife, but she had developed a drinking problem, and their marriage was never a storybook relationship, although it was depicted as such for years in the press. Still, Jackie Bone, his longtime companion later in life, maintained that he was more serious about Shelley than he was about most of his conquests. She also said, "Burt is a family man, he always was. He loved his mom and dad and his family life." So, he must have been terribly conflicted over the affair, especially after Norma gave birth to their third child, Susan, on July 5, 1949, at St. John's Hospital in Santa Monica.

On August 4, *Rope of Sand* opened. Burt's antipathy toward the project notwithstanding, it proved to be a stylish tale of adventure and a deadly game of one-upmanship between Lancaster, Rains, and Henreid, with the cache of diamonds—and ultimately Calvet—as the prizes. As Ruth Waterbury of the Los Angeles *Herald Examiner* put it, "So slick and smart is the original story and clever screenplay by Walter Doniger that it's as tense and holding a melodrama as ever chattered your teeth."

Lancaster, seen in a purely heroic good-guy role for the first time, gave a workmanlike performance, but his lack of inspiration showed—especially when compared to the zest that Henreid invested in the viscous, social-climbing commandant and Claude Rains' delight in the suave, amoral diamond-company director.

Rope of Sand ranked thirty-third among the year's biggest hits, second to *Sorry, Wrong Number* as Lancaster's most popular film to date.

• • •

The summer of 1949 offered a welcome distraction from the turmoil of Burt's love life—he had to prepare for his company's next project, known at the time as *The Hawk and the Arrow* (and released as *The Flame and the Arrow*).

After the modest success of *Kiss the Blood off My Hands,* Lancaster and Hecht had established a new coproduction arrangement with Warner Bros. Announced in March, just as Burt was finishing up *Rope of Sand,* the deal called for Hecht-Norma to produce six films for the studio over an indefinite time. Each picture was to have a budget of $1.1 million, the same as *Kiss the Blood,* and Burt was to star in all of them. The actor also agreed to appear in three of the studio's own productions (this was later reduced to two).

The Burbank home of Cagney, Bogart, Raft, and Robinson expected Lancaster to continue the tradition of crime melodramas that had formed the core of his film work to date. But, as Burt said many years later, "I was anxious to get into something different." What he and Harold chose was a swashbuckler, bringing derring-do back to the studio that had produced *Captain Blood* and *The Adventures of Robin Hood.* Hecht, having learned the ropes on *Kiss the Blood,* would coproduce the new picture, with Frank Ross, an independent producer whose credits included several films starring his then-wife, Jean Arthur.

The original screenplay about a hearty outlaw band's rebellion against the Hessians in twelfth-century Lombardy was written by Waldo Salt, a former college professor who turned to screenwriting in the late 1930s. One of Salt's inspired elements was the sidekick he created for Lancaster's mountaineer Dardo—a blacksmith by the name of Piccolo. Hecht and Lancaster decided to cast Nick Cravat in the role, so that Burt's former circus partner could assist with the many acrobatic stunts they were building into the film. Salt and members of the production team met for hours with the feisty acrobat in order to fashion the character to Nick's personality. Because he had no flair for dialogue, Piccolo became a mute.

Then, Nick and Burt got into one of their typical arguments, and the pint-size acrobat refused to do the role.

"You're just afraid to act," Burt asserted.

"That made me mad," Nick recalled, "so I did it, and I stayed mad all the way through the picture just to prove I could do it."

Filming began on September 26, 1949. Although the company would shoot some of the picture's forest sequences in Bronson Canyon and on the Corrigan Ranch, the vast majority of the work took place at Warners' Burbank studio. The massive sets included numerous castle interiors, some of which were borrowed from *The Adventures of Don Juan* and *The Adventures of Robin Hood*. Meanwhile the backlot was transformed into a large medieval town square. "To walk onto those sets, with all those extras, was an extraordinary experience," maintained Robert Douglas, cast as the dashing but traitorous nobleman Alessandro. "I had never seen sets like that on a stage."

Lancaster worked hard to get ready for the picture. As Cravat recalled, "We did roadwork every morning. We had to take up fencing and archery, and we had to practice climbing ropes until we had calluses as big as strawberries." That was not all. "I even had to take a few diction lessons from the professor of speech at the University of Southern California," Lancaster said. "I had played so many tough-guy roles that I was biting off my words and even talking out of the corner of my mouth."

Burt continued to exercise and train during the twelve weeks of shooting. He had to. His feats before the camera included a tightrope walk more than forty feet in the air and a re-creation of his old perchpole act with Nick (which ends with Dardo crowing to Piccolo, "I always said we should have been acrobats," a charming inside joke). The finale of the picture required him to do a joyous series of flips and somersaults along a scaffolding lined with flaming torches, a stunt so demanding that it was saved until the very end of shooting. Then, on December 17, after all of the other scenes had been filmed, the production shut down so that Burt and Nick could specifically train for and rehearse the sequence. It was slated for filming ten days later, but with injuries and poor weather, it did not go before the cameras until January 17 and 18. Kirk Douglas, who was present at the time, jokingly asked Lancaster to be his stunt double on his next film. Not surprisingly, Warners took out a $750,000 life insurance policy on Lancaster for the production.

Burt's costar, Virginia Mayo, had her own problems. Her gowns were so stifling under the heat of the arc lights that a low-pressure air hose was inserted in the back of her dress between takes.

The blond, twenty-nine-year-old Warners contract player enjoyed working with Lancaster but was amused by his intensity. One day, when they were doing a love scene, his energy got the better of him. "It was pretty forceful, that kiss," she said, laughing. "Oh my, it was wild. He nearly broke my teeth."

Robert Douglas was also impressed by Burt. "He had great charm," recalled the British actor. "He was wonderful with the crew. He was wonderful with the people he was working with." Douglas, who was a veteran of the London stage as well as Warners' *The Adventures of Don*

Juan, was also impressed by Lancaster's ability to orchestrate bits of business for the camera—including the wrestling moves that marked his own character's introduction to Dardo.

Although Douglas found Lancaster "wonderful" with the crew, the film's director, Jacques Tourneur, best known for the subtle 1942 horror classic *The Cat People,* walked off the set one day because, as he put it, "Burt had been incredibly rude to a technician, for no apparent reason. . . . I told him that if it happened again, I would walk off the picture for good, and he was very kind from then on."

The production wrapped in mid-January, twelve days over schedule. By then, a new decade had begun.

Ten years earlier, Burt Lancaster had been a circus acrobat with a bad right hand. He had had no direction, and his prospects were few. By 1950, he was a movie star—famous, loved, and rich. "Hollywood can remember few comets that have shot into brilliance as suddenly or have flamed as brightly as has Burt Lancaster," wrote Pete Martin in *The Saturday Evening Post.* Columnist Earl Wilson noted that when Burt played the Capitol with Nick Cravat at the end of 1948, "the young girls screamed for him just as they did for Sinatra." And, a month later, in January of 1949, Elizabeth Wilson wrote in *Liberty,* "All the ambitious feminine stars want him for their next picture. . . . 'The big brawny bird,' as Hellinger once called him affectionately, is just about the most wanted guy in Hollywood." And no wonder. His name on a marquee meant an additional $1 million in revenues for the picture playing inside. At a time when the highest-grossing movie of the year typically took in $4 to $5 million, that kind of earning power was impressive.

But, even as his star rose high in the Hollywood pantheon, he remained fixed on his ultimate objective. He wanted to be a director.

CHAPTER SIX

At Fox, MGM, Warners, and Columbia

Edward Mueller's story was perfect for Hollywood. For ten years, the elderly ex-janitor had maintained a counterfeiting operation on the Upper West Side of Manhattan without being captured by the Secret Service—despite poor engravings, the use of plain bond paper, and amateurish printing. That Mueller was something less than a master criminal was evidenced by his failure to expend his talent, limited though it was, on hundred-dollar bills or even twenties. He printed singles, about $40 a month, just enough to keep himself and his dog off the public dole.

In 1950, two years after Mueller's arrest, he was profiled in a series of *New Yorker* articles by St. Clair McKelway. Obtaining the film rights, 20th Century–Fox dubbed the project *Mister 880,* the name assigned to the case by the Treasury Department before Mueller was apprehended.

For the title role, Fox producer Julian Blaustein cast seventy-four-year-old character actor Edmund Gwenn, who had won an Academy Award as Best Supporting Actor for his delightful Kris Kringle in 1947's *Miracle on 34th Street.* To play Steve Buchanan, the fictitious Secret Service agent who finally nabs the old man, Blaustein wanted Lancaster. Burt encouraged Hal Wallis to agree to the loan-out.

Blaustein was eager to sign Lancaster because on its way to the screen, Mueller's story had become subordinate to that of the Secret Service agent. By focusing on the Treasury Department's investigation, screenwriter Robert Riskin had been able to, in his words, "goose the whole project by making a chase out of it." The result had a slightly Capraesque quality, not surprising since Riskin had written the screenplays for five of the director's pictures, including *It Happened One Night, Lost Horizon,* and *Mr. Deeds Goes to Town.*

Lancaster's love interest in the film was Fox contract player Dorothy McGuire, the petite thirty-one-year-old who had starred in *A Tree Grows in Brooklyn, The Spiral Staircase,* and *Gentleman's Agreement.* The costars did not know one another prior to the start of production on April 3, 1950, but they soon formed a solid friendship. As they lunched together at the studio commissary, discussing their lives, their families, and their careers, McGuire found Burt to be a captivating storyteller and was impressed by what she called his "remarkable sense of evaluation, not only of other people and events, but of himself." Adding to the joie de vivre was director Edmund Goulding, once described as a "husky, genial extrovert who sports screaming color combinations and cracks wise in stentorian tones slightly touched with British." Goulding's impressive list of credits included *Grand Hotel,* several of Bette Davis' best pictures—*Dark Victory, The Old Maid,* and *The Great Lie*—and McGuire's debut film, *Claudia.* Burt also came to admire Fox's often combative studio chief, Darryl F. Zanuck. Every day during shooting, the actor recalled the bantam mogul would "send down a memo about the previous day's rushes, and it contained the most brilliant analysis of what was wrong and what was right, about what had to be done."

Only one incident marred the production: during filming, Burt broke a finger in his left hand by catching it in the spokes of a steering wheel; incredibly, he had never broken a bone before. The injury did not delay production, however, and *Mister 880* wrapped on May 18. Eleven days later, Burt walked through the gates at Metro-Goldwyn-Mayer for his first film with the biggest studio of them all.

Vengeance Valley was Lancaster's first Western. To obtain his services, Metro paid Wallis $150,000 for eight weeks of filming and gave Hal the right to borrow one of its stars for a picture of his own. Thanks to such loan-outs, as well as Burt's commitments to his own production company, the actor would go virtually three years without working in a Hal B. Wallis production, an extraordinarily long time for someone under contract to a producer.

Vengeance Valley, a remarkably faithful adaptation of the novel by Luke Short, was a spin on the story of Cain and Abel. Burt was cast as Owen Daybright, the honest, hardworking ramrod of the Strobie ranch and the adopted son of its owner, Arch Strobie (Ray Collins). His foster brother, Lee Strobie, a wastrel, a cheat, and a liar, was played by Robert Walker—in a departure from Walker's usual boy-next-door roles. For the girl caught between them, Lee's wife, Jen, the studio chose Joanne Dru, a veteran of such notable Westerns as *Red River, She Wore a Yellow Ribbon,* and *Wagon Master.*

With Lee getting a girl pregnant, Owen romantically drawn to Jen, and the two stepbrothers vying for the future of the ranch, *Vengeance Valley* was as much a soap opera as it was a horse opera. But MGM contract director Richard Thorpe made sure that Western aficionados were not disappointed with the result. The fifty-four-year-old director, a quiet, easygoing man, was no stranger to the genre, with *20 Mule Team, Apache Trail,* and *Wyoming* among his credits.

Particularly outstanding were *Vengeance Valley*'s portrait of cowboy life at roundup time and its breathtaking vistas of the American West, the result of the company's location shooting in the Colorado Rockies. There were also several exciting fistfights. Hugh O'Brian, who played one of the villainous gunslingers in the film, gave Lancaster some of the credit for the success of those sequences, saying, Burt "didn't just sit in his chair and wait until everything was worked out and then say, 'I don't like that.' He worked very closely with the stuntmen."

O'Brian, then a virtual newcomer to films, was impressed with the way the star conducted himself: "Burt didn't demand it, but he got tremendous respect on the set. He handled himself extremely well. I mean, he had great respect for the crew, he knew his words, and he came in with very much a point of view." Lancaster's example would inspire O'Brian a few years later when he became the star of TV's *The Life and Legend of Wyatt Earp.*

Before *Vengeance Valley* went into production, Burt had arranged a leave of absence during the last half of July 1950 so that he and Nick could promote *The Flame and the Arrow.* Starting in Chicago on July 15—simultaneous with the film's release—they appeared in thirteen cities in twelve days.

The promotional campaign was orchestrated around the fact that Lancaster had done all of his stunts in the picture. To dramatize the issue, Warner Bros. offered $1 million to anyone who could prove that Lancaster did not execute Dardo's feats of derring-do. And to drive the point home, Burt and Nick displayed their acrobatic skills at many of the venues on the junket. In Chicago, for example, they re-created their perch-pole act at the intersection of State and Randolph in the Loop. In Cleveland, Burt could be seen atop the perch pole outside the Cleveland Press Building, answering the questions of a radio interviewer through an open window—while Cravat balanced the pole on his head in the street below.

The tour was wildly successful, as was the Technicolor production, which became the twelfth most popular picture of the year—and Burt's biggest hit to date.

The swashbuckler also marked a major turning point in Lancaster's career, for prior to *The Flame and the Arrow,* the cornerstones of his persona had included a deliberateness of movement, a slowness of speech, and a tough exterior masking the vulnerable, misunderstood man beneath. Above all, there was control; his characters held tight reins on their thoughts, their actions, and their emotions. But with *The Flame and the Arrow,* he reinvented himself. Instead of being methodical, he was expansive; instead of brooding, he was ebullient; instead of moving heavily and speaking slowly, he became light and graceful and lilting.

Remarkably, however, the picture's popularity did not inspire him to replace the old persona with the new. Nor did he blend the two. Rather, he kept them side by side, like twin books on a shelf, within easy reach as the occasion demanded. In the decades to come, the man of control would find expression in such films as *Sweet Smell of Success, Birdman of Alcatraz, The Leopard,* and *On Wings of Eagles,* while the expansive extrovert would extend from *The Crimson Pirate* to *Vera Cruz* to *Elmer Gantry* to *Cattle Annie and Little Britches.* It is difficult to think of any other major movie star who managed to sustain two personas as Lancaster did so consistently and so well and for so long, being recognized and appreciated by the public for both.

After the *Flame and the Arrow* promotional tour ended on July 29, Lancaster returned to MGM, finishing *Vengeance Valley* on August 9. In the meantime, Jules Garrison, an employee of the Los Angeles Water and Power Department, came forward to claim the $1 million offered by Warners in conjunction with *The Flame and the Arrow.* Garrison, who had worked as an extra during shooting, claimed that actor Don Turner was, in fact, responsible for Lancaster's stunt work. After Warner refused to pay the reward, he filed suit.

It took until July of 1953 for the case to come to trial—at which point the defense argued that Turner had doubled for Lancaster on only three minor occasions. Further, Jack and Harry Warner contended that the offer was invalid because it had never been approved by the studio's board of directors. Judge Ben Harrison, clearly disgusted by the whole matter, dismissed Garrison's claim.

• • •

Nine days after *Vengeance Valley* wrapped, Burt started work on *Jim Thorpe—All American*. It was the first film that he did for Warner Bros. under his quid-pro-quo agreement with the studio for backing his own projects.

James Francis Thorpe was arguably the best all-around athlete America has ever produced. Born in a one-room cabin in Prague, Oklahoma, in 1888, "Bright Path," as he was known by his tribe, the Sac and Fox, became an all-American football player at the Carlisle Indian School in Pennsylvania and a two-time Olympic gold medalist—for the pentathlon and the decathlon—at the 1912 games in Stockholm. (He was subsequently stripped of his medals because he had briefly played semiprofessional baseball while in college.[1]) Thorpe went on to careers as both a major league baseball player and a player-coach in the newly established professional football league. Off the field, he was not as successful, marrying three times and drifting through a series of odd jobs after retiring from sports.

Lancaster was perfect for the role. Walter Seltzer, who recalled taking him on a round of sporting activities for a forties magazine spread, asserted, "There wasn't anything physical that he couldn't do." Moreover, Burt had the hard edge the role required. Thorpe's alcoholism, his sullen disposition, his failed marriages, and his near-indigence in middle age were not the stuff of a typical Hollywood biography, but to their credit, screenwriters Douglas Morrow and Everett Freeman did little to soften the character's nature nor did they completely avoid his decline during his postathletic years.

Of course, Burt was not a Native American, but that was of no concern during the fifties; protests against actors taking roles outside their own racial groups were decades away. Moreover, as Burt saw the role, his race was less important than his character. "Thorpe had his bad breaks, but they weren't due to the fact that he was an Indian," the actor asserted. "As he realized in later life, his downfall as an athlete was largely brought on by weaknesses in his own nature—a feeling that the world was against him, unreasonable stubbornness, and the failure to understand the necessity for working as the member of a team."

Shortly after filming began, the company set out for Oklahoma to shoot Thorpe's college years—with Bacone, a junior college for Native Americans in Muskogee, substituting for the defunct Carlisle. It was there that

1. In 1982, the Amateur Athletic Union posthumously restored Thorpe's Olympic medals, which had been refused by the runner-up.

Burt shared his first scenes with Phyllis Thaxter, the twenty-eight-year-old Warners contract player who was cast as Thorpe's wife Margaret. Like Dorothy McGuire, Thaxter established an easy friendship with Lancaster during shooting. "We would go for walks on location after supper," she recalled. "We used to talk about our families, and our growing up." The highly trained Shakespearean actress was impressed by her costar's character and discipline: "He had great integrity. He was a very fair, kind person. And I thought he was very much a perfectionist, almost too much in a sense, because he would let it [his performance] bother him. He'd say, 'Well, I'll have to do that take again,' when the director thought it was fine." But the next take, she admitted, was often better.

Jack Warner had assigned the project to his star director, Michael Curtiz. Born in Budapest in 1889, Curtiz had given the studio a host of hits over the years, including *Captain Blood, The Adventures of Robin Hood, Casablanca,* and *Yankee Doodle Dandy.* His ability to fracture the English language was legendary. Once, when an assistant failed to execute an assignment, he said, "The next time I send a dumb son of a beetch, I go myself!" And during the making of *The Charge of the Light Brigade,* he called for a mount with no rider by saying, "Bring me an empty horse." But he was also known for being insulting and explosive on the set. A clash between Burt and the temperamental director seemed inevitable—and, according to Thaxter, one did occur. "Burt kind of let go about something," she recalled. "The next day he sent Curtiz flowers," after which "they kissed and made up." Otherwise, she said, the director and his star "got along very well."

The rapport between Curtiz and Lancaster may well have been grounded in the director's way of working. As Thaxter described it, "We would sit down and talk about each scene. We'd discuss it, to see if we liked the way it was written or if we wanted to change something. And after we talked about it a lot, we'd rehearse it, and then we'd shoot it." Thus, Burt had plenty of opportunity to voice his opinions.

After twenty-four days on location, the company returned to Los Angeles. Shortly thereafter, *Mister 880* opened—a scant four months after the production wrapped. On the whole, the critics were delighted with this offbeat picture, which *Newsweek* called "one of the most gratifying pieces of whimsy that has turned up since *Miracle on 34th Street.*" Lancaster received his share of the praise, which was justified by his engaging, unforced portrayal, but clearly the most interesting character in the piece was the old counterfeiter, whom Edmund Gwenn played with just the right twinkle and innocence. For his efforts, Gwenn would receive another Oscar nomination.

Meanwhile, shooting continued on *Jim Thorpe*. Occasionally, the great athlete watched his story take shape on film. "He was in pretty dire financial straits at the time," Lancaster recalled. "There was even a move by the producers to get his medals back: it would have been the perfect ending for the movie. My only personal contact with him during the filming was when he did the drop-kicking. He came out of the stands and tried to teach me. It was sort of touching. His life had gone to pot."

On November 10, Burt was shooting in North Hollywood Park when his second son, Billy, was rushed to Los Angeles County General. The boy, who was just a week shy of his third birthday, had contracted polio. Years later, Burt would recall the excellent treatment accorded his son by a staff that did not know at the time who his father was. "Now I had been pretty loudmouthed in criticizing our society up until then," the actor conceded. "I still criticize it because there are thousands of injustices that need to be corrected everywhere. However, when I came into that hospital that night . . . saw how the fine organization of a big city was working for the benefit of one small boy . . . well, then I knew that no man has the right merely to criticize."

This was not the first tragedy to strike one of Lancaster's children. According to Helen Itria of *Look,* his eldest son, Jimmy, had been born with clubfeet. To correct the deficiency, the appendages were put in casts, which had to be broken and replaced every two weeks for the first eight months of the child's life. Itria maintained that the deficiency caused Jimmy to withdraw from social activities later on: "He would hide from company or stand in a corner, hanging his head. Burt heard the boy called 'stupid' by enough misinformed people to bring him to a psychologist, where he learned that Jimmy was actually a superior youngster intellectually." Others have attributed Jimmy's behavior to some learning disorder or to a possible chemical imbalance. Whatever the root cause, he had difficulties adjusting to the world around him and was eventually placed in a private school for emotionally disturbed children. In time, he would go on to graduate from the Manhattan School of Music, and would get married.

Billy survived his battle with polio, but it left him with a limp. During the boy's recovery, Burt was advised by a physician to let his son pick himself up after falling—in order to help strengthen the muscles in the injured leg. It took extraordinary willpower for the actor to follow the doctor's orders. Even years later, tears would come to his eyes when he talked about this period in his life.

During the early weeks of Billy's recovery, Burt had no choice but to continue working on *Jim Thorpe*. How ironic it was that the athlete he was playing had also had to cope with a child's illness as well—but in Thorpe's case, the boy died.

Many of the remaining scenes were shot at the Warners lot, but the company also filmed at the studio's ranch (it served as the reservation where young Jim grew up) and at various locales around the metropolitan area. Bad weather caused frequent delays at these sites, as it had in Oklahoma, but finally the company wrapped on November 25—a dismal thirteen days behind schedule.

As 1950 wound down, Norma discovered that she was pregnant once again. When Shelley Winters read the announcement in the *Hollywood Reporter*, she was stunned. "I knew it was the end of my make-believe life with Burt," she wrote in her autobiography. She brought their affair to a close by throwing into the incinerator every photo of him that she possessed.

Shortly thereafter, on February 16, 1951, *Vengeance Valley* premiered. Several critics acknowledged the filmmakers' efforts to go beyond the routine horse opera. They also appreciated Lancaster's performance. But *Cue* spoke for many in the press when it noted, "The cast works mighty hard. . . . However, the Technicolor scenery takes first honors."

For Burt, there would be other, more memorable Westerns. Meanwhile, he was busy with a new production for Columbia. *Ten Tall Men* was one of two pictures that Hecht-Norma had agreed to produce for Harry Cohn, although Burt and Harold still had five films left on their agreement with Warners.

Originally, this adventure story, written by James Warner Bellah and Willis Goldbeck, focused on the conflict between the cavalry and the Apaches in the American Southwest. But that turf had been covered so well by other filmmakers that Hecht and Lancaster hired A. I. Bezzerides, known for his hard-hitting novels and screenplays, to reconfigure it as a tale of the French Foreign Legion. Then they decided that the project needed a lighter touch, for which they engaged Roland Kibbee, the author of several comedies including the Marx Brothers' *A*

Night in Casablanca, and Frank Davis, who had written additional dialogue for *Jim Thorpe—All American.*

Kibbee and Burt were nodding acquaintances, but after *Ten Tall Men,* they became fast friends. It was an unlikely combination. Where Burt was tall, athletic, and intense, Roland, one year younger, was, to quote actress Susan Clark, "a cuddly, Jewish teddy bear [who] . . . just kind of took everything in his stride." According to Jackie Bone, the actor's longtime companion, "Burt adored him."

In Kibbee's hands, *Ten Tall Men* evolved into a desert *Flame and the Arrow,* the story of a jovial band of legionnaires with Burt as their cocky, lighthearted, womanizing sergeant. Because a French accent is difficult to render, and Burt had no ear for dialects, his character, Mike Kincaid, became an American. Why this fellow was a member of the French Foreign Legion never became clear, but in the context of the rousing romp, such a detail was of little consequence.

Besides Roland Kibbee, *Ten Tall Men* introduced Burt to another enduring figure, Robert Aldrich. Assigned to oversee the production for Columbia, the thirty-three-year-old scion of a wealthy Rhode Island family would direct Burt in more pictures than any other individual except John Frankenheimer and would become the only filmmaker to extend his association with the actor from the 1950s through the 1970s.

Production on *Ten Tall Men* began in the desert around Palm Springs at the end of March, under the aegis of Willis Goldbeck, coauthor of the original story. Work on MGM's Dr. Kildare and Andy Hardy programmers had prepared him well for the comedic scenes, but he did not quite understand the combination of action, adventure, and lighthearted derring-do that Lancaster and Hecht wanted. As a result, the early rushes for *Ten Tall Men* lacked the punch of *The Flame and the Arrow.* Worse, the director was falling behind schedule. Finally, about midway through filming, he was replaced by Robert Parrish. "I was a brand-new director," Parrish recalled, but as an editor he had recut *All the King's Men* after it had bombed in previews. When it won the Academy Award for Best Picture, Cohn began to think of the thirty-five-year-old Georgian as a sort of Mr. Fix-It.

After Parrish took over, *Ten Tall Men* got on track. "Bob made things run a lot smoother," recalled Earl Bellamy, the film's assistant director. But the director was apprehensive about sharing Goldbeck's fate: "I remember thinking, 'Jeez, I hope I don't get thrown off the goddamn picture too.'" There was little reason for concern, however. Parrish, in his words, "got along very well with Burt." As a matter of fact, with his lack of experience, he welcomed any suggestions that the star had to offer.

In late April, after the company finished in Palm Springs, they began shooting interiors on the Columbia lot, and the picture wrapped—on schedule—on May 21. Despite Parrish's contribution, he was not listed as the film's director. Goldbeck, having shot about half the final footage and therefore entitled to screen credit by the tenets of the Directors Guild, received sole billing.

While *Ten Tall Men* was in production, so too was the second of Hecht-Lancaster's projects for Columbia, *The First Time*. It commenced shooting on April 1, 1951.

A domestic comedy about a husband, a wife, and their new baby, *The First Time* had initially been offered to Warners under its original name—*Small Wonder*—as a vehicle for Burt. But the studio, preferring to feature the actor in action-oriented fare, turned the property down. At Columbia, it went before the cameras with Robert Cummings as the husband and Barbara Hale as the wife, with Frank Tashlin directing.

When the film opened in early 1952, *Variety* aptly described it as "an unpretentious, entertaining domestic comedy," but this small, black-and-white picture had a hard time competing against that year's block-busters—*The Greatest Show on Earth, Quo Vadis?, Ivanhoe,* and *Singin' in the Rain.* Nevertheless, it signified that Hecht-Norma could mount a viable property without Lancaster as the star. Both partners wanted that. For Hecht, who produced the film (and *Ten Tall Men*), it represented the chance to get out from under Burt's shadow, and for Lancaster, it marked a down payment on the day when he could stop acting, an eventuality that he hoped would come soon.

After *The Flame and the Arrow* and *Ten Tall Men,* Hecht and Lancaster decided to bring their lighthearted approach to a pirate movie. It would become their jauntiest swashbuckler yet.

Given the roaring success of *The Flame and the Arrow,* Hecht logically engaged its author, Waldo Salt, to write what became known as *The Crimson Pirate.* But, after laboring on the project for six months, the screenwriter was fired. It may be that the script was unfinished when he was blacklisted by the House Un-American Activities Committee. Salt was replaced by Geoffrey Holmes, who, in turn, was replaced by Roland Kibbee, who got sole credit for the picture.

As the screenplay evolved, Lancaster was to play Captain Vallo, a gallant eighteenth-century buccaneer who involves his crew of brigands in a campaign to free the citizens of a Caribbean island from the tyranny of the Spanish king—while he romances the lovely daughter of the rebel leader. Lancaster himself discovered his leading lady, a beautiful twenty-three-year-old Hungarian named Eva Bartok, whom he saw in a stage musical in Rome. There was also a major supporting role for Nick Cravat, that of Vallo's lieutenant, Ojo, a mute in the tradition of *The Flame and the Arrow*'s Piccolo. *The Crimson Pirate* would turn out to be Cravat's last major film appearance, although Lancaster would find bits for his boyhood friend in many of his subsequent projects.

To direct the massive production, Hecht and Lancaster turned to Robert Siodmak. Given Siodmak's concentration on black-and-white film noir dramas, he was an odd choice for the lively, highly comedic Technicolor picture. Perhaps Lancaster had wanted to help a colleague who had seen better days, or perhaps he sought to dominate the proceedings by engaging a director who was inexperienced in the action-adventure genre.

Whether or not it influenced the decision to hire Siodmak, Lancaster did end up playing an aggressive part in the direction of the picture. As he would later assert, "I designed all the action sequences for *The Crimson Pirate,* all the comedy stuff. I worked with a comedy writer as well as with Siodmak himself. And as a matter of fact the whole last part of the film, the fight on the ship, which runs eighteen minutes of screen time, with all the gags and jokes, was shot by a writer and myself while Siodmak was in London shooting interiors for another part of the film."[2]

That Lancaster would extend himself so far beyond the actor's traditional role was unusual—even for him. But it provided wonderful experience for the day when he started directing.

Work on the picture commenced at the end of June 1951 on the Mediterranean island of Ischia, fifteen miles from Capri. It was a remarkably primitive place at the time, with no airport, only one good road, and no independent source of drinking water. At eight o'clock at night, the phone service shut down, isolating the island even further.

When filming began, the script was still unfinished. In fact, the first draft would not be completed for another month, and the final version would not be done until August 28. By that time, a third of the picture was in the can.

During the first two months, the company—about 125 actors, design-

2. No doubt, the writer was Kibbee.

ers, and technicians from the United States, Great Britain, Italy, and France (not counting extras)—concentrated on the sea sequences, including the picture's rousing opening, in which the pirates take over one of the king's ships by pretending to be dead. The principal settings for these episodes were a three-masted Spanish galleon and a two-masted pirate brig, which had recently made their debuts in *Captain Horatio Hornblower.*

As with *The Flame and the Arrow,* Lancaster was undaunted by even the most dangerous stunts. Christopher Lee, then at the start of his career, playing one of the king's men in the film, was enormously impressed. "I don't think I've ever seen a better-coordinated man," the British actor recalled. "He moved remarkably well, he was immensely strong and quite fearless." The actor remembered one particularly dangerous stunt for the final shipboard battle sequence. Lancaster had to cut a rope attached to a spar, which, when released, propelled him to the top of one of the ship's masts. "There was a camera on the ground to start him going up," Lee explained, "and there was a camera right at the very top of the mast shooting straight down, the idea being that when he cuts this rope and holds on . . . he comes to rest in a close-up right underneath the camera that was on the top. . . . Well, there wasn't more than about a foot to a foot and a half between the camera and the top of his head, and if anything had gone wrong, he would have hit that mast or the camera and undoubtedly would have been killed. It was one of the most courageous things I've ever seen an actor do."

Burt also agreed to an extended sequence involving a hot-air balloon. "The idea . . . seemed safe and simple when we originally planned it," he quipped. "But . . . the balloon seemed awfully high off the ground when I was clinging to the ropes. I would have liked to have backed gracefully out of doing the scene, but I couldn't."

The rigors of the production never became easy, but Burt found them more bearable in mid-August with the arrival of Norma and the children—including the infant Joanna, who had been born on July 3 and whom the actor had not yet seen.

Meanwhile, on August 24, *Jim Thorpe—All American* premiered back home. "The Warner Brothers, it should be noted, could not have assigned a better man to the title role than Burt Lancaster," asserted *The New York Times.* Indeed, in his skimpy track shorts and T-shirt, Burt looked every inch the "magnificent young stallion" described by Charles Bickford's Pop Warner in the voice-over narration. But, beyond the sports scenes, the role gave him little to do but look angry and talk tough.

Most of the critics correctly labeled *Jim Thorpe—All American* standard Hollywood fare. Even though the filmmakers had tried not to sugarcoat the athlete's personality or troubles, they set the story within the framework of a testimonial dinner, which muted its dramatic potential. Moreover, except for Thorpe, the characters were largely one-dimensional.

The biopic ended up a disappointing seventy-sixth among the year's most popular films.

Back on Ischia, Kibbee at last finished the script. But, by then, Gerald Blattner, an executive at Warners in London who served as the studio's eyes and ears during filming, and Steve Trilling, Jack Warner's executive assistant, were in a near panic over the production's delays and cost overruns. *The Crimson Pirate* had originally been allotted a sixteen-week shooting schedule; on August 28, Blattner advised Trilling that they would be lucky to finish up on Ischia in that amount of time—and they still faced some two months' studio work in Britain.

On September 1, Hecht cabled Burbank that they were doing every-thing they could to reduce the shooting time. Two days later, Burt joined Harold in another wire, pledging their willingness to make cuts, but, at the same time, cautioning the studio against decisions that would wreck what they fully believed was a terrific film.

Matters were not helped by the deteriorating relations between Lan-caster and Siodmak. At one point during shooting, according to colum-nist Sheilah Graham, the actor went so far as to brush past the director, saying, "Get out of my way, you silly old has-been." By late September, Siodmak was even threatening to quit. He blamed Hecht for the rift, claiming that Burt would be much easier to handle if the producer were not around. Blattner agreed, suggesting to Trilling that they send Hecht on an extended vacation. But Burt's partner remained in Ischia—as did Siodmak.

Finally, on October 15, to the great relief of the Warner executives, the *Crimson Pirate* company began shooting at Teddington, Warners' stu-dio in Britain.

Twelve days later, *Ten Tall Men* premiered in New York—only five months after the production had wrapped. *Variety* proclaimed it "a virtual tour de force for Lancaster. He bares his hairy chest, wrestles adversaries, and pitches woo in the best tradition of such roles." But several members of the press felt that, unlike *The Flame and the Arrow*, *Ten Tall Men* stepped too far over the line between adventure and spoof. As *Time* put it, "All that is missing—and it seems ready to appear any moment—is the sight of Bob Hope and Bing Crosby in burnooses with a few words to say about the script."

Ten Tall Men performed moderately well at the box office, but it did not come close to the success of *The Flame and the Arrow*.

At long last, *The Crimson Pirate* began to wind down.

On November 30, Kibbee left for the United States—to face the House Un-American Activities Committee, having been named a communist the previous September. In December, he would choose to meet in executive session with the committee's chief investigator, William Wheeler. Because he "cooperated," he was free to pursue his career. Nevertheless, the ugliness of the witch-hunt had struck the core of Lancaster's inner circle.

And it would get closer. On March 23, 1953, Hecht would be summoned. Like Kibbee, he would name names; in fact, he would name Kibbee. Although Lancaster would not have to testify before HUAC, he did not escape the horrors of the era unscathed. "I had my passport taken away," he said later. "I was reputed to be a card-carrying Communist. I was asked by Jack Warner to sign a loyalty oath and I refused. In a very small way, certainly not comparable to what others had suffered, I was on blacklists, but my position as a star was strong enough, and, of course, there was no evidence whatsoever that I'd had any Communist affiliations."

Finally, on December 7, 1951, Lancaster and Hecht headed for home, Hecht by plane and Burt, who had developed a fear of flying, by ship. The week aboard *La Liberté* gave him a chance to relax and to savor the luxury liner's haute cuisine. For once, he did not have to worry about his physique. He had lost fifteen pounds during the making of *The Crimson Pirate!*

CHAPTER SEVEN

Serious Acting and
South Seas Romps

After being away for half a year on a terribly difficult production, Burt was happy to be back in Bel-Air.

When he was not filming, he liked to potter around in his garden. Sometimes, he also played handyman, although the fruits of his labors were rarely satisfactory. He was not a proficient cook, either, but he did have one dish at which he excelled—spaghetti with marinara sauce—an appropriate specialty for a boy from Italian East Harlem.

Even when he was between pictures, he worked out religiously. An early riser, he typically warmed up for a half hour upon waking and then jogged several miles. Usually he skipped breakfast, preferring to have a sandwich and a glass of milk around eleven. In the early afternoon hours, he worked out in his gym at home and finished up later in the day with a gymnastics program—on riggings that he maintained in his back-yard, at Paramount, or at Warners. Cravat was usually on hand to help him train.

Evenings were primarily spent at home. Burt and Norma avoided the usual round of Hollywood nightclubs, premieres, and parties. "Sometimes we go out for dinner," Burt said in 1962, "but, frankly, my wife has to prod me to do that."

Their passion was bridge. "Saturday nights almost without exception there is a big bridge party at the Lancasters'," wrote Ruth Waterbury in 1956. In addition to the journalist, who was also a friend, the players included Roland Kibbee, Burt's business manager Jack Ostrow, Walter Doniger, producer Ross Hunter, actors Richard Conte and Barry Sullivan, and a young actress by the name of Julie Adams. "It was kind of a social thing," Adams recalled. "There were usually two or three tables, and after several hands, everyone would change partners and tables." But the players were expected to concentrate on the game; the Lancasters discouraged idle chitchat and eschewed sumptuous dinners.

"Whenever he would play with anybody," recalled Doniger, "and they made a mistake, he would macerate them." Another member of the group, actor Bob Quarry, recalled a time when Thom Conroy and Conroy's lover—"Joe something or other"—were playing at the Lancasters' house Joe was not proficient at the game. "This night there were just two tables," Quarry recalled. "I was sitting at the upstairs table. Well, suddenly from down below, [we heard] 'You dumb cocksucker. You wouldn't know how to play bridge if your mother came in and shoved the cards up your ass. You motherfucking dumb cocksucker.' " It was Burt yelling at Joe. The guest, his face drained of color, got up and left. Shortly thereafter, Lancaster came upstairs.

"Where's Joe?" he asked. When Quarry told him that Joe had gone home, Burt was genuinely confused. As with his flare-ups on the set, he had already put the incident out of his mind.

When William Inge's *Come Back, Little Sheba* opened on Broadway on February 15, 1950, virtually every critic found it, to quote John Chapman of the *Daily News,* "a work of great promise . . . which falls a little short of being a play." It was distinguished by its two principal characters: Lola Delaney, a blowsy, middle-aged housewife yearning for her little lost dog, Sheba, and her husband, an alcoholic chiropractor called Doc who is wasting away in a loveless marriage. Two spellbinding performances by Shirley Booth and Sidney Blackmer kept the play running for five and a half months.

On August 5, 1950, six days after the play closed in New York, Hal Wallis contracted it for the screen. The Paramount executives were, as he put it, "shocked at the thought of making a picture with beaten, unkempt, depressing people. . . . But the decision was mine."

To put the drama before the cameras, Wallis engaged the play's director, Daniel Mann, although the former actor and borscht-belt comedian had never directed a film before.[1] Wallis also wisely retained the play's star—after briefly considering Bette Davis. Although *Come Back, Little Sheba* would mark Shirley Booth's screen debut, the forty-five-year-old actress had been a Broadway luminary for two decades. She was also the voice of Miss Duffy on radio's *Duffy's Tavern.*[2] But *Come Back, Lit-*

---

1. Mann would go on to a distinguished film career, with credits that include *Teahouse of the August Moon, Butterfield 8, Our Man Flint,* and *Willard.*
2. Today, Booth is best remembered as the lovable maid in the TV situation comedy *Hazel.*

tle Sheba was her greatest triumph, for which she won both a Tony and a New York Drama Critics Circle award.

Although Wallis considered Booth's costar as well, he realized that he would need someone with greater drawing power than Sidney Blackmer to play opposite the largely unknown actress. His choice was Humphrey Bogart, who would have been ideal, but the actor's asking price was too high. Lancaster was desperate for the part, even though he was at least ten years too young for it. "I guess I wanted to play Doc Delaney in 'Sheba' more than any role I ever got close to," he said at the time. Michael Curtiz lent his support to the casting. Having seen the actor go from a shining teenager to an unhappy middle-aged has-been in *Jim Thorpe,* he encouraged Wallis to give Burt the role.

Finally, Hal decided to at least let Lancaster test for it. On the designated day, Burt showed up on the set wearing a conservative suit and no makeup and had his wild, wavy hair slicked down. "This result," to quote reporter Thomas Wood, "created such a plausible illusion of refinement that Wallis decided to look no further."

The economics of motion picture production rarely allow for extensive rehearsals before the cameras start to roll, but in the case of *Sheba,* Danny Mann insisted upon such an interval. Thus, on February 18, 1952, the cast gathered on the soundstage at Paramount, where the Delaney house had been constructed. Richard Jaeckel, the twenty-five-year-old actor who was playing the young, athletic Turk, was immediately impressed by the director's approach: "At the first rehearsal he told the actors not to come in with ideas etched in stone, but to be prepared to change and experiment. I looked around and everyone was paying strict attention, including the stars, Shirley and Burt." As an added benefit, Mann shot most of the film in sequence.

The quiet, bespectacled director had a manner that fostered good work, and Lancaster, playing so far from his normal age range and type, welcomed the help. "Burt was like a baby in Danny's hands," recalled Terry Moore, cast as the Delaneys' pretty, young boarder, "because he needed help. He was in unfamiliar territory." And the director responded. "Danny handled him with kid gloves," she asserted.

Mann was talented, but, according to Moore, "He always picked a scapegoat." In *Come Back, Little Sheba,* the actress, only twenty-three but a twelve-year movie veteran, became the target of his wrath. After a particularly rough day, Burt offered her words of encouragement and tried to help her see why an insecure director might need a scapegoat. "I never forgot that," said Moore. "I thought that was so wonderful and so big of Burt. And from then on, he was my protector. He went to Danny and said, 'Just cool it.' "

That Shirley Booth was delivering a rich, multilayered, and highly compelling performance became evident early on. No one was more impressed than her costar. "Now there's an actress I could talk about all day," enthused Burt. "She's an inspiration. This was her first picture and we expected her to be on edge, but she was so calm that she reassured all of us."

Of course, Booth had months of experience with Lola on Broadway, but, as she explained, "I had to adjust my Lola to Burt Lancaster's Doc. Burt was younger than Sidney Blackmer, it would have been silly to act the little girl for Burt that I had for the more comfortably mature Sidney. Burt's more restless interpretation, on the other hand, brought a more mature conception of Lola on my part."[3]

Lancaster was so impressed that, looking back on his career more than twenty years later, he would still assert, "Shirley Booth is the finest actress I have ever worked with."

For Burt, the challenge was to find a way to play a man considerably older than he, whose dreams had not come true, who had succumbed to a loveless marriage, and who was fighting against a powerful disease, alcoholism. He was, in Burt's opinion, "the most human, if imperfect, kind of guy ever written into a play or script." But Lancaster understood him. As he saw it, Doc "was doing the best possible job in an unfortunate marriage. Such people are legion. . . . Quietly, unsensationally, they go on year after year putting up with mates they never should have married in the first place." Although he could not—and would not—say so, he sounded like a man who was speaking from firsthand experience; after all, Burt had married Norma six months after she had given birth to his child.[4]

Clearly, Lancaster's own domestic situation helped him understand Doc's drinking problem. This too was not for public consumption. Instead, he noted another source of inspiration: the derelicts who congregated near the offices of Chicago's booking agents in his days as an acrobat.

3. Booth was twelve years younger than Blackmer; she was six years older than Lancaster.
4. In *Come Back, Little Sheba,* the audience discovers that Doc married Lola because she was pregnant, although she subsequently suffered a miscarriage.

To help the robust thirty-eight-year-old appear in late middle-age, the makeup department plastered down his wavy locks and added a bit of gray to his temples. Wardrobe also helped. "We dressed Burt in a sloppy, shapeless button-up sweater, padded his figure to flab out his trim waistline, and gave him baggy trousers that made him look hip-heavy," Wallis recalled. "He wore pale makeup over a stubble of beard, but we still had a problem hiding his magnificent physique. We had him stoop a little, hollow his chest, and walk with a slow scuffle in bedroom slippers." The producer was impressed by Lancaster's lack of vanity.

As Burt's performance took shape, he, like Booth, earned the respect of his costars. "I began to realize that this wasn't just a physical guy," recalled Jaeckel. "This guy was a very cerebral gentleman and, boy, was I wrong in thinking that he could only swing from one tree to another." To which Moore added, "I thought he was marvelous. I believed him always."

The production wrapped on May 22. It took a long fourteen weeks to shoot what was essentially a four-character, one-set drama that would run only ninety-six minutes in the final cut. That Wallis was willing to go so far beyond the standard eight-to-ten-week shooting schedule reflected the care to which *Come Back, Little Sheba* had been treated. For Burt it had represented a chance to stretch himself creatively beyond anything he had done before. As he put it, "Alas, for the first time since I can remember, I was called on to really act."

From the tight discipline of a typical Hal Wallis production, Lancaster returned to the organized chaos of his own company. Incredibly, the next Hecht-Norma project would suffer from the very same problems that had bedeviled *The Crimson Pirate*.

This time, Burt and Harold chose a South Seas adventure. Based on a novel by Lawrence Klingman and Gerald Green, *His Majesty O'Keefe* told a highly romanticized account of the real-life adventurer David Dean O'Keefe, an American who made a fortune in the 1870s by trading in copra, dried coconut meat with an exceedingly valuable oil extract. To direct, Burt and Harold chose Byron Haskin, who had stayed in touch with Lancaster since they had worked together on *I Walk Alone*. Haskin's previous film, *The War of the Worlds*, was arguably the best of his career.

As with *The Crimson Pirate*, the production would rely heavily on the splendors of a sun-drenched paradise, shot in glorious Technicolor. The producers chose the British-held Fiji Islands to serve as Yap and

O'Keefe's other stomping grounds, because the relative value of the pound to the dollar was exceedingly attractive.[5] *His Majesty O'Keefe* was only the third film to be shot there.

After the terrors of *The Crimson Pirate,* Jack Warner was hardly sanguine about sending Hecht and Lancaster to a remote locale with another expensive production. In early June of 1952, he cautioned the partners to economize in order to avoid the excesses that had proven so unfortunate on the previous production.

Although the company did not start shooting until July 21, Haskin, associate producer Norman Deming, and production manager Stanley Haynes arrived in the islands between mid-May and mid-June to audition actors from Australia and New Zealand and to supervise the construction of a production compound—including a large soundstage, a cutting room, and a recording studio—on the lush island of Viti Levu, about forty miles from the capital city of Suva.[6]

With Haskin's early departure for Fiji, it fell to Burt to test leading ladies in Hollywood for the role of the beautiful Polynesian girl who becomes O'Keefe's wife. "I didn't sleep a wink the night before the tests," Lancaster later said. "All I could do was toss and turn and think about what I was going to do the next day. I arrived on the set at eight o'clock in the morning before anyone else showed up. And I'm a guy who's never been early for anything in his life." After the tests were processed, they were shipped to Fiji for Haskin's review.

Among those under serious consideration were Dorothy Malone, Linda Christian, and Marisa Pavan, who would later play a featured role in the Lancaster–Anna Magnani film, *The Rose Tattoo.* But the role went to British actress Joan Rice, who had costarred as Maid Marian opposite Richard Todd in Walt Disney's *The Story of Robin Hood.*

As the start of production neared, Lancaster and Hecht faced the same problem that they had confronted with *The Crimson Pirate*—they had no script. The original version, written by Frank Nugent and Laurence Stallings, was rejected upon its delivery in early May. Several subsequent writers, including Roland Kibbee, Jim Webb, and Guy Trosper, had failed to produce a workable screenplay. No one could figure out where the problem lay. As production manager Stanley Haynes noted

5. Yap is now part of Micronesia.
6. After filming concluded, Warners and Hecht-Norma offered to donate the studio to the islands, but the colonial government asked that it be torn down because it threatened the islanders' primitive way of life.

shortly before shooting began, "I've had to pinch myself to believe that a great story could be in such bad shape after all the time spent on it."

Finally at the end of June, Hecht and Lancaster decided to hire Borden Chase, best known for the Western *Red River.* They were thrilled when he ad-libbed a brilliant new story line on the spot in a meeting with Jack Warner. But by the time he got to Fiji—to write the screenplay while the movie was being filmed—he had forgotten what he had said. Hecht and Lancaster quickly convened a story conference, the first of several. Present too were Haskin and James Hill, a former contract writer at MGM who was brought in to help with the script. "We were having a conference all right," recalled Haskin, "but nothing was ever written down. The MO was that when the slightest little bit of action was suggested, Burt would jump up and act it all over the room, breaking chairs and jumping over things, explaining as he went." Ten days before filming began, they still did not have word one on paper.

Chase soon reached the breaking point. One day he stormed out of the production compound, sword in hand, threatening to kill Burt, Harold, and Jim Hill. Hill found him in Suva—drunk. So the writers stayed there, in the city. Thereafter, a messenger would pass by their bungalow every day, pick up the completed pages that Hill secretly pitched through an open window, and deliver them to Hecht at the production compound. The producer would make changes, have the pages typed, and distribute them to the cast and the director for shooting. It would take Chase and Hill until September 15 to complete their task.

Filming in the tropics carried the ever-present threat of rain. It was, in fact, to avoid shutting down entirely during inclement weather that Hecht and Lancaster had built a soundstage. Otherwise, they could have shot the interiors later, in Burbank. But the torrential downpours made so much noise on the roof that shooting had to be halted until it could be soundproofed.

In August, Norma arrived with eldest son Jimmy, with Billy and Susan following shortly thereafter. (In September, the boys were enrolled at the Lomeri Catholic Mission School; three-year-old Susan was too young to attend.) Burt established his brood in a Fijian-type home constructed by a local crew; it featured electricity, indoor plumbing, and three bedrooms. To keep in shape, he ran every day from his cottage to the designated location. He also worked out on parallel bars brought all the way from Hollywood—to the great delight of the locals.

● ● ●

On August 27, nine days after Norma and Jimmy landed in the Fijis, *The Crimson Pirate* opened in New York. The ads boasted, "An astounding exhibition of daredevil deeds never before seen on the screen," and for once they were right. The messy, irritating, and woefully underbudgeted production had given rise to a joyful, entertaining romp, beautifully photographed in all of the Mediterranean's Technicolor glory. "It is the best fun conjured up by these derring-do dramas since the days of the fabled Douglas Fairbanks the elder," cheered Alton Cook of the *New York World-Telegram & Sun,* while *The Christian Science Monitor* proclaimed it nothing less than a "pirate film with everything."

The Crimson Pirate was a resounding personal triumph for Burt, whom *Time* called "the screen's most athletic swashbuckler" since Fairbanks. With his broad grin, billowing white shirt, and wavy hair, dyed blond and blowing in the sea wind, he made such an indelible impression that thirty years after the picture's release Richard Brooks announced plans to film a sequel, *The Son of the Crimson Pirate,* with Burt returning as Vallo and a younger actor—Mikhail Baryshnikov and Anthony Andrews were among those mentioned—as his offspring. The film, however, was never made.

The Crimson Pirate was a hit, but it failed to equal the success of *The Flame and the Arrow*—which made Jack Warner that much more nervous about *O'Keefe.* Once again, he cabled Burt and Harold to watch the budget.

Despite Warner's entreaty, it became obvious in early October that, without major cuts, the company would not finish on time. Indeed, Trilling estimated that, if they maintained their present rate, they would be a month behind schedule—at a cost of about $35,000 per week. To avoid such a catastrophe, he wanted to eliminate scenes and reduce the number of takes and setups. Burt cabled the Warners executive on October 21 to assure him that they had picked up the pace and had, indeed, made some cuts. To save time while Haskin was otherwise engaged, Burt even shot some of the remaining footage himself. But Trilling was not reassured.

Finally, on November 3, only six days behind schedule but seriously overbudget, the production wrapped. A week later, Haskin reflected on the ordeal. "Proudest I am of the fact I'm still here and on my feet at the finish," he wrote. "Few other directors would have lasted. . . . In my long career in this woeful racket, I can't recall a more classic endurance and nerve test."

• • •

The following month, on December 24, *Come Back, Little Sheba* opened. Notices for the production varied from muted criticism, such as Otis L. Guernsey Jr.'s assertion that it was "a photographed play" and a slow-moving one at that, to generous acclaim, with *Variety* calling it "a potent piece of screen entertainment." To no one's surprise, Shirley Booth was electrifying. Her performance would win her an Academy Award.

Far more startling was Lancaster's Doc. Just when audiences had come to accept the dour tough guy of the late 1940s as the toothsome, muscle-bound hero of genial action pictures, he had again thumbed his nose at typecasting. As he said later, "Suddenly they began to think of me as a serious actor."

For the moment, however, Burt was committed to a piece of total fluff. Warners' military service comedy, called *South Sea Woman,* was another of the quid-pro-quo projects that he made for the studio in return for its agreement to finance and distribute Hecht-Norma's productions. "I had to do it," he said later.

Based on a play called *General Court Martial* by William M. Rankin, *South Sea Woman* told the story of James O'Hearn (Lancaster), a gung ho gunnery sergeant, who helps his pal Pvt. Davey White (Chuck Connors) and Davey's perky fiancée, Ginger Martin (Virginia Mayo), escape from a Shanghai nightclub just two weeks before the bombing of Pearl Harbor.[7] What then ensues is an incredible series of mishaps that leaves O'Hearn facing a general court-martial for desertion, theft, and damage to private property.

Even though it was not a Hecht-Norma production, Lancaster was determined to make the slight comedy as good as it could be. He even arranged for his friend Roland Kibbee to do some rewrites—without credit. In return, Burt made an unbilled cameo appearance in *Three Sailors and a Girl,* a lightweight musical that Kibbee cowrote. It was shooting on the Warners lot concurrently with *South Sea Woman.* Lancaster did not even have to change out of his Marine uniform to do the bit.

During shooting, Burt also worked closely with the actor cast as his buddy, Chuck Connors. The lanky Brooklynite, seven and a half years Lancaster's junior, would go on to star in television's *The Rifleman,* but

7. O'Hearn was called O'Shanassey in the play.

in early 1953, he was the first baseman for the minor league Los Angeles Angels.[8] With only two small roles to his credit, he badly needed coaching. Lancaster "was always directing Chuck," asserted Virginia Mayo. Although Burt's tips and insights benefited the newcomer, whom he genuinely liked, they also helped Burt. Working with Connors—like shooting the battle sequence in *The Crimson Pirate* and directing the screen tests for *His Majesty O'Keefe*—provided valuable experience for the day when Burt would take charge of his own projects.

The film's director was Arthur Lubin, described as "a mild-mannered gentleman" with several Abbott and Costello and Francis the Talking Mule features to his credit. "I was a little intimidated when I started the picture," Lubin confessed years later, "because I was told that Burt was a very, very difficult man to deal with, but I found him very pleasant."

In part, the two men got along because Lubin was willing to indulge Burt's seemingly endless questions about character, motivation, and related matters. And because the director was generally disposed to take suggestions from his colleagues. As he put it, "A man or a lady who has a lot of experience comes up with valuable ideas and you must listen to them." Lubin was particularly impressed with Burt's input. He asserted during shooting, most "of the time, his suggestions are brilliant. But if I disagree, he'll give up his point without a struggle."

By a strange coincidence, *South Sea Woman* shared the general Polynesian locale of *His Majesty O'Keefe,* but it was filmed—between January 12 and the middle of March 1953—on the Warners soundstages in Burbank. There, the semblance of an entire tropical island was erected, with a 360-degree cyclorama depicting mountains and jungles and the sea behind them.

Although Lancaster tried to do his best with the material, he knew it for what it was. He also knew that another picture—with him again in uniform—was on the immediate horizon, and this time things would be much, much better.

They took to calling it "Cohn's Folly" because no one in Hollywood believed that a movie version of James Jones' sensationalistic first novel, *From Here to Eternity,* would ever be made. The joke was that Columbia studio chief Harry Cohn had acquired the property—for a hefty $85,000—because he was too crude to know how filthy it was.

8. While *South Sea Woman* was in production, Connors, then thirty-two years old, announced his retirement from sports.

Based on Jones' experiences in the infantry in the days just before the bombing of Pearl Harbor, the novel had garnered widespread critical acclaim, including the prestigious National Book Award for fiction, and was at the top of the best-seller lists for months. But how could it be made into a movie? Aside from its obscene language, the novel centered on two steamy sexual relationships, one involving a married woman, the other a prostitute—challenging material for Hollywood in the days of the Production Code. Moreover, it was more than eight hundred pages long, and it offered a jaundiced view of the military, which meant that the studio would have a difficult, if not impossible, time obtaining support for the picture in Washington. That was perhaps the biggest problem of all, for in the 1940s and 1950s, military films were not made without the cooperation of the Pentagon; the cost of obtaining authentic equipment, assuming one could find it, was prohibitive (the total budget for *From Here to Eternity* was a mere $2 million).

For all of these reasons, two studios had already given up on the project before Cohn entered the picture. Even Columbia, after announcing the acquisition in March of 1951 (as a vehicle for contract players Broderick Crawford, Glenn Ford, and John Derek), let it sit on the shelf for months while the studio tried to figure out what to do with it.

It took thirty-eight-year-old Daniel Taradash, himself a pre–Pearl Harbor inductee, to shape the material into a workable screenplay. As with Jones' novel, he focused on two principal characters: Pvt. Robert E. Lee Prewitt, a brilliant bugler and champion boxer who hung up the gloves after accidentally blinding a friend in the ring, and the "topkick" of Prewitt's company, 1st Sgt. Milt Warden, a tough, by-the-books noncom whom one colleague describes "as the best soldier I ever saw." There were also three major supporting characters: Prewitt's girlfriend, Lorene, softened from a prostitute in the novel to the hostess of a private men's club; Karen Holmes, the wife of Warden's commanding officer and the woman with whom the sergeant falls in love; and Pvt. Angelo Maggio, Prewitt's cocky friend.

It fell to the film's producer, Buddy Adler, who had been a lieutenant colonel in the Signal Corps during the war, to gain the cooperation of the Pentagon. He did so by addressing the Army's two major objections to the story. The first—Maggio's brutal treatment in the stockade—was made into a grudge match between the private and the sergeant of the guard rather than a reflection of Army policy. The second—the lack of retribution for the officer in charge of the regimental boxing squad for trying to force Prewitt to join the team—was changed; in the film, the officer would be forced to resign his commission. With these two compromises, Columbia garnered all the technical assistance and equipment that it needed from the Pentagon, as well as permission to shoot at Schofield Barracks, the Hawaiian setting for the story.

It was Taradash who suggested Fred Zinnemann to Cohn. The director was well respected, having been nominated twice for Academy Awards—in 1948 for *The Search* and again for *High Noon,* his film just before *Eternity.* But Zinnemann's relationship with Cohn was never easy. Among the battles that the director fought and won were the right to shoot the film in black and white ("color would have made it look trivial," Zinnemann wrote in his autobiography) and the casting of Prewitt. Cohn had wanted to use Aldo Ray, hoping that the role would make his contract player a major star, but Zinnemann insisted upon Montgomery Clift, who had made his film debut in *The Search.*

On one element the director and the studio chief were in complete accord: the casting of Jones' other principal character, Warden. They both wanted Burt Lancaster. Having traded away both of his options for Lancaster's services in 1952 and with only one chance to star Burt in a film in 1953, Wallis was a reluctant negotiator. But Cohn's assistant Milton Pickman and Columbia vice president Jerry Wald pressed hard. In the end, Wallis wound up with an extremely favorable deal: he received $150,000 for Burt. He also got Columbia to take over a mundane script entitled *Bad for Each Other* and to agree to star his contract players Charlton Heston and Lizabeth Scott in the picture.[9] The sale of this package earned Wallis an additional $180,000. Lancaster did not do too poorly either. "I knew he was getting the equivalent of $330,000 for me," Burt recalled, "so I asked for a bonus—I got my salary of $48,000 plus a $25,000 bonus."

For Burt's costar, Cohn cast Joan Crawford. But when the actress insisted that her usual designer create her wardrobe, he replaced her with Deborah Kerr. It was a strange choice. Not only was the thirty-one-year-old actress British (Scottish actually), she invariably played genteel ladies, and Karen Holmes was anything but that. "It was astounding— my getting the part," Kerr recalled. Cohn and Zinnemann also went against type for the other female lead, Prewitt's hardened girlfriend, Lorene, choosing the wholesome farm girl Donna Reed. Rounding out the major players was Frank Sinatra, then at the nadir of his career, as Prewitt's irrepressible pal, Maggio.

• • •

9. *Bad for Each Other,* directed by Irving Rapper, was released in 1953. Clive Hirschhorn, author of *The Columbia Story,* called it "predictable bilge."

The sweep and the richness of *From Here to Eternity* suggests an extensive production period, but, in fact, the film was shot in a whirlwind forty-one days. Lancaster reported to the Columbia lot on March 19, 1953, just forty-eight hours after he finished work on *South Sea Woman*. Shortly thereafter he and the rest of the company boarded a charter plane for Hawaii and three weeks of location shooting.

It was on the plane that Burt met his lovely costar. "It was a great help, really, to spend those hours chatting," Deborah Kerr recalled. "I'm a bit shy, particularly with a big noise as he was. He was sweetness itself. He couldn't have been more encouraging."

The onetime Sadler's Wells ballet dancer and the ex-acrobat soon found that their rapport translated extremely well on film. "There is a chemistry that happened between us," said Kerr. "I was not conscious of it and neither was he. But he had such a good and forceful attitude toward his part—and toward mine." It was this byplay, even more than the well-written script, that led to such a memorable on-screen relationship. As Kerr pointed out, "They [Karen and Warden] have very few scenes, and yet one feels that it's an enormous part of the movie."[10]

The best-remembered moment between the actor and the actress took place on Blowhole Beach in Oahu. There, they passionately kiss, lying on the sand in their bathing suits, while the ocean waves crash around them. As difficult as it is to imagine in retrospect, that celebrated embrace almost went unrecorded. According to assistant director Earl Bellamy, Zinnemann originally staged the kiss with Lancaster and Kerr standing up. After Buddy Adler watched it in rehearsal, he said to Bellamy, "Boy, we gotta change this." Seeing the producer's displeasure, Burt asked if they could show him another version, one with which they had experimented earlier in the day. The alternative staging was the one seen in the film, and the idea for it was Burt's.

Getting it in the can, however, took three days and involved more than one hundred people. "The challenge was timing the scene to the incoming waves," recalled Zinnemann, "so that they would break over the couple at the right instant." *Look* magazine maintained that the sequence set "a record in time, manpower, and equipment for a single movie love scene." But the result was one of the most famous romantic clinches in film history.

Fred Zinnemann and Montgomery Clift had a special rapport. When they worked together, they collaborated, they communed. Lancaster

10. In total, there are five scenes between Warden and Karen, including one brief encounter early in the film.

did not rely on the director the way Clift did. As Earl Bellamy put it, "You didn't have to talk with Burt about the character because he had it down to a gnat's eye."

The beach scene was not the only point of contention between the two men. "I don't think they got on awfully well," asserted Kerr. "Burt is very adamant and so is Fred, although in a sort of completely different manner." Zinnemann, once described as a "small, shy, unassuming man . . . who gives the impression that he is turning the pockets of his soul inside out each time he talks," made his points with quiet conviction. Lancaster, by contrast, was prone to argue loudly and vehemently.

Clift, it seems, was no more fond of Burt than Zinnemann. "Lancaster was not Monty's sort of man or actor," asserted Robert LaGuardia, one of Clift's two principal biographers. The other, Patricia Bosworth, quoted one of the star's friends to the effect that Monty considered Burt a "terrible" actor and "a big bag of wind" and deeply resented that he got top billing for the picture. Lancaster, however, had enormous regard for Monty. "The only time I was ever really afraid as an actor," he once said, "was that first scene with Clift. It was *my* scene, understand: I was the sergeant, I gave the orders, he was just a private under me. Well, when we started, I couldn't stop my knees from shaking. I thought they might have to stop because my trembling would show. But I'd never worked with an actor of Clift's power before; I was afraid he was going to blow me right off the screen." That Lancaster, by then a veteran of nineteen movies, could harbor such feelings of insecurity suggests that he had more in common with his sensitive costar than surface appearances would indicate.

So great was Lancaster's respect for Clift's talent that he sought other opportunities to work with him. If Monty disdained Burt as his biographers have suggested, he was at least willing to costar with him again if a suitable project developed.

Eternity wrapped in Hawaii around the middle of April, and the company returned to the mainland to complete the film on the Columbia lot. James Jones was able to watch much of the shooting in Burbank, thanks to Burt, who hired the author to adapt Max Catto's novel, *The Killing Frost* for the screen.[11] "Although he worked conscientiously on the script," wrote Jones' biographer Frank MacShane, "Jones felt he was in Hollywood mainly to be involved in the filming of *From Here to Eternity.*"

11. Burt's company would ultimately film *The Killing Frost*—although not with Jones' adaptation—as *Trapeze* in 1955.

The novelist was extremely enthusiastic about the footage that Zin-nemann was producing; so was everyone else associated with the pro-duction. But, as Lancaster said in retrospect, "None of us thought of the picture as really great while we were working in it. It was just one of those films that added up when it was put together."

On June 1, twenty days after Burt finished with *From Here to Eternity*, he had a kidney stone removed at Los Angeles' Cedars of Lebanon Hos-pital. The operation, which proved to be more complicated than ex-pected, took over three hours and left Burt hospitalized for about two weeks; he was unable to resume work for several months.

Although the operation may have served as a reminder, Lancaster had already come to realize that he was no longer a youngster. The pre-vious March, he had said, "I'll soon be forty and I feel that at best I have ten years left as an actor. I want to set up the future so that I won't have to depend on my looks or my physical agility. Besides, I've done just about all the films I care to." At the time, his plans included a six-week tour of Christopher Fry's epic 1948 verse play, *The Lady's Not for Burning*. The idea was to go on the road in the fall, playing college the-aters, civic auditoriums, and concert halls, but even before the Fourth of July, Burt preempted the tour for another film, his own company's production of a Western then called *Broncho Apache*. This decision may well have resulted from the precipitous end of Hecht-Norma's four-year relationship with Warner Bros.

The situation with Warners had come to a head in June. Clearly, Jack Warner, Steve Trilling, and other members of the executive staff had been sorely tried by the experiences of making *The Crimson Pirate* and *His Majesty O'Keefe*. To avoid similar delays and cost overruns in the future, they insisted that Burt and Harold budget subsequent pic-tures at $900,000 apiece. (The original agreement with the studio had called for ceilings of $1.1 million, but with overruns, *The Crimson Pi-rate* had cost $1.85 million and *O'Keefe* $1.55 million.) Furthermore, the studio restricted Hecht-Norma to shooting on the studio lot.

Burt and Harold rejected the conditions.

It did not take them long to find a new home, however. On June 23, just one week after they announced the end of the relationship with Warners, they formed a new partnership with United Artists.

Founded in 1919 by Charlie Chaplin, D. W. Griffith, Mary Pickford, and Douglas Fairbanks, UA was a production, releasing, and distribution company, which, in the early 1950s, had come under the control of two former attorneys, Arthur Krim and Robert Benjamin. "When we took over the company in '51," recalled Max Youngstein, who became executive vice president in charge of exploitation, "that company was insolvent. . . . We were looking for how to reestablish the name of United Artists, which had gone downhill by that time." Joining forces with Hecht and Lancaster was a step in the rebuilding process, but according to UA historian Tino Balio, to "capture its first big star, UA nearly had to give away the store." Specifically, the company offered Hecht and Lancaster "full financing, 75 percent of the profits, an overhead allowance to develop properties, and most notably, special distribution terms of 25 percent domestic." Because the industry standard was 30 percent, the extraordinary concession was, according to Balio, "kept a secret and referred to inside the company as the 'Lancaster terms.' "

United Artists yielded Hecht and Lancaster another advantage over their previous arrangements: UA did not have a studio of its own. As Burt later explained, "When you went to the big studios to make a film, there was a studio overhead imposed on you, which was somewhere in the area of fifty percent. . . . If you have a film for one million dollars, the studio automatically puts it on the books as a million and a half. Now the film has to make a million and a half in rentals before you get a profit area." At UA, by contrast, Hecht-Lancaster could rent equipment and facilities where they wished—for about 20 or 25 percent of what they had been paying. As a result, Burt asserted, "we were able to do our pictures for hundreds of thousands less than if we had gone to a major studio." In addition, UA gave Burt and Harold considerable autonomy. Said Bob Blumofe, then UA's vice president of West Coast operations and productions, "The approach that we took is that we are not picture makers, we don't make films. Once we know the basic elements of a film—the script, the budget, etc.—then it's yours to make as you see fit." After the intense scrutiny at Warners, Burt and Harold embraced their new freedom—but, in time, it would prove a curse.

The agreement with UA called for the company—now known as Hecht-Lancaster—to produce two pictures, the first of which was to be *Broncho Apache* (which they had been developing at Warners). Accordingly, Burt and Harold vacated their offices in Burbank on September 24 and moved into Keywest Studios at Santa Monica and Van Ness in Hollywood.

On June 3, while Burt was recuperating from his kidney-stone operation, *South Sea Woman* opened. The ads may have suggested a laugh riot, with tag lines like "From the brawls of Montezuma to the free-for-alls in Tripoli" and "Adventures of a Leatherneckin' Guy and His Hula-Hula Lady!" but Otis Guernsey Jr. of the New York *Herald Tribune* accurately called it "one of those random souped-up tales which gets out of hand early, races through all sorts of nonsense in search of a story, and winds up in a flurry of action, empty-handed."

Lancaster's hard work during shooting was apparent in the final cut, but it came off as just that—hard work. Rattling off jargon-riddled lines like "I don't want any bathtub jarhead beating his gums to save me," he was so robust—with his teeth flashing and his arms flailing—that he was almost a caricature of himself. The inexperienced Connors was worse. Only Mayo showed a hint of comedic skill as the perky but not-too-bright camera girl. On the picture's opening, *Variety* tersely noted, "The entertainment values are only fair and the business prospects appear about the same." That proved to be an accurate assessment.

Meanwhile, Fred Zinnemann, Buddy Adler, and editor William Lyon were working swiftly to ready *From Here to Eternity* for release. Harry Cohn, convinced that he had an enormous hit on his hands, had decreed that the picture would open in August, just three months after it had wrapped. "No one ever heard of releasing a major film in midsummer," Zinnemann asserted in his autobiography, because movie houses were not air-conditioned at the time. But Cohn was so sure of the picture's reception that, as his biographer Bob Thomas pointed out, "he did a remarkable thing. For the first time in his history, he allowed his name to appear in an advertisement for a Columbia picture. A message to the public over his signature conveyed the pride with which he was presenting *From Here to Eternity.*"

It opened on August 5, at the Capitol in New York. With virtually no publicity except for the ad with Cohn's endorsement, the picture drew an awesome 18,235 ticket buyers on its first day. Attendance continued to climb, netting box-office receipts of $171,674 for the first week, a record for any film house. "So great was the demand for seats at the Capitol in New York City," wrote Thomas, "that the theater remained open almost around the clock; it was closed briefly in the early morning so that janitors could sweep the floor." *From Here to Eternity* would go on to become the biggest moneymaker in Columbia's history to that point, earning $19 million in its first release (on total expenditures of $2.4 million, including prints and advertising). Only *The Robe*, Fox's Technicolor spectacle—the first picture in CinemaScope—would perform better in 1953.

From Here to Eternity was as successful critically as it was commercially. *Variety* asserted that it was "in many instances a much better motion picture than the novel was a book," while *Newsweek* proclaimed it "one of the most absorbing and thoroughly honest movies to cross a normal screen in years."

All those associated with the picture, including Zinnemann, Taradash, and cameraman Burnett Guffey, received acclaim, as did the five leading actors—especially Lancaster. Indeed, Burt seemed born to play Warden. His performance of a man who is tough, confident, and totally in control, and at the same time sensitive and fair, was his most compelling and believable to date. And his most romantic. Never before had he been as sensuous on film or as comfortable with a woman as he was with Deborah Kerr. The embrace on the beach is truly one of the classic moments in film history.

On December 28, 1953, *From Here to Eternity* earned the prestigious New York Film Critics award for Best Picture and Burt was named Best Actor. An Academy Award nomination for his performance—his first— seemed almost certain.

CHAPTER EIGHT

Working with United Artists

It was not until the 1970s and the advent of consciousness-raising that films such as *Little Big Man* and *Soldier Blue* attempted to depict the Wild West from the Native American's viewpoint. Before that, Hollywood had tended to portray Indians as either bloodthirsty savages or childlike primitives. A notable exception was *Apache*, in which Lancaster, a lifelong liberal, played the title character as a sympathetic, psychologically complex individual. With America on the cusp of the landmark *Brown v. Board of Education* decision, in which the Supreme Court would outlaw racial segregation in public schools, the picture also stood as what Burt later called "a broader statement on the injustice of racism." That was quite a leap from the lighthearted romps of the Warners years.

Massai, the Apache warrior that Lancaster portrayed in the film, was derived from a historical figure, a member of Geronimo's band who, in the late 1880s, waged a one-man war in the Southwest against white settlers and the Indians who collaborated with them. His story was told in a 1936 novel, *Broncho Apache* by Paul Wellman,[1] which Burt and Harold purchased in May of 1952. They assigned the adaptation to James R. Webb, who had been writing Hollywood Westerns since 1941 (he would win an Oscar for *How the West Was Won* in 1963).

The screenplay that Webb fashioned adhered to the basic tenets of Wellman's novel. Both began with Massai's escape from the train carrying Geronimo and his band to exile in Florida, then detailed the young warrior's extraordinary six-month trek from Illinois back to his starting point in Arizona and his raids against his enemies thereafter.

To put this story of social alienation on the screen, Burt and Harold

---

1. According to Wellman, broncho Apaches were "the wild, lone warriors who refused to acknowledge any chief, but remained in their own isolated camps."

turned to a director who came from the very heart of the American establishment, Robert Aldrich, a cousin to the Rockefellers. His family included a U.S. congressman, a senator, and, in time, the governors of New York and Arkansas. But Aldrich was a liberal, despite his background, and many of the films that he would make in his thirty-year career reflected an antiauthoritarian, even revolutionary, posture.

Since working with Hecht and Lancaster on *Ten Tall Men*, Aldrich had directed numerous episodic television programs and two inconsequential features, *The Big Leaguer* and *World for Ransom*. But Burt and Harold knew that he ran a smooth operation, which they sorely needed after their last two projects.

With Jean Peters as Massai's wife, Charles Bronson (then Charles Buchinsky) as a rival for her affections, and John McIntire as the scout determined to capture the renegade, *Apache* began principal photography on October 15, 1953. The picture's few interiors, as well as the bustling St. Louis sequence that highlighted Massai's long journey home, were shot at Columbia, but the vast majority of *Apache* was filmed around Sonora, California, and Sedona, Arizona. In all, nineteen locations were used, and this diversity was not lost in the final cut. *Apache* is replete with magnificent views.

Hecht and Lancaster were right about Bob Aldrich. Only two incidents marred the well-organized production. The first occurred on October 23: Lancaster was riding a horse along a narrow mountain pass when the animal slipped, plunging Burt sixty feet down the bluff. He was rushed to the Sonora hospital, where he learned that he had torn muscles in his right leg and hip. Since Massai was in almost every scene in the movie, this injury virtually shut down the production. At the time, Burt was expected to resume filming in a week, but in fact he was laid up for a month.

The other problem came at the conclusion of principal photography. The script called for Massai to be killed by federal troops. Just days before filming the sequence, United Artists, despite its usual hands-off approach to independent projects, insisted that Aldrich shoot an alternative ending, in which Massai would live. Aldrich refused to do so. For several days, Lancaster sided with the director, but finally, Harold convinced him to do as UA wished. "Now once Burt had changed his mind," Aldrich recalled, "it made little difference if I refused to direct the other ending because the next day they could have got someone who would." So he reluctantly directed the footage.

• • •

Apache wrapped on January 7, 1954. Twenty days later, *His Majesty O'Keefe* finally opened, more than thirteen months after the end of filming. The result was flawed but not without value, as Lancaster imbued the nineteenth-century freebooter with many of the qualities that had distinguished his previous swashbucklers. Nevertheless, O'Keefe was earthbound compared to Dardo and Vallo; the character gave rise to virtually no acrobatic feats of derring-do. Likewise, the film in general lacked the brisk pace and lighthearted air of its predecessors.

No one was more aware of its shortcomings than its director, Byron Haskin, who had written at the conclusion of shooting: "Under different conditions, *O'Keefe* could have been better. I'd say my own part is about 50 percent of what it could have been." He attributed most of the problems to the script, citing its "episodic structure, hasty expediencies, underdeveloped secondary characterizations, occasional feathery motivations, [and] oversimplifications."

Although the script for *His Majesty O'Keefe* had been found wanting, Burt and Harold were fully aware of the conditions under which the screenwriters had labored, and both were put to work on Hecht-Lancaster's second project for United Artists, *Vera Cruz*. Jim Hill, who was becoming a close buddy of Burt's, was elevated to producer, and Borden Chase was engaged to write the screenplay. Also on board was Robert Aldrich, who signed up for his second Lancaster film in a row before the first, *Apache,* was completed.

Vera Cruz marked the middle picture in a trilogy of Westerns that Hecht-Lancaster produced in succession, all starring Burt—thus signaling the end of the swashbuckling phase of the actor's career. But where *Apache* reflected a serious effort to address the plight of Native Americans in the twilight of the nineteenth century, *Vera Cruz* was strictly for fun, a tale of two adventurers out to steal a cache of gold from the French occupation forces in Mexico in the days following the American Civil War.

Although the plot bore some of the elements of a traditional Western, this was no ordinary shoot-'em-up. Instead *Vera Cruz* offered, to quote Arnold and Miller's study of Robert Aldrich's oeuvre, "an endlessly inventive game of one-upmanship. There are exaggerations, improbabilities, implausibilities, reversals, and variations throughout." Behind the game-playing lay, as film historian Pierre Sauvage observed, "a largely cynical, amoral attitude," highly unusual for the genre to that point. In its nihilism and seemingly random use of violence, *Vera Cruz* pointed the way toward Sergio Leone's violent 1960s "spaghetti" Westerns with Clint Eastwood. And as a "buddy picture" (before the advent of the term), it served as the precursor for the likes of 1969's *Butch Cassidy and the Sundance Kid* and 1985's *Silverado*.

Initially, Burt pictured himself as the hero of the piece, Benjamin Trane, a former Louisiana planter who had lost everything during the Civil War. He wanted Cary Grant for Joe Erin, the charming but amoral saddle tramp whom Trane befriends. "I don't go near horses," Grant replied.

Then inspiration struck: Lancaster could play the roguish but rotten Erin while a typical Hollywood leading man assumed the more conventional role of Trane. The obvious choice was Gary Cooper, still a top star twenty-eight years after the release of his first feature film and the winner of his second Oscar for *High Noon* the previous spring. But Clark Gable advised Coop to turn the role down. Having just seen *From Here to Eternity*, Gable predicted, "That young fella will wipe you off the screen, Gary." Finally, however, Cooper said yes.

It was in late January of 1954 that the one hundred members of the cast and crew journeyed into Mexico for principal photography (they were joined there by two hundred locals). Once again, Burt and Harold started without a completed screenplay. In addition to Chase, Hecht-Lancaster regulars James Webb and Roland Kibbee contributed to the final draft.

Often the intense pressure of creating a script on location produces a stilted drama, but with *Vera Cruz* a kind of freedom emerged. Still, the production was extremely difficult for Aldrich, who much preferred time for detailed preparation before the cameras rolled.

Although the company spent about two weeks at Churubusco, a studio in Mexico City, most of the picture was shot around Cuernavaca, fifty miles to the south. "We worked out in the friggin' desert," recalled Jack Elam, who played a member of Joe Erin's gang. "And it was hot and dirty." The rough country was even rumored to house an outlaw. Arnold and Miller maintained that "one of the film bandits, Charles Horvath, was mistaken for the desperado and arrested by the local militia."

This time, Aldrich had difficulties working with Burt. As Evelyn Harvey reported in *Colliers*, "From sunup to sundown, Lancaster was a one-man tornado, directing camera angles, fussing over details of script, makeup, music, wardrobe." The director was less than thrilled with his star's involvement in such matters. He considered *Vera Cruz* a significant career opportunity, and, as he put it, "When you're directing your first great picture, you don't welcome somebody else on hand with directorial notions."

Cesar Romero, cast as the principal villain, was equally struck by Lancaster's intensity. "He was very energetic in his work," the Latin actor recalled. "As a matter of fact, he was a little rough sometimes. He had one scene with Henry Brandon, and he had to tussle with him, knock him down on the ground. But he had to finish it up by giving him a big kick—and he gashed in the guy's forehead. It was unnecessary."

On March 25, while Burt was in Mexico, the motion picture industry's elite gathered for its annual rites, the Academy Awards. Lancaster had been nominated for Best Actor for *From Here to Eternity*—as had Montgomery Clift, Marlon Brando for *Julius Caesar,* Richard Burton for *The Robe,* and William Holden for *Stalag 17. Eternity* had garnered eleven other nominations, including one for Best Actress (Kerr), Best Supporting Actor (Sinatra), and Best Supporting Actress (Reed). Asked how he felt about his first-ever Oscar recognition, Burt, always the salesman, said from location, "Well, I wouldn't ask for it myself, but now that I am making this picture with Coop, think of the marquee: 'Last Two Academy Award Winners in *Vera Cruz.*' Think of the box office!"

But Holden won. According to Bob Thomas, the actor said at the time, "I really thought Burt would win. After I saw *From Here to Eternity,* I was so overwhelmed that I sent wires to everyone concerned with it. I honestly believed that Burt did the best acting of the year, and I told him so when I saw him one night at Chasen's." Lancaster returned the compliment. After the ceremony, he sent Holden a telegram that read, "Never had a doubt about the outcome for a moment."

Kerr also lost—to Audrey Hepburn for *Roman Holiday.* Otherwise, *Eternity* virtually swept the evening. Zinnemann won, as did Reed and Sinatra (whose sagging career was revived by the performance and the award). And the film was named Best Picture over *Julius Caesar, The Robe, Roman Holiday,* and *Shane.* In all, *From Here to Eternity* captured eight Oscars, tying *Gone with the Wind;* no one called it "Cohn's Folly" anymore.

Meanwhile, back in Mexico, Lancaster, playing an expert gunman, spent a considerable amount of time off-camera learning to twirl his six-shooter and perfecting his fast draw. One day, Cooper, who had appeared in his first Western when his costar was still in high school, said to him in his understated way, "Gettin' pretty fancy, aren't you, Burt?" Shortly thereafter, the Western veteran found an occasion to take his own gun from his holster and executed a series of dazzling spins. He then tossed the weapon into the air, caught it, whirled it back into his holster, nodded his head as he murmured, "Mm-hmm," and walked off the set. Cooper was usually such a quiet, self-contained man that on-lookers, including Ernest Borgnine, playing a member of the Erin gang, were enormously surprised and amused by the display.

Despite such antics, Lancaster and Cooper got along—although they had vastly different personalities and political views. But at the outset of their relationship, Burt had not known how to deal with the older actor's minimalistic acting style. "In the first few days of shooting, before the rushes came back to Mexico from processing," recalled Lancaster's friend Bob Quarry, "Burt thought Coop wasn't being very effective. He said, 'Coop is just throwing this away. Coop isn't doing anything. I have to compensate. I have to put energy in the scenes.' " Then the rushes came back and Burt told Quarry, "There I was, acting my ass off. I looked like an idiot, and Coop was absolutely marvelous." At Burt's insistence, his first three days of work were reshot.

As filming progressed, the bond between the two stars grew stronger. Years later, Lancaster said, "As far as I'm concerned, Coop was something special, a delightful man to work with. Quiet. Very insistent about what he was doing." Walter Seltzer recalled that Cooper, in turn, "was very, very open in his admiration of Burt." Lancaster would serve as an honorary pallbearer at Cooper's funeral on May 16, 1961.

In late June, *Apache* premiered at the Roosevelt Theater in Chicago. To mark the event, Hecht-Lancaster and UA sponsored an Old West parade down State Street, complete with covered wagons, cowboys doing rope tricks, and more than one hundred Native Americans decked out in tribal regalia.

Despite the festivities and the producers' ads, which linked the film to the artistry of *High Noon* and *Shane, Apache* received a decidedly mixed critical response, with Bosley Crowther of *The New York Times* calling it a "resounding clinker." The critics were not thrilled with Lancaster's performance either. Widespread opinion held, with Philip K. Scheuer of the *Los Angeles Times,* that "this athletic, blue-eyed Nordic is not the most convincing Indian in the whole world."[2]

With the passing of time, Lancaster came to regret his decision to

2. In 1954, there were no contact lenses that could enable Lancaster to alter the color of his eyes.

abandon the original ending, in which Massai was killed. "It was my opinion that we would have had something of a classic," he later reflected. But that alone would not have elevated *Apache* to some higher level of achievement. Still, the picture proved quite popular at the box office, grossing approximately $3 million in its initial release (on an expenditure of $900,000). It marked a bright start to Hecht-Lancaster's new relationship with UA.

Shortly after the premiere of *Apache,* Burt became a father for the fifth and final time. On July 7, Norma gave birth at St. John's Hospital in Santa Monica to a little girl, whom the parents named Sighle-Ann (pronounced Sheila). She weighed eight pounds six ounces.

The following month, Burt embarked on his directing debut. He chose as his maiden film *The Kentuckian,* the third in his company's trilogy of Westerns for United Artists. Based on the novel *The Gabriel Horn* by Felix Holt, the story was set in the 1820s, when Kentucky was on the edge of the frontier. Its hero, Eli Wakefield, was a strapping, buckskinned backwoodsman eager to pursue his future in Texas with his young son, Little Eli. Initially, Hecht and Lancaster saw the project as a musical, along the lines of Rodgers and Hammerstein's *Oklahoma!,* but they abandoned the notion in favor of a straight dramatic, albeit lyrical, screenplay by A. B. Guthrie Jr., whose epic novel *The Way West* they had optioned a few years earlier (*The Way West* would finally be produced as a film by Hecht in 1967).

The Kentuckian was the first project under Hecht-Lancaster's new agreement with United Artists. Announced on February 8, shortly before *Vera Cruz* went into production, the deal called for Burt and Harold to produce seven films over a two-year period at a total cost of $12 million. Two of the films were to be without Burt, but *The Kentuckian* was not one of them. "I don't like being in a picture I direct," the actor said at the time, "but I want to get my foot in as a director this year. I'm forty."

To assist him in his dual roles, Lancaster called on his friend, his story editor, and the producer of *Vera Cruz,* Jim Hill. "I'll stage all the scenes," Burt explained shortly before the start of shooting. "He'll be there. We'll discuss them. Another actor will play my part in rehearsals; for the final rehearsals, he'll step out and I'll step in." When the cameras were rolling, Hill would serve as what Burt called "my third eye." To expect such an arrangement to work, especially with a backup who had no directorial experience, reflected more a hope than a realistic approach to filmmaking. Playing a leading role in a major motion picture is terribly demanding. It becomes almost overwhelming when one is also directing—Charlie Chaplin, Orson Welles, Barbra Streisand, and Clint Eastwood notwithstanding. Moreover, the arrangement concentrates an inordinate amount of responsibility in one person's hands, especially if one is a first-time director. Nevertheless, before shooting began, Burt was supremely confident about the outcome, saying, "I will know if a scene—any scene—is right. You have taste or you don't; that's the guiding factor."

Burt was so arrogant, in fact, that shortly before he started scouting locations for the film, he launched an attack on the very fraternity that he was seeking to join. "Directors are the most irresponsible people I've seen," he told Philip K. Scheuer of the *Los Angeles Times*. "They think they're supermen . . . just try to show most of these directors where they may be wrong! They don't want the challenge; they're afraid of being exposed."

Then he applied for membership in the Directors Guild! Having read his remarks in the newspaper, the board of directors rejected his application, granting instead a waiver that would allow him to direct the picture without affiliation. He was invited to reapply after the production wrapped, however, when, it was hoped, his opinion of the profession would be better. Burt was furious. "I don't care whether I become a member of the guild or not," he fumed. "I know the idiots who are in the guild who are trying to stir up this trouble, and I'm not interested in making public issue of *The Kentuckian* or my directing of it."

Shooting began in August of 1954, with the Lincoln Pioneer Village, a living-history museum near Rockport, Indiana, and several places in Kentucky serving as backdrops for the action.

Following Danny Mann's example, Burt assembled the cast for three weeks of rehearsals before leaving Hollywood. He spent most of the time simply talking with his costars. "As an actor I've come to discover that lively discussions initiated by directors are not only stimulating but very valuable for character delineation," he wrote shortly before the picture opened. He even peppered his offstage conversation with remarks about religion, politics, and other lively topics in order to, in his words, "break down the inhibitions" of his costars—who included Dianne Foster, Diana Lynn, John McIntire, and Walter Matthau.

"He was an interesting director," recalled Matthau, a thirty-four-year-old veteran of the Broadway stage, who made his film debut as the town bully in *The Kentuckian.* He also thought Burt "was a nice fella," but confessed that every so often the star, who was a well-known practical joker, liked to make fun of his inexperience before the camera.

In addition to Matthau, a number of the leading players had kind words for Burt. Veteran character actor John McIntire, who had costarred with him in *Apache* and was playing his brother in *The Kentuckian,* found him "articulate and meticulous and [he] not only tells the players what to do but how and why. If necessary, he'll review the entire script to bring the actor up, emotionally, to the scene he's playing." Twenty-three-year-old Dianne Foster, making her fifth screen appearance with the Western, echoed the sentiment, saying, "Before he went into a scene he reminded me each time exactly how we felt about one another in the preceding sequence. Because it might have been shot three weeks before and therefore partly forgotten, Burt made certain that we arrived at the right mood before we would even rehearse it."

Of course, not all the talk was about character and motivation. As Burt recalled, "I used to sit at night in Kentucky . . . and say, 'Listen, there's this new writer—marvelous, just listen to this.'" And he would read to them from Paddy Chayefsky's *Marty.* The simple, tender story of a middle-aged bachelor had originally aired on May 24, 1953, on the NBC anthology series *Philco TV Playhouse,* starring Rod Steiger and Nancy Marchand with Delbert Mann directing. Burt and Harold decided to bring an expanded version to the large screen as one of the non-Lancaster vehicles for United Artists.

But, according to Walter Seltzer, then Hecht-Lancaster's vice president of advertising and publicity, "UA was never very hot for the project," even though it would only cost around $350,000 to make. Who, the studio asked, was going to want to see a story about a fat, middle-aged butcher and a homely spinster?

Then Burt brought his salesmanship to bear. "I think you people have a responsibility to underwrite new talent," he told UA executive Max Youngstein (third in command after Benjamin and Krim). "If you don't want to do it, fine—let's break up our relationship and you go your way and we'll go ours." UA gave in.

That Lancaster was willing to put his clout behind *Marty* may have been more a fight for principle—the belief that UA was not going to tell him what pictures he could and could not do—than a reflection of his devotion to the property, his memory of reading Paddy Chayefsky's script to the *Kentuckian* company notwithstanding. According to Jim

Hill, "From the beginning *Marty* was all Harold Hecht. He saw the thing on television and fell in love with it. Neither Burt nor I was that impressed." Further, a high-ranking member of the Hecht-Lancaster company who was on the staff when *Marty* was being filmed recalled, "During the production of the picture Burt was not terribly supportive and kind of made fun of it."

Once UA gave the project the green light, Burt and Harold engaged Chayefsky, a thirty-one-year-old writer from the Bronx, to nearly double the length of his forty-eight-minute teleplay and engaged the original director, Delbert Mann, to again put the script before the camera. The Kansas-born director had been working in television since 1948, when the medium was in its infancy, but *Marty* would be his first film. Indeed, he had never even been to Hollywood before.

Initially, Hecht and Lancaster considered Marlon Brando for the Bronx butcher, but the idea of engaging a major star was eventually abandoned. Mann and Chayefsky wanted Steiger and Marchand, but Burt and Harold feared that the presence of the two original stars would cause the film to become little more than an extended version of the television drama. Moreover, they intended to put under contract whoever played the title role, and Steiger would not sign. Thus, they turned to Ernest Borgnine, a thirty-seven-year-old character actor who had made his film debut in *China Corsair* in 1951. Burt knew him from *Eternity*, in which he played the sadistic sergeant of the guard, and from *Vera Cruz*, in which he was a member of Joe Erin's gang. To play opposite Borgnine, they cast Gene Kelly's wife, actress Betsy Blair.

Putting an actor under contract represented a major leap forward for Burt's production company; after the success of *Marty*, Borgnine loan-outs would add a tidy sum to Hecht-Lancaster's revenues. But there was something ironic about Burt, who was still under contract himself, having another actor working for him.

At Mann's request, *Marty* was accorded several weeks of rehearsal, some of which were held in New York prior to the three days of exterior shooting in the Bronx. The company then moved to Los Angeles, where the rest of the script was rehearsed and filmed. The whole movie was shot in sixteen days, plus three days of retakes, an incredibly short time for a feature even in 1954.

Borgnine later claimed that Hecht and Lancaster only took on the film for tax purposes, that, in fact, they had planned on shelving it halfway through filming until their accountant told them that it had to be shown at least once before it could earn any tax credits. No one else associated with the project supports this assertion. "I never heard a word of that," said UA's Bob Blumofe. "I can tell you from personal knowledge that

Harold—much more so than Burt, I think—was really, really head over heels convinced that he wanted to make that film." Delbert Mann agreed. Indeed, during the making of the picture, Mann came to like and respect Hecht. Harold was so supportive of the project that, after he and Mann watched the director's cut, he withdrew approximately $40,000 from his company's funds so that Mann could shoot a small added scene and several retakes (the ceiling that UA had placed upon the picture's financing had already been reached).

While *Marty* was in production, Burt was still in Kentucky—and starting to find directing far more rigorous than he had anticipated. As he recalled, "I had the problem of getting up terribly early in the morning to go out to the locations to set everything up. I got home late at night. I had to work with all the rushes and work with the editor, and then sit up until midnight or sometimes one o'clock in the morning, going over the scenes for the next day. I had no time for anything. It's no life really. Nobody works harder than a director, if he's at all serious. His work is never finished—simply never finished." And aside from all of that, Burt had lines to memorize and a performance to deliver, with his character in virtually every scene of the picture.

As the production neared its conclusion in mid-October, it appeared that Burt would have to go directly from *The Kentuckian* into the start of his next picture, Hal Wallis' *The Rose Tattoo,* which was to begin principal photography in Key West, Florida, during the week of October 25. On October 11, agent Herman Citron asked Wallis to change Burt's starting date to December 1.[3] The producer grew livid. "We made this deal last May," he told Citron on the phone, "and this is a very important property—we particularly brought a big star from Italy [Anna Magnani]—and everything is geared up and the plans are made and the reservations are made and we cannot do it. It's absolutely out of the question. There's no possibility at all."

Faced with an irate, resolute producer, Burt settled for going directly to Key West after *The Kentuckian* wrapped. Since he would then arrive

3. As Hecht became increasingly involved in producing, he could no longer serve as Burt's agent. The actor then signed with Lew Wasserman and Herman Citron of the powerful Music Corporation of America. When MCA was forced to withdraw from the agency business after it acquired Universal Pictures, Ted Ashley became Burt's agent. Ashley too leaped to the other side of the bargaining table, becoming the head of Warner Bros. in 1969. At that point, Burt went with Ben Benjamin, who had been part of Ashley's Famous Artists Agency and who stayed with the firm after it became International Creative Management (ICM). The gentlemanly, highly respected Benjamin continued as Burt's agent until his death at age eighty in 1991.

before the rest of the company, he could enjoy a few days' rest in the Florida sun. In the meantime, as Wallis' anger subsided, he juggled the schedule so that Burt's first call was not until November 8 (although the usual undemanding makeup and costume tests would be conducted the week before). In addition, the director, Daniel Mann, decided to fly to Key West early so that he and his star could talk before the day-to-day demands of production claimed their time.

That problem solved, Burt proceeded to bring *The Kentuckian* to a close. As the production wrapped, he felt fulfilled by the experience, although he realized that acting in and directing the same project had been a terrible mistake. "I find you cannot serve two masters; it's just too time-consuming," he said later. Still, he was fully intent on taking the helm of other projects in the future. "Much as I have enjoyed working as an actor in the past," he wrote in August of 1955, "it is now quite possible that I may soon quit that phase of show business altogether and concentrate only on being a director. That's been my real ambition ever since starting in motion pictures."

He would soon reverse that decision.

Tennessee Williams' Serafina Delle Rose was a fiery widow who rediscovers passion in the arms of a buffoonish truck driver. The author had written the role in his play *The Rose Tattoo* specifically for the earthy, volcanic Italian actress Anna Magnani. But she lacked a sufficient command of English to play it. It went instead to Maureen Stapleton, who drew raves when the play opened on Broadway on February 4, 1951— as did her costar, Eli Wallach, as the clownish suitor, Alvaro Mangiacavallo. The play was, in general, well received. Critics were particularly pleased with Williams' new and refreshing use of humor, although they were less enamored of his heavy-handed symbolism and the play's loose structure. Running for more than eight months on Broadway, *The Rose Tattoo* won a Tony Award for Best Play, with Stapleton and Wallach taking the acting honors.

"I first saw Tennessee Williams' powerful play *The Rose Tattoo* on its opening night in Chicago," Hal Wallis wrote in his autobiography, "and knew at once that I had to buy it. It was sure to be a great success. Audiences would identify with its earthiness, its sexuality, its deeply felt emotions and naturalistic dialogue." Williams insisted, as a condition of the sale, that Magnani be cast in the role that he had written for her. Her English had not improved perceptibly since she had turned down the stage assignment, but the nature of filmmaking, with scenes shot in small snippets, would allow her to work in the unfamiliar language as a live stage performance eight times a week would not.

The Rose Tattoo would mark Magnani's American film debut; she was a major star in Europe but was not well-known in the United States. Thus, Wallis turned to Lancaster to give the project some badly needed marquee value. By rights, Burt's 1947 contract with the producer should have expired on October 1, 1954 (while he was making *The Kentuckian*), but postponements and deferments at his request so that he could make films of his own (he did three Hecht-Lancaster productions in a row) had forced an extension. As of January 6, 1954, he was obliged to appear in three more Wallis films, of which *The Rose Tattoo* was the first. By this point, his salary had climbed to $100,000 per picture, a significant jump in his earnings but still $50,000 below the fee that Wallis commanded for loan-outs.

To write the screenplay, Wallis turned to Hal Kanter, then dropped the Georgia-born writer after receiving a treatment and thirty-five pages of screenplay. Kanter's replacement was Williams himself.[4] The playwright had previously coauthored the film version of *The Glass Menagerie* and had soloed on the adaptation of *A Streetcar Named Desire*—for which he had earned an Oscar nomination. As might be expected, he adhered closely to the original play, but opened it up to show more of the milieu of his Italian American protagonists. He also softened the play's sexual overtones to satisfy the Production Code.

Given Daniel Mann's success with *Come Back, Little Sheba,* he was the logical choice for *The Rose Tattoo*—which he had also directed on Broadway.

This time, Mann found Lancaster difficult to handle. "He had finished directing himself in *The Kentuckian*," recalled Ben Cooper, who played the boyfriend of Serafina's daughter, Rosa, "and he was still very full of himself as a director, so any suggestion that Danny Mann made, Burt wanted to discuss and change it around many times." Mann also had his hands full with Magnani, whom *Time* had called "the most explosive emotional actress of her generation." According to Cooper, she "had carte blanche in her contract, and if she wanted to do a scene standing on her head, Danny Mann could not have said don't do that." Magnani did not take advantage of her artistic license, but it was irritating. Mann could not simply take charge of the production.

---

4. Kanter would ultimately receive credit for his adaptation.

As he had done with Terry Moore during the making of *Sheba,* Mann took out his frustrations on the supporting players, in this case Cooper and Marisa Pavan, the young actress playing Rosa. "We were his whipping posts," said Cooper. "It was a very unhappy picture to work on because of that." On at least one occasion, Mann sent the twenty-one-year-old Pavan to her trailer in tears.

At the outset of filming, everyone wondered how the volatile Italian actress and her so-called temperamental leading man would get along. As it turned out, "Magnani fell head over heels for her costar, Burt Lancaster," Hal Wallis wrote in his autobiography. The feeling was not reciprocal, but Burt was enormously impressed by her talent. Years later, when he was asked to name his most gifted costars, he invariably cited Magnani—just after Shirley Booth.

Despite the one-sided ardor, Burt and Anna worked well together, at least in Key West. A clash finally developed back in Hollywood, however. Williams wrote his grandfather from Los Angeles that the costars got into a fight on the set "as she was directing the scene and he didn't like it." Burt, Williams continued, walked off the soundstage, and shooting resumed only after several intense discussions. "I shall just have to hope and pray that Danny Mann, the director, can keep peace between them long enough to finish the picture," he concluded.

As for Burt's relations with the rest of the cast, Cooper said, "He was not interactive with the other actors. He treated people kind of like they were props. You just felt no contact with him at all." Curiously, Cooper's appraisal was almost identical to that of Jack Elam during the making of *Vera Cruz.* "I don't think he ever made contact with anybody," said the character actor.

Burt's diffidence did not stem from snobbery or ego. When he was working, he was fully concentrated on the assignment at hand—and in the case of *The Rose Tattoo,* the role was a major challenge. Although Williams' male protagonists tended to be handsome, intelligent men of breeding gone to ruin, Alvaro Mangiacavallo was loud, uncouth, and foolish, the self-acknowledged "grandson of the village idiot of Ribera." But he was also the flame that rekindled Serafina's dormant sexuality. Maintaining the duality—oaf and sex object—was a major balancing act. Burt chose to concentrate on the character's foolish qualities—even to the extent of getting a close-cropped, unflattering haircut. He trusted that his innate sexuality would take him the rest of the way.

It was a risky choice, as bold as anything he had attempted before.

• • •

By the time *The Rose Tattoo* wrapped on January 25, 1955, *Vera Cruz* had been in release for a month. The picture, which opened on Christmas Day, baffled those critics who were expecting another *High Noon* or *Shane*. Bosley Crowther of *The New York Times* was the most vociferous, asserting, "The presence of both Gary Cooper and Burt Lancaster is a waste of potential manpower. Nothing that either is called to do in this big, noisy, badly photographed hodgepodge of outdoor melodrama is worthy of their skill." But Hecht, Lancaster, and Robert Aldrich had not set out to imbue their film with the high moral tone of its recent, highly regarded predecessors. *Cue* more accurately caught what they were after when it noted "the major concern here is with action—simple, unadulterated, uncomplicated."

Lancaster, argued *Time,* was "the virtuoso in this symphony of slam." Indeed, the actor was not far off the mark when he later asserted, "I ran away with the picture anyway—the character was the best thing in it."

The public embraced the rollicking Western. With earnings in excess of $9 million in its initial release (against expenses of about $3 million), it became Hecht-Lancaster's highest-grossing picture to date. In the intervening years, it has become something of a cult favorite. With its anarchistic point of view, seemingly endless rounds of one-upmanship, and antiheroic leading character, it has a more modern sensibility than most Westerns of the 1950s. It is also, to put it simply, fun.

Hecht-Lancaster followed one box-office bonanza with another. But, if the success of *Vera Cruz* was expected, *Marty* drew little in the way of fanfare when it opened on April 11, 1955. Even United Artists treated it as an art film, initially introducing it at select houses around the country rather than placing it in broad general release.

But the reviews were glowing. *The New York Times* was hardly alone in finding it "a warm and winning film, full of the sort of candid comment on plain, drab people that seldom reaches the screen." Then came the awards: the prestigious Golden Palm at Cannes in May of 1955, the New York Film Critics award for Best Picture of the year in December, and finally the Academy Award for Best Picture in March of 1956—with *Marty* besting *Love Is a Many Splendored Thing, Mister Roberts, Picnic,* and Lancaster's starring vehicle *The Rose Tattoo*.

With four Oscars to its credit (Ernest Borgnine, Delbert Mann, and Paddy Chayefsky also won), *Marty* ended its initial release with a gross of some $6 million; in terms of earnings to cost, it did even better than *Vera Cruz*. Its success was due in no small measure to the way its release was nurtured by Hecht and Lancaster, who spent $400,000 on promotion and advertising—$50,000 more than it cost to make the picture![5]

The glow of *Marty*'s reception was only slightly dimmed by a scurrilous article about Lancaster that appeared in *Confidential* magazine a month after the picture's release. The author, Charles Wright, alleged that Burt had a propensity for physically abusing women, citing two incidents to demonstrate his point. In one, the actor was reported to have ripped the clothes from and tried to force himself upon a Mrs. Bruce Cabot, who met him at his office on January 14, 1954, to test for a role in *Vera Cruz*. In the other, an international playgirl named Zina Rachevsky was supposedly treated in a similar fashion when she joined Lancaster in his bungalow at the Palm Springs Racquet Club in the spring of 1951. Zina, Wright maintained, bit the actor in an undisclosed body part, resulting in his hospitalization. "Burt's tendency toward clobbering cuties is rapidly becoming no secret at all among dames in the know in Hollywood," the reporter concluded.

As *Confidential* was hardly on a par with *Time* or *Life,* such a story would fail to merit serious consideration were it not for two factors. First, a prominent screenwriter who had been on the Hecht-Lancaster staff in the midfifties told this author that "Burt was living with a telephone switchboard operator and beating the shit out of her."

The second factor stems from an incident that took place in 1984, when Lancaster and actress Margot Kidder exchanged blows on the set of the film *Little Treasure.*[6] Kidder subsequently filed suit against the actor and won an out-of-court settlement, conditional to which was her silence on the subject. According to the film's director-screenwriter, Alan Sharp, the actress had "sent out feelers" to people she knew before filing the suit and got back reports that suggested she was not Burt's first victim.

It should be noted that what transpired between Kidder and Lancaster was in no way like the incidents described by Wright and that, in

5. According to *Inside Oscar: The Unofficial History of the Academy Awards* by Mason Wiley and Damien Bona, Hecht-Lancaster spent $400,000 solely to promote *Marty* for the Oscars, but Walter Seltzer, who was in charge of Hecht-Lancaster's advertising and publicity at the time, maintained that the sum represented the film's total ad budget. "I guess that we spent maybe seventy-five thousand dollars on the Oscar campaign," he recalled. But he also noted, "What we did was unprecedented at the time. We openly asked people to vote for our picture for the Oscar." As part of this effort, the company, for the first time in the award's history, made prints of its film available to any member of the Academy who wanted to view it in his or her home.

6. See pages 355–57.

Sharp's opinion, the actress was partly responsible for the fracas. But the fact that Burt struck a woman and that her case was settled out of court combined with the recollections of the Hecht-Lancaster employee suggests that perhaps the *Confidential* article should not be totally dismissed.

"For years I've been trying to find a good circus story," Burt said in March of 1955. But his choice of material was curious, for Max Catto's 1950 novel *The Killing Frost* hardly suggested a glitzy, blockbuster movie. Rather, it told the grim story of likable, handsome Tino Orsini, who is executed in London for the murder of a beautiful young woman. Thereafter, a priest seeking to determine the truth of his guilt discovers that Orsini's mentor, a cripple named Mike Ribble, perpetrated the crime. Along the way, the reader journeys with the priest into Orsini's world, that of a traveling European circus, in which he, Ribble, and the girl, Sarah Linden, are the members of a trapeze and wire-walking act. Even Burt acknowledged that "the acrobatics are incidental" to the plot, with less than half of the novel centering on Orsini's circus days.

That Lancaster originally gave the screen adaptation to James Jones suggests that at one time he and Hecht were considering a dramatization of Catto's entire novel. After the author of *From Here to Eternity* left the project, it was assigned at various times to Samuel Taylor *(Sabrina)*, Ernest Lehman *(Executive Suite)*, and Ruth and Augustus Goetz *(Carrie)*. "Eventually we decided the book was hopeless," recalled Sir Carol Reed, the film's director, and much of the plot was dropped. But screenwriter James R. Webb, who had scripted *Apache* and parts of *Vera Cruz*, retained the characters of Catto's romantic triangle—Orsini, Ribble, and Sarah (with the girl ultimately becoming an Italian, Lola, to accommodate the casting of Gina Lollobrigida). Webb added the film's other main plot element, Orsini and Ribble's quest to perfect the triple somersault.

For Burt, *Trapeze* represented a chance to get away from the type of big-top spectacle that Cecil B. DeMille had brought to the screen in *The Greatest Show on Earth*.[7] He wanted to portray what he called "the human-interest side [of the circus world], the drama and heartbreak behind the scenes." For this reason, he and Hecht engaged Carol Reed, a director who had demonstrated his command of character development and atmospheric detail in such films as *Odd Man Out, The Fallen Idol,* and *The Third Man*—called "three of the best British films of the post-

7. *The Greatest Show on Earth,* a dazzling spectacle with a soap-opera plot, won the Oscar for Best Picture in 1952.

war period" by Byron Forbes of the London *Observer.* Although he had been directing movies since 1930, Reed had never taken command of a big Hollywood project before and was so eager to do so—and to work with Lancaster—that he accepted the assignment without even reading the script. (He was, however, familiar with *The Killing Frost* and had an interest in circus life, to the point of exploring his own movie on the subject in the late 1940s.)

Lancaster would, of course, play Ribble, the embittered, crippled catcher, but the other major roles—Ribble's young partner Tino and the woman who comes between them—were uncast when Reed came aboard. It was, in fact, the director who persuaded the hot, sexy sensation Gina Lollobrigida to make her English-language film debut as the scheming female aerialist. She was offered $160,000, the highest amount ever paid a European film star to that point.

Burt had hoped to interest Montgomery Clift in Tino, but in the end the role went to Tony Curtis. Since the thirty-year-old actor had debuted in *Criss Cross,* he had become a star, mostly as the dashing hero of such costume dramas as *The Prince Who Was a Thief, Son of Ali Baba,* and *The Black Shield of Falworth.* Universal had initially been reluctant to loan out its popular contract player for the circus picture, but it finally relented in order to borrow Oscar-winner Ernest Borgnine from Burt and Harold for *The Square Jungle,* also starring Curtis. "*Trapeze* . . . wasn't my first outside movie," Tony noted in his autobiography, "but it was the most important of my career so far."

To kick off the start of filming in Paris, the company staged a parade up the Champs-Elysées on August 7. Nine hundred thousand Parisians lined the streets that Sunday morning to cheer the three stars and to applaud the circus troupers who would appear with them in the picture. Then the company settled down to work in the celebrated Cirque d'Hiver, a domed, five-thousand-seat arena that Hecht-Lancaster had rented. It was, in fact, the place where a Frenchman named Léotard had invented the flying trapeze in 1859.

Because *Trapeze* would be shot in CinemaScope, Reed decided to fill the very wide picture frame during the story's more intimate moments with troupers—clowns, equestriennes, jugglers, trained elephants, and so on—rehearsing in the background. Booking acts to perform these atmospheric roles—during the height of the summer touring season—was a major challenge for chief production manager Ruby Rosenberg. He had agents scouting talent throughout Western Europe. On one occasion, he even bought out an entire circus in order to make use of just three acts.

Hecht-Lancaster also had to secure the services of skilled aerialists who could double for the stars. "We have Eddie Ward of Ringling Brothers—the best catcher in the business—doubling for me and serving as technical adviser," said Burt at the time. Under Ward's watchful eye, Burt was able to do his own catching for the simpler tricks. Fay Alexander, who doubled for Curtis' flier and therefore had to entrust himself into Burt's hands, was impressed, noting that the star "was in great shape." He also found Burt to be "a great guy. He couldn't do enough for me. I had a personal masseur, a chauffeur, and four bodyguards."

Thanks to Ward and Alexander, the high-bar acrobatics in *Trapeze* were spectacular. "Some of the aerial stunts were so *dangerous* even the doubles had doubles," Curtis recalled. But capturing the magic on film was no easy matter. "It took all of [cinematographer] Robert Krasker's photographic know-how," reported Michael Mindlin, "to lick the problem of double images caused by the speeds in excess of seventy-five miles an hour at which the aerialists travel." Lighting the scenes was difficult as well. The powerful CinemaScope bulbs generated so much heat that cameramen working in the riggings high above the ground had to endure temperatures in excess of one hundred degrees, and special reflector hoods had to be devised to prevent the lights from blinding the aerialists as they performed their dangerous feats.

Tempers might easily have frayed during such a difficult production, but Reed, described by one reporter as a "quiet-spoken man who would obviously go far to avoid an argument," kept a firm but benevolent hand on the proceedings. His sensitive treatment of Lancaster, whom he recognized as a perfectionist, can be seen in their collaboration on an early scene. As the director's nephew, actor Oliver Reed, recounted the story, Sir Carol was satisfied with the first take. But at Burt's insistence, they shot it sixteen more times. After the final try, the director congratulated the actor, saying, "How right you were to have it reshot. That last shot was ideal." Then, he used the first take.

Although Burt's relationship with Reed was congenial, his association with Lollobrigida appears to have been less than ideal. "I don't know that they were thrilled with each other," recalled Mike Mindlin. But, since Burt's and Gina's characters spent most of the film bickering with one another, any off-screen antagonism may actually have worked in their favor. Lollobrigida also had difficulties with Katy Jurado (playing the equestrienne Rosa), so much so that the Mexican actress threatened to walk off the picture at one point.

In contrast, Burt enjoyed a wonderful rapport with Curtis. "Tony adored working with Burt, just worshiped the ground he walked on," recalled Lancaster's friend actor Bob Quarry. In his 1993 autobiography, Curtis remembered a night when he and Burt were shooting a bar sequence. They were sitting a short distance from one another, Curtis on the sidewalk, waiting for shooting to start: "We looked at each other, just kind of gazing. Then Burt took a cushion off one of the chairs and flung it toward me like you'd skip a pebble across water. The pillow hit the ground and bounced three or four times. I lifted up my ass and that thing just slid under me perfectly and stopped. I'll never forget that. It was such a perfect gesture of friendship." The actors became so close that, even before the picture's release, Curtis was signed to two future Hecht-Lancaster productions, *Sweet Smell of Success* and *Cat Ballou.*[8] Burt also wanted to work with Sir Carol again. They discussed a variety of projects, but none of them bore fruit.

After shooting concluded at the Cirque d'Hiver, the company filmed at night on the streets of nearby Versailles and at a small studio in Billancourt, a suburb of Paris. The long, eighteen-week production finally came to an end during the first week of December. Burt was so eager to get home after nearly six months in France that he decided to take a plane, despite his fear of flying.

8. Hecht-Lancaster never made *Cat Ballou.* In 1965, Hecht produced the picture without Burt or Curtis in the cast.

CHAPTER NINE

Independent Producer and Contract Player

On September 1, while Burt was filming *Trapeze, The Kentuckian* opened. Although most of the critics praised cinematographer Ernest Laszlo's pastoral images, they found the film slow-moving. Bosley Crowther of *The New York Times,* who had lacerated *Vera Cruz* the year before, was, if anything, even more hostile to the latest Hecht-Lancaster release. Not only did he find the screenplay "sprawling and overwritten," he also blamed Lancaster for "letting the whole thing run wild in mood and tempo with no sense of dramatic focus or control."

One of the few supportive voices was raised by *Time,* which proclaimed, "The good script . . . has had good direction and the credit goes to Actor Lancaster. . . . Furthermore, Lancaster directs himself with more sense for his own limits than most other directors have shown, and he gets an appealing, unaffected performance out of the boy who plays his son."

Ultimately, perhaps the worst that might be said of *The Kentuckian* is that it was amateurish. As *Newsweek* noted, "The picture rarely brings anything to mind at all but actors in costumes, posturing against a shiny replica of a backwoods village." Even Matthau said in retrospect, "It all came out like a high school production. It was cardboard."

For Burt, the tepid response was a terrible blow. So much so that, except for 1974's *The Midnight Man,* he never directed again. Late in life, he claimed that he stopped because "it's too exhausting. Too time-consuming." But before the release of the picture, when the production's intense demands were freshest in his memory, he gave every indication that he planned to continue working behind the cameras. He even announced his next directorial project, *Until They Sail,* from a story by James A. Michener.[1]

Why, then, did he stop after preparing so long and hard for a directing career? "Burt liked to do things perfectly," theorized Walter Seltzer, "and I think he realized that his talent as a director was lacking." Perhaps, with time, he could have improved. At the very least, he might have attempted a second project, one in which he did not also star. "I would have encouraged him to continue," said Seltzer. But Burt chose to abandon the dream.

On December 12, 1955, three and a half months after the premiere of *The Kentuckian, The Rose Tattoo* opened. As expected, Anna Magnani's performance drew superlatives from every quarter. More surprising were the several raves accorded Burt for his gutsy buffoonery. "Not the least of the film's amazements is Lancaster's portrayal," wrote Philip K. Scheuer of the *Los Angeles Times,* who liked Burt's Alvaro better than his Doc in *Come Back, Little Sheba.*

Still, Burt's performance, such a departure from his usual screen persona, had its detractors. Perhaps Arthur Knight of *The Saturday Review* articulated the viewpoint best, asserting that "one is always aware that he is acting, that he is playing a part that fits him physically but is beyond his emotional depth."

The Rose Tattoo was a major success, ranking an impressive sixteenth among the most popular films of 1956. It also garnered eight Oscar nominations and won three, including a Best Actress award for Magnani.

By January of 1956, Hecht-Lancaster had become an enormous success. Not only were *Vera Cruz* and *Marty* smash hits—with *Trapeze* on the horizon—*Marty* had brought Burt and Harold unprecedented prestige; never before had an actor's production company created an Oscar-winning film. "Hecht-Lancaster Productions is the largest and most important independent production organization in Hollywood," Burt proudly asserted. "We're worth twenty-five million dollars and have made five pictures, including *Marty,* have ten pictures in the works, employ thirty-five people, and own our own building."

Indeed, on December 5, 1954, he and Harold had acquired the former William Morris offices in Beverly Hills, for which they paid United

1. *Until They Sail* was eventually made by Robert Wise for MGM.

Artists $750,000. When they moved into their new quarters around the time of *Marty*'s premiere, the renovated building on N. Canon Drive had become a showplace. "It was paved with acres of white broadloom and furnished in the quasi-oriental style known as L. B. Ming and Metro-Goldwyn-Medici," observed Shana Alexander in *Life*. She also noted that Hecht's impressive office featured canvases by Corot, Utrillo, and other modern French masters and added, "Lancaster's office was more modest, though it did contain a half dozen Rouault paintings of circus acrobats, a barbecue, and a real waterfall." The pièce de résistance was the men's room, with its marble walls, onyx fixtures, and towels with *H-L* embroidered in gold.

The company also maintained less lavish offices in New York, which they opened in the United Artists Building in January of 1955. From there, they planned to mount their own Broadway shows (an ambition that they failed to realize) and to form their own music publishing company. Further, their presence in Manhattan enabled them to compete with the major studios for stage and book properties and for writers, directors, and actors working in television and the theater. According to Shirley Lantz (formerly Weingarten), who served as the head of Hecht-Lancaster's New York literary office, "We were very competitive. We covered everything everyone else was."

Lantz, who had worked as the Theatre Guild's casting director, was impressed by the budding moguls. "Burt and Harold were very smart and they read, unlike a lot of studio heads," she recalled. "And I think they had very admirable goals for this company. There was never any talk about just getting properties that would be hot at the box office. No one ever said, 'This is junky, but we should do it because it will be a hit.' They really wanted to make a contribution to the film industry." They did not plan on pursuing high-toned properties to the point of going broke, but, as Hecht argued in November of 1955, "Pictures with adult themes, intelligently approached and honestly executed, can be profitable."

In the six years since the making of *Kiss the Blood off My Hands,* Hecht had developed into a formidable producer. "People give Harold Hecht too little credit," said UA's Max Youngstein. "He was—at his best—one of the best producers I ever came across and had a real nose for product, for scripts, for writers." But Youngstein added that Harold could also be "a swift pain in the ass." Hecht-Lancaster writer John Gay agreed, saying, "He could be a very abrasive and abusive personality. He did not endear himself to a lot of people. He made a lot of enemies."

Given Hecht's personality and Burt's forthright manner and formidable temper, their offices were not unlike a war zone. "It was a very volatile company in terms of relationships," asserted Shirley Lantz. "People were not always treated very kindly. For me, it was like trying to keep a bit distant from a volcano." Life could be particularly rough on the company's writers, who at various points included Clifford Odets, N. Richard Nash, Paddy Chayefsky, Ernest Lehman, James Webb, John Gay, and J. P. Miller. "The partners could be harsh and unpleasant at times," said Lantz. "They were ambitious and demanding. Writers are frail. They have to be cushioned in order to write."

Dealing with Burt, Harold, and writer-producer Jim Hill (then the company's third man) could also be chaotic. "They had a routine that they did," recalled director Alexander Mackendrick. "You'd start off talking to Harold, and then Jim would walk in. So you'd recap for Jim, and then after a bit Harold would walk out. Then, while you were talking to Jim, in would walk Burt, you'd recap again, and Jim would walk out. And so on." Finally, in one of Mackendrick's meetings with them, "they all walked out. After a bit I got bored and went out into the corridor, and I saw all three of them having a little meeting at the end of the corridor."

Burt, Harold, and Jim played as hard as they worked. According to several employed by the company, Hecht and Hill drank excessively, with Burt not far behind (he was a heavy smoker as well). Burt and Hill were also said to have myriad liaisons with women. They often took staff members along with them on their jaunts—with Hecht's yacht a favorite hangout.

Burt was in no way a figurehead for the company that bore his name. According to J. P. Miller, he "had definite ideas about business, about publicity, about production. He understood what was going on when a picture was being produced."

Producing engaged Lancaster in a way that acting could not. "Some American actors think acting is unmanly," he acknowledged in 1969. "I felt that way myself for years—that I should be doing something else." By contrast, producing, with its air of command and element of risk, was macho. Moreover, he liked the challenge, saying, "I enjoy making decisions, like to sit in on story conferences, making suggestions—some of them good—and being part of the huge gamble that I can please audiences at the box office."

He was particularly interested in the company's choice of properties. "Burt loved to talk about stories," recalled Lantz. "He was fascinated with all things literary." Further, he was challenged by the development of screenplays. Sometimes he would become overly intellectual in his solutions to script problems, but story conferences usually found him acting out all the parts as he had done during the work on *His Majesty O'Keefe*. Said playwright N. Richard Nash, who worked with Hecht-Lancaster on an unproduced project, "He could tell you the truth of a scene instantly—by playing it for you right there. . . . That way he was a great producer." However, this technique was not always beneficial. "We'd talk a story or we'd talk a scene," asserted John Gay, "and he'd get up and do it with such enthusiasm and such artistry and everything, and I'd take notes and I'd say, 'Oh, yeah, yeah, yeah,' and I'd get it all down. And then, when I'd get upstairs to my typewriter, I'd say, 'Oh, my God, this doesn't work.' Then I realized that he'd sold me. When I watched him do it, it was wonderful, but underneath it all it didn't work."

Burt brought that same vigor to meetings with exhibitors and the executives at United Artists. In fact, his unflagging enthusiasm was probably his biggest contribution to the success of his company—after, of course, his drawing power at the box office. "He was a great salesman," recalled Walter Seltzer, "without being aggressively unpleasant or unctuous. It was something to see."

In public, Burt praised Hecht's skill. "Harold is the best executive I ever saw and an exceptional critic," he said in May of 1955. "He's not creative, but infallible when it comes to knowing what's good." In private, however, the association was volatile. "It was a love-hate relationship," said J. P. Miller. "It was a Freudian can of worms. Burt absolutely savaged Harold, and Harold was . . . kind of like a possum. If you scared him, he rolled up in a little ball. That did not mean that he was giving in or that he was backing off or anything else, but he just let the storm blow out." Sometimes the exchanges even turned physical. John Gay recalled a time when Burt, in a fit of temper, literally hoisted the producer into the air.

Hecht never lost sight of Burt's interests nor did he forget whose marquee value drove the company, but he wanted to forge his own identity. To his credit, Burt let Hecht enjoy the limelight during *Marty*'s night of triumph at the Oscar ceremonies. "I had nothing to do with *Marty* except I suggested Ernie Borgnine for it and our Hecht-Lancaster company made it," he told reporter Ruth Waterbury, forgetting the way that he had fought for the project with UA executive Max Youngstein. "Just because it has turned out to be a success gives me no right to go around taking any sort of bows for it."

Despite Burt's volatility and Harold's desire to be his own man, the partnership worked. "They needed each other," said Miller. "They bounced things off of each other. They listened to each other."

Indicative of their success was the new agreement they signed with United Artists on April 13, 1956. At $40 million for an estimated eighteen pictures over a four-year period, it was, according to *Variety,* the "biggest indie production-distribution deal in film history."

Although UA could no longer maintain its incredibly low 25 percent distribution fee for Hecht-Lancaster's films because the arrangement had become public and was putting the company at odds with every other independent producer in town, Krim and Benjamin devised a plan that achieved the same result. This new arrangement called for UA to give Hecht-Lancaster $50,000 for each million that their pictures (including the five already completed) earned over $45 million, the only stipulation being that each film had to break even first. Other incentives were provided as well, including a profit-sharing plan for key Hecht-Lancaster executives. "In essence," concluded UA historian Tino Balio, "UA subsidized Hecht-Lancaster's operations to the extent of $5,000 a week and indemnified the two partners against losses on the risks of running their business."

It was an extraordinary deal, signaling that, in less than a decade, Burt and Harold had become two of the leading filmmakers in Hollywood.

Lancaster was a budding mogul, but he was still under contract to Hal Wallis. He had two more films to go before he was free, and he started the first of them on March 12, 1956.

After the notable success of *Apache,* Wallis had eagerly sought a Western of his own for Lancaster. He found it in George Schulin's article "The Killer," which appeared in the August 1954 issue of *Holiday* magazine. "It is a story about Doc Holliday and Wyatt Earp," he wired his New York office, "and while both of these men have been dramatized to one extent or another in various Western pictures, I don't think the relationship between the two men, which makes this article interesting, has ever before been done."

Hollywood had, indeed, drawn inspiration from the legendary lawman and the consumptive dentist-cum-gunfighter. Arguably the best was *My Darling Clementine,* a 1946 John Ford film starring Henry Fonda and Victor Mature. Other versions include 1939's *Frontier Marshal* with Randolph Scott and Cesar Romero, 1967's *Hour of the Gun* with James Garner and Jason Robards, 1971's *Doc* with Stacy Keach and Harris

Yulin, 1993's *Tombstone* with Kurt Russell and Val Kilmer, and 1994's *Wyatt Earp* with Kevin Costner and Dennis Quaid.

Why the sixty-year fascination with the story? Part of it is due to the contrasting personalities of the two protagonists. Earp is typically seen as the plain, stoic, earnest upholder of the law, and Holliday as the ailing, cynical, flamboyant killer. Despite their differences, the marshal and the gunman are friends, and that camaraderie is also part of the appeal. And then there is the celebrated gun battle between, on the one side, Ike and Billy Clanton and Tom and Frank McLaury, and on the other, Wyatt, Doc, and Wyatt's two brothers, Morgan and Virgil. The encounter, which took place on October 26, 1881, in Tombstone, Arizona, has come to be regarded as the quintessential gun battle of the Old West.

The Wallis version was written by Leon Uris, who would gain fame as a best-selling novelist. Uris consulted Schulin's article and other published material but crafted much of his screenplay out of his imagination. "I would say it was my one happy experience in Hollywood," he asserted in 1993. "He [Wallis] had a tremendous respect for my ability to write."

Initially Lancaster refused to do *Gunfight at the O.K. Corral,* reflecting in all likelihood his usual, knee-jerk response to the properties Wallis chose for him. The producer began weighing alternatives, among them Gary Cooper, John Wayne, Gregory Peck, Charlton Heston, and Kirk Douglas. The first choice for Doc was Humphrey Bogart, who loved the idea, but after negotiations with the star fell through, Wallis considered Ben Gazzara and Jose Ferrer and, later, Frank Sinatra, Jack Palance, and Richard Widmark.

The producer then acquired the rights to the Broadway play *The Rainmaker.* "Burt telephoned me in the middle of the night," Wallis wrote in his autobiography, "to say that if I would let him play Starbuck, the lead in *The Rainmaker,* he would do *Gunfight at O.K. Corral* and that would take care of our two remaining commitments." Wallis agreed. With Burt on board, Kirk Douglas, once considered for Wyatt, signed on as Doc.[2]

• • •

2. Douglas, under contract to Wallis before Lancaster, had not sought Burt's extensions and delays. Consequently, he was a free agent by the time he signed to do *Gunfight at the O.K. Corral* and, as such, was paid considerably more for the film than his costar.

Nearly a decade had passed since Lancaster and Douglas had costarred in *I Walk Alone*. During the intervening years, Burt had matured considerably as an actor, and Douglas had become a major star. His portrayal of Vincent van Gogh in *Lust for Life*, shot just before *Gunfight at the O.K. Corral*, would earn him an Oscar nomination, as had his irrepressible film producer in *The Bad and the Beautiful* in 1952.

It was while filming the Western that the Lancaster-Douglas friendship was born. "We were really with each other night and day," Burt recalled. "We would sit up until one or two o'clock in the morning in this little hotel in Tucson, Arizona [where part of the film was shot], talking about our lives, our hopes, and our dreams. And Hal Wallis would always ask, 'What do you guys find to talk about?' The theory we used to have is that we spent so much time together because neither of us wanted to talk to Hal Wallis."

Lancaster perceptively realized that *Gunfight*, like *Vera Cruz*, was a buddy picture before Hollywood had a name for the genre. "We're playing two pre-Freudian fags," he told Kirk. "We're in love with each other and we don't know how to express ourselves that way—we just kind of look at each other and grunt and don't say very much, but you know we love each other." Douglas liked to recall a moment in the film that typified their relationship. It took place when Doc helps Wyatt subdue a saloon full of hostile cowboys. Afterward, the marshal thanks the gunfighter and Doc replies, "Forget it." "When I came to 'Forget it,'" Douglas asserted, "the ridiculousness of the scene—our great bravery, our machismo—made us howl. We did the scene over and over. It just made us laugh harder. Finally, we were laughing so hard, they had to stop shooting for the day and send us home like bad boys."

They liked each other, but some antagonism would always underscore the relationship. "We have a lot of controversy and conflict when we work," Burt explained, "because he's very much like me. He's conceited—he's opinionated. He tries to tell me how to act. I try to tell him how to act. And it goes this way." Then, the actor added, "And strangely enough out of this kind of feuding and fighting and fussing has come a great respect and mutual love that we've gained."

The "controversy and conflict" was not long in coming during the making of *Gunfight*. "From the start," Wallis recalled, "both stars asserted themselves. They reminded us constantly that they were directors as well as actors." It took a strong, self-confident director to keep two such volatile performers in check, but, as the producer asserted, "John [Sturges] was a match for them."

Two years older than Burt, Sturges had directed twenty-six pictures by 1956, including several Westerns. Uris was not only impressed by the director's skill, but also by his ability to work with independent actors. "He was a very good diplomat," recalled the writer. "He handled stars peaceably. I think that was as much his long suit as anything else."

It was the stars' attitude toward the script that perhaps challenged Sturges' diplomacy most. "They rewrote their dialogue at night," Wallis recalled, "but this was an exercise in futility, as I insisted that the lines be read exactly as Leon Uris had written them." Burt would later claim that he and one of his own company's writers (probably Jim Webb or A. B. Guthrie Jr.) extensively rewrote the script before filming began, forcing Wallis' complicity to such an extent that, in the actor's words, "I wouldn't let Wallis go out for lunch even; we had to send for sandwiches." There may be some truth to this story—Lancaster recounted it in such detail—but it is impossible to imagine him "letting" Wallis do anything; actors, even major stars like Burt, did not order him about. Moreover, Uris asserted that no changes were made to his text.

However, one alteration occurred, not in rewrites but in the way the film was cut. "When we started out," joked actress Rhonda Fleming, "it was going to be a love story between Burt and me with a strong relationship between Burt and Kirk, but as it went on, the relationship became stronger between Burt and Kirk, and I was kind of left holding the horse."

Fleming, a stunning, statuesque redhead, had been in films virtually since her graduation from Beverly Hills High School. In *Gunfight,* she played a gambler, Laura Denbow, whom Wyatt first arrests and then courts. She did not know her costar before filming began, but Burt charmed her from the outset. "He was like an old-world gentleman," she recalled. "He had a quality of class about him that I noticed immediately, because you don't work with many men who have that quality." She also found him "a lovely-looking man," but even more so, "a tender one."

Gunfight at the O.K. Corral was shot in several locales in Arizona and on the Paramount lot. For the climactic gunfight, Wallis considered going to the original site in Tombstone, "but we would have been cramped for angles," he said during filming. "There's a gas station on the corner now." The producer chose instead an adobe village in the Arizona desert, originally built by Columbia for its 1939 film *Arizona.*

The actual gunfight took about a half minute or so; essentially, the participants simply stood opposite one another and discharged their weapons. "We stretched ours to eleven minutes, and the excitement was terrific," enthused Wallis in his autobiography. During the course of the battle, the combatants moved from the corral to other parts of the town, with every bit of the action carefully choreographed and orchestrated so that the audience would know, to quote the producer, "at any given moment exactly where Earp and Holliday and the Clanton boys were." Filming the sequence took three days.

On May 17, after ten weeks of shooting, the production wrapped.

On May 30, just two weeks after Burt finished filming *Gunfight,* *Trapeze* premiered in Los Angeles, to benefit the Variety Boys Club. In the grand Hollywood tradition, the festivities included a two-ring circus on the sidewalk outside the theater, hosted by the reigning emcee of TV variety, Ed Sullivan, and a midnight party at the former Warners studio on Sunset Boulevard, with Lancaster, Curtis, and Carol Reed in attendance. The following week, Burt and Tony appeared on Sullivan's variety show. Working from a script by a television writer hired by Hecht-Lancaster, they were a smash. Wrote one reviewer, "Lancaster and Curtis, gag after gag, line after line, built up that tremendous TV audience's desire to see *Trapeze.*"

The special events were supported by a $2-million ad campaign—in an era when the norm for a top film was between $300,000 and $400,000. The gamble paid off—big. *Trapeze* took in $4.1 million at the box office for the week leading up to the Fourth of July. That was believed to be the largest seven-day gross in the history of the motion picture business to that point.

Trapeze was an enormous hit, but it failed to reveal the true-life backstage world of the circus as Burt had initially hoped. Burt and Curtis' early practice sessions on the riggings began to suggest what the actor had in mind, but as they gave way to the romantic triangle involving the picture's three stars, *Trapeze* became, to quote *The New York Times'* Bosley Crowther, "a hackneyed story that is almost as old and sawdust-littered as the one about the brokenhearted clown."

Still, the soap suds came wrapped in a spectacular package. To begin with there were the high-bar sequences, which Carol Reed had lovingly photographed from every conceivable angle. As *Variety* noted, "The aerial footage literally causes the hair to stand on end as the high fliers go through their death-defying stunts." Moreover, the Paris locales added a nice atmospheric touch. And, finally, as Reed had hoped, the screen was alive with elephants, horses, ballet dancers, midgets, and other circus folk. As a consequence, there was "hardly a dead spot for the eyes," to quote Philip K. Scheuer of the *Los Angeles Times.*

In the end, the picture would earn between $10 and $11 million in its initial release, making it the biggest moneymaker that Burt and Harold ever produced.

Lancaster barely had time to savor the response to *Trapeze* before he was summoned to Paramount for his second Wallis picture in a row—and his final contractual obligation to the producer.

The Rainmaker, set in Kansas in 1913, centers on the Curry family and, in particular, the slightly plain but loving woman of the house, Lizzie Curry. Lizzie, blessed with lively intelligence and a quick tongue, is in danger of becoming an old maid. It is through her involvement with a fast-talking con man named Starbuck, the title character, that she comes to realize her potential as a woman.

The play opened at the Cort Theater on October 28, 1954, with Geraldine Page and Darren McGaven in the leading roles. Despite glowing notices, it ran only fifteen weeks. No doubt, the relatively rapid closing distressed Hal Wallis, who paid a very sizable $350,000 for the film rights a month after the drama opened—disproving once again Lancaster's assertion that the producer was too cheap to expend any money for properties.

At the time of the acquisition, *Variety* noted, "Property was bought as a possible vehicle for Burt Lancaster." But in November of that year, after also considering Clark Gable and Bing Crosby, the producer announced that William Holden would be his Starbuck. By contrast, Wallis had only one candidate for the female lead: Katharine Hepburn.

Wallis engaged the original playwright, N. Richard Nash, to do his own adaptation. Nash created a prologue that showed Starbuck escaping from his previous con job, but "otherwise," said the playwright, "there aren't many differences between the film and the play. Except for that old expression, *opening out.*" As Wallis had done with *Come Back, Little Sheba* and *The Rose Tattoo,* he hired the play's director—in this case, Joseph Anthony—to put the adaptation before the cameras. It would mark Anthony's film directorial debut, but he was not a complete stranger to Hollywood. He had been an MGM contract player in the early 1940s.[3]

Hepburn was not happy about costarring with Holden. Not only did

3. Anthony would go on to direct several other films, including Shirley Booth in the adaptation of Thornton Wilder's play *The Matchmaker* in 1958. But he would also remain a very active stage director with comedies (*Mary, Mary, Under the Yum Yum Tree*), dramas (*The Best Man*), and musicals (*The Most Happy Fella* and *110 in the Shade*—from *The Rainmaker*) to his credit.

she think he was wrong for Starbuck, she also feared that, as his senior by eleven years, she was too old to play opposite him.[4] She was so distressed that, finally, on November 28, 1955, she asked Wallis to find someone else for Lizzie. But the producer urged her to reconsider, and two and a half months later, she did.

Then, Holden withdrew. According to Paul Nathan, the Oscar winner was "afraid of [the] part." And not without reason. Starbuck's blend of hokum and tenderness requires a special talent. It was when Lancaster read of Holden's withdrawal in Hedda Hopper's column that he called the producer and proposed himself as a replacement, offering to do *Gunfight at the O.K. Corral* to sweeten the deal. It was a fortuitous move, because Lancaster was perfect for the con man. "He naturally has all the braggadocio that Starbuck requires," asserted Nash. "It's part of his natural quality as a human being. . . . There is another very important requirement in Starbuck: his braggadocio should conceal an intense vulnerability, and Burt is a very vulnerable guy. He is touched by many things, although he pretends not to." No one could have been happier about the turn of events than Hepburn. At the end of February 1956, after seeing *The Rose Tattoo,* she wired the producer to praise the decision (as well as the film and Magnani's performance).

To round out the cast, Wallis chose Cameron Prud'homme of the original Broadway company and Lloyd Bridges as Lizzie's father and older brother respectively, and his contract player, Wendell Corey, for the deputy sheriff whom Lizzie fancies. For her younger, impulsive brother, he nearly hired Elvis Presley, which would have marked the teen idol's film debut, but the idea of Elvis as Kate Hepburn's sibling was too much of a stretch. The role went instead to Earl Holliman, who had turned in a commendable performance in *Gunfight at the O.K. Corral.*[5]

Strong-willed, opinionated, and intolerant of foolishness (but also kind and enormously sympathetic), Hepburn was quite different from the genteel leading ladies who had appeared opposite Lancaster in the past. He found that out on the first day of production—when he arrived late. According to Wallis, Hepburn "gave him hell. She walked into the center of the soundstage and said, 'I'm here; all these people are here; and if

4. Holden was four years younger than Lancaster.
5. Wallis would eventually put Elvis under contract and feature him in a number of pictures beginning with *Loving You* in 1957. But, by then, the singer had already made his film debut—in 1956's *Love Me Tender.*

you're not going to be here on time, we can't work.' He learned his lesson and was on time for the rest of the shooting."

Lancaster, himself a perfectionist who was rarely tardy, may have arrived late for reasons having nothing to do with punctuality. "I think he was scared to death to be playing with her," asserted Nash. But, in time, said the playwright, "she made him feel comfortable."

Kate's supportive prodding reached its zenith during the filming of the scene in which Starbuck tells Lizzie about his talented brothers. It is a long, poetic speech, one of the most important in the entire drama. When shooting started, Lancaster "was lying back, underplaying it quite considerably while she was playing full out," Nash recalled. He and Anthony were growing concerned when Hepburn dropped character, shook her finger at Burt, and whispered sotto voce, "Now look here, Burt, this is your scene, and if you don't play it full out, I'm going to take it away from you." Said Nash, "Now you know how selfless that actress was to have done that? And he responded to it. He saw that she was a decent person who cared about the film and about him too. And, boy, he played it full out, and he was wonderful in that scene."

After that, said the playwright, the costars "became deeply fond of each other. It became a very warm, warm friendship, full of respect and jokes and all the rest of it." Holliman agreed: "They looked to me like two people who really admired and respected each other professionally. And they seemed to like each other. . . . She thought Burt was marvelous."

It was not only the rapport between the stars that made *The Rainmaker* such a joyous experience. "The tone that Joe Anthony set was so relaxed, you couldn't wait to get to work," recalled Holliman.

Anthony also sought to, in his words, "create a very special and individual world for each vehicle." Unfortunately, he was unable to take advantage of *The Rainmaker*'s setting, the Great Plains. He could have benefited from several weeks of location shooting, but instead virtually the entire picture was filmed at Paramount. Three of the studio's largest soundstages were combined for the Curry farmhouse and tack room while the town scenes were filmed on the backlot, where Paramount had just erected a "Western Street" at the cost of half a million dollars.

Anthony, now deceased, told Hepburn biographer Charles Higham that he found Lancaster extremely difficult. Even before shooting started, he maintained that the actor "was grumbling, disagreeable, plainly rude. I decided if he stayed, I would not. Later, he apologized, to the limited extent of which he was capable, but it wasn't a very happy way to start a picture. I didn't think highly of him. I still don't." Anthony further asserted that, during filming, Lancaster "was butting into other people's business all the time, half-directing, suggesting things to the cameraman, insisting on key lights, interfering. He had to be completely in charge of everything or he wasn't satisfied." Holliman, on the other hand, said, "If there was anything unpleasant that went on between those two, it was well hidden. I was never exposed to it. All I ever saw was joy on that set." He went on to assert that Lancaster "really liked Joe Anthony. . . . He respected Joe's mentality, his creativity." Nash shared Holliman's viewpoint, maintaining that the actor and the director got along "wonderfully well. Sometimes Burt would stop after Joe had said something and be very still for a moment and then ask a question or two. And Joe might change a little bit of what he'd said or say something in furtherance of what he'd said, and then he'd go right back and do the scene practically the way Joe asked for it." Nash concluded by calling Lancaster "an absolute angel. He was very considerate of people around him."

Although Wallis typically took a year to release a film after the end of shooting, *The Rainmaker* premiered on December 13, 1956, only four months to the day that it had wrapped.

After Lancaster's intense performance as the embittered flier in *Trapeze,* Nash's engaging piece of Americana enabled him to return to the flamboyant, gregarious persona that had enlivened *The Flame and the Arrow* and *Vera Cruz.* As *Variety* noted, he played "the part with an infectious breeziness that's a major part of the entertainment."

More surprising was the tenderness that he brought to the intimate scenes between Starbuck and Lizzie. In these moments, he displayed an uncluttered simplicity that recalled his love scenes in *All My Sons*—but with a maturity that he had lacked in 1947 when the Miller drama was filmed. He was particularly moving during the tack-room scene, in which the con man convinces the spinster that she is beautiful. Hepburn, who had just appeared in a somewhat similar role in *Summertime,* worked wonderfully with her costar. She was not perfect casting—she was too old for Lizzie and from the wrong part of the country—but she was luminous nonetheless, well deserving of the Oscar nomination that she earned for her performance.

Despite mixed reviews, *The Rainmaker* ended up forty-sixth among the most popular films of 1957.

• • •

With the release of *The Rainmaker,* Lancaster's long association with
Hal Wallis came to an end. In the waning days of their relationship, the
tensions between the two men eased somewhat. Ruth Waterbury may
have gone a bit far when she wrote in *Photoplay* in 1956, "Hal Wallis,
whom he [Burt] once thought of as an enemy to conquer, had become
one of his most respected friends." But Burt asserted during the making
of *Trapeze,* "We're friendly—we have knockdowns and drag-outs—he's
not a bad man. . . . Several years ago I was bitter toward Wallis. Now I
feel sorry for him—he's in trouble; he's got forty million dollars and
doesn't know how to enjoy it."

People in show business tend to have long memories. Wallis' autobiography, *Starmaker,* published in 1980, nearly a quarter of a century after his relationship with Lancaster ended, clearly revealed his
smoldering resentment toward his former contract player. As for Burt,
he never stopped complaining about how cheap Wallis was.

The change in Lancaster's fortunes during his years as a Wallis contract
player was never more evident than on the very last day of 1956, when
Burt and Harold summoned the press to their sumptuous quarters in
Beverly Hills. Their purpose was to announce the company's highly ambitious program for the next two years.

Lancaster, seated in a corner, was silent as Hecht presented the com-
pany's impressive schedule, which included G. B. Shaw's *The Devil's
Disciple* (with Burt and Montgomery Clift); the $5-million *The Way
West,* which playwright Clifford Odets was scripting from A. B. Guthrie
Jr.'s novel and in which Burt, James Stewart, and (it was hoped) Gary
Cooper would star; *The Catbird Seat* by James Thurber, with a screen-
play by playwright George Axelrod; and *First Love* by Ivan Turgenev,
which playwright John Van Druten was adapting as a vehicle for Audrey
Hepburn.

When Hecht finished, Burt rose and said, "Before you go, boys, we
have one other bit of news. From now on the correct name of the firm is
Hecht-Hill-Lancaster."

Incredible as it may seem, Burt had made the decision to expand the
company's upper-management tier unilaterally. "When Hill became a
partner, it was a surprise to Hecht," recalled Walter Seltzer, who was
present when the announcement was made. Indeed, Lancaster's long-
standing associate was so stunned that, as Shana Alexander later reported in *Life,* "newsmen present say that Hecht's face drained white."

• • •

Few understood Hill's elevation to the senior-most level in one of the leading independent production companies in the industry. The forty-year-old native of Jeffersonville, Indiana, had simply been an MGM contract writer before he had joined Hecht-Lancaster.

"Burt and Harold thought he had a very fine story mind, and they leaned very heavily on him," acknowledged Walter Seltzer. But others in the company disagreed with their assessment of his abilities. "Everything that he thought about was a scene out of another movie," maintained writer J. P. Miller. "We were supposed to take some great scene from some other picture and duplicate it with our characters." To which Richard McWhorter added, "He didn't have any story sense to me." Actor Martin Milner, who was under contract to HHL, maintained, "I don't know what he brought to the company. I met Hill on a number of occasions and was with him a few times socially, and I never did exactly figure out where he fit."

Hill's rise—asserted colleagues in a position to know—was due to a more elemental factor than his story sense. "He was Lancaster's boy," maintained Julius Epstein, who wrote and produced Hecht-Hill-Lancaster's *Take a Giant Step.* "He and Lancaster were a team," echoed actor Jack Elam. "I think they were very close." So close that apparently Burt even involved himself in Jim's love life.

It was no secret that Hill, who was single until he married actress Rita Hayworth on February 2, 1958, liked to bed stars. "Jim Hill made fun of the people who screwed secretaries, because he was a snob," asserted writer J. P. Miller. "He was only interested in screwing big names." On at least one occasion, Lancaster assisted his friend in this ambition. According to one of the actor's costars, "Burt called me at home several times because Jim wanted to meet me, he wanted to take me out to dinner or something. And he [Burt] was rather ordering me [to go], and I thought this was very strange, because he didn't act like that on the set. But he was very determined that I was going to date Jim Hill." Eventually she did, though nothing much came of it. J. P. Miller was present when Hill asked Lancaster for help with the beautiful actress: "I heard Jim Hill telling him, 'Call her up. Tell her I'm a big producer. Give her a big line. I mean, I can't do that myself, but you can do it.' "

Hill did have his supporters at Hecht-Lancaster. John Gay credited him with "a very good story sense." He also found Hill "a lot of fun to be around." So did Jack Elam, who described Hill as "kind of pleasant, easygoing, had a sense of humor. I liked him."

Like him or not, Hill was Burt's friend, and as of the last day of 1956, he was a partner in an important production company. But the decision to make him so, announced without consultation, would have significant consequences for the future of the firm. As J. P. Miller put it, "His name went in between Harold's and Burt's, which was very symbolic."

CHAPTER TEN

Hecht-Hill-Lancaster

Before television and glossy magazines like *People* redefined the meaning of celebrity, New York's nationally syndicated columnists wielded enormous power. Those who were paid to keep their clients' names before the public would often do anything to get the ear of an Ed Sullivan or a Dorothy Kilgallen.

"That was my world," said screenwriter Ernest Lehman, who had once worked for big-time Broadway press agent Irving Hoffman. Lehman captured the milieu in a shocking, no-holds-barred novella entitled *The Sweet Smell of Success,* published in *Cosmopolitan* magazine in 1950. Lehman's protagonist—and narrator—was a sycophantic PR huckster named Sidney Wallace; the powerful columnist who plays Sidney like a puppet was called Harvey Hunsecker, a character clearly patterned after Hoffman's crony Walter Winchell.

Harold Hecht had handled the film rights to *Sweet Smell* while still an agent. After he became a producer, he tried to acquire the novella for himself, but Lehman rebuffed his offers. Finally, the success of *Marty* convinced the writer to make the sale—but he insisted on directing the picture as well as writing the screenplay.

From the outset Tony Curtis was tapped to play Sidney (whose last name was changed from Wallace to the more visceral Falco). "By his own admission, TC hounded Burt Lancaster for the part," wrote Barry Paris, coauthor of Curtis' autobiography. The role of a scheming, toadying, desperate PR flack was not what Universal had in mind for its popular all-American contract player. But Curtis, tired of costume melodramas and eager to display his talent, was determined to do the picture. Thereafter, he even helped finance it, through his and then-wife Janet Leigh's production company, Curtleigh.

For Hunsecker, whose first name was changed from Harvey to J.J.

and who was given a strong conservative political bias for the screenplay, Lehman considered Orson Welles, as well as Broadway actor Martin Gabel. The writer maintained that it was Burt—after sitting in on several story conferences—who proposed himself for the part. That may have been so, but the actor asserted that United Artists asked him to take the role to bolster the picture's drawing power. Whatever the reason, Lehman welcomed the casting.

Lehman, slight and relatively moralistic, had a difficult time adjusting to the rough-and-tumble world of Hecht-Hill-Lancaster. A major blow came when he was told that he would not be allowed to direct *Sweet Smell of Success* after all. UA, Hecht told him, was afraid of another first-time director in the wake of Burt's lack of success with *The Kentuckian.*

To replace him, the producers chose Alexander Mackendrick, the Scottish director who had distinguished himself with a series of comedies at the British studio Ealing, most notably *The Man in the White Suit,* starring Alec Guinness. Initially, Mackendrick had been engaged by Hecht-Hill-Lancaster to direct *The Devil's Disciple,* a project for which he was ideally suited. It was only when the Shaw comedy was put on hold that he was given *Sweet Smell of Success,* an assignment for which he was a far less obvious choice. But Mackendrick liked the project; it would enable him to prove that he could do something beyond what he called "cute British comedies." Moreover, he was challenged by the idea of "trying to capture on the screen the atmosphere of Manhattan," as well as the shady side of the newspaper business.

Despite the loss of the director's mantle, Lehman worked with Mackendrick on several drafts of the screenplay. But a few weeks before shooting was to begin, the writer developed an acute stomach disorder and had to withdraw from the project on the recommendation of his doctor.

When Lehman informed Burt of his condition, the actor expressed concern. Sometime after the film's release, however, they met at a party, and Burt reacted quite differently. As Lehman recalled it, Burt said, "Ernie, you weren't that sick. . . . If you had stayed, it would have been a much better picture. You know what? I ought to give you a punch in the jaw right now." The writer replied, "Go ahead, Burt, I need the money."[1]

1. Sheilah Graham recounted the incident in her book *Confessions of a Hollywood Columnist,* published in 1969, but attributed it to Odets. "She got it all wrong," said Lehman in 1993. "It was me, not Clifford."

Lehman was not disturbed by the threat; he saw it as a strange kind of compliment. "It wasn't that he was angry at me," the writer said. "He was angry that I left." Besides, he added, Burt "was always very kind to me, and gentle and respectful and nice, and I knew he wasn't really going to hit me."

By the time Lehman withdrew from *Sweet Smell of Success,* the screenplay simply needed polishing—or so the producers and Mackendrick believed. Hecht, Hill, and Lancaster wanted to assign the task to Paddy Chayefsky, but Mackendrick asked instead for Clifford Odets, the great liberal playwright of the 1930s, who was also on the HHL staff.

To everyone's surprise, Odets embarked on a complete rewrite. "What Clifford did, in effect," Mackendrick explained, "was dismantle the structure of every single sequence in order to rebuild situations and relationships that were much more complex, had much greater tension and more dramatic energy." The writing was exciting, but HHL could not wait for Odets to finish in order to put the picture before the cameras. Curtis and Lancaster had other commitments after *Sweet Smell* wrapped. Moreover, they could not change the complicated arrangements attendant to filming in Manhattan without considerable hardship. Thus, once more, Burt's company started a major project without a completed screenplay.

They began with three weeks of location work in New York during the winter of 1956. As soon as Odets finished writing a scene in his hotel room, he would deliver it to Mackendrick for filming that day. "It reached farcical proportions," recalled the director. "The mimeographed pages of script were usually distributed to the crew after the scenes had been shot." Final edits were made on the set, with the producers, the director, and the actors participating.

In addition to the script problem, the company had to contend with the rigors of shooting in the heart of America's busiest city. But capturing Manhattan's frenetic pace was crucial to Mackendrick's vision. As he maintained, "One of the characteristic aspects of New York . . . is the neurotic energy of the crowded sidewalks. This was, I argued, essential to the story of characters driven by the uglier aspects of ambition and greed." Given Hunsecker's and Falco's lifestyles, most of the shooting was done at night. "It was cold," recalled assistant director Richard McWhorter. "God, you needed all the clothes you could get on, and you were still cold."

• • •

Although Jim Hill was the film's producer, Martin Milner, cast as the musician boyfriend of Hunsecker's sister, Susan, asserted, "Burt was the central figure of the production. He always seemed to be in charge." Sometimes Lancaster would even, as Milner put it, talk "to me directly about the sort of values that he wanted in the scene."[2]

Mackendrick was apparently untroubled by such behavior. He said later, "In truth, at the time I found Lancaster very easy to work with as an actor. . . . He was extremely precise and well-disciplined." But he also felt that Burt was volatile, asserting that when the star entered the room, "the room temperature rises because he brings with him a sense of something that is . . . how shall I put it, 'dangerous!' There is that sense of something unpredictable."

To Odets, the star seemed downright schizophrenic. Later, he itemized Burt's many personalities for Shana Alexander: "No. 1 is Enigmatic Burt, the Inscrutable One, of whom a prominent Hollywood psychoanalyst once said, 'That man always gives me the creepiest feeling that I am in one room and he is in another.' No. 2 is Cocksure Burt, a man of total self-confidence, tinged with faint mockery and an edge of contempt. No. 3 is Wild Man Burt, a creature of enormous enthusiasms, exuberance, and inexhaustible physical energy. No. 4 is Old Father Burt, a kindly, paternal character who appears when older or weaker persons are present. No. 5 might be labeled 'Mr. Hyde,' cutting, searing Burt, who is remarkable not so much for his vulgarity—which can be spectacular— but for the destructive quality of his cruelty. No. 6 is the Marquis de Lancaster, a distinguished gentleman of the old school, rather mincing and prancing, who talks as if he'd just stepped out of the Congress of Vienna. No. 7 is Snake Oil Burt, con man, mischief-maker, and light-hearted rogue."

When *Sweet Smell* wrapped in New York, the company returned to Hollywood to shoot the interiors at the Goldwyn Studios. One of the major sets was an exact reproduction of Hunsecker's favorite hangout, the "21" Club, built at a cost of $25,000 on Soundstage 8. The set featured "wild walls"—partitions that could slide in and out—to allow James Wong Howe's camera to move in ways that would never have been possible on the actual site.

2. Milner won the role at the urging of Lancaster, who remembered him from *Gunfight at the O.K. Corral.* Like Ernest Borgnine, the twenty-nine-year-old actor was put under contract by HHL. He gained fame a few years later as one of the stars of television's popular drama series *Route 66.*

Mackendrick took maximum advantage of this flexibility. According to Lancaster, a scene that would run perhaps six minutes on the screen might have "thirty-five camera moves on a dolly. The whole floor was taped. We had to hit marks like crazy." Hours of rehearsal would be required just to coordinate the technical aspects of the shooting, and once the camera rolled, the concentration was fearsome, because even the tiniest error could ruin an entire take. Even if everything went like clockwork, Mackendrick typically called for retakes and then reorchestrated all of the camera positions. Sometimes Burt would argue that the budget could not support further experimentation, but otherwise, as he said, he "put up with it because you put up with Babe Ruth even if he's drunk. We respected Sandy; he was a little kooky, but he was good."

Mackendrick conceded that he overplotted some shots. "But my private reason," he added, "was that I had been warned by the editor, Alan Crosland, of the producer's intention to start drastic reediting of all the 'director's cut.' " Mackendrick believed that by creating a series of intricately photographed sequences, sequences that could only be pieced together as he intended before they were shot, he could preserve the integrity of his vision. He did not have much success, he said later. Worse, fear and chaos took their toll on the budget. By the time *Sweet Smell of Success* wrapped, a picture that should have cost $600,000 at most had become a $2.6 million white elephant.

While Burt and Jim concentrated on *Sweet Smell of Success,* Hecht focused on *The Bachelor Party.* Shot in New York and Hollywood beginning in late August of 1956 (before the Odets-Lehman drama), it reunited the producer, the director, and the author of *Marty* and, like its successful predecessor, had begun as a drama for television.

The Bachelor Party attempted to grapple with the institution of marriage. Specifically, the Manhattan-based drama centered on five men, including Charlie (Don Murray), a bookkeeper whose wife has just become pregnant; Eddie (Jack Warden), the office bachelor; and Arnold (Philip Abbott), a skittish groom-to-be. The two female leads were Charlie's sister (Nancy Marchand) and a liberated Greenwich Village intellectual whom Charlie picks up (Carolyn Jones).

"Burt certainly had nothing to do with the shooting of the film or the editing of it," recalled director Delbert Mann. "It was Harold all the way through." Don Murray noted, however, that Lancaster occasionally came by during the shooting in Los Angeles. "He would not assert himself in any way," recalled the actor, "except to offer encouragement, especially to a young actor playing a lead, like myself. . . . Here was a big star treating me as a coworker of equal stature. He was a very constructive, positive influence."

The Bachelor Party premiered on April 10, 1957, earning high marks from several quarters, including *Variety* and the *Los Angeles Times*. But *The Saturday Review* asserted that it "never wholly succeeds in engaging our sympathies. Its heroes are simply nice little guys—whereas *Marty* was a *person*," and *Newsweek* dubbed it "a movie which seems likely to strike many people as so dull that they will become positively angry about it."

The mixed reviews failed to send filmgoers rushing to their neighborhood theaters; consequently, *The Bachelor Party* did not remotely approach *Marty*'s grosses. Worse, it went so far over budget that it cost three times the first Hecht-Chayefsky-Mann collaboration.

On May 30, a month and a half after the premiere of *The Bachelor Party*, *Gunfight at the O.K. Corral* debuted. As with *Apache* and *Vera Cruz*, the critics were inclined to compare the picture to the likes of *High Noon* and *Shane*, sophisticated Westerns with high moral purposes. But, with *Gunfight*, some of the reviewers appeared relieved to be back on more elemental ground. As Hollis Alpert remarked in *The Saturday Review*, "The cowhand . . . is much more likely now to be a man ridden with guilt and haunted with ghosts of the past. . . . I bring all this up to show how original and even refreshing *Gunfight at the O.K. Corral* seems these days, now that the id and the superego have been made part of the Western pattern."

Lancaster was fine as the stalwart Earp. But, just as Burt nearly walked away with *Vera Cruz* in the flashier gunslinger role, so Douglas drew the eye as Doc Holliday in *Gunfight*. Alternately charming and deadly, he played the ailing, knife-throwing, fast-drawing, gentlemanly dentist as a coiled snake, a creature with a knack for irritating virtually everyone—including Wyatt—but who reserved his contempt for the one who loved him most, the poor, pathetic prostitute Kate Fisher (Jo Van Fleet). The contrasting rhythms between the volatile, emotional Douglas and the controlled, hardened Lancaster were particularly effective in this pairing, taking the "rip-roaring, gun-banging Western," as *Cue* called it, to twelfth place among the biggest hits of 1957.

On June 27, not even a month after the premiere of *Gunfight*, a very different Lancaster appeared on the nation's screens in *Sweet Smell of Success*.

Anyone expecting another *Trapeze* was sorely disappointed by the reteaming of the circus blockbuster's stars. "*Sweet Smell of Success* is such a sordid movie that you might want to go outside occasionally for a breath of fresh air," William Zinsser advised readers of the New York *Herald Tribune*. Then he added, "But it is so good that you will end up by keeping your seat." The film's pace, James Wong Howe's evocative camerawork, and Mackendrick's ability to capture the frenetic energy of Manhattan nightlife—just as he had hoped—all drew praise. So did the crackling dialogue, which was replete with gems like "You're dead, son. Get yourself buried" and "I'd hate to take a bite out of you. You're a cookie full of arsenic."

Dorothy Masters of the New York *Daily News* accurately recognized Sidney as Tony Curtis' "best performance to date" (it remains arguably the finest work of his career), and Lancaster was chilling as the powerful columnist. Without raising his voice or letting a hint of emotion cross his stone face, he created a portrait of raging ego and unbridled power that was alternately hilarious and terrifying. Wisely, he made no attempt to copy Winchell's inimitable style. He did not even focus on being a journalist. "I wasn't really portraying a columnist," he asserted, "but a heel. Otherwise I'd have spent time in newspaper offices, studying the characterization. No, I just played a heel who happened to be a columnist."

What gave his performance an unusually macabre aspect were the horn-rimmed spectacles that he wore throughout (Burt wore glasses in real life). According to Mackendrick, they were James Wong Howe's idea. The cinematographer used them as a focal point for light, with the shadows they cast giving the actor's chiseled features the aspect of a skeleton. "So throughout the entire film," said the director, "a light moved with Burt, just in front of him, often with Jimmy holding it himself, to produce this strange mask of a face."

In more recent decades, *Sweet Smell of Success* has become a cult favorite. Lehman's ruthless, power-mad, success-driven antiheroes are all too familiar to a post-Vietnam, post-Watergate society. The film is also regarded as among the best movies ever made about New York. But, in 1957, America saw itself in simpler, more positive terms. *Sweet Smell* was so out of sync with the times that, as UA executive Bob Blumofe said in retrospect, it almost seemed "as though it was made in defiance of the box office." Consequently, it lost millions, the first genuine flop that Hecht-Norma or its successors had ever produced. Burt later called it "a total disaster."

Ironically, the failure gave some measure of comfort to the HHL partner least involved in the picture's creation. According to reporter Ezra

Goodman, "Hecht had certain ideas about making the movie but was overruled by the combined Lancaster and Hill." After a preview of the picture in San Francisco, Hecht asked for Goodman's opinion, and when the reporter told him, "I thought that it was poor," he noticed the producer's surprising reaction: "Hecht was overjoyed. His face broke into a wide, CinemaScope-type smile and I became his buddy. *Sweet Smell of Success* was a flop and lost a great deal of money, but Hecht was happy. He had proved his point." That reaction did not augur well for the company's future.

During the early months of 1957—prior to the release of either *The Bachelor Party* or *Sweet Smell of Success*—Joseph Vogel, president of Loew's, Inc., got the idea of having Hecht, Hill, and Lancaster join Metro-Goldwyn-Mayer, Loew's subsidiary, as "special consultants." In addition, Vogel wanted Burt to play the title role in the studio's multi-million-dollar remake of the epic silent film *Ben-Hur,* then in preproduction.

Like all of the studios, MGM was struggling to survive in the post-TV age of declining box-office revenues and rising costs (the latter due, in no small measure, to the bigger-is-better approach to combating television's impact). MGM, once the most powerful studio in the industry, had fallen on particularly hard times because, after the 1951 ouster of production chief Louis B. Mayer, it lacked the continuity of leadership enjoyed by some of its competitors. Vogel thought that Burt, Harold, and Jim could give the company the new, brash air that it sorely needed. He could not, however, persuade his conservative board of directors, who bridled at the autonomy on which Lancaster, Hecht, and Hill insisted and at the partners' rather avant-garde program.

If they could not take over the studio, Burt, Harold, and Jim did the next best thing: they struck a one-picture deal with the biggest star in the Metro pantheon—Clark Gable. The film was *Run Silent, Run Deep.*

Typically, HHL acquired the properties that it wished to produce and then convinced United Artists to finance them. But it was UA that purchased the film rights to *Run Silent, Run Deep*—a *New York Times* bestseller—and then asked HHL to develop the property.

Written by Capt. Edward L. Beach, a thirty-year naval officer, the novel recounted the World War II exploits of its fictional narrator, Edward G. Richardson. Although the plot was episodic and overextended, it drew strength from Beach's vast, firsthand knowledge of submarine warfare. His characters, by contrast, were rather stock, with the book's primary conflict (apart from the war) stemming from the rivalry between Richardson and his protégé and executive officer, Jim Bledsoe. Gable would, of course, play Richardson, and Lancaster Bledsoe. To direct, HHL engaged Robert Wise, whose eclectic body of work included science fiction *(The Day the Earth Stood Still),* contemporary drama *(Executive Suite),* and biography *(Somebody Up There Likes Me)* and who would go on to guide two musicals *(West Side Story* and *The Sound of Music)* to Oscars for Best Picture.

John Gay, a New York television writer assigned to the adaptation, retained Beach's two principal characters, but he heightened the tension between them—with Richardson coming to represent a daring and innovative approach to combat and Bledsoe a steadier but more conservative style. Their encounters and the considerable telescoping of the plot gave the screenplay a sharper focus, greater dramatic tension, and a stronger narrative thrust than the book.

Gay was about two-thirds of the way through the screenplay when he attended a party at Lancaster's house. Burt, who had not yet read the script, pulled him aside and said, "John, you're too good a writer for this crap." Not knowing how to respond, Gay left the party fully convinced that Lancaster was not going to make the picture. "That was a Saturday night," the writer recalled, "and I was working weekends to get the thing done. So I was in the office the next morning, Sunday morning, working away and saying to myself, 'What am I doing? Burt doesn't want to do the film. He thinks it's crap.'" So Gay called Hecht and relayed what Burt had said the night before. The producer grew perceptibly agitated, but encouraged Gay to keep writing. A few hours later, Burt phoned the office. "John," he said, "maybe I had too much to drink last night or something, but forget what I said, just forget what I said. Just keep going, kid."

Despite the rocky beginning, the screenwriter and Lancaster got along well. "I think he really respected writers," Gay asserted. But Burt would occasionally ridicule the superficiality of his character in *Run Silent,* and finally Gay joined in. "In fact," the writer recalled, "we used to make fun of the lines. Burt had one line, 'Suppose we sink a couple [meaning enemy ships].' Well, that became sort of a catch phrase for us. Whenever anything went wrong on *Separate Tables* [which Gay coauthored] or something, he would say, 'Suppose we sink a couple.'"

During *Run Silent,* HHL was as chaotic as ever. One time, the lack of organizational efficiency nearly destroyed the producers' relationship with Gable. As Gay recalled it, the incident took place a few weeks before the start of production. "We were having a nighttime meeting at the

Hecht-Hill-Lancaster office on Canon Drive," said the writer. The meeting was scheduled for seven. Gay arrived about ten minutes early—to find Gable sitting on the front step with his wife. "What are you doing out here?" Gay asked.

"The fucking place is locked up," Gable answered angrily. "You can't get in. What kind of a cheesy, crummy outfit is this?"

Not having a key, Gay ran to the corner drugstore and phoned Hecht.

"The meeting's at eight o'clock," the producer informed Gay over the phone.

"Nobody told Clark, and nobody told me," replied the writer.

Hecht got the picture. "Oh, my God," he said. "I'll get down there right away." But, by the time he arrived, the damage had been done. As Gay put it, "That night, I think that kind of colored things a bit, you know, in his [Gable's] relationship with Hecht-Hill-Lancaster. He really was furious about that."

Gable had been the reigning king of Hollywood since the early 1930s, winning the hearts of filmgoers in *It Happened One Night, Mutiny on the Bounty, Gone with the Wind,* and a string of other hits. But since his return to Hollywood after a stint in the Air Force during World War II, he had seen his popularity slowly begin to decline. By 1957, he was fifty-six and no longer under contract to MGM. He may well have been a bit jealous of Lancaster, who was thirteen years younger, at the height of his popularity, and in excellent shape. Moreover, as Gay put it, "He just had this suspicion that Burt, because he was the producer, was going to get the best of the story." Gable's fears proved groundless. *Run Silent* turned out to be far more his picture than Lancaster's. Moreover, said Gay, "Burt looked upon Gable as anybody would, as a big star, as a solid, wonderful star. Behind his back, he and Hill made good-natured jokes about Gable's dentures and so forth, but Lancaster and Hill made fun of everyone."

Although he was generally congenial, Gable threw a fit over one scene in the screenplay. As written, his character was supposed to commit a judgmental error in a major encounter with a Japanese ship, causing Burt to take charge of the sub. About three weeks into the shooting, Gable announced, "I'm not going to do it. He's not going to take over the boat." Since the rest of the film turned on that plot development, Gay, the director, and the producers took pains to point out that he had approved the script with the scene in it, but Gable could not be swayed. With that, shooting came to a complete halt. For two days, Gay and Jim Hill tried to figure out a solution that would satisfy the star and, at the same time, still lead to the captain's relief from duty. Finally, they drew on an episode in the novel that they thought would work. "So we went to Gable and his agent," recalled Gay, "and we said, 'Look, Clark, supposing in that battle when things go wrong, you are severely injured, and you are incapable of going on to the next battle.' And he said, 'You mean, in that scene when I'm in the compartment with Burt, I get dizzy and pitch over,' and I said, 'That's it, that's it.' So the next morning," said Gay, laughing, "he was back on the set, working again."

The picture, which went into production on September 16, 1957, was shot in part at the naval base in San Diego, with the USS *Redfish* "playing" the sub in the picture. The interiors were filmed at the Goldwyn studios in Hollywood.

Given the ring of truth in Beach's novel, HHL wanted to insure a high level of accuracy for the film. "Every bit of dialogue is real submarine talk," asserted Lancaster, "every piece of equipment is in the right place and used the right way. Even the combat incidents in the John Gay screenplay . . . are taken from naval archives."

Don Rickles, cast as a member of the crew, recalled that Lancaster took the technical aspects of the production quite seriously: "He always wanted to know what the depth was and what this gear meant. . . . He'd say, 'Don, do you know what you're looking at?' I had no idea what I was looking at, but to humor him, I'd always say, 'Yes, I do. I do.'"

Rickles was impressed with the actor, saying, "Burt was bigger than life, he really was. And he was very strong in what he did. There was nothing wishy-washy about him." As with Ben Cooper on *The Rose Tattoo* and Jack Elam on *Vera Cruz,* the younger actor admitted that he found the picture's star somewhat aloof, but he understood, saying, "You remember that at that time it was Burt Lancaster's picture, and he was very involved, so I don't think he got too much time to socialize with the guys. But Lancaster was always a gentleman. I never found him annoyed or indifferent."

When *Run Silent, Run Deep* wrapped near the end of 1957, Burt went directly into another HHL project.

Separate Tables began as two one-act plays by Terence Rattigan, both set in a dreary residential hotel in Bournemouth, on the coast of England. The place is home primarily to retirees and pensioners, whose lives touch one another's but whose fundamental isolation is evoked by their dining arrangements: they eat at separate tables. Although several of the supporting characters appeared in both halves of the drama, the first act, "Table by the Window," centered on John Malcolm, an alcoholic

journalist who had once been a prominent politician before his impris-
onment for wife-beating, and his ex-wife, Anne Shankland, a fading
beauty who comes to visit him. Act 2, "Table Number Seven," focused
on a pompous ex-Army major named Pollack, who turns out to be a sexual pervert and a social poseur, and the painfully shy, mother-dominated
spinster Sybil Railton-Bell, who is drawn to him.

After a two-year run in London, *Separate Tables* debuted on Broadway on October 25, 1956, under the auspices of the Producers Theatre
in association with Hecht-Lancaster. It was called "spectacularly fine"
by Brooks Atkinson of *The New York Times* and "a triumph" by Richard
Watts Jr. of the *New York Post.*

It was Rattigan himself who suggested that the play's twin story lines
be merged into one seamless narrative for the film. The trick, as the picture's director, Delbert Mann, described it, lay "in trying to find the
crossover points between the two stories, where characters from one
story could impact on characters from another story." Five writers, said
Mann, took up the task at points along the way, but only Rattigan and
John Gay received screen credit.

Initially, the idea was to have two actors, Laurence Olivier and his
then-wife, Vivien Leigh, play the four principal characters in the film, as
Eric Portman and Margaret Leighton had done on the stage, with Olivier
also directing. Then, HHL decided to divide up the four roles. Olivier
would still play Major Pollack and direct, but Spencer Tracy would portray Malcolm. Ultimately, all three stars withdrew from the project. One
theory holds that Lancaster decided to play Malcolm himself, and the
Oliviers quit out of loyalty to Tracy. Another is that Leigh's deteriorating
mental condition precluded her and her husband's involvement. A third
is that Olivier decided to do *The Entertainer* by John Osborne on the
London stage instead.

Their departure left four major roles to cast and a director to hire.
For the latter, Harold Hecht turned to the man with whom he had
worked so well on *Marty* and *The Bachelor Party.* "I turned the picture
down when Harold first called me," said Del Mann, "because I felt it
needed an English director. It was much too English a project, and
Harold said, 'No, no, no, it's a people story, and if you need any back-
grounding, I will send you to Bournemouth to do your own research on
it.'" Mann accepted the offer. And, indeed, his visit to the English sea-
side town convinced him to accept the assignment.

As for the cast, two of the principal roles, the Major and Sybil, went to
British actors, David Niven and Deborah Kerr. Virtually all of the supporting players, including Wendy Hiller, Gladys Cooper, and Cathleen

Nesbitt, were British as well. But Malcolm and Anne were taken by Lancaster and Rita Hayworth, who would shortly marry James Hill.

Casting these two Americans forced the filmmakers to make difficult decisions. For starters, they had to consider whether Burt and Rita should attempt accents. Said Mann, "To try to get Burt to play with a British accent and Rita to play with a British accent and make it believable in the midst of people like Gladys Cooper and Deborah Kerr and David Niven and Cathleen Nesbitt would have come off as phony as could be."[3] Thus, the characters became Americans. According to the director, one version of the screenplay, drafted by John Michael Hayes, even changed Malcolm from a writer to a retired baseball player. "That script didn't last very long," he acknowledged. Gay took a less drastic approach, changing a couple of the play's references so that Malcolm went from growing up on the "Hull docks" to a youth in a "Pennsylvania steel town," and Anne's origins became "Park Avenue" rather than "Kensington Gore."

Separate Tables went into production in November of 1957. As with *Marty* and *The Bachelor Party,* Mann insisted on an extensive period of rehearsals before shooting began. That gave the actors adequate time to, as he put it, "explore the characters and their relationships" in a way that would not have been possible otherwise. Another aid to character development was Edward Carrere's evocative set. "They took the whole soundstage," said John Gay. "Upstairs, downstairs. There was the whole thing. You were at the hotel."

Lancaster enjoyed doing *Separate Tables*. Since it had begun as a play, Deborah Kerr thought that working on the production made him feel like "an actor in the theater more than a movie star." Mann recalled, "Burt did rehearse well, and he would do what I wanted him to do and as we talked it out together," but the director was not entirely satisfied with the actor's interpretation of the part. As he put it, "Burt brought a lot of bravura to the role, but it was Burt. . . . I wanted a little less of that overheartiness and found it hard to get in some spots."

Some of the actor's best moments in the picture came in his scenes with Wendy Hiller, who played the straightforward but empathetic hotel manager. Indeed, she would win an Oscar as Best Supporting Actress for her performance. But behind the scenes the relationship between the actor and the actress was puzzling. As Mann recalled, "Close to the

3. Proving Mann's point was Australian Rod Taylor, whose British accent in a relatively minor role was jarring in juxtaposition with the real thing.

end of the shooting, for whatever reason, Burt and Jim [Hill] took to tormenting Wendy Hiller, trying to embarrass her by telling dirty jokes, using [bad] language, saying things suggestively in the hearing of others. What triggered it I don't know. Whether one or the other of them had attempted to bed her and she had rejected him—it had that kind of quality about it, and it was ugly. It was insensitive and cruel, and she bore it silently and like the lady that she is, but I hated them both for it at that particular moment." Mann added that the treatment was sporadic, and that it always seemed to occur when Hill was present.

As shooting wound down, Mann, Gay, Hecht, and the actors continued to experiment with the best way to intercut the two plotlines. Then, Mann and editor Marjorie Fowler continued the process in the cutting room. Even after that, the struggle persisted. "We added two more days to the schedule," said Mann, "to reshoot the dining-room scene [the last scene in the picture]. This was after we had shot it and edited it and were still arguing about the placement of the two stories—when you cut from one to the other, which one you resolve first, what the relationships were."

But the problem was fundamentally beyond Mann's or Fowler's control; the two stories were simply unequal in their dramatic values. Onstage, when the pieces were separate, several critics referred to Act 1, the Malcolm-Anne story, as "a curtain raiser" for Act 2, the Major-Sybil story. John McClain of the *New York Journal-American* even asserted, "I think he [Rattigan] would have been advised to forget his first act." It was not until the filmmakers struggled with the resolution of the picture in postproduction that the dramatic inequity became fully apparent. "We died in the reel before the last," said Marge Fowler, "when Burt and Rita were going through all their moaning and groaning, and the audience was anxious for the Major and anxious for what was to come."

Worse, Fowler maintained that the producers influenced the cutting to favor Lancaster's performance. She even had to meter Burt's entrances and exits: " 'Mr. Lancaster makes his appearance at seventeen minutes in the picture, he goes in at twenty minutes . . .' I always had to come in with a time." She acknowledged that she did not have to report this information to the actor directly, but since it was his company, "I just assumed that the concern was coming from him in some way."

Mann was at pains to note that "through rehearsals and through shooting I never once felt the heavy hand of a coproducer, the owner of the company that was doing the picture, operating upon me. Burt rehearsed and performed very much in the manner of an independently hired actor." But after Mann, Fowler, and Hecht, who was the film's producer, finished editing, scoring, and dubbing, Hill and Lancaster, in the director's words, "reedited portions of the picture and cut chunks out of David and Deborah's early scenes, I'm quite sure with the aim of getting Burt and probably Burt and Rita on-screen sooner and building their two parts. I resented the manner in which it was done. It was the first time that that happened to me, that a picture was taken away and reedited without my participation in it."

Such behavior was not typical of Lancaster. Even on *Separate Tables,* John Gay said, "I never felt that he was out to put himself forward. I always felt that he wanted the picture to be as good as it could be with everybody involved."

On January 8, shortly after *Separate Tables* wrapped, Burt was rushed to Cedars of Lebanon Hospital with a ruptured appendix; the following day, he underwent surgery. On the tenth, as he was recuperating, a visiting reporter asked about his condition. Weak but combative as ever, the actor answered, "Fine. Good enough to jump out of this bed and lick you."

By March 26, Burt was sufficiently recovered to join Kirk Douglas on the Academy Awards telecast in a musical number written especially for the occasion by Sammy Cahn and Jimmy Van Heusen. Entitled "It's Great Not to be Nominated," it featured the cinema's two tough guys—each a former Oscar loser—doing a soft-shoe and patter as they taunted the year's nominees. The routine, which ended with Douglas doing a handstand onto the shoulders of Lancaster, who held him aloft while dancing offstage, was so popular that the following year Burt and Kirk kicked off the Oscar telecast with a taped reprise.

On March 27, 1958, one day after the Academy Awards, Lancaster could be seen on-screen, in his pairing with another of Hollywood's leading men, Clark Gable. But the official premiere of *Run Silent, Run Deep* came on April 1, when the film was screened aboard a submarine, the USS *Perch,* for an invited audience of senior Navy officers.

Most of the critics applauded the workmanlike efficiency of the Robert Wise-HHL production, which John L. Scott of the *Los Angeles Times* called "a tense, exciting submarine picture." Even *The New York Times'* Bosley Crowther, who had hated HHL's previous commercial films, *Vera Cruz* and *Trapeze,* asserted, "A better film about war beneath the ocean and about guys in the 'silent service' has not been made." Crowther liked the performances as well, and other critics agreed.

Despite the critical praise, one can see why Lancaster made fun of his role; Bledsoe, although admirable, forthright, and likable, was superficial, Wyatt Earp in a Navy uniform. Gable's Richardson, driven to avenge the sinking of his previous sub, was a more interesting figure. That Burt lent his drawing power to the film suggests his willingness to put the good of his company before his own predilections as an actor (he even gave Gable first billing, as he had done with Cooper in *Vera Cruz*). At the very least, he was inclined to trade a role like Jim Bledsoe for a J. J. Hunsecker. Indeed, as the former swashbuckler developed as an actor and unusual characters and projects became more readily available to him, he adopted the practice—a conscious choice made around 1957— to alternate his material. As Vincent Canby of *The New York Times* observed in 1981, "For each mass-market entertainment film he made, there was always one comparatively risky 'artistic venture.'" Or, as Burt told Peter Riegert, his costar in 1983's *Local Hero,* "I do one for the pope and one for me."

But, if *Run Silent, Run Deep* was to be one for the pope, the result was disappointing. It came nowhere near the success of *Trapeze* or Hal Wallis' *Gunfight at the O.K. Corral.* That was unfortunate for Hecht-Hill-Lancaster. At that point, the company could have used another smash.

CHAPTER ELEVEN

"*Marty* Was a Fluke"

"Shaw is my favorite author," Lancaster told columnist Sidney Skolsky. Perhaps it was the production of the Irish playwright's *The Devil's Disciple* starring Maurice Evans—which Burt caught at New York's City Center in 1950 and called "the best show of all he had seen"—that inspired him to bring the comedy to the screen.

First produced in London in 1897, *The Devil's Disciple* was set in New Hampshire in 1777, Shaw's only work to take place in America. With the Revolutionary War as a backdrop, the playwright centered his comedy on two contrasting personalities: Richard Dudgeon, a charming rogue who turns out to be a moralist of the highest order, and Rev. Anthony Anderson, an orderly man of peace who becomes the captain of the local militia. Thanks to a case of mistaken identity, the fates of the two men entwine in a lively encounter with "Gentlemanly Johnny" Burgoyne, the British general en route to Saratoga, New York, and what will become the first major American victory of the war.

Initially, HHL turned to Anthony Asquith, director of the 1938 film version of Shaw's *Pygmalion* starring Leslie Howard and Wendy Hiller, to direct and write the screenplay for *The Devil's Disciple*. The director was at work on the script when he was replaced by Alexander Mackendrick. "Why they decided they wanted to be rid of Asquith, I have no idea," Mackendrick said. "I admired Asquith's work very much." The original casting called for the teaming of two of Burt's former costars, actors who had never worked with one another: Montgomery Clift as Dudgeon and Gary Cooper as Anderson. Elizabeth Taylor, a close friend of Clift's, was being sought as the woman caught between the two. But a car accident on May 12, 1956, which badly disfigured Clift's face, put the project on hold.

It was not until February of 1958, when Kirk Douglas became interested in the role of Dudgeon, that the project was resurrected. By that point, Douglas had formed his own production company, Bryna Productions, and agreed not only to costar but also to coproduce. No doubt that offer pleased United Artists, which was not sanguine about the project's commercial prospects.

With Gary Cooper no longer in the picture, Burt decided to play Anderson himself. For good measure, a third star was added. According to Laurence Olivier's biographer Thomas Kiernan, the British actor had left *Separate Tables* with no ill feelings toward HHL. "Find a good property that I can appear in without Viv," he told the producers at the time, "and I'll do it with you." Clearly, Sir Laurence was ideally suited to the role of Burgoyne, the droll wit and most Shavian of *The Devil's Disciple*'s characters. After Elizabeth Taylor declined to make it a foursome, the producers tried to interest Carroll Baker, the blond bombshell of 1956's *Baby Doll,* in the role of Judith Anderson, but the role ultimately went to an unknown, nineteen-year-old Janette Scott. "I have the best of two worlds," she said before the picture's release. "Just think. I'm married to Burt—but have love scenes with Kirk."

When HHL replaced Asquith, the project lost its screenwriter as well as its director. The vacancy was filled by Burt's friend Roland Kibbee and Mackendrick's mentor John Dighton, whose credits included *Kind Hearts and Coronets* and *Roman Holiday.*

In addition to a change of stars, director, and screenwriter, the project would enjoy one more major shift in personnel before the cameras started to roll; Jim Hill, originally slated to produce, was replaced by Harold Hecht. According to Philip Kemp, author of a book on Mackendrick's films, the debacle of *Sweet Smell of Success,* produced by Jim, led to the change.

"We are committed to filming Shaw as honestly as possible," said an unidentified Hecht-Hill-Lancaster spokesman shortly after shooting began. "But what we are doing is turning a play of words into a play of action. If Shaw describes a battle, we show it." By definition, the act of "turning a play of words into a play of action" is to distort the original intent, especially if that author is the wordsmith and wit George Bernard Shaw. As the writing progressed, Mackendrick became convinced that Hecht and Lancaster were drawing further and further away from the integrity of the source material. "I was brought up on GBS," he said, and thus found the producers' choices highly distressing.

Then shooting began—at Elstree studios in July of 1958.[1]

Olivier came to *The Devil's Disciple* in poor spirits, thanks to his deteriorating marriage to Vivien Leigh and the recent demise of his own

1. For the exteriors, the company journeyed to Tring Park outside London.

independent production, a film version of *Macbeth,* due to escalating costs. That a former acrobat was able to mount a multimillion-dollar movie (*The Devil's Disciple* was budgeted at $2 million) where he could not smarted. Consequently, Olivier affected on *The Devil's Disciple* set what cameraman Gerald Fisher described as a "rather supercilious, superior manner." Moreover, he kept reversing the names of the two American stars, calling Burt "Kirk" and Kirk "Burt," which irritated Lancaster no end.

That Olivier could not distinguish Lancaster from Douglas went to the heart of another of Mackendrick's concerns over the project. As he explained, "The central device [of the play] is that you start off with two men who are complete opposites, and each one totally miscast. The parson just isn't a parson, he's really a dangerous fighting man. And the Disciple is a born preacher. So when they change over, you get this great burst of energy. But Kirk Douglas, he's another Burt, so you lose the temperamental thing." In order to distinguish Burt as much as possible from his rugged costar, Mackendrick tried to "inhibit him in every way possible from being the Burt Lancaster that we know . . . to make him play somebody who's gauche, clumsy, shy, and lacking in force." This approach clearly took its toll on the actor. "I was rather amused at the time," said Gerry Fisher, "by the athletic style of Kirk Douglas, which seemed to copy what I'd been used to seeing Burt Lancaster doing. . . . And Burt, playing the New England pastor, was shackled by his role and wasn't able to move his feet."

Between the discussions about the script and the discussions about Burt's character, shooting was proceeding in a desultory fashion. According to Burt, Mackendrick had been warned from the outset that money was tight, and the schedule—forty-eight days—was inflexible. As the actor recalled, "We said, 'Sandy, we're going to have to let you go if you don't stay on schedule—we just can't take it.' Well, we shot for one week and we had two days' worth of film—incidentally, the best two days of the picture."

Shortly thereafter, Mackendrick was fired.[2] The production's slow pace may have been the overriding factor, but, according to Gerry Fisher, the director had not been exhibiting the same degree of fussiness about setups and camera angles that had circumscribed his work

2. Just how long Mackendrick worked on *The Devil's Disciple* is a matter of some debate. It ranges from Burt's recollection of a week to the three weeks recalled by Mackendrick's replacement, Guy Hamilton. As *Variety* reported the director's withdrawal from the project on August 12, the best estimate is about two weeks.

on *Sweet Smell of Success*. In Mackendrick's opinion, speed had nothing to do with his dismissal; the cause was his interpretation of Lancaster's character. But, of course, the myriad off-the-set discussions about the role and about the script were indeed causing delays in the shooting.

Mackendrick was replaced by Guy Hamilton. Best known today for his James Bond films, starting with 1964's *Goldfinger,* Hamilton, once described as "a tall, laconic man with a finely honed sense of humor," made his feature debut in 1952 with a B picture called *The Ringer.* It had a three-week shooting schedule, which suggested that HHL would not have to worry about his ability to work quickly. *The Devil's Disciple* would be his seventh film.

"This transition was quite quick and professional," noted Gerry Fisher. "The crew knuckled down, once we got over the shock of realizing that Mackendrick wasn't going to be with us. . . . Most of us did know Guy Hamilton anyway. In fact, I had been the assistant cameraman on his first picture."

During Hamilton's first few days on the film, he drew support from his stars. "Both Burt and Kirk were very helpful," he recalled, "but the crunch came very rapidly, as I knew it would, when they had a scene together. Kirk had by far the flashier part and proposed to make it more so despite Burt's objections. 'What did I think?' Obviously, whoever I sided with, I would make an enemy of the other for the rest of the movie. I neatly sidestepped the question by replying, 'Fellas, don't ask me. If it were my picture, you, Burt, would be playing Dick Dudgeon, and you, Kirk, the Reverend Anderson.' For the rest of the day I could spot them in corners discreetly reading each other's parts, and I was never again faced with the question. Incidentally, I believed it and suspect that I was probably right."

Ironically, Hamilton shared some of Mackendrick's concerns about the film's concept, which he described as "an uneasy marriage of George Bernard Shaw meets *The Crimson Pirate.*" He believed that Burt's own ambivalence lay at the root of the problem, maintaining that on some days the actor took the "Shavian scenes very seriously, at other moments, 'Shit, kid, this is movies.' "

While Burt and Harold were refighting the American Revolution on the shores of Great Britain, their company was making three small, black-and-white films back home.

The first, *The Rabbit Trap,* was a genial slice-of-life by J. P. Miller. Like *Marty,* it had aired first on television—and the film version starred

Ernest Borgnine. The second, *Cry Tough,* based on a novel by Irving Shulman, offered a gritty examination of gang life in Spanish Harlem (substituting for the book's Lower East Side). The third, *Take a Giant Step,* from an off-Broadway play by Louis Peterson, depicted the trials of a black adolescent in a small white New England town.

Two of the three features—*The Rabbit Trap* and *Cry Tough*—were produced by Harry Kleiner (who also scripted the latter), while Oscar-winning screenwriter Julius Epstein wrote and produced the third. Thus, for the first time since *Kiss the Blood off My Hands,* Burt and Harold entrusted their projects to someone other than Hill or Hecht himself.[3] HHL's future anticipated growth mandated the delegation of such authority.

Of the three, perhaps *Take a Giant Step* was the most courageous, for in 1958 mainstream films about the black experience simply were not done. Ruby Dee, who was in the cast, later commended Lancaster, saying, "I thought it was a concerned thing to do. Burt did something about the exclusion of African-Americans from the Hollywood scene."

The following year, HHL would attempt one more small-scale picture without Lancaster in the cast (although it had originally been announced as a vehicle for Burt and Rita Hayworth). Called *Season of Passion,* it was based on an Australian play, *The Summer of the Seventeenth Doll* by Ray Lawler, and was shot on location in Australia with Leslie Norman producing and directing. Borgnine again starred, this time as a canecutter who finds that the city girl he sees during his annual layoff (played by Anne Baxter) wants a more meaningful relationship. John Mills and Angela Lansbury costarred.

One might question the selection of Borgnine in a romantic role originally meant for Lancaster. Indeed, J. P. Miller had found the burly actor miscast in *The Rabbit Trap* as well; he had wanted Jason Robards Jr., then just gaining a following among New York theatergoers. "They cast him [Borgnine]," Miller asserted, "because he was under contract, and they could get an Academy Award winner for fifty thousand dollars."

Borgnine was not happy about what he saw as exploitation. In fact, he had brought suit against Burt and Harold—in September of 1956—after the producers had negotiated several lucrative loan-outs for his services.[4] "There's a clause in the contract about loaning me out," he said at the time, "but nothing is said about them keeping the salary I earn, and

---

3. Frank Ross produced *The Flame and the Arrow* but with Harold.
4. When Borgnine was loaned to 20th Century–Fox, for example, for *The Best Things in Life Are Free,* Hecht-Lancaster received $75,000. The actor received $15,000.

they have. My attorney and I claim this is breach of contract." A few months later, Borgnine was back in court again, this time asserting that the profits for *Marty*—of which he was entitled to 2.5 percent—had been understated in the accounting reports by at least $250,000. Finally, at the end of November of 1957, both cases were settled out of court. Borgnine received a substantial cash payment, but he remained under contract.

Although HHL's four non-Lancaster films were widely divergent in theme and story line, they, like *Marty* and *The Bachelor Party*, reflected the company's desire to produce relatively inexpensive but meaningful adult fare.

But *Marty* had been a superbly crafted film. Although its successors had laudable elements, each was badly flawed. Of *The Rabbit Trap*, for example, *Newsweek* wrote, "The naturalism of this movie is unnaturally exaggerated, the sentiment sticky, the climactic irony obvious." Stanley Kauffmann of the *New Republic* asserted that *Take a Giant Step* was "very badly acted and directed." And, of *Cry Tough*, Bosley Crowther of *The New York Times* claimed, "What starts out as a promising picture about poor Puerto Ricans in New York . . . ends up as a routine gangster melodrama."

Not only did Hecht and his partners fail in their efforts to create intimate, sophisticated pictures of sustained high quality, their desire to replicate the success of *Marty* was all too readily apparent. UA historian Tino Balio reported, "The four pictures as a group went over budget $500,000 and they all lost money, demonstrating once again that there was no market for this kind of picture. *Marty* had been a fluke."

Hecht-Hill-Lancaster had better luck—critically and at the box office—with *Separate Tables*, which opened on December 18, 1958. The New York *Herald Tribune* spoke for most of the critics in asserting that it was "one of the year's finest achievements" and "a movie that nobody in his right mind will want to miss." All hands, including director Delbert Mann and screenwriters Rattigan and Gay, received their share of the praise—and, indeed, one must acknowledge their cleverness in interweaving the formerly independent stories.

None of the major critics seemed to mind—or even notice—the presence of two Americans in a story otherwise steeped in the atmosphere of a nondescript British hotel. But, in retrospect, the casting of Lancaster and Hayworth badly disrupted the picture's delicate balance. Although Burt did his best to portray the character's feisty independence, a British actor like Trevor Howard—who would subsequently play the role onstage with Deborah Kerr—would have more effectively preserved its place in the fabric of the drama, merely by his manner, mode of speech, and even his looks. As Kerr said of Lancaster's performance, "He was awfully good, Burt. But he wasn't quite the left-wing, rumbling angry man that the character was written." Although Hayworth had the easier job—she could simulate an aristocrat through poise and an effortless manner—there was something studied about her performance.

Separate Tables would go on to earn seven Academy Award nominations, with Niven and Hiller winning for Best Actor and Best Supporting Actress respectively.

Thanks in part to the Oscars, *Separate Tables* climbed to a surprising twenty-fifth place among the most popular films of 1959, higher than the previous year's ranking of HHL's far more commercial *Run Silent, Run Deep*. But *Separate Tables* could take HHL only so far. Given the company's considerable overhead—offices in Beverly Hills and New York (plus stringers in Europe), a staff of nearly forty full-time employees, and the partners' lavish way of doing business—plus several over-budgeted pictures that had performed from fair to poorly at the box office, they needed another *Trapeze*.

Burt, Harold, and Jim decided that *The Unforgiven* would have to be the blockbuster that would reverse their company's sagging fortunes.

The Unforgiven had started with loftier purposes. It was to be, according to the project's initial screenwriter, J. P. Miller, "a groundbreaking departure" from the traditional Hollywood Western. Its inspiration came from the novel of the same name by Alan LeMay, purchased by HHL for $75,000 in January of 1957, prior to the book's publication. LeMay was a highly regarded author of Western fiction, including *The Searchers*, which had already been made into a fine film by John Ford.

Like *The Searchers, The Unforgiven* was set in the Texas Panhandle in the decade after the Civil War. It told the story of a family of cattle ranchers named Zachary—the eldest son, Ben (the character Burt would play); Ben's brothers, Cash and youthful Andy; and their adopted sister, Rachel, who, unknown to them at the outset, was a Kiowa Indian by birth. The book was imbued with LeMay's feel for the parched, rugged country, the ways of ranching, the tenuous relationship between the white settlers and the Indians, and the delicate interplay among neighbors in such a treacherous environment.

With this earthy material, Miller sought to evoke, in his words, "real human beings in a specific time and a specific place, people relating to each other and the Indians, and the raw, unbeautiful, flat, arroyoed, dry land, an absolutely unfriendly environment with some of the most ferocious goddamn Indians that this country ever produced."

The director assigned to the project, Delbert Mann (this was well before the release of *Separate Tables*), shared Miller's strong affinity for the material. He too was eager to bring to the screen, as he put it, "a sense that this is what the West must have been like in those days."

At the outset, Burt, Harold, and Jim were in complete accord with Miller and Mann's vision. Then came the inescapable decision to commercialize. Specifically, the partners asked Miller to create a role for Kirk Douglas. Miller tried to comply, but, as he explained, "To write in a part for Kirk what you have to do is reimagine the entire thing with two brothers who are equal and who have a conflict with each other so there would be some kind of raison d'être for them both to be there and for them to move the story along." What he produced simply did not mesh. "So," said Miller, "I tore it all apart and started all over again, and I got about fifty pages into it and I said, 'Fellas, this doesn't work. This is crap.'" He not only withdrew from the project, he quit HHL and went back to New York. Mann shared the writer's assessment. "I thought the script was turning into a shambles," he said, and he too left *The Unforgiven.*

If gritty authenticity had been Miller and Mann's primary interest in the Western, John Huston, the celebrated director of *The Maltese Falcon, The Treasure of the Sierra Madre,* and *The African Queen,* was intrigued by another facet. "I wanted to turn it into the story of racial intolerance in a frontier town, to comment on the real nature of community 'morality,'" he wrote in his autobiography.

By the time Huston signed on to direct the picture in August of 1958, Ben Maddow had become its screenwriter. Indeed, Maddow was instrumental in involving Huston, who had previously collaborated with him on the hard-edged crime drama *The Asphalt Jungle.* Under the new screenwriter and director, several elements were added to the Western to heighten the story's racial tension (which was an ingredient in the book—LeMay's characters referred to the Kiowa as "red-niggers"—but had not been the novelist's main concern). First, Maddow made Cash Zachary a rabid Indian hater, which the character in the novel was not.

Second, he turned one of LeMay's minor figures, a Zachary ranch hand named Johnny Portugal, into a possible half-breed and, as such, the object of derision by Cash and the other local bigots. He also made the wrangler something of a rival with Lancaster's Ben Zachary for the affections of poor Rachel.

Lancaster shared Huston's desire to make *The Unforgiven* a statement about racial intolerance. The late fifties offered a particularly propitious moment for such a theme. Since the release of *Apache* in 1954, the quest for African-American civil rights had flowered into a major movement, with bus boycotts, sit-ins, and enforced school integration. But, first and foremost, HHL needed a commercial hit; what the picture might contribute toward harmonious race relations had to come second. To Huston, this translated into making *The Unforgiven* "a swashbuckler about a larger-than-life frontiersman," which he had absolutely no interest in doing. He considered quitting, but, as he later put it, "Quite mistakenly I agreed to stick it out, thus violating my own conviction that a picture-maker should undertake nothing but what he believes in—regardless." The director's biographer Axel Madsen maintained that the lure was Huston's $300,000 salary, which he needed to restore his imposing manor in Ireland, while Huston family chronicler Lawrence Grobel asserted that the director was attracted by the chance to hunt illegal pre-Columbian artifacts—his passion—while filming in Durango, Mexico.

It may be that shortly before shooting commenced, Burt, Harold, and Jim had grown as unsure of Huston as the director was about them. Grobel quoted HHL employee Jilda Smith (now deceased) to the effect that the producers had tried to force Huston into breaching his contract. "It was all a bit sinister," she concluded. But assistant director Tom Shaw maintained that at no time did HHL seek to replace John Huston.

Filming commenced on January 12, 1959. Durango, an old mining town in the badlands of central Mexico, was well suited to the making of Westerns. But it was rugged country. "It was really kind of like the Wild West," recalled John Saxon, cast as Johnny Portugal. "During the production, the pay office was stuck up at gunpoint, and they ran off with the company payroll."

The $300,000 set was constructed on a windswept prairie. At its center was a sod house with a steel frame and breakaway walls set into a man-made hillside. Not only would this serve as the Zachary household in the picture, it also became the cutting room for Huston, who edited the film as it was processed in London.[5]

As if to validate the wild, anything-goes atmosphere in which *The Unforgiven* was filmed, two of the picture's stars nearly died during shooting. The first was Audie Murphy, who inherited the "Kirk Douglas" role, Cash Zachary (which, in the interim, had gone to Tony Curtis and Richard Burton as well). Murphy almost drowned when he went duck hunting on a lake near Durango but was rescued by the company's still photographer, Inge Morath, who happened to be nearby and was an expert swimmer.

"Audie was a loose pistol," recalled Saxon, "not exactly a cannon, but a pistol." Not only was he always armed, he occasionally fired a shot above the heads of his costars. Moreover, there was a scene in the picture that called for Lancaster's Ben to slap his brother, and according to Murphy's biographer Don Graham, the moment so enraged the war hero that "Huston had to calm Audie down after the scene, walking back and forth with him, talking to him." One actor on the set was certain that Murphy would have killed Burt if the event had taken place in real life.

Then Audrey Hepburn was seriously injured. According to Doug McClure, who was playing young Andy Zachary, her mount became frightened when an assistant director signaled for it to stop. Instead, it bolted, and the actress, not an experienced horsewoman, went down. "When she landed," said McClure, "I didn't think she was hurt, but she landed flat on her back and she was frail." Rushed to a local hospital, she was treated for four broken bones, a badly sprained foot, and torn muscles in her back. Production had to be halted for three weeks—at an estimated cost of $250,000—while she recuperated sufficiently to resume work.

Even beyond Murphy's and Hepburn's mishaps, *The Unforgiven* was plagued by Huston's odd behavior. From the moment when he realized that his approach to the story was at odds with HHL's, his heart went out of the project. Inge Morath maintained that "half the time his head was not in directing the movie," and screenwriter John Gay agreed, saying, "I'm talking about one of the greatest directors we've ever had," but added, "On that film he was a real putz. He pitted people against each other. He was demanding and mean-spirited."

5. Huston chose a London processing center, although the firms in Hollywood were much closer to Durango, because he believed that the British produced a superior product. The daily shipments between Durango and London, via Mexico City, added considerably to the cost of production.

Gay also noted that Huston did not direct: "I never saw him in conversation with an actor. People would sometimes ask him for a reaction to a take, but usually he'd just say, 'Do it again.' " Saxon maintained that the director also delighted in finding challenges on the set, as if he were trying to stave off boredom or show his disdain for the producers or both. One time, for example, he spent an entire day trying to capture in one take a setup involving several disparate physical elements when virtually the same result could have been achieved far more efficiently by shooting each component separately and cutting them together. "I remember James Hill pacing the sidelines, going nuts," said Saxon.

As for the relationship between Huston and Lancaster, production designer Stephen Grimes said that the two men did not get along because the director resisted Burt's attempts to tell him where to place the camera.

In his autobiography, Huston refrained from expressing an opinion about Burt, but he did confess to pulling a diabolical practical joke on the actor. Lancaster and Murphy were among the participants in an invitational tournament at a new golf course outside Durango. To mark the occasion, Huston covered two thousand Ping-Pong balls with obscenities and anti-Mexican epithets and dropped them on the fairway from a rented airplane. "It was a triumph," the director crowed. "Nobody could possibly locate a golf ball. It took days to clean up the course, the tournament was canceled, and everybody was furious—especially Burt Lancaster, who was one of the tournament sponsors and took his golf quite seriously."

Still, if there was any genuine animosity between Huston and Lancaster, Tom Shaw never saw it. "I don't know how I would not have known it," said the AD. "I mean, I was there every day. Christ, from that experience I was with John for the next thirty-five years. He certainly would have told me, 'Lancaster is a prick.' He told me that about a lot of other people." Burt never expressed animosity toward Huston either. He later claimed that he even based part of his character in *Elmer Gantry* on Huston, whom he called "a wonderful actor, in addition to being a wonderful director." And he took a cameo in Huston's 1963 mystery, *The List of Adrian Messenger.*

If there was no overt hostility between Lancaster and Huston, the actor and director nevertheless had a great deal to say to one another during filming. On one occasion, Shaw recalled, "We were damn near four days before we did a goddamn thing while they ironed out a story point." John Saxon saw the same thing. "They were constantly having story conferences," said the actor. "And boy they were lengthy." The discussions finally reached the point where John Gay was dispatched to the location to effect uncredited script changes on the spot.

When it came to blocking, Lancaster's relationship with Huston was almost comic. As Doug McClure recalled the interaction: "Burt was intense. He would say something like, 'Here, John, look: The Indians come through here, and I take an ax and I hit this Indian, and he falls over. Then I grab this Indian and I throw him. How about that, John?' and John would go, 'No, no, that's not quite right.' 'Right, John. Then how about if I go over here and I do this and I do this. What about that, John?' And John would go, 'Well, no, that's not quite right, either.' " Amazingly, actor Peter Riegert would tell almost the same story about the way Lancaster related to director Bill Forsyth during the making of *Local Hero* more than twenty years later.[6]

McClure, at twenty-four and with only one prior film to his credit, developed an enormous regard for Lancaster. "He sent me to Lew Wasserman," recalled the actor, "and they [Universal] eventually put me under contract.[7] He really was helpful in getting my whole career started."

The dispute over the direction that *The Unforgiven* would take did not end after the completion of principal photography. Axel Madsen cited it as "another picture Huston walked away from during postproduction," which left it in the hands of the producers. Thanks to HHL, the Huston biographer argued, the picture lost much of its antiracist posture. The principal evidence of this was the disappearance of Johnny Portugal— the film's social outcast—about halfway through the final cut. But, according to Shaw, the theme had nothing to do the character's elimination; it was Portugal's relationship with Hepburn's Rachel. "What it boiled down to," the AD asserted, "was that Burt didn't want to believe that she could fuck somebody else. It was strictly a big ego thing."

Ironically, *The Unforgiven,* undertaken with the loftiest of purposes, ended up pleasing none of its creators. As the original screenwriter, J. P. Miller, put it, "I think the whole thing became a cynical exercise in 'let's make a movie that people are going to go see.' " As such, it was emblematic of the state of affairs troubling Burt's production company at the end of the 1950s.

Lancaster first met Richard Brooks in 1947, during the making of *Brute Force,* which the onetime sports reporter wrote. Over the intervening years, Brooks had leaped to the forefront of Hollywood filmmakers, thanks to such noteworthy pictures as *The Blackboard*

6. See page 349.
7. Wasserman's talent agency, MCA, acquired Universal in 1962.

Jungle, Something of Value, The Brothers Karamazov, and *Cat on a Hot Tin Roof.*

For years, the director-screenwriter had wanted to make a movie of *Elmer Gantry,* Sinclair Lewis' 1927 novel about a despicable minister. The epic story followed the title character from his student days at a midwestern Baptist college to his years as an evangelist preacher to his maturity as a nationally recognized spiritual leader.

In 1955, when Brooks acquired the rights to the novel, he saw Montgomery Clift in the title role. Then, one day, he asked Lancaster, "Did you ever read *Elmer Gantry*?" "Oh, yes, Sinclair Lewis was one of my heroes," Burt replied. And their collaboration on the film was born.

After three years, the writer completed his first draft. "It followed almost clinically the pattern of the book," recalled Lancaster. He told Brooks, "You can't show me as a twenty-two-year-old boy in school, that's out of the question. We have to start in the middle and somehow incorporate those early ideas into the script later."

Brooks was willing to comply—providing the actor would work with him on the changes. "So that's what we did," Burt said. "I went to his office and we'd kick this thing around and he'd say, 'Okay, go play golf for two days and then come back.' So I'd go play golf and come back and he'd have a series of scenes. The next few days we'd talk about them, tearing them apart, deciding what was right and what was wrong and so on. This went on for seven solid months and we got the screenplay you saw on the screen. It was a real collaboration, a labor of love."

What ultimately emerged was a rethinking of the title character. "Sinclair Lewis wrote him as a caricature," Lancaster explained. "He made him so one-sided and so bad that it was hard to identify with him." Indeed, that had been one of the critics' principal objections to the novel. "So we had him interested in dames and drinking," said Lancaster, "as well as hollering hellfire and brimstone. We weren't trying to uglify him. We were merely trying to make him a recognizable, full-blooded human being with common weaknesses and vanities."

The screenplay also softened Gantry's fellow evangelist, Sharon Falconer, who, in Lewis' hands, was as ambitious and manipulative as Elmer. In addition, Brooks eliminated numerous minor characters but enlarged the role of George Babbitt, the quintessential capitalist and arguably Lewis' finest creation. The result, as Arthur Knight noted in *The Saturday Review,* was "essentially a new work—a trenchant, virile screenplay that uses the novel primarily as a point of departure and perhaps secondarily as a source of verisimilitudinous detail."

• • •

Elmer Gantry had the trappings of a Hecht-Hill-Lancaster production. The company's story editor, Bernard Smith, produced the picture, although the ultimate authority rested with Brooks and Lancaster. Tom Shaw was assistant director, a role that he would perform on virtually every Brooks film thereafter. Gilbert Kurland, who had been the production manager of *The Devil's Disciple* and *The Unforgiven,* served in that capacity for *Gantry.* UA financed and distributed the picture—which was budgeted at $3 million. But *Gantry* was not an HHL project; neither Harold nor Jim was involved. As such, it reflected a new company policy, announced on April 3, 1959, just a few months before *Gantry* went before the cameras. From then on, HHL told the media, each of the three of the partners could take on outside properties. Industry insiders speculated on the implications of this decision, but, as the *Hollywood Reporter* noted, "Few facts on the new status were immediately available." In fact, HHL was crumbling. According to UA historian Tino Balio, Burt's company owed United Artists almost $7 million: $3 million for budget overages on *The Bachelor Party* and *Sweet Smell of Success;* $1.7 million for unabsorbed overhead charges; $700,000 for expenses on unproduced properties; $500,000 for writers' fees and royalties; and about $1 million for losses and cost overruns on the four low-budget pictures. As a consequence, the partners had to close their New York office, fire most of the California staffers, and lease their Beverly Hills showplace.

Then, on June 16, 1959, they announced that they would do two more films for UA and disband. The properties were *The Way West* and *Kimberly,* with Lancaster starring in both and Hill producing. Meanwhile, Hecht would produce a third picture, *Taras Bulba,* from the novel by Nikolay Gogol. "It is believed," wrote the *Hollywood Reporter* in the wake of this bombshell, "that, after Lancaster completes his next pic, UA's *Elmer Gantry* . . . Lancaster and James Hill will separately form a company and set up for themselves a UA financing and release arrangement."

In the meantime, Burt faced one of the most demanding roles of his career.

The filming of *Elmer Gantry* began in July of 1959 at the Columbia studios in Burbank. "After the first week," said Tom Shaw, "I knew we were making a great movie. I remember going to Bernard Smith and telling him that Burt was going to win an Academy Award."

It was, everyone agreed, an exciting performance in the making. Although Lancaster drew inspiration from John Huston—"his mannerisms, the charming demeanor he has," Burt said in 1981—he conceded that of all the roles he played in his long career, Gantry "was most like me." Numerous associates concurred. "It was not only his best picture," asserted screenwriter Leonardo Bercovicci, "it was the nearest thing to Burt. It was a wonderful, narcissistic holiday." And Shirley Jones added, "He was perfect for it and he was wonderful in it. Burt's a larger-than-life actor in everything he does, I think. And this was a larger-than-life character."

The twenty-five-year-old Jones was cast in the pivotal role of Lulu Bains, the vengeful minister's daughter, whose fall from grace at Elmer's hands put her on the road to prostitution. The actress had made her film debut in 1955 as Laurey in Rodgers and Hammerstein's *Oklahoma!* but by 1959, she later said, "My career was virtually over in motion pictures because I was considered a musical person. I was very typed in this town." It was Lancaster who saw her in a television drama and, in her words, "fought for me to do the role" in *Gantry* although Brooks had another actress in mind (Jones believes it was Piper Laurie).

Ironically, the actress had idolized Lancaster in her youth, so, as she put it, "this was a dream come true." She was not disappointed by the reality, finding him "wonderful to act with. He was easy to work with, and he gave a lot."

Lancaster also played extremely well with the picture's leading lady, Jean Simmons, cast as Sister Sharon Falconer. Simmons, an instinctual actor like Lancaster, recalled, "When he looks at you, he really looks at you. Sometimes [with an actor] you feel that you could be a lamp there, and you'd get the same performance." Like the rest of the company, she realized that he was creating something very special. "My God, it was wonderful to watch," she enthused in retrospect.

The British actress, who was thirty at the time, fell in love with Brooks during the making of the picture, but she admitted that the director could be intimidating: "The first three weeks I literally went home in tears because I didn't understand this lunatic. And one day he was carrying on about something—very noisy—and I suddenly caught the twinkle in his eye, and from then on it was a piece of cake." Jones also remembered Brooks' feisty nature, although she found him "wonderful to work with. He gave you what you needed, yet he allowed actors the freedom of doing it themselves."

With two strong-willed personalities like Brooks and Lancaster, contentious moments were bound to arise. Typically, Burt would take a stand on something, and Brooks would have to defend his position. "He'd wear Burt out," recalled Tom Shaw. "Right is right, and Burt's not a fool. If you finally convince him that you're right, then it's okay. But . . .

it might take a long time to convince him that what you're saying is true."

For the most part, however, the actor and the director got along. Said Patti Page, who played Sister Rachel, "On the set, Richard seemed to know what Burt was doing, and Burt seemed to know what Richard wanted. It was a very nice combination. They had a great respect for each other, and they admired each other."

Filming concluded with the climax of the picture, the raging fire that destroys the revivalist tent show and kills Sister Sharon. Shot on a Columbia soundstage, the studio's backlot, and the Santa Monica pier, the scene took five weeks or so to complete—but there was only enough money in the budget for six days. "Thank God, Burt Lancaster was one of the stars," said Brooks. He talked UA into advancing the cost of shooting the sequence—estimated at $200,000 or more—on the proviso that he and Brooks would let the company take the money out of their fees.

Next, they had to deal with the logistics of setting fire to a tent on a studio soundstage with the stars and hundreds of extras caught in the inferno. After prolonged negotiations with the local firemen, Brooks purchased dozens of cans of old, unwanted movies from Columbia, the nitrate component in motion picture film being extremely flammable. "Then," as he recalled, "we laid the film along the streamers, everywhere. . . . The cameras started going, the button was hit, and the fire went. 'Whoosh!' across the room. . . . I must say it was really terrific."

To Brooks, it was terrific. To Page, "It was so real that it was very, very frightening," and to Simmons, "It was really scary. When the people were screaming, you never knew if they were acting screaming or if they were really in trouble." But she added, "Richard had all the best stuntmen in the business stashed all over the tent to make sure nobody got hurt. And no one did."

Thus, *Elmer Gantry* wrapped.

On August 21, as Lancaster was filming in Burbank, *The Devil's Disciple* opened—and pleased virtually no one. Burt's fans found the picture overly verbose and bent toward some obscure philosophical point. The much smaller audience of Shaw devotees was horrified by the attempt to turn a comedy of wit into what Frank Morris of the *Toronto Globe and Mail* called "a horse opera." Like Morris, *The Saturday Review* was appalled, asserting, "Probably never before has a Bernard Shaw play, in its transference to film, been so cut up and virtually kicked around as *The Devil's Disciple*." Other critics agreed.

In addition to the script, the acting was seen as way off the mark—including Lancaster's performance, which *Time* called "stiff and starchy." The notable exception was Olivier in the plum role of General Burgoyne.

The Devil's Disciple would finish forty-eighth among the hit films of 1959, a remarkable testament to the popularity of Lancaster and Douglas in the face of such terrible notices and poor word of mouth. Still, it was far less successful than the duo's last pairing, *Gunfight at the O.K. Corral.*

CHAPTER TWELVE

A New Decade

Nineteen sixty. A new decade had arrived, bringing with it widespread hope for social and political change. Like many in the Hollywood community, the Lancasters were intrigued by the new chief executive, elected in November. One family friend noted, "Norma made a vow that if Kennedy got elected president, she would stay off booze for a year—and she did." For Burt as well as the country, the early years of the 1960s represented a period of growth and change—although, as with America itself, the transitions were not always by choice. He would lose his father, his home, and his company, and by the middle of the decade, he would all but end his marriage. But he would also finally come to terms with being an actor.

First, there was the business. With a swiftness that surprised even industry insiders, Hecht-Hill-Lancaster quietly came to an end in February of 1960. Despite the announcement of the previous June, Lancaster and Hill made neither *Kimberly* nor *The Way West* nor did they form their own production company (Hecht did produce *Taras Bulba*, as announced at the same time; it was released in 1962 with Yul Brynner and Tony Curtis). What had happened? How could a company that had reached the pinnacle of the industry fall so swiftly and so precipitously? There is no simple answer.

For starters, the company's tremendous growth fed upon itself. In the early years of Hecht-Norma, Burt and Harold had lovingly nurtured one property at a time—out of offices provided by whichever studio was then financing the operation. There was a minimal staff and virtually no overhead. As they became successful, they expanded without careful thought or planning. They established a lavish headquarters in Beverly

Hills, opened an office in New York, hired stringers abroad, financed Broadway plays, founded a music publishing company, put actors and directors under contract, and even created TV pilots of *The Bachelor Party* and *Vera Cruz* with the announced intent of turning them into weekly series. Such enterprise required a large staff—and there were some sixty or seventy people on the payroll by the end. "We had a nut of over one million dollars a year," Lancaster recalled, "paying secretaries and writers and things of this kind." Richard McWhorter noted that Hal Wallis, by contrast, "kept his personal staff lean and relied primarily on the staff at Paramount, the studio with which he was affiliated."

The partners were also lavish spenders. For proof, one needed to look no further than the Taj Mahal on Canon Drive, with the waterfall in Burt's office, the modern French masters on Hecht's walls, and the gold plumbing in the bathroom. They also spent a fortune on books and plays. "We'd purchase properties," said Burt, "but we wouldn't get into them." At the end, HHL had an inventory of $2.5 million worth of unproduced scripts.

The properties that *were* produced also contributed to the downfall. Through most of the company's first decade, it made popular entertainments centered on Burt's physical attributes and engaging persona. Then came *Marty* and the Oscar, and as Richard McWhorter put it, "They started getting into too much arty stuff." As Burt articulated the company's position in 1956, "We've reached the point now where we've stopped thinking about money. . . . The thing from now on is the fun of moviemaking." But Burt's pleasure came at a high price. The audience simply chose to skip HHL's esoteric black-and-white pictures. Instead of reevaluating their program when the first few films failed to perform as expected, the partners kept spending money as if the earnings would never stop.

Discord among the partners was yet another major reason for HHL's fall, and its origins stemmed from the last day of 1956, when Lancaster surprised Hecht by turning their company into a triumvirate. "Jim," said Delbert Mann, "was always siding with Burt against Harold and literally plotting to bounce Harold out of the firm and let it become Hill-Lancaster. So there was a lot of friction behind the scenes." McWhorter saw much the same thing. Lancaster and Hill even took to calling Hecht "The Mole," for his short, squat physique. Also, apart from Lancaster, Hecht and Hill had little to bind them together. "Hill was not an admirer of Hecht's," said an HHL executive. "Hecht tolerated Hill because he was a friend of Burt's."

Thus, divisiveness at the top, the company's incredibly rapid growth, the partners' lack of hands-on involvement with their properties, and above all, the pictures' disappointing grosses sounded the death knell for Hecht-Hill-Lancaster. "We should have stayed a small company," Burt said wistfully in 1975.

Then there was the home front. That Norma Lancaster could forswear alcohol for a year in the wake of JFK's election indicates that her drinking problem had not yet reached a debilitating state. Indeed, as the decade progressed, she was in sufficient health to take an active role in several political organizations, notably the League of Women Voters, which she had joined in the 1940s. She was particularly ardent in her support of interracial busing, becoming a "founding mother" of the Transport a Child program, which brought inner-city children to the schools in affluent Bel-Air and West L.A. She also served as president of the PTA at the Bellagio Road School, where her own children were enrolled.

Those who knew Norma spoke well of her. "She was just intelligent, full of life, full of flavor," said screenwriter Walter Doniger. "Norma was a very sweet person," added actress Julie Adams. "Down-to-earth and really a dear woman." To producer Ross Hunter, she "was a devoted, doting mother who adored Burt and did everything to make him a very happy man."

Such was Burt and Norma's public posture that for many years their union was regarded as one of Hollywood's most enduring. Many in the press were not even aware that Burt had been married previously—as, for that matter, had Norma—nor that their first child was born out of wedlock. But the marriage was not all that it appeared. First, as we have seen, Burt cheated on his wife. Still, as one friend put it, "She was blind as a bat to anything that was wrong. She refused to accept it. If somebody came to her and said, 'Norma, Burt's screwing Shelley Winters,' let's say, she didn't believe it. She'd just say, 'Oh, that's Hollywood gossip.' "

Then too there was Burt's temper. "One day," recalled J. P. Miller, "he told me that he had gotten drunk the night before and had a big fight with Norma and deliberately pissed all over [their] many-thousand-dollar white rug, left a yellow stain from one end to the other." Burt told Doug McClure that on another occasion he got angry at Norma "and called her a dirty name—a cunt or something like that." And then he saw his children watching them. "And I felt so bad," he informed the young actor. "Why did I call my wife such a lousy name? Who am I? In front of my children." To McClure, the anecdote "showed me that this wasn't a bully. This was a sensitive man who had a temper, volatile."

Finally, there was the awkwardness of being a private person married to a very public figure. "In those days in the world of this business," observed Walter Doniger, "you were treated as 'the wife.' I think it really devastated her that she was treated as an appendage." Norma and Burt's friend Bob Quarry recalled an occasion during the 1960s when a foreign film star called to invite the Lancasters to a party. As Burt was on location, Norma asked if she should come and bring a friend. But the star replied, "No, we'll see you when Burt gets back."

During the sixties, the Lancaster children entered adolescence. If Norma was the "doting" parent, Burt followed the stern ways of Elizabeth Lancaster, at least in the early years. But, in time, his approach to parenting softened. He was particularly induced to change after Jimmy saw him in the living room one day and shrank back in fear. Startled, Burt had to assure his son that he would cause him no harm. "I realized I was doing what Mother used to do," the actor recalled, "and vowed that I'd never spank the children again, that there must be a better way. Now we talk things out."

As a major movie star, Burt had less time for children than did the average nine-to-five worker. He made frequent public appearances in support of his career and the political and charitable causes close to his heart, notably the American Civil Liberties Union. And, of course, he was required to put in long hours before the cameras. Even when he took the family with him on location, shooting could mean twelve-hour stretches seven days a week (six on a studio lot). When he was not in production, he was at the office, tending to the myriad details associated with his production company. Or he was reading scripts or potential properties.

Still, he gave the children as much attention as he could. He often attended Little League games, cheering as loudly as any other proud father. He also sat in on classes at the Bellagio School. "I go down once a month or two," he said in 1955. Without spoiling them, he also made sure that his children enjoyed the advantages that his earnings could provide. He built a swimming pool in his backyard and acquired land next door, which he turned into a regulation-size baseball diamond. He also had 35-mm projection equipment installed in the living room, and on Saturdays a Warners projectionist, Julian Ullman, would come over and run pictures for the children and their friends. Perhaps the ultimate treat came in 1964, when Burt had the Beatles over for an evening with his family. The Fab Four were on their first American tour and could not go anywhere without being mobbed.

● ● ●

On April 6, while Lancaster recuperated from the rigors of making *Elmer Gantry* and the demise of his production company, *The Unforgiven* opened. Critic John McCarten caught the attempt to turn the conflict between settlers and Native Americans into a metaphor for contemporary times, asserting in *The New Yorker* that "Mr. Huston and Mr. Maddow have turned up a theme that is as up-to-date as Little Rock."[1] But Arthur Knight, as if knowing what had transpired behind the scenes, perceptively grappled with the film's failings: "Why make a picture that handles hot, controversial material in a manner that either blunts the edge or reduces everything to a noncontroversial cliché?" he asked readers of *The Saturday Review*. He also identified the postproduction evisceration of the Johnny Portugal subplot: "Characters appear and disappear with startling abruptness, suggesting that large chunks of the script were whacked out in the final editing. Sequences begin without motivation and end without resolution."

In retrospect, John Huston said, "Some of my pictures I don't care for, but *The Unforgiven* is the only one I actually dislike. Despite some good performances, the overall tone is bombastic and overinflated."

Although Lancaster had abandoned his plans to produce *The Way West* and *Kimberly,* he could not simply dismiss his obligation to United Artists. "I personally had to do four pictures," he said, "at a very minimal salary for me, one hundred eighty-five thousand dollars a picture, to write off that six million dollars [debt]" (UA simply added a quarter of the total, or $1.5 million, to the cost of each film).

The first of these was *The Young Savages,* for which Harold Hecht served as executve producer (with Pat Duggan producing). Based on a novel entitled *A Matter of Conviction* by Evan Hunter, it told the story of a conscientious Manhattan assistant district attorney, Hank Bell, who has to prosecute three Italian youths from his old neighborhood for the murder of a young, blind Puerto Rican boy.

Lancaster, who would play Bell, knew the turf; much of the picture would be filmed on West 117th Street, across Central Park and a few blocks up from where he was raised. Moreover, he responded to the attempt to confront the issue of juvenile delinquency, which had been the object of increasing national concern since the mid-1950s. Still, he was not keen to do *The Young Savages;* to him it represented working for low pay as part of an unpleasant obligation from his not-too-distant past.

1. In 1957, Little Rock, Arkansas, became a flash point in the civil rights movement when President Eisenhower sent federal troops to the city to enforce school integration, a policy opposed by many of the local citizenry and the governor of the state, Orval Faubus.

• • •

Evan Hunter was initially engaged to adapt his own novel for the screen, but he was replaced by Edward Anhalt, who had won an Oscar in 1950 for *Panic in the Streets*. It was Anhalt, in turn, who suggested that for director Hecht use an acclaimed television veteran, John Frankenheimer, after seeing Frankenheimer's live TV production of *For Whom the Bell Tolls*.

Born on Long Island in 1930, the tall, handsome director had emerged as one of the leading talents of television's golden age, averaging one *Playhouse 90* a month, including J. P. Miller's *The Days of Wine and Roses*. His feature debut came in 1956 with *The Young Stranger*, a quickie shot in twenty-six days; he hated the experience. But, five years later, he was ready to give movies another try.

Ironically, after Anhalt had suggested John for the job, the director brought in J. P. Miller to rework the *Young Savages* screenplay. Miller and Anhalt did not collaborate. As the former explained, "It's one of those cockamamie Hollywood deals where two guys share credit on a picture, and they never met."

As in the days of HHL, filming began without a script. "I rewrote it like one jump ahead of them," Miller recalled. "I was writing it while they were shooting it. I was dictating to two secretaries part of the time. And they would come up and say, 'What are the sets like for tomorrow? What are we going to build tonight?' "

Fortunately, Frankenheimer's television background enabled him to work quickly. The picture, which began filming on the streets of New York in May of 1960, had a shooting schedule of just thirty-five days.

At thirty, Frankenheimer was, to quote Miller, "a self-proclaimed genius and had self-confidence oozing from every pore. Part of Frankenheimer's arrogance was bravado to cover up a deep-seated insecurity." He and Lancaster, his senior by sixteen years and not exactly lacking in superficial self-confidence himself, had problems during filming. "John and I didn't get along very well when we did *The Young Savages*," Burt recalled. The actor blamed himself for the discord, which stemmed from his reluctance to do the film.

Eventually, Burt came around. As he put it, "I suddenly realized that this man was really very good. I started paying attention to him." Frankenheimer would return the compliment, calling Burt "a true professional" and adding, "I think he's one . . . of the few actors that I've met who really knows something about production. . . . I find it very easy to work with him."

There are those who assert that the ultimately good relationship was born of Frankenheimer's willingness to subordinate himself to Burt's wishes. By way of proof, the actor was once quoted as saying, "He's a wonderful director, absolutely wonderful. And he always does exactly what I say." But J. P. Miller disputed that John was Burt's patsy, at least during the making of *The Young Savages*. "Obviously the director is going to pay attention to what he says," asserted the screenwriter, "but I guarantee you that, in the scenes that were being shot when the acting came to be done, John was the one who made those decisions."

Whatever the basis for the relationship, the two men would go on to make four other films together in what would become the most extensive director-actor collaboration of Lancaster's career.

If Lancaster and Frankenheimer formed an enduring bond, the same could not be said of the director and Dina Merrill, who played Burt's wife. Merrill had been eager to work with the highly regarded television director. But she found herself at odds with him from the start of production. Acquaintances later told her that Frankenheimer, like Daniel Mann, picked out one person on each film to humiliate. Unfortunately, on this film it was Merrill.

As had Corinne Calvet and Terry Moore in similar circumstances, the actress turned to Lancaster for solace. "Burt was most sympathetic and helpful and tried to defend me in the best way he could," she asserted. "He would tell me in the scenes we had together, 'You're doing fine, doing fine.' He was very kind and nice and absolutely lovely to work with."

Burt's other leading lady in the film, Lee Grant, cast as his former girl-friend Mary di Pace, formed quite a different impression. Such was her antipathy for Burt that she walked off the picture. Her replacement was Shelley Winters, Lancaster's original choice for the role. Because the budget and the shooting schedule were so tight, Winters agreed to darken her hair to match Grant's. Thus, long shots of the original actress were used with Shelley dubbing the lines in voice-over.

As filming progressed, Winters came to believe that Lancaster had wanted her for the part because of their past history. "I almost never knew whether he was relating to me or the part I was playing or the Shelley of 1948 [*sic*]," she asserted. Indeed, there was something eerie about the real-life former lovers playing former lovers before the cameras. "I think we both enjoyed the acting," she noted, "but, off the set, we both were reserved and quiet with each other."

That is, until the last day of filming, by which point the company had returned to Los Angeles to shoot interiors on the Columbia lot. "We got into the scene," Winters recalled, "and suddenly we weren't acting anymore. We both began to break from the dialogue and call each other terrible names. . . . It got so bad that the crew, embarrassed, left their stations." Finally, the dialogue director pulled Burt and Shelley apart, and they went their separate ways. The next day, they returned to the lot, apologized to one another, and awkwardly completed the picture.

The man who refereed the Winters–Lancaster bout was Sydney Pollack, who would become one of the foremost directors of the seventies, eighties, and nineties. Pollack had previously been an actor, making his Broadway debut in 1955. He also taught acting at the noted Neighborhood Playhouse. But it was Pollack's casting in several of Frankenheimer's television dramas that led to his assignment on *The Young Savages*. He was engaged to coach the untrained New York street toughs cast as gang members in the film, so Frankenheimer could concentrate on the adults.

At the time, Pollack was not interested in directing, and it was Lancaster's influence that turned his career around. "Once in a while," Burt recalled, "you find a dialogue director who is basically a director—and I watched Sydney on the set rehearsing these three young kids and I thought to myself, 'This fellow is really talented.' "

As Burt's agency, MCA, moved into film and television production, the actor saw a way of helping Pollack get started. "One day I went to see Lew Wasserman," he recalled, "who was my agent, and told him I had a very interesting, very talented young man working on this picture. . . . Wasserman said, 'Have him come up and see me.' Well, Sydney . . . went to see him and he started directing television films for MCA. In about a year or so he won an Emmy."

Pollack would go on to direct such notable films as *They Shoot Horses, Don't They?*, *Tootsie*, *The Firm*, and the Oscar-winning *Out of Africa*.

After *The Young Savages* wrapped in June, Burt turned his attention toward the problems created by *Elmer Gantry*'s imminent opening, notably the objections of the Catholic censorship organization, the Legion of Decency.[2] As the film's editor, Marjorie Fowler, recalled, "One scene is chopped all to hell because we had to get out some [line] or other about the Virgin Mary." Lancaster recalled that he went to New York "and spent three days with a monsignor . . . discussing the final line of the picture." As the scene had been shot, a skeptical reporter played by Arthur Kennedy called, "See you around, brother," to Gantry as the

2. By 1960, the MPAA's Production Code had lost its once-authoritative grip on the industry.

preacher left the grounds of the burned-out revival meeting, to which Gantry replied, "See you in hell, brother." Burt said, "To me it represented the whole reevaluation of what Gantry had gone through and what he was doing, how he was corrupting people. But no dice." The line was dropped, and the film recut to exclude both the reporter's farewell and the revivalist's rejoinder. Burt remembered the line and used it years later in *Buffalo Bill and the Indians.*

As an added precaution, a disclaimer was added before the opening credits, which read: "We believe that certain aspects of Revivalism can bear examination—that the conduct of some revivalists makes a mockery of the traditional beliefs and practices of organized Christianity. We believe that everyone has a right to worship according to his conscience but Freedom of Religion is not a license to abuse the faith of the people. However, due to the highly controversial nature of this film, we strongly urge you to prevent impressionable children from seeing it!"

When the film finally premiered on July 7, 1960, several critics wondered what all the fuss was about. "As a commentary on religion," *Time* asserted, "the film is not so irreverent as it is irrelevant. Its redemption is achieved by Director Richard Brooks in the wonderfully gaudy, artfully graphic flavor of the production." And Stanley Kauffmann of the *New Republic* noted, "After a preliminary warning of its controversial nature . . . it doesn't even show clearly the virtues and faults of its subject."

Still, other members of the press found the message potent. A. H. Weiller of *The New York Times* called *Gantry* a "hard-hitting, briskly paced, often moving, and believable drama," and Arthur Knight of *The Saturday Review* dubbed it "a brilliant, provocative film."

While the critics debated the picture's power, few disputed the sweep of Lancaster's performance. The result was an indelible portrait of an irrepressible hyena, a crowing, sweating, brawling, lusty, fire-and-brimstone-spouting whirlwind. From the film's opening moments, he is a mesmerizing mass of flashing eyes, deftly floating fingers, tufts of wavy light brown hair blowing in all directions, and those incredible, gleaming white teeth. If one had to choose a single picture from the prime of Lancaster's career to define the essence of his stardom, *Elmer Gantry* would be that film.

But beyond the quality of the performance, one has to wonder where the personas of the actor and the preacher met. After all, Burt himself asserted that Elmer was the character most like him. Certainly, both were blessed with boundless energy and remarkable salesmanship skills, indomitable willpower, and an undeniable gift of gab. But beyond even that, what Burt and Elmer shared—and what made people forgive both of them their faults—was a fundamental kindness, a love of people, evidenced in Gantry's case by his concern for the prostitute who betrayed him (beautifully played by Shirley Jones) even at the moment of his worst public humiliation. In Burt's case, witness the numerous colleagues over the years, including Doug McClure and Sydney Pollack, whose careers benefited from his largesse, and old friends, like Nick Cravat, Irving Burns, and Thom Conroy, whom he kept continually employed. As his friend actor Bob Quarry put it, "Anybody and everybody who got into Burt's life—that he would let in, 'cause he didn't let a lot of people in—he was very, very loyal to and good to."

Elmer Gantry was a solid commercial hit, reaching thirteenth place among the top moneymakers of 1960. And in December, Lancaster received the New York Film Critics award for Best Actor of the year—for the first time since *From Here to Eternity*. As on the previous occasion, an Oscar nomination seemed a certainty.

When Robert Stroud died at the age of seventy-three on November 21, 1963, *The New York Times* described him as a "tall bald man who wore steel-rimmed spectacles" and characterized him as "an antisocial, nonconformist who discovered too late that he was by nature and talent a scholar and research scientist." Known as the Bird Man of Alcatraz, Stroud had been in prison for fifty-four years, forty-two of which were spent in solitary confinement.

As chronicled in a 1955 book entitled *Bird Man of Alcatraz* by Thomas E. Gaddis, Stroud had killed two men, one of whom was a guard in Leavenworth Federal Penitentiary. Then, he discovered a wounded sparrow in the prison exercise yard and experienced a remarkable transformation. By 1930, with more than three hundred birds in his charge, the incorrigible, poorly educated killer had become one of the world's leading authorities on the care and breeding of canaries. Eventually, he was forced to give up his aviary and was transferred to Alcatraz and later the Medical Center for Federal Prisoners in Springfield, Missouri. By then, he was sixty-nine and ailing. Still, he continued to apply for parole every year, and every year his petition was denied.

Two filmmakers tried—unsuccessfully—to bring Stroud's story to the screen. The first was director Joshua Logan, the second was producer Jack Cummings. When Cummings dropped the project because he could not win the support of the U.S. Bureau of Prisons, the author of the screenplay, Guy Trosper, took it to Hecht, who involved Lancaster. The actor was not only excited by the principal character, but also by the film's theme. "Using Stroud as our example," he asserted during filming, "we are trying to say that the initial concept of prisons—to send men away to be punished—is not only inhuman but outdated and out-moded. . . . And more essential than anything else is to return and stim-ulate the criminal to some kind of dignity. That is the essence of rehabilitation." Thus, *Birdman of Alcatraz* became the second of the films that Burt would undertake to reduce HHL's debt to United Artists.

Not since *Jim Thorpe* had Lancaster portrayed a twentieth-century character drawn from life. When he was finally allowed to visit the old con at the penal hospital in Springfield, Missouri, he found, in his words, "a very interesting, highly intelligent man" but also "a very mean, tough man—he made no bones about it."

The meeting was all that the Bureau of Prisons would provide. Hecht's requests to film at the institutions where Stroud had been incar-cerated were repeatedly denied by the agency's director, James V. Ben-nett. "Mr. Bennett is not the censor of what the American people shall see, nor is he paid for this purpose," Lancaster bristled. "The public in-terest must not be confused with the hurt feelings of a group, nor does any such group represent the public."

So, Burt and Harold built prisons of their own—on the Columbia lot, at a cost of about $150,000. "No concessions were made for the camera or the lighting requirements," said cinematographer Burnett Guffey, who reported that Stroud's cell "was constructed according to the di-mensions of the original." Positioning equipment in such cramped quar-ters proved exceedingly difficult, but Guffey would earn an Oscar nomination for his stark black-and-white photography.

Filming began in November of 1960 with Karl Malden, Neville Brand, Telly Savalas, and Thelma Ritter in supporting roles. Charles Crichton, a British comedy director, was at the helm, but his unsuitability for a bleak American prison drama soon became apparent. "At the end of a week he was fired," recalled Malden. Hecht suggested they hire Frankenheimer. "I thought for a while," Lancaster recalled, "and I said to myself, 'You know, even though we had difficulties and differences of opinion about things, he's the one to do something like this.' Because it needed someone with a great deal of fire and excitement to bring to it. Certainly John was noted for that."

By an odd coincidence, Frankenheimer had once hoped to tell Stroud's story as a live television drama for CBS. But, once again, the Bureau of Prisons had refused to cooperate. "I don't know what possessed me to think that I could have ever realized it on live television with the birds," Frankenheimer said in 1969, "because birds are very, very difficult."

The director was not, as he put it, "completely happy" during the making of the picture. "I felt the producer was trying to interfere, the writer was trying to interfere a great deal, and Burt was interfering." In Malden's view, the ultimate decision-maker on the set was Lancaster: "Guy was working for Burt. Frankenheimer was working for Burt. And I never saw Hecht."

Indeed, Burt became passionate about *Birdman;* the production turned into a genuine labor of love. He later confessed, "One of the problems an actor faces, and it's a very dangerous thing, is to get so involved in a role he loses control of what he is doing. With *Birdman of Alcatraz*—I couldn't stop crying throughout the film. I mean, if there was a line when someone said, 'Sorry, Stroud, you can't have your parole,' I'd burst into tears."

Karl Malden, who played Stroud's nemesis, Warden Harvey Shoemaker, did not share Burt's belief in the old convict. "I think he deserved what he got," said the Oscar-winning actor. "Burt went out and fought for his release. Unbeknownst maybe, we lived our parts."

In addition, Malden objected to the extensive rewrites during shooting. "The day's work would be done," he recalled, "and Burt and Guy would go off and start rewriting the scenes for the next day." The following morning, Karl and the other actors would arrive to find new pages of dialogue to memorize. "And I was embarrassed to not know what the hell I was doing," he said. Finally, on the third day, he insisted upon going to his trailer and studying his lines until he felt comfortable with them—despite pressure from Lancaster to start filming. "I sat in the trailer for two hours," Malden noted. "He didn't like that." But the actor admitted that his anger over the situation did not hurt when it came to the on-camera relationship between Stroud and Warden Shoemaker. "It gave us that tension that we needed," he said.

On January 27, 1961, while *Birdman* was still in production, Lancaster suffered a deep personal tragedy, the death of his brother James. After graduating from NYU, his oldest brother had become a highly decorated member of the New York police force. Upon James' retirement in 1954, he had moved to Los Angeles with his wife, Edna, to work as an assistant director on many of Burt's pictures. It was on the set of *Birdman* that he suffered a fatal heart attack and died at the age of fifty. According to the *Hollywood Citizen-News,* Burt had been preparing to shoot a difficult scene when James collapsed; he immediately rushed to his brother's side. Filming, of course, ended for the day, and the company was sent home.

Eighteen days after James' death, Burt took a hiatus from *Birdman* in order to play a featured role in Stanley Kramer's star-laden production *Judgment at Nuremberg.*

Nuremberg began as a television drama, airing on *Playhouse 90* on April 16, 1959. It was based on the series of war-crimes trials of Nazi officials conducted in Nuremberg, Germany, by the United States, Great Britain, the Soviet Union, and France between 1945 and 1949. Author Abby Mann chose not to dramatize the first big show trial, in which Hermann Goering, Rudolf Hess, Albert Speer, and Julius Streicher were prosecuted. Rather, he looked to the second trial, in which the defendants included judges, lawyers, industrialists, and diplomats, whom he called "the bulwark of what many thought to be the most enlightened culture in Europe—how could they have gone along? And if they had, how deep was their responsibility?" In attempting to answer these questions, Mann centered his drama on the trial of four fictional judges. He also added another layer to the story—by setting it in 1948, when the alliance between the United States and the Soviet Union turned to enmity, and Germany became a major pawn in the new world conflict.

Stanley Kramer, a native New Yorker just two months older than Lancaster, was a distinguished independent producer-director, of whom critic Bosley Crowther said, "In the aggregate, Stanley Kramer appears to have done as much as anyone now making pictures to raise the intellectual level of the screen." *Judgment at Nuremberg* was just Kramer's sort of fare. As he put it on the eve of the film's premiere, "This is not merely the story of the War Crimes Trials in which a new standard of international justice is established. This is the story of a moral challenge that faces a man of responsibility—whether to hew to a policy of expediency which might, in historical terms, one day subject him to the same charges as the defendants who face him in the dock." To play that "man of responsibility," Kramer turned to Spencer Tracy.

Fundamentally, the feature would follow the story line of the TV drama, but Mann added a significant new character, the widow of a German general, Mme. Bertholt, with whom Tracy's judge becomes involved. Through her, Mann could not only inject a bit of romance into the plot, but also give voice to the aristocratic Germans, the Junkers, who had supported Hitler's government but disdained the man. The role was played by Marlene Dietrich.

As Mann drafted the screenplay, Kramer assembled a remarkable cast of stars. In addition to Tracy and Dietrich, Maximilian Schell would re-create his role, defense attorney Hans Rolfe, from the television drama (as would Werner Klemperer as the venal defendant Emil Hahn), Laurence Olivier would play the principal defendant, Ernst Janning (created on TV by Paul Lukas), and Judy Garland and Montgomery Clift would portray the two primary prosecution witnesses.

Lancaster had been offered the role of the prosecuting attorney, but he turned it down (it would eventually go to Richard Widmark). Then, in early November of 1960, as Burt was starting work on *Birdman,* Olivier withdrew from the project.[3] Lancaster was intrigued by the character of Janning, whom he saw as "almost a symbol of the dilemma in Germany during the Nazi period . . . the man of good intentions who did things of which he did not approve" for the greater good of his nation. Neither Mann nor Kramer was sure about the casting. "He's an outstanding actor," asserted the director in retrospect. "It was only a question of whether or not he could play a German and make it believable." But, with time running short, Kramer set aside his apprehension and gave Burt the part.

The company started the five-day rehearsal period for *Judgment at Nuremberg* on February 15, 1961, at the Revue Studios in Universal City. There, art director Rudolph Sternad had erected a faithful replica of the courtroom in the Palace of Justice, where the actual trials had been conducted.

Because of the relatively static nature of the courtroom scenes, Kramer put the entire set on rollers, thereby enabling the camera to pan the space in a complete circle. The rehearsals were as much to work out the complicated maneuvers with director of photography Ernest Laszlo as to establish the actors' characters and relationships.

Because Kramer chose to shoot the film in lengthy continuous takes prescribed by changing camera positions rather than conventionally, with scenes shot in snippets from different angles, the actors had to be in position at all times during the courtroom scenes instead of relaxing offstage until needed. For Lancaster that meant weeks of sitting around

3. According to Kramer, Olivier's decision to marry Joan Plowright led to his withdrawal, but the wedding was not held until March of 1961. A press release issued by Kramer's office on November 4, 1960, cited the extended run of *Becket,* in which Olivier was then starring on Broadway.

with little to do. Because his character denied the legitimacy of the tribunal, the acting challenge, as he saw it, involved retreating "into another world. At the same time I must not be a man in a cataleptic state. I must be involved in the trial."

The relationship between Kramer and Lancaster was not the warmest. The director believed that the estrangement derived, at least in part, from his closeness with Spencer Tracy. In his opinion, Burt and Tracy "didn't see eye to eye." Indeed, columnist Joe Hyams had managed to stir up some trouble between the two stars even before filming began. In November of 1960, he ran a column in which he quoted Burt as saying that *Nuremberg* was "a picture that should be made, and even though I'll have a small part in it and I'll get paid very little money for it, I'd do the picture for nothing because I think it should be done. Actually I have only one good scene in the film—opposite Spencer Tracy, whom I admire."[4] For reasons of his own, Hyams then relayed these comments to Tracy and detailed the response in his column. First, the senior actor asserted, Lancaster was getting $500,000 for the picture, hardly a pittance, and second, their scene together consisted of seven pages of dialogue—all Burt's. Tracy concluded by suggesting that Hyams "go back and ask Mr. Lancaster about the billing he's going to get for his small, underpaid part." In fact, Burt was billed second—to Tracy.

The column seemed a petty, pointless exercise, but, if anything, it reflected worse on Tracy, who came across as petulant. He seemingly failed to recognize that Lancaster *did* sacrifice in order to be in *Nuremberg*—Burt typically commanded sole billing above the title, his usual asking price had risen to $1 million per picture, and he was carrying entire projects, major, noteworthy films. Abby Mann asserted that the column "really hurt Burt." But the actor continued to respect Tracy.

Burt did not exactly have a smooth relationship with Maximilian Schell either. The two men had little in common. Schell, born in Vienna and raised primarily in Switzerland, was thirty when *Nuremberg* went before the cameras and was enjoying the first flush of international success, his initial American film role having come in 1958 with *The Young Lions.* In *Nuremberg,* he was able to emote without restraint in a wonderful, flashy role, one that he knew intimately, having already played it on television (it would ultimately win him an Oscar for Best Actor). Burt, by contrast, was forty-seven, hardly a newcomer to films, and constricted by a character fifteen years older than he. Even the German accent, which Schell came by naturally, was a major constraint for

4. Actually, the scene takes place in the courtroom. Tracy was present, but so were many of the other cast members. Lancaster did a have a one-on-one encounter with Tracy, at the conclusion of the film, but that was not what he was thinking of when he was speaking to Hyams.

Lancaster. Above all, Burt could sense that the actor playing his attorney was less than thrilled with his work in *Nuremberg* (although he had admired past Lancaster performances). At the same time, Schell regarded Tracy with reverence.

Finally, the tension between the two actors erupted into a fierce argument on the set. At the time, Schell was off-camera, feeding lines to Burt for his close-ups. Suddenly, the star became enraged when the younger actor threw him what he thought was a wrong cue. Schell insisted that the delivery was correct. Later, the day's rushes proved Schell right, but Lancaster never apologized. In retrospect, Schell minimized the incident. "That just comes out of a frustrated moment," he said, adding that he remembered Burt "as a very kind man." At the end of shooting, Schell, a book collector, even gave Burt a first-edition copy of *Elmer Gantry*, which was thirty-four years old at the time.

Lancaster had been sitting in the dock in Universal City for a full month when, on March 28, he finally got his chance to do his big, seven-page speech.

As the moment unfolded, Judge Spencer Tracy asked him if he wished to address the court. A silence then descended on the set. The actor rose, his posture erect, his conservative suit, short, gray wig, and clipped mustache befitting the dignified jurist that he was playing, and he said, "Yes! Yes! I've been waiting four weeks for a chance to open my big mouth." As reporter Herbert Kamm later described the moment, "The jape broke up the set. Not only was Lancaster's timing superb, but the completely unexpected touch of levity brought a welcome break to the somber business at hand."

However, the speech itself was a serious matter indeed, one of the centerpieces of Mann's Oscar-winning screenplay. It was Lancaster's moment to explain how and why a decent, intelligent man, a man of breeding and position, could go along with the horrors of the Third Reich. "Where were we," he asks rhetorically, "when Hitler began shrieking his hate in the Reichstag? Where were we when our neighbors were being dragged out in the middle of the night to Dachau? Where were we when every village in Germany has a railroad terminal, where cattle cars are being filled with children on their way to extermination? Where were we when they cried out to us? Were we deaf? dumb? blind?"

Lancaster did his best with the material, but Mann felt, after watching the rushes, that it failed to resonate as it should. "And I went to Kramer," he recalled, "and suggested that he retake it. But Kramer didn't want to do it. You know, we had a big budget, big stars. But I went over his head to Lancaster and I said, 'Burt, I think you ought to look at it.' So Burt looked at it and he came in and said, 'Stanley, I'm embarrassed by it. We've got to do it over again.' " Even in the retake, however, Lancaster failed to do justice to the powerful message. It was not for lack of trying. As Mann put it, "He was bursting a blood vessel trying to get it right." But, as the writer added, "It was such a big reach, my God."

Lancaster completed his work on *Judgment at Nuremberg* on April 5 (the picture itself would not wrap until May). Then he headed back to Columbia—to finish *Birdman of Alcatraz.*

During the months that Burt had been at work on *Nuremberg*, Frankenheimer had assembled a rough cut of the picture. It turned out to be nearly four and a half hours long, the result of a badly overwritten script. To rectify the problem, the picture's early sequences were rewritten and the new versions shot upon Lancaster's return. Many of these sequences involved the birds, and as Frankenheimer said at the time, "It's really tough directing birds." The creatures are virtually impossible to train. It took about twenty-seven of them to play the sparrow that Stroud adopts and teaches to do tricks.

The first step was to keep them from flying away. To accomplish this, Burt explained, the trainer, Ray Berwick, "would take a few feathers and pluck them out of the wing." Next, to get a bird to respond to Burt, the actor would, in his words, "take some birdseed and I would put it right by him, and he would take some of it. Then I'd hold it a little bit away. . . . He'd see it and then he would make the jump. Then I'd place some of it on my shoulder, and he'd jump to my shoulder. So it was very simple for the bird to react to me." But matters did not always go quite so smoothly. Frankenheimer noted that sometimes "Burt would have to stand there with that birdseed in his fingers, and we'd have a thousand feet of film in that camera, and we'd start the film, and five minutes would go by, six minutes, seven minutes. He'd be standing there, and he'd say, 'Is this goddamn bird ever going to move?' and boom it would come." The hardest part, the actor confessed, was the sequence in which Stroud's canaries took sick and died. "And when we needed a bird to come in and be on his perch and become an actor and fall off, we had to do the real thing." In other words, another trainer, named Canard—"the Eichmann of the bird world"—Burt called him, would pour lighter fluid down the poor creatures' throats, causing them to keel over.

• • •

On April 17, while *Birdman* was in the final weeks of production, the Academy Award ceremonies were held at the Santa Monica Civic Auditorium. As expected, Burt had been nominated for *Elmer Gantry*. The film had scored in four other categories as well, including Best Picture and Best Supporting Actress (Shirley Jones). Brooks, who received a nomination for his screenplay, was overlooked as director.

It was impossible to gauge Burt's chances as the evening progressed. Shirley Jones captured the Best Supporting Actress statuette, and Brooks won for his screenplay (based on material from another medium). But Billy Wilder had been named Best Director for *The Apartment;* his screenplay with I. A. L. Diamond was also honored (for material written directly for the screen). Would Jack Lemmon complete the honors for the black comedy with his fine performance as the ambitious junior executive? Perhaps, but the Best Actress presentation offered a hopeful sign for Lancaster fans: Elizabeth Taylor claimed the prize for *Butterfield 8* over a field that included Shirley MacLaine, costar of *The Apartment* (Jean Simmons had not been nominated for *Gantry*).[5]

Finally, the moment arrived. Greer Garson announced the five nominees: Trevor Howard for *Sons and Lovers,* Burt Lancaster for *Elmer Gantry,* Jack Lemmon for *The Apartment,* Laurence Olivier for *The Entertainer,* and Spencer Tracy for *Inherit the Wind.* And the winner was . . . Burt Lancaster! As the British actress announced the result, she added, "This is really rightly deserved." At the age of forty-seven, the former acrobat who had never dreamed of a career as an actor and had never taken a lesson in the craft had captured the highest honor that his profession could bestow. Bounding up to the podium, he flashed that toothsome smile and said, "I'd like to thank all those who voted for me. I'd even like to thank those who voted against me."

"People in the community were very, very happy when he won his Oscar award," recalled actor Don Murray. "It was a very, very popular selection." Early the following morning, as the actor returned home, he saw a sign that his Bel-Air neighbors had erected. Earlier it had read, "Good luck, Burt." Now it said, "Congrats, Burt." Inside, he found a telegram from David Niven, who had won two years earlier for Lancaster's own *Separate Tables.* "Congratulations," the British actor had written, "and welcome to the most exclusive club in the world."

5. *The Apartment* would go on to capture the evening's final and most important award, that for Best Picture, besting not only *Elmer Gantry* but also *The Alamo, Sons and Lovers,* and *The Sundowners.*

CHAPTER THIRTEEN

At the Top

On May 24, 1961, five weeks after the Academy Awards ceremony, *The Young Savages* premiered.

Virtually all of the critics agreed that the melodrama was well crafted and suspenseful, but that it shed little light on the problem of disaffected youth. "Superficially," to quote *The Saturday Review*, "it resembles just about every other study of juvenile delinquency recorded on celluloid since the days of the Dead End Kids."

Lancaster rendered what was generally regarded as a solid, workmanlike portrayal of a dedicated assistant DA, but from the twilight of his career Burt would look back on the picture and give it surprisingly high marks. "The work was good," he said in 1989, "the acting was good, what the story was about, what it had to say, was said rather well." And Frankenheimer added, "I think Burt Lancaster is terrific in this movie."

At the time of the picture's release, Lancaster's stature within the industry could not have been higher. Three months later, he was even named—for the first time—the number one male box-office star by the Motion Picture Exhibitors of America, with Doris Day as the number one female. On September 10, however, his elation turned to sorrow. His father had suffered a heart attack and passed away at the age of eighty-four.

"Burt was very devoted to his father," said Walter Seltzer. The two Lancasters had grown particularly close after James had come to live with his youngest son in 1947. As with Burt's older brother William, who died in 1946, James' remains were shipped to New York for burial beside Burt's mother, Elizabeth, at the Cypress Hills Cemetery on Long Island.

Two months later, on November 6, tragedy struck again; this time, Burt's home burned to the ground. It was one of three hundred houses lost in Bel-Air and Brentwood during a raging inferno. In Burt's case, virtually everything went up in smoke. Spotted by newsmen as he arrived to inspect the damage, he quipped, "I just came to mainly pick up my *Variety* in the mailbox." Fortunately, his extensive art collection was then on loan to the Los Angeles County Museum of Art.

In the aftermath of the fire, Lancaster gave serious thought to moving his family to Portland, Oregon, or Seattle, Washington, where they could lead more normal lives, but Norma and the kids elected to stay and to rebuild on the grounds of their lost home.

When construction was finished, the new place turned out to be far more expansive than the first. "It was like a castle," to quote projectionist Julian Ullman, who worked there on weekends. Made of stone and cement, its centerpiece was a swimming pool that flowed from the outside into the living room. Actress Julie Adams said that "whereas the other one was sort of like a family house, this one was rather grand." It may have been a little too sumptuous for the unpretentious Lancasters. As Jackie Bone put it, "It was huge and elegant, and it just wasn't them."

The world premiere of *Judgment at Nuremberg* was held in West Berlin in December of 1961. The gala was a public relations bonanza, with more than one hundred film critics and newspaper columnists flown in for five days at an estimated cost of $200,000.

On the evening of the fourteenth, the screening was held in the Kongresshalle, the home of the Berlin Film Festival. Introducing a movie about the darkest side of the Third Reich in the very city that had housed its ministries was enormously bold. Afterward, however, the mayor of West Berlin, Willy Brandt, called the premiere "an important political event" and maintained that "the roots of the present position of our people, country, and city lie in the fact that we did not prevent right from being trampled underfoot during the time of Nazi power."

Many among the press gave the picture rave reviews. *The New Yorker* called it a "bold and, despite its great length, continuously exciting picture," Bosley Crowther of *The New York Times* found it "brilliantly constructed and directed," and Richard L. Coe of *The Washington Post* proclaimed it "an extraordinary film, both in concept and in handling."

As might have been expected, the lion's share of the acting honors went to Tracy, the picture's sober, earnest anchor, and Schell in its flashiest role. Garland and Clift were also memorable, she shockingly overweight and terribly vulnerable, he awkward, frail, and odd-looking (all four actors would receive Oscar nominations).

Lancaster was praised in numerous quarters for what Richard Coe called "a solidly restrained performance," but others shared the assessment of *Variety,* which asserted that "he never quite attains the cold, superior intensity that Paul Lukas brought to the part on TV." In retrospect, Lancaster deserves more praise for his willingness to stretch himself as an actor than for the performance itself. As Abby Mann noted, "Casting him as a German intellectual was just a bit of a reach."

Five days after the picture's premiere in Berlin, it debuted in New York. Although some among the American press questioned its box-office appeal, it became the eleventh most popular picture of 1962. Not until Steven Spielberg's *Schindler's List* in 1993, a film of very different style and affect, would an examination of the horrors of the Third Reich find such commercial success.

Judgment at Nuremberg gave rise to *A Child Is Waiting,* a sober examination of mentally retarded children and the spectrum of adult attitudes toward them. It reunited Lancaster with Stanley Kramer, Abby Mann, and Judy Garland.

Like *Nuremberg, A Child Is Waiting* began as a teleplay, airing on *Studio One* on March 11, 1957. At the time, mental retardation was still a "closet" subject. Mann's interest began when he visited a classmate who worked at a facility for such youngsters. "And there was a little boy there," he recalled, "who waited every Wednesday afternoon for his mother to come, and she hadn't come for years and years."

The child's plight became a central element in the drama, as did a conflict between Jean Hansen, a teacher's aide with a strong attachment toward the youngsters, and hospital administrator Dr. Matthew Clark, a stern disciplinarian who believes that mentally retarded children should be pushed to realize their full potential. On TV, Pat Hingle had played the doctor and Mary Fickett the aide, with Vincent J. Donohue directing.

"There are two reasons I'm making the picture," Kramer said. "First, to entertain. It is a powerful drama. Second, to throw a spotlight on a dark-ages type of social thinking which has tried to relegate the subject of retardation to a place under the rocks." Lancaster, having endured the mental aberrations of his own son Jimmy, was a sympathetic ally. To play the hospital administrator, he even agreed to a 50 percent cut in his then-asking price of $1 million per picture (in exchange for a share of the profits).

Kramer wanted to direct *A Child Is Waiting* himself, but he had a schedule conflict, so he chose Jack Clayton. The British director had leaped to the forefront of international filmmakers with his first full-length feature, 1958's *Room at the Top*. David Shipman, author of a 1993 biography of Judy Garland, maintained that Clayton and Ingrid Bergman, who had been expected to play Jean Hansen, "left the film when Lancaster was cast." But Mann and Kramer said otherwise. Bergman, the screen-writer asserted, had never been firmly committed. When she started "waffling," he and Kramer began to look elsewhere, principally at Katharine Hepburn and Elizabeth Taylor. As for Clayton, the director's attorney, Christopher Mann, wrote Kramer a letter dated April 19, 1961, to express his client's pleasure at Burt's casting (and at the possibility of hiring Elizabeth Taylor for the female lead). Clayton's withdrawal resulted solely from scheduling difficulties; in demand after *Room at the Top*, he could simply not hold himself available indefinitely while Kramer struggled to find the right leading lady.

It took until the middle of September before the producer settled on Lancaster's costar—thirty-nine-year-old Judy Garland. The once-endearing child actress had grown into a troubled adult, constantly battling a weight problem and addictions to pills and liquor. Although she had turned in a stunning cameo performance in *Judgment at Nuremberg*, she had not starred in a movie for seven years. She was not up to the challenge physically or emotionally in late 1961 and early 1962 either. But Judy, like Burt, related to the project on a personal level; she had been befriended by a mentally disturbed child during her hospitalization for a nervous breakdown in 1948. Although she was a friend, Mann did not think she was right for the part, but Kramer had exhausted his options.

Several weeks after Garland's casting was announced, the producer engaged thirty-one-year-old John Cassavetes to direct. The Long Island–born son of a Greek-immigrant travel agent had already made a name for himself as an actor. His directing debut came in 1959, with an independent, low-budget "new wave" piece entitled *Shadows*. Lancaster had reservations about the choice, but Mann, a friend of Cassavetes', told Burt, "You'll like him. I think it'll work out."

A Child Is Waiting went into production at the Revue Studios in Universal City on January 16, 1962. As with *Nuremberg*, production designer Rudy Sternad lent verisimilitude to the proceedings by closely modeling his sets for the fictional Crawthorne State Mental Hospital on an actual locale, the Vineland Training School in New Jersey, one of the world's foremost institutions for the care and treatment of mentally retarded children.

Lancaster had diligently prepared for his role. As he recalled, "For three weeks before the start of shooting, I visited almost daily at the Pacific State Hospital, to become acquainted with the operations and techniques of such an institution. I became acquainted too with scores of the young patients." The facility in Pomona, California, just east of Los Angeles, also lent the production fourteen of its charges, ages nine to twelve, to play student-inmates in the film. The only "pro" among the young cast members was Bruce Ritchey, who had appeared in bit parts in two commercials and one previous feature; he played Reuben, the abandoned child who wins the heart of Garland's Hansen.

To use actual mentally retarded children in the picture was a big gamble. Some felt that Kramer had no business exposing the public to such unfortunates. But the producer was pleased with his decision. "It was exciting," he recalled. "They surprised us every day in reaction and what they did."

Burt was also pleased. "We have to ad-lib around the periphery of a scene," he said during shooting, "and I have to attune and adjust myself to the unexpected things they do. But they are much better than child actors for the parts. They have certain gestures that are characteristic, very difficult for even an experienced actor." Lancaster worked well with the youngsters. On one occasion, for example, they grew upset when the script called for him to admonish Reuben. Burt gave them a group hug and then explained that he was not really angry, that he was only pretending for the movie.

The actor was perhaps less forthcoming with his adult costars. Elizabeth Wilson, who played one of the hospital's teachers, echoed the sentiments of several supporting players from previous films when she said, "I didn't care for him. I mean, he was not the least bit friendly. I have no recollection of ever having a conversation with him."

By contrast, Wilson adored Cassavetes. The director, a fervent proponent of improvisational acting, ran a loose set. As he explained, "I think that players should be allowed to let their personalities, abilities, and concepts speak for themselves in translating a writer's thoughts and words to the screen. A director then should concern himself largely with the overall image of the author's intention."

But on one occasion—an argument between Burt's and Garland's characters—Cassavetes insisted that Lancaster do the scene his way, with fury. "John, I can't do that," Burt told him. "I'm playing a doctor, a man of enormous responsibility; even if I felt that anger, I'd have to handle it." Nevertheless, the actor agreed to comply with Cassavetes' wishes. "The next day," Burt recalled, "Stanley Kramer comes in and says, 'I just saw the rushes, what were you doing in that scene? You look ridiculous.' I looked over at John and John was very sweet. He said,

'Burt didn't want to do it that way, but I asked him to.'" The scene was reshot.

Although Burt later asserted that he and Cassavetes became "very good friends" during filming, the star was not impressed with his director. He told Mann, "This kid doesn't really know what he's doing." The writer agreed. Mann also asserted that "Garland grew to hate" Cassavetes. But Judy had problems that went far beyond a lack of rapport with her director. According to Burt, "Garland was drinking a great deal, and it was a big effort to get herself together and get in shape to work." Elizabeth Wilson, who loved Judy, agreed, saying, "I think she was very, very rocky at that point." Indeed, a glance at the production log reveals frequent absences and late arrivals. When she did appear, according to Mann, she was "ill prepared" and "surly."

Lancaster tried to be supportive. "Really Burt was very kind to her," said Mann. "Burt was trying to help her." The actor later recalled, "There was no personal problem in working with her, but she was in a period of her life where she just wasn't together. I had to kind of nurse her along with it. And because of her mental condition at the time, she wasn't terribly involved in the part." As a result, Garland's character became tearful, overly emotional, and ineffectual, and what should have been a battle between equally valid but opposing points of view collapsed. Moreover, the resultant delays and postponements caused the filming, which had been scheduled for ten weeks, to last fourteen. Finally, however, on April 13, *A Child Is Waiting* wrapped.

Eleven days later, on April 24, Lancaster appeared on a local New York TV program entitled *PM* to promote *Birdman of Alcatraz,* scheduled for release in July. (Since Burt would be in Europe at the time, he embarked on a four-city junket in April, visiting San Francisco, Chicago, New York, and Washington, D.C.)

The host of *PM,* Mike Wallace, saw the actor just prior to taping. "I remember that we stood in the men's room, talking ahead of time," the journalist said. "And I think I asked him if there was anything he didn't want to talk about and he said no, he wasn't particularly anxious to talk about his family and things of that nature, but it was perfectly cordial, perfectly pleasant." Then, on camera, Wallace decided to delve a bit into Lancaster's character. "In my research," he remembered, "I had found that he had a monumental temper, and so I thought that it would be sort of interesting to ask him about it and see what happened." As Wallace began to raise the subject, actor Ossie Davis could see his fellow guest bristle. "Right away I said to myself, 'This is not a guy to be played with,'" the actor recalled, laughing. Wallace noticed Burt's reaction too. "I could see a kind of smile," he said, "but not a funny smile or a happy smile, sort of a calculating [smile] . . . It worried me." Nevertheless, the host persisted with his inquiry, at which point Lancaster reminded him that he had come on the show to talk about *Birdman.* Wallace told him, "We're going to get to *Birdman* right away, as soon as this next commercial break is finished." But Burt replied, "The hell we are." He then stalked off the set and left the studio.

The following day, Lancaster staged a small, informal press conference in his room at the Plaza Hotel, at which he said that he had no idea that Wallace would ask about his personality, and when the host did so, it made him "sick to my stomach."

If Wallace had wanted to find out if Lancaster had a temper, he got his answer. Burt offered further proof the following month in Rome. At around 2 A.M. on May 13, he was coming out of a posh restaurant on the Via Veneto in the company of a beautiful Italian starlet named Beatrice Altariba. When the paparazzi started to take the couple's picture, Lancaster asked them to stop. But they persisted, and he started swinging. The principal object of his fury was Umberto Spagna. Although the photographer was over six feet tall and weighed 260 pounds, Lancaster managed to knock him to the ground and then, according to Spagna, kick him. When Eleanor Packard of the New York *Daily News* questioned Burt about the incident, which was covered by the paper later the same day, she asked if he had been provoked, and the actor snapped, "That would be putting it mildly."

The incidents in New York and Rome were anomalies; to that point, Burt had managed to restrict his outbursts to his private world—the home, the office, and the set. He had also closely guarded his extramarital liaisons. Although his evening with Beatrice Altariba may have been perfectly innocent, his fury with the paparazzi probably stemmed from the desire to protect himself from the hint of indiscretion.

In addition, Burt was anxious over the role that he was about to undertake, one that he had said he could not play when it was first offered to him. The picture would mark a turning point in his career. Indeed, it would change his way of looking at acting and, for that matter, the entire process of filmmaking.

It was called *The Leopard.*

• • •

The Leopard had begun as a novel by an impoverished Sicilian prince named Giuseppe Tomasi di Lampedusa. He was sixty and dying of cancer when he decided to write about the decisive moment in his nation's history, the 1860 uprising by which Giuseppe Garibaldi and the Red Shirts toppled the Bourbon dynasty in what was known as the Kingdom of the Two Sicilies (Sicily and Naples) and set the stage for the unification of the entire Italian peninsula. The Risorgimento, or unification movement, signaled the end of Lampedusa's class, the landed aristocracy, which had ruled for centuries in untroubled splendor. *Il Gattopardo* was published in 1958—to great acclaim. In America, *The Leopard,* the English translation by Archibald Colquhoun, was on *The New York Times* bestseller list for thirty-eight weeks.

The Leopard was primarily a psychological study of one man, Don Fabrizio, the prince of Salina, a character based on the author's great-grandfather. Strong, proud, and powerful, he is known as the Leopard, from the haughty, crowned feline at the center of his family crest. Unlike many of his peers, Don Fabrizio acknowledges the whirlwind that is engulfing his class and accommodates himself to the new order by wedding his beloved nephew, Tancredi Falconeri, to Angelica Sedara, the irrepressible daughter of a prosperous merchant.

In 1961, producer Goffredo Lombardo acquired *The Leopard* for the screen and engaged Luchino Visconti to cowrite and direct the adaptation. Visconti, who had scored a resounding international triumph with Lombardo's production *Rocco and His Brothers* in 1960, was ideally suited to take charge of *The Leopard,* having been born—in 1906—to the highest-ranking family of Milan.

"I developed an affection for that extraordinary character Prince Fabrizio di Salina," said Visconti. But he believed that the Leopard's "world had to go and that is what I want to show in the film." He also sought to express through the turbulent events of the Risorgimento his disillusionment with his own time, where, as he put it, "everything, despite a little modernization, remains what it was."

To play the dashing Tancredi and his engaging fiancée, Visconti cast the twenty-six-year old French actor Alain Delon and the Tunisian-born beauty twenty-three-year-old Claudia Cardinale, both of whom had been in *Rocco and His Brothers.* For the all-important role of the prince, he considered a Russian actor, Nikolai Cherkassov, as well as Laurence Olivier and Marlon Brando, but for varying reasons the role remained uncast.

While Visconti struggled to find his Don Fabrizio, producer Lombardo's budget difficulties with another film forced him to turn to Hollywood to help finance *The Leopard.* He received the requisite capital, $3 million, from 20th Century–Fox—with the provisos that the Sicilian epic star an American actor and that it be shot in English. Visconti refused to accede to the latter, so, by way of compromise, the parties agreed that the prince's dialogue would be in English, and the rest of the picture would be dubbed from the Italian (or, in Delon's case, French) for the American-British release.

While in Hollywood, Lombardo also attempted to secure Lancaster's services for a different project. Burt was not interested, but when the producer saw a copy of Lampedusa's novel on the star's desk, he asked, "Would you like to play the role?" Burt demurred, saying, "It calls for a real Italian." Nevertheless, when Lombardo returned home, he mentioned Burt to Visconti. According to the actor, the director said, "No, no, cowboy actor, gangster, terrible, ridiculous." But Visconti was no more enamored of the candidates suggested by Fox, Spencer Tracy and Anthony Quinn. Ironically, it was Burt's performance in *Judgment at Nuremberg*—in the role originally intended for Olivier—that swung the decision in his favor.[1]

"Of course I was far from certain that I was capable of playing the prince of Salina when the part was offered to me," Lancaster said. Growing up in Italian East Harlem, he knew plenty of Sicilians, but all of them were of peasant stock. He had to "discover and make real for myself the mannerisms and attitudes born of centuries of belonging to a ruling class." It was a discovery that he was eager to make. As he put it, "I had been fascinated by the Leopard long before I was offered the part. I think it is the best-written and most perceptive study of a man and his social background that has appeared for many years."

The film went into production in Palermo on May 14, 1962. But even there, in comparatively rural Sicily, telegraph poles had to be removed and cobblestones overlaid on asphalt roads in order to preserve the nineteenth-century atmosphere of the picture. Moreover, permission to film had to be obtained from the local Mafia chieftains.

Visconti's passion for accuracy extended to *everything,* down to the smallest detail. "Even in my purse that nobody saw," recalled Claudia

---

1. When Lancaster publicly recounted the story of his casting in *The Leopard,* as he often did, he invariably said that Visconti was also persuaded by his performance in *Birdman of Alcatraz.* If so, Visconti arranged to see a rough cut of the picture; Burt had already been filming *The Leopard* for months when *Birdman* was released in the United States.

Cardinale, "I had real perfume of the period." Each extra for the street-fighting sequence had to physically resemble the people of the region from which he was supposed to come—short, dark-haired men for the Bourbons and tall blonds for the Red Shirts—and each was given a basic course in military training.

The director had such absolute control over the entire enterprise that, according to Cardinale, even "the producer had trouble gaining admission to the set."

Lancaster arrived in Sicily eager to acquaint himself with the country and the people that were in Don Fabrizio's blood. He hoped that Visconti would assist him in his preparation, but Suso Cecchi D'Amico, coauthor of the screenplay and one of the director's close friends, asserted, "Visconti didn't help him at all." Cardinale agreed, describing the director's manner with Burt as "almost rude." As Visconti saw it, there was no reason to extend himself to an American film star who had been foisted on him as the price for making the picture. Surely, that "cowboy" would never lend himself to Visconti's rigorous approach to moviemaking.

Visconti began with a major battle sequence, for which Lancaster was not needed. But, when Burt was finally called to work, his relations with the director remained cool. For starters, Alain Delon, whom Visconti adored, was the only actor to rate a private dressing room. By contrast, as the director's biographer Gaia Servadio noted, "poor Burt Lancaster stood around for hours, waiting."

Atypically, Burt refused to be provoked by Visconti's evident disdain. For once, he recognized that he was working with someone of enormous talent. Years later he said, "I didn't for one moment pretend that I could do what he was doing better than Visconti could do it himself in the framework of the film, in the setup of the camera, in terms of how it should be shot, in terms of the style." He also acknowledged that "the ideas he wanted me to get across were brilliant. They were far superior to anything I had in mind."

Above all, Lancaster admired Visconti's quest for perfection, saying, "He potters round the set interminably and nothing escapes him. He controls everything from the camera and the lighting down to the most insignificant prop—even a visiting card lying on a desk must be impeccably authentic. For him everything contributes to the atmosphere, and you feel it." A case in point was a scene in which Burt had to remove some money from a dresser drawer. "And when I opened it," he recalled, "I found magnificent silk shirts that had been made for me. I said to the cameraman, 'Does the camera see these?' He said, 'No.' I said to Visconti, 'Why are they there?' He said, 'You're the prince. Is for you to touch.' " It was a moment that stirred Burt deeply; he would recount the incident often, in private as well public, throughout the rest of his career.

If, in the early stages of shooting, Burt had failed to win over his director, he had at least impressed the rest of the company. As Cardinale put it, "To do this kind of part, a prince, in Sicily, and to change completely his personality and physicality—he changed completely—he is really a great actor." She noted that Delon felt the same way. "In fact," she said, "in the film, when Alain looks at Burt with great love for his uncle, I think it was also for what Burt was personally."

In August, work began on the ball sequence, which comprises roughly the last forty-five minutes of the film and captures the dying gasp of a world that is about to vanish forever. Shot at the Gangi Palace in Palermo, it took forty-eight days to complete, with the cast and crew working every evening from seven until dawn. "It was terribly hot," recalled Suso Cecchi D'Amico. "They worked only at night because it was impossible to work during the daylight." Visconti's passion for detail reached its zenith in this exquisite, visually stunning sequence. The palace was filled with fresh flowers; the myriad chandeliers were lit by genuine candles, which had to be replaced every hour; cooked foods were carried by extras with the steam still rising from them, thanks to the production unit's kitchens, purposely set close to the ballroom. Even a laundry was established on the ground floor of the palace so that the men's white gloves could periodically be cleaned of sweat. Moreover, the "guests" were played by genuine princes and princesses.

During the filming of the ball sequence, Visconti's ire with Lancaster reached its zenith. As Don Fabrizio, the actor had to dance with Cardinale's Angelica, and Visconti, in characteristic fashion, wanted their waltz together to be perfect: the audience should see the aging prince become young again as he whirls his nephew's beautiful, vivacious fiancée around the floor. The director had even arranged for the actors to rehearse their interlude with a ballet master. But Lancaster had injured his knee in the rugged Sicilian terrain, and when it came time to shoot the scene, he was in considerable pain. He asked the director if the dance could be postponed, but he was rudely rebuffed. As Cardinale recalled, "Luchino said, 'Mr. Lancaster, when you are ready, you call me,' and then he—Luchino—took me, and we went to his apartment in this marvelous palace. We had a cup of champagne and we talked for hours really. I was very embarrassed. I didn't know what to do, because I knew Burt was there waiting for us." Finally, an assistant arrived to tell them that Lancaster was ready. Visconti and Cardinale then joined him on the set and filmed the waltz—with Burt masking his pain quite effectively.

Given the forty-eight days of filming in the Gangi Palace, Visconti could easily have postponed the prince's waltz. Cardinale said that he refused to do so because "I think Luchino wanted just to show Lancaster that *he* was the master of the set." Afterward, Lancaster met with Visconti. The substance of the conversation went unrecorded, but according to Suso Cecchi D'Amico, "Some very high voices were heard." Still, from that encounter—and Lancaster's willingness to submit himself to Visconti's harsh discipline—a new relationship emerged between the director and the star.

"It was the moment when the great friendship started," said D'Amico. In time each man grew to love and respect the other. For Visconti's part, as Cardinale explained, "Luchino admired Burt's power, his integrity, and his professionalism. . . . He knew perfectly what he was supposed to do. And Luchino loved these kinds of actors."

As for Lancaster, the actress said that he "admired the novelty of Visconti, his intelligence, his preparation. Luchino . . . could talk about everything—about classical music, about rock and roll, about opera, about costumes, hairdo, makeup. . . . He came from a very old family in Italy, and he had all this past, and of course, Burt, being an American, was fascinated by that." So much so, in fact, that Lancaster ultimately modeled Don Fabrizio on the director; those who knew Visconti say that they can see his mannerisms in the actor's performance.

Superficially, the American actor and the Italian director could not have been more different, but Suso D'Amico came to feel that the two men were alike in many ways—intellect, passion, love of work. "They were born on the same day [November 2]," she noted, "and that's maybe why they were so similar in character." In fact, during filming, Visconti gave a party at his villa in Rome to celebrate their joint birthdays. (By then, interiors for *The Leopard* were being shot in the Eternal City.) "And it was very funny," D'Amico recalled, "because Lancaster arrived with a big painting by Guttuso he had bought for Visconti, and Visconti had bought a Guttuso for Lancaster."[2]

● ● ●

2. Born in Sicily in 1912, Renato Guttuso was a modern figurative painter.

In all, it took seven months to film *The Leopard,* but Lancaster's presence was not required the entire time. On September 5, he was present at the screening of *Birdman of Alcatraz* at the Venice Film Festival, where the picture was the only American entry. At the conclusion of the festival, Burt was named Best Actor, and the picture was awarded the San Giorgio Prize.

By then, *Birdman* had been playing to receptive audiences in America for a month and a half, having opened on July 18 to generally favorable reviews. *Variety* called it "the finest prison picture ever made," but the film was hardly typical of the genre, which usually boasted tough, jargon-filled dialogue, fights between inmates, escape attempts, and macho performances by the likes of James Cagney and Humphrey Bogart. Instead, *Birdman* went about the telling one man's actual incarceration with deliberateness, a low-key manner, and clarity of focus. Still, a few critics found the picture overly long at 147 minutes and argued, with some justification, that the story lacked punch in the latter half, after Stroud lost his canaries. Even costar Karl Malden asserted that "the most effective relationship in the picture was between Burt and the birds."

Lancaster brought a restrained intensity to his performance that drew praise from virtually every quarter. Even Stanley Kauffmann, the *New Republic* critic who rarely extended a kind word to the actor, called Stroud "one of his few good performances." Indeed, if *Elmer Gantry* stands as the quintessence of Lancaster's larger-than-life, bravura persona, *Birdman* may well offer the best example of that bottled-up, tightly controlled, excruciatingly deliberate character who had intrigued audiences from the Swede to Ernst Janning. As Stroud, Lancaster not only had to carry much of the film, although he had fine support from Telly Savalas as another con (for which Savalas earned an Oscar nomination), he also had to age from a hotheaded adolescent to a sexagenarian. He even shaved his head and used three different wigs to emphasize the character's maturation.

Birdman brought Burt his third Academy Award nomination, but the award went to Gregory Peck for *To Kill a Mockingbird.* Peck, the sentimental favorite, had never won an Oscar before.

Although Burt may not have invested quite so much of himself in *A Child Is Waiting,* it was also close to his heart, and he monitored its postproduction progress while he was in Sicily and Rome.

Matters were not going well. The picture's producer, Stanley Kramer, and director, John Cassavetes, simply could not agree on how the film

was to be edited. Finally, Kramer fired Cassavetes and cut the film himself. Cassavetes, however, would retain sole director's credit.

Later, after the picture's release, Cassavetes said, "I didn't think his film—
and that's what I consider it to be, his film—was so bad, just a lot more sentimental than mine." But the picture's editor, Gene Fowler Jr.,
maintained that point of view was not at the heart of the problem: "It was
a fight of technique. Stanley is a more traditional picture-maker, and
Cassavetes was, I guess, called Nouvelle Vague. He was trying some
things, which frankly I disagreed with, and I thought he was hurting the picture by blunting the so-called message with technique." By way of example, Fowler cited footage in which the picture was jumpy because the
camera had run over a cable during filming. He automatically chose another
take. "My God, you damn Hollywood people," Cassavetes said. "All you can
think of is smoothness of camera. What we want is to get some rough edges
in here." Worse, Cassavetes' passion for improvised dialogue made it difficult, if not impossible, to use different takes of the same scene. "If one person said something [in a two-shot]," Fowler explained, "you had to
search [the other character's close-ups] to find an answer, and it was
an intricate and terribly difficult thing to put together."

When Lancaster learned of the postproduction difficulties at the end
of September, he sent Kramer a sympathetic note. Clearly, in the dispute between Kramer and Cassavetes, he sided with the producer. Two
weeks later, having encountered Abby Mann in Rome in the interim, he
wrote again, volunteering to view the rough cut and lend a fresh perspective to the editing. Kramer declined the offer with thanks, explaining that the picture had been scored and dubbed and could not be
altered without major expense. He assured Lancaster that he had
worked "to the very best of my ability with film which was not always
shot with the impact which we all desired," but confessed that in some
instances he had "to compensate for what is not there." Burt replied
graciously, expressing every confidence in Kramer's editing choices.

Shortly after dispatching his second missive to Kramer, Lancaster took
another brief hiatus from *The Leopard* to do a cameo in *The List of
Adrian Messenger,* which Kirk Douglas' Joel Productions was making
in England and Ireland for Universal. Directed by John Huston from
a screenplay by Anthony Veiller, *Adrian Messenger* was a black-
and-white British mystery in the classic tradition, with George C. Scott
as an intelligence officer on the trail of a murderer, played by Douglas.
Kirk was required to don several disguises, for which makeup wizard Bud
Westmore had devised elaborate latex masks, wigs, and prostheses. Since

the audience would not know until the denouement that Douglas was, in fact, the killer and, by extension, the fellow in disguise, producer Edward Lewis decided to have several other male stars appear briefly at strategic points in the story—also in disguise. These "red herrings," as he called them, would not only fuel suspense over the killer's identity, but also set the audience to guessing about which star was playing which cameo. In an epilogue, each actor would be revealed as he peeled off his makeup before the camera.

Burt was cast as an old woman, an animal-rights activist. Joining him in the fun were Tony Curtis, Robert Mitchum, and Frank Sinatra.

Finally, in late November, work on the long, grueling *Leopard* came to an end. The production had been hard but exhilarating. "We knew we were doing something important," said Cardinale, "part of the history of the cinema. Because everything around us was so magnificent—the costumes, the palace—I mean, everything was just the perfect thing."

No one had been more inspired than Lancaster. Over the ensuing years, several of his costars would experience the special glow that came over him when he talked about *The Leopard*. "I think Visconti did something for Burt that was really very, very important to him," said screenwriter Alan Sharp, "which was . . . I think Burt always felt he was a performer and not an actor, and Visconti, who came from the European tradition, treated him as one of the great diva actors. I don't know if this was out of respect for Burt or just Visconti's sense of mise-en-scène reality, but for Burt it was very impressive. He had moved to where he wasn't a circus performer." Lancaster himself acknowledged the pivotal role that *The Leopard* played in his career. Visconti "was the most important director I worked for," he said in 1976, "because he opened for me a new world and a new way of doing things."

No longer would Burt be ashamed to call himself an actor.

CHAPTER FOURTEEN

Turning Fifty

On December 6, shortly after Lancaster's return to America, he attended a special preview of *A Child Is Waiting* at the Statler Hilton Hotel in Washington, D.C. The screening was part of the First International Awards dinner for "outstanding achievement in research, service, and leadership in mental retardation" sponsored by the Joseph P. Kennedy Jr. Foundation. It was a glittering affair, attended by JFK with U.N. ambassador Adlai Stevenson as the master of ceremonies. During the evening, Lancaster was able to chat with the president, who subsequently told Abby Mann, "I really like Burt. He has rough outer edges, but he really cares about these things, doesn't he?" JFK's sister Eunice and her husband, Sargent Shriver, were also taken with the actor. Mann recalled Lancaster telling Kennedy's brother-in-law, "You keep the Peace Corps [which Shriver headed], and I'll take Eunice."

A Child Is Waiting officially opened on February 13, 1963. Amazingly, the agonies endured by Kramer and Fowler in the editing room did not show in the final cut. The dialogue hardly seemed improvisational, and numerous scenes were enlivened by Cassavetes' interesting and unconventional—but hardly radical—camera angles.

Time asserted, "Lancaster has never been better," and, indeed, the actor deftly assayed the myriad sides of Clark's character, displaying remarkable gentleness in sequences with the problem child, Reuben Witticombe. But most critics spent little time on the picture's artistic merits, preferring instead to discuss the appropriateness of the subject, thereby indicating the extent to which mental retardation was a taboo topic in the early sixties. Brendan Gill spoke for many of his colleagues when he maintained in *The New Yorker,* "It is almost unbearable to be made to observe and admire the delicacy of the acting skill of Mr. Lancaster and Miss Garland as they move—the charming, the successful, the gifted ones—among that host of pitiful children. Despite the purity of their motives, as actors they have no business being there; simply as moviegoers, we have no business watching them."

Looking back on *A Child Is Waiting,* Kramer said, "My dream was to jump the barrier of ordinary objection to the subject matter into an area in which the treatment of it and the performance of it would be so exquisite that it would transcend all that." But, as he admitted, "Somewhere we failed."

As 1962 gave way to the new year, Lancaster once more turned his attention toward *The Leopard,* because Visconti had asked him to supervise the English-language version of the film. With Sydney Pollack, his *Young Savages* protégé, to help him, Burt assembled a strong cast of character actors for the dubbing, including Thomas Gomez, Kurt Kasznar, Howard DeSilva, and Donald Madden (Lancaster, of course, had originally performed his scenes in English). The Italian director also gave Lancaster the authority to edit approximately fifty minutes from the European version, including some scenes dealing with the Risorgimento that would have meaning only for the Italians.

For Burt, bringing Visconti's masterpiece to the English-speaking pubic was a labor of love. According to Shana Alexander, he spent fourteen weeks "sitting in a movie dubbing room and sometimes climbing the walls trying to record, rejigger, and wrench *The Leopard* sound track into something resembling English." Alexander called him the "one man in the world with the patience and fortitude, as well as the ability, to render this auditory antipasto acceptable, or at least comprehensible, to American audiences."

Finally, in mid-April, he returned to acting. The film was *Seven Days in May.*

The 1962 novel on which the picture was based had been written by Fletcher Knebel and Charles W. Bailey II, reporters for the Washington Bureau of Cowles Publications. It presented a chilling scenario in which Gen. James M. Scott, the chairman of the Joint Chiefs of Staff, a man of MacArthur-like stature, popularity, and ego, attempted to lead an American coup d'état. His purpose was to remove from office the president of the United States, Jordan Lyman, whose disarmament treaty with the Soviet Union was—in Scott's opinion—tantamount to treason.

At the time of the book's publication, some signposts suggested that *Seven Days in May* was more than pure fabrication. In 1961, for example, outgoing president Dwight D. Eisenhower warned the public of a vast military-industrial complex that carried the "potential for the disastrous rise of misplaced power." Later that year, Gen. Edwin Walker, a Korean War hero and staunch conservative, was fired for attempting to politically indoctrinate troops in West Germany. And, in 1963, President Kennedy instigated a treaty with the Soviet Union to prohibit the atmospheric testing of nuclear weapons. This was a popular move, unlike the treaty in the novel, but one that prompted Adm. Lewis Strauss to say, "I am not sure that the reduction of tensions [between the superpowers] is necessarily a good thing."

Among those who saw a prophetic vision in the Knebel-Bailey novel was director John Frankenheimer, who had just scored an enormous triumph with another tale of political intrigue, *The Manchurian Candidate.* It was producer Edward Lewis who had brought the galleys of the as-yet-unpublished novel to John's attention. He and Lewis acquired it jointly, in concert with Lewis' partner, Kirk Douglas. Then, according to Douglas, the deal nearly fell through when Frankenheimer learned that Lancaster would costar. "He had just finished working with Burt on *Birdman of Alcatraz,* " wrote Douglas in his autobiography, "and swore he'd never work with him again." But Kirk reassured the director, and the issue was settled.

Douglas would not only produce the picture, he would also costar— as Col. Jiggs Casey, the director of the Joint Chiefs who seeks to stop the coup. Douglas had offered Lancaster his choice of roles, Casey or Scott, and took the one that Burt rejected. It was good casting, given Lancaster's imposing mien and bearing and Douglas' higher emotional pitch. The rest of the cast was also solid: Fredric March, Martin Balsam, John Houseman, and two of Lancaster's costars from *The Killers,* Edmond O'Brien and Ava Gardner. The taut script was by Rod Serling, best known for TV's *The Twilight Zone.*

Portions of *Seven Days in May* were shot in California and Arizona, and, appropriately, in the District of Columbia. The company was even able to stage a riot outside the White House for the opening scene— thanks to Kennedy's support for the project. But they knew that they would receive no cooperation from the Pentagon—they did not even ask for it. Thus, all of Lancaster's scenes were filmed at Paramount.

Despite Frankenheimer's concerns about Burt, they got along well once the cameras started to roll. Indeed, to Hal Polaire, *Seven Days*' assistant director, it was evident that the actor had come to think of John as a "talented director and brilliant guy." Kirk was another matter. According to Whit Bissell, who played the film's archconservative Senator Prentiss, Douglas "was a bit of a prima donna on the set. Much more so than Burt."

By 1963, Douglas was arguably as big a star as Lancaster. Like Burt he was fiercely dedicated to his craft and articulated strong opinions about how scenes should be played and shot. He too invested his performances with enormous energy. But, despite Douglas' obvious gifts and success, some maintained that he was jealous of his oft-time costar. Among them was Frankenheimer, who asserted that Douglas "wanted to be Burt Lancaster. He's wanted to be Burt Lancaster all his life." Why? For starters, numerous colleagues claim that Douglas lacks Lancaster's way with people. Kirk himself noted in 1986, "I see a certain loyalty in Burt that I envy. I find that I have very few friends, whereas Burt has people around him who have been with him for years." Second, Lancaster, while hardly secure, was far more emotionally stable than Douglas. For this, Burt could thank his loving parents and a supportive family environment; Kirk had a considerably less wholesome upbringing.

In addition, Burt was six foot two, Kirk much shorter. According to one colleague, "Douglas was so touchy about his height that he said he never wanted to see an extra on the set who was taller than him. Never." He wore shoes with thick heels—which made him appear taller but also affected his gait. "Burt," noted the colleague, "would imitate his walk. And Kirk would come in and get very angry."

Finally, according to Frankenheimer, Douglas was convinced that Lancaster's role in *Seven Days in May* was better than his. Frankenheimer thought so too—although why is unclear. Jiggs, the hero of the piece, had much more screen time than the general and was a less constraining character. As Casey, Douglas was even able to display an on-screen affability that he rarely got to show.

For Lancaster, the major acting challenge in the picture was the opposite of Kirk's, to find a viable way of portraying the villain. He had done so only twice before, in *Vera Cruz* and *Sweet Smell of Success,* and in both instances the characters had been far more mannered than General Scott. He explained the problem to the novel's coauthor Fletcher Knebel during filming: "In the book, you didn't examine the general's motives and character because you told the story from the president's point of view. But on the screen, General Scott is seen and the audience must understand him and sympathize with the feelings that motivate him." The actor's solution was, in Knebel's words, "to invest him with a dignity and patriotism, however misguided, as strong as those motivating the president."

It was in the face-to-face confrontation between Scott and the chief executive—the climax of the picture—that the character's righteous indignation was needed most, for Lancaster had to stand his ground with two-time Oscar winner Fredric March. Knebel, who was present during the filming of the sequence, noted, "Rehearsing the tense scene depleted the actors. Frequently, they had to break off and relax. Then they bantered."

For Lancaster, May of 1963 brought the premiere of two films. One was *The List of Adrian Messenger,* which opened in New York on the twenty-ninth. Instead of relishing the guessing game, the critics tended to find Burt's bit as an old woman and the other star cameos distracting. As for the larger murder mystery, critical opinion diverged widely, with Penelope Gilliatt of the London *Observer* calling *Adrian Messenger* "a riveting thriller, put together like a game of poker," and *Esquire* asserting that it was "hard to believe that the man who made *The Maltese Falcon* [John Huston] also set this turkey waddling."

On May 20, the actor joined Luchino Visconti and Suso Cecchi D'Amico in Cannes for the annual film festival and the world premiere of *The Leopard.* Several days later, the judges awarded the picture their top prize, the Golden Palm. *The Leopard* went on to enjoy a smashing success in Europe, critically and at the box office.

The result was considerably different in America, where the English-language version debuted on August 12. Not only was it forty-three minutes shorter, but the Italian- and French-speaking actors had been dubbed into a polyglot of accented and nonaccented English, with the lip-synching often quite poor—despite Burt's best efforts. In addition, the prints had been processed by DeLuxe with considerable less subtlety and richness than the European Technicolor version.

Visconti, who attended the American premiere, was terribly disappointed. In fact, when *The Leopard* opened in Britain, he sent a letter to the London *Times* urging that the French or Italian version be shown instead. He even threatened to sue Fox. "If there is any suing to be done," replied studio vice president Seymour Poe, "we may be forced to initiate action against Visconti, who seems dedicated to harming his own picture with a series of negative statements which seek to denigrate the film." As for Burt, he stood by his work. Years later, he said, "The English version as far as I'm concerned is very good too." But one can hear a certain defensiveness in his words.

Despite the flaws in the English-language release, few American critics failed to appreciate Visconti's stunning production values. But, on the whole, they did not respond well to *The Leopard*. *Newsweek* dubbed it "an egregious catastrophe," while Judith Crist of the New York *Herald Tribune* found it "a major disappointment."

Lancaster also drew a mixed response. It was generally conceded that he looked splendid with his thick mustache, muttonchop whiskers, and hair parted just off the center, and that he presented a magisterial figure. But there were those who complained about his American speech, and *Newsweek* suggested venomously, "Burt Lancaster looks as if he were playing Clarence Day's 'Father' in summer stock."

It might be fairer to say that the role of the prince demanded relatively little of Burt beyond the loan of his imposing presence; so controlled was Don Fabrizio that the range of emotions the actor had to display was almost nil. In a curious way, he was asked more to be than to act. Thus, it is surprising that Lancaster often cited the prince as his best role. One can only conclude that he was not necessarily the best judge of his own creativity. And it was easy for him to confuse process with result. After all, he—an untrained actor, an American movie star— had been able to go to a foreign country and hold his own in an important European production, meeting the rigorous standards of one of the greatest filmmakers of all time. That was triumph enough.

To Visconti's great disappointment, Burt had been unable to attend the New York premiere of *The Leopard*. He was France, working on a new picture, *The Train*. He did return to the United States, however, for a single day—to participate in the civil rights March on Washington on August 28, attended by more than two hundred thousand people.

Bearing a petition of support with the signatures of two thousand Americans living in Paris, Burt joined a contingent of other Hollywood notables, including Marlon Brando, Paul Newman, Joanne Woodward, Tony Curtis, Sidney Poitier, James Garner, Blake Edwards, and Sam Peckinpah. "We were a small group numerically," observed Charlton Heston, who had organized the film community's contingent, "but with a lot of well-known figures in it and thus perhaps disproportionately important." The March on Washington has since become a mythic event, in large measure because of Martin Luther King Jr.'s unforgettable "I Have a Dream" speech, but Heston pointed out that participation "was not a wildly popular move at the time in the [film] industry," adding that "a lot of people you would expect to be there were not there." That Lancaster was willing to travel from France just for the day—when he had such an easy explanation for his absence—said much about his willingness to stand by his political beliefs, an act made all the more courageous by his terrible fear of flying.

The Train was based on an incident from *Le Front de l'art* by Rose Valland, an employee of Paris' Jeu de Paume, then the home of the world's richest collection of impressionist masterpieces.[1] The author had described a Resistance action during the waning days of the Nazi occupation of France that prevented a railroad shipment of priceless paintings from reaching its intended destination in Czechoslovakia. The script by Franklin Coen, Frank Davis, and Walter Bernstein had been acquired by producer Jules Bricken, who had, in turn, engaged Arthur Penn to direct. Burt, brought in to play the Resistance leader who reluctantly saves the cargo, took the project to United Artists, where it served as another vehicle in his debt-reduction program with the company. Thus, in effect, *The Train* became a Burt Lancaster production.

Filming began—on a seemingly generous fifteen-week shooting schedule—with the internationally renowned French actress Jeanne Moreau in a featured role and Paul Scofield as the Nazi colonel in charge of the art shipment. It was the distinguished British actor's first major film assignment.

Penn, a veteran of live television drama and the Broadway theater, was a highly regarded director whose film credits included *The Left-Handed Gun* with Paul Newman and *The Miracle Worker*, from the Broadway play, which he had also directed. But shortly after work began on *The Train*, it became evident that he and Lancaster had radically different views of the project, and three days into production, Penn was fired.

"Burt called me and asked if I would come over to France and direct it," recalled John Frankenheimer. "I'd just finished *Seven Days in May*.[2] I was quite tired. I didn't want to do it, yet he asked me to do it as

1. Today the paintings are housed in the Musée d'Orsay, France's national museum of nineteenth-century art, which opened in Paris in 1986.
2. Although Burt had finished working on *Seven Days in May* in the spring—the studio scenes having been shot first—the production did not wrap until the very end of July.

a favor to him. And also, I wanted to go to Europe." By August 19, the director and his A.D., Hal Polaire, were en route.

Taking over a big action picture, a period piece with a predominantly French cast and crew, was no simple matter. As Polaire recalled, "We had to shut down for a period of time after Penn was released from the film in order to look at all of the film that he had shot, to see if any of it could be saved. Frankenheimer wanted none of it."

The director not only hated the footage, he also disliked the script. "The damned train didn't leave the station until page one hundred and forty," he recalled. He particularly wanted to eliminate the verbiage. "Half of the film now has no dialogue at all," *Newsweek* later reported. To help him cut and reshape the material, he imported Ned Young and Howard Infell, who labored without screen credit.

Another major production problem, according to the director, was that "none of the locations worked." A case in point was the rail line between Paris and Lyon, which he described as "far too heavily trafficked to permit adequate shooting." Finally, Frankenheimer found a little village in Normandy called Acquigny, which seemed to meet his needs. He went to Lancaster and said, "You know, Burt, we've got to figure out how to make this picture without ever moving this company." The option did not seem possible. After all, the train was supposed to travel hundreds of miles. "What happens if they start here," the director finally suggested, "and the Resistance paints out the signs and changes the town and we end up back here."

"Well, that didn't happen," the actor replied.

"Who's to know?" the director retorted.

So, the bold gambit was employed and it became one of the major twists in the plot.

However, not all of the picture was filmed in Acquigny; the company also traveled to Paris and numerous other locales—with the script being rewritten as the cameras turned. The director described the process as "chaos." Finally, a rough winter brought a halt to production, which was resumed the following spring. Given the rewrites, delays, and other upsets during filming, it is surprising that, according to Frankenheimer, the production's total expense—$5.8 million—was only about $600,000 over budget.

Lancaster was, as we have seen, a veteran of chaotic productions with uncompleted scripts. But even he was impressed by Frankenheimer's command over *The Train,* especially the railroad sequences. As he put it, "I looked at him and I said to myself, 'Son of a bitch, he's really good.' "

Frankenheimer returned the compliment, noting upon the picture's release, "Lancaster is built for his part in *The Train* as a Resistance fighter," and later asserting that the actor *lived* the role. But Burt did not idealize his character, saying, "Those Resistance workers were not heroes at that stage of the war; they were tired, many suffered malnutrition, depressed by so many deaths in their organization." Speaking specifically of the attempt to save the paintings, he added, "They had no heart for this assignment, but it was a job to be done and they put their hearts into it and did it heroically."

As usual, Burt threw himself into the job, performing many dangerous stunts without a stand-in. But one feat, which called for him to jump from the moving train and roll down a hill, did not go as planned, and he badly reinjured the knee that he had hurt during the making of *The Leopard.* Such was the damage that a limp for his character, Labiche, had to be written into the script. After that, he left the film's stunts to the experts.

Finally, on June 9, the production wrapped. What had begun the previous August as a fifteen-week shoot had lasted ten months. "What do I do now?" asked Lancaster rhetorically in response to a question from reporter Leo Mishkin. "I'm going home, that's what. I'll stop off in New York for a few days and then on to California." He grinned wickedly. "It's about time, isn't it?"

Lancaster had been in France so long that, by the time he returned home, *Seven Days in May* had already opened in, and disappeared from, the nation's movie houses.

The picture, which debuted on February 20, 1964, had been an enormous popular and critical success, drawing cheers from nearly every quarter. Although a few journalists took issue with the screenplay's preachy sentiments in the final reel, and some asserted that the plot was, to quote Bosley Crowther, "a bit far-fetched," most shared *The New York Times* critic's overall assessment, that the picture was "taut and exciting melodrama, as loaded as a Hitchcock mystery."

Lancaster succeeded in his task, credibly underscoring General Scott's messianic zeal. As expected, his confrontation with Fredric March was the highlight of the piece, the two skilled pros sparring with one another in lightning-quick exchanges. Some in the audience may even have been reminded of a real encounter between a president and a general, the Wake Island confrontation between Harry Truman and Douglas MacArthur during the Korean War.[3]

A month after *The Train* wrapped, Lancaster was before the cameras again—this time for *The Hallelujah Trail.*

A Mirisch Brothers production released by United Artists, *The Hallelujah Trail* reunited Lancaster with two former colleagues, John Sturges and John Gay.

Since *Gunfight at the O.K. Corral,* Sturges had directed ten films, but it was two blockbuster entertainments, 1960's *The Magnificent Seven* and 1963's *The Great Escape,* that gave him virtually carte blanche for his next project. Why he chose to do a comic Western is a mystery. "He was not a funny man, and he didn't have much of a sense of humor," observed Tim Zinnemann, Fred's son and *Trail's* second assistant director. Nevertheless, Sturges produced as well as directed the picture.

Like the Bill Gulick novel on which it was based, John Gay's script told the story of the fictional Battle of Whiskey Hills, a bizarre 1867 engagement that arose when a wagon train full of liquor became a prize in the wrangling between a band of Indians, a group of temperance women, a citizen's militia, the Irish teamsters who were driving the train, and the cavalry troop who served as their escort. To Sturges it was pure situational comedy. Accordingly, since, in his words, "it isn't the people who are funny, but a matter of people being put in funny situations, we selected actors who are actors, rather than comedians."

In addition to Lancaster, cast as the blustering cavalry commander, Col. Thadeus Gearhart, Sturges selected Lee Remick as the ardent temperance leader who ultimately succumbs to his charms, and character actors Brian Keith, Donald Pleasence, and Martin Landau. Only Jim Hutton and Pamela Tiffin as the young romantic interests were well versed in light comedy.

Filming began in Gallup, New Mexico, on July 6, 1964. "It was a very big picture logistically with a huge cast," recalled Tim Zinnemann. Indeed, the company totaled 289. The scale of the production was epic, with a final cut that would run 165 minutes. But Sturges kept a firm hand on the proceedings. "It was really tough to do logistically," asserted Martin Landau. "He was the right director for the action aspect of it."

3. After which, on April 11, 1951, the president fired the general for insubordination.

Work proceeded smoothly, but life after hours was another matter. As Zinnemann explained, Gallup in the early sixties was "a truck stop on the old Route 66. It was a very rough town. . . . There were a lot of bars, and everybody went to all of them, and everybody got into trouble." By way of distraction, Sturges staged shrimp and saki parties, Remick took up needlepoint, and Lancaster flew back to Los Angeles whenever the shooting schedule gave him a few days off. On one such occasion, Zinnemann said, "My boss [the first assistant] told me to tell him [Burt] that he was dismissed and that he could go back to LA for a hiatus. So I went to find him in the bar." Zinnemann gave Burt the news, but the star responded with anger. "I think he was going to hit me actually," the AD asserted, "and said that he'd known this four hours ago and . . . started cursing me. Basically he was drunk, I think. Or mad and drunk. . . . After that I stayed away from him, and he stayed away from me."

At work, Zinnemann found Lancaster more restrained. "As I remember," the AD said, "he was pretty courteous to all the other actors, and they were all courteous to him." He did not get along with Brian Keith, however. Nor was he especially fond of Lee Remick—or she of him. According to Pamela Tiffin, Remick's disdain extended to the rest of the company as well. "I had the feeling," Tiffin said, "that she thought she was too good an actress to be involved in this."

As for Tiffin herself, the young, perky beauty considered Burt "dazzlingly charming" with "his medicine-tent smile." Twenty-one at the time, but a veteran of eight films, she also found him unlike other major stars that she had known: "Burt was not worried at any time about other actors and if they had more lines, if they had close-ups, if they had more screen time. That was one of the most wonderful things about him when I knew him. There was no pettiness in him whatsoever. And that's rare."

Landau was also somewhat fond of his costar, saying, "I liked the fact that he was very prepared, and he was very willing to work." The actor did concede, however, that occasionally Burt would "step outside of his realm, so to speak." He recalled an instance in which Lancaster suggested a bit of business for him that he did not think was funny. He did not want to start a fight. "So," as he recalled, "I did it full out the way Burt wanted me to do it, and then I did it full out the way I wanted to do it. . . . I knew my way was better, and I knew that John [Sturges] would know that, even though he came from the Mount Rushmore school of comedy." Sturges, in fact, preferred Landau's solution, but since the actor had at least tried Lancaster's approach, Burt was mollified.

While in Gallup, Lancaster "pretty much hung out by himself," to quote Zinnemann. "I think he had a girlfriend he found on the picture, and he seemed to be spending most of his time with her."

That "girlfriend" was Tiffin's hairdresser, Jackie Bone, and she would become Burt's companion for the next twenty years.

The pretty, voluptuous brunette was born in Temple, Texas, in 1928, but her family moved to Redondo Beach, California, in the early 1930s. "I didn't go to college," she recalled. "We were too poor." Instead, she married a commercial fisherman by the name of William Bone. "Billy, I can say truthfully," she asserted, "is the only other love besides Burt, the only other one that meant anything to me truly down deep."

Billy died in a fishing accident when Jackie was twenty-two. To support herself, she became a hairdresser, eventually freelancing within the motion picture industry. She also remarried twice, but neither union lasted more than six months.

"Jackie was a pioneer Texas girl," Tiffin recalled, "not loud at all, but just plainspoken and very direct and very much a good companion to everyone. She wasn't a sycophant. She did her work, did it well, without ego but without submission either."

It did not take Lancaster long to notice the pretty thirty-six-year-old, fifteen years his junior. Bone was drawn to the star as well. "I had seen him in person before on the golf course," she recalled. "And I'd seen his films. . . . He's a very attractive man, and also he had a great personality." In very short order, they were an item.

As we have seen, Burt had not been faithful to his wife, but it is doubtful that anyone since Shelley Winters had meant anything significant to him. With Jackie, he fell in love. "They were so happy together," Tiffin recalled. "It was such a healthy kind of sexual attraction and pleasure of being together. . . . There was a cleanliness about that love affair. There was nothing smarmy or sordid about it."

Still, Lancaster was very much a married man and a public figure; he had to be careful. "They were trying to be very discreet," said Landau, "as much as they could, but it was pretty clear. I mean, I just saw them together a lot. They wouldn't tend to be together that much if there wasn't something going on."

Remarkably, despite the hundreds of people associated with *The Hallelujah Trail,* word of the affair did not leak. Indeed, not until Burt's divorce from Norma in 1969 did the press become aware of Jackie's existence, and even then, several journalists would get her name and/or background wrong. As late as January of 1973, in fact, columnist John J. Miller was able to write a piece called "Burt Lancaster: A Secret Love" and to speculate about Jackie's identity.

• • •

Lancaster "loved the part" of Colonel Gearhart, recalled John Gay, "he loved doing it. He got a big kick out of it." One could see why. Although Burt's fifties swashbucklers were rendered with a light touch and there were humorous moments in *The Rose Tattoo,* he had never done a genuine comedy before.

However, the filming was not going smoothly. "There was bad weather continually," Landau recalled. "The day would usually start beautifully, and then the afternoon storms would come up." Finally, the company was forced to return to Los Angeles, shoot the interiors at the Goldwyn Studios and the town scenes on the Paramount backlot, and then return to Gallup to finish up.

They were back in New Mexico on November 13—a Friday—when tragedy struck: a forty-three-year-old stuntman named Bill Williams was crushed by the wheels of a wagon and killed. Lancaster was not on call that day; neither were most of the actors. The following Monday, the picture wrapped—some six weeks behind schedule.

It was nearly a year before Lancaster made another picture, his longest hiatus by far. He had earned a rest, having been in production from August of 1963 to November of 1964—sixteen months—with little more than four weeks off, and had been involved in two extremely arduous location shoots, one in a foreign country. That sort of schedule would have been taxing for a twenty-year-old; Lancaster had turned fifty-one just before *The Hallelujah Trail* wrapped.

As well as rest, Burt needed time to consider his personal life. He had, on the one hand, an exciting, new love, and on the other, a wife and five children. Meaningless affairs were one thing; they threatened no one. As one friend put it, "The fucking around he did was sort of a matter of Hollywood macho pride." But a serious extramarital relationship was another matter. Burt valued family. He would not throw away his life with Norma lightly.

There was no question, however, that the marriage was falling apart, and at the root of the problem was Norma's alcoholism. Dr. John Fitzpatrick, director of Alcoholism and Substance Abuse Services at the Lutheran Medical Center in New York and president of the Unified Alcoholism Constituency of New York State, observed that, although self-help groups like Alcoholics Anonymous emerged in the 1930s, an understanding of the causes of alcoholism and appropriate methods of treatment only began to mature in the 1970s. When Norma and Burt were trying to cope with her disease, "there was," as Fitzpatrick put it, "much more stigma attached to it, much more secrecy attached to it, much more perplexity—particularly if the individual was a woman." He pointed out that many then subscribed to "the 'moral defect theory,' that there was something wrong with them that they needed to have a drink, and it was simply a matter of control."

Within the limits of what was known at the time, the Lancasters explored all of the appropriate forms of treatment—AA, psychiatric counseling, hospitalization. "She tried so hard to get it together for Burt and the kids," observed one family friend. And for periods of time she was perfectly functional. The problem was that one never knew when an alcoholic binge cycle would start.

Of course, the Lancaster children could not help but be affected by Norma's condition. "She was a very concerned mother," said a family friend, "a very sweet mother. But her alcoholism got in the way. The kids didn't hate her, they got impatient with her, because you couldn't communicate with her when she got drunk." Actress Anita Gillette, who dated Burt's son Bill in the 1970s, said simply, "According to the kids, life with their mother was pretty awful."

Burt was also badly impacted by his wife's disease. "Unfortunately, the codependent partner begins to feel helpless about the situation," Dr. Fitzpatrick explained, "that in trying to hide the bottle, control the situation, stop the drinking, set limits, it becomes increasingly clear that the partner has a greater love of the substance than they have an investment in the relationship." He pointed out that "most of the time the males would leave their female partners rather than put up with this."

Given his home environment, it is not surprising that the actor basked in the first blush of his new romance with Jackie. One of the things he liked about her was her willingness to join him in his favorite pastimes, including drinking, an activity that he obviously could not share with his wife. Further, she credited Burt with introducing her to classical music. "He loved being like a Pygmalion," she recalled, "educating us ladies. He loved to see people develop to their fullest potential." She even tried to learn his beloved bridge, but, as she put it, "Burt was a yeller and a screamer at the bridge table, and it floored me. I couldn't take it, so I quit."

One area of his life that she did not wish to share was that involving other women. In the formative period of their relationship, he talked to her about prior affairs until she asked him to refrain from doing so, a decision that she later regretted. "It closed him off," she said, "and he became secretive. I should have let him be the buddy to me that he seemed to find me. He needed that. I didn't want to hear it though."

(Left) At age four and a half, Burt *(right)* made a reluctant model. He is seen here with his brother William and his sister Jane. Although they were poor, the Lancasters were a proud, close-knit family. (The Kobal Collection)

(Below) In his senior year in high school, Lancaster *(front, second from left)* won a spot as a forward on the varsity basketball team. He helped the Red and Black Courtmen take the championship of the Bronx for the 1929/30 season. (*The Clintonian,* DeWitt Clinton High School)

(Right) Burt and Nick Cravat posed backstage in 1937, when they were with the Federal Theatre Circus. The youngsters had been friends since the early 1920s, when they met at summer camp. (American Theater Collection, Special Collections & Archives, George Mason University, Fairfax, Virginia)

(Above left) Lancaster hardly looked his age—thirty-one—when this photo was taken in the fall of 1945. But he had good reason to smile: he was just about to start rehearsals for his professional acting debut in *A Sound of Hunting*. (The Kobal Collection)

(Above right) To help him cope with a host of offers after *A Sound of Hunting* opened on Broadway, Burt signed with a relatively insignificant agent, Harold Hecht. Within two years, he and Hecht were producing their first film together. (United Artists/The Kobal Collection)

(Below) In his first picture, *The Killers,* Lancaster played an ex-boxer who is led astray and then double-crossed by a beautiful woman. Both he and his leading lady, Ava Gardner, became stars upon the film's release. (Universal/The Kobal Collection)

(Above) On December 28, 1946, Burt married Norma Anderson in Yuma, Arizona. The couple is seen here a few months later, with Burt sporting the eyeglasses that he wore off camera. (The Bettmann Archive)

(Below) Lancaster and Kirk Douglas costarred for the first time in 1948's *I Walk Alone*, playing former pals battling for control of a swanky nightclub. Lizabeth Scott was the sultry singer caught between them. (Hal Wallis Productions/The Kobal Collection)

(Left) After he became a star, Burt stayed in top physical condition by working out every day on the horizontal bars. In this 1949 photo, he and Nick Cravat are readying their old act for a guest engagement with the celebrated Cole Brothers Circus. (UPI/Bettmann)

(Below) In *The Flame and the Arrow,* released in 1950, Burt traded in his dour tough-guy image for that of a smiling, ebullient swashbuckler—and audiences were thrilled! (Warner Bros./The Kobal Collection)

(Above) With *The Crimson Pirate,* Burt and Nick Cravat took the acrobatics and lighthearted tone of *The Flame and the Arrow* to even greater heights. The picture was a hit, but executives at Warners were dismayed by the chaos and cost overruns during production. (Warner Bros./The Kobal Collection)

(Left) "I guess I wanted to play Doc Delaney in [*Come Back, Little*] *Sheba* more than any role I ever got close to," Burt said. Although he was far too young for the part, his performance as the alcoholic trapped in a loveless marriage brought him his first acclaim as a serious actor. (Hal Wallis Productions/The Kobal Collection)

(Above) Among the most famous love scenes in film history is this one between Lancaster and Deborah Kerr in *From Here to Eternity*. It was Burt's idea to film the clinch on the sand with the waves crashing around them. (Columbia/The Kobal Collection)

(Right) After years of anticipation, Lancaster finally got his wish—to become a director. But the picture, 1955's *The Kentuckian,* in which he also starred, was not a success, and he abandoned the dream. (United Artists/The Kobal Collection)

(Left) Although the picture's romantic triangle was trite, 1956's *Trapeze* was a smash hit, the biggest in the history of Lancaster's production company. Burt, playing an embittered, crippled catcher, costarred with Gina Lollobrigida and Tony Curtis. (United Artists/The Kobal Collection)

(Below) In 1956, a decade after becoming a Hal Wallis contract player, Lancaster completed *Gunfight at the O.K. Corral,* his last picture for the producer. He is seen here on location with Wallis and costar Kirk Douglas. (Hal Wallis Productions/The Kobal Collection)

(Left) In *Sweet Smell of Success,* Lancaster presented a chilling portrait of a powerful newspaper columnist. Tony Curtis was the ambitious press agent who caters to the journalist's every whim. (United Artists/The Kobal Collection)

(Right) At the end of 1956, Burt shocked many industry insiders—including his own associate, Harold Hecht—by naming Jim Hill a partner in his production company, thereafter called Hecht-Hill-Lancaster. Friction among those at the top contributed significantly to the enterprise's ultimate demise. (The Kobal Collection)

(Below) Burt proudly showed off his children upon landing in England for the filming of *The Devil's Disciple* in July 1958. They are *(left to right)* James, William, Susan, Joanna, and Sighle. Whenever possible, Lancaster took his family with him on location shootings. (UPI/Bettmann)

(Left) As the fiery title character in *Elmer Gantry,* Lancaster promises his radio audience, "As long as I've got a foot, I'll kick booze. As long as I've got a fist, I'll punch it. And as long as I've got a tooth, I'll bite it. And when I'm old and gray and bootless and toothless, I'll gum it till I go to heaven and booze goes to hell." (United Artists/The Kobal Collection)

(Below) On April 17, 1961, the Academy of Motion Picture Arts and Sciences awarded Lancaster an Oscar for his performance in *Elmer Gantry.* Elizabeth Taylor was named Best Actress for *Butterfield 8.* (UPI/Bettmann)

(Above) Lancaster was deeply moved by the plight of Robert Stroud, a two-time murderer who became a leading authority on diseases in birds. The actor's intense portrayal of the convict in *Birdman of Alcatraz* earned him his third Academy Award nomination. (United Artists/The Kobal Collection)

(Below) Director Luchino Visconti fought against Lancaster's casting as Don Fabrizio, the prince of Salina, in *The Leopard,* but ultimately he and the star become extremely close friends. Burt considered his performance in *The Leopard* the best of his career. (20th Century–Fox/The Kobal Collection)

(Above) At the climax of *Seven Days in May,* an egomaniacal chairman of the Joint Chiefs of Staff—played by Lancaster—engages in a no-holds-barred showdown with the man he seeks to replace, the president of the United States, portrayed by the formidable Fredric March. (Joel Productions/The Kobal Collection)

(Right) To show his support for the civil rights movement, Lancaster flew from Paris, where he was filming *The Train,* to take part in the March on Washington on August 28, 1963. There he joined Harry Belafonte *(center)* and Charlton Heston *(right)* and other members of the Hollywood contingent. The next day, he returned to France. (UPI/Bettmann)

(Above) Lancaster's support for civil rights could also be seen on the screen, in 1968's *The Scalphunters,* which climaxed with a muddy slugfest between Burt and Ossie Davis. The "issue," said Davis, "was how are we going to have a top-box-office white fighting with somebody who was not his equal and black. It really wasn't done. Of course, Burt's response was, 'Bullshit.'" (United Artists/The Kobal Collection)

(Below) In *Valdez Is Coming*, released in 1971, Lancaster attempted to segue into character roles by portraying a mild Hispanic constable. The gambit failed. He is seen here at a climactic moment with costars Susan Clark and Jon Cypher. (United Artists/The Kobal Collection)

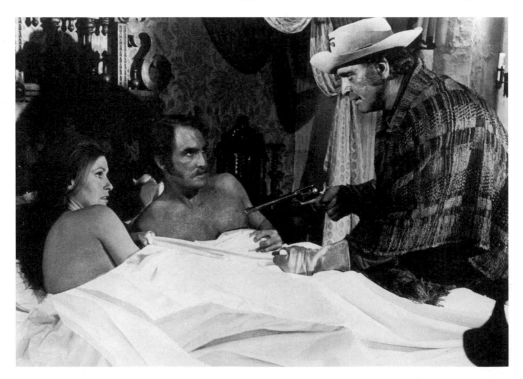

(Above) Anthony Burgess' earthy, humanistic script attracted Lancaster to *Moses, the Lawgiver,* a six-part miniseries that aired in the United States during the summer of 1975. It was Burt's first acting job for television. (Avco Embassy/The Kobal Collection)

(Below) Among Lancaster's most courageous performances was that of the senile, decaying old padrone in Bernardo Bertolucci's *1900*. Because the director could not meet Burt's usual acting price, the actor did the role for free. (PEA/The Kobal Collection)

(Above) Burt brought a refreshing droll wit to one of Hollywood's first Vietnam films, *Go Tell the Spartans*. The young actors in the cast—including Craig Wasson *(third from the left)* and Marc Singer *(right)*—were thrilled to work with the old pro. (Avco Embassy/The Kobal Collection)

(Below left) Burt and Jackie Bone enjoy a sumptuous meal at L.A.'s Blue Ribbon Room in 1972. The couple met on location during the making of *The Hallelujah Trail* in 1964 and remained together for nearly twenty years. (Larry Bessel/*Los Angeles Times* Photo)

(Below center) Tough Guys, released in 1986, reunited Lancaster and Kirk Douglas one last time. Their love-hate relationship in the film was closer to their real-life rapport than that of any of their previous pairings. (Touchstone/The Kobal Collection)

(Above) Lancaster's rich performance as the silly, weak-willed petty criminal in *Atlantic City* injected new life into his faltering career—and earned him his fourth and final Academy Award nomination. (Paramount/The Kobal Collection)

(Below right) Burt and director Daniel Petrie discuss a scene during the filming of *Rocket Gibraltar*. The two men endured a rocky beginning, but, said Petrie, "All the rest of the way through the picture we had a great relationship. I loved working with the guy." (Columbia/The Kobal Collection)

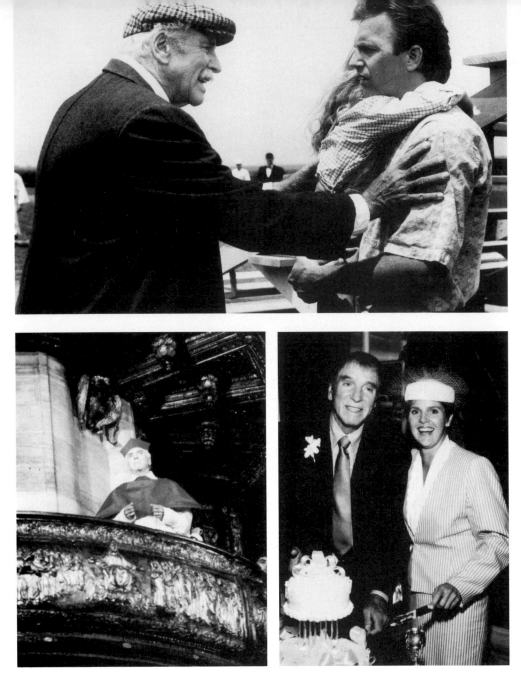

(Top) This moment from *Field of Dreams* kicks off the last scene in Lancaster's long big-screen career. After saving young Karen (Gaby Hoffman) from a fall, Burt (as Doc Graham) bids farewell to her dad (Kevin Costner), walks into a cornfield, and disappears. (Universal/The Kobal Collection)

(Above left) On hiatus from *Field of Dreams,* Lancaster went to Milan to play the role of Cardinal Federigo Borromeo in *The Betrothed*. Here, in the Duomo, he sermonizes at the pulpit from which the real cardinal spoke 359 years earlier. The TV miniseries never aired in the United States (The RAI Corporation)

(Above right) On September 10, 1990, Burt married his former secretary Susie Scherer in Los Angeles. The following day the newlyweds departed for South Carolina where Lancaster began work on the last project of his career, the TV film *Separate but Equal*. (Eric Brooks/Shooting Star)

Although Lancaster found comfort with the feisty hairdresser, he nevertheless remained ambivalent about the future of their relationship. "Burt was very protective [of Norma]," Jackie recalled. "He had a great deal of guilt feeling after he left home. In fact, he went back to her in the early part of our relationship to see if he couldn't work it out. But she was an alcoholic. He just couldn't do it. It was finished." The Lancasters would not separate, however, until 1967 and would not divorce until two years after that.

During the eleven months of Lancaster's hiatus, the two pictures that he had previously made reached the nation's movie screens, *The Train* on March 17, 1965, and *The Hallelujah Trail* on July 1.

Given its enormous problems, *The Train* proved to be a remarkably fluid and suspenseful melodrama—although several critics found it overly long at 133 minutes and slow to get moving. Photographed in black and white, the film had an almost documentary quality to it. Appropriately, given its title, the director's work with the trains was particularly impressive; for some sequences up to fourteen cameras were used.

Lancaster's decision not to try an accent—a wise choice in the face of his inability to do one well—caused several journalists to assert along with *Time* that "not for a moment does he seem to be a French patriot named Labiche." But *The Saturday Review* argued, "Burt Lancaster is perhaps the only American star both physically and psychologically endowed to play the hard, knowledgeable, and durable railroad man." Moreover, the actor brought a weary cynicism to the role, which contrasted nicely with the cold efficiency of the Nazi colonel, well played by Paul Scofield. Burt also established a moving bond with Jeanne Moreau as the stalwart hotelier who gives him shelter. It was a tender relationship, born less of passion than of fear and a hatred for the Nazis who occupied their homeland.

The Train did quite well at the box office. *The Hallelujah Trail* was another matter.

Most of the critics simply hated it. Perhaps the New York *Herald Tribune*'s Judith Crist best summed up her colleagues' views when she called it a "heavy-handed, flat-footed, subsophomoric spoof" that hadn't "a chance from the outset . . . since neither the director nor cast seem to have either a nodding acquaintance with comedy or the ability to acquire one in action."

There is no question that the spoof suffered by comparison with *Cat Ballou,* another Western comedy, released only one week earlier. Ironically, as noted earlier, *Cat* had once been a Hecht-Hill-Lancaster property and was produced by Burt's former partner, Harold Hecht.

Moreover, *Trail* was released in Cinerama, the gigantic three-camera-three-screen process that had initially lent scope to travelogues but had come into use for mainstream features with *How the West Was Won* in 1962. *Trail*'s New Mexico scenery looked breathtaking on the massive, slightly concave screens, but consequently, as Leo Mishkin pointed out, "a good deal of the fun seems to get lost in its own immensity."

Also, in retrospect, Sturges erred in casting Lancaster and Remick. The comedy needed truly gifted farceurs. The role of Colonel Gearhart would have been much better served by the likes of Rock Hudson or James Garner, and Remick's temperance leader was ideal for Doris Day, who, according to John Gay, had been interested in the part.

CHAPTER FIFTEEN

The Ennui of the Age

After two heavy dramas—*Sweet Bird of Youth* and *Lord Jim*, the latter an expensive failure—Richard Brooks wanted to get back to basics. Of his next project, he said, "This picture won't surprise the avant-garde with anything new; it's an exercise in entertainment, a real fast-moving action picture." Indeed, *The Professionals*, based on Frank O'Rourke's novel *A Mule for the Marquesa*, was a slam-bang tale about a band of rugged individualists hired to retrieve the wife of a rancher from a ruthless *bandito* in the waning days of the Old West.

When Burt and Richard Brooks acquired the movie rights to the novel in March of 1965, Lancaster assumed that he would play the leader of the gritty band. But Brooks told him that when he portrayed authority figures, he was boring. "This guy you'll play," said the director, "is a dynamiter, a clown, he's funny."

"Dynamiter?" Burt replied. "There's no dynamiter in the book."

"There will be by the time you get to do the movie," Brooks retorted.

Filming began on October 20, 1965, on an eighty-day production schedule, an incredibly short shoot for such a sprawling action picture (*The Hallelujah Trail*, by contrast, had been budgeted for thirteen weeks and took nineteen). What made the compact schedule possible was that the action was mostly confined to just four actors, the hardened soldiers of fortune. In addition to Burt, Woody Strode played an expert tracker, Robert Ryan a formidable horseman, and Lee Marvin, fresh from his triumph in *Cat Ballou* (for which he would win an Oscar the following year), was the gang's leader. "This picture is about a bunch of cynics," said Burt during filming, "but it has a sort of Elmer Gantry humor. Elmer Gantry out west." For Lancaster, the affable, womanizing, cigar-smoking, easily corruptible Bill Dolworth would represent something of a swan song, a final portrait in the gallery of grinning, lighthearted rogues that he had been etching into the American consciousness since *The Flame and the Arrow*. He would make other Westerns after *The Professionals,* but they, like the remainder of his oeuvre, would reflect the posture of a much more mature man.

Initially, Brooks had hoped to shoot *The Professionals* in Mexico, where the action of the picture occurs. But, he said, "We couldn't find the changes of terrain we needed without traveling three thousand miles." Thus, he settled for several remote locations in California and Nevada.

"It was a very difficult movie to do," recalled Claudia Cardinale, Burt's costar from *The Leopard* who was cast as the rancher's kidnapped wife, "shooting all around in the desert in difficult places. And the heat was terrible." In fact, according to Brooks, the temperature climbed to as high as 115 degrees. The director appreciated the efforts of his cast. "Some of them waited for three, four, and sometimes five hours to do their scenes without complaint," he said.

When the locations were not blistering hot, they were drenched with rain, snow, and sleet. The worst of the weather fell while the company was filming in the Valley of Fire, about fifty miles north of Las Vegas. On December 13, a flash flood swept through the area, trapping cast and crew in a box canyon until workers with the requisite road grader and shovel loader could rescue them.

Like Frankenheimer before him, Brooks was impressed by Burt's agility. According to reporter Philip K. Scheuer, the star pulled off stunts, such as a climb up a fifteen-foot cliff by means of a rope, "like a young man and better than a stuntman." To do so, he continued to work out like a thirty-year-old. "Burt was fantastic," enthused Cardinale. "Every morning he was doing his gymnastics. . . . Of course, he always had a marvelous body." But, even beyond the derring-do, there was gen-uine respect between Burt and Brooks. "They were very close," said Cardinale, "and there was a complicity between them. This I could see."

The same could not be said of the relationship between Burt and Mar-vin. "There was kind of an important scene on top of a rock, which was shot in the Valley of Fire outside of Las Vegas," recalled Tom Shaw, who served as the film's assistant director. "Lee comes up there drunk out of his mind. And Burt was so mad. Burt said to me, 'If this cocksucker does this one more time, I'm going to throw him off the fucking rock.' They had to stop shooting for the day, and the next time they returned to the scene, Marvin was drunk again. I think we did it three times."

• • •

Beginning December 16, the company enjoyed a brief respite from the elements, filming for a week at Columbia, which was producing the picture with Lancaster and Brooks. While at home, Burt attended the wedding of his son Bill to Kippie Kovacs, the daughter of the late comedian Ernie Kovacs. The couple had actually married in Tijuana, Mexico, the previous June, but there was some question about the legality of the ceremony, because both of them were underage at the time. The second wedding was performed by a Superior Court judge, with Kovacs' widow, actress Edie Adams, also present. The following year, the young couple would make Burt a grandfather.

During the year-end interval, Lancaster invited Cardinale to his home. Indeed, she asserted that Burt watched over her throughout the production: "He knew that here was this woman coming from Europe, from Italy, and among these men. He wanted to protect me all the time. He was extremely nice."

At the end of January, after shooting south of Palm Springs and the completion of the interiors at Columbia, the picture wrapped.

As the sixties progressed, opposition to the Vietnam conflict gave rise to a youth counterculture whose bywords were "Tune in, turn on, drop out" and "Don't trust anyone over thirty." In this tumultuous climate, even long-standing liberals found themselves out of touch, and society seemed more stratified than ever along the lines of race, age, and class.

Perhaps no character represented the confusion and malaise of the era's establishment better than Ned Merrill, the protagonist of John Cheever's 1964 short story "The Swimmer." To Lancaster, the tale of a middle-aged suburbanite who decides to swim home by way of his neighbors' pools was, as he put it, "a tragedy based on the American way of life, with its emphasis on success and a misguided notion that a man can get by on charm alone."

The Swimmer had found its initial champions in screenwriter Eleanor Perry and her then-husband, director Frank Perry. They had previously collaborated on 1962's acclaimed *David and Lisa,* a sensitive study of two mentally disturbed teenagers, for which they were both nominated for Oscars.

Initially, Frank had wanted to produce *The Swimmer* himself, as an independent project, but after failing to secure the financing, he took it to Sam Spiegel, the producer of *The Bridge on the River Kwai* and *Lawrence of Arabia,* who had recently formed his own independent production company. Spiegel insisted that Perry relinquish complete artistic control to him. The director had to accede in order to get the project under way, but he would later regret ever becoming involved with Spiegel.

Adapting Cheever's story for the screen took nearly two years and five script revisions. Ultimately Eleanor had to invent virtually all of the dialogue and create two important supporting characters, a young boy and a voluptuous teenage girl, each of whom accompanies Ned on part of his journey. She also enlarged Cheever's brief exchange between Merrill and his ex-mistress into the scathing climax of the film.

Finding the right actor to play the pivotal lead role proved just as challenging as the scripting. "Ned Merrill is the Cheever man," explained the director, which meant that he was a WASP, educated at prep schools and Ivy League colleges, well bred, and riddled with puritan guilt. Burt, raised in poverty in Italian East Harlem, was, in Perry's words, "positively antithetical to Ned Merrill." A more appropriate choice, the director thought, was William Holden—with whom Spiegel had worked on *The Bridge on the River Kwai*. But Holden turned the role down; so did Paul Newman and Glenn Ford.

Finally, at Spiegel's behest, they approached Burt. He might not have been perfect, but he was eager to do it. And his marquee value was crucial, because he would be the only name actor in the piece; the rest of the cast would be drawn from the New York theatrical community, although several of them, Dolph Sweet, Joan Rivers, and Diana Muldaur, would subsequently find notable careers in television. To play the important role of Merrill's ex-mistress, the director selected Barbara Loden, the then-wife of director Elia Kazan, who was concurrently starring in her husband's Broadway production of Arthur Miller's *After the Fall*. Casting Loden would prove to be a fateful decision.

Ned Merrill offered Lancaster a nearly overwhelming acting challenge. The character, so charming and confident at the outset, disintegrates physically and psychologically as the film progresses until, by the shattering conclusion, he has been reduced to a pathetic shell, shivering in the doorway of his ruined home. Making Ned's decline believable yet poignant without specific plot points to mark the changes would not be easy, especially in the short-take way that movies are produced. At least, Perry would endeavor to shoot the scenes in sequence, which was rare in filmmaking.

That Burt was willing to attempt the difficult, and none too sympathetic, character says much about his lack of concern for his public image, at least where his craft was concerned. "It was a major risk for Lancaster at that time," recalled Michael Herzberg, who served as the film's assistant director and later became a producer. "Here was this Hollywood swashbuckler . . . doing something that was pretty esoteric. I thought it was very brave of him." Burt explained at the time, "Action pictures are hard, tough, mechanical work, but as an actor you're not even cutting through the first layer. . . . A role like this is tremendously rewarding to an actor. I know I'm right for it physically. I hope I'm right for it artistically too."

To be sure he was "right for it physically," he immediately went into training, engaging Robert Horn, the head swimming and water-polo coach at UCLA, to assist him. Perry thought Lancaster would have been better advised to, as he put it, "immerse himself in Cheever's world" by visiting the "enclaves of high WASP-dom" in New York and Connecticut. "But," the director added, "it was not of interest to him."

Filming began in Westport, Connecticut, Perry's hometown, on June 23, 1966. A total of fourteen locations, most of them actual residences, were used during the eight weeks of production.

Although Lancaster was willing to embrace the challenge that Ned Merrill represented, he was, as he confessed, "scared to death" of the real acting jobs. He was so nervous, in fact, that, when Herzberg arrived on the set for the first day of shooting, he saw the actor throwing up outside his trailer. "I thought that that was endearing, honest to God," the assistant director confessed.

Burt's concern over his own performance translated into giving direction to his fellow players, an old and sometimes unfortunate habit. In her autobiography, comedienne and talk show host Joan Rivers, an aspiring actress in 1966, recalled that she, Burt, and Perry rehearsed her scene together. After Perry left, Burt proceeded to redirect her "so that," as she wrote, "there would be no sympathy for me." Indeed, Perry had envisioned her character as a happy party girl while Lancaster wanted her to play the scene as a bitch. "I was going back and forth between line readings," she recalled, "and nothing made sense." She also accused Lancaster of upstaging her in their two-shots.

Diana Muldaur claimed the same thing. "Actually Lancaster directed our scene," she recalled. "He just took me aside and said, 'Okay, this is the way we're doing it.' And I said, 'Yes, sir. Yes, sir.' " It was, Muldaur pointed out, her first movie. Although the actress obliged the star, she was not exactly crazy about him. "He lacked warmth, let's put it that way," she said. "But I was very happy to be working with him."

Perry would not feel the same. A self-proclaimed "Method director," he liked to take actors into the past lives of their characters through improvisations, discussions, and sensory exercises. Lancaster created characters in a radically different way. As he explained in 1962, "I approach acting at an intellectual level. That permits me to act with intelligence, not emotion. I don't like displaying myself." He *did* enjoy discussing his characters and their worlds, ruminating on the ideas behind the story, and debating how a scene should be shot or staged, but that was not what Perry had in mind. He wanted to engage all of Burt's senses, not just his brain. Consequently, he found the star superficial. Worse, he did not consider Lancaster skilled enough to do justice to the part.

Not surprisingly, as Perry confessed, their "relationship had a lot of conflict." But even their style of arguing was at odds. The director cited, as an example, their first major dispute—which came within the first few days of filming: "Burt wanted to have it out in front of the whole cast and crew, and I kept saying, 'Burt, let's take a walk. I'll fight this out with you, but I do my fights in private.' And he said, 'I have balls. I do my fights in public.' So he made me do it in front of people. And his crowning blow was, 'Look, kid, do you know how much I'm making on this picture?' And I said, 'Yeah.' And he said, 'Well, I'll tell you just in case you don't. I'm making seven hundred and fifty thousand dollars plus a deferment, and you're making fifty thousand dollars. Now that means I'm getting paid fifteen times as much as you are. And I think I know what I'm talking about, and you're still green'—or words to that effect." In the end, Perry thought that the point of the argument had been of little consequence to Lancaster. "But he had a strong streak of sadism," the director asserted, "and I think he wanted a confrontation for the sake of the confrontation."

However, the disputes may not have been all Burt's fault. One member of the company said, "Perry wasn't the easiest guy to get along with. Very mercurial. If Perry perceived a problem with Lancaster, it was Perry's, not Lancaster's." Ultimately, assistant director Michael Herzberg was probably correct when he said, "My take is that, in this case, there was nothing wrong with the director, and there was nothing wrong with the actor, but they were just wrong for each other."

Remarkably, in spite of everything, Perry became, in his words, "rather fond of Burt." In fact, when *The Swimmer* wrapped, he and Eleanor and Burt and Jackie went on a vacation together in Jamaica. According to the director, "We had a wonderful time together."

But the dispute over the direction of *The Swimmer* was not over.

• • •

On November 2, 1966, *The Professionals* opened and became an enormous hit. Richard Brooks had set out to make a slam-bang entertainment, and that is precisely what he delivered. Indeed, the rigors that Lancaster and his fellow players endured were put to impeccable effect on film; one could almost feel the heat coming off the screen.

As for Lancaster, it was a delight to see him flash once more that Starbuck grin and display that Elmer Gantry bravado, but ultimately *The Professionals* was an ensemble piece. It was the macho camaraderie *between* Lancaster, Marvin, Ryan, and Strode and their skill in the arts of combat that accounted for the picture's considerable success and made it a fitting precursor for the likes of 1967's *The Dirty Dozen* and 1969's *The Wild Bunch.*

Burt was pleased with the Western. He said later, "*The Professionals* is a good film—highly entertaining. . . . People can't live in the darkness of life all the time. . . . We have to be able to laugh, you know, and have a little fun."

But real life was not "fun" for Burt as 1966 came to an end. He waited until after the holidays, but on January 4, he separated from Norma. They had been married for just over twenty years.

Did his relationship with Jackie precipitate the breakup? "I think it had a lot to do with it," she said in 1993. "I said to him one time, 'Burt, this is ridiculous. Your marriage is a mess. You've got to decide what you want to do. . . . I don't care if we stay together or not, but you've got to do something about yourself.' " He did not answer, but he did not disagree.

Would Burt have left his wife if he and Jackie had not met? "Maybe, but maybe not," said Bone. Still, she observed that the couple's problems were deep, going beyond Burt's infidelities—or, for that matter, Norma's alcoholism. "They had drifted away from each other," the actor's companion recalled. She further maintained that Burt wanted Norma to seek the divorce, and it took more than a year for her to accommodate herself to the idea.

A friend of Norma's disagreed with Bone's assessment. "Jackie had nothing to do with the divorce at all," he asserted. "Booze did." He was not even sure that Burt wanted the marriage to end, but believed rather that it was Norma's decision. "She was miserable," he said. "She wanted to get away from here."[1]

---

1. By "here" he means the United States. After the divorce in 1969, Norma moved to Rome.

Regardless of who initiated the decision, Lancaster packed his bags and left. And whether it was his choice or not, he was unhappy about the turn of events. As Jackie put it, "Burt is a family man, he always was. He loved his mom and dad and his family life, and I think it went hard for him to have to see his marriage break up."

By the time Burt left home, Perry had completed his rough cut of *The Swimmer;* it was approximately ninety-four minutes in length. But, by the time Spiegel removed what he did not like, only about fifty-four minutes remained. To make up the deficit, he then called for reshoots in California. Surprisingly, he persuaded Eleanor Perry to go to the West Coast to work on rewrites. He also elicited Lancaster's support for re-opening the production. In fact, the actor eventually paid for the last day of filming—which cost $10,000—out of his own pocket, Spiegel having exhausted his own resources by then.

"My impression," said Perry, "is that, when Spiegel went to Lancaster to say, 'We want to do some more shooting,' Lancaster said, 'My condition for doing more shooting is to redo the Barbara Loden scene.'" Columnist Sidney Skolsky concurred.

Burt's reason for wanting another crack at the climactic encounter between Ned Merrill and his ex-mistress was obvious—at least to Perry: "Barbara Loden . . . destroyed him as a character, which was the way it was supposed to be, and many people felt she destroyed him as an actor. . . . There was not a single climactic take of hers at which the crew did not give her—give *her*—a standing ovation. It drove Lancaster crazy." For the reshoot, Spiegel and Lancaster chose another actress, Janice Rule. Rule was stunningly beautiful but not particularly noted for emotionally charged performances. And to direct the sequence—without credit—Burt prevailed on his friend Sydney Pollack.

Oddly, Lancaster gave a completely different version of how the scene came to be reshot. "It was simply not done the first time," he asserted, then added, "Barbara Loden, who was very unhappy on the film for many reasons, didn't feel a rapport with Frank. She didn't want to do it [the reshoot]." Of course, Loden's attitude toward Perry would not have been a factor if Pollack was going to direct the scene. Later, Burt said that they had "shot some of the scene [in Connecticut], but not all of it." His explanations simply do not ring true.

The Lancaster-Pollack-Rule sequence was the most significant post-production alteration to *The Swimmer,* but not the only one. Little bits were directed by commercial director Michael Nebia, who received screen credit as a cameraman, and by a fourth, unnamed director. In the end, about 30 or 40 percent of the picture was different from Perry's rough cut. The director said, "I considered running an ad in the *Times* saying, 'This is not my picture.' [But a]fter all, I had relinquished my right of final cut, so legally I had no bitch."

First came *The Defiant Ones,* Stanley Kramer's 1958 film in which a black escaped convict, played by Sidney Poitier, was every bit the equal of his reluctant white partner, played by Tony Curtis. In 1967, Lancaster decided to take the idea and transport it back to the pre–Civil War West, when the prospect of slavery threatened the black character's every move. *The Scalphunters* would be Lancaster's third Western in three years.

Not only was *The Scalphunters* William Norton's first script, the forty-one-year-old was not even a professional writer. But, as Burt would later say, he "had a funny, backwoods way of talking and he had posed this exceptionally interesting idea." Specifically, *The Scalphunters* centered on a trapper named Joe Bass, who loses his cache of furs to a band of Kiowa. By way of trade, the Indians leave him with a runaway slave named Joseph Lee. Bass and Lee then set off to retrieve the furs, which, in the meantime, have fallen into the hands of a band of cutthroats who collect bounties for Indian scalps. This unsavory gang is led by the ruthless Jim Howie and his blowsy girlfriend, Kate.

Lancaster acquired the property for his newly formed production company, Norlan. For production support, he brought in the team of Levy, Gardner, and Lavan, who had been producing such television Westerns as *The Rifleman* and *The Big Valley,* and for financing and distribution he turned to United Artists.[2] Thus, *The Scalphunters* became the fourth and final project in Burt's long struggle to reduce HHL's old debt with the company.

For Kate and Jim Howie, he engaged his old amour, Shelley Winters, and his *Young Savages* and *Birdman* costar, Telly Savalas. The pivotal role of Joseph Lee went to Ossie Davis.

Four years Burt's junior, Davis had made his Broadway debut in 1946, but had scored his biggest triumph in 1961, with the title role in his own play, *Purlie Victorious,* a part that he repeated in the 1963 film version, entitled *Gone Are the Days!* Davis liked the script for *The Scalphunters,* saying in retrospect, "I was aware of the pioneering nature of

2. Levy, Gardner, and Lavan returned the favor by giving Burt's son Bill his first acting role, in *The Big Valley.*

the film, and I was aware that this was the kind of film that would only be made if somebody like a Burt Lancaster insisted that it be made."

The Scalphunters marked Lancaster's return to Durango, eight years after the making of *The Unforgiven.* The company also shot in Torreón, some 150 miles to the northeast. The temperatures there were so fierce that special permission had to be obtained from the Screen Actors Guild so they could start working around 5 A.M., before the intense heat set in. "Instead of breaking for lunch," explained assistant director Charles Scott, "we would work right on through, and the caterers would be coming around with melons and tacos and all that stuff, so everyone could eat as they wanted to, and then at one we'd pull the plug and go back to Torreón."

Burt and Shelley Winters apparently put their volatile past behind them during filming. Said Davis, "Their relationship seemed not only professional but cordial as far as I could see." As for the actor's own relationship with Lancaster, Davis put it simply: "He liked me, and I liked him, and that made it easier for us to relate to each other." Charles Scott confirmed that the duo "worked very well together. They just seemed to click." Which was fortunate, for the bantering between their characters and the constant reversals in their on-screen relationship were the Western's principal distinguishing features.

The association climaxed—as did the picture itself—with a knock-down-drag-out fight that had Joe Bass and Joseph Lee tumbling about in a pool of mud; Lancaster choreographed the action himself. It was shot on a mesa high in the mountains in temperatures of 110 degrees. "In order to get the mudhole," Davis remembered, "they had to pipe in water from much further down, and it was absolutely chilling." When the actors came out, they were so cold they had to be wrapped in blankets, despite the sizzling heat. But to Davis at least, the result far outweighed the effort. In 1967 terms, he noted, the "issue was how are we going to have a top box-office white fighting with somebody who was not his equal and black. It really wasn't done." Then he added with a chuckle, "Of course, Burt's response was, 'Bullshit.' "

Although the chemistry between Lancaster and Davis was crucial to the success of *The Scalphunters,* Burt's most important relationship on the picture was with its director, Sydney Pollack, who some maintain was being rewarded for helping reshoot *The Swimmer.* If so, Lancaster did himself no disservice; Pollack was a major talent in the making. In addition to *The Slender Thread,* the director had completed a second feature by 1967, *This Property Is Condemned,* which marked the start of his long collaboration with Robert Redford. He had also won an Emmy for "The Game," starring Cliff Robertson.

Although the bond was personal—Lancaster felt almost like a father or an older brother toward the director, who was twenty years his junior—the kinship colored their professional collaboration as well. "He was the man who really worked me the hardest and the man I best communicated with," Lancaster would say nearly a decade later.

Of course, at times the two men disagreed. But, unlike the public arguments between Burt and Perry during the making of *The Swimmer,* these disputes took place in private. Neither Davis nor Scott nor the film's cinematographer, Duke Callaghan saw any discord between them.

The same could not be said of Lancaster's relationships with other members of the company. "Burt is a no-nonsense actor," Scott asserted. "He would be the first one to get his hackles up if he thought [someone else in the company] was bumbling." Callaghan further asserted that in the off-hours the star "kept pouring booze in," which made him even more dangerous. On the set, however, the cinematographer conceded that Lancaster "was very, very professional—hardworking, ready, frequently the first one out there in the morning, in costume, knowing the dialogue, and ready to go. No matter how hard he had been drinking the night before. I marveled at it."

Before *The Scalphunters* began filming, Lancaster and Pollack had decided to form their own production company, with Roland Kibbee and a friend of Pollack's, writer David Rayfiel. A short time later, a novel caught Rayfiel's eye. Called *Castle Keep,* it was a semisurrealistic tale about a group of eccentric GIs forced to take up residence in a medieval castle after being separated from their unit during the winter-laden Battle of the Bulge. The author, William Eastlake, was a veteran of the World War II engagement and had served in just such an oddball outfit.

Rayfiel, Pollack, and Lancaster were all enthusiastic about the novel, which they saw as an opportunity to create a subtle metaphor for the ongoing conflict in Vietnam. Years later, Pollack would concede, "*Castle Keep* was certainly as much of an antiwar film as I could make."

But the film rights to *Castle Keep* had been acquired by producer Martin Ransohoff, who had, in turn, engaged Daniel Taradash, the Oscar-winning screenwriter of *From Here to Eternity,* for the adaptation. Ransohoff's Filmways Corporation would produce the film, with financing and distribution provided by Columbia Pictures.

Burt let Columbia know of his interest in playing the commander of the ragtag outfit, the eye-patched Major Falconer. The studio, still basking in the success of *The Professionals,* was delighted, and the casting was announced in July of 1967. Burt also arranged for Pollack to direct and for Rayfiel to undertake a rewrite of the script—although Ransohoff advised them that he liked the screenplay as it was.

The producer felt the same way after reading the new treatment. "I looked on it [the novel] as a romantic fable," he said, while Lancaster, Pollack, and Rayfiel saw it in much more surrealistic, satiric terms. Ransohoff wanted to continue with the project as he envisioned it, even if that meant replacing his star and his director, but Columbia backed Burt. Thereafter, he would be listed as the film's producer, but, according to Rayfiel, "He didn't have anything to do with the production." Neither, for that matter, did Taradash. However, in keeping with the rules of the Writers Guild, the Oscar-winning screenwriter would receive partial credit for the script.

In effect, Lancaster, Pollack, and Rayfiel had gotten involved in another team's project and taken over. They were either extremely dedicated filmmakers or utterly ruthless depending upon one's point of view.

Jackie accompanied Burt to Yugoslavia when *Castle Keep* went into production in early January of 1968. One evening, in fact, they got into a very public argument in a local restaurant. "She took exception to the fact that Burt was looking in the direction of a Viennese actress," noted a magazine at the time, "and decided to cool his interest by spilling ice water over him and then breaking the pitcher over his head." The incident made the international papers, but the journalists attributed it to Burt's wife. (They obviously did not know Norma on sight; she and Jackie looked nothing like one another.)

They were staying in Novi Sad, the fortress city some forty-five miles north of Belgrade that served as the company's base of operations. "It was out in the tulies," said Bruce Dern, cast as a ragtag solider-cum-religious-fanatic. Nearby, designer Rino Mondellini had erected the film's principal set, the art-laden castle that served as the GIs' refuge. It cost $1 million, an enormous sum at the time.

When shooting began, temperatures were well below zero, but a few weeks into production, a very early spring produced record highs—and melted the snow and ice around the company's castle. Since the Battle of the Bulge had been fought in inclement weather, an artificial snow machine had to be quickly dispatched from Hollywood. It was capable of producing seventy-five tons a day, but as the temperatures continued to climb, even that was insufficient. Finally, the resourceful moviemakers decided to create a wintry effect by draping the castle in marble dust.

In addition to the castle exteriors, the early weeks of filming involved scenes in what was supposed to be the Ardennes town of St.-Croix. The quaint village set, also constructed specifically for the picture, occupied a ten-block area in Petrovaradin, a small town across the Danube from Novi Sad. Although production designer Mondellini lined the main thoroughfare with shops, inns, and homes, his most compelling concoction was the Red Queen brothel, a fantastic oddity decorated entirely in scarlet and outfitted with a vintage pipe organ, an antique German piano, and a sixty-year-old gramophone. In the picture, it would become the favorite haunt of the GIs played by Scott Wilson, Al Freeman Jr., Michael Conrad, and James Patterson.

Even after Pollack emerged as one of the most celebrated directors in Hollywood, he rarely, if ever, started production with a completed script. "I don't know how to prepare," he would say in 1990. "I don't really prepare until I get there. It produces terrible anxiety, because I go into a movie not quite knowing what I'm going to do, always." That was certainly the case with *Castle Keep*. "The script was being written while we were shooting," asserted Rayfiel. He remembered, for example, redrafting lines for one scene just moments before it was shot. But no matter what changes were wrought, the screenplay remained, to quote the writer, "very, very faithful to the novel." Burt was invariably present during script conferences, but, Rayfiel noted, "He never pulled any star stuff; he was never overbearing. He just made suggestions"—which, the writer added, were "generally good."

One time, however, Rayfiel and Lancaster got into a fight because the star asked the film's technical adviser to rewrite some of the dialogue. After Rayfiel told Burt off, the star replied, "Well, I didn't mean to offend you," and no doubt that was so. In typical fashion, he had acted impulsively, without thinking. But Rayfiel clearly remained upset. A few moments later, Burt went up to him, put his arm around his shoulder, and without reference to the argument said, "You know, I was thinking, once you finish this scene and the next one, you'll be able to go home." As the writer saw it, "He was attributing my outrage to the fact that I'd been away from home for so long. He's unbelievable. He's a very, very sensitive guy."

Throughout his career, Lancaster was not particularly social on location, preferring to read or listen to opera records during the off-hours instead of chatting with members of the company. Still, during the making of *Cas-*

tle Keep, he occasionally mingled with the "kids." Bruce Dern recalled one evening when Burt, having had a few drinks, joined him, Scott Wilson, and a few of the others as they sat around the Novi Sad hotel, talking. "It was really pissing down snow," said Dern, "and Scott Wilson was bragging about the fact that he had placed in his Georgia State meet when he was in high school in the one-hundred-yard dash." Dern was just the opposite of a speed runner, an ultramarathoner. But Lancaster said to Wilson, "I'll bet you that we could go outside and run a one-hundred-yard dash in the snow in the street and that Dern could beat you." Wilson took the dare, so the actors went outside, where Lancaster drew a line to mark the finish of the race. Then, just as they were about to start, a car pulled up. Said Dern, "He went berserk, you know, to move the car out of the way, because this race had become a whole play for him. . . . Anyway we ran the race, and I beat Scott Wilson by a hair or something. I don't how I ever did. I think he was a little drunk, too, probably. But anyway Burt got a big kick out of that, he really liked that." Thereafter, Lancaster behaved differently toward Dern. "He treated me with a certain kind of fondness that I hadn't felt before," said the actor.

Although Dern was the veteran of eleven features and numerous episodic television roles by the start of 1968, Lancaster had a profound impact on him. Twenty-five years later, Dern was eloquent on the subject: "Burt Lancaster was like an enormous tower. He was powerful, he was strong, he had original ideas, he had great insight into acting, he was a wonderful actor, he had done everything there was to do in show business. He was a great star." And what did Dern take away from the relationship? "He left me with a whole feeling of 'dare to achieve bigger things, dare to risk.' And I like that."

Although the budget for *Castle Keep* had originally called for four months of production, the company was running behind schedule. Considerable work remained on April 26, when the castle was consumed by fire, the result of an explosion set near the drawbridge entrance as part of the picture's long, climactic battle sequence.

There was no choice but to rebuild. In the meantime, the cast and crew shot the castle's interiors at the Avala Film Studios in Belgrade. When construction on the new facade was completed, they returned, finished the battle sequence, and wrapped the picture.

While Lancaster was abroad, two of his movies opened back home.

The first was *The Scalphunters*. After a Beverly Hills preview on

February 16, 1968, to benefit Norma's busing effort, the Transport a Child Program, the picture debuted in New York on April 2. A few critics argued that the script meandered, but the general consensus held that the film was, to quote Ann Guarino of the New York *Daily News,* "a first-rate comedy Western for adults." Lancaster looked a bit grizzled as mountain man Joe Bass, but as Archer Winsten of the *New York Post* wrote, "at his age [he] can still move like a man of the frontier who lives by his muscle, eyes, and other senses." Even more remarkable in light of *The Hallelujah Trail*—he was funny!

Much of the humor sprang from the contrast between Burt's plainspoken man of common sense and Davis' well-educated runaway—with each man totally convinced of his superiority over the other. But when faced with a common enemy—the scalphunters—they join forces, and a mutual respect begins to emerge. "Throw you in a pigpen," Bass says grudgingly after Lee steals some whiskey from the outlaw band, "and you'd come out vice president of the hogs."

With plenty of action and rugged scenery to go with the laughs, *The Scalphunters* seemed to have the makings of a major hit. Instead it performed modestly. Two years later, however, one critic called it "the only respectable picture in recent memory to come from a major studio and deal honestly with the relationship between a white man and a black man. Badly promoted as an action picture, the film left town before anyone noticed it was here." It would not be the last time that such a complaint would be raised over the selling of a quirky Lancaster film.

Burt's second release of 1968, *The Swimmer,* fared even worse than *The Scalphunters.* The picture had baffled producer Sam Spiegel and his associates at Columbia to such an extent that it sat on the shelf for more than a year while they decided what to do with it.

"I happened to like it very much," wrote Vincent Canby in *The New York Times* upon the picture's debut on May 15, 1968. But the critic also conceded that it was "an uneven, patchy kind of movie, occasionally gross, and mawkish." That was a rave compared to the comments of most of his colleagues. Lancaster's performance fared no better. The kindest notice again came from Canby, who wrote that Burt was "essentially miscast."

Over the years, *The Swimmer* has grown in stature. Virtually all of the present film and video guides give it their second-highest rating and endow it with such adjectives as "absorbing," "totally engrossing," and "unfailingly watchable and sharply evocative." Mark Martin and Marsha Porter assert that "Burt Lancaster is excellent in the title role," while

Leonard Maltin, who dubs the picture "fascinating, vastly underrated," finds him "superb." Most impressive is Lancaster's use of body language. In a wardrobe consisting entirely of seventeen identical pairs of dark blue nylon swimming trucks (all supposed to be the same pair), he sports at the outset the body of a man in his prime. By the end, he is limping, withered, and old beyond his years.

Hollywood rarely makes films like *The Swimmer*—frank, unvarnished examinations of daily life. Without question, the effort was flawed, but it offered much to admire. Perhaps the good points were harder to see amid the political and social upheavals of the late sixties when Ned Merrills seemed to be everywhere. Even so, it must have been terribly disappointing for Lancaster, Perry, and the others who believed in the project to see such a rich opportunity go so unrewarded. Looking back on it in 1975, the actor said simply, "The whole film was a disaster."

"It's about choice and self-destruction," said John Frankenheimer of *The Gypsy Moths*, his fifth and final collaboration with Burt Lancaster.

The Gypsy Moths was a product of the production company that John had formed with Edward Lewis. Although the novel by James Drought had been published—to virtually no interest—in 1955, the story of three rootless sky divers during a climactic Fourth of July layover in a small midwestern town was much more in keeping with the spirit of the late 1960s. It reflected the ennui of the age.

At the outset, Frankenheimer had hoped to use Steve McQueen, then at the height of his popularity, as the most daring of the sky divers, Mike Rettig, the role that would eventually go to Burt. If ever a star was the strong, silent type, McQueen was it; he may well have spoken fewer lines of dialogue during his career than any other major actor in Hollywood since the advent of talkies. Lancaster never made a film in which he said less.

Once Burt was in place, Frankenheimer was inspired to cast Deborah Kerr as the local matron with whom Rettig has a brief affair, thereby reuniting the costars of *From Here to Eternity*. For the two remaining sky divers, he chose Gene Hackman, fresh from his triumph as gangster Buck Barrow in 1967's *Bonnie and Clyde*, and John Phillip Law, a young featured player in *The Russians Are Coming! The Russians Are Coming!*, *Hurry Sundown*, and *Barbarella*. (Law, injured early in the production, was replaced by Scott Wilson, one of the motley soldiers in *Castle Keep*.)

• • •

Portions of *The Gypsy Moths* were shot on the soundstages at MGM, which served as the film's distributor, but the heart of the picture was filmed—starting in July of 1968—in Kansas. In particular, Abilene lent its frontier aura to the fictional community of Bridgeville. El Dorado and the Nelson Air Field outside Wichita were also used.

Working with Frankenheimer could be trying. Kerr found him a "fascinating character, but disturbing in many ways, a little difficult to understand his why and wherewithal." Assistant director Lynn Guthrie was far blunter, saying, "Frankenheimer is not a nice man. He's a tough hombre."

Burt, however, saw a different side of the director than the rest of the company. According to a colleague on another Lancaster-Frankenheimer picture, John showed Burt a deference that he did not accord others. Bruce Dern, who lived near the director in Malibu and would star in his *Black Sunday* some years later, cast the relationship in a more positive light, saying, "John loved Burt, and Burt loved him, and they were very good for each other. And when you look at their films together, it was good stuff."

Although Burt made it clear that he would play his scenes in *The Gypsy Moths* as he thought they should be played, Lynn Guthrie saw a lot of kidding between the two men. For starters, the star called the director "Frankie. Frankie Frankenheimer." He was also not above playing a practical joke on his colleague.

"We were doing a scene once outside a hangar," Guthrie recalled. "It was a dialogue scene with two people about one hundred and fifty yards, two hundred yards, from a hangar. In that hangar was Burt Lancaster, and he was folding parachutes in the background. Maybe he was pissing, saying, 'What am I doing folding things one hundred yards away. They can hardly see. Anybody could be doing this.' But anyway, he was in there, and every time Frankenheimer started to roll the camera we heard a radio. And Frankenheimer has got a short fuse, and he's just not really a sweet guy, and every time he would scream out, 'God damn it. Find out where that radio is.' And I was the guy who had to find out." But, search as he could, Guthrie could not locate the source of the music. Eventually, it would stop, and the company would get ready for another take. "And as soon as they'd get up to speed and yell, 'Action,'" Guthrie asserted, "the radio would come on again. This happened about six times. By the sixth time, Frankenheimer had absolutely gone ballistic. I got the other assistant to roll the camera, and I decided to go near where the radio was coming from, which was around the hangar. So they rolled the camera, and Burt starts singing opera! He'd been doing this every time. . . . It was a great joke and it was great fun. So I said to him, 'Burt, you're getting me in a lot of trouble.' But I'm laughing, and he's laughing, and it was a great joke."

Guthrie's recollection might suggest that Lancaster was having a wonderful time during the making of *The Gypsy Moths*, but such was not the case. "He was pretty quiet, I have to say," the AD recalled, adding that Burt often displayed a "sullenness on and off the set." In part, this attitude reflected the state of the actor's personal life at the time—his separation from Norma, the excessive drinking, the realization that his years as a leading man were perforce drawing to a close. Then too he was playing a dour, fundamentally inarticulate man, a man bent on self-destruction, and the character's ennui may have unconsciously colored Burt's state of mind.

The full extent of Lancaster's funk can be seen in an incident that took place on September 24, 1968, shortly after *The Gypsy Moths* wrapped.

It was around eleven at night, and Burt was driving along the Pacific Coast Highway in Malibu, doing fifty-five miles per hour in a forty-five-mile-per-hour zone. He was spotted by John Lilly and P. C. Miller of the California Highway Patrol, who set off in pursuit. When the officers turned on their lights, however, Burt accelerated to sixty-five instead of pulling over. Finally, after about a three-mile chase, he stopped in the driveway of his rented home. There, Lilly and Miller issued him a citation—which he refused to sign. When asked why, he reportedly said, "To get an education." The officers were willing to oblige, placing him under arrest and holding him overnight at the County Central Jail. Finally, about five the following morning, he posted bail and went home in a taxi.

It was a bizarre incident, perhaps, but in keeping with the times, when liberals like Burt considered the police to be the ultimate symbols of authority. Never was that more so than at the Democratic Party's national convention in Chicago—just a month before Burt's arrest—when the police used brutal force to break up the concurrent antiwar demonstrations.

In keeping with Lancaster's posture of civil disobedience, the actor was elected the following February to the chairmanship of the Roger Baldwin Foundation of the American Civil Liberties Union of Southern California, an organization named for a longtime director of the ACLU and established, to quote the organization's literature, "to support the day-to-day work of the civil liberties organization by creating long-range educational programs and filing test cases to challenge unconstitutional laws." The cochairmen were Frank Sinatra and Irving L. Lichtenstein, and the members of the advisory board included actors Tony Curtis, Paul Newman, and Sidney Poitier and director Robert Wise.

For decades thereafter, Lancaster would remain an ardent supporter of, and fund-raiser for, the ACLU. Linda Burstyn, who worked closely with him during the late 1980s when she was with the ACLU's southern-California branch, said, "He really wanted to spend his time doing things that helped society. He felt strongly about freedom of speech [and] First Amendment rights."

Ironically, in light of Lancaster's antiestablishment credentials, the last movie that he would complete during the turbulent 1960s would cast him as a pillar of the social order. For the first time in forty-six films, he would be shown as a working business executive, appearing on screen in a suit for the first time in seven years. Although the picture would be nominated for an Academy Award, he called it "the biggest piece of junk ever made." Nevertheless, it would earn him a small fortune, more than any other movie of his career.

It was called *Airport*.

"We knew that it would be a bestseller," the film's producer, Ross Hunter, said of the novel, which he read in galley form prior to its publication. But even Hunter and his partner, Jacques Mapes, were surprised at how popular the book became. It was published in the spring of 1968 and quickly climbed to the top of *The New York Times* bestseller list, where it stayed for sixty-five weeks.

Novelist Arthur Hailey's special province was to take readers inside a major industry, providing nuggets of information about how it worked and what innovations lay on its horizon, and at the same time juggle an array of major characters, each of whom was engaged in a soap-opera-like crisis. In the case of *Airport*, the fictional Lincoln International—clearly based on Chicago's O'Hare—became the backdrop.

For the film version, Hunter decided that he wanted to create what he called "an old-fashioned *Grand Hotel* of the air,"[3] which was perfectly in keeping with his previous body of work, slick, melodramatic films such as *Magnificent Obsession, Imitation of Life,* and *Back*

3. Based on the novel by Vicki Baum, *Grand Hotel,* released by MGM in 1932, intermixed the personal stories of a disparate group of guests at a plush Berlin hostelry.

Street. To write the screenplay—as well as direct—he turned to George Seaton, a onetime actor who had won Oscars for his screenplays of *Miracle on 34th Street* and *The Country Girl,* both of which he also directed. Like Hunter, Seaton headed his own production unit at Universal, the studio that was financing and distributing *Airport.*

Seaton was well aware of *Airport*'s enormous readership. "You can't take a property like that," he said, "and purposely alter it to suit your own purposes." His only major departure was the elimination of a major character, an unstable air-traffic controller, who he felt slowed down the action. So successful was the adaptation that only the most minimal of rewrites took place during filming, and few scenes were left on the cutting-room floor.

The first star that Ross Hunter secured for *Airport* was Dean Martin, who would play the skilled but arrogant airline pilot. Martin would later be joined by Oscar-winner George Kennedy as the expert mechanic, Helen Hayes as the stowaway, Jean Seberg as the passenger relations agent, Van Heflin as the mad bomber, and Jacqueline Bisset as the stewardess. For the harried airport manager, Mel Bakersfield, the producer wanted his old bridge-party crony Burt Lancaster. "There were very few men then," he explained, "who I thought had both the macho and the sensitivity that the role needed."

Burt's agent, Ben Benjamin, agreed, but Lancaster turned the project down. So, Hunter started to consider other candidates, in particular Gregory Peck. Still, Benjamin continued to push for Burt. Finally, the agent won his client over—after persuading Hunter to give the star a percentage of the profits, an approach that the producer also employed with Seaton and Dean Martin. "If the picture was a success," said Hunter prophetically, "Burt Lancaster was going to make millions."

Before the deal was finalized, however, Seaton wanted to meet the actor. "I'd never worked with Burt," he recalled in 1974, "but he has a reputation of wanting to direct, to produce, and be the cameraman." At a meeting arranged by Hunter, Seaton insisted upon control over the project. "I must say he took it all very graciously," the director recalled. "He said, 'Well, you don't mind if I make a suggestion now and then?' I said, 'Burt, not on the set, but beforehand, we'll go into my dressing room or yours and we can talk about character, relationships, or anything else. I'll talk as long as you want. But once we arrive on the set, I'm the boss.'"

Lancaster told a very different version of the encounter, claiming that over lunch he told Seaton of his concerns about his character's relationship with his estranged wife. "I imposed the idea on him of 'What can I do to help?' " Burt recalled. "And the next thing you know, I got him to rewrite all my scenes. I know how to handle a man like that. You live and learn and, with luck, you mature."

Regardless of how it happened, Lancaster and Seaton came to terms. The director never regretted the decision. "I must say he was just absolutely superb," George later said of Burt.

Shortly after the star's casting was announced on October 31, 1968, Sydney Pollack saw a copy of the script in Burt's office.

"You're not going to do this, are you?" the director asked with disdain.

"Oh, yes," Lancaster replied. "That's how I can do pictures like *Castle Keep.*"

Some of *Airport*'s sequences were filmed on soundstages, but for the runways and terminal shots, the company needed the real thing. O'Hare was too busy. LAX and any other warm-weather airport was also out, because a huge snowstorm figured in the plot. Finally, to quote the director, "Minneapolis gave us exactly what we wanted. Between nine o'-clock at night and four in the morning, there were only two flights coming in and going out, so it gave us time to work on the field and also in the terminal." Hunter also arranged to rent a Boeing 707 from Flying Tiger Lines, along with a flight crew. The jet would serve as both an imperiled plane in the air and one stuck in the snow.

On January 20, 1969, the day before shooting was to begin, Seaton took sick with pneumonia. "The studio wanted to replace him," Hunter recalled, "but Jacques and I . . . called upon a friend of ours, Henry Hathaway, to sit in for about two weeks." According to Seaton, Hathaway shot "second-unit stuff, planes doing takeoffs and landings and the like." Then, in mid-February, the original choice was well enough to take over.

Lancaster agreed to star in *Airport,* but that did not mean he liked it. According to Hunter he "was very nice, very professional, he always knew his lines. But he was just not with the group. He seemed to be above it all. I didn't think he was that much interested in the picture, which bothered me, because I've never worked with people who did a picture unless they wanted to." By contrast, the producer asserted that other members of the cast, including Dean Martin, "really threw themselves into it."

Lancaster's disaffection arguably reached its height with Jean Seberg, playing his character's love interest, Tanya Livingston. Hunter conceded that his own choice had been Angie Dickinson, saying, "I needed that sort of sly kind of sex appeal for the role, and I wanted someone with a little more stature to play opposite Lancaster." But Universal had Seberg under a two-picture, pay-or-play contract and insisted that she be used. The beautiful, blond actress had become something of an international figure, thanks to her role in Jean-Luc Godard's *Breathless* and her marriage to novelist Romain Gary. For many years, she lived abroad. Then, in the late sixties, she returned to the States, starring just prior to *Airport* in the Western musical *Paint Your Wagon,* a total disaster.

"She was a darling little girl," said Hunter, "but sort of a broken sparrow, you know. She was having an affair with someone, and it was not someone that she should have been having an affair with. Plus, she felt inadequate in the role. And she knew the studio had forced her on us, although we did everything we could to make her happy." Everyone, perhaps, except Lancaster, who was twenty-five years her senior. "I think she was very inhibited by him," asserted the producer. "I don't think he helped her in the least. I think he thought she was very inadequate."[4]

After about six weeks, the company wrapped in Minneapolis–St. Paul and returned to Los Angeles to film interiors on the soundstages at Universal. Five weeks later, Lancaster finished his work on *Airport.* Hunter was not terribly sorry to see him go. "Burt was the only one in the cast who never said good-bye," he recalled, "never said thank you, never came to the big cast party, never did anything to promote the picture. I kept saying to myself, 'You're a schmuck. You should have gotten someone else.'"

Burt's divorce became final on June 27, Norma having finally filed in Santa Monica, charging her husband with extreme cruelty. She was awarded custody of the three minor children, and they divided the community property, valued at least $2 million.

Burt, usually so articulate in public, offered the press a few tortured words. "I have had, for whatever reasons, rightly or wrongly, a desire for a long time to sort of . . ." He stopped and then started again. "I found marriage somewhat stifling. Frankly, I don't know that I am the kind of man who ought to be married. Mind you, I certainly don't regret it. I've

4. On August 30, 1979, Seberg would die of an overdose of barbiturates, a suicide in all likelihood. She was forty years old.

had many happy years in my marriage. My former wife is, in my opinion, a truly wonderful person; so it's not easy."

Electing, as any gentleman would, to avoid mentioning Norma's drinking problem, he added, "I can't say we split up because she's a difficult woman and I couldn't live with her or vice versa. But if I'm going to get married again"—he paused—"and I'm not sure either that I'm the kind of man to live alone . . ." Then, he finished softly, "I will undoubtedly take up with someone similar."

In spite of the divorce, Lancaster felt a great sense of responsibility toward Norma, a family friend asserted. Thereafter, he said, "Burt came over for certain Christmas things, he stopped by with the family. And he always watched out for her, always. Her whole staff was kind of like Burt's minions, they kind of reported what was going on. But he always watched out for her. With a lot of love. Booze just wrecked the marriage." Jackie Bone, however, asserted that after the divorce "Burt was very uncomfortable around her [Norma]. He didn't want to be around her." It may well be that both parties are right.

A month later, on July 23, *Castle Keep* opened.

Far from the hesitant figure who talked about the breakup of his marriage, Lancaster appeared absolutely fearless on the screen. He and the young actors in his "platoon" got to enjoy myriad moments of existential humor arising out of fantasies, non sequiturs, and the absurdity of their situation. But because the whimsy was lost when the climactic battle finally began, no one knew what to make of the picture when it debuted, a confusion made worse by Columbia's publicity campaign. "They sold it as a Burt Lancaster war movie," decried Bruce Dern. It fell to Vincent Canby to correctly assess the effort and articulate its failings, noting in *The New York Times* that it "begins as a satire on war, eventually runs out of madness, and concludes by glorifying the very things it has been satirizing."

Castle Keep ended up a disappointing sixtieth among the top releases of 1969. "It was a terrible flop," recalled David Rayfiel.

Still, with only one failure between them—and a noble effort at that—it is surprising that Lancaster and Pollack never worked together again. According to Rayfiel, they tried. "We kept coming to him to talk about future projects," the writer recalled, "and Burt would say, 'You guys better hurry up.' " But nothing ever came to fruition. Instead, Pollack would go on to forge a major screen collaboration with another, younger actor, Robert Redford.

• • •

Castle Keep soon found itself competing for the attention of Burt Lancaster fans with *The Gypsy Moths.*

With the pretentious advertising tag line "When you turn on by falling free . . . when jumping is not only a way to live but a way to die too . . . you're a Gypsy Moth," the John Frankenheimer film debuted at New York's Radio City Music Hall on August 28. It was a curious booking because, with its stage show featuring the Rockettes, the giant mid-Manhattan picture palace typically drew family audiences, and *The Gypsy Moths* was decidedly adult fare. Not only did it show the death of one of the central characters—Lancaster's Mike Rettig—who failed to open his parachute after a jump, it also featured a nude love scene between Burt and Deborah Kerr, and a striptease by Sheree North, who played Gene Hackman's love interest. Several excisions were made for the booking in order to qualify the picture for a rating of M (for "mature audiences," meaning parental discretion was advised).

Frankenheimer would later blame MGM's James Aubrey for the choice of theater and the cuts, saying, "I sued him; I got it out of the Music Hall, got it cut back to my version, and then he took it out of all of the theaters and it opened in the airport in Los Angeles."

Frankenheimer was exaggerating about the subsequent booking, but the picture was withdrawn after the end of its engagement at Radio City on September 24 and was not rereleased until November. At that point some of the excised footage, including North's striptease, was restored, and the picture was given an R rating, meaning that children under the age of seventeen could only be admitted when accompanied by a parent or an adult guardian.

Frankenheimer also asserted that the studio did nothing to promote the picture. "I want to do all kinds of things to help with it," he said at the time. "But I cannot find anyone in authority at MGM whom you can reach. Burt Lancaster was also willing to help promote the film, but he wasn't asked."

The skydiving sequences were, without question, the highlight of the picture. "We did over a thousand jumps to get the footage," recalled assistant director Lynn Guthrie, and the parachutists endured considerable risks in the process. According to FAA regulations, the stunt doubles and the divers photographing them were supposed to pull their chutes at two thousand feet, but, Guthrie recalled, "We had guys pulling at eight hundred feet. . . I was standing almost directly under them, and I could see their eyes and their fingers when they reached for their rip cords."

Despite the spectacular aerials, *The Gypsy Moths* was not an action picture. Even Frankenheimer said at the time, "If anybody tells me this is a film about parachute jumping, I'll feel like hitting them on the head." But when the drama was on the ground, it was, to quote *Variety*, "a lackluster affair."

No one fared worse than Lancaster. The film needed someone who could convey his character's malaise, which is never articulated, someone who could fill the brooding silences with palpable emotion—anger, rage, frustration, something. Perhaps Frankenheimer's original choice for the part, Steve McQueen, could have made the silences work, but Lancaster, a verbal person and a cerebral actor, did not know how to play off the lines, to convey what was not in the script. All he could do was look weary, resigned, unhappy, and that was not enough. Even Kerr said in retrospect, "I don't think he himself quite got it. I don't know what he was after."

In the end, Lancaster himself recognized the flaws in the movie. In 1989, he would assert, "*The Gypsy Moths* unfortunately was just not a good picture. An interesting idea, not well done, not well written, I would say."

It was his last release of the turbulent 1960s.

CHAPTER SIXTEEN

"A Fallen King"

As the 1970s dawned, Lancaster had gone three years without a hit. Moreover, time was no longer on his side. He still looked fit, but the phrase "for a man of his age" was increasingly coloring observations about his looks. Even he had to concede, "My romantic leading days are over, so I have to look for strong character portraits." Moreover, the great physical stunts of the previous decades came harder. For one thing, the knee that he had injured during the making of *The Leopard* had never healed properly, forcing several operations. For another, his alcoholic intake had increased dramatically over the years. Although he never faced the prospect of alcoholism—as had Norma—the heavy drinking took its toll on his physical resources. And, finally, as he confessed in 1977, "I don't do as much exercise as I used to. . . . Now I just go out and read a line and see if I can get away with it."

Many actors who are forced to confront the loss of their looks—and the often commensurate decline in popularity—go into a deep depression. Lancaster was no exception. "He told me about how terrible it is to get old," recalled one friend. Burt had relished the attention from fans, including the women who threw themselves at him. "And suddenly that all began to stop. Younger people didn't recognize him. He didn't find the same adulation. And he found it very, very difficult."

Jackie Bone acknowledged the depth of Lancaster's midlife crisis. "There was a point, near his sixtieth birthday," she recalled, "when he said, 'I can't do anything. This is all I have, and it's nothing.' He felt like a failure." She was shocked. "I really didn't understand that he was that distressed," she admitted. Nor did she fully know how to cope with his attitude, saying in retrospect, "See, I was thrown into a whole world that I didn't understand, and it was very difficult for both of us." At the same time, her influence led him to become more introspective, and, as she said, "I think he saw a lot of things that he didn't like."

Was his career one of those things? The actor could not seem to decide. At the end of the 1960s, he admitted that he had thought about quitting but had changed his mind, adding, "All I want to do is go on as long as I can making films that touch people emotionally and express what I feel about life." But, in 1975, he would say, "I've been bored with acting for years. I never had that usual kind of actor's mentality anyway." His ambivalence was not helped by the radical change within the industry, for, as the 1970s progressed, Hollywood increasingly tailored pictures to attract the powerful new youth market, a group beyond Burt's reach.

Despite these personal and professional obstacles, he would persevere, appearing in fourteen feature films during the decade, plus a television miniseries, a made-for-television movie, and a stage musical.[1] It was an enormous body of work, more than that produced by any of his contemporaries. Kirk Douglas, for example, did twelve pictures during the decade, as did Robert Mitchum. William Holden made nine and Gregory Peck six.

Why did Burt drive himself so? Actor Jon Cypher, who would costar with him in *Valdez Is Coming,* offered a thoughtful appraisal: "I think Burt is an intellectual, but there is only so much time you can spend in your den reading. You need outside contact. You need some recognition from other people, people who can say, 'I know who you are. I know what you can do and have done.' And you need some structure. Actors have minimal structure. The only structure they have is when they're working. And when they're working, they say, 'Oh, I can't wait to stop. I can't wait to take that vacation,' or whatever, but pretty soon, without structure, you start feeling like you're adrift. I think that's why he stayed."

Burt would remain busy, but the seventies would be the worst decade in his long career. In retrospect, most of the fourteen pictures were well crafted, but too many carried a sour tone, with Burt cast more often than not as either someone outside the system or a product of the system's worst elements. To be sure, some of the most popular pictures of the decade were antiestablishment, reflecting the public's increasing rejection of the Vietnam War and, in the first half of the decade, the persistence of the counterculture movement. But there was an ebullience to the likes of *M*A*S*H, Little Big Man, One Flew Over the Cuckoo's Nest,* and *All the President's Men* that Lancaster's movies lacked. Ap-

---

1. Not counting two pictures made in 1979, which were not released until 1981.

pearing at times to have been drained of energy—the hallmark of his screen persona—he projected a posture of world-weariness cloaked in a mantle of wisdom (albeit, often misguided wisdom) that was not particularly appealing. To fans, it was not the Burt of old, and for the new generation, it carried no resonance.

A case in point was *Valdez Is Coming,* which commanded Lancaster's attention as the decade began.

The project had originated in late 1967, when MGM producer Ira Steiner acquired the novel of the same name by Elmore Leonard. Set in Arizona in 1890, it introduced a different type of Western hero, a humble Hispanic constable who wages a private war against a wealthy Anglo, Frank Tanner, after the rancher engineers the death of a black soldier at Valdez' hand.

Steiner sent the book to Lancaster, who agreed to coproduce it through his own Norlan Productions, in association with United Artists. Originally Burt was going to play Tanner with Marlon Brando as Valdez. Burt's crony Sydney Pollack was slated to direct, and David Rayfiel would write the script.

Then, in November of 1968, Burt announced the postponement of the project, so that he could do *Airport.* When he turned his attention toward *Valdez* once more, Pollack, Brando, and Rayfiel were no longer involved. Accordingly, Lancaster decided to play the title character himself and engaged Roland Kibbee to tailor the script for him.[2] Ultimately, Rayfiel would get cocredit for the screenplay, but he conceded, "They didn't use anything" he wrote.

To replace Pollack, Lancaster made a bold choice—Ed Sherin. The onetime actor and stage director had never been involved with a film before, but his 1969 Broadway debut, *The Great White Hope* by Howard Sackler, had bought him instant cachet within the motion picture industry. Disappointed when the movie version of *The Great White Hope* went to Martin Ritt, the director found consolation in the Elmore Leonard Western, but he also saw, in his words, "things in this story . . . that offered a chance to say something important."[3]

Susan Clark, who would costar in the picture, asserted in 1993 that Lancaster hired Sherin "because he wanted a fresh look, I think, and to

2. In the 1990s, a character like Bob Valdez would go to the likes of Raul Julia or Edward James Olmos or Jimmy Smits. But even as late as the early 1970s, Anglo actors were regularly playing members of ethnic or racial minorities without protest from special interest groups.
3. By coincidence, *The Great White Hope* would be in production in Spain concurrently with *Valdez;* the two Hollywood units were about five hundred miles apart.

find out how a big-hit Broadway director would deal with actors and who he would choose. And, indeed, Ed chose some very talented, young New York actors to be in that movie, to give it kind of a different look, to give it a little different kind of energy."

Among those whom Sherin cast were Richard Jordan, Jon Cypher, and Hector Elizondo, each of whom would make his film debut in *Valdez*. Cypher was especially fortunate, winning the role of the principal villain, Frank Tanner.

Clark, cast as Cypher's fiancée, also had a strong theatrical background, having trained at the Royal Academy of Dramatic Arts in London. The Canadian actress, who was twenty-nine years old at the time, had already costarred in several films, notably *Madigan* with Richard Widmark, *Coogan's Bluff* with Clint Eastwood, and *Tell Them Willie Boy Is Here* with Robert Redford.

The company commenced production in Almería, Spain, about 260 miles from Madrid, in November of 1969. "We had an English sound crew," recalled Clark, "an Italian camera crew, French designers, and Spanish workers, and Americans heading up each department. So there was a constant friction between how it's done in Hollywood, and how they were going to do it in Europe." None of which helped Sherin in his debut effort. Nor did the weather. "Here we were doing a film that was supposedly taking place in Sonora in the desert heat," he recalled, "and the fucking rain was just pouring down on us."

While Lancaster waited for breaks in the precipitation, he played bridge. With Kibbee as the film's executive producer, Thom Conroy as the dialogue director, and Nick Cravat in a small role, he had all the hands he needed. As Susan Clark astutely observed, "He took what parts of his life he needed with him." That included Jackie too. In fact, Burt arranged for the only hotel in Almería to knock down a wall separating two rooms so that she and he could share a suite. "I liked Jackie," said Clark. "Good lady. She was there for him. She had no illusions about him. She loved him. And he loved her, at that particular time."

"My sense of Burt when I worked with him," said Jon Cypher, "was that he was a fallen king, because it was clear that he had had three flops, and now he was doing this. He had stumbled, and there was a certain sadness about him." Cypher recalled that for a time Burt was not even sure he could arrange financing for the picture, although at about $6 million it had a relatively small budget.

One day Clark caught a glimpse of Lancaster's melancholy. They were sitting atop a mountain, waiting to be called for a scene, "and out of the blue, he said, 'Never let them take your dream away. . . . They'll try, you know. Those bastards'll try. Never let them, never give them one hundred percent.' " Clark took him to mean, in her words, "never show how vulnerable you are to the business aspect, because it is a business, it's not an art form."

Lancaster freely advised Cypher as well, focusing especially on how to work more economically for the screen. The younger actor, accustomed to performing for the stage, welcomed the help. As he put it, "I thought it was very generous of him to take me under his wing like that."

Meanwhile Burt was grappling with his own role. In terms of age, manner, and temperament, Bob Valdez was as big a stretch as any he had previously undertaken.

For starters, there was Burt's appearance. He sported a thick mustache and long gray sideburns, his skin darkened by makeup, and a paunch creeping over his usually trim waistline. At Sherin's urging, he even replaced the beautiful white caps on his teeth with stained ones made especially for the film. Cypher, for one, was impressed, saying, "It was a big thing for him to say, 'I'm of an age where I'm not totally a leading man anymore. I'm going to allow myself to play this older guy.' "

Burt also focused on his speech and manner, meeting with linguists and members of the Hispanic studies program at Los Angeles City College before leaving for Spain. He even quizzed the production company's script boy, who was Mexican.

Since character development was one of Sherin's strengths, he helped Lancaster flesh out his performance, something that rarely happens during filmmaking. The director tried to move him away from the usual gestures and mannerisms. When Burt saw the result of his efforts in the dailies, he was "thrilled," to quote Sherin, "because he had an enormous desire to act well and truthfully." The director cited the sequence leading up to Valdez' killing of the black man as an example of how the collaboration worked: "I was trying to get Burt to open up to him . . . to disarm him with a sense that he would be safe in his hands. And Burt had some problems with that because it was one of the first days we were shooting, and Burt had a kind of natural, coarse aggressiveness toward him. When he finally got it, it was effortless. . . . He had taken his armor off as an actor, he had shown his softness."

Still, Burt was insecure—as evidenced by the good-natured way that he referred to Cypher as "New York actor." Clark got the treatment too. "He used to tease me about the Royal Academy," she recalled. "What does the Royal Academy have to say about this, what does the Royal Academy have to say about that?"

That Lancaster and Sherin worked in tandem on Burt's performance did not mean that they never disagreed. "I love him, but as in all good love affairs, there is an element of hate too," Burt said during filming. "We often had arguments on the top floor of the Grand Hotel in Almería where the whole hotel shook," the director recalled, laughing. "They were head-to-head arguments, and at some points I thought he was going to lift me up and throw me out the window." Sherin did not mind. "I love fighting," he said. "The truth will out. It's in the synthesis that this bastard art form finally realizes itself."

As with Pollack, Lancaster railed against the director in private, but the company knew that Burt had the power on the set—which was not wholly inappropriate since his company was producing the picture. Moreover, he had decades of film experience to Sherin's none. Said Clark, "Burt would know without even seeing dailies when an action scene worked, just by talking to the cameraman. He would know when an actor or a stuntperson or whatever had had it, and you weren't going to get anything more, and Sherin at that point thought that just by doing a lot more takes and a lot more coverage he would make it better." Thus, if it came to a choice of whom to listen to, Clark knew where to turn. "I intuitively trusted Burt for the whole project," she said.

Despite the battles royal, the director and the actor remained, to quote Sherin, "very fast friends."

On March 5, while *Valdez* was nearing completion in Madrid, *Airport* opened at Radio City Music Hall in New York. "It is doubtful there will be the kind of stampede necessary to bail out Universal's investment of $10,000,000," *Variety* predicted. Despite the book's enormous readership, *Airport,* with its star-studded cast, lush production values, and stock characters and situations, was like a dinosaur compared to such concurrent pictures as *M*A*S*H, Bob and Carol and Ted and Alice,* and *Five Easy Pieces.*

Virtually every major critic commented on the antiquated nature of the melodrama. To Joe Rosen of the *New York Morning Telegraph* it seemed "as though it had been made years ago and then immediately was stored away in a vault with a time lock." But, he asserted, "For a change of pace, it is nice." People everywhere thought so too. The Ross Hunter production was not just a hit, it was a blockbuster, the biggest moneymaker in the history of Universal Pictures to that time.

Despite Lancaster's antipathy toward the project, no one could complain about his performance. He was precisely the well-meaning but firm businessman the role required. Ultimately, however, it was the character actors—Van Heflin, Maureen Stapleton, Lloyd Nolan, and above all Helen Hayes—who stole the acting honors. Hayes even won an Academy Award as Best Supporting Actress.

Burt's string of box-office failures ended with *Airport,* but the film was not perceived—nor should it have been—as a Burt Lancaster picture. It did very little, if anything, to boost his stature with the public or within the industry. It did, however, do wonders for his pocketbook. Burt's friend actor Bob Quarry was present when one of his profit participation checks arrived. It was for millions of dollars, and said Quarry, it was only "the first of several."

Lancaster had no sooner returned from Spain than he was back in another Western—as yet another law enforcement officer. But where the Hispanic hero of *Valdez Is Coming* was a champion of the underdog— and an underdog himself—the protagonist of *Lawman,* Jered Maddox, represented the cold, efficient, brutal arm of the law, a man determined to bring to justice the gang of cowboys who shot up his town and killed an old man.

The project came to Burt by way of its thirty-five-year-old British producer-director, Michael Winner.

Winner, who did not know Lancaster, traveled to California to persuade him to do the picture. To his great surprise, Burt reviewed the entire screenplay with him. "It took so long we went into a second day of it," the director recalled, chuckling. But, as they worked, the actor made clear that he was not going to do the picture. "I'm just getting the script better for Gregory Peck," he asserted.

At the end of the first day, Winner went to a Hollywood store that sold movie star photographs and purchased a still of Peck. Then, as he put it, "I drew a big bubble coming out of Gregory Peck's mouth, and it said, 'Thanks, Burt, you're doing a great job.' " The following day, as they began their second working session, he put the envelope with the photo on the actor's desk and waited for him to notice. "Eventually the phone rings," he recalled, "and while he's talking on the phone, he sees the envelope. So, with one hand, he opens it and he takes out the photo and sees Gregory Peck with the bubble coming out of his mouth. And I'm sitting there, trembling. I'm thinking, 'This was not such a good idea.' And he looks at me absolutely icy. Not a flicker. Not a flicker on his face of any kind. And he puts the photo back. He puts the envelope very neatly on his desk. He puts the phone down. And he's about to go through the script, and then he looks at me and he says, 'Did you do that, Winner?' And I said, 'Yes, sir. Yes, sir.' Nothing. And then he says, 'Now here, on page thirty-eight, this line . . .' And he just carried on with the script. . . . His secretary said to me, 'That's absolutely typical.' "

But Winner's larger gambit paid off. By the end of the second day, Lancaster had agreed to do the film.

That Michael Winner had chosen to direct a Western seemed odd. The London-born, Cambridge-educated filmmaker had made a name for himself with impish British pictures, such as 1966's *The Jokers* and the following year's *I'll Never Forget What's 'Is Name*. In 1969, he had tried a more Hollywood-like project, *The Games,* a behind-the-scenes drama about Olympic runners with Ryan O'Neal among the cast, but it was not a success.

Lawman, his first film since *The Games,* had originated with a Canadian named Gerald Wilson—who had convinced Winner to let him write what he later described as "an almost rigidly archetypal Western" but one pushed "to a sense of extreme." Wilson also wanted to make a statement about America in the 1970s. As he explained, "*Lawman* was conceived and written at a time when there was a great deal of law-and-order policy in the United States. I certainly wanted to say that law and order is not the way to administer justice."

Winner, who would arguably make the ultimate film statement about the difference between law and justice in 1974's vigilante movie *Death Wish* (and then beat the subject into the ground with several unfortunate sequels), was drawn to Wilson's theme, but conceded, "It may seem unusual for a British director to want to tackle as American a subject as a Western, but this brief period of American history seems to have a universal and endless allure. Possibly because it was a time when complex actions and emotions could be settled in a simple man-to-man combat in a rather classic way."

Filming took place near Durango, marking Lancaster's third trek to the northern-Mexico locale in search of quintessential images of the Old West. Winner came to love the location, saying, "It was very primitive.

The surrounding countryside was very untouched. It was absolute heaven." Joining the director and the star was an impressive cast that included Lee J. Cobb as Maddox's principal antagonist, rancher Vincent Bronson, and Robert Duvall, Albert Salmi, and J. D. Cannon as three of the ranch hands faced with Maddox' retribution. Several of the other actors had worked with Lancaster before, including Robert Ryan, Sheree North, and, from *Valdez Is Coming,* Richard Jordan. According to Winner, Burt specifically asked for Jordan as the young aspiring gunslinger, and the chemistry between the two actors would serve as the most engaging relationship in the picture.

Winner was an intense worker with a strong sense of his own vision. "Team effort is a lot of people doing what I say," he once proclaimed. A number of actors and technicians found him difficult, but the director genuinely liked Burt. "He's the kindest, dearest man you could ever meet," Winner said in 1994. "He's the most loyal friend. And very humorous. He can occasionally be bad-tempered. He has threatened to kill me a couple of times, but it lasts all of half an hour." The regard was mutual. Lancaster said in 1975 that Winner was a "fast, intelligent director" and "was always in command."

To begin with, the director, like Frankenheimer and Brooks half a decade earlier, was impressed by the actor's physical investment in his role. As Winner recalled, "One day, he came up to me and said, 'Michael, have I got twenty minutes? I'd like to practice falling off my horse.' We were shooting on the Western street in Durango, and I looked up the street and here was this man—he must have been fifty-five or fifty-six then [he was fifty-six]—just getting on the horse, and throwing himself off the horse, getting back on the horse, throwing himself off the horse. And I thought, 'I don't believe this.' I mean, the man is an absolute wonder."

Unlike Ed Sherin, Winner did not work with Lancaster on character development. Of course, Jered Maddox was not a physical and emotional stretch like Bob Valdez. But also Winner was not interested in acting coaching. "You don't take an actor and give him a lesson in acting," the director asserted. "You make him feel comfortable. You suggest the moves, where they might be standing for the camera. And with Burt, you just kind of, as it were, set him down, and he did it."

To Winner, making Burt feel comfortable meant fostering the kind of environment in which he could flourish. "Burt likes a very quiet, controlled set," the director explained. "He likes great order—which is very

Scorpio.[4] He likes everything just so. If the cameraman took too long to set up, he'd say, 'I think he should be ready now, Michael. Let's go,' and we'd walk up in front of the lights, and amazingly, everything would suddenly be ready."

As the director recalled it, he and the star had only one fight while in production. It came when they were filming a scene in which Burt had to "shoot" Robert Duvall's horse. For the first couple of takes, he used a pistol. But on the third, he grabbed his rifle, a Winchester .73. When Winner pointed out the inconsistency, Burt, to quote the director, "went absolutely hysterical. He said, 'What do you know about Westerns?' He screamed hysterically, you see. And he grabbed me by the lapels, and he said, 'I'll kill you, I'll kill you. What did I shoot this horse with?' And I said, 'A Winchester .73, sir, there's no doubt of it. You're absolutely right.' And the script girl said to me, 'But, Michael, it won't cut together.' And I said, 'Well, I'm not going to die on a mountain in Mexico over which gun this fellow shoots the horse with. As far as I'm concerned, he can blow it up with a hydrogen bomb. Let's just carry on living.' He then came in for the looping—this is about four months later—and I said, 'Burt, if you look very closely you'll see a hint of the wrong gun here, but it's all right. We cut away to a passing buzzard. Because you threatened to kill me over changing the gun.' And he said, 'I don't remember that, Winner. That's very careless of you.' "

After shooting *Valdez* and *Lawman* back-to-back, Lancaster took a nineteen-month hiatus from filmmaking. During that interval, he kept busy with a variety of personal and professional endeavors.

For starters, he sold his home in Bel-Air. "I realized I was living in a house that required five servants and cost seventy thousand dollars a year to maintain, including taxes," he said. "All that for two people [him and Jackie]! So I sold the house and I'm renting a house at the beach. It's not cheap—three thousand dollars a month—but I can manage with only one servant."

Next, he lent his distinctive baritone to two documentaries, a government short on malnutrition in impoverished children and a feature-length biography of Martin Luther King Jr., *King: A Filmed Record . . . Montgomery to Memphis*.

Then, on April 9, *Valdez Is Coming* opened. Although it offered the novelty of a humble Hispanic constable as its hero and attempted to make a thematic statement about racism, it was widely regarded, to

4. People born in early November are, astrologically, Scorpios. Winner would remember that when choosing a name for his second feature with Lancaster.

quote Leo Mishkin of the *New York Morning Telegraph,* as "a cliché-ridden, machine-made, assembly-line product." Kevin Thomas of the *Los Angeles Times* even argued that it was Lancaster's "first real comedown."

Burt's transition to a character role did not go unnoticed, and as *Variety* put it, "He certainly retains both physical and thespic charisma for such a move." But, his work with Sherin notwithstanding, he never truly disappeared into the role as genuinely gifted character actors do, and his accent—especially compared with those of his fellow players, Frank Silvera and Hector Elizondo—failed to ring true.

Just as *Valdez* was debuting in New York, Lancaster went into rehearsal in Los Angeles for what was by far the most ambitious endeavor of his long hiatus, playing Peter Stuyvesant, the crusty, peg-legged governor of New Amsterdam, in *Knickerbocker Holiday* for the San Francisco Civic Light Opera. He chose the Kurt Weill–Maxwell Anderson musical over another, concurrent offer: playing Harold Hill, the fast-talking salesman, in a Las Vegas production of *The Music Man.* "I was getting bored," said the actor on his decision to return to the stage. "Very rarely do I get something I want to do in films. I wouldn't give up movies, but I wanted to do something different."

The role of Stuyvesant had been created in 1938 by Walter Huston, and according to Joshua Logan, the director of the original Broadway production, the show "became a smash hit because of Walter singing 'September Song,' " one of the most haunting ballads in the history of the American musical theater. But Logan also recalled that the show "got terrible reviews" and rightly so. Even in an era when musicals tended to be loose amalgams of song, dance, jokes, and story, *Knickerbocker Holiday* was pretty flimsy.

Behind the corn librettist/lyricist Maxwell Anderson had used the political situation in 1647 to comment upon the rise of fascism in his own day. To bring the allusions up-to-date—specifically with regard to the ongoing conflict in Vietnam—Lancaster, the show's director, Albert Marre, and Burt's friend Roland Kibbee rewrote the book. The strife between the whites and the Indians, for example, became "Algonquinization," an unmistakable reference to Vietnamization, the policy in Southeast Asia of then-president Richard Nixon. They also tried to forge a greater integration between the book and the score, in keeping with the modern notion of a musical. But there was only so much they could do, given the underpinnings of the thirty-two-year-old material. "Presentationally, there was not a lot of difference between it and, say,

The Great Waltz,[5] which I did for the same people," said Anita Gillette, who costarred as the musical's ingenue. "It was not handled in any kind of modern way."

Lancaster had not worked in the legitimate theater for twenty-five years. Film acting, done in short takes with close-ups and no audience to worry about, places very different demands on an actor than does a stage performance, which must be larger-than-life so that it will "read" at the back of the house—and then be repeated night after night. Lancaster embraced the challenge. For guidance, he had a seasoned veteran in Albert Marre, who had directed three major musicals on Broadway: *Kismet* in 1953, *Milk and Honey* in 1961, and *Man of La Mancha* in 1965. According to the director, the biggest challenge in working with Lancaster was—not surprisingly—getting him to adjust to the demands of the stage. He said that he had the actor's trust right from the start and, in 1993, remembered their association as pleasant, albeit professional.

To strengthen his singing voice, Burt consulted his old friend Frank Sinatra, but according to Gillette, a veteran of Broadway musicals dating back to 1959, the star never quite felt comfortable with his numbers. "He had problems with the singing," said the actress, "because he was nervous about it. When he wasn't nervous, he actually sang quite well. He has a very sweet voice and on pitch." Marre encouraged him to talk-sing some of the material, à la Rex Harrison in *My Fair Lady,* but, said Gillette, "He kept trying to sing it more than he spoke it," as if it were a point of honor.

Learning to walk on a peg leg, with his real leg tied behind his back, was also a drain. "That strap becomes a sack of cement," said Burt at the time. "I simply have to defeat it. Then it isn't there anymore." Sometimes, when his knee was particularly bothering him, Gillette had to help him offstage after their second-act scene together. Even then, Burt would remain focused on his singing. "He was constantly checking with me," she asserted. " 'Was it okay? Did I do it right? What could I do to make it better?' "

Burt and the pretty, lively young actress struck up a friendship during the run of *Knickerbocker Holiday*—which opened at the Curran Theatre in San Francisco on May 11, 1971. Eventually, Gillette became a friend of Jackie's as well. When the company moved into the Dorothy Chandler Pavilion for its eight-week stint in Los Angeles—commencing

5. *The Great Waltz* was an operetta derived from the music of Johann Strauss.

June 29—Gillette even stayed occasionally at Burt's rented house in Malibu.

As for his performance in *Knickerbocker Holiday,* Dan Sullivan of the *Los Angeles Times* said, "Oddly enough, his singing isn't at all bad. It's the acting side of the role that gives him trouble. . . . He is simply not at home in sly, twinkling, mock-ferocious comedy. Lines that ought to come out with deft irony sound like heavy camp." *Variety* maintained just the opposite: "He . . . handles the tyrannical personality of Stuyvesant with aplomb, but the show's highlight ('September Song') is his weakest point." Leo Mishkin of the *New York Morning Telegraph* probably summed up the experience best when he wrote, "The net impression given by the film star in such an assignment puts one in mind of the classic line about the talking dog: it's not how well he does it, but that he can do it at all."

On August 6, while performing *Knickerbocker Holiday* in Los Angeles, Burt was arrested for drunk driving. It happened in Malibu as he and Jackie were coming home from a performance. According to the *New York Post,* he had been "weaving across a double line while driving his sports car" and was taken into custody after refusing to submit to a sobriety test.

In retrospect, Jackie said that he was not drunk that night but tired. However, she added that he did not have to be inebriated to perform erratically behind the wheel, because his mind tended to drift to other concerns. "He would slow down and speed up," she recalled, "and sometimes he'd wander all over the road. I mean, it was nutty. And he was stone-cold sober when he did those things."

On the night in question, she said he lost his temper because the officer was, in her words, "kind of smart-assy." It was Lancaster's attitude that precipitated the arrest. Eventually, the case went to trial, and Burt was acquitted.

Two days before the incident in Malibu, *Lawman* debuted. It was even less successful at the box office than *Valdez Is Coming.*

The Durango locations and production designer Stan Jolley's sets lent a wonderful, authentic texture to the picture, but the *New York Post's* Archer Winsten was correct when he called it "a Western of simple confrontations." From the opening sequence, in which Robert Duvall, Albert Salmi, and their cronies shoot up Lancaster's town—a scene that immediately calls to mind Frederic Remington's great sculpture *Comin'*

Through the Rye—to the final bloody confrontation on Main Street, *Lawman* is basically a compendium of previous Westerns rolled up into one violent homage.

There was, however, a kernel of intrigue, never fully developed, in the byplay between Lancaster's Maddox and Lee J. Cobb's Bronson. The rancher, ostensibly the villain of the piece, was portrayed as a rational, peace-loving businessman who believes that every problem can be solved at the bargaining table. By contrast, the lawman, ostensibly the hero, was so obsessed with finding his quarry that he lost all perspective. Lancaster added to the character's antiheroic posture by playing him ramrod straight, with a hawklike countenance and steely eyes.

Finally, on January 17, 1972, Burt resumed his film career—with yet another Western, his third in a row. But *Ulzana's Raid* was as different from *Lawman* as the Michael Winner film had been from *Valdez Is Coming*.

"It was about Vietnam," said Lancaster's costar Bruce Davison.

It had been four years since the making of *Castle Keep* and still the war dragged on—with America's military might rendered impotent in the face of a small but fiercely independent indigenous population. *Ulzana's Raid* addressed the implications of such a conflict. The film's screenwriter, Alan Sharp, hailed from Scotland and could thus view the U.S. position in Southeast Asia from a European perspective. "To me, the Vietnam War was just another imperial war," he said in retrospect. "The Americans were getting stuck defending their vital interests as they defined them. Like the British had done, and the Germans had done."

Sharp, whose first feature had been a crime drama, 1971's *The Last Run,* fashioned his allegory in the form of a cavalry patrol in the wilds of Arizona during the 1880s, with the troopers in pursuit of a band of marauding Apaches led by the cunning Ulzana (played by Joaquin Martinez). The troop is commanded by a young, idealistic lieutenant, DeBuin, played by Davison, with the assistance of a veteran sergeant (Richard Jaeckel) and two scouts, an inscrutable Indian, Ke-Ni-Tay (Jorge Luke), and a grizzled, world-weary Anglo (Lancaster).

"I had been very, very interested in the frontier Apache West," Sharp recalled. "If somebody said, 'Tell me the three places you don't want to be,' I didn't want to be Armenian in Turkey in 1917, I didn't want to be Jewish during the Third Reich, and I didn't want to be a soldier in fucking Arizona in the 1880s."

Sharp took the position that neither the whites nor the Indians were inherently good or bad. They were simply different from one another, and neither could get past its own ethnocentricity. It would fall to Lancaster's character, McIntosh, to articulate Sharp's philosophy. The scout accepts the inscrutability of the Apache without hatred. As he tells De-Buin, "It's like hating the desert because there ain't no water on it. I can get by just by being plenty scared of them." It was a notion that appealed to Lancaster. Not only would *Ulzana's Raid* give him the chance to make a subtle comment on Vietnam, but he could also articulate his own sense of cultural relativism. McIntosh, he said later, "reflected my own feelings about life."

Ulzana's Raid reunited Burt with Robert Aldrich.

It had been eighteen years since *Vera Cruz* wrapped. During the interim, the director had made nineteen pictures, including *What Ever Happened to Baby Jane?, Flight of the Phoenix,* and *The Dirty Dozen.* He had also opened his own studio but had been forced to sell it—at a loss—in 1971. *Ulzana's Raid* was his first work-for-hire job since then, and he had to take the assignment at a terrible drop in salary. In a noteworthy act of generosity, Lancaster contributed $50,000 out of his percentage of the picture's gross to enhance the director's earnings.

Initially, Aldrich and Lancaster had wanted to film in Mexico, as they had done with *Vera Cruz,* but Sharp, who also served as the picture's associate producer, said that Universal, which released the film, insisted on the use of U.S. locations in order to pacify Hollywood's technical guilds. The majority of the action would be filmed around Nogales, Arizona, on the Mexican border, but the film's climax would take place in the Valley of Fire, Nevada, the locus of *The Professionals.* Said Richard Jaeckel, who had not worked with Lancaster since *Come Back, Little Sheba,* "It was a tough location, very tough." Because of the cost differential between U.S. and Mexican film production, the original shooting schedule was reduced by two weeks. This was particularly galling to Lancaster, who insisted that the quality of filming not be affected by the change. Aldrich, by contrast, was determined to finish on time. Their diverse agendas put the star and the director on something of a collision course, and the first clash came swiftly.

They were shooting an early expositional scene, set on the cavalry outpost before the troopers go after Ulzana, and at the end of the day, Burt did not think the scene had been adequately covered. Aldrich disagreed. Finally, the director offered to ask Universal to keep the set intact, and if after viewing the dailies, they still felt they needed more footage, they would go back and reshoot. "And Burt," Sharp recalled, "let it be known that that was total, fuckin' bullshit, that nobody was ever going to go back to Universal, reconstruct the set, get the actors in, and shoot it again. This was Bob jerkin' him off, basically, was how he saw it."

The two men met in Aldrich's hotel suite the following Sunday, their day off, to discuss the matter. Sharp, who was present as well, described the encounter: "Burt came in the door like *Brute Force,* and the first thing he said was, 'You little fat cocksucker, do you think I believed that shit about keeping the sets? Do you think I was born yesterday?' And Bob was just sittin' there, grinning like 'I told you. I knew this bastard from way back.' So they argued, and Bob won, if you like." But Sharp understood Lancaster's attitude, saying, "He knew the business. He probably knew Bob's problem, but that wasn't *his* problem. His problem was to get the movie the way he wanted to get it." The screenwriter added that Burt had reduced his usual asking fee to be in the picture in return for a percentage of the profits—"points," to use the parlance of the industry. That, in essence, "made him a silent producer, with a big financial stake in the piece and a lot of clout."

Other disagreements between Lancaster and Aldrich would follow. Typically, when disputes arose, the company would take a short break while the director and the star, at some remove from everyone else, thrashed out the problem. Jaeckel respected Lancaster for voicing his opinions because, as he put it, "Here was a star who was only interested in doing it better." He also noted that Lancaster was not intransigent. If someone could "show Burt that it was better this way than what he was doing, Burt would go for it." To Lancaster, such conflicts were really nothing more than the normal course of moviemaking and had no bearing on his regard for Aldrich—nor, for that matter, did they affect Aldrich's attitude toward him. "I think that they respected each other deep down inside," said Jaeckel, "because each represented to the other a way to get things done at a pretty fair level [of craftsmanship]."

Lancaster's quest for excellence caused him to lose patience occasionally while *Ulzana* was in production—as he had so often in the past. One member of the company said during filming, "Lancaster was very pleasant, the perfect gentleman, his first few days on the set, but it is a different story now. We keep away from him."

As usual, Burt was toughest on himself. "He started asking me if I thought he was being too much Burt Lancaster," recalled Sharp. The screenwriter was impressed by the star's desire to depart from his screen persona. Bruce Davison was less so—at least in the early days of production. "He's not doing anything," the young actor thought. "I'm going to steal this movie right away from him." Ironically, Burt had drawn the same conclusion early in his relationship with Gary Cooper during the making of *Vera Cruz*. And just as he changed his mind when he saw Coop in the rushes, so Davison said about Burt, "But then you see the movie, and you realize that he doesn't have to do anything. He just stands there."

On their last day together, Lancaster gave Davison a bit of advice. Calling the young man over during a break between takes, he said, "You're a hell of an actor. That goes without saying. But I have to tell you something. You don't use your rehearsal time properly. You try to please the soundman. You try to please the extras. And you shoot your wad, so by the time we get to the shoot, *the* moment, you're already over the top, you're falling all over yourself. Son, it's like making love to a woman. You can't try to come all at once."

On that note, the picture wrapped on March 11.

Scorpio was prophetic, maintained Michael Winner in 1994. "It showed the CIA doing things that nobody at the time believed they did. And that now everybody believes they do." Specifically, it was about a longtime CIA operative named Cross earmarked for assassination by his own agency. It falls to a young friend and former colleague—the title character—to carry out the execution. As he follows Cross on a cat-and-mouse chase across Western Europe, a Russian, the so-called enemy, tries to save the aging operative.

United Artists, which had acquired the property by television writer David W. Rintels, lined up Lancaster to play Cross. Winner, with whom the company had struck a multipicture deal at the time of *Lawman*, would direct with Walter Mirisch producing.

Winner liked Rintels' idea, but he hated the screenplay, which contained incidents that the director simply could not credit. One, for instance, had someone garroted in view of hundreds of people. Rintels rewrote, but Winner was still dissatisfied. Unable to effect further changes because producer Mirisch did not share his concerns, he decided to withdraw from the project. Lancaster was sorry to lose him but understood. It was only after, in Winner's words, "United Artists removed Walter Mirisch from the project and they handed the whole thing to me" that he agreed to stay on.[6]

6. Mirisch, however, retained the producer's credit for the picture. That was part of UA's arrangement with Winner.

Now that he was in charge, Winner brought in Gerald Wilson, the screenwriter of *Lawman,* for a major overhaul of the script. Although Rintels would be given screen credit, Wilson essentially started from scratch, retaining only the original idea and some of Rintels' characters.

It is surprising, in light of Winner's dissatisfaction with the original property, that Lancaster agreed to do it. "By that time I don't think he was getting, in truth, alternatives that were much better," the director conceded. Even Burt admitted that the picture was "nothing incisive, just a lot of action," and referred to it as "one of those things you do as part of your living, but you try to avoid doing them as much as you can."

Given Lancaster's previous experience with the federal government during the making of *Birdman of Alcatraz* and *Seven Days in May,* he no doubt expected the CIA to balk at cooperating with a film that cast the agency in such a dubious light, but, said Winner, "They gave us permission [to film there] immediately, and without even asking to see the script." Burt was, to quote the director, "very impressed indeed."

Filming began in Washington, D.C., on May 29, 1972, roughly two and a half months after *Ulzana's Raid* wrapped. In addition to the CIA's headquarters, the company shot scenes at the Watergate hotel and office complex—where Lancaster, Winner, and Alain Delon, who was cast as the young assassin, were lodging. At the time—the late spring and summer of 1972—the place had yet to lend its name to the worst political scandal in American history. "In fact," said Winner, "we were staying in Watergate the night it was robbed."[7] Not only that, but according to Fred Emery, author of 1994's *Watergate,* the burglars encountered Lancaster and Delon in the hours preceding the break-in.

Shortly after the infamous burglary, the *Scorpio* company wrapped in Washington and headed for Europe, where filming would take place in London, Vienna, and Paris. In Vienna, Burt and Delon—working together for the first time since *The Leopard*—were joined by the picture's third major star, Paul Scofield. Lancaster's colleague from *The Train* was playing the Soviet spy who tries to help Cross. Burt had enormous respect and affection for the distinguished British thespian, saying during filming, "I'm a movie star. He's a great actor. That's the difference." Indeed, according to Winner, Burt "was very keen to have Paul Scofield" in the picture. Scofield, in turn, cited his friendship with the American as a major reason for accepting the role. So congenial, in fact, were the three stars and Winner with them that the director said in ret-

7. June 16, 1972.

rospect, making *Scorpio* "was really very nice. Because everybody liked everybody."

By the time the company wrapped in mid-August, *Ulzana's Raid* had been cut and scored. Burt reviewed the footage and then insisted on reediting. It is not often that a star who is neither the producer nor the director of a picture can make such a demand. But perhaps because of Burt's association with *Airport,* Universal's giant moneymaker, the studio agreed to let him do what he wished, providing no rescoring was required.

Burt invited Alan Sharp to join him. "And in the cutting room," said the screenwriter, "if I ever had any doubts about Lancaster's knowledge of the business, they were soon put to rest. I mean, he wasn't there to fuck over Bob's film, but he had ideas that he wanted to express." Sharp agreed with the changes, although he conceded, "At the end of the day, because he was still working with Bob's footage and he couldn't go too far because of the score, it all got to be fairly minor."

The picture opened on November 15. Virtually none of the critics caught the Vietnam analogy. Because the conflict had ended for the Americans only weeks earlier, they may have lacked the requisite distance to see how the Western paralleled the situation in Southeast Asia.

As a Western, several critics found it wanting. Frances Herridge of the *New York Post,* for example, noted that it lacked "some of the sizzling adventure common to such Army-Indian confrontations." But the more astute agreed with Vincent Canby of *The New York Times,* who found it "so consistently unsentimental and provocative that it should restore some measure of faith in the future of the action film, which, except for the films made for black audiences, would be practically extinct today."

As for Burt's performance, *Variety* noted, "Lancaster's physical appearance may draw some gasps from those who recall his early roles, where his imposing and manly grace lent a virile elegance to his characterizations. Herein, a deliberate attempt has been made to strip away what remains of the past, and it provides the basis for a credible and effective shift into a wide range of future castings." Andrew Sarris asserted simply in the *Village Voice,* "Burt Lancaster gives the performance of his career as the world-weary scout." Given *Elmer Gantry* and *Birdman of Alcatraz,* and other noteworthy efforts, Sarris may have gone too far, but Burt's performance was clean, simple, and honest. He had, in fact, realized his own ambition—to become a character actor.

Unfortunately, *Ulzana's Raid* failed to find its audience. But at least two critics, Sarris and Gene Siskel, remembered it when it came time to put together their year-end lists of the best pictures of 1972.

The string of box-office disappointments was starting to add up. Jon Cypher recalled that, a year or so after *Valdez* wrapped, a producer asked him, "Do you think Burt Lancaster is still bankable?" Taken aback, Cypher replied, "Sure, he's still a major star." But, in retrospect, the actor said, "The perception was that his career had really stalled."

Arguably, Burt reached a low ebb with his next two projects, *The Midnight Man* and *Executive Action*.

"It was a concession to me, because I wanted to make some money," Roland Kibbee said of *The Midnight Man*. "It certainly wasn't the kind of project Burt would have picked out for himself."

Based on a mystery novel entitled *The Midnight Lady and the Mourning Man* by David Anthony, the project focused on an ex-cop named Jim Slade. Just released from prison for killing his wife's lover, he becomes involved in a murder investigation at the college campus where he is employed as a night watchman. Lancaster described it as "a straightforward whodunit but with some light comment on police corruption."

Not only would Burt be playing for the first time a gumshoe in the old Bogart tradition, he would cowrite the screenplay—with Kibbee. The friends would also share the producer's duties on the $2.5-million project, which would be released under the auspices of Burt's Norlan Productions in association with Universal Pictures. And, most surprising of all, Lancaster would direct the picture, nineteen years after *The Kentuckian*. "I've sort of been directing ever since," he conceded with self-deprecating humor before *The Midnight Man* went into production, "but this one's official. I'm cutting my ancient eyeteeth on it." On a more serious note, he said during the making of *Scorpio*, "When you reach my sort of age and have done so much acting-wise, you begin to look around and wonder what to do next. I feel it's about time I made a move towards directing again." As with the writing and producing, Kibbee was listed as the codirector.

As *The Midnight Man* was set in a college town, Lancaster and Kibbee chose to film in Anderson, South Carolina, and on the campus of nearby

Clemson University. It was not the liveliest of locations. Said Harris Yulin, who was playing the local sheriff in the picture, "It was southern bars and Holiday Inns where everybody gathers. I feel like I've been in a thousand of them." Supporting the leading actors, which, in addition to Burt and Yulin, included Susan Clark, Cameron Mitchell, and Burt's son Bill, were such local amateurs as Sen. Weems Oliver Baskin III, who portrayed a bartender, and Eleanor Ross, the superintendent of the local board of education. For the pros, filming with such an eclectic cast and crew offered a welcome change of pace. Yulin, for example, found the company "an interesting group, all kinds of people, people from different disciplines and different worlds. So it was kind of nice."

By the time filming began on February 18, 1973, nearly three years had elapsed since *Valdez* had wrapped. Susan Clark, playing Lancaster's parole officer/love interest in *The Midnight Man,* found Burt even more subdued than he had been in Spain. "And he was under a lot of stress," she added.

Yulin thought that Burt, like his character in *The Midnight Man,* was "a man betrayed," that he had been disappointed by numerous friends and colleagues over the years—perhaps because of his keen sense of loyalty combined with his exacting professional standards. "I don't think he felt at ease with people," Yulin concluded. To which Clark added, "There was a part of Burt that nobody was going to get."

Still, Yulin liked the star. "We had a very good working relationship," he said years later. "He was very generous. I felt that there was this mutual respect." But Lancaster was not above teasing the younger actor, as he had Jon Cypher during the making of *Valdez* and perhaps for the same reason—both had strong theatrical backgrounds, Yulin having done Shakespeare, Shaw, Chekhov, and other classics on the stage. "Does it bother you that I'm a millionaire?" Burt would ask his costar, gloating. Then, he would cajole in mock deference, "Mr. Yulin, do you mind. I don't mean to rush you. Are you ready? Mr. Yulin is ready. Let's shoot."

Obviously, the many hats that Lancaster wore during filming prevented him from concentrating as fully on his performance as he had with roles in the past. Even Burt recognized that, saying at the time, "There's a big problem in directing yourself. You become so immersed in a scene as the director that you don't respond on the same acting level as the other actors when you switch from directing."

In theory, Kibbee was his codirector, but, as Yulin put it, "Kibbee was not about to step forward and take charge when Burt was around." It was highly unusual for two people even to attempt to direct a film, because a director's primary role is to infuse an entire production with his or her vision; by definition, that is a one-person job. Why Lancaster and Kibbee decided to share the position is a mystery. Most likely, Burt had hoped to use his friend for a backup, as he had Jim Hill on *The Kentuckian*. In any event, although the project was billed as a collaboration, Yulin maintained, "Kibbee did most of the writing, and Burt did most of the directing."

Yulin also noted that the two men "would fight like sons of bitches on the set. I mean, Burt would go ballistic at Kibbee. . . . And Kibbee would throw up his hands and walk off." Then Yulin added, "But it didn't mean anything. I mean, they were together five minutes later. I think Kibbee allowed Burt that room, because that was his nature." Indeed, no matter how much they argued, Lancaster and Kibbee were the dearest of friends. Clark observed a "mutual respect and mutual need" between them. With Kibbee, she said, Burt "got somebody who could actually sit down and write the script. He got somebody to whom he could bounce ideas off of—what would and wouldn't work. He got an ally as well as a friend. I think Kibbee loved him, and Burt loved *him*."

As for Lancaster's directing, Yulin said, "He enjoyed setting up the shots. He enjoyed deciding what shot we were going to do, and how we were going to cover the scene, and so on and so forth, the nuts and bolts of directing." But by the end of filming, the work was taking its toll. As Susan Clark found out.

As she recalled it, they met one evening to review the final scene of the picture. "And he was really tired," she said. "I think the stress had gotten to him." Still, the discussion was relaxed and friendly—until Burt started to drink. Then, Clark continued, "He went off, and it was like a missile, and it was [aimed] at me. I don't remember quite why, but I remember the shock of being attacked, viciously attacked—verbally, viciously attacked. Screaming at me from one end of this dining table to the next. . . . And I was comatose. It had come from nowhere."

The company shot around Clark for a couple of days. Finally, Lancaster apologized. "He knew he was apologizing for unconscionable behavior," she asserted, "but he wasn't quite sure what he'd said. It was on such a visceral level that the words were irrelevant." Thereafter, Clark's relationship with Lancaster was not the same. As she put it, "It was kind of sad, because what happened in that attack was a loss of trust. Not respect. I mean, other people have lost their temper, and I've lost my temper too. But trust." Reflecting on the incident, Yulin agreed that the star's reaction had been totally out of proportion. It prompted the actor to say with a rueful grin, "I was very glad that Burt liked me. I would really not want to be in the position where he didn't like me."

The Midnight Man wrapped around the beginning of April. Several weeks later, on the nineteenth, *Scorpio* debuted.

The critics hated it. Judith Crist even advised readers of *New York* that the screenplay "sounded like a *Get Smart* script but took itself seriously."[8] No one, however, quibbled with Lancaster's performance. As Jay Cocks observed in *Time,* "If *Scorpio* does little else, it proves that Lancaster, after all this time, still has an enviable store of vigor. At fifty-nine, he is a little paunchier, a little slower, and he breathes harder on the run; but he can still haul himself up a scaffold with the best of them."

In retrospect, the picture was not as bad as the critics made it out to be. The script offered several clever gambits plus an exciting chase scene that followed Burt and Delon through the warehouse district of Vienna. Moreover, Winner made excellent use of the film's myriad locales, with cafés, parks, broad avenues, back alleys, apartment complexes, and other colorful venues serving as backdrops for the action. But, despite its strong points, *Scorpio* came at the end of a long string of spy thrillers—from the lavishly produced, arch-toned entries in the James Bond series (which that same year saw Roger Moore take over from Sean Connery) to the hip, mocking Bond rip-offs featuring Dean Martin and James Coburn to the ostensibly realistic melodramas like *The Spy Who Came In from the Cold* and *The Ipcress File. Scorpio* was simply not strong enough to rise above the apathy. The new game in town—thanks in large measure to Lancaster's own *Airport*—was the disaster picture. In 1973, the year of *Scorpio's* release, *The Poseidon Adventure,* about a capsized luxury liner, grossed $40 million.

While *Scorpio* sought to cast doubt on the moral integrity of the CIA, *Executive Action,* which Lancaster started filming a few weeks after the spy thriller's release, cast a net of suspicion over the nation's entire power elite, arguing that the assassination of President Kennedy had been the result of a right-wing conspiracy.

Executive Action had been in development as far back as 1970, when

---

8. *Get Smart* was a 1960s television sitcom that spoofed the spy genre with comic Don Adams as an inept agent named Maxwell Smart.

Donald Sutherland commissioned the screenplay from attorney Mark Lane, one the foremost critics of the Warren Report, and Donald Freed, who had written a play about the Rosenberg spy case. Among those to whom Sutherland gave the script was Edward Lewis, the producer (with Kirk Douglas) of *Seven Days in May* and (with John Franken- heimer) of *The Gypsy Moths.* "The screenplay knocked me over," Lewis recalled. So much so that he took over the project when Sutherland was unable to secure financing.

Concerned that Lane and Freed's screenplay offered too much un- substantiated theory, Lewis sought a rewrite from Dalton Trumbo, who had written five screenplays for the producer, starting with the 1960 epic *Spartacus.* "I've never believed in the conspiracy theory of his- tory," Trumbo recalled. "When Ed Lewis came to me with some material on the assassination and said he wanted me to do a script that sug- gested conspiracy, I told him I just wasn't his boy." But a perusal of the Warren Commission report and the other literature in the field changed his mind. He was particularly impressed by the home movie shot by Abraham Zapruder during the assassination. As Trumbo put it, "The public has never seen the uncut version of that film, which is a shocking convincer. It clearly shows Kennedy was hit from two different direc- tions. If that's the case, there must have been at least two assassins— hence, a conspiracy." What Trumbo produced was a drama that placed responsibility for the assassination in the hands of a group of powerful businessmen (played by Robert Ryan, Will Geer, and John Anderson) who were opposed to Kennedy's stands on civil rights, Vietnam, and the nuclear test-ban treaty with the Soviets.

In addition to script problems, Lewis faced the prospect of being un- able to insure the production against potential libel suits. "Eventually," explained Steve Jaffe, the film's associate producer and technical ad- viser, "after the producers had submitted a document several hundred pages long that contained all their material about the assassination, Lloyds of London insured the film." Then there was the budget. After encountering the same studio indifference that had discouraged Sutherland, Lewis managed to raise $500,000 by putting up his house as collateral—against which even the $2.5 million for *The Midnight Man* looked expansive.[9] Finally came the matter of casting. What star would be willing to work on such sensitive material for a percentage of the profits instead of a large fee? An obvious choice was Burt, whom Lewis cast as Farrington, the conspirators' operations director. "I struggled with the idea as to whether I should do this kind of thing or not," Burt

9. *Executive Action* would ultimately be distributed by National General.

confessed later. Like Lewis and Trumbo he was persuaded by the ever-expanding literature on the assassination.

Under what *Variety*'s Steve Toy called "a rare cloak of secrecy," *Executive Action* went before the cameras in May of 1973. Lewis and director David Miller had wanted to film in Dallas, the site of the assassination, but, said production designer Kurt Axtel, "We couldn't get a film permit." A small crew sneaked into the Texas community to get some badly needed footage for overviews and establishing shots, but otherwise, the picture was filmed in the greater Los Angeles area. "We used more than ninety different locations," said Miller, "and I've never heard of such a thing before, although I have directed thirty motion pictures."

Four years older than Lancaster, Miller had started as an editor; his first feature as a director, *Billy the Kid* starring Robert Taylor, came in 1941. But it was his work on Lewis' *Lonely Are the Brave* that led to his hiring for *Executive Action.* Although Lancaster was occasionally irked by the cut-rate nature of the production—on which many members of the crew were holding down several jobs—he and Miller enjoyed a good rapport. In Axtel's opinion, the star even "became [like] a director-producer on the film. He was very assertive. He suggested this, this, and this, and David Miller listened." Axtel added, "I think a good director listens to a good actor—and Burt has so much experience, he knows what he's talking about." Later Miller would say Burt "was marvelous to work with. He never acted like a star on the set—he was one of the family. He had terrific teamwork with the other actors, and he made some very helpful suggestions to me." In particular, Miller noted Lancaster's relationship with Robert Ryan, with whom Burt had previously costarred in *The Professionals* and *Lawman,* saying they "were very close friends, and that contributed to both their performances."

Thirty days after shooting began, *Executive Action* wrapped—on budget and two days ahead of schedule. A few weeks later, Robert Ryan died of cancer.

Lewis and Miller put *Executive Action* through its postproduction paces with unusual speed, and by November 22, 1973, the ten-year anniversary of Kennedy's assassination, the picture was on the nation's movie screens. "A year ago, our big problem would have been credibility," said Lewis. "Who would have believed in a criminal political conspiracy in the United States?" Then, he added, along "came Watergate and the credibility of the film increased a millionfold."

Many of the critics did not think so. Charles Champlin of the *Los Angeles Times* found *Executive Action* "surprisingly unconvincing," while his counterpart on *The New York Times*, Vincent Canby, argued that "even to people who are prepared to accept some sort of conspiracy theory, including myself, this manner of fiction simply isn't good enough. In spite of the rather pious, unexciting, low-keyed professionalism with which *Executive Action* has been put together, it is fiction of a gross and shabby order." Several also found the timing of the release unfortunate. "Aren't we having enough presidential troubles at the moment?" asked Stanley Kauffmann in the *New Republic*.[10]

Beyond the issues of credibility and timing, there was the quality of the execution. Here too many found *Executive Action* wanting, notably Pauline Kael of *The New Yorker,* who called it "so graceless it's beyond using even as a demonstration of ineptitude."

Thus, the picture disappeared without a ripple. It would take until 1991 and Oliver Stone's *JFK,* a better-written, better-executed, and more probing conspiracy-theory drama, to spark the kind of national debate that the makers of *Executive Action* had hoped to engender.

10. Just a month before the film's release, the Watergate scandal had reached a crisis with President Nixon's firing of then-Watergate special prosecutor Archibald Cox, an act that resulted in the concurrent resignations of his attorney general, Elliot Richardson, and, the deputy attorney general William Ruckelshaus. Immediately thereafter, the clamor for Nixon's impeachment increased dramatically.

CHAPTER SEVENTEEN

"As Superstardom Fades"

Around mid-1973, Burt and Jackie moved to Rome, a decision probably precipitated by the actor's next project, *Moses, the Lawgiver,* which would be partly filmed there. "Burt loved Rome very much," said Claudia Cardinale. "After *The Leopard,* he fell in love with the country. He loved the culture, the art, the painting. I think he wanted to understand, to know better, the people of the country." Moreover, the Italians loved *him.* Playing the prince of Salina had made him a national hero.

The apartment that Lancaster acquired was in the old part of the city, near the celebrated Trevi fountain. Given its location, said Burt, "we couldn't do anything to the outside; you're forbidden to make any exterior changes that will alter the look of antiquity, even to adding a balcony or an extra room." In time, however, he would completely redesign the interior, using mostly local artisans.

Burt relished the energy, the language, and the foods of the local people. They were familiar. After all, he had grown up among Italian immigrants in East Harlem. By the time *The Leopard* had wrapped, he could speak a bit of the language, and as he would boast in 1982, "I've mastered the skill of preparing pasta, which so many Americans ruin by overcooking. And all of my sauces are authentic, whether I'm serving spaghetti carbonara or *matriciana.*" Many a coworker over the years got to savor his cooking, and actor Rod Steiger spoke for them all when he said, "He makes a hell of a plate of spaghetti." Burt also did a bit of gardening. As he said proudly, "I grow my own herbs—basil, rosemary, oregano—just as the Italians do, and I plant flowers in between, which is an Italian custom."

His relationship with Jackie, however, was not quite as placid as his lifestyle. She was not the kind of woman to live blithely in Burt's shadow. Alan Sharp described her as "kind of tough and kind of practical and kind of street and kind of common, and Burt would occasionally say things like, 'You don't want to cross swords with Jackie. She'll fell you as soon as look at you.' "

Given Jackie's independent streak and Burt's temper, they were bound to clash—and they did. "He and Jackie had terrible, terrible knock-down-drag-out, hitting-people-over-the-head-with-a-bottle kind of fights, which mostly she would win," recalled Anita Gillette. "In restaurants. In public places. She's a real hot-tempered woman." To which a friend of Burt and Norma's added with some bias, "Oh, God, that was horrible, that whole relationship. They were the Maggie and Jiggs of the world."[1] Susan Clark recalled, by way of example, that during the making of *Valdez,* Burt and Jackie had gotten into a fight in their hotel suite in Almería and in Clark's words, he "put his fist through a wall and had to have it repaired."

In addition to the battles royal, Burt cheated on Jackie, just as he had on Norma. "He loved to go to bed with his leading lady," Bone recalled. "He would say, 'Remember, I love *you.*'" But she was not pacified. Moreover, she was not allowed the same latitude. At one point, after they had been together for years, Burt thought she was having an affair. He told her, "I don't care what I've done. I can't take this."

Burt's liaisons may not have been restricted to women, for colleagues have speculated over his possible bisexuality for decades. "That was a rampant rumor," conceded Alexandra King, who costarred with the actor in *La Pelle* in 1980, but she added, "There was nothing to indicate that on the set, really." Idalah Luria, an American dialogue coach who worked on several Italian productions starring Lancaster in the 1970s and 1980s (including *La Pelle*), noted, "In Italy, Burt is known as a bisexual." She recalled a small dinner party during the making of *Marco Polo* in 1981, when Burt happened to remark, "The most beautiful thing I've ever seen and I think the most beautiful thing that exists is a man on a horse." Luria was taken aback "because even though I'd heard stories about Lancaster having had dalliances with men, I thought he was your American he-man. But I think a statement like that is almost an admittance [*sic*] that he preferred the aesthetic of a man to the aesthetic of a woman."

Moreover, an actress who worked with Lancaster in the 1970s maintained that when her husband met with Burt at the star's home to discuss some business matter, Burt insisted upon showing off his Jacuzzi and demonstrating wrestling moves. The man was so nervous, he could not wait to leave. Robert Steadman, the director of photography for *On Wings of Eagles,* which Burt made in 1985, volunteered, "He would do

---

1. Maggie and Jiggs were the perpetually battling husband and wife in the popular comic strip, "Bringing Up Father," created in 1913 by George McManus.

a lot of sort of over-the-top gay impersonations. I thought it was very, very strange for a man of that age to have found humor in that way, you know. I thought, 'Jesus, is this guy gay or what?' Well, ultimately I guess not, but he sure did a lot of it."

In any event, Burt and Jackie would remain a couple for about a decade more, but long separations would color the final years of their relationship. To Anita Gillette, who visited Burt and Jackie in the autumn of 1973, "The split was really starting then. Bad."

Moses, the Lawgiver, a coproduction of Italy's RAI Television and ITC, the British firm of flamboyant Lew Grade, began filming in August of 1973. The plan was to air the miniseries in Italy, Great Britain, and the United States, then release a truncated version theatrically. Given TV's stricter censorship standards, especially in America, the footage shot for the big screen would contain more sex and violence than that intended for the living room.

Initially, Burt had not been interested in playing the Hebrew patriarch. First of all, he was an atheist. Secondly, he did not think much of biblical pictures. As for Moses in particular, he said, "It's been done. I could still see Heston parting the Red Sea."[2]

Then he read the teleplay, which was by the noted British novelist Anthony Burgess, best known in America for *A Clockwork Orange.* He loved it, saying, "Anthony Burgess wrote a magnificent script—full of genius and wonder." He was particularly impressed by its lack of pretension and rhetoric. "Burgess gets down to the people," he said. "He deals with those simple desert people out of whom this kind of enormous religious thing arose. This is what really happened."

Burt was hooked.

Until *Moses, the Lawgiver,* Lancaster had limited his television work to rare, nonacting guest shots. Such was the way with most film stars—then and now. In the hierarchy of Hollywood, features rank well above episodic TV and, for that matter, made-for-TV movies and miniseries. The salaries for movies are much greater—as are the projects' budgets—and the shooting schedules are far more expansive. Where an average feature might complete two or three script pages a day, a made-for-TV movie has to tackle ten.

2. Charlton Heston starred as Moses in the 1956 epic *The Ten Commandments,* Cecil B. De-Mille's remake of his own 1923 silent version of the story of Exodus.

Moses, the Lawgiver fell somewhere in between the two media. At a cost of $6 million, it was, to quote *Variety*'s Frank Meyer, "probably the most expensive property ever shot for TV." Still, Burt had to drop his asking price to do it. It was less a case of a down-on-his-luck movie star turning to the lesser medium in order to keep working—although he probably would not have considered the project under any circumstances a few years earlier—but more an example of Lancaster's willingness to do something that he wanted to do, even if that meant a reduction in his earnings. It was not the first time that he had made such a sacrifice nor would it be the last. Still he was not completely eleemosynary. "I drove a hard bargain," he said of his salary for the miniseries.

Although Lancaster had enormous regard for Burgess' teleplay, he was not above supplying his own editorial contributions during filming. That was "easy to do," asserted Burgess, "when the director knew no English." The writer cited as an example Moses' final words to the pharaoh. As written, the prophet was to explain that thereafter he would use his brother as his interpreter "because I am slow of speech." Instead, Burt said, "Because I am uncircumcised of lips." Burgess, unaware of the change until he saw it in the editing room, was appalled. By that time, however, the production had wrapped. Finally, they found a shot of the back of Burt's head, which was inserted into the appropriate moment, with the correct line read by the film's American editor, Michael Billingsly.

Burgess also recalled footage in the dailies that showed the celebrated Lancaster temper. In one shot, the writer could see Burt, as he put it, "dissatisfied with a scene and visibly if inaudibly growling, 'Fuck it,' viciously hitting a porous rock with his staff." Some of Burt's anger was reserved for the director, Gianfranco De Bosio, whom he thought was overshooting. According to director George Cosmatos, who also lived in Rome, "He'd say to the director, 'You already took here [pointing to a place where the camera had been] and took there [pointing to another camera angle]. What do you want from me?' And he walked off the set."

But the biggest disturbance during filming had nothing to do with Lancaster. In September, after filming several weeks at the Cinecittà Studio in Rome, the company had moved to Israel and was shooting in Jericho, near Jerusalem, on October 6 when the Yom Kippur War erupted. "We woke one morning to find tanks moving down the street in front of our hotel," Lancaster recalled, referring to the King David in Jerusalem.

The company took a vote on whether to remain in Israel or go back to Rome, and according to one of the producers, Ali Koren, "Ninety-nine percent voted to stay." Said Burt, "After the fourth day of the war we started to shoot again without the Israeli crew, who had joined their military units. We chose locations away from the borders, using Jerusalem and Ashkelon." But, finally, they ran out of scenes that could be shot under such restricted conditions, and they went back to Rome. That very day, the armistice was signed. When it appeared that, indeed, Israel had returned to its normal state of nervous anticipation, they went back to Jerusalem.

In all, it took six months to film *Moses, the Lawgiver.* As it turned out, Burt's criticism of De Bosio was not wholly without foundation. The director had shot more than five hundred thousand feet of film—of which a mere thirty thousand ended up in the miniseries.

For Burt, one of the great pleasures of living in Italy was the chance to be with Luchino Visconti. But the director was in poor health as a result of a major stroke in 1973. "It was very bad," recalled Claudia Cardinale. "He was in an armchair.[3] He was very sick. He couldn't hardly talk. For all of us who loved him, it was terrible."

Visconti still wanted to work, but in his weakened condition, he needed an intimate story that could be shot entirely in a studio in Rome. It was screenwriter Enrico Medioli—a friend as well as a colleague— who came up with the idea of an elderly professor living alone in a house in Rome, surrounded by his books, his music, and his paintings, who reluctantly leases the top floor to a rich, demanding countess and her entourage—her lover, her daughter, and her daughter's boyfriend— and then watches in horror as the wildly eccentric foursome wreak havoc on his solitude. The picture was called *Conversation Piece* (in Italian, *Gruppo Di Famiglia in Un Interno*)—from the professor's favorite paintings, a series of eighteenth-century family groupings of that designation.

The model for the professor was, in part, an art critic named Mario Pratz and, in part, Visconti himself; the director would even coauthor the screenplay, with Medioli and Suso Cecchi D'Amico. Although the result was largely a character study, it would resonate, as did *The Leopard,* with the politics of the day. Italy in the early 1970s was beset by terrorists of both the left and the right. In the film, the nation's turmoil

3. She means wheelchair.

would bring death and destruction to the professor's home through the countess' boyfriend, Konrad, a left-wing activist.

Ironically, a right-wing producer by the name of Edilio Rusconi agreed to finance *Conversation Piece*. The relationship with Visconti was born of mutual need. Rusconi, a highly successful book and magazine publisher, wanted a major filmmaker to give his new $16-million enterprise credibility, and the ailing director needed someone who was willing to take a chance on him, despite his poor health. But it was an unusual match, to say the least, one which, asserted Visconti's biographer Gaia Servadio, "produced fierce controversy" within the Italian artistic community.

When the Visconti-Rusconi association was announced in the fall of 1973, Henry Fonda was expected to star in *Conversation Piece*, with Anne Bancroft as the countess. But arrangements with both stars fell apart. In the meantime, insuring the frail director was becoming a major barrier to any production. Medioli and D'Amico decided to seek Lancaster's help. Not only did Burt agree to star in the film, he also stipulated for insurance purposes that if anything happened to Visconti, he would direct the rest of the picture himself. It was this pledge, said D'Amico, as well as Lancaster's marquee value (which was still considerable in Europe), that allowed them to go forward. Visconti never learned of the proviso with the insurance company.

For a time, it appeared that Audrey Hepburn would costar with Burt, marking a reunion of the stars of *The Unforgiven*, but by year's end Italy's Silvana Mangano had been signed to play the countess. Costarring as Konrad would be Helmut Berger, the Austrian actor who had gained international recognition in Visconti's 1969 film, *The Damned*.

For Lancaster, the role of the professor was a major risk. Even in a career marked by bold choices, he had never attempted a character so sedentary. Moreover, the professor was unmistakably gay. Although he and Konrad never consummate their relationship, a homoerotic undertone clearly pervades their feelings for one another.

Burt tried to argue otherwise in 1975, asserting that Visconti "didn't want to open up the homosexual angle completely." But, as Visconti biographer Laurence Schifano put it, "Lancaster is manifestly wrong in saying that Visconti was afraid to bear down on homosexual relationships and explore these complex feelings. He constantly did precisely that in all his work. But never had Visconti dealt with a homosexual relationship more gently, never was it more religiously purified of any desire for possession, than at this period when fate forced him to live alone in an ivory tower from which he tried desperately to escape."

Burt had to know that this was so; his performance was infused with the knowledge. It is tempting to argue, in light of the allegations over his own bisexuality, that he had a strong personal reason for wanting the character's sexual orientation to go unacknowledged. He realized, however, that the professor was based largely on Visconti, and it was no secret that Visconti was gay. Burt even said of him, "Now, here's a man who loves little boys. It's as simple as that. He's a throwback to the old Roman emperors." In point of fact, Lancaster modeled his performance on Luchino. As Suso D'Amico put it, "That's Visconti. The movement of the hands, the way he walked, sort of in a very decided way." Cardinale, who appeared in a very brief flashback, agreed, saying that watching Burt act, "you think of Visconti." She considered the performance a tribute, reflecting the star's love for the director.

Filming began on April 8, 1974, at the Dear Studios on the outskirts of Rome. A second studio, De Paolis, was also used. To accommodate the director, shooting took place from around 1 P.M. to around 9 P.M.

Although Luchino was ailing, he had not lost his fanatical attention to detail. Burt remembered the day that the director stopped shooting entirely because he saw three antennae on some buildings in the distance—after he had asked that such unsightly objects be removed from view. He told Lancaster, "I stopped shooting so my producers and crew learn I'm serious when I say no antennae. At times like this you must be intransigent."

As filming progressed, the director became increasingly fatigued, but he refused to give in to his infirmity; he would not even sit in his wheelchair on the set. Invariably there was Lancaster, ready to lend support. In particular, Burt made it his business to keep Berger in line. "At that moment, Helmut was very wild, very strange," explained D'Amico. Sometimes, he would report to work with a hangover. Often, he would look fatigued, his face bloated from the effects of drink. Which would infuriate Visconti. The actor might have been tempted to argue with the old man, but, asserted D'Amico, "Berger didn't want to anger Lancaster. After all, he was a big star, very important." Given Visconti's pride in the face of his disability and Burt's gentle concern, it must have been moving to watch the two men at work. Said D'Amico, "Lancaster was really a father to him, he was so sweet with him, helping, helping, helping."

Conversation Piece wrapped on July 15.

•　•　•

On June 14, while Burt was working on *Conversation Piece, The Midnight Man* debuted. It was not a success. In fact, Vincent Canby of *The New York Times,* a long-standing Lancaster booster, called it "the second worst film of 1974" (he did not specify what was number one). To be sure, it was a pedestrian affair. For a writer of Kibbee's flair, the dialogue was curiously flat, devoid of all humor, and the plot was hopelessly byzantine. Even Susan Clark said in retrospect, "The script never worked. I mean, when you have to have a fifteen-minute summation of what this plot was all about to a totally confused audience, something got lost somewhere."[4]

However, several critics had kind words for Burt, with *Time*'s Richard Schickel noting that he was "turning into an attractive, hardworking actor as superstardom fades." Moreover, the rapport that he and Harris Yulin enjoyed off-screen gave rise to some sparks before the cameras. And finally, those with an eye on the cast list could enjoy watching Burt interact with his son Bill. They shared a particularly engaging scene together on a park bench when Lancaster the younger, playing a long-haired college kid, tries to help the old man decipher a vital clue.

The Midnight Man marked the last time that Burt attempted to direct. Neither of his principal costars mourned the loss. Clark found him intolerant as a director, asserting, "He had it in his head what he wanted and [lost patience] if you didn't get it right away." On the other hand, Yulin remarked, "I don't think he was confident enough in his abilities as a director to direct again. . . . He was okay on *Midnight Man,* but he was too careful on it or something. He wasn't really going for something."

A month after the mystery's debut, Lancaster went back to work. If playing an elderly, gay recluse in *Conversation Piece* had been daring, he arguably topped himself with his next role, that of a decadent, senile padrone in *1900,* a film directed by Bernardo Bertolucci.

Once described as "a cross between the neurasthenic aesthete and a lumberjack posing in a Skoal tobacco ad," Bertolucci was the hottest director in Europe in 1974, thanks to the masterful, erotic, and highly controversial *Last Tango in Paris* starring Marlon Brando, which was released the previous year when Bernardo was thirty-two.

Unlike *Last Tango*'s contemporary story, *Novecento,* as *1900* was called in Italy, traced the history of Bertolucci's native Emilia, a province in the north-central region, during the first half of the twenti-

---

4. To make a point, Clark exaggerated the length of Lancaster's voice-over plot summary shortly before the film's climax, but it *felt* like fifteen minutes.

eth century, using two families to tell the story: the landowning Berlinghieris and the peasant Dalcos. At the center of the drama were two sons, one born to each of the families on the same day in the summer of 1900. Initially, it had been planned as a six-part miniseries for television, but the director said that as the project took shape, "we began to feel that for political, social, and narrative reasons it belonged on the large screen."

The young sons would be played by two rising international stars, Robert De Niro (the landowner Alfredo) and Gerard Depardieu (the peasant Olmo). But, briefly, before they take command of the film, the focus would be on the boys' grandfathers. "I wanted to give this kind of epic size to these grandparents," said Bertolucci. For the peasant Leo Dalco, he cast Sterling Hayden, who had recently distinguished himself as the corrupt police chief in *The Godfather.* For the landowner Alfredo senior, he considered Orson Welles, then thought of Lancaster. Not only was Burt, in Bertolucci's opinion, part of "the patriarchy of the old Hollywood," he was also Don Fabrizio. Like *The Leopard, 1900* was largely about class conflict, although in this case the strife was between the bourgeoisie and the peasants; old Alfredo, like the noble prince of Salina, had to grapple with the changes swirling about him.

While Bertolucci was casting, Lancaster was conveniently in Rome, working on *Conversation Piece.* Moreover, he was definitely interested in *1900.* "Ever since I saw *Last Tango in Paris,* I had wanted to work with Bertolucci," he said later. But, despite the mutual admiration, there was a problem. Even with a budget of $6.5 million—the largest in the history of the Italian cinema to that point—Bertolucci could ill afford to meet Lancaster's usual asking price. They were deadlocked until Burt made an unbelievable offer: he would do the movie for free! "I wasn't doing anything at the time," he said later, "and it was only two weeks' work. . . . I treated the whole thing like a vacation." To Bertolucci, it was "an absolutely incredible, very gratifying act of generosity."

Filming started in the summer of 1974 in the lush Po Valley, Bertolucci's birthplace, with the Villa Saviola, east of Parma, serving as the Berlinghieri estate. Once the home of a count, it had been abandoned and had fallen into disrepair, but a crew of sixty-five spent three months returning it to its former glory for the film.

Bertolucci, the genial host, was inclined to open his villa to members of the company, including Lancaster during his brief sojourn in Emilia. The director remembered, in particular, one Saturday night when Burt came to visit. Sterling Hayden was also there. "And he [Hayden] was

drinking a lot of vodka," said Bertolucci, "and smoking and listening ob-
sessively to an album, which I remember was called the *Love Unlim-
ited Orchestra.* He was putting it on and on for two hours. Then the
padrone, the master, the landowner came; Burt came. And I saw Sterling hiding his bottle behind the speaker and stopped playing [the
record]. Like the relationship between the two characters was transmit-
ted to the two actors. It was so strange."

Bertolucci considered Lancaster a cerebral actor. "With Burt," he recalled, "I was forced—and I thank him for that—I was forced to look at
the character in more practical terms."

An extraordinary case in point occurred when they were shooting the
sequence in which old Alfredo wistfully watches a group of peasants
making merry in the fields. Suddenly, Bertolucci spied three piglets in a
nearby cart and, on an impulse, asked Burt to pick up one of the animals
and French-kiss it on camera. Disgusting as the notion was—and
Bertolucci *knew* it was—Lancaster was amenable, as long as the director could give him a reason for the action. "So he forced me to motivate
that direction I gave him," Bertolucci recalled, "and I was forced to
think. Because it was only pure intuition, which I really didn't know the
meaning of. I was like that very often, you know. I'd do something, and
then I'd understand it months later. Or maybe I will never understand
it." As for the explanation, "I told him I wanted to show this conflict between the kind of lyrical scene, to enjoy what he was seeing, and in the
meantime be full of despair. And this French-kissing a pig, it was a way
of showing the despair. Like degrading himself."

Satisfied with the director's logic, Burt kissed the pig. Bertolucci was
impressed. "There are things that many actors would be unwilling to do
simply for the sake of a movie," he conceded. "It takes guts for a director to ask Burt Lancaster to do that, and it takes guts for Burt Lancaster
to do it. He was facing risky things with great bravery."

Among the other "risky things" was Lancaster's final sequence in the
picture. By then, the old padrone has become senile and impotent, a decline that is evident in his pathetic attempt to make love to a young
peasant girl in his barn. It is a scene redolent of decay and degradation.
For a major movie star to humble himself in that way was as commendable as it was rare.

The knee that Lancaster had injured during the making of *The Leopard*
had never truly healed. It "was so bad I'd be walking along the street

and it would suddenly cave in on me," he said in 1975. Finally, in May of that year, he returned to the United States for surgery. The following month, he would be able to report, "I'll be walking all right in two months."

Meanwhile, he used the time—cane in hand—to publicize *Moses, the Lawgiver.* The miniseries had been a resounding success in Italy, where it had drawn the largest TV audience in that country's history, an average of 23 million viewers per episode. But CBS, which had paid $2.5 million for the U.S. rights, decided to air the program on six consecutive Saturday nights starting in June. "People go away weekends this time of year," an angry Burt asserted. "They might catch one part or two and miss the rest." Then he added, "But then I was told they were having sponsor problems and couldn't go for the big treatment. The sponsors were apparently saying, 'Who wants to see a Bible story on TV?' These are the people who buy stuff like *Mod Squad.*"[5]

Lancaster left little doubt about his attitude toward the miniseries. "I must tell you very candidly—it's tremendous," he told one TV critic. "It's so superior to the DeMille epic *The Ten Commandments,* there's no comparison." He was proud of his own work as well, saying, "My Moses is just a frightened guy with no confidence in himself." He saw it as a marked departure from Charlton Heston's heroic portrayal in the DeMille picture. But, then, Heston had been in his early thirties at the time; Burt was fifty-nine. The critics agreed with the star's assessment. "Lancaster imbued his role with stoic strength," noted *Variety.* To which Marvin Kitman of the *New Leader* added, "The Moses he gave us was an angry, repressed, middle-aged man."

Audiences had to wait until the second episode to judge Burt's performance. The introductory segment, which dealt with Moses' youth, featured Burt's son Bill. While proud of his offspring, Burt thought the producers had erred. "They should have had me in the first show somehow," he asserted. "People have a right to expect to see me. It's my name they're selling the show with, and hell, even though my son is in it, the thing could have been handled differently." Nevertheless, viewers tuned in the following week when Burt took over. Indeed, despite his concern, CBS estimated that an impressive 25 million viewers watched each episode.

As planned, a theatrical version of *Moses, the Lawgiver* opened on March 24, 1976, some eight months after the miniseries concluded. It did not equal the success of the TV version. As Anthony Burgess put it,

5. *The Mod Squad,* an episodic series about three young former criminals (Michael Cole, Peggy Lipton, and Clarence Williams III) who made up a special police unit, debuted on ABC in 1968. It was decidedly intended for the youth market.

"The large screen showed up the insufficiency of the resources, less than epic. It was sort of a shoestring *Ten Commandments*."

As the title character in *Moses, the Lawgiver,* Lancaster obviously dominated the proceedings. But, for the remainder of his career, he often followed the modus operandi of *1900,* albeit not for free: he would lend his still considerable presence to important but nevertheless supporting roles that could be filmed in relatively brief, highly concentrated spurts. Hollywood calls them "and/as" roles, because the billing typically reads "And (actor's name) as (character's name)." These assignments fulfilled Burt's ongoing need to work, kept his name before the public, and usually added a tidy sum to his bank account. At the same time, they did not overtax his diminishing physical resources as he moved through his sixties and seventies.

Such a role was Ned Buntline in *Buffalo Bill and the Indians.*

As far back as October of 1969, *Variety* had announced that Paul Newman would play Buffalo Bill Cody in the film adaptation of Arthur Kopit's play *Indians,* which had opened that very month on Broadway. George Roy Hill, who had worked with Newman on *Butch Cassidy and the Sundance Kid,* was slated to direct. But it was not until May of 1975 that the project truly got under way, with Dino De Laurentiis producing and Robert Altman directing (in what was to be the first of a three-picture deal between the producer and the director).

By 1975, the fifty-year-old Altman had established a special place for himself among the industry's filmmakers. Through movies such as *M*A*S*H, McCabe and Mrs. Miller,* and *Nashville,* he had forged a highly distinctive style, a form of cinema verité circumscribed by an ever-shifting visual perspective and overlapping, often improvised dialogue. Frank Rich of the *New York Post* considered him "so unique . . . that even casual moviegoers can immediately separate Altman's films from the rest of Hollywood's product."

Like *Nashville,* Altman's Oscar-nominated look at the world of country music, *Buffalo Bill* would use show business as a vehicle for examining the American condition. In this case, the focus was on William F. Cody and his Wild West Show and Congress of Rough Riders, the sensation of the 1880s, and, by extension, the contrast between America's myths and realities. As such, the screenplay by Altman and Alan Rudolph had a markedly different affect than Kopit's play, which railed against the mistreatment of Native Americans. In fact, the director would later assert that he and Rudolph drafted the screenplay without even looking at Kopit's text.

The Buffalo Bill of legend was largely fabricated by Ned Buntline. Born Edward Zane Carroll Judson in 1823, Buntline penned more than two hundred dime novels about the Old West, including *Buffalo Bill—The King of the Border Men,* which made Cody a star. Not only did he give the young scout his nickname, he put him in show business, featuring him in an 1872 melodrama called *The Scouts of the Prairie.*

Although the men remained friends in real life, Altman's version found Cody resentful of Buntline, so much so that the showman assiduously avoids the writer when he comes to visit the Wild West Show's encampment. Consequently, as the troupe rehearses, Buntline sits in a saloon, drinking and regaling anyone who will listen with tales of the real Buffalo Bill. In this, he serves as something of a Greek chorus, undermining, to quote film historian Gerard Plecki, "the very image that the man created."

Who better to play this spinner of hokum than the actor who had brought Starbuck and Elmer Gantry to the screen? Ironically, Lancaster had already portrayed Wyatt Earp, another of Buntline's heroes, and in 1980's *Cattle Annie and Little Britches,* he would play outlaw Bill Doolin, who also inspired Buntline's pen.

For Burt, the challenge in *Buffalo Bill* was unique, for the role was punctuated with "grandiloquent stories," as he called them, that were basically delivered to the camera (only in his final scene would he share the screen with Newman). He had to find a way to come across as, in his words, "extraordinarily entertaining" to the cinema audience while appearing to bore the patrons of the saloon. So he prepared mightily before filming began, working for weeks with a dialogue coach. "Every day for three hours a day at my house in Malibu, we went over these lines, these stories," he recalled. "It was very dull, very boring work, but very essential."

Filming began on August 11, 1975, at the Stoney Indian reservation in Calgary, Alberta, Canada, and would continue there until late October, when the picture wrapped. But all of Lancaster's scenes were shot in roughly a four-day period. "He showed up," said the assistant director, Tommy Thompson, "and he had a rather gruff, exacting exterior. You know, he kinda knew what he wanted and didn't want to be bothered. And what I found out all that was—or I felt I found out what that was—he was becoming Ned Buntline."

Altman quickly earned Lancaster's respect. Later, the actor would describe the director as "a highly creative man and wide open to ideas," adding, "However, he's an absolute, solid, one hundred percent authority figure—and there's no question when he says, 'Well, that's a lovely idea but I don't think we can use that.' That's the end of it, period."

Burt was glad that he had put in all those hours in Malibu, for Altman never rehearsed. Instead, said the actor, "He'll set up the scene, we stand there and talk about it," roughing out the character's moods and actions. Then he would bring in the saloon extras and tell them go about their business without paying any attention to Burt—which Burt found, by his own admission, "totally confusing." Finally, they would start to film. Typically, after about three takes, Altman would be satisfied, and they would go on to the next setup. Without the time Lancaster had spent in Malibu, he would never have been able to keep up.

The highlight of Burt's brief stay in Calgary was his scene with Newman. The two stars knew one another; they had served together on the ACLU foundation. But they had never worked together professionally. Newman, twelve years younger than Lancaster, came from a different film generation and a different school of acting, having studied the Method at the Actors Studio. Moreover, *Buffalo Bill* was *his* picture; he was the title character and the central figure. At the same time, Lancaster had been a star for nearly a decade by the time Newman made his first feature. So, in a sense, their interplay was not unlike that between their characters. "It was exciting for everyone on the set to see these people working together," recalled Thompson.

On September 26, *Conversation Piece* kicked off the 13th New York Film Festival at Lincoln Center's Avery Fisher Hall. The picture had done well—commercially and critically—in Italy and France. Lancaster's performance as the professor had even earned the Donatello Davidas Award, the Italian equivalent of the Oscar, for Best Foreign Actor (an honor that he shared with Jack Lemmon and Walter Matthau for their remake of *The Front Page*).

But the American premiere—with the dialogue dubbed into English—was a total disaster, sparking derisive laughter from many in the audience and inspiring others to walk out. "Nothing, absolutely nothing that I had endured for the past twelve years prepared me for the ruinous debacle of Opening Night 1975," asserted Andrew Sarris in the *Village Voice.*

Variety, which reviewed the picture months before, liked it, calling it "a touching tale of the generation gap and the loss of life-contact of an intellectual" and asserting that Lancaster was "highly effective as the professor." But most of those who caught the film at the festival were not so kind. "*Conversation Piece* is a disaster," argued Vincent Canby of *The New York Times,* who also took issue with Burt's performance. So did Pauline Kael of *The New Yorker,* who asked, "Whose idea can it have been to cast Burt Lancaster as a gentle intellectual? He is as extroverted as an actor can be." She then proceeded to launch an attack that included such scathing observations as "Whatever goes on inside that man, he doesn't use as an actor: he doesn't draw on himself" and "When he's serious, he is sexless and almost obsequiously conscientious."

In the aftermath of the New York Film Festival, *Conversation Piece* struggled to find an American distributor. Finally, at year's end, New Line Cinema agreed to pick it up. Using a freelance editor, Fima Noveck, the company attempted to eliminate the film's shortcomings, cutting it by half an hour and rewriting some of the clichéd dialogue. But the new version failed to win critical approval when it debuted in London in February of 1976. Thus, it was the original Italian version with subtitles that opened in New York in September of 1977. Even then, Vincent Canby asserted that the picture contained virtually the same flaws as that screened at the film festival, "though," he wrote, "the Italian dialogue, translated by subtitles, does have the effect of slightly distancing some of the screenplay's banalities."

By that time, three years had elapsed since the film was shot, and it quickly disappeared from view.

By the mid-1970s, disaster pictures were hot—thanks to Ross Hunter and George Seaton. Without intending to do so, the producer and director of *Airport* had given rise to a new genre, circumscribed by a host of stars playing relatively stock characters caught up in soap-opera-like crises, lush production values, state-of-the-art special effects, and a catastrophe of major proportions. Producer-director Irwin Allen staked a special claim to the turf with 1972's *The Poseidon Adventure,* 1974's *The Towering Inferno,* and 1978's *The Swarm.* Other entries in the field included *Earthquake, Meteor,* and the sequels to the original *Airport, Airport 1975, Airport '77,* and *The Concorde—Airport '79.*

The genre's enormous popularity had not been lost on George Pan Cosmatos, a thirty-one-year-old Greek-Italian director. In the wake of his first major film, 1973's *Massacre in Rome* starring Richard Burton and Marcello Mastroianni, he decided to make his own disaster film. What he and screenwriter-novelist Robert Katz devised was the story of a plague-infested train. Thus, *The Cassandra Crossing* was born.[6]

Cosmatos wanted Lancaster for the picture. The young director already knew Burt. "All the foreigners around Rome know each other," he explained. In fact, Lancaster had helped him interest Richard Burton in *Massacre in Rome.*

Initially, George saw Burt as the eminent doctor who takes charge of the passengers' safety. But the actor felt he was too old for the part, which called for a romance with the character's ex-wife. Moreover, it would require fourteen weeks of filming, and he did not want to devote that much time to the project. He opted instead for Col. Stephen McKenzie, an American attached to the World Health Organization who is placed in charge of the crisis. As McKenzie spends virtually the entire film in a command center, monitoring the progress of the train, all of Burt's scenes could be shot in a brief, concentrated period on one set— the control room—which would be built at the Cinecittà Studio in Rome.

While the obligatory star-studded cast included Richard Harris (as the doctor), Sophia Loren, Ava Gardner, Martin Sheen, Lee Strasberg, and O. J. Simpson, all of Lancaster's scenes were with John Phillip Law, who played his aide, and Ingrid Thulin as a consulting physician. Law, who had begun *The Gypsy Moths* with Lancaster but had been forced to withdraw due to an injury, had been eager to make up for the lost opportunity. As he put it, Burt "was always a favorite of mine as a kid. My God, I loved *The Crimson Pirate.* . . . As a matter of fact, they offered me the part that Martin Sheen played [one of the passengers on the train], but I wanted to work with Burt."

Law was not disappointed. "I found him to be very generous and very open," the actor recalled. "If someone wanted some advice from him, he was very direct and very sincere." Burt did, however, take time to occasionally needle Thulin, who had previously played his sister Miriam in *Moses, the Lawgiver.* "He'd try to get her goat," Law said, laughing. " 'You look like hell today' or something. I was never sure if it was personal or if he was trying to stir up something as far as their relationship

6. The title derived from a dangerously defective bridge in Poland that the train would have to cross on its way to quarantine.

in the film was concerned." Later, Burt would say, "Actually I enjoyed sitting with the marvelous Ingrid Thulin and talking for ten straight days."

Lancaster's most difficult moments lay in the numerous telephone conversations that he had with Richard Harris. Because Burt's scenes were shot before the rest of the company started filming, he did not have the other actor's responses to inspire him. "I had Harris put some of the scenes on audiotape so Burt could have something to act with," Cosmatos recalled, "but it didn't work. It didn't have the same spontaneity. We had to have another actor read the lines to him." Still, Law was impressed with the way Lancaster handled those moments. Said the younger actor, "He knew how to . . . set his face and ask the question. Bam. Bam. Bam. He just had that kind of directness about his acting that people respond to. It's manly."

Meanwhile, Cosmatos was amazed at Burt's technical knowledge, saying, "He knows from your lenses if you're fucking up." That is unusual for an actor. The sixty-two-year-old star and the thirty-one-year-old director had a special rapport, a bond that had been formed before they started working together. "He would look at me with a twinkle in his eye," Cosmatos recalled, "and say, 'So, you're a big director, right, George? You want to go to Hollywood, eh?' "[7]

While they were making the film, Lancaster would often cook pasta at the director's house. Then, one night, Cosmatos had dinner at Burt's apartment, and Sydney Pollack was also present.

"How is Burt with you?" Pollack asked Cosmatos. "Is he difficult? Is he tough?"

"No, I think he is wonderful and gracious," George replied.

Pollack turned to Lancaster and said, "Ah, Burt, you're becoming wiser."

Not all of the actors in his next movie would think so.

In the novel *Viper Three*, Walter Wager depicted the takeover of a U.S. missile installation by a gang of criminals. Director Robert Aldrich thought it was a routine thriller, but he had an idea that would make it different: he wanted to make the ringleader of the plot a former officer in Vietnam who was using the threat of nuclear holocaust to force the government into revealing the truth about the war.

Seven drafts and several screenwriters later, he had the script he wanted—thanks to Ronald M. Cohen and Edward Huebsch. The two

7. Cosmatos would indeed get to Hollywood, where he would direct such large-scale action films as *Rambo: First Blood, Part II* and *Tombstone*.

writers had never worked together before, but, as Cohen explained, Aldrich "knew Eddie knew about the politics, and he knew I could write action, so he put us together." The script, said Cohen, was written in a whirlwind eighteen days with the writers working around the clock in an office that Aldrich provided.

Lancaster, intrigued by the political angle, agreed to play the deranged officer, an ex–Air Force general named Laurence Dell.

For the other principal character in the melodrama, the Kennedy-like American president, David Stevens, Aldrich wanted Paul Newman. He even asked Burt to appeal to his *Buffalo Bill* costar—which Burt did— but Newman was not interested. So the director reconceived the character as what he later called "a smart, classy, uptown [Richard] Daley"[8] and cast Charles Durning. The talented company also included Melvyn Douglas and Joseph Cotten as cabinet members; Richard Widmark as the general trying to regain control of the missile silo; newcomers Paul Winfield and Burt Young as Dell's confederates; and Vera Miles as the First Lady, a role that would end up on the cutting-room floor.

Although *Twilight's Last Gleaming,* as the picture was called, was produced by a U.S. TV production company, Lorimar, one of the principal financial backers was the Bavaria Film Studio. Thus, the company elected to shoot at the studio's home base in Munich, which lent a surreal air to the American drama, much of which was set in the White House. However, as Edwin T. Arnold and Eugene L. Miller noted in *The Films and Career of Robert Aldrich,* "The Germans were able to construct not only an enlarged and exact replica of the president's Oval Office, but also an approximation of the underground silos which seemed extremely authentic because, as Aldrich wryly remarked, they 'had better research than we have. They had all the photographs down to the minutest detail.' "

Lancaster arrived in Munich on March 20, by which time the White House scenes and those involving Widmark had been completed. Dell was not exactly an "and/as" role. In fact, Burt would receive top billing in *Twilight's Last Gleaming.* But the film's construction was virtually identical to that of *The Cassandra Crossing* in that it dealt with several disparate groups, physically separated but in contact by phone. Thus, all of Burt's scenes could be ganged up and shot together in a con-

8. Richard Daley, mayor of Chicago from 1955 to 1976, was the boss of one of the last of the big-city political machines.

centrated period. As Ronald Cohen put it, "This was not a big deal for Lancaster. . . . He showed up, he did it, and he left."

With this, their fifth and final collaboration over a twenty-two-year period, Lancaster and Aldrich came together as old friends. "I think they really enjoyed each other," said Morgan Paull, now a talent agent, then an actor playing one of the soldiers in the missile complex. Still, Paul Winfield maintained, "Aldrich was well aware of the fact that you had to keep him in tight rein or he would start to manipulate everything."

Winfield, who had won an Oscar nomination as Best Actor for 1972's *Sounder,* often found Lancaster, in his words, "very charming," but he had difficulties working with the star. In particular, he resented Lancaster's attempts to give him line readings. Said Winfield, "I first let him know it wasn't welcome. I said, 'Well, you know, we have a director. And you should tell *him* that I should do it this way, and he will tell me.' " But Burt persisted. Winfield also had a problem with Lancaster during the filming of his close-ups. Burt was off-camera feeding him his cues. "Well, it didn't take me very long," Winfield recalled, "to realize that he was actually mouthing my words as I said them. It really distracted me. After the first take, Aldrich came up and said, 'Is something wrong?' " Winfield took the director aside, described the problem, and Aldrich, in turn, spoke to the star. Burt then apologized to his fellow actor. "So we did it again," Winfield continued, "and sure enough there he was doing it again. And this time, Aldrich was watching him instead of me and cut the scene. Anyway, it went about three or four times before Lancaster could control himself enough not to say the lines along with me. But, by then, of course, I wasn't focusing on him anymore." So the value of the actor being off-camera, throwing him cues, was lost.

Winfield did not consider Lancaster's actions malicious. Said he, "I really think he was so involved with getting everything right that he felt he had to be in control—of everything." That was indeed Burt's modus operandi. But mouthing a costar's lines seems more a reflection of the star's advancing age than his quest for perfection. Further evidence was manifest in Lancaster's difficulty with the general's long monologues—so much so that some of the speeches had to be trimmed on the set. Indeed, as the years progressed, Lancaster, like many an aging actor before him, would have increasing difficulty memorizing lines. It would become a source of major embarrassment for him.

The flip side of Lancaster's loss of concentration was his renewed physical vigor in the wake of his knee operation. He was even jogging again, which, according to Burt Young, made him "proud as a bastard. He had to beat that thing. He'd come back and say, 'Yeah, I did the half hour.' And when he did the half hour, it was quicker than most joggers do it. He was a very fit, strong man."

Young, who was about to make an indelible impression in the then-unreleased *Rocky,* was also given line readings by Lancaster. But he reacted differently than Winfield. "I thought it was funny as hell," he asserted. "He would reduce the scene to where he was it. He wasn't giving someone inspirational work. He was worried about how he was looking in a scene with that other party." Nevertheless, Young liked Lancaster, saying, "I used to get a kick of him, to tell you the truth."

Lancaster completed his scenes for *Twilight's Last Gleaming* on May 5. Twelve days later, he was in Cannes, paying tribute to Luchino Visconti, who had died two months earlier. After the screening of the director's final picture, *The Innocent,* Burt took the stage to acknowledge the auteur's very special place in his life and work. He "gave a beautiful speech," noted Bernardo Bertolucci years later.

CHAPTER EIGHTEEN

Back Home

After Cannes, Burt and Jackie returned home. Although he would maintain the Rome apartment well into the 1980s and would undertake several more Italian productions, he was once more rooted in the United States.

Burt's return was metaphorically echoed in his subsequent films. Where the pictures during the first half of the 1970s had largely concerned themselves with the dark side of the American dream—from racism *(Valdez Is Coming)* to the price of Manifest Destiny *(Ulzana's Raid)* to the treachery of national institutions and public figures *(Scorpio, Buffalo Bill and the Indians, The Cassandra Crossing, Twilight's Last Gleaming)*—he would look elsewhere for material thereafter. Only twice more in his career—in *Go Tell the Spartans* and *The Osterman Weekend*, released in 1978 and 1983 respectively—would he again address the flaws in the American political system. It was almost as if the return to normalcy that swept the nation in the post-Watergate bicentennial year found its counterpart in Burt's own psyche. Both settled more comfortably, though hardly passively, into maturity.

Bernardo Bertolucci had been in Cannes in 1976 for the screening of *1900,* which came the week after the tribute to Visconti. Although Lancaster had finished working on the picture in the summer of 1974, the director had continued filming until the end of May 1975. By that point, the cost had climbed to more than $8 million. But, at least, Bertolucci's producer, Alberto Grimaldi, could see the money on the screen; at Cannes, *1900* ran five and a half hours—and was a resounding success.

In Europe, the film was shown in two parts, released simultaneously. In the United States, however, Paramount, which was the distributor, insisted upon a single English-language film with a running time of no more than three and a quarter hours. That set off a legal battle between Grimaldi, who cut the picture to the requisite length, and Bertolucci, who felt that the result violated his "civil right of expression."

Finally, a compromise four-hour-and-ten minute version premiered at the New York Film Festival on October 8, 1977—where it was deemed a fiasco. The critical comments ran from "so overdone as to be ludicrous" to "scales new heights of dreadfulness in film." Still, many of those who condemned it did so with awe at the breadth and sweep of Bertolucci's vision. As Jack Kroll wrote in *Newsweek,* "It's a huge work and its faults are the excesses of a huge talent, perhaps even genius."

Moreover, the reviews for Lancaster's performance were quite respectable. It may have given the star some satisfaction to note the praise from Canby and Kael, after their damning responses to his work in *Conversation Piece.*

By the time *1900* arrived at the New York Film Festival, *Buffalo Bill and the Indians* had come and gone from the nation's movie screens. In what was one of the most ill-conceived openings in the history of film, the picture, which debunked a great American hero and made ignoble the conquest of the West, debuted on July 4, 1976, the very day when the entire nation was glorying in its bicentennial.

Even before the premiere, *Buffalo Bill* was steeped in controversy, the third Lancaster picture in a row to endure—through no fault of Burt's—major postproduction difficulties.

In this case, the dispute was something of a replay of *1900:* producer De Laurentiis wanted a shorter film than director Altman was willing to deliver. In America, Great Britain, and France, the director had the right of final cut, but elsewhere De Laurentiis removed twenty minutes from the two-hour picture. He then entered it in the Berlin Film Festival over Altman's objections. It went on to win the festival's grand prize, but the jury made clear that the award was for the uncut version.

In America, the critical response to *Buffalo Bill* was also reminiscent of that for *1900:* both were seen as failures of excess by masterful filmmakers. Although Richard Schickel of *Time* would praise Altman's picture as "a sly, wry, wise study of what fame does to people cursed with that most mixed of blessings," the *Nation*'s Robert Hatch spoke for the majority of his colleagues when he wrote that it was occasionally "exhilarating" and "entertaining. But on close acquaintance Bill Cody is a bore."

In the wake of the tepid notices, *Buffalo Bill* quickly disappeared from view. Still, Lancaster was proud of the picture, saying before its release, "It's very sad, rather poignant, but it's a highly entertaining film and a meaningful one." He could take pleasure in his contribution, which Charles Champlin of the *Los Angeles Times* called "a well-modulated, ironic performance." It ends wonderfully—with Burt raising his glass to Paul Newman and saying, "Buffalo Bill. It's the thrill of my life to have invented you." He then bounds out of the saloon, gets on his horse, leaps a red fence, and disappears.

Although *Buffalo Bill* was a major disappointment, Burt could still draw some satisfaction from the box-office grosses of 1976: *The Bad News Bears,* written by his son Bill, was a smash hit. In fact, the lighthearted film about a juvenile baseball team, with Burt's *Kentuckian* costar Walter Matthau and young Tatum O'Neal, would become the fourth most popular film of the year, with rentals of $22.3 million.

Lancaster senior, who had lavished such attention on the scripts of his own projects, was understandably bursting with pride over his son's achievement. At the time he told the press, "Recently I said, 'Billy, I have an idea for a screenplay. Would you write it for me?' 'No, Dad,' he said. 'You'll have to make it on your own.' " Unfortunately, young Lancaster was never able to build on his early success as a writer.

On the very day of *Buffalo Bill*'s debut and America's two hundredth anniversary, Israel celebrated the successful rescue of 250 Air France passengers from the clutches of a terrorist organization known as the Popular Front for the Liberation of Palestine. Several days earlier, on June 27, their jet, which had been en route from Tel Aviv to Paris, had been hijacked and diverted to the airport in Entebbe, Uganda. There, under the protection of dictator Idi Amin, the terrorists tried to use the passengers and crew to effect the release of fifty-three imprisoned Arab terrorists. The daring rescue by Israeli commandos ended the negotiations.

The raid on Entebbe inspired two television docudramas. One of them was produced by the eminent David Wolper, who had given viewers the acclaimed miniseries *Roots* earlier in the year. Working in concert with Warner Bros., Wolper was determined to see his version air first. He also intended to prepare a virtually simultaneous theatrical release, somewhat in the manner of *Moses, the Lawgiver.* That was targeted for European movie houses in December, only five months after the raid.

Ernest Kinoy, who was engaged to write the teleplay, believed that although "the actual raid itself was a moment of high tension and action, it was really only a part of the overall story." Thus, his script would focus on two groups caught up in the drama—the passengers being held hostage in Entebbe and the members of the coalition Israeli government seeking a solution to the crisis. Among the latter, he would lavish considerable attention on the deliberations between the defense minister, Shimon Peres, and the prime minister, Yitzhak Rabin, Peres' political opponent.

Lancaster was eager to play Peres. So much so that he even postponed the start of his next film, *The Island of Dr. Moreau,* in order to do the project. Other members of the quickly assembled, star-studded cast included Anthony Hopkins as Rabin, Godfrey Cambridge as Idi Amin, Richard Dreyfuss as the commander of the raid, Helen Hayes and Linda Blair as hostages, and Elizabeth Taylor and Kirk Douglas as Israeli parents (Burt and Kirk shared no scenes together; they were not even filming at the same time).[1]

To direct, Wolper chose Marvin Chomsky, who had directed half the episodes of *Roots* and had numerous made-for-TV movies to his credit. The director would need all the experience he could muster, for the three-hour *Victory at Entebbe* would have a shooting schedule of eighteen days. That meant completing eighteen to twenty pages of script a day, approximately twice the pace of a typical television movie and ten times that of a feature film. Said the director in retrospect, "Logistically, it was—I don't want to say 'nightmare,' because it worked—but it was as fast as I ever want to work, and I never want to work that fast again."

Shooting took place in the fall of 1976 at the Warners lot in Burbank.[2] As with *The Cassandra Crossing* and *Twilight's Last Gleaming,* all of the scenes involving each disparate group—the hostages, the cabinet members, the commandos—were ganged up together. They worked in videotape because the format required no developing time and was easy to edit. In fact, Chomsky would cut together each day's work at night, and by the following day, the result was already being scored. Eventually, the final cut was transferred to film for a smoother, more polished look.

As one of the major figures in the drama, Lancaster faced an enormous challenge. Said Chomsky, "He knew that in a matter of four or five

1. Cambridge suffered a heart attack and died on his first day of work on *Victory at Entebbe.* He was replaced overnight by Julius Harris.
2. Except for the scenes on the Air France jet, which were filmed in Long Beach, south of Los Angeles.

days—which is all he worked on that picture—he would have to do a tremendous page count, something that he would normally do in a matter of three weeks." Moreover, he was going to be working in television, a medium with which he was unfamiliar, with cameras shooting from different angles at the same time and few opportunities for retakes. It would be as close to the live TV dramas of the 1950s as he would ever get. Recognizing the obstacles before him, he decided to place his trust in Chomsky. "What he based it on, I really don't know," said the director, "but he decided early on that he was going to follow my lead."

Moreover, when the situation called for it, he brought one of his costars into line. Chomsky explained, "We were doing a rather intense scene, during which Rabin and Peres were meeting with the military command." Peres had learned that the terrorists had not placed explosives around the Entebbe airport and was relaying this crucial piece of information to those planning the raid. "At this point," Chomsky continued, "a young actor said, 'Wait a minute. How do *I* know there are no explosives.' And we immediately came to a screeching halt 'cause this actor needed motivation." Nothing Chomsky could say proved acceptable. Meanwhile, the precarious schedule was in serious jeopardy. Chomsky was on the verge of losing his temper when, as he put it, "Burt caught the eye of this young actor and nodded, 'Yes. He's right.' And this young actor swallowed his pride, took the good advice of Burt Lancaster, and we got on with the day's work. . . . For this, I am perpetually indebted to Burt. Burt saved the day for me."

Wolper won the race. *Victory at Entebbe* aired on ABC on Monday, December 13, while NBC's *Raid on Entebbe* was held until January 9, 1977, when it was seen in the coveted spot after the Super Bowl.

Given the speed with which the Wolper-Chomsky production was created, it was a laudable effort. Kinoy was particularly effective at dramatizing the strife within Israel's coalition government, but he was less adept at portraying the hostages, who tended to come across as stereotypes.

Comparisons with *Raid on Entebbe,* in which Jack Warden played Peres and Peter Finch Rabin, were inevitable. Each had strengths and weaknesses, but there was a volatility to the Lancaster-Hopkins exchanges that the latter film lacked.

A week after *Victory at Entebbe* aired, Lancaster began work on *The Island of Dr. Moreau.*

Burt was to play the title character, a mad scientist living in the remote tropics where his experiments in genetics have turned animals into humanoids. The story originally saw life as an 1896 novel by H. G. Wells and then as a 1933 film entitled *Island of Lost Souls,* which featured Charles Laughton as Moreau, Bela Lugosi as one of his half-animal-half-human creatures, and Richard Arlen as a young man shipwrecked on the island. The film also introduced a character not in the novel, Lota, a panther-woman who was used by the doctor as a sexual lure for Arlen.

Although Metromedia Productions had announced its remake of the property in 1972, three years later it was the hands of independent producer Sandy Howard and American International Pictures. Founded in 1954, AIP had spent its first two decades turning out inexpensive exploitation films such as *I Was a Teenage Werewolf* and *How to Stuff a Wild Bikini,* but in 1975, the company switched to mainstream, big-budget offerings.

By the time Burt's casting was announced on September 13, 1976, the script was being written by John Herman Shaner and Al Ramrus, who adhered rather closely to the novel—although they kept *Lost Souls'* woman-animal as a romantic interest for the young man, changing her name to Maria. Shaner and Ramrus also introduced a new, highly intriguing plot twist: when the young man, whom they called Andrew Braddock, attempts to thwart Moreau's plans, the doctor tries to turn him into a half-animal.

Lancaster had never before acted in anything remotely approaching horror or science fiction, but he felt that the picture carried an important message. As he explained, it dealt "with the responsibilities of science towards mankind. Or, if you will, how far can they go before the dehumanization of man takes place? How can they toy with the cosmic forces—or God or whatever you care to call it? How far can they go doing mutations?" Moreover, he did not see Moreau as the quintessential mad scientist, with eyes bulging and hair standing on end. Rather, he thought of him as "an unusual man, a man involved in his career, a strange man. So we played him dead straight on."

Given Lancaster's view of the material, it is not surprising that he fought the producers' temptation to heighten the story's horror elements once filming began on the Caribbean island of St. Croix. So did his costars Michael York, as Braddock, and Nigel Davenport, as the doctor's overseer. The element that stirred the biggest controversy was the ending, in which young Braddock and Maria are confronted with Moreau's death and the revolt of his creatures. "There were about three or four endings that I remember," said Barbara Carrera. "In one of them, Maria, my character, turned back into a cat." In another, they were discovered by a boat and taken back to England. A third found Braddock remaining with Maria on the island and continuing Moreau's work. And a fourth had Maria give birth to a kitten. That version was favored by coproducer John Temple-Smith, but the actors hated it. Said York, "You're asking the audience to accept an awful lot as it is. . . . It's totally wrong and I for one will not do it." To which Davenport added, "Personally, I think it's in the worst possible bad taste, and I've told them [the producers]." No doubt Lancaster agreed—as did the director, Don Taylor. According to Taylor, the birth scene was never shot. "I never took it seriously," he said in 1993, "because I never had any intention of doing anything like that."

In addition to the rewrites, Taylor would remember *Moreau* as a "tough picture" to shoot because of the four hours of makeup that had to be applied to the fifteen man-animals before each day's work (one of whom was Nick Cravat) and the intermixing of these humans with real wild animals.

Lancaster, who had points in *Moreau* and therefore was something of an unnamed producer, was a major force during filming. Said Carrera, "He just came on [the set] and said the way it was. No questions. Done." As a newcomer, with only two films to her credit, she welcomed his involvement. "I didn't even know who my character was," she explained, "she was so ambiguous on those pages. One wanted the character of Maria a certain way. Another wanted her another way. And, of course, I wanted to please everyone. Finally, Burt came up to me and said, 'Listen, kid, forget everything they're saying. Just be there. And if you're in doubt, look at me.' He was very, very supportive." His conviction, she added, enabled her to follow her instinct and "play her [character] as simple, naive, very elemental."

Lancaster's relationship with Michael York was not as sanguine. "They worked together very well," Carrera asserted, "but they had rough jokes, you can call them, with each other. Little daggers thrown out." Cameraman Gerald Fisher, who had last worked with Lancaster on *The Devil's Disciple,* believed that "Burt thought he [York] was a sort of lightweight." But, in all likelihood, the senior actor felt a bit threatened by his costar. Not only was York highly trained, with years of stage experience, he was also twenty-eight years younger and the picture's romantic lead. No doubt Burt could recall the time when his presence had evoked a similar response from Clark Gable and Spencer Tracy.

As for Burt's rapport with his director, one might suspect, in light of his frequent suggestions on the set, that the relationship was tinged with tension, but such was not the case. Although they were not close friends, he and Taylor had known each other from their earliest days in Hollywood, when they were both contract players under Mark Hellinger. Taylor, six years younger than Burt, had made the switch to directing through episodic television, with his first feature, *Ride the Wild Surf,* coming in 1964. Said Carrera, "They got along well because Don Taylor knew how to get along with him. Don Taylor would just sort of joke with him and say, 'Oh, so you're the director today.' " Moreover, said Gerald Fisher, Taylor indulged Lancaster's passion for intellectual discussions about character and scene construction. Taylor himself would fondly recall the association, saying, "He was marvelous. He gave me everything. And he took chances. I had no problem with Burt at all."

Working swiftly, Taylor and editor Marion Rothman readied the picture for a summer release. Not surprisingly, the biggest problem was the ending. Ultimately, they opted for the version in which Maria turns back into a cat. But, said Taylor, "When we previewed it, nobody liked the ending. I was shocked. I'd planted seeds all along. But they'd bought the love story, and they didn't want this to be." Taylor had no choice but to recut. However, he lacked the footage to do a proper job. Consequently, what remained was the hint of a transformation, but one so subtle that filmgoers could make of it what they wished.

Variety called *Moreau* "a handsome, well-acted piece of cinematic storytelling for all ages" with Lancaster a distinguished villain, if one somewhat "sluggish," to quote Rex Reed of the New York *Daily News.* But Charles Champlin of the *Los Angeles Times* correctly diagnosed the problem with the picture when he called it "just a little too polite to be a bloody good yarn and a little too bloody to reach the level of myth or fable." Ultimately, it seemed more akin to the 1959 adaptation of Jules Verne's *Journey to the Center of the Earth* and 1960's *The Time Machine,* from another Wells novel, than such recent horror/science-fiction excursions as *The Exorcist, Jaws,* and *The Omen*—to say nothing of *Star Wars,* George Lucas' epic space adventure, which had debuted the previous May. In retrospect, even Taylor saw the inherent problem with the material, and the way it was handled. "I needed horror," he said in 1993. "I needed suspense. I needed to get to the audience and get them involved. I never did completely succeed."

Lancaster finished with *The Island of Dr. Moreau* around February 7, 1977. Two days later, in a peculiar accident of timing, two of his films—

The Cassandra Crossing and *Twilight's Last Gleaming*—opened in New York.[3]

The critics found the pictures silly but somewhat entertaining. Referring to *Twilight's Last Gleaming,* John Simon of *New York* spoke for the majority about both films when he wrote, "You giggle, get faintly repelled, feel infinitely superior to the obvious idiocy, but are not bored."

Of the two, Robert Aldrich's political thriller was launched with far more serious purpose. Yet not even Charles Durning's effective performance as the not-too-bright but well-meaning president could elevate this examination of venality in the corridors of power. The problem lay in the secret memo that Lancaster's Dell was forcing the president to reveal. Although the audience was asked to believe that its disclosure would devastate the government, even Burt Young said in retrospect, "It wasn't a secret that made everyone go, 'Oh, no, we did that.' " Better, argued Vincent Canby in *The New York Times,* to have kept the contents obscure in the manner of Alfred Hitchcock. The master of suspense knew that whatever set his plots in motion—the McGuffin as he called it—should go undisclosed because, in Canby's words, "nothing can seem as important as it's been built up to be."

As for Lancaster's performances, both films essentially called upon him to be authoritative, and he was. But neither *Cassandra* nor *Twilight* were actors' pictures.

Burt had done *Cassandra, Twilight,* and *Moreau* for money, but his next project, a Vietnam war film entitled *Go Tell the Spartans,* was a labor of love. As he well knew, a movie about the U.S. experience in Southeast Asia was enormously risky in 1977. *The Deer Hunter,* the first commercially successful examination of the war, would not be released for another year, and the Oscar-winning *Platoon* was nearly a decade away. But he considered *Spartans* "one of the best scripts I've read, and certainly the best I've had for myself in a few years." And, for him, that was reason enough to commit to the project. He even withdrew from a thriller, *The Wild Geese* costarring Richard Burton and Roger Moore—which proved to be an international blockbuster—in order to do the film.

It had taken Wendell Mayes seven years to see the project come to fruition. The screenwriter of *Anatomy of a Murder, The Poseidon Ad-*

---

3. A preview of *Twilight's Last Gleaming* was held on February 6 at the Kennedy Center in Washington, D.C., to benefit the National Press Club.

venture, and *Death Wish* had acquired the rights to the novel *Incident at Muc Wa,* by Daniel Ford, in 1970. Like the book, the screenplay was set in 1964, when a mere twelve thousand Americans were serving as military advisers in South Vietnam. But the folly of the escalating conflict could be seen even then. Mayes drew his title from an incident in the ancient war between the Greeks and the Persians. In 480 B.C., three hundred Spartans died in order to hold a vital pass at the Battle of Thermopylae—for which Herodotus penned the epitaph: "Go tell the Spartans, thou that passeth by, / That here, obedient to their laws, we lie."

In 1972, it looked as though the project might finally go forward, with Ted Post directing and William Holden as the lead, the commander of a ragtag assistance advisory group named Maj. Asa Barker. The budget was a mere $1 million, but even so, the money could not be raised.

Five years later, Post made a two-picture deal with independent producers Allan F. Bodoh and Mitchell Cannold of Mar-Vista Productions: in return for directing a Chuck Norris film, *Good Guys Wear Black,* which held little interest for him, they would produce *Go Tell the Spartans.*[4] The only problem was that Holden, whose career had skyrocketed in the wake of 1976's *Network,* was unavailable for some time, and the producers could not wait until he was free.

"My next thought was Burt," Post recalled. The director not only knew Lancaster—having met him during World War II, when they were both stationed in Italy—he was also closely related to the star's longtime business manager and friend, Jack Ostrow. Post arranged to forward a script to Lancaster at La Costa (near San Diego), where the actor was recuperating from another knee operation. A few days later, Burt was in Los Angeles, helping cast his costars.

Costs of production having risen since 1972, *Spartans* was now budgeted at $1.5 million—which still made it an extremely cut-rate affair. (The budget for a nearly concurrent Vietnam film, *Apocalypse Now,* was $26 million.) Instead of filming in a remote tropical locale, the company set up shop—on September 14, 1977—in Valencia, California, just north of the San Fernando Valley. The site, across Interstate 5 from Magic Mountain, the giant amusement park, included, to quote Post, "tigerish terrain, natural streams, and dense forests" that were "an eerie ringer for Vietnam." For extras, the production company drew on the large population of Vietnamese refugees who had settled in southern California, many of whom had served in the army of the Republic of Vietnam.

4. With Avco Embassy as the film's distributor.

Although the terrain was perfect, Post recalled, "Everything had to be shot with tight angles, otherwise the rides from the amusement park would show in the background." Moreover, the budget only allowed for forty days of filming. "There was only one take on every scene basically," recalled Craig Wasson, age twenty-three and making his third film appearance, as a young draftee. Still, Wasson said it was a happy set, noting, "Everybody was impressed by the script and felt that we were doing something important."

Much of the credit for this atmosphere went to Post. The gentle, sensitive director was well suited to psychological and social dramas, but for the most part he found himself directing action films, including Clint Eastwood's *Hang 'Em High* and *Magnum Force,* and *Beneath the Planet of the Apes.* Said Marc Singer, playing the amiable Captain Livetti, "When we would film, he would clasp his hands together and wring them with enthusiasm. He would rock from foot to foot, like a coach from the sidelines, and watch with delight at every line that was spoken."

Post particularly relished his work with Lancaster. "I was alerted to the fact that he was a little difficult," the director said in retrospect. "Not on my picture. He was just tremendous on my picture. He had a great sense of humor, and we took advantage of that." Indeed, the droll wit that Burt brought to Major Barker would be one of the great joys of the film. Moreover, Post admired the effort that the star put into the work. As he put it, "I loved him because this was a craftsman. He really poured every corpuscle he could gather in his system into what he did."

Arguably the film's young costars derived even more pleasure from their interaction with Burt; many of them had thrilled to the likes of *The Crimson Pirate, Apache, Gunfight at the O.K. Corral,* and *Trapeze* as youngsters. According to Post, Singer, a stage actor with a Lancastrian physical presence, had even been offered his choice of roles in *Spartans* and asked for the one that had the most screen time with Burt.

Years later, Singer remembered his first on-screen moment with the star—which was, additionally, the first scene that Lancaster filmed for the picture. "Standing behind the camera," Singer explained, "was the entire production company: there was every young actor who was in this film, there was the entire crew. And all of this attention was being focused toward us, Burt Lancaster and this young actor standing beside him." Singer was so nervous that he had to silently give himself words of encouragement "in order to stop my knees from knocking," the same syndrome in reverse that Burt had experienced in his first scene with Montgomery Clift in *From Here to Eternity.* Singer continued, "The director, Ted Post, calls, 'And action,' and as the cameras started to roll, Burt Lancaster takes this little cigar out of his mouth, and he looks up at me with this old and wrinkled and seamed face, with these beautiful crystal blue eyes in it, he blows a little puff of smoke and says, 'You know, when I was a younger man, all I had to do was walk out on a set and say, 'Hey, baby, what's going on. Ha! Ha! Ha!' And he does a parody on himself. And suddenly as he says, 'Hey, baby, what's going on,' his face transforms itself and he becomes young again. And he's gorgeous. He's gorgeous to the extent that you can't take your eyes off him, you're mesmerized by that beauty. And then his face relaxes, and he says, 'But, as I've become older,' and he takes another puff, 'it forced me to learn how to act.' Then there's a huge silence. And the director says, 'Cut.' And at that instant I fell deeply in love with him, and that was it. A man of his stature and his experience saying such a thing and revealing himself in such a way and making everything all right with everybody was someone you had to adore."

Craig Wasson also recalled *his* first scene with Lancaster: "We'd been rehearsing it, and I was really a bit tense, acting with Burt Lancaster. He took me aside, and he said, 'Listen, do you know your lines?' And I said, 'Yeah.' And he said, 'Well, look, you've got a great script here. You've got a director, you've got a cinematographer, you've got me. Son, you don't have to do a goddamn thing.' It was great advice really. I was trying so hard to do the right thing that I wasn't doing the scene, I wasn't just speaking. And I think the scene went well based on that direction."

Burt evidenced even greater generosity toward the end of filming when the company ran out of money. According to Post, the shortfall resulted from embezzlement. When the director made the discovery, he was stunned. He knew he was on schedule and fully believed that he had ample funds to complete the work. Instead, he was short $150,000! With considerable embarrassment, he reported the discovery to Lancaster. At first, Burt was shocked too. Then he recovered, wrote a personal check for the requisite amount, and enabled Post to complete the picture.

Eight months would elapse before Burt started work on his next project, *Zulu Dawn,* but in typical Lancaster fashion, he kept busy, narrating three different documentaries, including a ninety-minute NBC special entitled *Psychic Phenomenon: Exploring the Unknown,* and a twenty-part series of one-hour episodes examining the Eastern Front during World War II—for which Lancaster spent three weeks shooting

in the Soviet Union. It was produced by Air Time International and entitled *The Unknown War.*

Then, on June 14, 1978, *Go Tell the Spartans* opened. Burt Lancaster is
"in solid command of the best starring role he's had in years," proclaimed Richard Schickel in *Time.* Kevin Thomas of the *Los Angeles
Times* agreed, going on to note, "How rewarding it is to realize that despite the various mediocre movies of recent years Lancaster's dramatic
instincts are sharp as ever and his characterizations—when given the
opportunity, as here—are only enriched by maturity." Indeed, Burt's
Asa Barker is a profane, frustrated, sarcastic career officer who, as he
puts it, has "the feeling we're in a goddamn loony bin." It is a memorable
character, enlivened by Lancaster's droll comic timing.

The picture also garnered notices the likes of which Lancaster had
not seen in years. *Newsweek* called it "the best movie yet made about
the Vietnam War," a sentiment echoed by, of all people, Stanley Kauffmann.

But, despite the fine work by all hands, the public was simply not interested in Vietnam, and *Go Tell the Spartans* quickly disappeared
from view. Nine years later, in the wake of *Platoon* and *Rambo: First
Blood Part II* (and in anticipation of *Full Metal Jacket* and Clint Eastwood's *Hamburger Hill*), an independent producer named Martin Cohen sought to rerelease *Spartans,* in association with Dino De
Laurentiis, who had obtained the rights to the picture as part of his acquisition of Avco Embassy. But nothing much came of the attempt. Lancaster was philosophical about the matter, saying at the time, "I thought
it was a marvelous movie. You hope it makes some money, but that's always a mysterious thing. . . . Life goes on. You die and you're forgotten.
For me, it's gone and over."

Like *Go Tell the Spartans,* Burt's next project, *Zulu Dawn,* struggled
to reach production.

The project had its origins in a 1964 film entitled *Zulu,* which had
starred Stanley Baker, Michael Caine, and Jack Hawkins and had detailed an engagement in the 1879 war between the Zulus and the British
colonials who controlled their homeland, Natal.

Ten years later, Baker and Cy Endfield, who had coproduced the hit
film, decided to make a prequel, *Zulu Dawn,* which would cover the
origins of the Zulu uprising and the disastrous British defeat at

Isandhlwana on January 22, 1879. Endfield, who had written and directed *Zulu,* drafted the new script with Anthony Storey, but by the time Samarkand Motion Picture Productions decided to make the film in 1978, both he and Baker were dead.

To replace Endfield as director, producer Nate Kohn chose Douglas Hickox, a forty-nine-year-old Londoner whose films included *Theatre of Blood* with Vincent Price and Diana Rigg and *Brannigan* with John Wayne. Hickox, in turn, amassed an impressive cast of British actors, notably Peter O'Toole as Lord Chelmsford, the commander of the forces in Natal, John Mills as the high commissioner, and Simon Ward, Nigel Davenport, Michael Jayston, Denholm Elliott, and a then-unknown Bob Hoskins as officers and enlisted men in the local British outpost. Lancaster, the lone American, would portray the one-armed Colonel Durnford, a rebel who runs afoul of Chelmsford. It was the role Baker was to have played.

On June 20, 1978, Lancaster, O'Toole, and Ward arrived in Johannesburg, South Africa, and made their way to KwaZulu—Zulu trust land—where filming was to take place, on what was to be a twelve-week schedule. In the manner of Burt's own *His Majesty O'Keefe* twenty-seven years earlier, the producers of *Zulu Dawn* had spent $1 million to erect a city out of prefabricated ski huts roughly thirty miles from the Isandhlwana battle site. Maintaining the facilities cost roughly $40,000 a day.

Samarkand, a novice company that primarily served as an outlet for European investors, wildly underestimated the costs of production. So much so that what had originally been budgeted for $7.5 million ended up running $15 million. To meet the deficit, the producers had to return to the original backers during filming. From them, they obtained a quarter of the overage; the rest came from German and Swiss banks. Said producer Nate Kohn, "They saw what we had and . . . gave us the go-ahead to make the film the way we envisioned it in the beginning."

Indeed, *Zulu Dawn* was being crafted with considerable care. Hickox was determined to show the overconfidence of the military, which led to the slaughter at Isandhlwana, and to portray the arrogance of the colonial administrators, which had fostered the rebellion in the first place. Said the director, "Historically it's fascinating, because the English did to the Zulus what Hitler did to Poland—provoked a war with a perfectly reasonable race." Ultimately, he felt that the best way to shed light on the engagement was to focus on the major participants. As he put it, "There's absolutely no point in hacking a thousand faceless people to death. We go to great lengths to establish the character of each person, and we have an extraordinarily good English cast, all superlative actors."

Hickox's approach was what drew Lancaster to the project. "This is an honest film full of action and courage," the star said. "It is very realistic with an almost documentary approach that follows the course of history accurately. It makes a real change from some of the films being made today. I've turned down a lot of garbage lately."

Although Durnford was much like *Ulzana's Raid*'s McIntosh, the role offered a few unique challenges. First, Burt had to learn to fight and ride a horse with one arm. Second, he had to contend with a Scottish accent. And third, he had to hold his own with one of the great actors of the British stage and screen, Peter O'Toole, a fitting complement to his previous film appearances with Laurence Olivier, Paul Scofield, and Anthony Hopkins.

Looking back on the experience in 1994, O'Toole remembered Lancaster with great fondness: "He was a pleasure, he was a delight. . . . It's always easy to be with someone one admires. And we just got on."

Lancaster was sixty-five at the outset of 1979, a bit old for cowboys and Indians, but he had a final Western in him.

Cattle Annie and Little Britches had been conceived by Robert Ward in 1973 while he was teaching college in upstate New York. The title characters were two adolescents who joined the notorious Doolin-Dalton gang in the waning days of the Old West. "The girls were orphans who hung out in Guthrie, Oklahoma," explained the screenwriter, "and who literally lived through what they read in dime novels, the way kids today live through video games. Meanwhile, the Doolin-Dalton gang were media freaks who wanted to be as famous as the James gang." The dichotomy between myth and reality would supply much of the picture's humor, as would the outlaws' attempts to maintain their old ways in the face of civilization's advance.

Although *Cattle Annie and Little Britches* was something of a cross between *True Grit* and *Butch Cassidy and the Sundance Kid,* Ward's screenplay "was turned down by every studio," asserted Rupert Hitzig, an independent producer who championed the project in 1975 as a vehicle for Jodie Foster and Tatum O'Neal. Finally, after three years, Hitzig and his partner, comedian Alan King, were able to finance the $5.1-million picture through Britain's Hemdale Leisure Corporation and the United Artists Theatre Circuit. By then, Foster and O'Neal were too old for the roles, so director Lamont Johnson cast Amanda Plummer and Diane Lane, newcomers with only one, as-yet-unreleased, film between them.[5]

With unknowns in the title roles, a major older star was needed as Bill Doolin. John Wayne, the obvious choice, was interested, but he was ill. The producers waited a year for him before turning to Lancaster. Said Johnson, Burt "really adored that character." Moreover, it was fitting that the star, having played Ned Buntline in *Buffalo Bill and the Indians,* give life to one of the legend-maker's creations.

Cattle Annie would take Lancaster back to Durango, Mexico, one last time. The town had not changed much since he first saw it twenty years earlier. "Everybody in Durango walks around with a .45 in his belt," recalled Rod Steiger, who would costar as Sheriff Bill Tilghman. "I mean, that's one place where you're not going to flirt with anybody's girlfriend, I can tell you that."

Filming began on April 2, 1979, on a nine-week schedule. Lancaster quickly antagonized his director, a thirty-year veteran of stage, film, and television, first as an actor and later as a director, with several breakthrough made-for-TV movies to his credit (*My Sweet Charlie, That Certain Summer,* and *The Execution of Private Slovik*). As Johnson recalled, on their first day together, they were shooting an action scene. "And I laid it out and he said, 'Very good, Monty.' " He then started giving bits of business to the other actors. Johnson interrupted, saying, "Burt, let's talk about this. I'm the director. If you have some ideas, let me pass them on." Lancaster agreed to do so. But, in the days that followed, the directorial comments continued, with Johnson, in his words, growing "tenser and tenser." Finally, he said, "I just blew up in front of everybody. I said, 'Burt, stop directing. You have a director.' And *he* blew up at me." The source of Johnson's rage was obvious, but what had angered Burt? As Johnson saw it, he "was mad that I was interfering with his prerogative as a great old action star to know what to do about things, and he refused to accept the fact that he was possibly confusing the actors by giving counterdirections." They argued for several moments, then repaired to the director's trailer where, to quote Johnson, "we yelled at each other for like two hours. I mean, we were mad, and we screamed."

Finally, having exhausted themselves, they rejoined the company and shot the scene in question. After that, Johnson said, Lancaster worked

5. Lane had made her debut in George Roy Hill's *A Little Romance.*

hard to restrain himself. When he occasionally slipped, the director would grin, wink, and ask, "Burt, are we getting into that?" and the star would stop. Otherwise, Johnson found Lancaster a pleasure. "He was wonderful in it," the director recalled. "And interpretively, he would listen to me when I would say, 'Not quite as broad as that,' 'Let's try a little of this,' 'What if you went after the scene as though that were happening.'" And he added, "We parted great friends, and we've had warm times since."

Burt also earned the respect of his costars. "I admired him because of his discipline," said John Savage, cast as a member of the gang, while Steiger, an actor of very different training and style, called him "a very wonderful, professional actor. He was very polite to me. He was very nice. And a man of dignity and intelligence." As for Lane and Plummer, Johnson said, "He loved them both, and they loved him. They had scenes together that they adored doing because it was like working with grandpa, you know?"

The esteem in which Lancaster was held made what happened on his last day of filming that much more frightening. He was slated to do a chase scene on horseback after lunch—in the hot June sun. Johnson cautioned him to eat sparingly, but, as the director recalled, "One of his stunt buddies cooked a massive lunch—lots of tortillas and beans—and Burt ate his fill. Shortly after lunch, we were getting set up for the scene, and Burt came over, looking sort of gray. He started to mount up, and he fell flat on the ground. And was absolutely ashen. His eyes were open, and he was having a hard time breathing. And he looked like he was dying." Finally, Lancaster's stunt double and several other members of the crew took him to a hospital—leaving the company devastated. Said Johnson, "We were all standing around with tears coming down our faces, like we're seeing the end of Burt Lancaster."

Ultimately, Lancaster rallied. Later, he would tell the director that when he arrived at the hospital, he awoke long enough to hear his stunt double ordering the Mexican physicians to give him a "KGB."[6] "That's all I needed," Burt quipped, "was a Soviet secret-service man crawling all over me."

According to Lamont Johnson, Lancaster's near-death experience left him "ill for a long, long time. He had to have an operation some weeks later." In this, the director may have been somewhat mistaken. Burt never made public mention of an operation in 1979, nor did any news-

6. Obviously meaning an EKG.

papers report such an eventuality. In January of 1980, however, some six months after *Cattle Annie* wrapped, he went into Cedars Sinai Medical Center for serious gallbladder surgery. In fact, he nearly died on the operating table.

But, before that, he passed the rest of the summer of 1979 quietly and uneventfully. Then, in September, he gave serious thought to running for the presidency of the Screen Actors Guild, a powerful position that had, in fact, launched Ronald Reagan's political career.

The current president, Kathleen Nolan, had decided not to seek re-election. But she wanted to insure the continuity of her policies by choosing her replacement. "And I came up with Burt Lancaster," she recalled. "I felt that he was somebody who people respected." Moreover, he was a devoted unionist. As she put it, whenever "there was a picket needing people who were highly visible or people to speak, he was always there."

Nolan arranged a meeting to sound Burt out. He was interested, but before he made a final decision on his candidacy, he undertook a thorough investigation of the union's affairs. Said Nolan, "He wanted to look at the books, he wanted to know about the financial situation at the Guild, what the structure was. He talked to the executive secretary. We went over contracts and proposals for where we were going." Then, he decided to run.

"There was absolutely no question that he would have been the next president of the union," Nolan asserted—except for one technicality. Although Burt had not produced a film since *The Midnight Man* five years earlier, he had never disbanded Norlan Productions, and Article V, Section 13, of the Guild rules stipulated that "no person who has an interest in motion picture production . . . shall be eligible to become or remain an Officer of the Guild." On that basis, Lancaster's candidacy was rejected by the Elections Review Committee.

Said Nolan in 1993, "I always felt—I still feel today—that the opposition to the production company, which was dormant, was something that could have been worked out." Nevertheless, Burt's political career, such as it was, came to an abrupt end.

The actor wasted little time brooding over the defeat. The end of September found him in Spain, golfing, attending bullfights with friends, and attending film festivals in San Sebastián and Deauville, France. Then, in October, *Zulu Dawn* opened in London—where it was a dismal failure. Philip French of the London *Observer* called it "a distinctly uncomfortable affair," although he noted that as "spectacle it isn't all bad."

Viewing the film in the 1990s, from an American perspective, it is hard to see why it did so poorly. Although depth of character was sacrificed to the sweep of events and Lancaster sported what French called "a rather ill-fitting Celtic accent"—no surprise in light of *Judgment at Nuremberg* and *Valdez Is Coming*—the picture shed light on a little-known and interesting period of British and African history. Time and again, director Hickox juxtaposed scenes of the two cultures, leading to the inevitable conclusion that the Zulus and the British colonialists did not understand each other any better than had the Apaches and the cavalry in the American Southwest, a point made quite differently but not more effectively in *Ulzana's Raid*. Hickox was especially adroit at showing the power and majesty of the Zulus; his opening sequence, which starts with villagers going about their routines, silhouetted against the rising sun and ends with thousands of warriors dancing, is mesmerizing. Moreover, *Zulu Dawn* is peppered with informative vignettes of nineteenth-century army life, and the battle sequences are extremely well done.

Given the negative response in Britain, *Zulu Dawn* was not picked up for distribution in America. Finally, nearly three years after its premiere, Roger Corman's New World Pictures made it available in the States on a limited, short-run basis.

As October of 1979 drew to a close, Lancaster started work on another film, his final project of the decade. But, in all save chronology, it would more appropriately belong to the 1980s.

The seventies had been the worst decade of Burt's career. Most of his pictures, produced on small budgets after they had been rejected by numerous producers, had opened with a minimum of advertising support and quickly disappeared from view. Consequently, by 1979, through good pictures and bad, the vast majority of filmgoers had simply grown accustomed to tuning Burt out.

All that was about to change, however. The actor's long career would enjoy one final burst of glory, a comeback in the true Hollywood tradition, thanks to a small picture about a resort community that was itself on the brink of a glorious renaissance.

On October 31, *Atlantic City* went into production.

CHAPTER NINETEEN

"Floy-Floy"

Atlantic City began for the most prosaic of reasons: Canadian producers John Kemeney and Denis Heroux of the International Cinema Corporation had a tax-shelter group that wanted to invest in a picture, and they had nothing to shoot. Worse, they only had six months before the money would disappear.

It was French director Louis Malle and American playwright John Guare who suggested they do a film about the old New Jersey resort community, once home to gangsters and bootleggers, that had just legalized gambling. "For both of us," said the director, "it was very obviously a metaphor for America itself."

It was somewhat odd that a filmmaker born to a wealthy family in Thumeries, France, would be drawn to such subject matter, but Malle had come to America in the mid-1970s because he felt his work was stagnating. Being an outsider, he thought, would give him a fresh perspective. "It's not that I see things that others don't," he said, "but I'm curious about things that, probably if I were born here, I would take for granted, which is the case in my own country."

The plot of what was first called *The Neighbor* and then *Bamboozle* and then *Atlantic City, U.S.A.*[1] centered on two characters: Lou, a small-time gangster reduced to playing nursemaid, errand boy, and lover to a cantankerous widow; and Sally, a young, pretty oyster-bar waitress who aspires to a career as a dealer in Monte Carlo. They, in fact, represented the past and future of the city, but Guare, known for his quirky characters, made them two highly distinctive individuals.

Malle knew precisely whom he wanted for Sally: Susan Sarandon. The thirty-two-year-old actress, who had made her film debut in *Joe* in 1970,

1. The "U.S.A." was eventually dropped.

had already worked with him in his previous film *Pretty Baby.* She was also his girlfriend. For Lou, he had two actors in mind, Robert Mitchum and Burt Lancaster—with a decided preference for Mitchum, whom he had always admired.

Malle arranged to see both actors in Los Angeles on the same day. First came Mitchum, who struck him as disinterested. Next, he met with Burt. Early in the conversation, they discovered their mutual admiration for Visconti—whom Malle had known. That, said the director, "started us very much on the right foot." Then, they talked about the script, and Lancaster won Malle over by saying, "This is the kind of a part for an actor of my age that comes along once every ten years." The role was his.

When the company assembled at the Resorts International Hotel and Casino in Atlantic City at the end of October 1979, a mere three months had elapsed since the project's initiation. Burt was thrilled to be in New Jersey, only a few hours' drive from Manhattan. He said at the time, "It's like a homecoming for me. . . . I haven't worked on the East Coast since *The Young Savages* with Shelley Winters in 1960."

Malle was experiencing a different emotion. "We were really short of time and I was quite scared," he later confessed. Since the script was not finished, Guare was on hand for further drafting as well as rewrites. The plan was to shoot for about three weeks on location, then complete the picture at the Sono Lab production center in Montreal. In the end, however, Malle got several extra weeks in New Jersey because, in his words, "we never had the right weather."

While *Atlantic City* was in production, the town was undergoing radical change. So much so that filming there became like trying to hit a moving target. For example, the beach house that was rented for a key Lancaster-Sarandon scene was destroyed immediately after the company finished with it. On another occasion, Malle heard about a building that was going to be torn down and moved production to the site so that he could get the demolition in the background.

While Malle coped with logistics, Lancaster wrestled with his role. Creating Lou was a major challenge because the character was a nonentity whose biggest thrill was watching his pretty neighbor run lemons over her naked torso. Moreover, he lives in the past, when, as he puts it, "Atlantic City had floy-floy coming out of its ears." Said Burt, "I've never tried anything like this—a weak character. It's good to reach out to try something different." He was not intimidated, however. As he put it, "I know the Atlantic City story. I know these characters. I . . . lived among them in New York."

In the first few days of production, Malle feared that the star was, as he put it, "too heroic" in the role. But as filming progressed, he began to realize that Burt's power would, in fact, work to the picture's advantage. "Because it's very hard to play this little wreck of a man," he explained, "and be touching and be funny and be somebody you want to watch. But he could do that because of his image, because of his past." Still, Malle wanted to keep Lancaster from relying on his usual mannerisms, especially his trademark smile. "I cut a lot of that grinning in the cutting room," he asserted. "I used to say to the editor, 'We're going to degrin Burt.' "

In some respects, Malle enjoyed working with Lancaster. "His approach was never intellectual," said the director, "which, I must admit, I liked. Coming from Europe, I'm not used to actors who say, 'Let's talk about the motivations.' Usually that drives me crazy." Typically, they would do a couple of takes, then discuss what was happening and make adjustments. The director was pleased to find Burt open to his suggestions.

Sarandon was more of a Method actor. "It was really funny to see these two together," said the director, "because they were obviously a different generation, a different style of acting, a different sensibility." But, as he pointed out, the characters were different as well, so, on the screen, the dichotomy worked. In life, it produced tensions. Malle felt that, to some extent, Lancaster was suspicious of Sarandon because she was the director's girlfriend. Conversely, neither Malle nor Sarandon found Burt, in the director's words, "a barrel of laughs." He pointed out that the actor was particularly difficult at night "because he was drinking. When he was drinking, his Irishness would come out, and he would get very mean."

There was tension between Lancaster and Sarandon, but there was downright hostility between Burt and the actress playing the old lady, Kate Reid. Originally Malle and the producers had hoped to cast a major star; in 1994, the director, with some uncertainty, believed that they had sought Ginger Rogers. Reid, primarily a stage actress, was virtually unknown to the general public. Moreover, she was unaccustomed to working for the camera. But she was attractive on two counts: she was talented, and she was Canadian, a plus in light of the picture's financing.

Reid's lack of celebrity may have partly roused Lancaster's ire. Said

Malle, "I think Burt was expecting that this horrible character he had to deal with would be at least as famous as he was, because that would have made it easier. But the fact that we cast this woman he never heard of . . . from the beginning he was not happy." Reid did not help matters. On the first day of filming, she threw herself at Lancaster's feet, which drew a big laugh from the company, but Burt was less than thrilled.

The off-screen hostility, however, was perfect for the on-screen pairing. Reid was inspired to, in Malle's words, offer "certain details and suggestions to make their relationship even worse than it was written in the script." And Lancaster, he argued, laughing, "was great in those scenes because he was so pissed."

Malle himself got into a heated argument with the star late in the production, as they were filming the final scene between Lancaster and Sarandon. The sequence takes place in a motel outside town. She volunteers to pick up a pizza, but has no intention of returning. According to Malle, Burt wanted his character to end the relationship. As the director put it, "After having spent a night with him, for him it was inconceivable that a woman would leave." But Malle insisted that they do the scene as written. Years later, John Guare reminded him that (to quote Malle) Burt "sort of exploded and said, 'All right, we're going to do it the way the froggie wants it, and then we'll do it the way I want it.'" Which they did. But, in the cutting room, Burt lost.

By the time *Atlantic City* wrapped, 1979 had given way to a new decade.

The eighties would bring significant changes in Lancaster's life. To the good, he would meet a new woman and fall in love. Less happily, his health would start to fail; the gallbladder operation at the outset of the decade was a serious portent of things to come. But, incredibly, he would keep working at a daunting rate. More often than not, he no longer carried his projects, but he was a realist about the nature of the business. As he said in 1985, "It's a natural diminution of power, energy, things of that kind, and the realization that new people are coming up who will take the spotlight. You have to step aside for them."

Still, he intended to be selective in what he did. As late as 1988, when he was seventy-five, he was proclaiming, "As an actor, selfishly perhaps, I want a role that gives me an opportunity to explore different dimensions, to show sides of me, Burt Lancaster, that maybe people haven't seen before. You always strive for something that's a little beyond you and maybe not quite attainable, but you have to reach for it." The man who had once been ashamed of acting now declared, "The joy of creativity is delicious. The moment-by-moment experience of doing it."

For starters, there was *La Pelle (The Skin),* which took him back to Italy. Like *Ulzana's Raid* and *Zulu Dawn,* the picture would examine the clash of two disparate cultures, in this case the American GIs who invaded Italy in 1943 (a force that included one Burton Lancaster) and the residents of Naples, the first city on the mainland to be occupied by the Allies. Based on the book by Curzio Malaparte, a onetime supporter of Mussolini who became a liaison with the Allies in the final stages of the war, *La Pelle* was to be a showcase for Gaumont Italia (an affiliate of France's Gaumont S.A.). As such, it would have a budget of $6 million, lavish by European standards, and would be shot in English (except when the Italians spoke to one another, in which case they would use their native language). The title derived from Malaparte's assertion, "Our country is our skin."

Directing was Liliana Cavani, who wrote the screenplay with Robert Katz, coauthor of *The Cassandra Crossing.* As she saw it, occupied Naples was something of a modern Sodom and Gomorrah. Said American model Alexandra King, who made her movie debut in *La Pelle,* "What she really tried to portray in this film is . . . how whorish the Italians are sometimes and how naive the Americans are sometimes." Born in 1936, Cavani made her first feature in 1966, but it was 1974's *The Night Porter,* the highly controversial story of an ex-Nazi and a concentration camp victim, that brought her international recognition.

To play Malaparte, she cast Marcello Mastroianni, symbol of the Latin sophisticate in such classics as 1960's *La Dolce Vita* and 1963's *8½.* But she needed an American for General Cork, the head of the occupying forces (patterned after Mark Clark). Burt read the script and liked it. He was intrigued by Cork, whom Cavani described as "slightly comic . . . pompous, lacking in humor, and incapable of understanding the Neapolitan people."

But, through a misunderstanding in real life, the star nearly passed up the project. According to Robert Katz, Enrico Medioli, who had cowritten *Conversation Piece,* hosted a luncheon while Burt was considering *La Pelle,* at which Katz and Cavani were present. Lancaster was convinced that the affair had been set up to pressure him into doing the film. "That night he called me up," Katz recalled, "and said, 'You fucking cocksucker. What the fuck are you doing to me?' . . . No one had ever talked to me like that in my life." Katz was just about to hang up when Burt calmed down. Then, in a complete about-face, he asked, "How much money do you think they have?"

In the end, said Cavani, "The amount requested [by agent Ben Benjamin] for the four weeks of work for Burt Lancaster was one-third of the entire budget." Her producer, Renzo Rossellini, Roberto's son, told her to hire another actor, but she said, "I couldn't think about anybody else." Finally, Lancaster came up with a solution: he would do what he had done in *1900,* work for free! "I asked myself," Cavani recalled, "was this not the gesture of a prince?"

Filming started in Rome on August 18, 1980. The company also traveled to Cavani's native Capri, where Malaparte had his home. But the majority of the scenes were shot—appropriately—in Naples.

Although the production was scheduled for twelve weeks, Cavani ganged up Burt's scenes in the manner of his recent projects so that they could be filmed in a month. Thus, the company had been shooting in Rome for several weeks by the time he joined them. There was considerable anticipation as his arrival became imminent, and when he finally appeared, said Alexandra King, he was treated like royalty. "We were all walking on eggs around him," she recalled. According to her, he never did become a familiar presence. "We didn't have dinner with him or anything like that," she asserted, "whereas with Marcello, all of us often went out together. He was really alone, and you got the impression that he really wanted to be left alone." Katz and Cavani had more favorable impressions of Burt's impact on the cast and crew. Said the director, "He was loved by the members of the company because he never acted like a star." Still, she admitted that she did not socialize with him away from the set.

More importantly perhaps, Cavani was enormously pleased with Burt's work. Despite the intense heat during filming and the lack of adequate air-conditioning in his trailer, she found him "giving the best of himself just like it was the first movie of his career." Moreover, she said, "He would grasp immediately the sense of what a scene required." Such was their rapport that she felt "as if we had made other movies together and had known each other a long time."

Cavani was not, in fact, an old friend. But someone who was—Shelley Winters—gave Lancaster quite a surprise that summer. In her autobiography, *Shelley, Also Known as Shirley,* published by William Morrow in

June, she detailed at great length her affair with Burt in the late 1940s, a relationship that had gone unreported to that point. The prose was punctuated with the likes of "We gazed into each other's eyes. I guess we threw off such an aura of success, desire, and beauty that everyone who was anyone in the restaurant came up to talk to us, wanting to be included."

At the time, Burt did not say much about the autobiography, even to close friends. Looking back, however, Jackie Bone asserted, "I think Burt was very hurt—maybe surprised—that she said the things that she did in that book." Six years later, when he appeared on *Donahue,* a member of the audience asked about it. Burt answered somewhat evasively, "Yes. I was uncomfortable with some of the things that have been written about me, and like everything written about me, they are half-truths at best." Then he added, "She's a wonderful actress and a great girl."

Burt's presence in Italy for *La Pelle* led to his next assignment, a guest appearance in the lavish, ten-hour miniseries *Marco Polo* being coproduced by Procter & Gamble, RAI-TV, and the newly formed Chinese Cinematographic Company. The most compelling component of the project—which at $30 million was the most expensive TV program in history to that point—was that it would film for six months in mainland China.

The thirteenth-century explorer was played by a virtual unknown, Ken Marshall, who took on the role after Mandy Patinkin quit a couple of days into production. Marshall was in Italy thanks to his costarring role in *La Pelle,* but as far as can be determined, Lancaster had no hand in his casting. Marshall's principal costars, Marco's father and uncle, were taken by Denholm Elliott and Tony Vogel respectively, with Ying Ruocheng as Kublai Khan. But, in the fashion of such extended dramas, a battery of familiar faces were given cameos in the hope of bolstering the ratings. In addition to Lancaster, cast as Teobaldo Visconti, also known as the warrior pope, Gregory X, the list of luminaries included John Houseman, John Gielgud, Leonard Nimoy, Anne Bancroft, Tony Lo Bianco, F. Murray Abraham, Sada Thompson, and Ian McShane.

According to the project's director, Giuliano Montaldo, Burt's scenes took about three weeks to shoot and were primarily filmed at the basilica of Fassanova in southern Italy, which Montaldo described as "a very austere building of the twelve hundreds in naked stone. It was very cold, and it was impossible to warm up those immense spaces."

Even though the role was small, Lancaster, to quote Montaldo, "arrived on the set very well prepared." In fact, the director was impressed by his in-depth knowledge of Gregory X. Montaldo was also moved by the actor's insistence upon wearing original armor from the period—which weighed about seventy-five pounds—instead of the much lighter costume created for him. Moreover, he found Lancaster a joy to work with. "Perhaps even a little too meticulous," he added, "but adorable. I never had with him an argument during the three weeks of work on *Marco Polo.*"

By the time Lancaster finished with the miniseries, *Atlantic City* had opened, debuting in New York on April 3, 1981. According to Louis Malle, "When we made the film, we didn't have an American distributor, and it took months to convince Paramount to release it." Even after the picture won the Golden Lion at the Venice Film Festival (sharing the honor with John Cassavetes' *Gloria*), it opened with a minimum of publicity in only a few cities. But the critics raved about it and Burt's performance as the two-bit gangster. Perhaps *Newsweek*'s David Ansen summed up the reaction best when he asserted that "the movie's sweet, elegiac heart belongs to Lancaster. Lou may be the role of his lifetime and he carries it gently, obviously cherishing the gift."

The critical enthusiasm inspired Paramount to send *Atlantic City* into wide, general release, but according to Malle, the picture never really took off at the box office. "It sort of stayed in a few theaters and became a cult movie," he said. "I think it was very unpredictable and very original. It doesn't play out there when it's too original."

Burt went on to pick up most of the year's acting awards, including those of the Los Angeles Film Critics and the British Academy of Motion Picture Arts and Sciences. And he earned his fourth Academy Award nomination—nineteen years after he was cited for his performance in *Birdman of Alcatraz.* The picture also garnered nominations for Best Picture, Best Actress, Best Director, and Best Original Screenplay. But it failed to win in a single category. Perhaps the biggest disappointment came with Burt's loss; unfortunately, 1981 was Henry Fonda's year. The great American actor had never won an Oscar, and many in Hollywood feared—rightly, as it turned out—that *On Golden Pond* would be his last chance.[2]

Still, Lancaster's performance in *Atlantic City* will endure. He was funny, pathetic, flamboyant, charming, endearing, maddening—and old.

---

2. Fonda died five months after the awards ceremony, on August 12, 1982.

Indeed, although he had been looking grizzled on the screen for some time, *Atlantic City* marked his official transition to senior roles. It was a brave step to take.

In 1993, more than a decade after the film's release, many of his colleagues were still cheering his magnetic performance. Former HHL writer John Gay spoke for them all when he said that it represented "the accumulation of all the things that he was working for over the years. That was his lifetime achievement."

On May 15, just five weeks after the premiere of *Atlantic City*, *Cattle Annie and Little Britches* made its debut in New York. Nearly two years had elapsed since the picture had wrapped. For a long time the producers had struggled to a find a distributor. Then when Universal finally picked up the film, it kept it on the shelf for more than a year while trying to figure out how to market it. "They kept saying, 'What kind of a movie is it?' " recalled director Lamont Johnson. " 'Is it a Western, is it a comedy?' I said, 'It's a brand-new thing. It's a woman's switch on the desperado story, and if that isn't a fresh item to exploit, what is?' " Even when the picture did finally appear, Pauline Kael noted that it "wasn't really released: it was just dropped into a Broadway theater for a week to plug up a hole before *Outland* arrived."[3]

Usually a movie with that sort of history is absolutely terrible, but the Johnson-Lancaster Western was a delight—as several critics noted. *The New York Times'* Vincent Canby, for example, called it "a funny, sweet, mock-Western," while his counterpart in Los Angeles, Kevin Thomas, dubbed it "a very handsome film."

As with *Atlantic City*, much of the praise went to Lancaster—although Stanley Kauffmann could not resist the chance to assail him once more, writing, "His acting has always seemed to me that of an amateur imitating actors, as if he had hired a professional to do his role privately and was now showing us, as best he could, what he had learned from the pro." Canby more accurately asserted, "The Lancaster who presides over the twilight of the once-notorious Doolin-Dalton gang in *Cattle Annie* is in much closer connection with his resources as an actor than even the Lancaster who twenty years ago won an Oscar for his flamboyant performance in *Elmer Gantry*."

But the critical acclaim could not save *Cattle Annie* in the face of virtually no publicity. Coproducer Alan King was appalled. "As far as I'm

3. *Outland* was an outer-space melodrama, liberally adapted from *High Noon*, with Sean Connery in the Gary Cooper role.

concerned, it's become a cause célèbre," he said three months after the film's debut, "and I want it back to release independently." But, instead, the Western rode into cable-TV sunset.

Also in May, *La Pelle* was shown at Cannes. "At the end people booed and stamped their feet," recalled Robert Katz. "It was really embarrassing." At the time, *Variety* called the film "mostly a poorly staged creepshow travesty with little to redeem it. Performances, dialogue, and especially direction are embarrassingly inadequate."

Although the picture went on to enjoy box-office success in Italy, it was not picked up for distribution in the United States, making it the first Burt Lancaster movie never to play in the actor's native land.

In late spring, 1981, after finishing his work in *Marco Polo,* Burt returned home. By that point, his relationship with Jackie was in serious trouble. As she later put it, "We were really quarreling too much. It was a very uncomfortable situation."

"Jackie felt that she was being treated as his slave," asserted Anita Gillette. "She was there to cook for him, to have his meals ready when he came home, keep the house, be a companion on the road, service him. Jackie felt that she wanted to do something on her own. She took up any number of courses—just ask Burt, and he would wax eloquently on the subject of how many courses she took and didn't finish: interior design, she was going to learn a language, flower arrangements, landscape gardening." Gillette was surprised that Lancaster was not more supportive of these efforts. "He encouraged me," she pointed out.

"There was also a power struggle," Jackie added, "who's going to dominate who. I'm a strong lady, and he liked that in me, but it worked against us." Furthermore, Gillette maintained, "Once the passion was gone, once the sex disappeared, which I think it did, there was nothing there. They didn't communicate on the same level."

Although they had never wed, in all except the legalities they *were* married. "He gave her anything she wanted financially," recalled Gillette. "He took care of her sister, her family. He bought her a house. He gave her anything she wanted in the way of clothes and set up some sort of fund for her." The financial support, in fact, continued after the breakup. "She didn't have to go to court to sue for palimony," noted one of Burt's friends. "He was more than generous."

Moreover, they had established a strong emotional bond. "We weren't able to make the decision on our own to let it go," said Jackie, even though "we had hurt each other terribly." They even consulted a psychologist to help them break-up, although Lancaster did not usually like to involve outsiders in such matters. The first step was to live apart. When they returned from Italy, Jackie continued to reside in Malibu while Burt purchased a condominium in Century City, near Westwood and Beverly Hills. Once the backlot of 20th Century–Fox, the 176-acre complex came to encompass office buildings, shopping centers, dozens of restaurants, several hotels, a legitimate theater and cinema multiplex, a hospital, and two thousand condominiums and town houses. It would serve as Lancaster's home for the rest of his life.

Burt and Jackie had separated, but they would remain a couple—although on a less intense basis—for several more years.

Meanwhile, Lancaster's thoughts turned once more toward the stage, specifically *The Boys in Autumn,* Bernard Sabath's two-character speculation on the adulthood of Mark Twain's Tom Sawyer and Huckleberry Finn. Although it had humorous moments, the play was hardly a sunny reminiscence of youthful frolics and old friendships. Huck, now known as Henry Finnegan, had become a staid businessman who had performed a mercy killing on his wife, and Tom, called Thomas Gray, was a vaudevillian who had been arrested for child molesting.

The play reunited Burt with Kirk Douglas. It "was an inspired idea," said the play's director, Tom Moore. "I can't think of two people who would be more interesting playing an adult Tom Sawyer and Huck Finn." A sixth teaming of Hollywood's two tough guys[4]—live and in person—was not bad box office either, although Sabath maintained that the project "wasn't something they expected to make money on." Indeed, the actors primarily approached the play as a workshop for their own edification. "We don't want to do anything that isn't fun," Douglas cautioned all hands at the outset.

The Boys in Autumn enjoyed an unusually long rehearsal period—about eight or nine weeks—instead of the usual four. For starters, the stars wanted to shake out the material; the play, lacking a linear plot, particularly lent itself to tinkering. Moreover, they needed time to adjust to the physical and vocal demands of the stage. Because it was a two-character play, such extended work was possible: the producers did not have to finance a large roster of rehearsal salaries. Initially, the director was Ed Hastings, a fifty-one-year-old associate of San Francisco's American Conservatory Theatre (ACT). But after about five weeks,

4. Not counting *Victory at Entebbe,* in which they had no scenes together.

Hastings was fired. As Sabath put it, "I think a director has to be a powerhouse to direct stars," and Hastings was not.

As a replacement, they chose Tom Moore, a bright thirty-eight-year-old with a graduate degree from Yale and experience at the Guthrie, the Arena Stage, ACT, and the Mark Taper Forum, plus the Broadway productions of *Grease* and *Over Here.* "I was intimidated at the idea," he said, "but who's going to turn down the chance to direct these two men?"

Sabath was impressed with the choice, saying, "Tom is a marvelous director. . . . He comes in knowing the material, seeing what he wants to create, and seeing that it can be done. . . . So he was the powerhouse that any play wants." But even with Moore at the helm, rehearsals proceeded with considerable discussion and debate. "It was never totally comfortable," the director recalled, "because I always felt like I was a kind of an arbiter—between the play, myself, and two people [Burt and Kirk], all of whom had a slightly different take on what it should be." Surprisingly, of all those involved, Moore said, "Burt was actually the most willing to do the author's original intent. . . . He was usually the one who was fighting for us to stop tearing it apart."

Indeed, the star was starting to mellow. "I think Burt had reached a sort of peace with who he is," Moore said. By contrast, the director felt that Douglas was "still in the battle to have a major career. That's not a negative, but they're very different in what they want." Sabath also saw differences in the stars' personalities: "Kirk is very exterior, fire and music. And Burt knows how to suffer in silence." Moreover, both playwright and director noted the actors' competitive spirits. As Sabath put it, "They wanted to make sure things were fifty-fifty." As for their rapport, Burt said at the time, "We've got what I call a love-hate relationship." To which Moore added, "I got the impression that they both led their own lives, that they didn't socialize much, that they were never bosom buddies. They had a healthy respect for each other, but also a realization that they had different interests and different purposes. Even socially."

Moore gravitated toward Lancaster. In retrospect, the director said, "I feel that I got to be friends with Burt. . . . I think he respected me, and I really respected him and grew to love him." Moreover, he "found him so gentle and considerate and touching in his wish to make this play work."

The Boys in Autumn premiered on September 3 at the Marines Memorial, a small proscenium theater in San Francisco, for a four-week engagement. It was not a hit. Gerald Nachman, drama critic for the *San Francisco Chronicle,* complained about the lack of plot, asserting "by

Act II it's plain that nothing is happening onstage except show-biz charisma" and saw little to call to mind Twain's Huck and Tom, arguing, "Their random reminiscences could be a reunion of any two old pals." Of the acting duo, he found Douglas more comfortable onstage. "Lancaster," he wrote, "never knows quite where to turn—where the 'camera' is." Even Moore conceded, "Kirk had had the more legitimate training, and I think could manipulate language onstage more readily. . . . When an actor isn't used to projecting, he feels forced. I think that was a real frustration for" Burt. But, despite the poor notices, the play was sold out for the entire run. *Variety* described it as "a theatrical event not theatre," meaning that the crowds came to see the stars not the drama.

Initially, the hope had been to carry the production to Broadway, but Lancaster and Douglas stopped after the Marines Memorial engagement. Burt later asserted that they found the piece too tiring to pursue, but the tepid critical response was no doubt a contributing factor. Still, he looked back on the experience in a positive light, saying, "Although it was a flawed play, I enjoyed working on *The Boys in Autumn*. . . . It was very rewarding because people loved seeing Kirk and I together. There were some very fine moments for both of us from an actor's point of view."

Five years later, the play would finally come to Broadway via the not-for-profit company Circle in the Square, with George C. Scott as Huck and John Cullum as Tom and Theodore Mann directing. It would not be a success.

One plus emerged from the demise of *The Boys in Autumn:* it freed Burt for the role of the eccentric oil tycoon Felix Happer in *Local Hero*—which would have been precluded by an extended Broadway engagement. No one was more pleased than Bill Forsyth. "He was my favorite choice from the word go," said the picture's writer-director. "As I was writing it, I began to hear him saying the lines. But I didn't really think we would get him." Even though accepting the role in the $4.5-million comedy meant reducing his usual asking price (in exchange for points), Lancaster knew a good thing when he saw it. "One of the privileges of being my age," he explained, "is that you get to choose the roles you like. It's amazing the junk that's sent to me. The same sort of 'tits and sand' epics I did thirty years ago. I turn them down, of course. But when a good script comes along—like *Atlantic City* or this one—I get the urge to go back to work."

The project had been inspired by a news story about a man in the Hebrides who had wrangled a highly favorable deal out of an American oil company. "I wondered how the rural Scots and the Texas oilmen would get along," recalled British producer David Puttnam, whose most recent picture, *Chariots of Fire,* had beaten *Atlantic City* for the 1981 Best Picture Oscar. "Somewhere in there was the idea for a movie. But it needed a gentle comic approach, the sort of thing Frank Capra and Preston Sturges did so well. Few filmmakers have that touch in this day of going for the big laugh."

One who did was Forsyth. Born in Glasgow in 1946, he had only written and directed two features, one of which, 1981's *Gregory's Girl,* a $400,000 tale of adolescent love, had become a sleeper hit in America. In Forsyth's hands, *Local Hero* became a fable about a town of quaint locals who become rich by outnegotiating a young go-getter from Houston; he called it "a Scottish *Beverly Hillbillies.*" To play the sharp urbanite MacIntyre, Forsyth cast Peter Riegert, an amiable thirty-five-year-old New Yorker who had made his film debut in 1978's *National Lampoon's Animal House.* The other major parts would be assumed by Scots.

For Burt, Happer would be another "and/as" role, demanding a bit of shooting in Houston and three weeks in Scotland. But it was the best "and/as" role of his career. As the actor noted, "Felix Happer is just a little mad. When he's not putting his business rivals literally over a barrel, he's shoring up his psyche with 'abuse therapy' or indulging his passion for astronomy." The character, even more than Asa Barker in *Go Tell the Spartans,* was funny without meaning to be, and Lancaster would deliver lines like "I want you to keep an eye on Virgo for me, will you do that?" and "Good sky you've got here, MacIntyre. Well done" with complete deadpan, thereby maximizing their comic potential.

Filming began in Houston in April of 1982, but the bulk of the work took place in Scotland, principally the town of Pennan on the east coast. The locals were awed by Lancaster's presence. To Riegert, it was, in his words, "pretty fascinating to watch Burt walk the streets and have different people yelling after him different movies that they liked him in. 'Ah, *Crimson Pirate,* loved it, fantastic, great. Ah, *The Train, The Train.*' It's a way of the world being turned into a village. I mean, suddenly you're the mayor of a village."

Riegert was not above awe himself. A child of the fifties, he had caught Burt's pictures at his local Brooklyn movie theater, and his own attitude toward his costar flowed naturally into MacIntyre's for Happer. As he put it, "I had the good fortune of playing a character who was overwhelmed by Lancaster's character. So . . . I didn't really have to do any work. It was already within me, because that's how I saw him anyway."

In a funny sort of way, Burt and Peter even adopted something of the quirky rapport between their characters. As the young actor explained, "Whenever we would see each other—and this was totally without ever having discussed it—if I was standing around the tea truck or if I was getting my costume or if I was going to my dressing room, if we crossed paths, he would begin by saying the first line of the scene of that day, and that's how we rehearsed."

"Mrs. Vineburg," Burt said to him on one such occasion.

Confused, Riegert replied, "I'm sorry, Burt, what did you say?"

"Mrs. Vineburg."

Riegert, frantically trying to place the scene—with no luck—asked him to say it once more. Which Burt did.

" 'Mrs. Vineburg'?" Riegert asked, finally giving up. "Is that a new line?"

"No, no. Your cousin Anna Vineburg, she sends her regards."

"Apparently, my cousin Anna Vineburg," Riegert explained, "worked for his lawyer's firm and, through his lawyer, sent her regards to me." That could have been a scene from the movie.

Watching the rising young actor and the elderly star communicate must have been a treat, but no more so than seeing Burt with Bill Forsyth. "Bill is practically nonverbal," Riegert explained. "I mean, if you came to the set, you would be hard-pressed to discover who the director was." One night, the actor observed the sphinxlike Scot and the verbose American as they set up a scene. Riegert described the exchange thus: "[Burt said,] 'I think I'll gesture to the sky, and then I'll put my other arm around MacIntyre, and then I'll move in this direction,' and he went on like this for forty-five seconds, a minute, describing everything he was going to do physically. And Bill just sort of listened to him and didn't say anything, and then when Lancaster was finished, Bill said, 'Um, I think a little bit less.' And without missing a beat Lancaster said, 'All right, how about this: instead of putting my right arm around him, I'll put my left arm around him, and I'll move him in this direction, and maybe I'll gesture this way,' and he went on for another forty-five seconds. And Bill patiently listened, and after Lancaster finished, Bill said, 'Um, a wee bit less, a wee bit less.' And this went on for like five minutes, and I thought this is the meeting of two absolutely opposite people."

What the actor did not know was that virtually the same exchange between Burt and another director—John Huston—had been witnessed by another youngster, Doug McClure, on the set of *The Unforgiven* some twenty-three years earlier.[5]

While *Local Hero* was filming in Scotland, *Marco Polo* was airing in the United States—on NBC over four nights, May 16, 17, 18, and 19. The lavish production managed to capture its time slot each night, but it fell far short of such blockbusters as *Shogun* and *Roots*.[6] Most viewers tended to agree with Henry F. Walters of *Newsweek*, who found that it displayed "all the standard ingredients of the overworked miniseries formula—stock characters, banal dialogue, end-of-episode cliff-hangers, and all-too-brief cameos by heavyweight actors passing through on their way to meatier roles."

As one of those "heavyweight actors," Lancaster had little invested in the success of the production, but Walters noted that "Burt Lancaster appears so delighted to be playing Pope Gregory X that one can almost hear a heavenly chorus every time he parades on-screen." *Variety* went even further, stating, "Burt Lancaster's natural authority constitutes an international acting treasure, and despite the fact that he looks like no pope that ever existed, his moments on the screen were overwhelming and unforgettable."

Three months to the day after *Marco Polo* debuted, Burt announced that he needed a bypass operation. "I'm suffering from a damaged heart muscle or else I'd have gone in for surgery before this," he said. "They're just waiting for it to strengthen before the operation."

The surgery—a quadruple bypass—took place on August 26 at Cedars Sinai Medical Center; it lasted five and a half hours. A week later, the star quipped, "I feel great. I've been leading the life of a saint, no smoking, no drinking, no sex." He paused, then added, "I cheat a little."

His recovery also meant no acting, at least for several months. Which necessitated his withdrawal from several upcoming projects, including *Firestarter* (from the Stephen King novel) and *Kiss of the Spider Woman*.

• • •

5. See page186.
6. *Shogun,* the twelve-hour miniseries set in feudal Japan, was a smashing success when it aired on NBC in September 1980. *Roots,* which aired on ABC in January 1977, was the most popular miniseries of all time.

Burt's eagerness to get back to work may explain his decision to take an "and/as" role in *The Osterman Weekend,* a thriller based on Robert Ludlum's novel about a group of friends who turn on each other when they learn that one of them may be a Soviet spy. It would start filming in mid-October, close enough to his operation to doubtlessly distress his doctor, but the role was so small and sedentary that it would present a minimal risk to his health. What it would do for his career was another matter. Maxwell Danforth, the manipulative director of the CIA, was merely an extension of the characters Burt had played half a dozen years earlier in *The Cassandra Crossing* and *Twilight's Last Gleaming.*

The Osterman Weekend was a production of Peter S. Davis and William N. Panzer with a screenplay by Alan Sharp. In fact, Sharp had already tried his hand at another Ludlum novel, *The Gemini Contenders,* which had gone unproduced. "And the thing that I discovered as I began to read Ludlum," he recalled, "is that the plots don't actually make sense," although he conceded that with all the twists and red herrings, "they're great when you're reading them." For *Osterman,* he adhered to Ludlum's basic plot, but given the time constraints of a feature film, he lost the wheels-within-wheels-whom-can-I-really-trust essence of the material. Instead, the screenplay became a more conventional portrait of morally bankrupt power brokers. As such, it was more in keeping with the paranoia of the Watergate period than the optimism of the Reagan years.

After Sharp completed the job, he figured that *The Osterman Weekend,* like several other scripts he had done for Panzer and Davis, would never be produced. When he learned otherwise and that Sam Peckinpah was going to direct, he was, as he put it, "astonished . . . I mean, the story was incoherent."

In a business with no shortage of oddballs and characters, Sam Peckinpah was a legend. Described by one reporter as a "crusty, taciturn, gray-haired man with white mustache," the director had forged his reputation with such graphically violent essays as *Major Dundee, The Wild Bunch, Straw Dogs,* and *The Getaway.* But abuse of alcohol and drugs and a heart attack in 1979 had left him a shadow of his former self. He had not directed a film since 1977, and he desperately wanted to work again. *The Osterman Weekend* "was kind of like Sam's last chance," explained the film's production manager, Don Guest, who had worked with the director on *The Getaway.* "He was difficult to work with, and people weren't offering him a lot of deals."[7]

7. *The Osterman Weekend* was, in fact, Peckinpah's last film. He died on December 28, 1984.

Once Peckinpah had the job, he waged war with the producers over everything: the script, the budget, casting, his lack of creative control over the production, the number of days in the shooting schedule, the tardiness of his incremental paychecks, what he saw as the producers' lack of professionalism. By the time filming started, he was not even speaking to Panzer and Davis.

On September 4, only nine days after his surgery, Lancaster met with Peckinpah to discuss the script. Before the actor made a final commitment, he wanted a rewrite, to make the character more integral to the plot and to give it greater depth. Sharp was willing to try, but he thought that what Burt wanted was impossible, because Danforth had but a single function in the piece—to set up the big lie that pits all of the major characters in the picture against one another. In the end, the changes were slightly more than cosmetic. As Sharp put it, "We basically repainted the room. We didn't really rearrange the furniture very much."

This having been done, Burt agreed to play the part—which amounted to a rehearsal on October 6 and ten days of filming and videotaping (the latter for sequences in which the CIA chief appears on TV). "He was very professional," recalled Guest. "He did his work, and he was not a problem." The production manager also saw no discord between Burt and Sam. As he put it, "There was great respect between these two men. They're both kind of old warriors, you know."

After finishing his scenes in *The Osterman Weekend* on November 2 (the picture would continue in production until December 31), Lancaster took the extended rest that his heart condition warranted. In 1983, the year in which he turned seventy, he accepted no acting roles at all.

However, he did host and narrate PBS's six-part series *The Life of Verdi*, which aired on Monday evenings from October 24 through November 28. The project once again united Burt with RAI, the Italian TV company that had produced *Moses, the Lawgiver* and *Marco Polo*. As a lifelong opera enthusiast, Burt's involvement in the $10-million project was a labor of love. It even took him back to Italy—to film at Verdi's birthplace in Busseto and at La Scala, the celebrated opera house in Milan. "It was a happy time when we were taping it," the actor recalled.

Also in November, the Nuart, a film revival house in Los Angeles, presented "An Evening with Burt Lancaster," which kicked off a six-night retrospective of films. Dressed in blue jeans and a blue cotton shirt, Burt took the stage for his first public appearance since his heart surgery. "I like the opportunity of talking like I am to you people here," he told the audience of more than three hundred. "I do a lot of this. I go to schools around the country and talk to students that are in cinema classes."

While the Nuart celebrated Lancaster's past triumphs, 1983 saw the release of *Local Hero* and *The Osterman Weekend.*

First came the engaging Bill Forsyth comedy, which opened on February 17. The critics dubbed it "an effortlessly charming, contemporary comic fable," which is "dominated by a constantly surprising sense of whimsicality" in which "everything is unexpected and nothing is forced." And they were justifiably captivated by Burt's performance—with Pauline Kael, as she had with *Atlantic City* and *Cattle Annie,* waxing eloquent on the subject: "A stargazing reserve has become apparent in Lancaster's recent performances; it's as if he finally felt free enough to be himself on the screen—to let us see that he has thoughts he feels no need to communicate. The welcome familiarity of his speech rhythms tells us something: he, too, is one of a kind. There's nobody else in the world with a voice like that—the smoothness with the remnant of toughness underneath."

Despite the glowing notices, this delightful comedy failed to ignite at the box office—at least in the United States. As Louis Malle had said about *Atlantic City,* "It doesn't play out there when it's too original." Puttnam's biographer, Andrew Yule, reported, however, that "the film turned a tidy profit with cable and TV sales," and it was a success in foreign markets.

By contrast, *The Osterman Weekend,* which debuted in New York on November 4, nearly nine months after *Local Hero,* left the critics baffled. It "makes you work so hard trying to figure out what's really going on at any given moment," asserted Kevin Thomas of the *Los Angeles Times,* "you start wondering whether the effort is worth it, especially when the points that finally do emerge are pretty familiar by now." *The New York Times'* Vincent Canby even speculated, "It's as if Mr. Peckinpah read the book and Alan Sharp's screen adaptation and decided that the only way to deal with so much outrageously unbelievable plotting was to make it, if possible, totally incomprehensible and then stuff it so full of gratuitous sex and violence that the audience wouldn't notice anything else."

The Osterman Weekend turned out to be one of the shabbiest films in Burt's long career. As Sharp put it, "It was a sad business all around really."

Sandwiched in between the releases of *Local Hero* and *The Osterman Weekend* came 20th Century–Fox's reissue of *The Leopard*. Debuting in New York on September 2, 1983, the new print addressed all of the problems in the original English version: it was in Italian with subtitles, the prints were beautifully struck in Technicolor rather than DeLuxe, and twenty-two minutes that had been cut in 1963 were restored.

The changes forced a critical reappraisal of the picture and of Burt's performance. Vincent Canby, noting the shock he experienced when a rather gruff Italian voice came out of the star's mouth, asserted, "This may or may not be his greatest performance—there's no way of telling without the voice—but it's a visually arresting one, and one that points the way to the great performances later in his career."

Burt was unimpressed by the reappraisal. As he said at the time, "When *The Leopard* first came out . . . the critics laughed at me. I was a bum. Twenty years later they're saying, 'It's his chef d'oeuvre, his great acting piece.' I don't know what happened to these people, but suddenly I've become a hell of a performer."

CHAPTER TWENTY

"The Guy Who Works in the Field"

When Burt finally went back to acting in February of 1984, after a fifteen-month hiatus, it was to play a small but pivotal role in *Little Treasure*. The picture would mark the directorial debut of Alan Sharp, who also wrote the screenplay.

Burt was cast as an old bank robber named Teschemacher, who had been hiding out in Mexico for decades, having left his wife and daughter, Margo, back in the States. Dying of blood poisoning, he summons Margo—who has grown into a foulmouthed topless dancer—in order to give her a map that will lead her to his hidden loot. After Teschemacher dies, Margot is joined in her treasure hunt by a carefree American expatriate named Eugene, with whom she falls in love.

Sharp had waited a long time to see *Little Treasure* reach production. In fact, Lancaster had read a draft of the script in 1972, when he and the screenwriter were making *Ulzana's Raid;* at that point, Burt was still young enough to have played Eugene. Sharp thought it was the best script he had written, but it was quirky. It took a new production company, Tri-Star—formed by CBS, Home Box Office, and Columbia Pictures, with Sydney Pollack as the creative consultant—to take a chance on it.[1] In fact, it was one of a series of low-budget, $5-million films that Tri-Star bankrolled.

When the company offered Sharp the opportunity to direct, he grabbed it. He figured that no one knew the material better than he. Moreover, it was essentially a three-character piece and could be shot in sequence—which made the director's task much easier.

There was never any question about Lancaster playing Teschemacher. Sharp would even get a second member of the family in the

---

1. Tri-Star's first feature, *The Natural,* was released in 1984.

bargain: Burt's daughter Joanna, who had gone into film production, would serve as the picture's executive producer (with Richard Wagner). But finding the right actress for Margo, the story's principal character, proved difficult. At various times it had been seen as a vehicle for Julie Christie, Susan Tyrrell, and Ann-Margret, but it ultimately went to Margot Kidder. For Eugene, Sharp cast Ted Danson, who could sandwich the production between seasons of his hit sitcom, *Cheers.*

The company would shoot in Lancaster's old stomping grounds, Durango, Mexico, but all of Burt's scenes were filmed in Cuernavaca. As Sharp said, "Burt was coming in for two weeks, so it was an in-and-out job."

When Lancaster arrived, he dramatically altered the dynamics of the production. "Before that . . . there was kind of a collective," explained Sharp, meaning that he, Kidder, and Danson were making choices as a group. Once Lancaster joined them, there was, in Sharp's words, "kind of an apex." Burt even started taking charge of the rehearsals. "He didn't humiliate me," Sharp explained. "He didn't do anything rude to me, but he just took over. And I didn't have the skill, the knowledge, or the energy to start struggling with him."

Sharp found Lancaster's attitude disconcerting, but his performance even more so. Thanks to his long hiatus, Burt had not only gained weight, he had become unusually lethargic. He was not interested in stretching himself as he had been during the making of *Ulzana's Raid.* Thus, said Sharp, "All I could do is let him be Burt Lancaster." Moreover, there was tension between Burt and Margot Kidder. Said Sharp, "Margot just did not like him at all. From word one." Moreover, she hated acting with him because he would not open himself up to her. She was so upset that she even campaigned to have him replaced, which was impossible; his name was too important to the selling of the picture. But the director sympathized with the actress. "When I looked at the two of them," he recalled, "I thought, 'There is nothing happening.' There was no chemistry between the two of them."

Finally, after Burt had been with the company for about ten days, the friction with Kidder produced an explosion.

It happened one night as the actors were trying to set their blocking for their climactic encounter. At one point, Kidder wanted to grab Lancaster by the front of his shirt, pull him toward her, and tell him off.

Burt said that he did not think his character would let her do that. Kidder insisted, and Lancaster, equally adamant, refused. Finally, Burt rose from the chair in which he was sitting, Kidder yanked him toward her—and he hit her. Kidder retaliated by kicking him, while continuing to hold on to his shirt. "They ended up on the fuckin' floor," said Sharp, "and Margot split her head." The combatants were finally separated by the director and other members of the company, at which point Kidder said, "How dare you?" to Burt, and fled the set. There was, to quote Sharp, "a stony hush in the amphitheater."

In the director's opinion, Burt had not intended to hit Kidder. As he put it, "It was just reflexive." Indeed, the star told his daughter after the fracas was over, "I don't know what came over me." It was hard, however, not to remember reports in days gone by—unsubstantiated though they were—of his physical abusiveness toward women.[2]

After the set was cleared, Sharp went to each of the actors and offered to wrap for the night, but they both wanted to continue. Thus, the scene was shot—with neither star speaking to the other except in character. "Now Sam Peckinpah would have used that to get a great scene," the director concluded. "I just wanted to get through the fuckin' thing." After that night, Lancaster still had about three days' work on the film. Both he and Kidder managed to restrain themselves sufficiently to produce the requisite footage. "And as soon as Burt went off," Sharp recalled, "Margot collapsed and went to the hospital. We shut down for a week."

Meanwhile, word of the incident had leaked to the press, via a UPI reporter who learned of the fracas from a Cuernavaca local. The unit publicist, John Langley, tried to deny that the fight had taken place, saying Kidder had bumped her head on a post and that the source of the story, a Mexican woman, was not fluent in English and had misunderstood what she had witnessed. But essentially, the press got the facts right.

Even with Kidder's hiatus, *Little Treasure* wrapped on schedule. When the actress returned to Los Angeles, she refused to let go of the incident with Lancaster, checking into the star's past and thereby learning of the previous allegations of brutality. "So Margot was able to convince herself that Burt was abusive to women," said Sharp, "and she was one in a sequence. My attitude was, 'Yeah, but I think both of you cooperated here. Burt gave you a few clues that he didn't want to play the scene

2. See pages 136.

that way, but you wanted to go on and do that. It got out of hand, okay, but there was a point at which I didn't think you were listening to what he was saying.' " In any event, the actress brought suit against the actor, and the matter was settled out of court. Among the terms of the settlement was that she not discuss what had transpired in Mexico.

It was a livelier, more focused Burt, by far, who showed up in November of 1984, six months after he left Cuernavaca, for the start of his first made-for-TV movie, *Scandal Sheet*.[3]

Burt's presence in the film was clever casting, for in a sense it was an extension of *Sweet Smell of Success*. Celebrity journalism had come a long way since the days of Walter Winchell and Dorothy Kilgallen. By the eighties, there were several weekly newspapers devoted solely to the tawdry side of human life, reveling in everything from freaks of nature to aliens from outer space to the private lives of the rich and famous. Leading the pack was the *National Enquirer*, with a devoted readership in the millions.

The idea for the project had, in fact, originated with a former member of the *Enquirer* staff. As scripted by Howard Rodman, the plot centered on a mainstream journalist, played by Pamela Reed, who is enticed into working for the fictional rag *Inside World*, after which she is spurned by her former colleagues. Drawing her into the dark side of journalism is the paper's publisher and editor, Harold Fallen, the role Lancaster would play. To quote actor Henry Winkler, whose company produced the project, the character is "the living incarnation of the devil," because he is totally dedicated to his publication and the trash it publishes.

Initially, Lancaster's agent, Ben Benjamin, turned the project down, saying that his client did not do TV. But Burt had to modify his posture if he wanted to continue working; TV movies, the stage, and commercials are the principal venues for movie stars past their box-office peak. Moreover, in this case, Winkler was fiercely determined to land Lancaster for his film. As he told Burt, "I think there's probably no one else who can play it. I can't take no for an answer." He was even willing to meet the star's salary demands, which were considerably above the norm for television. So Burt acquiesced. Later, as the film was about to air, he put his own spin on his decision to take the role, saying, "Televi-

---

3. Arguably, *Victory at Entebbe* was a made-for-TV movie, but it was conceived and concurrently produced as a European theatrical release, so in a sense it was also a feature. Burt's other previous projects for television, *Moses, the Lawgiver* and *Marco Polo*, had been miniseries.

sion . . . dramatizes subjects today that wouldn't have been seen by viewers in the home years ago."

• • •

As Winkler put it, "Television is the theater of the fast. You get it done, you get it on the air, you move on." *Scandal Sheet,* like most made-for-TV movies, was filmed in a mere nineteen days—at a variety of locations in the Los Angeles metropolitan area. To his credit, Lancaster, an Oscar winner with decades of major features behind him, brought no movie-star baggage to the set. "There was no bullshit," said Winkler. "There was no conning. There was no attitude. There was just this great professional." The sentiment was echoed by a young character actor, Peter Jurasik, who was cast as Fallen's star photographer and eager disciple: "Burt was not a show-offy guy, and he could have been. He had a confidence and a pride about him, but he was not a strutter."

To illustrate the point, Jurasik, who would soon distinguish himself in a continuing role in the acclaimed police drama *Hill Street Blues,* recalled the first night that he and Lancaster worked together. Jurasik's photographer was supposed to place a call to the publisher from a pay phone. Thus, all the star would have to do is feed the costar his lines off-camera, something an assistant director could have done. Said Jurasik, "It was late at night, it was cold out on the desert, and there are plenty of stars who would not stay around to do the off-camera stuff. And, believe me, I did not expect it—I had not even met Burt at that point." That Lancaster was willing to extend himself indicated, in Jurasik's words, "a respect for me, a respect for the script, and the picture. It speaks to what kind of actor you are if you do that."

Several times thereafter, Burt gave the younger actor the benefit of his expertise. For example, said Jurasik, "He made me understand that I had to take this horrible, reprehensible character I was playing and find something within me that said this is positive. At least he works hard, doesn't he? Or, he sure is tenacious about getting the story." Burt applied the same logic to his own character, a truly despicable man. "Actually Fallen thinks of himself as a wonderful fellow," said the star. "He imagines he's doing everyone a big favor by producing the kind of reading material they want. It doesn't bother him that many people are being destroyed in the process."

In fact, Lancaster had to articulate Fallen's chilling philosophy to his staff in his first scene in the picture, through a long, *Elmer Gantry*–like speech. Jurasik recalled, "For the most part, the people in that movie were just television actors, run-of-the-mill actors, meaning we're the workers in the field. Burt is really on another level as an actor, so there was a lot of excitement about him being there, in that scene." But, when the moment came, said Jurasik, "He just could not get through it. He would start it, get a couple of lines into it, get lost, and then stop. Do a little more, get lost, and stop."

Each time Burt faltered, director David Lowell Rich, a veteran of the medium since the live dramas of the fifties, would call, "Cut," giving the star a moment to regroup. But the difficulty persisted. By then, Jurasik explained, "You could feel people were starting to worry for him and care about him. And then Burt did something that I thought was so extraordinary. He addressed the problem. He said, 'This is a problem I'm having now as an actor, doing long speeches and keeping all the lines in my head.' He kind of cursed it a little bit." Finally, director Rich offered to shoot the speech in sections, pointing out that inserts of the listening staffers would give the effect of cut-and-paste anyway. But Lancaster, to quote Jurasik, "hung in there and did the whole speech." Nothing that Burt did thereafter impressed the young actor more. As he put it, "It was painful, but it was just courageous to watch him do that, that he had enough pride and care about his work and his relationship to this film and knowing who he was that he hung in there and did that. The whole veneer of Burt Lancaster the movie star totally dropped away, and all at once you had Burt the actor, the guy who works in the field like me."

On January 21, 1985, less than two months after the end of filming, *Scandal Sheet* aired on ABC. Not only was it a noble effort to explore a facet of contemporary popular culture that had not been examined on film—television or theatrical—before, it occasionally rose to moments of genuine horror, as when Lancaster's Fallen forces Pamela Reed's journalist to write an exposé on her movie-star friends (played by Lauren Hutton and Robert Urich), which leads to their ruination.

But perhaps the film's most memorable moment is that lengthy, early speech of Burt's when he characterizes his public: "You hunger and you thirst for the true lives of the glamorous, the important. Not your uncle Phil nor your aunt Beatrice because you know all there is to know about their lives, and what they do doesn't thrill you or excite you, doesn't make your life richer. So you go into a supermarket and after you buy your orange juice and your steak because your belly is empty, you stand before the rack where the tabloids are because your whole life is empty." That is not the stuff of most TV scripting, and Burt, his difficulties during shooting aside, relished the words. Jon Anderson of the *Chicago Tribune* called him "terrific," and Kay Gardella of the New

York *Daily News* asserted that he gave "a fine performance, skillfully underplayed to offset the villainy of the character."

Looking back on the experience, Lancaster said, "I enjoyed it tremendously. The demands of TV are hard. I think we waste more time in movies." And Winkler was thrilled. Said the actor-producer, "The intellect that he brought to the character, the technique that he brought to the character, the thirty-five years or forty years in the business that he brought to the character was all there.[4] A little present that was wrapped up and given to me."

Far less effective was Lancaster's appearance in *Little Treasure*—which was not a surprise in light of the events in Cuernavaca. The picture opened in New York on May 1, 1985, where it garnered universally negative notices. "Nothing in *Little Treasure* quite comes together," noted Vincent Canby in *The New York Times*. "The performances weren't bad in themselves, but no one seems to be playing to the other actors in the same scene." Rex Reed of the New York *Daily News* called it simply "a jaundiced mess."

Based on its reception in New York, *Little Treasure* quickly disappeared. Apparently, it played nowhere else.

Sandwiched in between the broadcast of *Scandal Sheet* and the release of *Little Treasure* was Burt's appearance on the March 25 Academy Awards telecast, in which he joined Kirk Douglas to present the Oscars for screenwriting. There was nothing unusual about the appearance; it was part of the usual pairing of stars for the annual affair. But, as director Jeff Kanew would later note, "Everyone saw the charm and chemistry between them and started talking about another film." Particularly inspired were two Canadian writers, James Orr and James Cruickshank, who had been partners in scripting youth-oriented projects for about seven years. Looking for a change of pace, they set out—without knowing either Burt or Kirk or having any contact with them—to write a script that would reunite the old costars for one more feature.

In the meantime, Lancaster, having surmounted the hurdle of television movies, made two more forays into the field.

Sins of the Fathers brought the actor back to the Bavaria Film Stu-

4. When *Scandal Sheet* was shot, thirty-nine years had elapsed since Burt's Broadway debut.

dio, where he had made *Twilight's Last Gleaming.* Shot in English in Prague; Leuna, East Germany; and the Faber-Castell castle near Nuremberg—which had housed American prosecutors and journalists during the war crimes trials—the eight-hour miniseries, written and directed by Bernhard Sinkel, offered a portrait of a fictional German family, the Deutzes, between 1911 and 1947. Clearly patterned after the Farbens, the Deutzes would become involved in the manufacture of poison gases, thereby contributing to the chemical warfare of World War I and the Holocaust during World War II. Burt was the patriarch of the clan, Carl Julius Deutz, strong-willed but fair. Costarring were Bruno Ganz as the son-in-law who involves the family in its nefarious enterprises and Julie Christie as his daughter.

Sins of the Fathers would not air in the U.S. until 1988, not a good sign. Reduced to four hours, it was carried on the premium cable channel Showtime, starting July 10, and was broadcast in two parts (Burt's character died at the end of the first half). At the time, David Bianculli of the *New York Post* wrote, "While the casting sounds good, the show itself is horrible. In fact, it's the dumbest, slowest, most unwatchable miniseries since—well, in a long time." *Variety* found it "ponderous," and Kay Gardella called it "lavish and illuminating but sometimes plodding," although she acknowledged that "Burt Lancaster gives a commanding performance."

Lancaster had somewhat better luck with *On Wings of Eagles,* a two-part, five-hour telemovie based on the best-selling 1983 book by Ken Follett. Like *Sins of the Fathers,* it was drawn from actual events, specifically a daring American raid into the heart of the Ayatollah Khomeini's fundamentalist regime in Iran. The mission was sponsored by Texas billionaire H. Ross Perot after two employees of EDS, his computer data-processing company, were imprisoned in Teheran in December of 1978. The unit's "commandos" were amateurs, executives in Perot's firm, but they were led by a pro, retired Army colonel Arthur D. Simons.

A veteran of guerrilla combat in World War II and Vietnam, Simons had earned celebrity—and the Distinguished Service Cross—when he tried to free American prisoners of war in a camp near Hanoi in July of 1970 (no prisoners were rescued—they had all been moved). A true hero, Simons was told by John Wayne, "You're the man I play in the movies."

Aside from Wayne, who had died in 1979, there were not many stars who could fill Simons' shoes. Lancaster was one of them. "I took the part," Burt explained later, "because I like the whole idea of what Simons stood for. He has a phenomenal record of bravery. . . . As tough as he was, though, he never ignored what was going on personally with his soldiers. He had a soft, compassionate side that provoked great loyalty. And those are the qualities he used when he organized a civilian group to free the Americans in Iran."

The makers of *On Wings of Eagles* faced two difficult obstacles. The first was where to shoot, since the actual sites in Iran would obviously be unavailable. They selected Mexico City. That the ten weeks of filming began shortly after the devastating earthquake of September 19 did not hurt; the rubble added to the sense of a city in the throes of revolution.

The second problem was the static nature of much of Sam Rolfe's screenplay. During the first three hours in particular, when Perot and his associates attempt to negotiate the release of their comrades and then plan and train for the raid, there were, to quote the project's director of photography, Robert Steadman, "endless scenes of guys sitting around in hotel rooms talking about what the hell they were going to do." Such moments demanded multiple camera angles—to inject movement through a shifting visual perspective—but, at the same time, the requisite actors had to be kept in the picture frame. Looking back, Steadman recalled, "I had a real photographic problem in trying to make this interesting. And [the director] Andrew [McLaglen] did as well." Under such circumstances, the actors' choices became rather limited. Steadman said, "When you have six actors in a room together, you all better just say the lines as written or it's just going to be a mess, you're never going to get through it."

Lancaster intuitively understood the problem and was remarkably cooperative. "He wasn't trying to change his characterization through the rearranging of lines or substitutions or anything like that," asserted Steadman. "He just generally did it." The same, however, could not be said for a young actor playing a participant in the raid. The latter was, to quote the director of photography, "always trying to tinker with the script," and, in his words, it "drove Burt nuts." The star kept telling him, "Jesus Christ, we don't have time for this. We're on a TV schedule here." On one occasion, McLaglen recalled that "Burt cut loose and really let him have it, told him to wake up and become a professional." In the director's opinion, the outburst was fully justified, and thereafter the actor's attitude improved.

Other than that, Burt got along well with his *Eagles* costars, particularly Richard Crenna, the handsome, talented veteran of such feature films as *Wait Until Dark, Star!,* and the *Rambo* series, who was cast as H. Ross Perot. (The billionaire jokingly told the actor later, if Crenna had played him during the 1992 presidential campaign, he would be the nation's chief executive today.) Crenna, thirteen years younger than Lancaster, had long admired the senior actor for the chances he had taken with his career. Looking back in 1993, he remembered their association with affection and respect. Burt also established a warm rapport with young, cocky Esai Morales, who played a sympathetic Iranian EDS employee. As McLaglen put it, "I think Burt got a kick of out of the kid." In fact, the youngster may have reminded Burt of another cocky up-and-comer forty years earlier—himself.

Burt also enjoyed a good working relationship with McLaglen. Son of actor Victor McLaglen, the director was no stranger to male movie legends, having worked with James Stewart, Robert Mitchum, Kirk Douglas, and Richard Widmark—and John Wayne in several films, including *McLintock!* and *Chisum.* Of Lancaster's work in *Eagles,* the director said, "I thought he kept the Burtisms to a minimum. He was really trying to do the character."

Still, age was continuing to take its toll. Said McLaglen, "Learning lines was not as easy for him as it had been in the past, and he was a little self-conscious about it. . . . I've seen that before. As you grow older, the old memory just doesn't click as easily as it did before." Because the director was sympathetic, he would simply call for additional rehearsals when he sensed Burt struggling. Thus, no one else in the company knew of his difficulty—or so the director maintained. Moreover, the problem did nothing to diminish his regard for the star. "Burt was always really so professional," he asserted. "He had a good sense of humor, nothing was too much trouble, no star complex. There were times in the past when you heard that Burt Lancaster was not the easiest guy to work with, but I found him to be just great."

By the time *On Wings of Eagles* went into production, there was a new woman in Burt's life.

Susie Scherer had been born Susan June Martin in California on May 3, 1942. Her father, David Richard Martin, was a public relations executive in the motion picture industry, notably with MGM. Her mother, the former Violet Geraldine Percha, hailed from Michigan. Like Burt, Susie dropped out of college, but she managed to complete her sophomore year. Then she married and had a son, John.

Although the pretty young woman aspired to an acting career, she had trained as a legal secretary, and it was in that capacity that her relationship with Lancaster began. After they met at a party early in 1985, he asked her to go to work for him. About six months later, said one friend, "Burt started to open up to her more and more. Before they knew it, they were in love."

"It was as big a shock to me as to anyone that Burt and I became romantically attached," Scherer told one friend. "I never even dreamed about that when he hired me. I expected to be just doing a job for a movie star. But he turned out to be a wonderful, tender, loving man."

Burt's romance with the secretary, then forty-three years old and twenty-nine years his junior, marked the final blow to his relationship with Jackie. For all the passion and support that Burt derived from that long affair, he seemed to have found something in Susie that he had not known with a woman before—calm. Andrew McLaglen, who saw the couple in the early throes of romance, said of the future Mrs. Lancaster, "We got to know her a bit while we were shooting *On Wings of Eagles*. She's really a super, super lady. I mean, a really nice lady." To which director Daniel Petrie added, "I think she was a joy for him. She was very supportive, very adoring. She was a tonic, a real tonic, to him. I just thought it was a lovely relationship."

But, as the year came to an end, neither knew where their relationship would take them. For starters, Susie was still married.

While *Sins of the Fathers* and *On Wings of Eagles* were in production, the two Canadian screenwriters Orr and Cruickshank were working on their reunion vehicle for Lancaster and Kirk Douglas. The result was a story about two gangsters, Harry Doyle and Archie Long, released after thirty years in prison for armed robbery and coping with life on the outside as senior citizens.

The property, which was called *Tough Guys,* was acquired by independent film producer Joe Wyzan, who, in turn, took it to Disney for the studio's adult division, Touchstone. To direct, he engaged Jeff Kanew, best known for the hit youth-oriented feature *Revenge of the Nerds.* Kanew had worked with Douglas before—on 1983's *Eddie Macon's Run.*

When the director signed on for *Tough Guys,* neither Kirk nor Burt had even seen the script, much less agreed to do the picture. It was Kanew, in fact, who sent the screenplay to Douglas. The actor, who loved it, passed it on to Lancaster, who was also enthusiastic. "It seemed to suit our talents," Burt explained shortly thereafter, "and it allows us to spoof many of the heroes we've played in the past." Lancaster, more than Douglas, was also drawn to the project's depiction of senior citizens. As he put it, "Nobody in our society wants to deal with older people. They've outlived their usefulness and everyone wants to bring on the young. . . . That was the underlying concept that appealed to me in *Tough Guys.* That's what takes it beyond farcical comedy."

There was never any question about who would play what. Said Kanew, "Burt plays [Harry], the brains of the outfit. He is often exasperated with Archie, who is the more energetic and impulsive of the two. In the other movies they've done, like *Gunfight at the O.K. Corral,* they've essentially played the same characters. Burt is the anchor and Kirk is the flier." Nevertheless, each star thought the other's role was better. "In Kirk's mind," recalled Kanew, "the thinker and the leader was the great part, and in Burt's mind, the crazy, impetuous guy was the great part." Lancaster, however, was willing to give Kirk the edge in one respect: he did not want to have any punch lines. "The irony about Burt," said screenwriter Orr, "is that he has no confidence in his ability to be funny when, in fact, he's funny without trying." But they could not convince him of that, so Harry's jokes were cut.

Other changes in the screenplay followed. Initially, recalled Kanew, Harry and Archie "had a more harmonious relationship. And the two actors said that wasn't real. Part of the magic between Kirk and Burt is the friction as well as the love." But the most significant alteration came with the film's climax. As written, Harry and Archie, unable to cope with life on the outside, engineered a robbery in order to return to prison. "But when you looked at Kirk and Burt," explained Kanew, "you said, 'These guys willingly going back to prison? Doesn't seem right.' So everybody agreed we should find a different way of ending the movie." What emerged was the old-timers' attempt to hold up the train they had robbed thirty years earlier. The addition of this sequence—and, in particular, the wreck of the train—would add considerably to the cost of the project. As Jeffrey Lantos noted in *American Film,* "By December [1985], what had been a $5-million buddy picture with a heartfelt ending had become a $10-million caper with an incendiary ($2-million) ending." It had been many a year since Lancaster had received top billing in a studio-backed film with such a budget. The opportunity would not come again.

In fact, it almost did not happen at all. Shortly before filming began, Lancaster decided not to do *Tough Guys.* Said Kanew, "Burt had just worked on several projects and a miniseries, and he was tired. . . . I called Kirk, and I said, 'Well, it looks like it's over. Burt doesn't want to do it.' " Douglas phoned Lancaster and told him, "It's not fair. We have this long relationship, and one day one of us is going to be doing the other guy's eulogy, and we need to do this last film together." The next day, Kirk reported, "He's doing it."

• • •

Principal photography began on February 10, 1986, on a fifty-one-day schedule. All of the filming would take place in the Los Angeles area, except for the train sequence, which would be shot along a spur line in the desert south of Palm Springs. Originally, Tony Curtis was to have joined Burt and Kirk as an aging hit man with a beef against the duo. Curtis had not only appeared in three films with Lancaster (including his cameo debut in *Criss Cross*), he had also costarred in *The Vikings* and *Spartacus* with Douglas. But the three-way reunion failed to materialize, and the role went to Adolph Caesar, the African-American actor who had won an Oscar nomination in 1984 for his electrifying supporting role in *A Soldier's Story*. Caesar, however, suffered a heart attack and died after only one day of filming; he was replaced by Eli Wallach. Also in the cast were Charles Durning, Dana Carvey, and Alexis Smith as Burt's love interest.

As with Tom Moore, Kanew brought the right combination of strength and flexibility to his association with Burt and Kirk. "For me it's really about knowing the material really well," the director explained, "not trying to come off like I have all the answers, and having a real open dialogue with the actors, because the actors have a lot to contribute I think." Naturally, he felt more comfortable with Douglas, whom he had directed before. He was also more simpatico with the expansive, energetic star. He found Burt "reserved." Moreover, Lancaster was not in the best of shape during filming. Said Kanew, "He told me one day. 'I like making movies, but I don't know if I have the energy for this anymore. I'm finding everything about this process annoying.'" In particular, Burt was again plagued with memorization problems.

Nevertheless, Kanew could recall only one occasion when he and Burt got into an argument: "I was creating an extra scene for each character, because I felt that each needed one more indignity to drive them back to their life of crime." Burt disagreed. To break the impasse, Kanew went to Lancaster's home on a Sunday, their day off. Instead of discussing the matter, however, they ended up working together on the extra scene for Harry. Thus, Kanew eliminated the objection by involving Burt in the solution.

As for the relationship between Burt and Kirk, it was volatile as always, a mirror of that between Harry and Archie. "Off-screen, they're constantly bickering," said Kanew. "They're like an old married couple. They know how to push each other's buttons. They're like Laurel and Hardy with muscles." Part of the tension stemmed from their different ways of working. "Burt, his process as an actor and as a person, is keep it simple, less is more," explained the director. "Kirk tends to put a lot out there, and sometimes it creates great energy, and sometimes he has to be reined in a little bit. You never have to rein Burt in; he's always reining himself in." Production manager Penelope Foster added, "I think that when they were on-screen together or in front of the camera, they were very professional, and the relationship worked. I think off-camera, they didn't have too much in common. I did not see them spending a great deal of time together off the set." Even Kirk said after the picture wrapped, "Some people think we're the closest buddies. We're not, though I think we have a wonderful friendship. Sometimes I don't see Burt for a year or two, but he's there if I need him and I'm here if he needs me. We have a respect for each other that we don't voice."

Still, after their seventh collaboration, Lancaster decided he was too old for Kirk's never-say-die approach. As Charles Durning put it, "Burt told me after *Tough Guys* that he would never, ever do another picture with Kirk. He said, 'He's a pain in the ass, and I can't deal with it anymore. In my youth, I could deal with it, but I can't deal with it now.' "

Tough Guys wrapped at the end of April, just one day behind schedule. Two weeks later, on May 18 and 19, *On Wings of Eagles* aired on NBC. Lancaster seemed stiff and wooden in the early sequences, reflecting perhaps an attempt to capture Bull Simons' ennui in the face of retirement and the death of his wife. By the second night, however, as the colonel got caught up in the preparations for the raid, the actor had loosened up considerably, prompting Doug Hill of *TV Guide* to proclaim, "Burt Lancaster fits the part of Bull Simons as snugly as the old pea coat he wears in the film." Burt evidenced, in particular, an engaging chemistry with Esai Morales, reflecting their off-screen rapport, and with Paul LeMat, who played one of the principal EDS executives-turned-commando. The film, while rising occasionally to moments of gripping tension, was long at five hours (the first night's airing ran three hours). "Dull to the point of stupor" was the somewhat excessive verdict of *Variety.*

On TV, Lancaster went from one historical figure, Bull Simons, to another, P. T. Barnum—for the two-hour movie *Barnum.* How appropriate that, in the twilight of his career, the former circus acrobat would portray the founder of the Greatest Show on Earth, the Ringling Bros.–Barnum & Bailey Circus.

Lancaster was seventy-two when filming commenced in Montreal on

July 30, 1986.[5] He would portray the title character as an old man, narrating the drama from the campgrounds of his circus, and he would appear in the flashbacks once Barnum reached the age of thirty-three; the younger Phineas would be played by John Roney. Roney was Canadian, like most of the cast (except Hanna Schuygulla as Jenny Lind). The project's director, American Lee Phillips, himself a former actor and the director of numerous TV movies, was impressed by the way Burt interacted with his costars, all of whom were unknown to him before the start of filming. "He was available to the actors at all times to rehearse," the director recalled. "He was always off-camera for their close-up lines. There was never any of that star shit. He just did his work."

As usual for Burt, "doing his work" meant coming to Montreal with a well-defined notion of his character and the production's theme. As he saw it, "Barnum epitomized the force and drive and sense of free enterprise that our society stands for." Phillips' primary role (with Burt) was to harness the actor's energy for the scenes depicting Barnum the showman and to, in the director's words, "sit on it sometimes when it was a very quiet and soft scene, to get the variety in the man that he was capable of." As an example of the latter, Phillips cited the moment in which Barnum appears in the wings of a theater, relishing the lush tones of Jenny Lind. He remembered that Lancaster "just stood there with the tears streaming down his face, listening to this beautiful voice."

"I had a good time with him," Phillips recalled. "I appreciated his gifts and what he tried to do with the part. And when it was all over, we shook hands and hugged and said good-bye and went on to the next project."

Barnum wrapped on September 10, after thirty-one days of filming, a bonus over the usual eighteen-to-twenty-day TV-movie schedule. Two days later, Lancaster made an unprecedented appearance on a television talk show—as the sole guest on *Donahue,* briefly airing from Los Angeles. As usual in question-and-answer sessions with the public, Burt demonstrated his affability as well as a surprising openness, fielding inquiries on a range of subjects, from his mother's kindness toward blacks and Jews to his audition for *A Sound of Hunting* to the shooting of the beach scene in *From Here to Eternity.* When someone asked him if he would do Frank Gorshin, the impressionist well known for his Lancaster imitation, the star replied, "I can't do an impression of Burt Lancaster,"

5. By the 1980s, Montreal had become a magnet for American TV movies because pictures could be produced there far less expensively than in the States.

which got a big laugh. He even gave viewers some insight into his psyche, explaining, "I enjoy acting when I get into it. I grumble and grouse about it. It's not good enough, how are they going to make this picture, I think the writer is terrible, the director doesn't know what he's doing, the other actors are ordinary, the girl isn't beautiful enough. I go through all of this nonsense and then I get in and I love it. I'm a pain in the neck, I try to direct the picture, I try to tell the other actors how to act, all that. People hate me, and when it's all over, they wind up loving me. I don't know why." Of course, the *Donahue* audience loved him too.

Best of all, from Burt's perspective, the talk show gave him an opportunity to publicize *Tough Guys*, which was to open on October 3. Most of the critics identified the comedy for what it was, "a chance," to quote Michael Wilmington of the *Los Angeles Times*, "to see them [Burt and Kirk] strutting their stuff one more time." Wilmington added, "On that level it's a success: a rousing tribute and, hopefully, a not-quite-last hurrah." Rex Reed of the New York *Daily News* agreed, arguing, "The old pros are still the best, and in *Tough Guys* two of the all-time greats give it all they've got."

Moreover, of all Burt and Kirk's joint efforts, *Tough Guys* most closely approximated their off-screen relationship, and watching them play together—as devoted friends who drive each other nuts—was the picture's redeeming feature. Otherwise, it lacked the stature of the two classic Burt-Kirk pairings, *Gunfight at the O.K. Corral* and *Seven Days in May.* As Wilmington put it, "This movie needs Lancaster and Douglas. It's really nothing much without them."

The film performed moderately well at the box office, but prerelease rumors of a sequel came to an end, and with them the screen collaboration that began in 1947. The link between the two stars would continue, however, with Burt playing host to an American Academy of Dramatic Arts tribute to Kirk at the Majestic Theatre in New York in April of 1987. Douglas would return the favor, presenting the Screen Actors Guild's Achievement Award to Burt in a moving ceremony in Los Angeles on December 15, 1991. (The award was accepted by Burt's wife, Susie, and daughter Joanna, the star being too sick by then to attend.)

By the time *Tough Guys* premiered, Lancaster was at Cinecittà in Rome, filming a small "and/as" role in a TV movie called *Control.* Directed by Giuliano Montaldo, with whom Burt had worked on *Marco Polo,* the picture hypothesized what would happen to fifteen individuals who volunteered to inhabit a bomb shelter for twenty days—only to find during the experiment that an actual nuclear war was imminent. Burt played the scientist conducting the experiment. His *Moses* and *Cassandra Crossing* costar, Ingrid Thulin, was his associate, a well-meaning foundation director, and Ben Gazzara, Kate Nelligan, and Burt's *Atlantic City* bête noire, Kate Reid, were among the volunteers.

As with numerous projects in the past, it was the idea behind *Control* that intrigued Lancaster. "It has an antinuclear theme," he explained, "which says that if the bomb doesn't kill us, we'll kill ourselves anyway." Of his own work, he said, "I play a nuclear scientist in *Control* and the truth of the matter is, I don't know how you prepare to be one if you're not really a scientist. . . . What I try to do is be myself in the situation, which I think is generally true of all acting."

On November 30, *Barnum* aired on CBS. As with *Tough Guys*, the critics found Burt's presence the saving grace of an otherwise routine affair. To quote Daniel Ruth of the *Chicago Sun-Times*, "Looking fit and robust, Lancaster is nothing short of joy." Otherwise, wrote Kay Gardella of the New York *Daily News*, the film was "pedantic and plodding."

Two and a half months later, on February 14, 1987, Lancaster could again be seen on the small screen, as *Control* started airing on the premium cable channel Home Box Office. If anything, the critical response was worse than for *Barnum*, with Gardella calling it "a tedious, disappointing film" and Ruth finding it "a heavy-handed opus on nuclear war." Given Lancaster's relatively small role, which took only a week to film, his presence did little to enliven the drama.

When Lancaster told Peter Riegert in 1982 that he chose projects by doing one for the pope and one for himself, he was not speaking literally. But *The Jeweler's Shop* was not only *for* the pope, it was *by* the pope. That is, the 1960 play on which the film was based had been written by John Paul II, then Karol Wojtyla, bishop of Kraków.

The story of *The Jeweler's Shop* was simple. Two young couples— Stefan and Anna and Andrej and Teresa (respectively played in the film by Ben Cross and Jo Champa and Andrea Occipinti and Olivia Hussey)—meet and marry in Kraków in 1939, then flee Poland in the wake of the Nazi invasion (which results in Andrej's death). Years later, in Canada, their children fall in love and return to Kraków to marry. The character who links the couples' stories is the old jeweler who sells them their wedding rings. A wise, mystical figure, he serves as the pontiff's spokesman, voicing the theme that the film's director, Michael Anderson, stated as: "You don't put a wedding ring on unless you mean it to be an enduring and lasting bond."

Anderson, born in London in 1920 but a citizen of Canada, was probably best known for his 1956 Oscar-winning film, *Around the World in 80 Days*. But it was his 1968 picture about a fictional pope, *The Shoes of the Fisherman,* that earned him Vatican approval for *The Jeweler's Shop.*

One can readily see why he would want Lancaster for the old jeweler. But why Burt chose to do the vehicle is difficult to fathom. Not being a Catholic or religious or even monogamous, he could not have been drawn by the theme. Moreover, he must have known that the script was terribly old-fashioned and lacking strong character development. Perhaps he was attracted by the challenge of humanizing the jeweler, essentially an allegorical figure, who had to render lines like "Love is a constant challenge. It is given to man so that he can challenge fate. The future depends on love." Or perhaps he wanted to do a favor for RAI, with whom he had worked several times since the making of *Moses, the Lawgiver.* The Italian firm was producing *The Jeweler's Shop* as a $9-million television movie in conjunction with PAC of Italy and a consortium of French, Canadian, and American companies.

In any event, Lancaster and Susie arrived in Kraków in early July to film his scenes, which had been ganged together as an accommodation and would consume roughly a week's time (the company, without Burt, would later shoot in Montreal as well).

Grappling with the source material was difficult. Olivia Hussey recalled, "The script was always changing, which meant checking each time with the pope's friend and representative on the set, Msgr. Janusz Paierb. Paierb, in turn, had to consult with the Vatican. "Even for a word change," Hussey asserted.

Moreover, making a movie behind the Iron Curtain was a novel experience for all hands, including Lancaster. Actress Jo Champa remembered Kraków as "a beautiful town" but one that "was totally polluted. All of us got sick." In addition, she said, "We had the KGB spying on us. We even had a government person assigned to us."

Anderson had little tolerance for complaints about the working conditions, saying later, "I feel that one has to take what is there with good grace," and adding, "We received tremendous cooperation from the people in Kraków." Of Lancaster's response to the location, he asserted, Burt is "such a professional, he never let on whether he liked it or not.

He was there to do a job . . . and if he felt uneasy or uncomfortable, not so much by a word did he let anybody know." Champa noted, however, "On the set they said he was pretty grouchy and stuff, that he was very upset about the situation."

Although Champa and Anderson disagreed on Lancaster's response to Kraków, they shared similar feelings about their association with him. Said she, "I'll tell you, Burt was great to work with. I mean, this is like a real movie star. The minute I arrived on the set, he'd get up, kiss me on both cheeks [knowing that that is what they do in Italy, where she worked most of the time], and he was always behind the camera for my close-ups [feeding her his lines]. I would have understood if Burt Lancaster had left, because he was tired, and he was an older man and a legend. But, no, he stayed right there. He waited for the lights to be put on me, and he waited for the makeup to be done. Which is very kind, I thought." Likewise, Anderson found Burt "so disarming, he just put me and everyone else at their ease right away, and we just had a very good, professional relationship that I remember very fondly." The director was particularly impressed by Burt's desire to, as Anderson put it, "get the meaning behind the author's words, and so we would discuss at length what the pope had meant when he had written it. And then he would go away and come back and try different readings in order to get the full meaning. As always a perfectionist."

Before *The Jeweler's Shop* aired on Italian television, it was previewed at the Vatican. "I had been told there would be a small screening," Anderson recalled. "We thought that there would be thirty or forty people there." There were six thousand. Afterward, the pope congratulated the director. "He was very complimentary, touching, and surprisingly humorous," Anderson said at the time.

The TV movie was not picked up in the United States, either by a network or a premium cable channel, and one can see why. Its affect was too much like that of a Sunday-morning morality drama to appeal on a mass level to American audiences. It was eventually acquired for syndication by New Line Cinema and, as such, appeared as afternoon or late-night fare on various local channels around the country.

CHAPTER TWENTY-ONE

Twilight's Last Gleamings

By the 1980s, Lancaster was among the last of a breed—a star from the golden age of the studio system. He had worked for L. B. Mayer, Harry Cohn, and Jack Warner, had been directed by Robert Siodmak and William Dieterle, and had costarred with Clark Gable, Gary Cooper, Peter Lorre, and Edward G. Robinson as well as Ava Gardner, Barbara Stanwyck, and Deborah Kerr. As much as the motion picture industry glories in the latest trend and the current box-office sensation, its members venerate their past.

Nowhere was Lancaster's stature in Hollywood more closely mirrored on film than in *Rocket Gibraltar.* "He was the patriarch of the story," recalled the picture's assistant director, Matthew Carlisle, "and he was the patriarch of the movie too."

Rocket Gibraltar was written by Amos Poe, a thirty-eight-year-old New Yorker with rock videos and several funky, low-budget independent features to his credit. *Rocket Gibraltar* was his entry into the big time. The comic drama centered on the members of the Rockwell clan, who gather on Long Island over a summer weekend to celebrate the seventy-fifth birthday of Levi Rockwell, a bearded writer, teacher, and liberal thinker. Included are his grown son and daughters, their spouses and children, his doctor, and the African-American housekeeper with whom he is having an affair. "It's a story about a family," Burt said later. "In a very simple way, it's almost not a story. You're just seeing how people behave."

Poe sold the screenplay to a friend, Jeff Weiss, a former entertainment lawyer who had recently formed an independent production company; *Rocket Gibraltar* was to be its first venture. Finding investors proved difficult, however, until the comedy-drama was championed by *Local Hero* producer David Puttnam, who had recently taken charge of Columbia Pictures.

Given Weiss' budget—$3 million, less than a third of that for *Tough Guys*—most of the characters would be played by unknowns. Poe, who had insisted upon directing the property himself, selected John Glover, Bill Pullman, Kevin Spacey, Suzy Amis, and, in his screen debut, six-year-old Macaulay Culkin, all of whom have gone on to major success since. The role of the housekeeper, originally awarded to supermodel Iman, was recast with Pam Grier a few days into production.

But Puttnam wanted a star for Levi. Initially, Poe chose John Huston, but the ailing director proved uninsurable. Puttnam then suggested James Stewart—who refused to play a character who died. "Burt was always on the list," Poe recalled, "but his agent at the time said he wouldn't read it without an offer." Then apparently Kirk Douglas mentioned it favorably, because Burt decided to take a look. "I immediately wanted to do it," he recalled. "It was the same experience as when I first read *Atlantic City*. It was a film with some depth, some meaning, a lot of powerful emotions. I don't often get the really good parts nowadays because I'm long past my so-called motion picture prime in terms of the box office. So I have to wait and hope something good comes along now and then." The money was good as well. Agent Ben Benjamin was able to secure $750,000 for Lancaster, three times what Huston was to have been paid. Poe considered the money well spent, saying, "What we needed was somebody who was larger than life, and that's what he brought. There were other actors we considered who were very good actors [Eli Wallach, for example], but they didn't have that dimension."

With a seven-week production schedule, filming began in Westhampton, Long Island—about sixty miles from Manhattan—on August 4, 1987.

When Burt and Susie Scherer arrived, Poe was at pains to introduce the star to young Macaulay Culkin. Not only because their characters enjoyed a special rapport, but also because, in the director's words, "The buzz among the crew and the cast was that Macaulay Culkin was like this genius kid actor. You could see Mac was special." When Burt and the youngster met, the star said, "I've heard good things about you. I'm sure I'll enjoy working with you. I hope you'll enjoy working with me." Then he asked Culkin if he could give him any advice. The boy thought for a moment, then called upon Poe's instruction from the previous day. "Don't step on my lines," he replied. "And Burt's blood pressure just like shot up out of his head," the director recalled. "I thought his head was going to go through the fucking chimney." Despite the rocky start, however, the old man and the kid got along fine.

About three weeks into production, Poe was fired. "Everybody knew that it wasn't going well," John Glover maintained, citing as an example the scene in which Levi's children visit their mother's grave. "Everybody was just lined up in a line," he explained. "We felt that we were doing *Our Town*. It was just static, and we started realizing then that . . . we needed an experienced director to guide us." In his defense, Poe said in 1993, "They didn't let me have any rehearsal time, which really killed the schedule. I became the bad guy, because I was falling behind schedule." The situation was distressing for all hands, in part because, to quote Glover, "Everybody loved Amos."

By all accounts, Lancaster played no role in the decision to fire Poe. Given his history, his lack of involvement in such an important decision is curious. "Maybe because he was playing a man who was dealing with his own mortality and basically dying," theorized Glover, "he wasn't as aggressive as he may have been other times." To which Carlisle added, "Well, I think, as you get older, perhaps you want to get less involved. You're just there to concentrate on your performance."

Poe's replacement was Daniel Petrie. Described by one reporter as "a happy leprechaun," the Nova Scotia–born director began as an actor, then cut his directorial teeth on the live TV dramas of the fifties. Since then, he had freely intermixed projects for the small and big screens, including *A Raisin in the Sun, Fort Apache, the Bronx, Eleanor and Franklin,* and *Sybil*. When asked to take over *Gibraltar,* Petrie, in his words, "had sort of like fifteen minutes to make up my mind." What persuaded him was the script. "I thought it was rather a unique look at life in the eighties in America," he recalled, "and the values of the current generation being contrasted with the values of the very young, and much older, generations."

The production, having shut down for a week or so after Poe's departure, reopened on September 1. Said Carlisle, "Dan . . . came in and made everybody very happy and worked everybody very hard, which was very rewarding." Glover agreed. At the end of his long week, the director felt tired but good about what they had accomplished. Then, to his great surprise, Burt attacked.

It happened during a scene between Lancaster and Culkin. Before wrapping for the night, Petrie announced two more setups, including a close-up of the star. "And," said the director, "Burt went berserk. He started yelling and swearing. 'Why the fuck do you need a goddamn close-up? I'm sick to death of that crap. You need the ambience, you need the feeling of the room.' He was loud. He was really angry, in an absolute rage. I was really shocked. Everybody was shocked."

Not knowing what to do, Petrie ignored the outburst and proceeded to film the setups, including Lancaster's close-up—with the actor glaring at him when he was not on camera. But the situation, Petrie felt, needed to be addressed. The next day was Sunday, the company's day off, so he called the cottage where Burt and Susie were staying and asked for a late-afternoon meeting. The actor cheerfully okayed the get-together, the temper tantrum largely forgotten by then.

Came four o'clock. Petrie arrived, and a genial Lancaster offered him some coffee. "Oh, yes, Burt, that would be nice—if it's made."

"Just made it, just made it," the actor replied as he went into the kitchen. He quickly came back out. "How do you like it? Black or cream and sugar?"

"Black, please."

Again, the star exited only to return. "Listen, about last night," he said, having clearly reflected upon Petrie's mission as the director had hoped when he set the meeting for late in the day. "I really feel terrible. You came in and you rescued this thing, and you're doing such a great job, and for me to take off on you like that, that was really rotten."

"Well, Burt, that's why I'm here. Because I was very upset by it, and I wanted to confront you with it."

At which point, Burt started to cry. "The tears just rolled down his cheeks," Petrie recalled. "And he said, 'I don't know why I do things like that, that's really, really rotten of me. I really, really owe you an apology.'" By then, the director's anger had vanished completely. "He almost made me cry," Petrie asserted. "So I went over to him and put my arms around him—he's a great, big guy, great, big shoulders—so I patted him. Then he kind of wiped off the tears, and he said, 'Black, right?' And he walked into the kitchen."

After that, said Petrie, laughing, "we had a great relationship. And I loved working with the guy. He was great."

Lancaster ended 1987 on a mixed note. In November, he saw his brother Jim posthumously inducted into the New York University Sports Hall of Fame. "Burt had great admiration for his brother," recalled the university's director of athletics, Dan Quilty. "He spoke very highly of him. That brotherly love just came across so beautifully."

The following month, however, he was fired from *Old Gringo,* which Columbia had scheduled for filming in early 1988. Burt, who was to have played the title character, writer Ambrose Bierce, was deemed uninsurable because of his weak heart and the high altitudes in Mexico where shooting was to take place. Jane Fonda, whose company was coproducing, asserted that she had offered to "put up my part [ownership of the film] . . . as guarantee. Just like I did, along with Katharine Hepburn, for *On Golden Pond* when my father couldn't get insurance." But with no success. "It was one of the hardest things I've ever been through," the actress recalled. "I love him very much." Gregory Peck assumed Lancaster's role.

"That really hurt a lot," asserted one of Burt's friends, because an uninsurable actor has no career. "He immediately went out and made like seven movies to prove the point."[1] He also filed a breach-of-contract suit against Columbia in late May of 1988. According to the *Hollywood Reporter*, Burt and his attorney, Robert S. Warren of the firm Gibson, Dunn & Crutcher, alleged, "Columbia had no right to terminate the agreement between the parties based on an inability to obtain cast insurance . . . until it first notified [Lancaster] or his representatives of any potential problem . . . and allowed them to resolve it by various measures." To which Burt added, "The suit also contends that Columbia negotiated with Peck even before I was fired." He asked for $1.5 million, his full salary for the picture, having received at the time of his dismissal $196,428 for preproduction work, "which included rehearsing in Mexico and taking riding lessons."[2] The check had been returned to the studio.

The case was settled out of court on September 15, 1989. By that point, Lancaster had made four more films (one theatrical and three for television); clearly, the firing was having no effect on his earning power. By a strange coincidence, *Old Gringo* opened the following month, after sitting on the shelf for nearly a year. It was not a success.

By contrast, Burt's next feature would prove to be the most popular movie he ever made, in terms of box-office receipts, taking in nearly $64 million in its initial release.

Field of Dreams was the pet project of writer-director Phil Alden Robinson, who had wanted to adapt the novel *Shoeless Joe* by W. P. Kinsella since its publication in 1982. After writing *Rhinestone* for Sylvester Stallone and Dolly Parton and *All of Me* for Steve Martin and Lily Tomlin and earning his director's stripes with *In the Mood,* a small comedy about a teenage Romeo, he had the stature to command a $13-

---

1. This is a slight exaggeration. Lancaster may have contracted for that many projects, but he would appear in only five more films during his career.
2. Unaware of any problem, Lancaster had gone to Mexico to start rehearsals on December 13.

million budget for the project from producers Lawrence Gordon and
Charles Gordon and Universal Pictures—providing he changed its
name. Thus, it became *Field of Dreams.*

Robinson, once likened to "an assistant professor of English," wrote a
powerful screenplay. "The script brought you to tears," asserted the picture's executive producer, Brian Frankish. The venture had one other
major plus: the lead, Ray Kinsella, an Iowa farmer who plows under his
corn crop to build a baseball field because an unseen voice tells him to,
would be played by Kevin Costner. The thirty-three-year-old actor was
hot, thanks to *Silverado, The Untouchables,* and *No Way Out,* and he
would grow even more popular after *Field of Dreams* started filming in
May of 1988 with the release of *Bull Durham.*

The story featured two important supporting characters: Terrence
Mann, a reclusive writer whom Kinsella brings to Iowa (he was J. D.
Salinger in the novel) and Archibald "Moonlight" Graham, an elderly
doctor (actually he is deceased) who spent half an inning in the major
leagues as a youth. For Mann, Robinson chose James Earl Jones. For
Doc, the director explained that he had wanted an old-time movie star,
but also "somebody who in their youth was a jock." As he put it, "Burt
Lancaster certainly fills those requirements."

Frankish was delighted to have Lancaster in the cast. Said he, "Burt
was almost like the validation for me of the picture. . . . Everyone else is
a newcomer, but here's the tent pole to our canvas." The executive producer also remembered Burt's concern about the insurance question:
"He was really upset with the fact that he was not insurable on *Old
Gringo.* . . . I remember him saying, 'Now, Brian, if anybody wants to
charge you any more money to insure me on this movie, I want to pay
for that.' I said to him, 'No, don't worry about it, Burt.' In fact, it did cost
me an extra five grand for his insurance policy, I just never told him
about it."

The bulk of the eight-week production schedule was centered on
Dubuque, Iowa. Among the first sequences to be shot was one involving
Lancaster. Although it was set in Chisholm, Minnesota, it was filmed in
Galena, Illinois, a historic nineteenth-century community just south and
east of Dubuque.

The challenge in this scene, as with the entire picture, was expressed
by producer Charles Gordon: "When you have a film where the lead
character hears voices, you have to base the rest of the movie in as
much reality as you can." Specifically, Burt as old Doc was to explain to

Costner's Kinsella—with whom he has an instant connection—his life-long ambition, to bat in the major leagues. He does so in a lyrical speech that underscores the theme of the picture, which Lancaster later described as, "If you don't have dreams of some sort, ambitions, whatever you choose to call them, that you never test and never try, then something's missing from your life."

The scene, one of the key moments in the film, depended in large part on the chemistry between the two actors who appear in it. Frankish recalled how Costner and Lancaster, separated by forty years and different eras of filmmaking, tried to establish the bond to make it work: "Ray Kinsella wanted to be tuned to Doc Graham. He was looking for him, he wanted to find out about him. So Kevin approached Burt just exactly like Ray Kinsella would approach Doc Graham. They spent time together. In between takes, they shared moments with each other." Because the scene came so early in the schedule, the executive producer asserted, "Nobody knew what we were doing yet. So how those guys focused on each other was an important study. It was professional performer to professional performer: 'I have a problem here, I have a problem here, let's solve it together.' Or, 'I have an opportunity here, I have an opportunity here, let's make value of that opportunity.' And I think they did. I think they did it quite beautifully." Second assistant director Grant Gilmore agreed, saying, "The scene was so good, I just sat there in awe, going, 'My God, this is something we're going to remember.' "

About four days were required to film the scene. Thereafter, Lancaster was free to leave Iowa while the company continued shooting. "Burt was what they call a 'drop and pick up' actor," explained Frankish, "which means that I hire him at the beginning of the show with firm dates, and then I release him for, like, a four-week period, five-week period of time, and I give him a hard date that I need him back again."

During his hiatus from *Field of Dreams*, Lancaster busied himself with a five-hour miniseries for RAI entitled *The Betrothed (I Promessi Sposi)*, based on the panoramic 1827 novel of the same name by Alessandro Manzoni. Manzoni "is sort of like Dickens for the English, except Dickens was a much more prolific writer," explained Phyllis King, who served as liaison between the production's director, Salvatore Nocita, and the non-Italian-speaking members of the cast. Set in 1629 when a deadly plague, introduced by the invading Spaniards, was decimating northern Italy, this classic of Italian literature encompassed more than a half dozen major characters, including a pair of poor young lovers (played by Delphine Forest and Danny Quinn, Anthony Quinn's son) and the arrogant aristocrat who comes between them (Gary Cady).

Lancaster was to play Cardinal Federigo Borromeo, a historical figure born in Milan in 1564 (and who died there in 1631, two years after the plague). It was not a large role, but it required an actor with maturity and dignity. "Apparently the director always worshiped Lancaster as a child," recalled King. "So when he knew that he was going to do a film with the financial availability of this—which was quite massive—and could employ someone like Burt Lancaster, he immediately turned to him for the very important part of this elderly cardinal."[3]

The making of *The Betrothed* would take eight months, but Lancaster was called for only seven days—from June 20 to June 28. He and Susie arrived in Milan, headquarters for the production, about a week early, to get acclimated, study the script, and see the city. Shortly thereafter, he fell ill. "He became very allergic," recalled Danny Quinn, "all red and puffy"—a consequence of the dye that he had used to turn his salt-and-pepper hair white before leaving the United States.

By the twentieth, he had sufficiently recuperated to begin work. While most of his scenes would be shot at a studio in Yugoslavia (with one day of exteriors there as well), he started in the Duomo, the famous old cathedral in Milan, rendering the same sermon that his character had delivered from the same pulpit 359 years earlier. "It was beautiful," recalled Nocita. "In that moment, Burt Lancaster take the part very well."

According to Quinn, the director was not an easy collaborator. The young American found him not only "mean-spirited," but also disdainful of actors. King concurred, saying, "He's a difficult director. Some of them aren't overindulgent to actors, let's say, and Nocita certainly isn't."

Nocita was more temperate with Lancaster and Murray Abraham, cast as an evil nobleman. Nocita did not care for Burt personally, however, feeling that the star failed to appreciate his special attempts to please him. A case in point was the lavish book that he had prepared on the cardinal and presented to Burt with great ceremony upon the star's arrival in Milan. But, as King saw it, Lancaster was not inconsiderate. It was that Nocita wanted his boyhood idol to feel as he did about the import of their association, and Burt simply considered the miniseries, as she put it, "a well-paying job like any other that he had to get on with."

3. The budget for *The Betrothed* was approximately $15 million.

Still, she asserted that there were no arguments between the two men nor even an undercurrent of tension on the set.

It was in Yugoslavia that Lancaster filmed his most important scene—arguably the most dynamic encounter in the miniseries—that in which the cardinal consoles the powerful count, who is on the brink of madness after recognizing his own evil. Only a skilled veteran could have held his own against the histrionics of Murray Abraham, the eccentric New York character actor who had captured the 1984 Best Actor Oscar for his riveting performance in *Amadeus,* but Lancaster matched Abraham's frenzy with calm, his torment with inner strength. King aptly described the encounter as "a challenge. The challenge of an old lion who realizes that he's got to face up to a mature tiger," adding that both actors were "old hands at the film business. They both knew exactly how to skirmish around each other and jostle for the lights and the position and everything like that, so it was quite an education watching them."

Although *The Betrothed* was based on an Italian classic and produced by an Italian production company, it was shot in English and intended for viewing in Great Britain and the United States. But it aired in neither country—which, in retrospect, is not terribly surprising. Although the production was sumptuous and beautifully photographed, it was plodding and long—even in the three-hour version prepared for the Anglo-American market. Moreover, the novel was virtually unknown in the English-speaking world and the drama's historical context too remote to be of interest outside Manzoni's native land, at least as it was obliquely presented in the film. Finally, the romance of the two lovers—which should have transcended all else—was simply not compelling.

In Italy, the production aired over five successive weeks, commencing on November 12, 1989. It did quite well, averaging nearly a 50 percent share of the total viewing audience per episode—although many journalists and viewers protested the original use of English.

While Lancaster was filming *The Betrothed,* the *Field of Dreams* company was struggling with the weather in Iowa. The problem was that a severe drought had precluded the growth of a successful crop in the corn-field-cum-baseball-diamond that the company had rented from two farmers, Don Lansing and Al Ameskamp. Fortunately, Frankish had thought to insure the corn, so he was able to pay for intense fertilization and irrigation and thus keep the company on schedule.

Burt returned for a scene late in the film when the young Graham, having realized his wish to bat against a major league pitcher, becomes old again to save the Kinsellas' little girl.[4] It only took about two days. Looking back, Frankish fondly remembered his association with the star, saying, "He was very easy to work with, he was a pro." To which Gilmore added, "He was a total gentleman . . . he was all class."

At the time, however, neither man knew how prophetic that final scene with Lancaster would be.

By an odd coincidence, in July of 1988, as Burt was consumed with a film about lost chances and death, Norma Lancaster passed away at the age of seventy-one. The date was July 21. Although the official causes were pneumonia and a stroke, her death certificate also revealed alcoholic liver disease. According to one friend, her drinking had progressively worsened during her final years. "She was as hopeless an alcoholic as you could ever run into towards the end," he recalled. "She had serious things happen to her where doctors would tell her, 'Now, Norma, if you take another drink, you're going to die.' And she'd stop for two weeks, and then she'd go back to drinking by degrees."

On July 26, her body was cremated at the Angeles Abbey under the auspices of the Neptune Society. Her children held a memorial service for a gathering that included members of the local school boards and municipal government. Burt, a friend recalled, came late and stayed briefly, but his appearance was appreciated.

On September 2, *Rocket Gibraltar* debuted in New York, marking Lancaster's first big-screen appearance since *Tough Guys* nearly two years earlier. Pam Grier was absent in the final cut, Dan Petrie having edited out the story line involving Levi Rockwell and the African-American housekeeper. "I thought it cluttered it up," the director recalled. "I hated [to do] it because Pam was a good friend and a wonderful actress."

But even with the deletion, the Chekhovian nature of the family comedy-drama was diluted by the presence of too many characters coping with too many problems; a six-hour miniseries would have been needed to adequately dramatize all of the story lines. Consequently, at only one hundred minutes, *Rocket Gibraltar* did not, to quote Michael Wilmington of the *Los Angles Times,* "get far past the surface." Not surprisingly, the standout in the large cast was the old pro. "No one on the screen today plays old men of emotional and intellectual gravity more appealingly or

4. Young Doc was played by Frank Whaley.

convincingly than Lancaster," asserted *Variety.* To which Janet Maslin of *The New York Times* added, "Lancaster is so touching that he makes it a disappointment every time the story wanders off elsewhere."

But few would see the performance. *Rocket Gibraltar* was probably too fragile to find a mass audience in any event, but lacking a major, contemporary star—a Tom Cruise or a Kevin Costner—to draw the public's attention, it needed strong studio support to make its presence felt. Perhaps such backing would have been forthcoming if David Puttnam, the film's champion at Columbia, had remained in power, but he had been replaced by Dawn Steel, who, to quote one member of the *Gibraltar* company, "had no interest whatsoever in that movie." Consequently, it quickly disappeared from view.

The public did not have to wait another two years to see Lancaster. On April 21, 1989, seven months after the debut of *Rocket Gibraltar, Field of Dreams* opened in New York (following its world premiere in Dubuque, Iowa, the previous day).

As with the Poe-Petrie picture, the makers of *Field of Dreams* were not happy with the way the studio—in this case Universal—handled the release. "Universal really didn't know what to do with the picture," recalled Brian Frankish, "so they only released four hundred prints initially." A blockbuster, by contrast, will usually open in a thousand theaters or more. "That first weekend," the executive producer continued, "that picture did twenty-five thousand dollars per screen for those four hundred prints. . . . The average is three thousand dollars per screen." The studio quickly started making more prints, tripling the amount by the third weekend, but, as Frankish asserted, "The momentum was lost at that time." Had the picture been handled differently, he contended, *Field of Dreams* would have cleared $100 million in its initial domestic release. "The guys at Universal just didn't know what they had," he concluded sadly.

Not only was Universal baffled by *Field of Dreams,* so were some of the critics. While Caryn James of *The New York Times* found it "a work so smartly written, so beautifully filmed, so perfectly acted, that it does the almost impossible trick of turning sentimentality into true emotion," and Mike McGrady of *Newsday* asserted, "*Field of Dreams* goes beyond fantasy into the realm of pure magic," *The New Yorker's* Pauline Kael dubbed it "a crock . . . there's no competitive excitement in it, and no rhythmic beauty," and *Time's* Richard Corliss said it was "a male weepie at its wussiest."

But *Field of Dreams* captured the hearts of moviegoers. So much so, maintained Frankish, that the field itself, retained by the farmers who owned it, became a tourist attraction, drawing some seventy thousand visitors in the year of the picture's release. *Field of Dreams* was also nominated for three Oscars—Best Picture, Best Screenplay from Another Medium, and Best Score—but won no awards.

As Doc Graham, Lancaster made an indelible impression although, in fact, he had but two scenes. In his final moment, the old man heads for the cornfield and oblivion, shaking hands with the ballplayers on his way. Then he reaches the outfield. The camera cuts to the legendary slugger Shoeless Joe Jackson, who calls out, "Hey, rookie, you were good." The camera then returns to Doc for a final close-up, after which he disappears into the stalks. This would prove to be Burt's final moment in feature films—coming nearly forty-three years after the premiere of *The Killers.* In retrospect, Jackson's accolade to Doc acquired a chilling double meaning, as though the young actor playing him, Ray Liotta, were giving one last pat on the back to the old star. "Hey, rookie, you were good." It was a fitting tribute.

On October 7, 1985, four terrorists from the Palestine Liberation Front captured the *Achille Lauro,* an Italian luxury liner, and held its five hundred passengers hostage for fifty-two hours, killing one—an elderly American invalid named Leon Klinghoffer—before taking flight in an Egyptian jet. Surrounded in the air by F-14s of the U.S. Navy, they were ordered to land in Sicily, where they were taken into custody.

Hollywood had already dramatized the story once, in a 1989 TV movie entitled *The Hijacking of the Achille Lauro,* with Karl Malden as Klinghoffer and Lee Grant as his wife, Marilyn. That same year, the Tribune Premiere Network, an international consortium composed of Italian, German, and French companies, decided to produce its own version, again for television, with much of the filming to take place on the *Achille Lauro* itself. In what would become his last Italian project, Burt agreed to play Klinghoffer. For his wife, director Alberto Negrin chose Eva Marie Saint, the cool blonde who had made her film debut in 1954's *On the Waterfront.* Also in the cast were Robert Culp as the American general tracking the hostages and Rebecca Schaeffer as one of the passengers. The young actress would be killed by a stalker on July 18, shortly after the picture wrapped.

Filming on the four-hour, $10-million project called *Voyage of Terror: The Achille Lauro Affair* began in May of 1989, a year after the start of *Field of Dreams.* En route to Rome, Burt met Klinghoffer's daughters in New York.

Lancaster and Negrin enjoyed a solid working relationship, but as with other projects in the 1980s, the star suffered from occasional memorization problems during shooting. "The first time it happened," Negrin recalled, "I just stopped and we started again, and he was very embarrassed, very nervous." Thereafter, the director treated the impediment with the same sensitivity that Andrew McLaglen had shown during the making of *On Wings of Eagles.* "I just gave the stop to the camera milliseconds before Burt could become without words," he explained, typically blaming the halt on himself or a mechanical error. "I tried to avoid Burt the embarrassment of losing the memory. And also the fear of losing the memory."

Despite Burt's difficulty with the lines, his age, and his heart condition, he remained a perfectionist. When, for example, the company was shooting the scene in which the terrorists bring the passengers on deck and the wheelchair-bound Klinghoffer has to try to climb a flight of steps, he insisted on getting the moment right. "For Burt to jump on the stairs was very, very difficult," Negrin asserted, "because he had a heart, how you say, bypass." The director was satisfied after two or three takes, but the star insisted on so many reshoots that Negrin finally begged him to stop. Still, Burt persisted. "He did another one, probably the twelfth," Negrin explained, "and this was really extraordinary. It's the one that is in the movie, and everyone started clapping hands to him, applauding. And he was like a child, very, very happy."

Lancaster went swiftly from Italy to Paris for the making of a new four-hour television version of *The Phantom of the Opera.*

The 1911 novel by Gaston Leroux, a classic of horror fiction, was about a deformed creature who "haunts" the Paris Opera House, terrorizing its management and patrons while falling in love with a beautiful ingenue in the ensemble, Christine Dáae. It had inspired five previous film and TV versions dating back to the 1925 silent classic starring Lon Chaney, plus a popular 1986 musical by Andrew Lloyd Webber. One feature starring *Nightmare on Elm Street*'s Robert Englund was released the year in which the new TV version was filmed.

The Lancaster treatment had also started as a musical—by composer Murray Yestin and playwright Arthur Kopit, but the score had been jettisoned years earlier. What distinguished it, rather, was the absence of horror, for Kopit chose to depict the phantom as sensitive, cultured, and urbane—which made his love for the pretty, talented singer Christine Dáae all the more poignant.

Lancaster's role, theater manager Gérard Carrière, was, to quote Kopit, "a composite of two characters from the novel, the opera manager and the Persian, a man who always knows the phantom's whereabouts." To which the writer added a twist of his own—he made the manager the phantom's father and sole link with the outside world. This relationship helped humanize his protagonist, as Burt later explained: "The phantom had to react to things. He couldn't go to other people and say, 'Hey, wait a minute, what's going on here?' He had to come to me. Or I could go to him." The relationship was so poignant that the drama became not only a romance between a man and a woman, but, as Lancaster put it, "a love story between a father and a son." Said Charles Dance, the forty-three-year-old, classically trained British actor who played the lead, "I thought it worked very well. If the intention was to actually make it [the story] as believable as possible . . . that sort of bridge [to reality] was absolutely vital."

One of Burt's principal reasons for accepting the assignment was the relatively long production schedule—eleven weeks—with much of the filming taking place at the Paris Opera House itself (the stage was being renovated so some sequences had to be shot in another theater, the Odéon). "We did it like a movie," the star recalled, "none of that television rush."

Another attraction was the project's director, Tony Richardson, one of the leading lights of post–World War II Britain, with such stage productions as *Look Back in Anger, The Entertainer,* and *A Taste of Honey* to his credit, as well as the Academy Award–winning Best Picture *Tom Jones.* Thin, hawk-nosed, and, to quote one reporter, "with a voice like a run-down foghorn," Richardson was in Dance's opinion "outrageous, privately and professionally. And he would come straight to the point. I can remember a blazing row on the roof of the Paris Opera at three o'-clock in the morning when one of our producers was silly enough to approach him . . . and Tony said to him, 'Will you fuck off. You're an amateur and you're ruining my film, and if you don't go away, I'm not going to do any more.' "

But there was no disharmony between the director and Lancaster. Later, the star would maintain that Richardson "does his own thing, and it's right. Marvelous director, brilliant ideas." Tony would return the compliment, saying of Burt, "He's wonderful."

So cooperative was Lancaster during the making of *Phantom* that Dance could not fathom the star's previous history with writers and directors. He only saw an actor who was content to perform his scenes as written and leave the rest of the production to those in charge. Dance did observe, however, Burt's tendency to "minimize the dialogue," which probably reflected the star's ongoing memorization problem.

On September 13, while Burt was in Paris, the Public Broadcasting System aired a one-hour documentary entitled *Dawn's Early Light: Ralph McGill and the Segregated South,* with Lancaster providing the voice of McGill, who had died in 1969.

Born in 1898, McGill had served for thirty-one years as the editor of the *Atlanta Constitution* and the author of its daily front-page column. He had started out as a segregationist but in time became one of the South's most eloquent spokesmen for integration. "McGill represented the best attributes of the ideal newspaper editor," wrote Daniel Ruth of the *Chicago Sun-Times.* "He was bold, decisive, and ready to take a stand on unpopular issues and defended himself with forcefulness and clarity." It was fitting that Burt, a long-standing public proponent of civil rights, read his words. The documentary, which Rick Kogan of the *Chicago Tribune* called "inspirational," also included on-camera interviews with newsman Tom Brokaw, Atlanta mayor Andrew Young, and the former Georgia state senator Julian Bond.

NBC aired *The Phantom of the Opera* in two two-hour segments on March 18 and 19, 1990, some five months after the production wrapped.

Sight unseen, one might question the point of doing a horror story without the horror, but the production worked, resulting in, to quote *The New York Times,* "an odd but fascinating prime-time diversion."

Among the film's principal charms were its sumptuous production values—sumptuous even for its generous $10-million budget—plus Teri Polo's sweet, engaging Christine, and Charles Dance's suave, dashing, and ultimately pathetic phantom.

Lancaster, decked out in a full mustache, sideburns, and evening clothes, brought his usual magisterial air to the proceedings. "In a performance of grace and grandeur," wrote Rick Kogan of the *Chicago Tribune,* "he takes the nifty Kopit composite and gives it sensitive life." Especially memorable was his final scene with Dance, in which Carrière admits to being the younger man's father. "He was terrific," Dance recalled. "It was a joy because he just gave himself to the situation." Indeed, when Burt leaned down and kissed the masked forehead and then placed his cheek against the phantom's, the love between the father and son superseded even the sweet sadness of the young man's unrequited ardor for Christine.

• • •

Two months after the airing of *The Phantom of the Opera, Voyage of Terror: The Achille Lauro Affair* was shown in syndication—on May 1 and 2 in most markets. In contrast to the dignified, nineteenth-century theater manager of *Phantom of the Opera,* the docudrama featured a down-to-earth, highly contemporary Burt. Indeed, from the moment he first appeared, parting the ship's passengers in his wheelchair while sporting a windbreaker and yachting hat and flashing his celebrated smile, he effectively evoked the typical loud but nonetheless likable American tourist. Watching the telefilm several years later—with the knowledge of what happened to Burt a scant six months after it aired— is truly bizarre, for as he copes with his character's paralysis, the result of a stroke, he foreshadows his own subsequent condition.

Most of the critics found *Voyage of Terror* "gripping," to quote Kay Gardella of the New York *Daily News.* Leonard Maltin even found it "head and shoulders above" the earlier *Hijacking of the Achille Lauro,* and Daniel Ruth of the *Chicago Sun-Times* agreed, describing the newer, longer docudrama as "a more thorough account of the takeover and the U.S. government's efforts to bring the terrorists to justice."

Four months after the airing of *Voyage of Terror,* Burt surprised many in Hollywood by getting married, Susie's divorce having become final on January 5, 1989. It had been twenty-one years since his relationship with Norma had come to an end, and five years since the onetime secretary had entered his life.

An acquaintance told one of the tabloids that "Burt had been telling Susan for the past five years that he was too old to get married. He said he was in failing health . . . and didn't want to go through with a third wedding." According to this source, Susie forced the marriage after Gene Kelly wed a much younger woman. Perhaps that was so, but Lancaster was reported to have told a friend, "Some people might think I'm too old to get married, but age has nothing to do with it. I feel like a kid again—thanks to Susan!"

The civil ceremony, held September 10, 1990, was simple and re- stricted to family members. The following day, the newlyweds em- barked for Charleston, South Carolina, and the final role of Lancaster's long career.

Like *Voyage of Terror, Separate but Equal,* Burt's third two-part TV film in a row, was drawn from contemporary history. And like *Dawn's*

Early Light, it focused on the civil rights struggle of the 1950s. Specifically, it dramatized the seemingly impossible effort by Thurgood Marshall, chief counsel of the NAACP Legal Defense Fund, and his associates to overturn the 1896 Supreme Court decision making racial school-segregation legal. Their victory in the 1954 case *Brown v. Board of Education* was a milestone in American history. "*Separate but Equal* is about black people winning their own fight," asserted George Stevens Jr., who wrote, directed, and coproduced the telefilm. Stevens, the founder of the American Film Institute and head of the Kennedy Center in Washington, had initially conceived the story as a feature, "but," he said, "what interested me was the sweep of it, and you need the four hours to cover the landscape."

The docudrama promised to be high-caliber fare. In addition to Stevens, whose *The Murder of Mary Phagan* had won the Emmy for Outstanding Mini-Series of 1988, the coproducer was Stan Margulies Jr., whose credits included *Roots* and *The Thorn Birds*. Moreover, the cast featured Sidney Poitier as Thurgood Marshall and Richard Kiley as Chief Justice Earl Warren. The drama would mark Poitier's first TV role in thirty-five years.[5]

Once the Oscar-winning Poitier had signed on, Stevens needed a star of comparable stature to play John W. Davis, the opposing counsel before the Supreme Court. "This was a story, in part, of a great contest between two great lawyers," the director explained. "I mean, John W. Davis was the greatest lawyer in America; he had that reputation. He had been the Democratic candidate for president in 1924. He was the head of the biggest law firm. He was a friend of presidents. He was this tremendous force. And he was a respected force." As the voice of segregation, the role would not carry the audience's sympathies. Nevertheless, asserted Richard Kiley, "They didn't want to have an obvious heavy. They wanted Davis to be a thoughtful, warm man who simply was on the wrong side." Thus, Stevens turned to Lancaster. The star was hardly sympathetic to Davis' views, but as Stevens put it, "I don't think Burt was always looking for the good guy [to play]. He looked for projects that had some value, and roles that he thought he could bring something to."

By the time Burt and Susie arrived in Charleston, the company had been shooting for some five weeks—on what was to be a generous ten-week production schedule. Burt's scenes would take roughly three weeks to complete and would carry him from Charleston, which gave

5. He had last appeared in 1956 in a drama entitled *A Man Is Ten Feet Tall.*

rise to the sequences in Davis' home and office, to Washington, D.C., for the Supreme Court exteriors, and finally to the Disney production studio in Orlando, Florida, where the court interiors were shot.

"I must say it was such a nice experience to work with him," recalled Stevens. "I'd known him for a long time. I never really expected that I would be directing him. It was good. He was fun."

As for their professional association, Stevens felt that his most important contribution toward the actor's performance was, as he put it, "making him comfortable." Which was no mean feat, given Lancaster's memorization problem and the wordy nature of the role. Kiley remembered that "Burt was worried about the massive chunks of dialogue, really a monologue, that he had to spout in the courtroom scene." But Stevens told him, "It's not a huge problem. We'll just take the time, and we'll do it." And, indeed, the director arranged for teleprompters to be installed in strategic locales around the courtroom; they proved so effective that Poitier and Kiley used them as well. Not only were these sequences the climax of the drama, they marked the sole moments when Lancaster and Poitier shared the screen. At the time, the African-American actor, Burt's junior by thirteen years, said, "He's incredible. . . . I was looking forward to working with that talent and I wasn't disappointed. He sparks you."

As Burt relaxed into the court sequences—or perhaps to mask his fear—he joked from time to time with the crowd of extras seated behind him in the gallery. In 1994, Stevens recalled those lighthearted moments and Lancaster's imposing mien, saying, "He looked quite beautiful in his white hair and his morning clothes." It was a warm memory—of what turned out to be the last sequences Lancaster ever filmed. In fact, Burt's final lines came with Davis' closing remarks to the justices in his second appearance before the bench: "But I entreat them to remember the age-old motto: that the best is often the enemy of the good."

About seven weeks later, on the evening of November 29, 1990, Burt and Susie attended a concert at the Dorothy Chandler Pavilion, with the Los Angeles Philharmonic under the direction of Kurt Sanderling offering a program of Haydn's Symphony no. 39 in G Minor and Mahler's Symphony no. 9. Earl Holliman, Lancaster's costar from *Gunfight at the O.K. Corral* and *The Rainmaker,* bumped into the couple at intermission. Having decided to collect autographed photos of the greats with whom he had worked, Holliman asked Burt for a picture. The star said that he would be happy to oblige if Earl would send him a reminder the next day. It would be Lancaster's last public appearance.

The following morning, the thirtieth, he drove to Los Alamitos, just south of Los Angeles, to visit actor Dana Andrews at the John Douglas French Center for Alzheimer's Disease, There, around eleven forty-five, he began to feel something amiss. "He was heading towards the dining room . . . downstairs," explained one of the center's nurses, Cheryl Hunter, "and he started wobbling a little bit, and he got to a chair and said, 'Help me, help me.' " A 911 call was placed, and moments later an ambulance was transporting him to the Los Alamitos Medical Center, a block away. There, physicians determined that he had suffered a major cerebral hemorrhage, a stroke.

For several days, the extent of his condition was unknown as he underwent tests at the behest of his personal doctor, Gary Sugerman. By his side were family members and longtime associates Ben Benjamin and Jack Ostrow. Reporters clamored for news, but the family remained mute. Then, on December 3, nursing supervisor Ardis Smith announced, "He's having some difficulty with his speech. But at the request of the family I'm not able to say more." What Smith did not mention was that Burt was also experiencing paralysis on his right side. For the next nine days, he remained in intensive care as therapists tried to help him regain his motor skills—with minimal success. Finally, on the thirteenth, he was transferred to a long-term treatment center for, in the words of a hospital spokesperson, "extensive physical and speech therapy."

Thereafter, updates on Burt's condition would be few and vague. On March 15, 1991, for example, Ben Benjamin asserted that the star—at home by then—was "in fine spirits at the moment and is really deeply touched by all the support, cards, and letters he's been getting." The agent also held out the hope that Lancaster would someday return to work. Nearly three months later, on June 4, the Associated Press reported that the star, confined to a wheelchair, could still not speak or walk. The wire service's source, an anonymous assistant of Benjamin's, added, "He's doing as well as can be expected after such a serious stroke. We all knew it would take a long time, but he says he's going to lick this." The assistant also noted, "He's been looking at some of his old movies. He particularly enjoys seeing these old films." Finally, on September 20, Susie said, "Burt's very strong physically and mentally and that's a great help in the long haul. . . . There's a lot of laughter going on at the house. Burt's constantly saying something to make us all laugh. And that's a very good part of the medicine too."

After that, as the anniversary of the stroke came and went, the updates more or less ceased.

●　●　●

But, fortunately, one last, new Lancaster performance remained. On April 7 and 8, 1991, *Separate but Equal* aired on ABC. "It is absorbing TV," enthused *Variety*. Kay Gardella of the New York *Daily News* agreed, calling it "a meticulous lesson, no question about it." Burt earned his share of the praise. To John O'Connor of *The New York Times*, he was "the soul of courtly but tough dignity," while *Variety* called his performance "lovely . . . with depth and awareness." His *Separate but Equal* colleagues also spoke glowingly of his work. "I thought he was just thrilling," said Kiley of Burt's courtroom appearance. "I thought it some of the most wonderful work he had done . . . it had such dignity and intelligence behind it." To which Stevens added, "He brought to that film precisely what the film needed from him. From a filmmaker's standpoint, you can't ask for more."

Separate but Equal went on to win the Emmy for the Best Mini-Series of the 1990/91 season.

Meanwhile, Lancaster persevered. But justifiably proud of his image, he chose to remain in seclusion in Century City rather than expose himself to public view.

Anytime a celebrity vanishes behind a veil of secrecy, professional associates, colleagues, and the media inevitably speculate on the true nature of his or her condition. In Burt's case, rumor had it that he lay in bed reciting lines from his old movies—or that he had become a vegetable. Such was not the case. A friend who saw him in the fall of 1993, three years after the stroke, asserted that he was still working with a therapist and described the effort as "the most valiant, wonderful thing." He remained partially paralyzed and his speech continued to be impaired, but he could be understood. "For an eighty-year-old man, he looks pretty fuckin' good," the friend concluded.

The aftereffects of the stroke were not Burt's only concern. According to friends, he suffered several heart attacks and ensuing periods of hospitalization in the years following his confinement, incidents that went unrecorded in the press. To those who knew him, who remembered the incredible vitality, the beautiful physicality of the man in his prime, it was a sad way to end up. Editor Marjorie Fowler spoke for many of his colleagues when she said, "Of all the people in the world who should not be physically incapacitated, it's that man." George Stevens Jr. agreed, asserting, "I remember him saying, 'I love to get up in the morning, to go to the door and get the newspaper and bring it in and to put the coffee on and to fix breakfast and to read the paper.' You know, he was just talking about the details. He enjoyed living. And that always kind of haunted me a little bit over these last years when he was disabled, that a man who had such zest and appreciation for life should be impaired in that way."

On November 2, 1993, Lancaster turned eighty. While the family celebrated quietly on Friday, November 5, the world remembered. TNT, Ted Turner's cable network, devoted a full day and evening to Burt's films, starting with *Castle Keep* at 9 A.M. and running through *Vengeance Valley, Apache, Vera Cruz, Birdman of Alcatraz, Ten Tall Men,* and *Trapeze.* Meanwhile, the Arts and Entertainment channel broadcast *All My Sons,* the American Movie Channel aired *The Rose Tattoo* and *Rope of Sand,* and Showtime featured *Separate Tables.*

It was the last birthday. On October 20, 1994, nearly nine months after the passing of his lifelong friend Nick Cravat and only two weeks shy of his eighty-first birthday, Burt Lancaster died.[6] He was at his home, with his wife at his side, when the fatal heart attack struck. "This last week he'd been better than ever," Susie told the press. "It came as a complete surprise." She added, "He went very, very peacefully. We were together, thank God. He was patting my hair and touching my face and he took a sigh and that was it."

6. Nick Cravat died of lung cancer at the age of eighty-two on January 29, 1994.

Epilogue

"He was a dreamer when he was a little kid," his father recalled. "He could be off in his own world for hours, and he wouldn't hear a thing you'd say."

But even Burt Lancaster could not have imagined the journey that his life would take. The signposts form an enduring legacy, a body of work encompassing eighty-five movies—theatrical and for television—plus three stage productions. Arguably no star in motion picture history has done better. From *The Killers* to *From Here to Eternity* to *Elmer Gantry* to *Atlantic City*, he put his stamp on a host of films that will endure for as long as people enjoy sitting in darkened theaters and thrilling to the evanescent images flickering before them.

Moreover, in an industry that loves to pigeonhole, he simply refused to be typecast. Consider the remarkable diversity of his roles: the bright young man in *All My Sons*; the king of derring-do in *The Flame and the Arrow*; the ineffectual alcoholic in *Come Back, Little Sheba*; the huckster who can sell anybody anything in *The Rainmaker*; the malevolent newspaper columnist in *Sweet Smell of Success*; the embittered convict capable of loving a simple sparrow in *Birdman of Alcatraz*; the proud but fading Sicilian nobleman in *The Leopard*; and the eccentric billionaire in *Local Hero*. Not to mention Wyatt Earp, Moses, and P. T. Barnum. It is hard to find another major star who displayed a greater range. As *The New York Times* critic Vincent Canby observed in 1981, "The Lancaster career, more than that of any actor I can think of, demonstrates the growth of a talent as well as the intelligence that commands that talent."

His maturation was no accident. "It's like this," he said at the outset, "the idea of being the best at whatever I'm doing at the moment has been sort of an obsession with me all my life. If I were making chairs, I would want to learn how to make the best in the world." Fortunately, he found something he liked better than carpentry. As one of his directors, Andrew McLaglen, put it, "He loved his craft. He loved making movies."

Perhaps that is why he endured long after his youth and beauty had faded. It is well to remember that when he began, Hollywood was in the final days of its golden age. By the end, the miniseries and the made-for-television movie had come of age. In the early years, he costarred with the likes of Gary Cooper and Clark Gable. His later offerings featured Robert De Niro and Kevin Costner. And his leading ladies spanned the generations from Katharine Hepburn, Ava Gardner, and Rita Hayworth to Susan Sarandon and Amanda Plummer.

Even if he had not persevered so long as an actor, his contribution as a film producer deserves remembrance. Through light entertainments like *The Crimson Pirate* and small, intimate, meaningful dramas like *Marty* and *Separate Tables,* he set the mark for other stars, like Costner and Clint Eastwood, to follow.

As for the man, he was guarded. He did not let many people in. Even Luchino Visconti said, "I sometimes think that Burt is the most perfectly mysterious man I ever met in my life." Like many creative people, he was an amalgam of contradictions. He came on brash, but he was really insecure. He could be incredibly insensitive and amazingly generous. He was, at times, rambunctious and playful and always verbose, but he valued his privacy and was content to enjoy the solitary pursuits, such as reading and listening to classical music. Without question, he had a terrible temper, but he softened with age. "Well, you know, you mature and you mellow and you realize scenes don't solve anything," he said in 1975. "So you try other ways."

Ultimately, stars become legends because they leave behind a lifetime of entertainment that intertwines with a mass of individual experiences. No doubt there are those who recall seeing *Gunfight at the O.K. Corral* at the Saturday matinee and wanting to be like Wyatt or Doc. Others remember that first date when they went to see *From Here to Eternity* and held hands during the scene on the beach. Some may even have been inspired to become actors themselves thanks to the power of *Birdman of Alcatraz* or *Atlantic City.* If so, then Lancaster's life will have come full circle: the little kid who had been prompted to feats of living-room derring-do by the cinema exploits of Douglas Fairbanks will, in turn, have passed the creative spark on to others.

Above all, Burt Lancaster endures even beyond death because for nearly fifty years he has been the stuff of our fantasies. Tall, feisty, always speaking his mind, a he-man if there ever was one, he was larger than life. Perhaps an anonymous fan, quoted upon the release of *Tough Guys,* put it best: "Burt Lancaster is what got me in love with Hollywood. He's part of the whole fantasy of moviemaking. I watch his movies over and over. Burt Lancaster *is* Hollywood."

Filmography

Unless otherwise indicated, dates reflect the American premiere. An asterisk indicates the film's availability on videotape.

FEATURE FILMS

1. *The Killers* (Mark Hellinger Productions/Universal). August 29, 1946. Produced by Mark Hellinger. Directed by Robert Siodmak. Screenplay by Anthony Veiller, based on the short story by Ernest Hemingway. With Ava Gardner, Edmond O'Brien, Albert Dekker, Sam Levene, Jeff Corey, William Conrad. 105 minutes. b&w.

2. *Brute Force* (Mark Hellinger Productions/Universal). June 30, 1947. Produced by Mark Hellinger. Directed by Jules Dassin. Screenplay by Richard Brooks, based on the story by Robert Patterson. With Hume Cronyn, Charles Bickford, Yvonne De Carlo, Ann Blyth, Ella Raines, Anita Colby, Sam Levene, Howard Duff, Jeff Corey. 96 minutes. b&w.

3. *Desert Fury* (Hal Wallis Productions/Paramount). September 24, 1947. Produced by Hal B. Wallis. Directed by Lewis Allen. Screenplay by Robert Rossen, based on the novel *Desert Town* by Ramona Stewart. With John Hodiak, Lizabeth Scott, Wendell Corey, Mary Astor. 96 minutes. color.

4. *Variety Girl* (Paramount). October 16, 1947. Produced by Daniel Dare. Directed by George Marshall. Screenplay by Edmund Hartmann, Frank Tashlin, Robert Welch, and Monte Brice. With Olga San Juan, Mary Hatcher, DeForest Kelley, William Demarest (Lancaster was a "guest star"; other "guest stars" included Bing Crosby, Bob Hope, William Holden, Lizabeth Scott, Robert Preston, Veronica Lake, Sterling Hayden, Macdonald Carey). 83 minutes. b&w and color.

5. *I Walk Alone* (Hal Wallis Productions/Paramount). January 22,

1948. Produced by Hal B. Wallis. Directed by Byron Haskin. Screenplay by Charles Schnee, based on the play *The Beggars Are Coming to Town* by Theodore Reeves, adapted by Robert Smith and John Bright. With Lizabeth Scott, Kirk Douglas, Wendell Corey. 98 minutes. b&w.

6. *All My Sons* (Universal). March 27, 1948. Produced by Chester Erskine. Directed by Irving Reis. Screenplay by Chester Erskine, based on the play by Arthur Miller. With Edward G. Robinson, Mady Christians, Louisa Horton, Howard Duff, Frank Conroy, Arlene Francis. 94 minutes. b&w.

7. *Sorry, Wrong Number* (Hal Wallis Productions/Paramount). September 1, 1948. Produced by Hal B. Wallis and Anatole Litvak. Directed by Litvak. Screenplay by Lucille Fletcher, based on her radio play. With Barbara Stanwyck, Ann Richards, Wendell Corey, Ed Begley, Leif Erickson, William Conrad. 89 minutes. b&w.*

8. *Kiss the Blood off My Hands* (Hecht-Norma/Universal). October 30, 1948. Produced by Richard Vernon. Directed by Norman Foster. Screenplay by Leonardo Bercovicci, based on the novel by Gerald C. Butler, adapted by Ben Maddow and Walter Bernstein. With Joan Fontaine, Robert Newton, Lewis Russell. 80 minutes. b&w.

9. *Criss Cross* (Universal). March 12, 1949. Produced by Michael Kraike. Directed by Robert Siodmak. Screenplay by Daniel Fuchs, based on the novel by Don Tracy. With Yvonne De Carlo, Dan Duryea, Stephen McNally, Richard Long. 87 minutes. b&w.*

10. *Rope of Sand* (Hal Wallis Productions/Paramount). August 4, 1949. Produced by Hal B. Wallis. Directed by William Dieterle. Screenplay by Walter Doniger, additional dialogue by John Paxton. With Paul Henreid, Claude Rains, Corinne Calvet, Peter Lorre, Sam Jaffe. 105 minutes. b&w.

11. *The Flame and the Arrow* (Hecht-Norma/Warner Bros.). July 15, 1950. Produced by Harold Hecht and Frank Ross. Directed by Jacques Tourneur. Screenplay by Waldo Salt. With Virginia Mayo, Robert Douglas, Aline MacMahon, Frank Allenby, Nick Cravat. 88 minutes. color.*

12. *Mister 880* (20th Century–Fox). September 29, 1950. Produced by Julian Blaustein. Directed by Edmund Goulding. Screenplay by Robert Riskin, based on articles by St. Clair McKelway. With Dorothy McGuire, Edmund Gwenn, Millard Mitchell, Howard St. John. 90 minutes. b&w.

13. *Vengeance Valley* (Metro-Goldwyn-Mayer). February 16, 1951. Produced by Nicholas Nayfack. Directed by Richard Thorpe. Screenplay by Irving Ravetch, based on the novel by Luke Short. With Robert Walker, Joanne Dru, Sally Forrest, John Ireland, Carleton Carpenter, Ray Collins, Hugh O'Brian. 82 minutes. color.*

14. *Jim Thorpe—All American* (Warner Bros.). August 24, 1951.

Produced by Everett Freeman. Directed by Michael Curtiz. Screenplay by Douglas Morrow and Everett Freeman, based on the story by Morrow and Vincent X. Flaherty and the autobiography by Jim Thorpe and Russel J. Birdwell. With Charles Bickford, Phyllis Thaxter, Steve Cochran, Dick Wesson. 105 minutes. b&w.*

15. *Ten Tall Men* (Hecht-Norma/Columbia). October 26, 1951. Produced by Harold Hecht. Directed by Willis Goldbeck. Screenplay by Roland Kibbee and Frank Davis, from a story by Goldbeck and James Warner Bellah. With Jody Lawrence, Gilbert Roland, Kieron Moore, George Tobias, Mari Blanchard. 97 minutes. color.

16. *The Crimson Pirate* (Hecht-Norma/Warner Bros.). August 27, 1952. Produced by Harold Hecht. Directed by Robert Siodmak. Screenplay by Roland Kibbee. With Eva Bartok, Nick Cravat, Leslie Bradley, Torin Thatcher, Margo Grahame, Christopher Lee, Dagmar Wynter, Frank Pettingill. 104 minutes. color.*

17. *Come Back, Little Sheba* (Hal Wallis Productions/Paramount). December 24, 1952. Produced by Hal B. Wallis. Directed by Daniel Mann. Screenplay by Ketti Frings, based on the play by William Inge. With Shirley Booth, Terry Moore, Richard Jaeckel, Philip Ober. 96 minutes. b&w.*

18. *South Sea Woman* (Warner Bros.). June 3, 1953. Produced by Sam Bischoff. Directed by Arthur Lubin. Screenplay by Edwin Blum, based on the play *General Court Martial* by William M. Rankin, adapted by Earl Baldwin and Stanley Shapiro. With Virginia Mayo, Chuck Connors, Arthur Shields, Veola Vonn. 89 minutes. b&w.

19. *From Here to Eternity* (Columbia). August 5, 1953. Produced by Buddy Adler. Directed by Fred Zinnemann. Screenplay by Daniel Taradash, based on the novel by James Jones. With Montgomery Clift, Deborah Kerr, Donna Reed, Frank Sinatra, Philip Ober, Ernest Borgnine, Jack Warden, Mickey Shaughnessy. 118 minutes. b&w.*

20. *Three Sailors and a Girl* (Warner Bros.). November 23, 1953. Produced by Sammy Cahn. Directed by Roy Del Ruth. Screenplay by Roland Kibbee and Devery Freeman, based on the play *The Butter and Egg Man* by George S. Kaufman. With Jane Powell, Gordon MacRae, Gene Nelson, Sam Levene, Jack E. Leonard, Veda Ann Borg (Lancaster had a cameo). 95 minutes. color.

21. *His Majesty O'Keefe* (Hecht-Norma/Warner Bros.). January 27, 1954. Produced by Harold Hecht. Directed by Byron Haskin. Screenplay by Borden Chase and James Hill, based on the novel by Lawrence Klingman and Gerald Green. With Joan Rice, Andre Morrell, Abraham Sofaer, Archie Savage, Benson Fong, Tessa Prendergast, Lloyd Berrell, Charles Horvath. 90 minutes. color.*

22. *Apache* (Hecht-Lancaster/United Artists). Late June 1954. Produced by Harold Hecht. Directed by Robert Aldrich. Screenplay by James R. Webb, based on the novel *Broncho Apache* by Paul I. Wellman. With Jean Peters, John McIntire, Charles Buchinsky, John Dehner, Paul Guilfoyle. 87 minutes. color.*

23. *Vera Cruz* (Hecht-Lancaster/United Artists). December 25, 1954. Produced by James Hill. Directed by Robert Aldrich. Screenplay by Roland Kibbee and James R. Webb, based on a story by Borden Chase. With Gary Gooper, Denise Darcel, Cesar Romero, Sarita Montiel, Ernest Borgnine, Jack Elam. 92 minutes. color.*

24. *The Kentuckian* (Hecht-Lancaster/United Artists). September 1, 1955. Produced by Harold Hecht. Directed by Burt Lancaster. Screenplay by A. B. Guthrie Jr., based on the novel *The Gabriel Horn* by Felix Holt. With Diana Lynn, Dianne Foster, John McIntire, Una Merkel, John Carradine, Walter Matthau, Donald MacDonald. 101 minutes. color.*

25. *The Rose Tattoo* (Hal Wallis Productions/Paramount). December 12, 1955. Produced by Hal B. Wallis. Directed by Daniel Mann. Screenplay by Tennessee Williams, based on his play, adaptation by Hal Kanter. With Anna Magnani, Marisa Pavan, Ben Cooper, Virginia Grey, Jo Van Fleet, Sandro Giglio. 114 minutes. b&w.*

26. *Trapeze* (Hecht-Lancaster/United Artists). May 30, 1956. Produced by James Hill. Directed by Carol Reed. Screenplay by James R. Webb, based on the novel *The Killing Frost* by Max Catto, adaptation by Liam O'Brien. With Tony Curtis, Gina Lollobrigida, Katy Jurado, Thomas Gomez, Johnny Puleo, Minor Watson. 106 minutes. color.*

27. *The Rainmaker* (Hal Wallis Productions/Paramount). December 13, 1956. Produced by Hal B. Wallis. Directed by Joseph Anthony. Screenplay by N. Richard Nash, based on his play. With Katharine Hepburn, Wendell Corey, Lloyd Bridges, Earl Holliman, Cameron Prud'homme. 122 minutes. color.*

28. *Gunfight at the O.K. Corral* (Hal Wallis Productions/Paramount). May 30, 1957. Produced by Hal B. Wallis. Directed by John Sturges. Screenplay by Leon Uris, based on the story *The Killer* by George Schulin. With Kirk Douglas, Rhonda Fleming, Jo Van Fleet, John Ireland, Frank Faylen, Earl Holliman, Lyle Bettger, Ted De Corsia, Dennis Hopper. 122 minutes. color.*

29. *Sweet Smell of Success* (Hecht-Hill-Lancaster/United Artists). June 27, 1957. Produced by James Hill. Directed by Alexander Mackendrick. Screenplay by Clifford Odets and Ernest Lehman, based on the novella by Lehman. With Tony Curtis, Susan Harrison, Martin Milner, Sam Levene, Barbara Nichols, Jeff Donnell, Lurene Tuttle, Edith Atwater, Queenie Smith. 93 minutes. b&w.*

30. *Run Silent, Run Deep* (Hecht-Hill-Lancaster/United Artists). March 27, 1958. Produced by Harold Hecht. Directed by Robert Wise. Screenplay by John Gay, based on the novel by Edward L. Beach. With Clark Gable, Jack Warden, Brad Dexter, Don Rickles, Nick Cravat, Hoe Maross, Mary LaRoche, Eddie Foy III, Rudy Bond. 93 minutes. b&w.*

31. *Separate Tables* (Hecht-Hill-Lancaster/United Artists). December 18, 1958. Produced by Harold Hecht. Directed by Delbert Mann. Screenplay by Terence Rattigan and John Gay, based on the play by Rattigan. With Rita Hayworth, Deborah Kerr, David Niven, Wendy Hiller, Gladys Cooper, Cathleen Nesbitt, Felix Aylmer, Rod Taylor. 98 minutes. b&w.*

32. *The Devil's Disciple* (Hecht-Hill-Lancaster/Bryna/United Artists). August 21, 1959. Produced by Harold Hecht. Directed by Guy Hamilton. Screenplay by John Dighton and Roland Kibbee, based on the play by George Bernard Shaw. With Kirk Douglas, Laurence Olivier, Eva Le Gallienne, Harry Andrews, Basil Sydney, George Rose, Janette Scott, Neil McCallum. 82 minutes. b&w.*

33. *The Unforgiven* (Hecht-Hill-Lancaster/United Artists). April 6, 1960. Produced by James Hill. Directed by John Huston. Screenplay by Ben Maddow, based on the novel by Alan LeMay. With Audrey Hepburn, Audie Murphy, Lillian Gish, John Saxon, Charles Bickford, Albert Salmi, Joseph Wiseman, Doug McClure, June Walker. 125 minutes. color.*

34. *Elmer Gantry* (Elmer Gantry Productions/United Artists). July 7, 1960. Produced by Bernard Smith. Directed by Richard Brooks. Screenplay by Brooks, based on the novel by Sinclair Lewis. With Jean Simmons, Arthur Kennedy, Shirley Jones, Dean Jagger, Patti Page, Edward Andrews, John McIntire. 145 minutes. color.*

35. *The Young Savages* (Contemporary Productions/United Artists). May 24, 1961. Executive producer, Harold Hecht. Directed by John Frankenheimer. Screenplay by Edward Anhalt and J. P. Miller, from the novel *A Matter of Conviction* by Evan Hunter. With Dina Merrill, Shelley Winters, Edward Andrews, Telly Savalas, Vivian Nathan, Larry Gates, Pilar Seurat, Jody Fair. 103 minutes. b&w.

36. *Judgment at Nuremberg* (Roxlum Productions/United Artists). December 19, 1961. Produced and directed by Stanley Kramer. Screenplay by Abby Mann, based on his teleplay. With Spencer Tracy, Richard Widmark, Marlene Dietrich, Maximilian Schell, Judy Garland, Montgomery Clift, Ed Binns, Werner Klemperer, William Shatner. 183 minutes. b&w.*

37. *Birdman of Alcatraz* (Norma Productions/United Artists). July 18, 1962. Produced by Stuart Miller and Guy Trosper. Directed by John Frankenheimer. Screenplay by Guy Trosper, based on the book by

Thomas E. Gaddis. With Karl Malden, Thelma Ritter, Betty Field, Neville Brand, Edmond O'Brien, Telly Savalas, Whit Bissell. 147 minutes. b&w.*

38. *A Child Is Waiting* (Larcus Productions/United Artists). February 13, 1963. Produced by Stanley Kramer. Directed by John Cassavetes. Screenplay by Abby Mann, based on his teleplay. With Judy Garland, Gena Rowlands, Steven Hill, Bruce Ritchey, Gloria McGehee, Paul Stewart, Lawrence Tierney, Elizabeth Wilson. 104 minutes. b&w.*

39. *The List of Adrian Messenger* (Universal). May 1963. Produced by Edward Lewis. Directed by John Huston. Screenplay by Anthony Veiller, based on the novel by Philip MacDonald. With Kirk Douglas, George C. Scott, Clive Brook, Dana Wynter, Gladys Cooper, Herbert Marshall, John Merivale (Lancaster had a cameo. Other cameos by Tony Curtis, Robert Mitchum, and Frank Sinatra). 98 minutes. b&w.*

40. *The Leopard (Il Gattopardo)* (Titanus/20th Century–Fox). August 12, 1963. Produced by Goffredo Lombardo. Directed by Luchino Visconti. Screenplay by Suso Cecchi D'Amico, Pasquale Festa Campanile, Massimo Franciosa, Enrico Medioli, and Luchino Visconti, from the novel by Giuseppe di Lampedusa. With Claudia Cardinale, Alain Delon, Paolo Stoppa, Rina Morelli, Romolo Valli, Serge Reggiani, Leslie French, Ivo Garrani. 205 minutes. color.

41. *Seven Days in May* (Seven Arts–Joel/Paramount). February 20, 1964. Produced by Edward Lewis and John Frankenheimer. Directed by Frankenheimer. Screenplay by Rod Serling, based on the novel by Fletcher Knebel and Charles W. Bailey II. With Kirk Douglas, Fredric March, Ava Gardner, Edmond O'Brien, Martin Balsam, George Macready, Whit Bissell, Hugh Marlowe, Andrew Duggan, Christopher Todd, John Houseman. 120 minutes. b&w.*

42. *The Train* (Ariane/Dear/United Artists). March 17, 1965. Produced by Jules Bricken. Directed by John Frankenheimer. Screenplay by Franklin Coen and Frank Davis, based on the book *Le Front de l'art* by Rose Valland. With Paul Scofield, Jeanne Moreau, Michel Simon, Suzanne Flon, Albert Remy, Wolfgang Preiss, Charles Millot. 133 minutes. b&w.*

43. *The Hallelujah Trail* (Mirisch-Kappa/United Artists). July 1, 1965. Produced and directed by John Sturges. Screenplay by John Gay, based on the novel by Bill Gulick. With Lee Remick, Jim Hutton, Pamela Tiffin, Donald Pleasence, Brian Keith, Martin Landau, John Anderson, Tom Stern, Whit Bissell. 165 minutes. color.*

44. *The Professionals* (Pax/Columbia). November 2, 1966. Produced and directed by Richard Brooks. Screenplay by Brooks, based on the novel *A Mule for the Marquesa* by Frank O'Rourke. With Lee Marvin,

Robert Ryan, Claudia Cardinale, Jack Palance, Ralph Bellamy, Woody Strode. 117 minutes. color.*

45. *The Scalphunters* (Bristol/Norlan/United Artists). April 2, 1968. Produced by Jules Levy, Arthur Gardner, and Arnold Laven. Directed by Sydney Pollack. Screenplay by William Norton. With Shelley Winters, Telly Savalas, Ossie Davis, Armando Silvestre, Dabney Coleman. 102 minutes. color.*

46. *The Swimmer* (Horizon/Dover/Columbia). May 15, 1968. Produced by Frank Perry and Roger Lewis. Directed by Frank Perry. Screenplay by Eleanor Perry, from the short story by John Cheever. With Janet Landgard, Janice Rule, Tony Bickley, Marge Champion, Nancy Cushman, Bill Fiore, John Garfield Jr., Kim Hunter, Diana Muldaur, Joan Rivers, Jan Miner, Louise Troy, Dolph Sweet. 94 minutes. color.*

47. *Castle Keep* (Filmways/Columbia). July 23, 1969. Produced by Martin Ransohoff and John Calley. Directed by Sydney Pollack. Screenplay by Daniel Taradash and David Rayfiel, based on the novel by William Eastlake. With Patrick O'Neal, Jean-Pierre Aumont, Astrid Heeren, Peter Falk, Scott Wilson, Tony Bill, Al Freeman Jr., Bruce Dern, Michael Conrad, James Patterson. 106 minutes. color.

48. *The Gypsy Moths* (Frankenheimer-Lewis/Metro-Goldwyn-Mayer). August 28, 1969. Executive producer, Edward Lewis. Directed by John Frankenheimer. Screenplay by William Hanley, based on the novel by James Drought. With Deborah Kerr, Gene Hackman, Scott Wilson, Sheree North, William Windom, Bonnie Bedelia. 110 minutes. color.

49. *Airport* (Ross Hunter Productions/Universal). March 5, 1970. Produced by Ross Hunter. Directed by George Seaton. Written by Seaton, based on the novel by Arthur Hailey. With Dean Martin, Jacqueline Bisset, Jean Seberg, George Kennedy, Helen Hayes, Van Heflin, Maureen Stapleton, Barry Nelson, Dana Wynter, Barbara Hale, Lloyd Nolan. 137 minutes. color.*

50. *Valdez Is Coming* (Norlan/United Artists). April 9, 1971. Produced by Ira Steiner. Directed by Edwin Sherin. Screenplay by Roland Kibbee and David Rayfiel, based on the novel by Elmore Leonard. With Susan Clark, Jon Cypher, Barton Heyman, Richard Jordan, Frank Silvera, Hector Elizondo. 90 minutes. color.*

51. *Lawman* (Scimitar/United Artists). August 4, 1971. Produced and directed by Michael Winner. Screenplay by Gerald Wilson. With Robert Ryan, Lee J. Cobb, Sheree North, Joseph Wiseman, Robert Duvall, Albert Salmi, J. D. Cannon, John McGiver, Richard Jordan, John Beck. 99 minutes. color.

52. *Ulzana's Raid* (Universal). November 15, 1972. Produced by

Carter DeHaven. Directed by Robert Aldrich. Screenplay by Alan Sharp. With Bruce Davison, Jorge Luke, Richard Jaeckel, Joaquin Martinez, Lloyd Bochner, Karl Swenson. 103 minutes. color.*

53. *Scorpio* (Scimitar/Mirisch/United Artists). April 19, 1973. Produced by Walter Mirisch. Directed by Michael Winner. Screenplay by David W. Rintels and Gerald Wilson, based on the story by Rintels. With Alain Delon, Paul Scofield, John Colicos, Gayle Hunnicutt, J. D. Cannon. 114 minutes. color.*

54. *Executive Action* (Wakefield Orloff/National General). November 7, 1973. Produced by Edward Lewis. Directed by David Miller. Screenplay by Dalton Trumbo, based on the story by Mark Lane and Donald Freed. With Robert Ryan, Will Geer, Gilbert Green, John Anderson, Paul Carr, Colby Chester, Ed Lauter. 91 minutes. color.*

55. *The Midnight Man* (Norlan/Universal). June 14, 1974. Produced, directed, and written by Burt Lancaster and Roland Kibbee, based on the novel *The Midnight Lady and the Mourning Man* by David Anthony. With Susan Clark, Cameron Mitchell, Morgan Woodward, Harris Yulin, Robert Quarry, Joan Lorring, Lawrence Dobkin, Ed Lauter, Mills Watson, Charles Tyner, Catherine Bach, William Lancaster. 117 minutes. color.

56. *Conversation Piece (Gruppo Di Famiglia in Un Interno)* (Rusconi Film/Gaumont International SARL/New Line Cinema). September 26, 1975 (New York Film Festival). Produced by Giovanni Bertolucci. Directed by Luchino Visconti. Screenplay by Visconti, Suso Cecchi D'Amico, and Enrico Medioli. With Silvana Mangano, Helmut Berger, Claudia Marsani, Stefano Patrizi, Elvira Cortese, Dominique Sanda, Claudia Cardinale, 119 minutes. color.*

57. *Buffalo Bill and the Indians* (Dino De Laurentiis Productions). July 4, 1976. Executive producer, David Susskind. Directed by Robert Altman. Screenplay by Alan Rudolph and Robert Altman, based on the play *Indians* by Arthur Kopit. With Paul Newman, Joel Grey, Geraldine Chaplin, Kevin McCarthy, Harvey Keitel, Denver Pyle, John Considine, Pat McCormick, Shelley Duvall, Will Sampson. 123 minutes. color.*

58. *The Cassandra Crossing* (International Cine Productions). February 9, 1977. Produced by Carlo Ponti. Directed by George Pan Cosmatos. Screenplay by Robert Katz and Cosmatos with Tom Mankiewicz. With Sophia Loren, Richard Harris, Ava Gardner, Lee Strasberg, Martin Sheen, Ingrid Thulin, John Phillip Law, Ann Turkel, O. J. Simpson, Lionel Stander. 129 minutes. color.*

59. *Twilight's Last Gleaming* (Geria/Lorimar-Bavaria). February 9, 1977. Executive producer, Helmut Jedele. Directed by Robert Aldrich. Screenplay by Ronald M. Cohen and Edward Huebsch, based on the

novel *Viper Three* by Walter Wager. With Richard Widmark, Charles Durning, Melvyn Douglas, Joseph Cotten, Paul Winfield, Burt Young. 146 minutes. color.*

60. *The Island of Dr. Moreau* (Skip Steloff/Sandy Howard/Major Productions/American International). July 13, 1977. Executive producers, Samuel Z. Arkoff and Sandy Howard. Directed by Don Taylor. Screenplay by John Herman Shaner and Al Ramrus, based on the novel by H. G. Wells. With Michael York, Barbara Carrera, Nigel Davenport, Richard Basehart, Nick Cravat. 98 minutes. color.*

61. *1900 (Novecento)* (PEA/Artistes Associés/Artemis/Paramount). October 8, 1977 (New York Film Festival). Produced by Alberto Grimaldi. Directed by Bernardo Bertolucci. Screenplay by Bertolucci, Franco Arcalli, and Giuseppe Bertolucci. With Robert De Niro, Gerard Depardieu, Dominique Sanda, Donald Sutherland, Sterling Hayden, Alida Valli. 248 minutes. color.*

62. *Go Tell the Spartans* (Spartans/Mar-Vista). June 14, 1978. Produced by Allan F. Bodah and Mitchell Cannold. Directed by Ted Post. Screenplay by Wendell Mayes, based on the novel *Incident at Muc Wa* by Daniel Ford. With Craig Wasson, Marc Singer, Jonathan Goldsmith, Joe Unger, Dennis Howard, David Clennon, Evan Kim, John Megna, Dolph Sweet. 114 minutes. color.*

63. *Zulu Dawn* (Lamitas/Samarkand). October 1979 (Great Britain). Produced by Nate Kohn. Directed by Douglas Hickox. Screenplay by Cy Endfield and Anthony Storey. With Peter O'Toole, Simon Ward, Nigel Davenport, Michael Jayston, Denholm Elliott, John Mills, Bob Hoskins. 117 minutes. color.*

64. *Atlantic City* (A Denis Heroux and John Kemeney Production/International Cinema Corp./Selta Films/Paramount). April 3, 1981. Executive producers, Joseph Beaubain, Gabriel Boustany. Directed by Louis Malle. Screenplay by John Guare. With Susan Sarandon, Kate Reid, Robert Joy. 105 minutes. color.*

65. *Cattle Annie and Little Britches* (King-Hitzig/Universal). May 15, 1981. Produced by Rupert Hitzig and Alan King. Directed by Lamont Johnson. Screenplay by Robert Ward. With Diane Lane, Amanda Plummer, Rod Steiger, John Savage, Scott Glenn. 95 minutes. color.

66. *La Pelle (The Skin)* (Opera Film/Gaumont-Italia). May 1981 (Cannes Film Festival, France). Executive producer, Manolo Boligini. Directed by Liliana Cavani. Screenplay by Robert Katz and Cavani, from the novel by Curzio Malaparte. With Claudia Cardinale, Marcello Mastroianni, Ken Marshall, Alexandra King. 131 minutes. color.

67. *Local Hero* (Enima/Goldcrest/Warner Bros.). February 17, 1983. Produced by David Puttnam. Directed and written by Bill Forsyth. With

Peter Riegert, Denis Lawson, Peter Capaldi, Fulton MacKay, Chris Rozycki, Jenny Seagrove. 111 minutes. color.*

68. *The Osterman Weekend* (Osterman Weekend Productions/20th Century–Fox). November 4, 1983. Produced by Peter S. Davis and William N. Panzer. Directed by Sam Peckinpah. Screenplay by Alan Sharp, based on the novel by Robert Ludlum. With Rutger Hauer, John Hurt, Craig T. Nelson, Dennis Hopper, Chris Sarandon, Meg Foster, Helen Shaver, Cassie Yates. 105 minutes. color.*

69. *Little Treasure* (Tri-Star/Vista). May 1, 1985. Executive producers, Joanna Lancaster and Richard Wagner. Directed and written by Alan Sharp. With Margot Kidder, Ted Danson. 95 minutes. color.*

70. *Tough Guys* (Touchstone/Silver Screen Partners II). October 3, 1986. Produced by Joe Wyzan. Directed by Jeff Kanew. Screenplay by James Orr and Jim Cruickshank. With Kirk Douglas, Eli Wallach, Charles Durning, Dana Carvey, Alexis Smith, Darlanne Fluegel. 102 minutes. color.*

71. *Rocket Gibraltar* (Ulick Mayo Weiss/Columbia). September 2, 1988. Executive producers, Michael Ulick, Geoffrey Mayo, Robert Fisher. Directed by Daniel Petrie. Screenplay by Amos Poe. With Suzy Amis, Patricia Clarkson, Frances Conroy, Sinead Cusack, John Glover, Bill Pullman, Kevin Spacey, Macaulay Culkin. 100 minutes. color.*

72. *Field of Dreams* (Carolco/Universal). April 21, 1989. Executive producer, Brian Frankish. Directed by Phil Alden Robinson. Screenplay by Robinson, based on the novel *Shoeless Joe* by W. P. Kinsella. With Kevin Costner, Amy Madigan, James Earl Jones, Ray Liotta, Timothy Busfield. 106 minutes. color.*

TELEVISION MOVIES AND MINISERIES

1. *Moses, the Lawgiver* (RAI/ITC/CBS). June 21, 28, July 5, 12, 16, August 2, 1975. Produced by Vincenzo Labella. Directed by Gianfranco De Bosio. Teleplay by Anthony Burgess, Vittorio Bonicelli, and Gianfranco De Bosio. With William Lancaster, Anthony Quayle, Irene Papas, Ingrid Thulin, Laurent Terzieff, Yousef Shiloah, Aharon Ipale, Marina Berti, Melba Englander. Narrated by Richard Johnson. 360 minutes (theatrical release: 141 minutes). color.*

2. *Victory at Entebbe* (David Wolper/Warner Bros./ABC). December 13, 1976. Produced by Robert Guenette. Directed by Marvin Chomsky. Teleplay by Ernest Kinoy. With Anthony Hopkins, Richard Dreyfuss, Helen Hayes, Linda Blair, Elizabeth Taylor, Kirk Douglas, Harris Yulin, Stephen Geirasch, Helmut Berger, Julius Harris. 180 minutes (theatrical release: 119 minutes). color.

3. *Marco Polo* (RAI Radiotelevisione Italiana/Cristaldi-Labella/NBC). May 16–19, 1982. Produced by Vincenzo Labella. Directed by Giuliano Montaldo. Teleplay by Montaldo, Labella, and David Butler. With Ken Marshall, Denholm Elliott, Tony Vogel, Anne Bancroft, John Gielgud, John Houseman, Tony Lo Bianco, Sada Thompson, David Warner, Ying Ruocheng, Ian McShane, Leonard Nimoy, Kathryn Dowling, Mario Adorf, F. Murray Abraham. 600 minutes. color.

4. *Scandal Sheet* (Fair Dinkum/ABC). January 21, 1985. Produced by Roger Birnbaum. Directed by David Lowell Rich. Teleplay by Howard Rodman. With Pamela Reed, Lauren Hutton, Robert Urich, Max Wright, Peter Jurasik. 120 minutes. color.

5. *On Wings of Eagles* (An Edgar Scherick Production/Taft Entertainment/NBC). May 18, 19, 1986. Executive producer, Edgar J. Scherick. Directed by Andrew W. McLaglen. Teleplay by Sam Rolfe, based on the book by Ken Follett. With Richard Crenna, Paul LeMat, Esai Morales, Louis Giambalvo, Jim Metzler, Larry Pressman, Cyril O'Reilly, James Sutorius, Constance Towers. 300 minutes. color.*

6. *Barnum* (Academy Entertainment/CBS). November 30, 1986. Produced by Robert Halmi and David Patterson. Directed by Lee Phillips. Teleplay by Norman Norell. With Hanna Schuygulla, Laura Press, John Roney, Lorena Gale, Sando Raski, Patty Maloney. 120 minues. color.*

7. *Control* (Alliance Entertainment/Cristaldi Films/Les Films Ariane/HBO). February 14, 1987. Executive producer, Denis Heroux. Directed by Giuliano Montaldo. Teleplay by Brian Moore and Jeremy Hale. With Kate Nelligan, Ben Gazzara, Kate Reid, Erland Josephson, Cyrielle Clark, Andrea Occipinti, Andrea Ferreol, Jan Benguiqui, Lavinia Serguirin, Ingrid Thulin. 90 minutes. color.*

8. *Sins of the Fathers* (Bavaria Atelier/Bernhard Sinkel/Jorn Schroeder/Helmut Krapp/Showtime). July 10, 11, 1988. Directed and written by Bernhard Sinkel. With Julie Christie, Tina Engel, Bruno Ganz, Dieter Laser. 240 minutes. color.

9. *The Jeweler's Shop* (PAC/RAI/Alliance/IMP). 1989 (Italy). Produced by Mario Bregni. Directed by Michael Anderson. Teleplay by Mario di Nardi and Jeff Andrews, based on the play by Karol Wojtyla. With Daniel Olbrychski, Ben Cross, Olivia Hussey, Andrea Occipinti, Jo Champa. 90 minutes. color.*

10. *The Betrothed (I Promessi Sposi)* (RAI/UNO, Hermes Film, Bayerischer Rundfunk Gevest Holding B.V., RTV Ljubljana). November 12, 19, 26, December 3, 10, 1989 (Italy). Executive producers, Alessandro Calosci and Anna Maria Denza. Directed by Salvatore Nocita. Teleplay by Enrico Medioli, Roberta Mazzoni, with the collaboration of Salvatore

Nocita and Pier Emilio Gennarini, based on the novel by Alessandro Manzoni. With Helmut Berger, Gary Cady, Mathieu Carrière, Valentina Cortese, Delphine Forest, Danny Quinn, Fernando Rey, Jenny Seagrove, Gisela Steinn, Franco Nero, Alberto Sordi, F. Murray Abraham. 300 minutes. color.

11. *The Phantom of the Opera* (Saban Schenck Productions/NBC). March 18, 19, 1990. Executive producers, Edgar J. Scherick and Haim Saban. Directed by Tony Richardson. Teleplay by Arthur Kopit, based on the novel by Gaston Leroux. With Charles Dance, Teri Polo, Ian Richardson, Adam Storke, Andrea Ferreol. 240 minutes. color.

12. *Voyage of Terror: The Achille Lauro Affair* (Tribune Entertainment/Beta Taurus Group/Filmalpha Productions/T-F1/Syndicated). May 1, 2, 1990. Executive producers, Mario Gallo, Fabrizio Castellani. Directed by Alberto Negrin. Teleplay by Sergio Donati and Negrin. With Eva Marie Saint, Robert Culp, Renzo Nontagnani, Dominique Sanda, Bernard Fresson, Gabrielle Ferzetti, Adriana Innocenti, Said Amadis, Brian Bloom, Jochen Horst, Rebecca Schaeffer. 240 minutes. color.*

13. *Separate but Equal* (A New Liberty Production in association with Republic Pictures Television/ABC). April 7, 8, 1991. Executive producers, George Stevens Jr. and Stan Margulies. Written and directed by Stevens. With Sidney Poitier, Richard Kiley, Cleavon Little, Gloria Foster, John McMartin, Graham Beckel, Ed Hall, Lynne Thigpen, Macon McCalman, Cheryl Lynn Bruce, Henderson Forsythe, Randle Mell, Tommy Hollis, John Rothman, Danien Leake, Albert Hall, Mike Nussbaum, Hallie Foote, William Cain, E. Katharine Kerr, Tom Aldredge. 240 minutes. color.

THEATER

1. *A Sound of Hunting* (Lyceum Theatre, New York City). November 20, 1945. Produced by Irving Jacobs. Directed by Anthony Brown. Written by Harry Brown. With Sam Levene, Frank Lovejoy, Carl Frank, George Tyne, Bruce Evans. Ran three weeks.

2. *Knickerbocker Holiday* (Curran Theatre, San Francisco; the Dorothy Chandler Pavilion, Los Angeles). May 11, 1971. Produced by the San Francisco Civic Light Opera Company; Edwin Lester, general producer; Glenn Jordan, producer. Directed by Albert Marre. Music by Kurt Weill. Book and lyrics by Maxwell Anderson. With Anita Gillette, David Holiday, Jack Collins, Dale Malone, Eric Brotherson, Jerry Marin, John Ferante, Robert Miller Driscoll, Ruth Kobart, John Wheeler, Gino Conforti. Ran fifteen weeks.

3. *The Boys in Autumn* (Marines Memorial Theatre, San Francisco).

September 3, 1981. Produced by James McKenzie, George Stevens Jr., and the John F. Kennedy Center for the Performing Arts. Directed by Tom Moore. Written by Bernard Sabath. With Kirk Douglas. Ran four weeks.

SELECTED DOCUMENTARIES AND SERIES WITH LANCASTER AS HOST AND/OR NARRATOR

1. *King: A Filmed Record . . . Montgomery to Memphis* (Eli Landau). March 1970. Directed by Joseph Mankiewicz and Sidney Lumet. With (in voice-over) Harry Belafonte, Ruby Dee, Charlton Heston, James Earl Jones, Paul Newman, Anthony Quinn, Clarence Williams III, Joanne Woodward. 153 minutes. b&w.*

2. *The Unknown War* (Air Time International/Syndication). Started October 7, 1978 (twenty episodes). Executive producer, Isaac Kleinerman. Directed by Roman Karen. Written by Fred Weiner, Roman Karmen, John Lord, and Rod McKuen. 1,200 minutes. color and b&w.

3. *The Life of Verdi* (RAI-Radiotelevisione Italiana/PBS). October 24, 31, November 7, 14, 21, 28, 1983. Executive producer, Alessandra Altieri. Directed and written by Renato Casellani. With Ronald Pickup, Carla Fracci, Daria Nicolodi, Margherita Barezzi, Giampiero Albertini, Omero Antonutti, Eva Christian. 360 minutes. color.*

4. *Dawn's Early Light: Ralph McGill and the Segregated South* (South Carolina Educational Television Network/Center for Contemporary Media/PBS). September 13, 1989. Directed by Kathleen Dowdey and Jed Dannenbaum. 57 minutes. color and b&w.

HECHT-LANCASTER FILMS WITHOUT LANCASTER IN THE CAST

1. *The First Time* (Hecht-Norma/Columbia). Early 1952. Produced by Harold Hecht. Directed by Frank Tashlin. Screenplay by Jean Rouverol, Hugo Butler, Frank Tashlin, and Dane Lussier, from a story by Rouverol and Butler. With Barbara Hale, Robert Cummings, Jeff Donnell, Mona Barrie, Cora Witherspoon. 89 minutes. b&w.

2. *Marty* (Hecht-Lancaster/United Artists). April 11, 1955. Produced by Harold Hecht. Directed by Delbert Mann. Screenplay by Paddy Chayefsky, based on his teleplay. With Ernest Borgnine, Betsy Blair, Joe Mantell, Joe De Santis, Esther Minciotti, Augusta Ciolli, Karen Steele, Jerry Paris, Frank Sutton. 91 minutes. b&w.*

3. *The Bachelor Party* (Hecht-Lancaster/United Artists). April 10,

1957. Produced by Harold Hecht. Directed by Delbert Mann. Screenplay by Paddy Chayefsky, based on his teleplay. With Don Murray, Carolyn Jones, E. G. Marshall, Jack Warden, Philip Abbott, Nancy Marchand, Larry Blyden. 93 minutes. b&w.

4. *The Rabbit Trap* (Hecht-Hill-Lancaster/United Artists). June, 1959. Produced by Harry Kleiner. Directed by Philip Leacock. Screenplay by J. P. Miller, based on his teleplay. With Ernest Borgnine, David Brian, Bethel Leslie, Kevin Corcoran, June Blair, Jeanette Nolan, Russell Collins, Christopher Dark, Don Rickles. 72 minutes. b&w.

5. *Cry Tough* (Hecht-Hill-Lancaster/United Artists). September 17, 1959. Produced by Harry Kleiner. Directed by Paul Stanley. Screenplay by Harry Kleiner, based on the novel by Irving Shulman. With John Saxon, Linda Cristal, Joseph Calleia, Arthur Batanides, Paul Clarke, Joe De Santis, Don Godron, Perry Lopez, Barbara Luna, Frank Puglia, Penny Santon, Harry Townes. 84 minutes. b&w.

6. *Take a Giant Step* (Hecht-Hill-Lancaster/United Artists). Late 1959. Produced by Julius Epstein. Directed by Philip Leacock. Screenplay by Julius Epstein and Louis S. Peterson, based on the play by Peterson. With Johnny Nash, Estelle Hemsley, Ruby Dee, Frederick O'Neal, Beah Richards. 100 minutes. b&w.

7. *Season of Passion* (Hecht-Hill-Lancaster/United Artists). December 16, 1961. Produced and directed by Leslie Norman. Screenplay by John Dighton, based on the play *The Summer of the Seventeenth Doll* by Ray Lawler. With Ernest Borgnine, Anne Baxter, John Mills, Angela Lansbury, Vincent Ball, Ethel Gabriel, Janette Craig, Deryck Barnes, Tom Lurich, Al Thomas. 93 minutes. b&w.

Notes

Research for this book was taken from three principal sources: (1) interviews conducted by the author, principally between July and November of 1993. These are indicated by "AI" (Author Interview) in the citations below; (2) books and periodicals. Minor reviews, announcements, and articles are cited below. Otherwise, information on the sources cited below can be found in the bibliography; and (3) primary-source materials. The Hal Wallis Collection (HWC) and Sam Peckinpah Collection (SPC) are found in the Margaret Herrick Library of the Academy of Motion Picture Arts and Sciences, as is an (as yet) unpublished oral history with Gene Fowler Jr. and Majorie Fowler, Douglas Bell interviewer, which is part of the library's Oral History Program (Bell). The 20th Century–Fox Collection (TFC) and the Stanley Kramer Collection (SKC) are in the Department of Special Collections, University Research Library, University of California, Los Angeles. There too are *An Oral History of the Motion Picture in America: Recollections of Edward Anhalt,* Estelle Changas, interviewer, Regents of the University of California, 1969 (Changas) and *An Oral History of the Motion Picture in America: Recollections of Abby Mann,* Stephen Farber, interviewer, Regents of the University of California, 1969 (Farber). Two oral histories were produced by the Directors Guild. The one with Byron Haskin is published and information pertaining to it may be found in the bibliography. The other is *A Directors Guild of America Oral History: Arthur Lubin, December 1976–January 1977,* James Demaris, interviewer (Demaris). The Mark Hellinger Collection (MHC) is in the University of Southern California Cinema-TV Library, Doheny Library. Included therein is the producer's 1946 manuscript for an article for *Photoplay,* which may or may not have been published (MHP). Also at USC's Cinema-TV Library are the Universal Pictures Collection (UPC) and the Warner Bros. Collection (WBC). At the Louis B. Mayer Library of the American Film Institute are the Robert Aldrich Collection (RAC) and the AFI's *Oral History with George Seaton, January–June, 1974,* David Chierichetti, interviewer (Chierichetti). The archives of the Union Settlement House in Manhattan contain two unpublished remembrances, *As I Remember Union Settlement* by Ellen S. Martin, circa 1945 (Martin), and Gaylord S. White's *Twenty Years in South Harlem* (White). In addition, Multimedia Entertainment, Inc., of Cincinnati, Ohio, provided a transcript of Lancaster's appearance on *Donahue,* transcript #09126 (Donahue) and American Cinematheque provided cassette recordings of the question-and-answer sessions conducted by Lancaster and John Frankenheimer during a retrospective of the director's films in November of 1989 (ACR). Those who helped the author gather this information can be found in the acknowledgments.

CHAPTER ONE

The ethnic evolution of East Harlem (Orsi). "I'm told that" (Pomeroy). "used to talk" (Waterbury, 1961). The high incidence of births through midwives in East Harlem (Martin). Burt's birth (Mitchell, Mitgang). Description of the Lancaster apartment (Waterbury, 1961). "Though I came" (UPI, 11/20/61). "used to stand" (Jamison). James Lancaster's memories of Burt and the family (James Lancaster). "a gentle, kind" (Windeler). James Lancaster's amateur act (James Lancaster). "a strong-willed, formidable" (Windeler). "Mother beat hell" (Itria). "When he lost" (Callaghan/AI). The milk story (Hopper, 6/11/48). The $20-bill story (ibid.). "Bums were forever" (Waterbury, 1961). "I saw the" (Donahue). "Mentally, Burt was" (Cravat). Burt's tardiness (Liza Wilson). "I read the" (Itria). "When he wasn't" (Holliman/AI). "He read constantly" (Carrera/AI). Burt and Nick's trips to the Metropolitan Opera (Champlin, 1990). "Out on the" (Windeler). "We boys had" (Pomeroy). Burt's automobile injuries (Itria). Sunday outings with James Lancaster (James Lancaster). "The life of" (Waterbury, 1961). "One night I" (ibid.). The murder in Burt's backyard (Mitgang). "You'd take your" (ibid.). The goals of the Settlement movement (Husock). The history of Union Settlement (White). "Burt showed lots" (Mitchell). "For a kid" (Windeler). "spent her life" (Martin, 1948). "He was the" (Thomasetti/AI). Burt's appearance in *Three Pills in a Bottle* (Marsh; Waterbury, 1961; Crist; Demaris). The recollections of Abe Platt (AI). The recollections of Clement Segal (AI). "He adored his" (Bone/AI). "Mom was like" (Hopper, 6/11/48). "He's uneasy with" (Sharp/AI). "I've watched him" (Jones/AI). "At fourteen, I" (Waterbury,

1961). "[S]he instilled concepts" (Windeler). Burt's basketball exploits (*Clinton News,* 11/15/29 and 12/20/29). "We hope that" (A. Mortimer Clark, *DeWitt Clinton Yearbook,* 1930).

CHAPTER TWO

Information about Lancaster's circus years was drawn from interviews with Ernestine Baer Clark, Mary Ernst Burdick, Bill Powell, Frank Robie, and a letter to the author from Harold Barnes (summer 1993), which recounted Bob Ketrow's recollections as well as Barnes' own. Other sources: "One of the" (Gow, 1973). "I was an" (telegram from Lancaster dated 5/31/61, Elmer Holmes Bobst Library, Office of University Archives, New York University). "When he used" (Ourgourlian/AI). Burt and Curley Brent (Demaris). Burt and Nick's visits to the Ringling Brothers Circus (Lancaster, 1951). "I was amazed" (Sala/AI). "one of the" (Harris, Union Settlement newsletter, Union Settlement House archives). Burt's stabbing (ibid.). "I was pretty" (James Lancaster). "Burt never knew" (Sternberger/AI). The site of the audition with Kay Brothers (Martin, 1948; Cravat; Barnes). "On my first" (Oppenheimer). "When Burt nervously" (Cravat). "that's when you" (Lancaster, 1951). "a little circus" (ibid.). "We were a" (Lancaster, 1951). Nick and Burt's separation from Kay Brothers (Cravat). "achieving nothing" (ibid.). The holes-in-the-floor problem (Martin, 1948). Lancaster's involvement with the Russell Brothers (*Billboard,* 5/19/34, in which a "B. Lancaster" was listed as "boss props"). The Russell Brothers 1934 season (Webb). Burt, Nick, and June's departure from Gorman Brothers (Martin, 1948). The Federal Theatre Circus (the circus' press releases, Lincoln Center Library for the Performing Arts). "We never had" (Martin, 1948). "It was a" (Demaris). "wonderful girl" (ibid.). The Newton Brothers Circus (Bradbury, 1972). "In 1938, the" (Dahlinger/AI). The demise of circuses during the 1930s (demographics compiled by Prof. Marcello Truzzi, Robert L. Parkinson Library and Research Center, Circus World Museum). Lancaster and Cravat on the fringes of the circus world (The biographies of Burt released by the studios over the years maintained that he eventually joined the Ringling Brothers–Barnum & Bailey troupe, which was the zenith for American circus performers, but this author could locate no evidence to support that contention. "I'm sure he was never with Ringling-Barnum," asserted Fred D. Pfening Jr., editor of *Bandwagon: The Journal of the Circus Historical Society,* in a letter to this author during the summer of 1993. And Tim Spindler, archivist at the Circus World Museum library, concurrently wrote this author, "I was not able to find any reference to Burt Lancaster or Lang and Cravat working for Ringling Bros. and Barnum & Bailey Circus. I would consider this highly unlikely because through the thirties they [Ringling Brothers] had the Concellos and later in the forties there were the Clarkonians.") Burt's booking on the Poli circuit (Martin, 1948). "Nick Cravat held" (Alexander/AI). The Ozzie Nelson loan story (*Modern Screen*, 7/57). The booking at Shea's Buffalo (Marx). Burt's visit to Warner Bros. as a vaudevillian (Hedda Hopper column, circa early 1948) "We worked one" (Liza Wilson). "We went over" (Martin, 1948). "We're not getting" (Cravat). "They were like" (Atkinson/AI). "A more violent" (Warner Bros. press release for *His Majesty O'Keefe*). Selling men's furnishings (Lancaster, 1957). "Don't look down" (20th Century–Fox press release for *Mister 880*). Burt's job with the Fulton Market Refrigeration Company (Martin, 1948). Jobs as highway laborer and fireman (Universal press release, circa 1946). Burt's involvement with Columbia Concerts (United Artist press release, 3/22/55; Martin, 1948). Burt's job at the Torch Club (ibid.). Lancaster's service record (Unless otherwise indicated, this information is derived from a summary of Lancaster's service record provided by the National Personnel Records Center, Military Personnel Records, St. Louis, Missouri). Lancaster's wish to serve in the Engineers (Oppenheimer). The prestige of the Engineers compared to Special Services (William McKale, Museum Specialist, Fort Riley, KS/AI). The 21st Special Service Unit (Unless indicated otherwise, information about this unit is derived from the unit history submitted to the adjutant general on 11/28/45 by Capt. Hubert W. Freeman, Historical Records Section, National Archives). Burt's problem with the lieutenant (Martin, 1948). The Allied forces in North Africa in summer, 1943 (Peret). The creation of *Stars and Gripes* (Oppenheimer). Burt and Irving Burns' rendition of "Sonny Boy" (Post/AI). "It took a" (Shipp). "[H]e seemed to" (ibid.). "what he considered" (Itria). "fine pianists with" (ibid.). "We often went" (Oppenheimer). Background on the Andersons and Carrols (Cora Everson Graham letter to author, fall, 1993). "were a close-knit" (ibid.). Norma Anderson's high school years. (Miami Edison High School yearbook, 1933). Norma Anderson's involvement with the USO (Hoffman). "shuffling along a" (Universal press release, 3/15/47). "At first I" (Oppenheimer). Burt's courtship of Norma. (Universal press release, 3/15/47)

CHAPTER THREE

Nick Cravat's loan to Lancaster (Martin, 1948). The Jack Mahlor elevator story (Earl Wilson). "He was the" (Bercovicci/AI). "Look, I'm wasting" (Donahue). Burt's casting announcement (*The New York Times,*

10/21/45). Lancaster's "working vocabulary" as an acrobat (Shipp). "I never took" (Lancaster, 1951). "I never dreamed" (Windeler). "We rehearsed twenty-four" (Pendleton). The Philadelphia reviews of *A Sound of Hunting* are dated 11/7/45. The New York reviews are dated 11/21/45. "kind of unformed" (Mann/AI). "I yelled each" (Universal press release, 1945). "They were offering" (United Artists press release, 3/22/55). "I was scared" (Hoffman). "a rather short" (Darr Smith, 1/50). "I know everybody" (Hopper, 1955). The *Red River* offer (United Artists press release, 3/22/55). The Wallis offer (Wallis). Walter Seltzer's recollections (AI). "one suit to" (Scheuer, *Los Angeles Times,* 1959). "was a brilliant" (Heston/AI). "profit participation, a" (Wallis). Burt's diatribe with Haskin (Shipp). "Stenographers, office boys" (Hopper column, 1948). "We rehearsed the" (Scott/AI). The terms of Lancaster's contract with Wallis (HWC). Huston's coauthorship of *The Killers* screenplay (MHC). Hellinger's interest in casting Morris and Tufts (MHP). Hellinger meeting with Juroc (ibid.). Hellinger's version of the meeting with Lancaster (ibid.). "You know what" (Martin, 1948). Lancaster's version of the meeting with Hellinger (Gow, 1973). "Hal," he said (MHP). "A glass slipper" (Universal press release, 3/28/46). "Today's best bet" (John Todd column, 4/27/46). "had a great" (Brown/AI). "he likes to" (MHP). Jeff Corey's recollections (AI). "It was lucky" (ibid.). "Siodmak and Hellinger" (Higham, 1974). "One thing I" (Gardner). "easily one of" (Donahue). "So help me" (Bishop). "I didn't recognize" (Marsh). "I have never" (MHC). "I could be" (Gow, 1973). "He knocked them" (Mayo/AI). "I'm afraid you're" (MIIC). "four old, beat-up" (MHP). "a hard-hitting example" (Bron., *Variety,* 8/7/46). "taut and absorbing" (Crowther, *The New York Times,* 8/29/46). "a polished and tantalizing" (Guernsey Jr., New York *Herald Tribune,* 8/29/46). "It also justifies" (MHC).

CHAPTER FOUR

"I woke up" (Sidney Skolsky syndicated column, 7/13/50). Walter Seltzer's recollections (AI). Wallis expanded Burt's role in *Desert Fury* (Gow, 1973). "We'd go into" (Strassberg). Lizabeth Scott's recollections (AI). A "sweet" man (Crist). Lancaster's blowup with Allen (ibid.). "Burt has had" (McWhorter/AI). "He wasn't like" (Polaire/AI). "I don't want" (Hopper, 1951). "I think Burt" (Singer/AI). Lancaster's decision to become a director (Wallis). De Carlo's fling with Lancaster (De Carlo). "Kirk is very" (Durning/AI). "I got the" (Adamson). "Burt was so" (ibid.). "A lot of" (Brooks/AI). "the human mud" (Production notes for *Brute Force*). "embarrassed eating with" (ibid.). Incident with

Sheilah Graham (Graham). "I was amazed" (Corey/AI). "This kid has" (unknown periodical, 1947). "If you're just" (Blowen). "I was so" (unknown periodical, 1970). Burt's late arrival on the set (Universal press release for *All My Sons*). "a very good" (Cronyn/AI). "could excite new" (Gow, 1973). "Julie did not" (Corey/AI). Hellinger's fight with Breen (MHC). "But this was" (Gow, 1973). "brooding, effective performance (Guernsey, New York *Herald Tribune*, 7/17/47). "It was very" (Gow, 1973). The meeting between Lancaster and Irene Mayer Selznick (Selznick). The Lancaster-Wallis contract despute (HWC). "Wallis was very" (Doniger/AI). "He had nothing" (Windeler). "His ploy would" (Crist). Wallis' fees for *Come Back, Little Sheba* and *The Rose Tattoo* (HWC). "Very consciously, I" (Wallis). "Harold has assured" (HWC). "a magnificently decorated" (Winston, *New York Post*, 9/24/47). "dark, intense young" (Hobart). "Why, it's a" (Production notes for *All My Sons*). "I was so" (Lancaster, circa 1947/48). Burt's salary for *All My Sons* (Pryor). Universal's agreement to finance *Kiss the Blood* (HWC). "The theme of" (Hobart). *All My Sons* production schedule (UPC). Edward G. Robinson's political difficulties (Gansberg). "He was quite" (Gardella). "Hollywood is gutless" (Bishop).

CHAPTER FIVE

The New York reviews for *I Walk Alone* are dated 1/22/48. "tougher than he" (*Newsweek*, 1/26/48). Lancaster's conversation with Wallis about *Sorry, Wrong Number* (Gow, 1973). Litvak's working style (Eyles and Pattison). McWhorter's feeling about Lancaster's cooperativeness (McWhorter/AI). "There was a" (Seltzer/AI). The twelve days of shooting with Stanwyck alone (Diorio). "He had an" (Gow, 1973). Mark Productions' resolution of the *Criss Cross* project and the settlement of Lancaster's contract (MHC; UPC). Independent film production in 1959 (*Variety*, circa 1959). "a bouncy little" (Darr Smith, *Los Angeles Daily News*, 4/20/49). *Kiss the Blood*'s budget (UPC). *Kiss the Blood*'s sets (ibid.). Leonardo Bercovicci's recollections (AI). Fontaine's absences during shooting (UPC). "Instead of thinking" (Universal press release for *Kiss the Blood*). The *New York Times* review of *All My Sons* is dated 3/29/48. "more direct and" (Edwin Schallert, *Los Angeles Times*, 5/20/48). "I believed in" (Jesse Zunser, *Cue*, 6/8/57). Curtis' recollections (Curtis). The *Criss Cross* shooting schedule (UPC). The location shooting and sets for *Criss Cross* (Universal press releases for *Criss Cross*). "He's just the" (ibid.). Lancaster's move to Bel-Air (ibid.). The $150,000 valuation (Itria). The number of rooms and the home's valuation in 1961 (Mitchell). Alberta and Adele (Waterbury, c. 1956).

The kitchen as the Lancasters' hangout (Ullman/AI). The *Kiss the Blood* title changes (UPC). The New York reviews of *Sorry, Wrong Number* are dated 9/2/48. The year-end ranking for *Sorry, Wrong Number* (*Variety,* 2/5/49). "a somber, penetrating" (*Cue,* 10/30/48). "dismal" (*Time,* 11/8/48). "Burt is never" (Windeler). "I want to" (Martin, 1948). Wallis's initial plans to start *Rope of Sand* (HWC). "I read an" (Doniger/AI). "When I think" (Richard). Wallis' agreement to consult Lancaster on projects during preproduction (1950 letter from Lancaster to Wallis, HWC). "thought he could" (Doniger/AI). Calvet's recollections (Calvet). "William Dieterle was" (McWhorter/AI). Henreid's recollections (Henreid). "Burt and I" (Doniger/AI). "Lancaster is almost" (Barstow Jr., New York *Herald Tribune,* n.d.). "verbose, redundant, and" (Pryor, *The New York Times,* 3/12/49). Lancaster's relationship with Winters, except as noted (Winters). "one of the" (*Variety,* 3/23/49). "all fixed up" (United Artists press release, 3/22/55) Lancaster's Cole Brothers engagement (John Scott). Bone's assessment of Lancaster's feelings for Winters (AI). "Burt is a" (ibid.). "so slick and" (Waterbury, Los Angeles *Herald Examiner,* 9/26/49). Hecht-Norma's agreement with Warner Bros. (Thomas F. Brady, *The New York Times,* n.d.; *Hollywood Reporter,* 6/16/53). "I was anxious" (Gow, 1973). The development of the Piccolo character and Cravat's near-refusal to do it (Smith, 7/50). "We did roadwork" (Kirkley). "I even had" (Warner Bros. press release for *The Flame and the Arrow*). Lancaster's stunts in *The Flame and the Arrow* and the shooting schedule for them (ibid.). Virginia Mayo's costuming and use of an air hose (ibid.). Virginia Mayo's recollections (AI). Robert Douglas' recollections (AI). "Burt had been" (Tavernier). "Hollywood can remember" (Martin, 1948). "the young girls" (Earl Wilson). "All the ambitious" (Elizabeth Wilson). Lancaster's marquee value (Pryor).

CHAPTER SIX

Edward Mueller's background (*Life,* 9/11/50). "goose the whole" (Smith, 10/50). McGuire and Lancaster (20th Century–Fox press release for *Mister 880*). "husky, genial extrovert" (Philip K. Scheuer, *Los Angeles Times,* 5/18/47). "send down a" (Farber). Lancaster's broken finger (Carroll, 1950). Hugh O'Brian's recollections (AI). Burt's *Flame and the Arrow* promotional tour (Warners press release; *Motion Picture Herald,* 7/29/50). The year-end ranking of *The Flame and the Arrow* (*Variety,* 1/3/51). The Garrison lawsuit (*Los Angeles Times,* 7/22/53; 7/24/53). "There wasn't anything" (Seltzer/AI). "Thorpe had his" (Hopper, 1951). Phyllis Thaxter's recollections (AI). Curtiz's malapropisms (George Frazier, *True*, 10/47). "one of the most" (*Newsweek*, 9/25/50). "He was in" (Windeler). "Now I had" (Pomeroy). Jimmy Lancaster's problems (Itria). Burt's reaction to Billy's polio in later years (Bone/AI). The end of the Winters-Lancaster affair (Winters). "The cast works" (*Cue*, 2/17/51). Hecht-Norma's deal with Columbia (*Variety*, 12/14/50). The original setting of *Ten Tall Men* (Brady, 1950). "a cuddly Jewish" (Clark/AI). "Burt adored him" (Bone/AI). Goldbeck's difficulties in directing *Ten Tall Men* (Bellamy/AI). Robert Parrish's recollections (AI). "Bob made things" (Bellamy/AI). The offer of *The First Time (Small Wonder)* to Warners (Memo from Walter MacEwen to Steve Trilling, 12/6/50, WBC). "an unpretentious, entertaining" (*Variety*, 1/25/52). Lancaster's interest in 1951 in concentrating on producing and directing (Lancaster, 1951). The writers involved with *The Crimson Pirate* (WBC). Lancaster's discovery of Bartok (Cleveland *Plain Dealer Pictorial Magazine*, 9/14/52). "I designed all" (Gow, 1973). Ischia in the early 1950s (Warners press releases for *The Crimson Pirate;* Watts). The ships' debuts in *Captain Horatio Hornblower* (Watts). "I don't think" (Lee/AI). "The idea . . . seemed" (Warners press release for *The Crimson Pirate*). "The Warner Brothers" (Weiller, *The New York Times*, 8/25/51). The year-end ranking of *Jim Thorpe—All American* (*Variety*, 1/2/52). Communications between Trilling and Blattner and between Trilling and Hecht and Lancaster (WBC). "Get out of" (Graham). Siodmak's difficulties with Lancaster and Hecht during shooting (WBC). "a virtual tour de force" (*Variety*, 10/24/51, Gilb.). "All that is" (*Time*, 11/26/51). Kibbee's involvement with HUAC (Navasky). "I had my" (Crist). Burt's weight loss during shooting (Warners press release for *The Crimson Pirate*).

CHAPTER SEVEN

Lancaster's home regimen (Sidney Skolksy syndicated column, 7/14/50). "Sometimes we go" (Oppenheimer). Information about the Lancasters' bridge nights was drawn from interviews with Julia Adams, Walter Doniger, Bob Quarry, plus Waterbury, c. 1956. "a work of" (Chapman, New York *Daily News*, 2/16/50). "shocked at the" (Wallis). Wallis' interest in casting Bogart in *Sheba* (United Artists press release, 3/22/55) "I guess I" (Paramount press release for *Sheba*). Curtiz's role in Lancaster's casting in *Sheba* (Brownell, 1/53). "This result created" (Wood, 1952). Richard Jaeckel's recollections (AI). Terry Moore's recollections (AI). "Now there's an" (Brownell, 1/53). "I had to" (*Los Angeles Daily News*, 5/23/53). "Shirley Booth is" (Gow, 1973). "the most human" (Paramount press release for *Sheba*). "was doing the" (ibid.). The drunks who inspired Lancaster's Doc (ibid.). "We dressed Burt" (Wallis). "Alas, for the" (Paramount press release for *Sheba*). Why Fiji was chosen for *O'Keefe* (Carroll, 1952). Jack Warner's June warning to Hecht and Lancaster (Letter from Jack Warner to Burt and Harold, 6/2/52, WBC). Unless otherwise indicated, information pertaining to *His Majesty O'Keefe* (Warners press releases, WBC). The studio facilities in Fiji (Lancaster, 1954). "I didn't sleep" (unidentified publication, 1/31/54). Consideration given to the casting of Marisa Pavan in *O'Keefe* (Connolly, *Hollywood Reporter,* May 6, 1953). Consideration given to the casting of Dorothy Malone and Linda Christian (Schallert, 1953). "I've had to" (Haynes memo to Steve Trilling, 7/12/52, WBC). Chase's ad-libbed story line and the writing of the *O'Keefe* screenplay in Fiji (Adamson). Hecht-Norma's anticipation of the rain in Fiji (Lancaster, 1954). "It is the" (Cook, *New York World-Telegram & Sun*, n.d.). "pirate film with" (*The Christian Science Monitor,* n.d.). "the screen's most" (*Time*, 9/15/52). Brooks' plan for *Son of the Crimson Pirate* (Martin Beck, unknown publication, 5/26/82). The communications between Jack Warner, Steve Trilling, and Hecht-Lancaster during the making of *O'Keefe* (WBC). The footage Lancaster shot for *O'Keefe* (Scheuer, 1952). "Proudest I am" (Haskin letter to Trilling, 11/11/52, WBC). "a photographed play" (Guernsey Jr., New York *Herald Tribune*, 12/24/52). "a potent piece" (*Variety*, 12/3/52, Brog.). "Suddenly they began" (Gow, 1973). "I had to" (ibid.). Unless otherwise indicated, information pertaining to *South Sea Woman* (WBC). "was always directing" (Mayo/AI). "a mild-mannered" (Warners press release for *South Sea Woman*). "I was a little" (Demaris). "A man or" (ibid.). "of the time" (Carroll, 1953). The island set and cyclorama (ibid.). The aphorism "Cohn's Folly" (Zinnemann). The acquisition price of *From Here to Eternity* (*Variety,* 3/5/51). The joke about Cohn being crude (Thomas, 1967). *Eternity*'s budget (ibid.). Two studios having given up on *Eternity* before Columbia (Zinnemann). Columbia's letting the project idle (Mitgang, 1953). The Army's objections (Zinnemann; Mitgang, 1953). Taradash's fight for Zinnemann (Zinnemann). "color would have" (ibid.). Casting Clift (Thomas, 1967). The deal for Lancaster (ibid.). "predictable bilge" (Hirschhorn). "I knew he" (United Artists press release, 3/22/55). Crawford firing (Thomas, 1978). Deborah Kerr's recollections (AI). The forty-one-day shooting schedule (Zinnemann). The original staging of the beach scene (Kerr/AI; Bellamy/AI). "The challenge was" (Zinnemann). "a record in" (*Look*, 8/25/53). "You didn't have" (Bellamy/AI). "small, shy, unassuming" (Studio bio of Zinnemann, 1950). "Lancaster was not" (LaGuardia). Clift's attitude toward Lancaster (Bosworth). "The only time" (Goldman). Lancaster's hiring of

Jones for *The Killing Frost* (MacShane). "Although he worked" (ibid.). "None of us" (Erskine Johnson). "I'll soon be" (unknown publication). The end of Hecht-Norma's relationship with Warners (*Hollywood Reporter*, 6/16/53). "When we took" (Youngstein/AI). Hecht-Lancaster's first deal with UA (*Daily Variety*, 6/24/53). "capture its first" (Balio). "When you went" (Crist). "we were able" (ibid.). "The approach that" (Blumofe/AI). Hecht-Lancaster's move to Keywest Studios (*Daily Variety*, 9/24/53). "one of those" (Guernsey Jr., New York *Herald Tribune*, 6/4/53). "The entertainment values" (*Variety*, 6/3/53, Brog.). "No one ever" (Zinnemann). "he did a" (Thomas, 1967). *Eternity*'s opening day and record week (*Variety*, n.d.). *Eternity*'s success (Thomas, 1967). "So great was" (ibid.). "in many instances" (*Variety*, 7/29/53, Brog.). "one of the" (*Newsweek*, 8/10/53).

CHAPTER EIGHT

"a broader statement" (Arnold and Miller). "the wild, lone" (Paul I. Wellman, *Broncho Apache*, Macmillan Publishing Company, 1936). Burt's injury (*Beverly Hills Citizen-News*, 10/23/53; Brownell, 12/53). "Now once Burt" (Arnold and Miller). "Under different conditions" (Haskin letter dated 11/11/52, WBC). "an endlessly inventive" (*Time*, 2/15/54). "a largely cynical" (Arnold and Miller). Burt's pursuit of Grant (Windeler). Gable's warning to Cooper (Crist). The status of the script for *Vera Cruz* before and during shooting (Arnold and Miller). "*Vera Cruz* was" (ibid.). "We worked out" (Elam/AI). "From sunup to" (Evelyn Harvey). "When you're directing" (Arnold and Miller). "He was very" (Romero/AI). "Well, I wouldn't" (Wiley and Bona). "I really thought" (Thomas, 1983). "Never had a" (Wiley and Bona). Cooper's gunmanship (Ben Cooper/AI). "In the first" (Quarry/AI). "As far as" (Kahn). Walter Seltzer's recollections (AI). "resounding clinker" (Crowther, *The New York Times*, 7/10/54). "this athletic, blue-eyed" (Scheuer, *Los Angeles Times*, 7/22/54). "It was my" (Arnold and Miller). Hecht-Lancaster's second agreement with UA (*The New York Times*, 2/8/54). Lancaster's scheme for directing *The Kentuckian* (Scheuer, 1954). "Directors are the" (ibid.). The Directors Guild's response (Joe Hyams, New York *Herald Tribune*, 12/10/54). "I don't care" (unknown publication). "As an actor" (Lancaster, 11/55). Walter Matthau's recollections (AI). John McIntire's and Dianne Foster's impressions of Lancaster as director (United Artists press release for *The Kentuckian*). "I used to" (Crist). "I think you" (ibid.). "From the beginning" (Considine). "During the production" (anonymous/AI). *Marty*'s shooting schedule (*The Christian Science Monitor*, 3/27/56). Borgnine's assertion that H-L only planned to shoot half of *Marty* (Considine). "I never heard" (Blumofe/AI). Delbert Mann's denial of Borgnine's assertion (Mann/AI). "I had the" (Gow, 1973). Burt's attempt to delay the start of *The Rose Tattoo* (HWC). "We made this" (transcript of Wallis-Citron phone conversation, 10/11/54, HWC). "I find you" (Lancaster, 8/55). "I first saw" (Wallis). Lancaster's revised contract with Wallis (HWC). Ben Cooper's recollections (AI). "the most explosive" (*Time*, 2/19/55). "Magnani fell head" (Wallis). Burt and Magnani in Key West (Grady Johnson). "as she was" (Phillips). "I don't think" (Elam/AI). "The presence of" (Crowther, *The New York Times*, 12/27/54). "the major concern" (*Cue*, n.d.). "the virtuoso in" (*Time*, 1/10/55). "I ran away" (Demaris). "a warm and" (Crowther, *The New York Times*, 4/12/55). H-L's $400,000 Oscar campaign (Wiley and Bona). The *Confidential* article (Charles Wright, *Confidential*, 5/55). "I knew and" (anonymous/AI). Alan Sharp's recollections (AI). "For years I've" (United Artists press release, 3/22/55). "the acrobatics are incidental" (Philip K. Scheuer, *Los Angeles Times*, n.d.). "Eventually we decided" (Wapshott). "the human-interest" (Burt Lancaster, New York *Herald Tribune*, n.d.). "three of the" (Forbes, London *Observer*, 9/30/90). Reed's reasons for doing *Trapeze* (Wapshott). Lollobrigida's fee (UA production notes for *Trapeze*). Burt's interest in Clift (Schallert, 1955). Curtis' recollections (Curtis). The Cirque d'Hiver as the place where the flying trapeze was invented (UA press release for *Trapeze*). Reed's desire to have performers fill the background (Wapshott). Buying out an entire circus for three acts (Mindlin). "We have Eddie" (UA release, 3/22/55). "was in great" (Alexander/AI). "It took all" (Mindlin). The heat from the bulbs and special reflector hoods for the lights (UA production notes for *Trapeze*). "quiet-spoken man" (Paul P. Kennedy, *The New York Times*, 11/30/47). Reed's patience with Lancaster (Reed). "I don't know" (Mindlin/AI). Lollobrigida's difficulty with Jurado (Wapshott). "Tony adored working" (Quarry/AI). Curtis signed for *Sweet Smell of Success* and *Cat Ballou* (UA production notes for *Trapeze*). Burt and Reed's desire to work together again (Wapshott).

CHAPTER NINE

"sprawling and overwritten" (Crowther, *The New York Times*, 9/2/55). "The good script" (*Time*, 9/26/55). "The picture rarely" (*Newsweek*, 8/8/55). "It all came" (Matthau/AI). "it's too exhausting" (Mark Shivas, unknown publication, 1970). "Burt liked to" (Seltzer/AI). "Not the least" (Scheuer, *Los Angeles Times*, n.d.). "one is always" (Knight, *The Saturday Review*, n.d.). *The Rose Tattoo*'s year-end ranking (*Variety*, 1/2/57). Information about Hecht-Lancaster was derived from interviews with John Gay, Shirley Lantz, J. P. Miller, N. Richard Nash, Walter Seltzer, and Max Youngstein, plus "Hecht-Lancaster Production" (Hyams, 1956). Hecht-Lancaster's New York offices and plans for Broadway and music publishing company (*Variety,* c. 1955). "Pictures with adult" (Hecht). "They had a" (Kemp). "Some American actors" (Hal Boyle, AP, 7/26/69). "I enjoy making" (Lancaster, 1951). "Harold is the" (Hopper, 1955). "I had nothing" (Waterbury, c. 1956). The size of Hecht-Lancaster's deal with UA (*Variety,* 4/13/56). The terms of Hecht-Lancaster's 1956 deal with UA (Balio). "It is a" (Wallis telex, 7/30/54, HWC). Leon Uris' recollections (AI). Alternatives for Wyatt and Doc (Paul Nathan memo, 2/23/55, HWC). "Burt telephoned me" (Wallis). "We were really" (Farber). "We're playing two" (Crist). "the ridiculousness of" (Douglas). "We have a" (Donahue). "From the start" (Wallis). "They rewrote their" (ibid.). "I wouldn't let" (Crist). Rhonda Fleming's recollections (AI). "but we would" (Wood, 1956). Shooting on the locale of *Arizona* (ibid.). "We stretched ours" (Wallis). "at any given" (ibid.). *Trapeze*'s premiere (Edwin Schallert, *Los Angeles Times,* 5/31/56). "Lancaster and Curtis" (W. R. Wilkerson, *Hollywood Reporter,* 6/6/56). The ad campaign for *Trapeze* (*Hollywood Reporter,* 5/29/56). *Trapeze*'s record gross for the week before July 4 (*Variety,* 7/11/56). "a hackneyed story" (Crowther, *The New York Times,* 6/5/56). "The aerial footage" (*Variety,* 5/30/56). "hardly a dead" (Scheuer, *Los Angeles Times,* 5/20/56). Wallis' purchase price for *The Rainmaker* (*Variety,* 11/26/54). "Property was bought" (ibid.). The casting of William Holden (Thomas M. Pryor, *The New York Times,* circa 11/55). N. Richard Nash's recollections (AI). Hepburn's response to the casting of Holden (HWC). "afraid of [the]" (Nathan telegram, HWC). Hepburn's response to Lancaster and *The Rose Tattoo* (Hepburn letter, 2/28/56, HWC). Wallis' interest in Presley for *The Rainmaker* (Earl Holliman/AI). "gave him hell" (Wallis). Earl Holliman's recollections (AI). "was grumbling, disagreeable" (Higham, 1975). "was butting into" (ibid.). "the part with" (*Variety,* 12/12/56, Brog.). *The Rainmaker*'s year-end ranking (*Variety,* 1/8/58). "Hall Wallis, whom" (Waterbury, c. 1956). "We're friendly— we" (United Artists press release, 3/22/55). Hecht-Lancaster's program at 12/31/56 (*Variety,* n.d.; Alexander). "Before you go" (Alexander). "Newsmen present say" (ibid.). Information about Lancaster's relationship with Hill was drawn from interviews with Jack Elam, Julius Epstein, Richard McWhorter, Martin Milner, Michael Mindlin, and anonymous sources.

CHAPTER TEN

Ernest Lehman's recollections (AI). "By his own" (Curtis). Universal's opposition to Curtis' loan-out and his investment in *Sweet Smell* (Kemp). UA asking Burt to play J. J. (Richard). The picture's original budget (Crist). "trying to capture" (Kemp). Sheilah Graham's version of the "punch in the jaw" story (Graham). How Odets came to replace Lehman (Kemp). "What Clifford did" (ibid.). Unless otherwise indicated, Mackendrick's recollections (Mackendrick's letter to author, 8/23/93). "One of the" (Kemp). "It was cold" (McWhorter/AI). Martin Milner's recollections (AI). "Number one is" (Alexander). the reproduction of the "21" Club (UA press release for *Sweet Smell*). "thirty-five camera" (Windeler). "put up with" (idid.). The final cost of *Sweet Smell* (Crist). Delbert Mann's recollections (AI). "He would not" (Murray/AI). "never wholly succeeds" (*The Saturday Review,* 4/27/57). "a movie which" (*Newsweek,* 4/22/57). "The cowhand . . . is" (Alpert, *The Saturday Review,* 6/22/57). "rip-roaring, gun-banging" (*Cue,* 6/1/57). *Gunfight*'s year-end ranking (*Variety,* 1/8/58). "*Sweet Smell of*" (Zinsser, New York *Herald Tribune,* 6/28/57). "best performance to" (Masters, New York *Daily News,* 6/28/57). "I wasn't really" (Leonard Lyons, "The Lyons Den," n.d.). "So throughout the" (Kemp). "as though it" (Blumofe/UA). "a total disaster" (Crist). "Hecht had certain" (Goodman). The MGM-HHL connection (Higham, 1993). John Gay's recollections (AI). "Every bit of" (UA press release for *Run Silent*). Don Rickles' recollections (AI). The New York reviews of *Separate Tables* on Broadway are dated 10/26/56. Five writers worked on *Separate Tables* (Morley, 1985). The Oliviers' withdrawal (Morley, 1985; Cottrell; Kiernan). Deborah Kerr's recollections (AI). Marjorie Fowler's recollections (Fowler/AI). "a curtain-raiser" (McClain, *New York Journal-American,* 10/26/56). "Fine. Good enough" (unknown publication). "a tense, exciting" (Scott, *Los Angeles Times,* 4/3/58). "A better film" (Crowther, *The New York Times,* 3/28/58). "For each mass-market" (Canby). "I do one" (Riegert/AI).

CHAPTER ELEVEN

"Shaw is my favorite" (Sidney Skolsky syndicated column, 8/23/59). "the best show" (Warners press release for *The Flame and the Arrow*). Unless otherwise indicated, Mackendrick's recollections (Mackendrick's letter to author, 8/23/93). The original casting ideas for *The Devil's Disciple* (Kemp). "Find a good" (Kiernan). The attempt to cast Baker (Kemp). "I have the" (Whitcomb). Hecht's decision to replace Hil'

(Kemp). "We are committed" (*Beverly Hills Citizen-News*, 8/5/58). Olivier's inability to produce *Macbeth* (Cottrell). Olivier's love life (Kiernan). Gerald Fisher's recollections (AI). Olivier's difficulty with Burt's and Kirk's names (Holden). "The central device" (Kemp). "inhibit him in" (ibid.). "We said, 'Sandy' " (Crist). "a tall, laconic" (Gordon Gow, *Films & Filming*, 7/73). Guy Hamilton's recollections (Hamilton letter to author, summer, 1993). "I thought it" (Dee/AI). Miller's interest in Robards (Miller/AI). Borgnine's loan-out for *The Best Things in Life Are Free* (Dick Williams, *Los Angeles Mirror-News*, 9/26/56). "There's a clause" (ibid.). Borgnine's suit over the profits for *Marty* (*Los Angeles Times*, 12/3/56). "the naturalism of" (*Newsweek*, 8/10/59). "very badly acted" (Kauffmann, *New Republic*, 3/20/61). "What starts out" (Crowther, *The New York Times*, 9/17/59). "The four pictures" (Balio). "one of the" (P.V.B., New York *Herald Tribune*, n.d.). *Separate Tables*' year-end ranking (*Variety*, 1/6/60). Information about *The Unforgiven* derived from interviews with John Gay, Delbert Mann, Doug McClure, J. P. Miller, John Saxon, and Tom Shaw; plus, the acquisition of Alan LeMay's novel (*Variety*, 1/29/57). Burt's support for *The Unforgiven*'s racial theme (Alpert). "a swashbuckler about" (Huston). "Quite mistakenly I" (ibid.). Money as Huston's motivation (Madsen). Pre-Columbian artifacts as Huston's motivation (Grobel). Jilda Smith's recollections (ibid.). Huston's predilection for London film processing (Madsen). Murphy's accident (Don Graham). "Huston had to" (ibid.). Stephen Grimes' recollections (Grobel). "It was a" (Huston). "a wonderful actor" (Donahue). "another picture Huston" (Madsen). "What it boiled" (Grobel). Brooks' initial interest in Clift (Weiller). "Did you ever" (ibid.). "It followed almost" (Crist). "So that's what" (ibid.). "Sinclair Lewis wrote" (Martin, 1961). "So we had" (ibid.). "essentially a new" (Knight, *The Saturday Review*, 6/25/60). The HHL announcement about taking on outside projects (*Hollywood Reporter*, 4/3/59). "Few facts on" (ibid.). HHL's indebtedness (Balio). The announcement of HHL's closure after two more Lancaster pictures (*Hollywood Reporter*, 6/16/59). "It is believed" (ibid.). Information about *Elmer Gantry* derived from interviews with Shirley Jones, Patti Page, Tom Shaw, and Jean Simmons; plus, "his mannerisms, the" (*Drama-Logue*). "was most like" (Richard). "It was not" (Bercovicci/AI). "Thank God, Burt" (interview with Brooks, *American Film*, 10/77). How Brooks staged the fire sequence (ibid.). "a horse opera" (Morris, *Toronto Globe and Mail*, 11/6/59). "Probably never before" (*The Saturday Review*, 8/15/59). "stiff and starchy" (*Time*, 8/31/59). *The Devil's Disciple* year-end ranking (*Variety*, 1/6/60).

CHAPTER TWELVE

"Norma made a" (anonymous/AI). The extent of the HHL payroll (Alexander). "We had a" (Crist). "We'd purchase properties" (ibid.). The $2.5-million inventory (Alexander). "They started getting" (McWhorter/AI). "We've reached the" (*Time,* 9/3/56). "Jim was always" (Mann/AI). McWhorter's impression of the friction behind the scenes (McWhorter/AI). "Hill was not" (anonymous/AI). "We should have" (Crist). Information about Norma Lancaster and her relationship with Burt was drawn from interviews with Walter Doniger, Julie Adams, Ross Hunter, J. P. Miller, Doug McClure, and anonymous sources. "I realized I" (unknown publication). "I go down" (United Artists press release, 3/22/55). The Lancasters' evening with the Beatles (Wanda Hale, New York *Daily News,* 2/15/65). "Mr. Huston and" (McCarten, *The New Yorker,* 4/16/60). "Why make a" (Knight, *The Saturday Review,* 4/16/60). "Some of my" (Woodward). "I personally had" (Crist). Lancaster's attitude toward *The Young Savages* (ACR). Anhalt's suggestion of Frankenheimer (Changas). J. P. Miller's recollections (AI). *The Young Savage*'s shooting schedule (ACR). "John and I" (ibid.). "I suddenly realized" (ibid.). "a true professional" (Pratley). "He's a wonderful" (Windeler). Dina Merrill's recollections (AI). Burt and Grant (Winters, 1989). The use of Grant in long shots (ibid.). Winters' recollections (ibid.). "Once in a" (Crist). "One day I" (ibid.). "One scene is" (Bell). "and spent three" (Crist). "To me it" (ibid.). "As a commentary" (*Time,* 7/18/60). "After a preliminary" (Kauffmann, *New Republic,* 8/15/60). "hard-hitting, briskly paced" (Weiller, *The New York Times,* 7/10/60). "a brilliant, provocative" (Knight, *The Saturday Review,* 6/25/60). "Anybody and everybody" (Quarry/AI). *Elmer Gantry*'s year-end ranking (*Variety,* n.d.). "tall bald man" (*The New York Times,* 11/22/63). Logan's attempt to make *Birdman* (*Hollywood Reporter,* 6/6/56). Cummings' attempt to make *Birdman* (*Hollywood Reporter,* 7/24/58). The U.S. Bureau of Prisons' refusal to cooperate with Cummings (*Variety,* 11/28/60). Trosper took *Birdman* to Hecht (ACR). "Using Stroud as" (Waugh). "a very interesting" (Crist). Bennett's refusal to cooperate and Lancaster's response (Dick Williams). The cost of the prison sets (ibid.). "No concessions were" (Lichtman). Karl Malden's recollections (AI). "I thought for" (ACR). "I don't know" (Pratley). "I felt the" (ibid.). "One of the problems" (Crist). James Lancaster's death (*Beverly Hills Citizen-News,* 1/28/61). "the bulwark of" (*Judgment at Nuremberg* program). "In the aggregate" (ibid.). "This is not" (*Hollywood Examiner,* 12/3/61). Olivier's withdrawal to wed Plowright (Kramer/AI; Spoto). Olivier's withdrawal because of *Becket* (UA press release, 11/4/60). "almost a symbol" (Schumach). Unless otherwise indicated, Stanley Kramer's recollections (AI). "into another world" (Schumach). The Hyams column (Hyams, New York *Herald Tribune,* 11/13/60). Unless otherwise indicated, Abby Mann's recollections (AI). The incident between Lancaster and Schell (Oppenheimer). "That just comes" (Schell/AI). The book that Schell gave Burt (ibid.). The way Lancaster started his big speech (Kamm). The first rough cut of *Birdman* and subsequent rewrites (Pratley). "It's really tough" (Waugh). "would take a" (ACR). "Burt would have" (ibid.). The lighter-fluid story (ibid.). "People in the" (Murray/AI). The neighbors' signs and Niven's telegram (Wiley and Bona).

CHAPTER THIRTEEN

"Superficially it resembles" (*The Saturday Reviw,* 5/31/61). "The work was" (ACR). "I think Burt" (ibid.). "Burt was very" (Seltzer/AI). The Bel-Air fire (Arthur Berman, *New York Post,* 11/8/61). "I just came" (unknown publication). Lancaster's interest in moving to Portland or Seattle (Lorraine Gauguin, *Movieland,* n.d.). "It was like" (Ullman/AI). The swimming pool (Vincent Canby, *The New York Times,* 7/16/66). "whereas the other" (Adams/AI). "It was huge" (Bone/AI). The Berlin press junket (*Variety,* 12/13/61). "an important political" (New York *Herald Tribune,* 12/15/61). "bold and, despite" (*The New Yorker,* 12/23/61). "brilliantly constructed and" (Crowther, *The New York Times,* 12/24/61). "an extraordinary film" (Coe, *The Washington Post,* 2/15/62). "he never quite" (*Variety,* 10/18/61, Tube.). "Casting him as" (Farber). *Nuremberg*'s year-end ranking (*Variety,* n.d.). Abby Mann's recollections (AI). "There are two" (United Artists press release for *A Child Is Waiting*). The terms of Lancaster's employment for *A Child Is Waiting* (SKC). "left the film" (Shipman). Clayton's reaction to Lancaster's casting (letter from Christopher Mann to Stanley Kramer, SKC). Clayton's withdrawal from the project (letter from Christopher Mann to Stanley Kramer, 8/2/61, SKC). Garland's condition in 1961 (Edwards). The child that befriended Garland (Lorna Smith). The inspiration for Sternad's design (United Artists press release for *A Child Is Waiting*). "For three weeks" (ibid.). Pacific State Hospital's involvement with the film (ibid.). "It was exciting" (Kramer/AI). "We have to" (Glenn). Elizabeth Wilson's recollections (AI). "I think that" (United Artists press release for *A Child Is Waiting*). "John, I can't" (Crist). "very good friends" (ibid.). "Garland was drinking" (ibid.). Garland's absences and late arrivals (*A Child Is Waiting* production logs, SKC). "There was no" (Crist). Mike Wallace's recollections (AI). "Right away I" (Davis/AI).

Lancaster's Plaza Hotel press conference (Richard K. Doan, New York *Herald Tribune,* 4/26/62). The incident with Beatrice Altariba (Eleanor Packard, New York *Daily News,* 5/13/62). Burt's initial belief that he could not play Don Fabrizio (Chase). "I developed an" (Schifano). "world had to" (Servadio). "everything, despite a" (Schifano). Considering Brando for the prince (Servadio). Lombardo's need for Hollywood financing and the deal he struck (ibid.). "No, no, cowboy" (Chase). Visconti's lack of interest in Tracy and Quinn (Servadio). Why Visconti chose Lancaster (Chase; Crist). "Of course I" (Prouse). "discover and make" (ibid.). "I had been" (ibid.). Except where noted, Claudia Cardinale's recollections (AI). "the producer had" (Schifano). Suso Cecchi D'Amico's recollections (AI). "poor Burt Lancaster" (Servadio). "I didn't for" (Gow, 1973). "the ideas he" (ibid.). "He potters round" (Prouse). "And when I" (Chase). The ball sequence (Schifano). "the finest prison" (*Variety,* 6/20/62, Tube.). "the most effective" (Malden/AI). "one of his" (Kauffmann, *New Republic,* 8/13/62). "I didn't think" (Shipman). Gene Fowler Jr.'s recollections (AI). The Lancaster-Kramer correspondence (letters from Lancaster to Kramer, 9/28/62, 10/15/62, 10/26/62; Kramer's reply, 10/22/62, SKC). "I think Visconti" (Sharp/AI). "was the most" (*Film Today,* 5/17/76).

CHAPTER FOURTEEN

"I really like" (Mann/AI). "You keep the" (ibid.). "Lancaster has never" (*Time,* 2/8/63). "It is almost" (Gill, *The New Yorker,* 2/23/63). "My dream was" (Kramer/AI). "sitting in a" (Alexander). "one man in" (ibid.). "potential for the" (Manchester). "I am not" (ibid.). "He had just" (Douglas). "talented director and" (Polaire/AI). "was a bit" (Bissell/AI). "wanted to be" (Higham, 1974). "I see a" (Farber). "Douglas was so" (anonymous/AI). Douglas's and Frankenheimer's assessments of Douglas's and Lancaster's parts (Higham, 1974). "In the book" (Knebel). "to invest him" (ibid.). "Rehearsing the tense" (ibid.). "a riveting thriller" (Gilliatt, *London Observer,* 5/26/63). "hard to believe" (*Esquire,* October 1963). "If there is" (Robert Salmaggi, *Variety,* 12/20/63). "The English version" (Chase). "an egregious catastrophe" (*Newsweek,* 8/26/63). "a major disappointment" (Crist, New York *Herald Tribune,* 8/13/63). "Burt Lancaster looks" (*Newsweek,* 8/26/63). Charlton Heston's recollections (AI). "Burt called me" (Pratley). "We had to" (Polaire/AI). "The damned train" (Pratley). "Half of the" (*Newsweek,* 4/25/64). "none of the locations" (ACR). "far too heavily" (ibid.). "You know, Burt" (ibid.). "chaos" (ibid.). The final cost of *The Train* (Vincent Canby, *Variety,* 2/17/65). "I looked at" (ACR). "Lancaster is built" (Shea, *The Film Daily,* 1/26/65). "Those Resistance workers" (Hale). "They had no" (ibid.). "What do I" (Mishkin). "a bit far-fetched" (Crowther, *The New York Times,* 3/1/64). Information about *The Hallelujah Trail* and the meeting of Lancaster and Jackie Bone was drawn from interviews with Jackie Bone, John Gay, Martin Landau, Pamela Tiffin, and Tim Zinnemann; plus, "it isn't the" (*Beverly Hills Citizen-News,* 7/6/65). The size of the company (United Artists production notes for *The Hallelujah Trail*). Sturges' parties, Remick's needlepoint (Art Seidenbaum, *Los Angeles Times,* 11/1/64). The conflict between Burt and Brian Keith (Zinnemann/AI). Lancaster's lack of fondness for Remick (Zinnemann/AI; Tiffin/AI). "Burt Lancaster: A" (John J. Miller, unknown publication, 1/4/73). The death of Bill Williams (*Variety,* 11/18/64). "The fucking around" (anonymous/AI). Dr. John Fitzpatrick's insights into alcoholism (Fitzpatrick/AI). "She tried so" (anonymous/AI). "She was a" (ibid.). "According to the" (Gillette/AI). "not for a" (*Time,* 7/16/65). "Burt Lancaster is" (*The Saturday Review,* 3/13/65). "heavy-handed, flat-footed" (Crist, New York *Herald Tribune,* 7/16/65). "a good deal" (Mishkin, *New York Morning-Telegraph,* 7/2/65).

CHAPTER FIFTEEN

"This picture won't" (Scheuer, 1966). "This guy you'll" (Windeler). "This picture is" (Carroll, 1966). "We couldn't find" (Scheuer, 1966). Claudia Cardinale's recollections (AI). "Some of them" (*Hollywood Reporter,* 11/5/65). The flash flood (Los Angeles *Herald Examiner,* 12/14/65; the New York *Herald Tribune,* 12/15/65). "like a young" (Scheuer, 1966). "There was kind" (Shaw/AI). "a tragedy based" (Gelmis). The terms of Spiegel's association with Perry (Gross). Information about *The Swimmer* was drawn from interviews with Michael Herzberg, Diana Muldaur, and Frank Perry; plus "Action pictures are" (Stang). "scared to death" (ibid.). "so that there" (Rivers). "I approach acting" (Kamm). "Perry wasn't the" (anonymous/AI). *"The Professionals* is" (Windeler). Jackie Bone's recollections (AI). "Jackie had nothing" (anonymous/AI). Burt's expenditure of $10,000 for *Swimmer* reshoots (Champlin, 1988). Skolsky on the reshoot of the Loden scene (Sidney Skolsky column, n.d.). "It was simply" (Crist). "I considered running" (*The New York Times,* 4/12/70). "had a funny" (Crist). Information about *The Scalphunters* was drawn from interviews with Duke Callaghan, Ossie Davis, and Charles Scott; plus, "He was the" (Ken Ferguson, unknown publication, 6/76). Information about *Castle Keep* was drawn from interviews with Bruce Dern, Martin Ransohoff, and David

Rayfiel; plus, "*Castle Keep* was" (Susan Royal, *Premiere*, 8/80). "She took exception" (*Modern Screen*, 7/68). The castle set, the impact of the weather on filming, the village and brothel sets (Columbia production notes for *Castle Keep*). "I don't know" (Stephen Schiff, *Vanity Fair*, 12/90). "a first-rate" (Guarino, New York *Daily News*, 4/3/68). "at his age" (Winsten, *New York Post*, 4/3/68). "the only respectable" (Deac Rossell, unknown publication, 3/11/70). "I happened to" (Canby, *The New York Times*, 5/16/68). "absorbing" (Steven H. Scheuer, ed., *Movies on TV and Videocassette*, Bantam Books, 1993–94). "totally engrossing" (Tom Milne, ed., *The Time-Out Film Guide*, 3rd ed., Penguin, 1993). "unfailingly watchable and" (Ron Castell, ed., *Blockbuster Video Guide to Movies and Videos, 1995*, Island Books, 10/94). "Burt Lancaster is" (Mark Martin and Marsha Porter, *Video Movie Guide, 1995*, Ballantine, 10/94). "fascinating, vastly underrated" (Leonard Maltin, *Leonard Maltin's TV Movies and Video Guide, 1992*, Signet Books, 10/91). "The whole film" (Crist). "It's about choice" (Pratley). Frankenheimer's interest in McQueen (Army Archerd, *Variety*, 2/9/67). Deborah Kerr's recollections (AI). Lynn Guthrie's recollections (AI). Frankenheimer's deferential attitude toward Lancaster (anonymous/AI). "John loved Burt" (Dern/AI). Burt's arrest for speeding (*Los Angeles Times*, 9/26/68; *New York Post*, 10/1/68). "He really wanted" (Burstyn/AI). "the biggest piece" (Crist). Ross Hunter's recollections (AI). "You can't take" (Vernon Scott, UPI, 4/9/70). Unless otherwise indicated, Seaton's recollections (Chierichetti). Lancaster's version of the meeting with Seaton (Crist). The announcement of Lancaster's casting in *Airport* (*Variety*, 10/31/68). "You're not going" (Rayfiel/AI). Seaton's return to the production (*Variety*, 2/17/69). "I have had" (unknown publication). "Burt came over" (anonymous/AI). "Burt was very" (Bone/AI). "begins as a" (Canby, *The New York Times*, 7/24/69). *Castle Keep*'s year-end ranking. (*Variety*, n.d.) "I sued him" (Larry Gross and Robert Avrech, *Millimeter*, n.d.). "I want to" (Ron Pennington, *Motion Picture Herald*, 11/5/69). "If anybody tells" (Pratley). "a lackluster" (*Variety*, 8/27/69). *"The Gypsy Moths"* (ACR).

CHAPTER SIXTEEN

"My romantic leading" (Loynd, 3/77). "I don't do" (Train). "He told me" (anonymous/AI). Jackie Bone's recollections (AI). "All I want" (Hal Boyle, AP, 7/26/69). "I've been bored" (Hall and Crawly). Information about *Valdez* was drawn from interviews with Susan Clark, Jon Cypher, David Rayfiel, and Ed Sherin; plus, Ira Steiner's acquisition of the property (*Variety*, 11/6/67). Putting *Valdez* on hold for *Airport* (*Hollywood Re-*

porter, 11/4/68). "I love him" (Byrne). "It is doubtful" (*Variety,* 2/18/70, Rick.). "as though it" (Rosen, *New York Morning Telegraph,* 3/6/70). The $13-million check (Quarry/AI). Information about *Lawman* was drawn from interviews with Sheree North, Stan Jolley, and Michael Winner; plus, "an almost rigidly" (Harding). "*Lawman* was conceived" (ibid.). "It may seem" (United Artists press release for *Lawman*). "Team effort is" (Harding). "fast, intelligent director" (Crawly). "I realized I" (unknown publication). "a cliché-ridden, machine-made" (Mishkin, *New York Morning Telegraph,* 4/10/71). first real comedown" (Thomas, *Los Angeles Times,* 8/1/71). "He certainly retains" (*Variety,* 3/10/71, Murf.). "I was getting" (Duston Harvey). "became a smash" (Grobel). "got terrible reviews" (ibid.). Information about *Knickerbocker Holiday* was drawn from interviews with Anita Gillette and Albert Marre; plus, Burt seeking help from Sinatra (Hartford). "That strap becomes" (ibid.). "Oddly enough, his" (Sullivan, *Los Angeles Times,* n.d.). "He . . . handles the" (*Variety,* 7/1/91). "The net impression" (Mishkin, *New York Morning Telegraph,* 7/9/71). "weaving across a" (*New York Post,* n.d.). "a Western of" (Winsten, *New York Post,* 8/5/71). Information about *Ulzana's Raid* was drawn from interviews with Bruce Davison, Richard Jaeckel, and Alan Sharp; plus, "reflected my own" (unknown publication). Burt's contribution toward Aldrich's salary (RAC). "Lancaster was very" (Micheline Keating, *Tucson Daily Citizen,* 2/19/72). Unless otherwise indicated, Michael Winner's recollections of *Scorpio* (AI). "nothing incisive, just" (Windeler). "In fact we" (Crawly). The Watergate burglars' encounter with Lancaster and Delon (Emery). "I'm a movie" (Sydney Edwards, *London Evening Standard,* 6/16/72). Why Scofield took the role (UA press book for *Scorpio*). "some of the" (Herridge, *New York Post,* 11/16/72). "so consistently unsentimental" (Canby, *The New York Times,* 12/3/72). "Lancaster's physical appearance" (*Variety,* 10/18/72, Murf.). "Burt Lancaster gives" (Sarris, *Village Voice,* 11/30/72). "Do you think" (Cypher/AI). "It was a" (Windeler). "a straightforward whodunit" (Clinch). "I've sort of" (Windeler). "When you reach" (Clinch). Information about *The Midnight Man* and the relationship between Lancaster and Kibbee was drawn from interviews with Susan Clark and Harris Yulin; plus, the locals who appeared in the film (Universal press notes for *The Midnight Man*). "There's a big" (ibid.). "sounded like a" (Crist). "If *Scorpio* does" (Cocks, *Time,* 5/7/73). Sutherland's involvement with *Executive Action* (*Hollywood Reporter,* 10/26/70). "The screenplay knocked" (Kilday). Lewis' belief that the Lane-Freed script went too far (*Boxoffice,* 12/10/73). "I've never believed" (Production notes for *Executive Action*). "The public has" (ibid.). The $500,000 Lewis raised on his house (*Boxoffice* 12/10/73; 12/17/73). "I struggled with" (Production notes for *Executive Action*). "a rare cloak" (Toy, *Daily Variety*, 6/6/73). Kurt Axtel's recollections (AI). "We used more" (Production notes for *Executive Action*). "was marvelous to" (ibid.). "were very close" (ibid.). That *Executive Action* wrapped on budget and two days ahead of schedule (*Boxoffice*, 12/17/73; production notes for *Executive Action*). "A year ago" (Kilday). "surprisingly unconvincing" (Champlin, *Los Angeles Times*, 11/7/73). "even to people" (Canby, *The New York Times* 11/25/73). "Aren't we having" (Kauffmann, *New Republic*, 11/24/73). "so graceless it's" (Kael, *The New Yorker*, 11/19/73).

CHAPTER SEVENTEEN

Claudia Cardinale's recollections (AI). "we couldn't do" (Christy). The redesign of Burt's apartment (ibid.). "I've mastered the" (ibid.). "He makes a" (Steiger/AI). "I grow my" (Christy). "kind of tough" (Sharp/AI). Information on the relationship between Lancaster and Bone (interviews with Anita Gillette, Jackie Bone, and an anonymous source). "That was a" (King/AI). "In Italy, Burt" (Luria/AI). "The most beautiful" (ibid.). The actress' husband who met with Burt (anonymous/AI). "He would do" (Steadman/AI). "It's been done" (Cecil Smith). "Anthony Burgess wrote" (ibid.). "Burgess gets down" (ibid.). "probably the most" (Meyer). Burt dropped his asking price for Moses (Unger). "I drove a" (ibid.). "easy to do" (Burgess). "dissatisfied with a" (ibid.). "He'd say to" (Cosmatos/AI). "We woke one" (Cecil Smith). "Ninety-nine percent voted" (Harris). "After the fourth" (Meyer). The amount of footage shot by De Bosio (Adams). The basis for the character of the professor (Schifano). "produced fierce controversy" (Servadio). The original casting of Fonda and Bancroft in *Conversation Piece* (*Andy Warhol's Interview*, 9/73). Suso Cecchi D'Amico's recollections (AI). The near casting of Hepburn in *Conversation Piece* (*Variety*, 11/21/73). "didn't want to" (Crist). "Lancaster is manifestly" (Schifano). "Now, here's a" (Crist). "I stopped shooting" (Rex Reed). "the second worst" (Canby, *The New York Times*, 6/15/74). "The script never" (Clark/AI). "turning into an" (Schickel, *Time*, 6/17/74). "He had it" (Clark/AI). "I don't think" (Yulin/AI). "a cross between" (Mark N. Grant, *Los Angeles Times*, 6/25/77). "we began to" (Production notes for *1900*). Unless otherwise indicated, Bernardo Bertolucci's recollections (AI). Bertolucci's consideration of Welles (Idalah Luria/AI). "the patriarchy of" (Kolker). "Ever since I" (Rex Reed). The $6.5-million budget (*Time*, 9/9/74). "I wasn't doing" (Rex Reed). The use of the Villa Saviola (Production notes for *1900*). "was so bad" (Gardella). "I'll be walking" (ibid.). *Moses*' Italian viewership (Meyer). CBS's payment for the U.S.

rights (Bob Williams, 1975). "People go away" (ibid.). "I must tell" (Gardella). "My Moses is" (Unger). "Lancaster imbued his" (*Variety*, 7/2/75, Bok.). "The Moses he" (Kitman, *New Leader*, 9/15/75). "They should have" (Kaufman, *Newsday*, 6/15/75). The American viewership for Moses (Adams). "The large screen" (Burgess). The announcement about Newman in *Buffalo Bill* (*Variety*, 10/22/69). "so unique . . . that" (Rich, *New York Post*, 6/26/76). Drafting the screenplay without Kopit's text (Sarris, 1976). "the very image" (Plecki). "Every day for" (Crist). Tommy Thompson's recollections (AI). Lancaster's recollections of working with Altman (Crist). "Nothing, absolutely nothing" (Sarris, 1975). "a touching tale" (*Variety*, 3/26/75). *"Conversation Piece* is" (Canby, *The New York Times*, 10/5/75). "Whose idea can" (Kael, *The New Yorker*, 9/29/75). New Line's plans for revising *Conversation Piece* (Verrill). "though the Italian" (Canby, *The New York Times*, 6/24/77). Information about *The Cassandra Crossing* was derived from interviews with George Cosmatos, Robert Katz, and John Phillip Law; plus, "Actually I enjoyed" (Rex Reed). Information about *Twilight's Last Gleaming* was drawn from interviews with Ronald Cohen, Charles Durning, Morgan Paull, Paul Winfield, and Burt Young; plus, the seven drafts of the script (*Variety*, 1/20/77). Burt's attempt to involve Newman (RAC). "a smart, classy" (Arnold and Miller). "The Germans were" (ibid.).

CHAPTER EIGHTEEN

The final cost of *1900* (*Variety*, n.d.). The dispute between Bertolucci and Grimaldi (Bertolucci). "so overdone as" (Canby, *The New York Times*, 11/16/77). "scales new heights" (Kauffmann, *New Republic*, 11/26/77). "It's a huge" (Kroll, *Newsweek*, 10/17/77). The dispute between De Laurentiis and Altman (Sarris, 1976). *Buffalo Bill*'s reception at the Berlin Festival (*Variety*, 4/7/76). "a sly, wry" (Schickel, *Time*, 7/19/76). "exhilarating . . . entertaining. But" (Hatch, *Nation*, 7/31–8/7/76). "It's very sad" (Crist). "a well-modulated" (Champlin, *Los Angeles Times*, 6/30/76). "Recently I said" (unknown publication). "the actual raid" (Bob Williams, 1976). Marvin Chomsky's recollections (AI). Information about *Moreau* was drawn from interviews with Barbara Carrera, Gerald Fisher, and Don Taylor; plus, Metromedia's announced remake (Allen Rich, *Hollywood Reporter*, 11/8/72). Burt's casting (*Boxoffice*, 9/13/76). "With the responsibilities" (Train). "an unusual man" (ibid.). Lancaster's opposition to making *Moreau* more horrific (ibid.). "You're asking the" (Loynd, 2/77). "Personally, I think" (Hall). "a handsome, well-acted" (*Variety*, 7/13/77, Mack.). "sluggish" (Reed, *New*

York Daily News, 7/15/77). "just a little" (Champlin, *Los Angeles Times*, 7/13/77). "You giggle, get" (Simon, *New York*, 2/14/77). "It wasn't a" (Young/AI). "nothing can seem" (Canby, *The New York Times*, 2/10/77). "one of the" (Press release for *Go Tell the Spartans*). Information about *Go Tell the Spartans* was drawn from interviews with Ted Post, Marc Singer, and Craig Wasson; plus, the budget for *Apocalypse Now* (Aljean Harmetz, *The New York Times*, 6/24/87). "tigerish terrain, natural" (*Hollywood Reporter*, 10/28/77). The Vietnamese extras (Press release for *Go Tell the Spartans*). "in solid command" (Schickel, *Time*, 9/25/78). "How rewarding it" (Thomas, *Los Angeles Times*, 9/6/78). "the best movie" (*Newsweek*, 10/2/78). Kauffmann's review of *Spartans* (Kauffmann, *New Republic*, 6/24/78). "I thought it" (Harmetz, 1987). The *Zulu Dawn* "city" (Kocian). "They saw what" (Austin). "Historically it's fascinating" (Lukk). "There's absolutely no" (ibid.). "This is an" (Clinch). "He was a" (O'Toole/AI). Information about *Cattle Annie* was drawn from interviews with Lamont Johnson, John Savage, and Rod Steiger; plus, "The girls were" (*Soho News*, 3/9/82). "was turned down" (Harmetz, 1982). The financing for *Cattle Annie* (Rainer). The interest in John Wayne for *Cattle Annie* (ibid.). Kathleen Nolan's recollections (AI). "no person who" (*Articles of Incorporation, Constitution and By-Laws, Rules, and Regulations of Screen Actors Guild*). "a distinctly uncomfortable" (French, London *Observer*, 10/28/79). "a rather ill-fitting" (ibid.).

CHAPTER NINETEEN

The financing for *Atlantic City* (*Variety*, 10/31/79). "For both of" (French). "It's not that" (William Wolf, *New York*, 6/1/81). Unless otherwise indicated, Louis Malle's recollections (AI). "It's like a" (Buckley). "We were really" (French). "I've never tried" (Windeler). "I know the" (Demaris). Reid throwing herself at Lancaster's feet (Elizabeth Wilson/AI). "It's a natural" (Press release for *Scandal Sheet*, 1/10/85). "As an actor" (Demaris). "The joy of creativity" (*Drama-Logue*). Information about *La Pelle* was drawn from interviews with Robert Katz and Alexandra King and a letter to the author from Liliana Cavani (fall 1993) translated from the Italian for the author by Gaia Striano. "We gazed into" (Winters). Burt's reluctance to talk with friends about Winters' book (anonymous/AI). "I think Burt" (Bone/AI). "Yes. I was" (Donahue). Giuliano Montaldo's recollections (Montaldo letter to author, fall 1993, translated from the Italian for the author by Gaia Striano). "When we made" (French). "the movie's sweet" (Ansen, *Newsweek*, 4/6/81). "the accumulation of" (Gay/AI). "They kept saying" (Johnson/AI). "wasn't really released" (Kael, *The New Yorker,* 6/15/81). "a funny, sweet, mock-Western" (Canby, *The New York Times,* 5/15/81). "a very handsome" (Thomas, *Los Angeles Times,* 9/14/81). "His acting has" (Kauffmann, *New Republic,* 6/6/81). "The Lancaster who" (Canby). "As far as" (Marilyn Beck, New York *Daily News,* 8/27/81). "mostly a poorly staged" (*Variety,* 6/3/81, Werb.). Jackie Bone's recollections (AI). Anita Gillette's recollections (AI). Information about *Boys in Autumn* was drawn from interviews with Tom Moore and Bernard Sabath; plus, "We've got what" (Cathleen McGuigan Douglas). "by Act II it's" (Nachman, *San Francisco Chronicle,* n.d.). "a theatrical event" (*Variety,* 9/4/81). Why Burt and Kirk did not pursue *Boys in Autumn* after San Francisco (Richard). "Although it was" (ibid.). "He was my" (Sutherland). The budget for *Local Hero* (Michael Billington, *The New York Times,* 8/22/82). "I wondered how" (Production notes for *Local Hero*). "a Scottish *Beverly*" (Falk). "Felix Happer is" (Press release for *Local Hero*). Peter Riegert's recollections (AI). "all the standard" (Henry F. Walters, *Newsweek,* n.d.). "Burt Lancaster's natural" (*Variety,* n.d.). "I'm suffering from" (unknown publication). "I feel great" (Chase). Alan Sharp's recollections (AI). "crusty, taciturn, gray-haired" (Michael Sragow, *The Movies,* 10/83). Don Guest's recollections (AI). Peckinpah's war with Panzer and Davis (SPC). Lancaster's demands for a rewrite for *Osterman* (SPC). "It was a" (unknown publication). "I like the" (Richard). "an effortlessly charming" (Sheila Benson, *Los Angeles Times,* 3/18/83). "dominated by a" (*Variety,* 2/16/85, Cart.). "everything is unexpected" (Kael, *The New Yorker,* 3/21/83). "A stargazing reserve" (ibid.). "the film turned" (Yule). "makes you work" (Thomas, *Los Angeles Times,* 11/4/83). "It's as if" (Canby, *The New York Times,* 11/4/83). The rereleased *Leopard* (Leogrande). "This may or" (Canby, *The New York Times,* 9/11/83). "When *The Leopard*" (Chase).

CHAPTER TWENTY

Alan Sharp's recollections (AI). "I don't know" (*Los Angeles Times,* 3/2/84). Langley's denial of the Lancaster-Kidder fight (Frank Swertlow, Los Angeles *Herald Examiner,* 3/2/84). Information about *Scandal Sheet* was derived from interviews with Henry Winkler and Peter Jurasik; plus, "Television . . . dramatizes subjects" (Press release for *Scandal Sheet,* 1/10/85). "Actually Fallen thinks" (unknown publication). "terrific" (Anderson, *Chicago Tribune,* 1/21/85). "a fine performance" (Gardella, New York *Daily News,* 1/16/85). "I enjoyed it" (unknown publication). "Nothing in *Little*" (Canby, *The New York Times,* n.d.). "a jaundiced mess" (Reed, New York *Daily News,* n.d.).

"Everyone saw the" (unknown publication). "While the casting" (Bian-culli, *New York Post*, 7/8/88). "ponderous" (*Variety*, 7/27/88). "lavish and illuminating" (Gardella, New York *Daily News*, 7/8/88). Information about *On Wings of Eagles* was drawn from interviews with Richard Crenna, Andrew McLaglen, and Robert Steadman; plus, "You're the man" (unknown publication). "I took the" (Press release for *On Wings of Eagles*). "Burt started to" (*The Star*, 9/25/90). "It was as" (Noel Botham and David Perel, *National Enquirer*, n.d.). "I think she" (Petrie/AI). "It seemed to" (Lantos). "Nobody in our" (Farber). Unless otherwise indicated, Jeff Kanew's recollections (AI). "The irony about" (Lantos). "By December [1985], what" (Lantos). "I think that" (Fos-ter/AI). "Some people think" (Farber). "Burt told me" (Durning/AI). "Burt Lancaster fits" (Hill, *TV Guide*, 5/17/86). "Dull to the" (*Variety*, 5/21/86). Lee Phillips' recollections (AI). "Barnum epitomized the" (un-known publication). "I can't do" (Donahue). "I enjoy acting" (ibid.). "a chance to" (Wilmington, *Los Angeles Times*, 10/2/86). "The old pros" (Reed, New York *Daily News*, n.d.). "It has an" (Tuber). "I play a" (HBO press release, 1/30/87). The reviews for *Barnum* are dated 11/28/86. The reviews for *Control* are dated 2/13/87. Unless otherwise indicated, Michael Anderson's recollections (AI). *The Shoes of the Fisherman* earned Anderson Vatican approval (*Variety*, 5/20/87). "The script was" (Mann). "Even for a" (ibid.). Jo Champa's recollections (AI). "He was very" (*Los Angeles Times*, 1/8/89).

CHAPTER TWENTY-ONE

Information about *Rocket Gibraltar* was drawn from interviews with Matthew Carlisle, John Glover, Daniel Petrie, and Amos Poe; plus, "It's a story" (Park). "It was the" (ibid.). "a happy leprechaun" (Marshall Berges, *Los Angeles Times Home Magazine*, 7/30/78). "Burt had great" (Quilty/AI). "put up my" (*Variety*, 5/22/89). "It was one" (*Vari-ety*, 6/3/88). "That really hurt" (anonymous/AI). "Columbia had no" (*Hollywood Reporter*, 5/25/88). "an assistant professor" (Bernard Weinraub, *The New York Times*, 9/15/92). Brian Frankish's recollec-tions (AI). "somebody who in" (Production notes for *Field of Dreams*). Grant Gilmore's recollections (AI). Information about *The Betrothed* was drawn from interviews with Phyllis King, Salvatore Nocita, and Danny Quinn. "She was as" (anonymous/AI). "get far past" (Wilmington, *Los Angeles Times*, 9/2/88). "No one on" (*Variety*, 8/31/88, Cart.). "Lancaster is so" (Maslin, *The New York Times*, 9/2/88). "had no inter-est" (anonymous/AI). "a work so" (James, *The New York Times*, 4/21/89). "*Field of Dreams* goes" (McGrady, *Newsday*, n.d.). "a crock

. . . there's" (Kael, *The New Yorker,* 5/1/89). "a male weepie" (Corliss, *Time,* 4/24/89). Alberto Negrin's recollections (Negrin cassette tape to author, fall, 1993). "a composite of" (unknown publication). "The phantom had" (ibid.). "a love story" (ibid.). Charles Dance's recollections (AI). "We did it" (Champlin, 3/18–24, 1990). "with a voice" (Kathleen Tynan, *Vanity Fair,* 2/92). "does his own" (Champlin, 3/18–24, 1990). "He's wonderful" (Army Archerd, *Variety,* 10/23/89). "McGill represented the" (Ruth, *Chicago Sun-Times,* 9/13/89). "inspirational" (Kogan, *Chicago Tribune,* 9/12/89). The reviews of *Phantom* are dated 3/16/90. "gripping" (Gardella, New York *Daily News,* 5/1/90). "head and shoulders" (Maltin, *Leonard Maltin's TV Movies and Video Guide, 1992,* Penguin Books, 10/91). "a more thorough" (Ruth, *Chicago Sun-Times,* 5/1/90). "Burt had been" (*Star,* 9/25/90). "Some people might" (Noel Botham and David Perel, *National Enquirer,* n.d.). *"Separate but Equal"* (Gamorekian). "what interested me" (ibid.). Unless otherwise indicated, George Stevens Jr.'s recollections (AI). Richard Kiley's recollections (AI). "He's incredible . . . . I" (Gardella, New York *Daily News,* 4/7/91). Earl Holliman's encounter with Lancaster on 11/29/90 (Holliman/AI). "He was heading" (*Hollywood Reporter,* 12/3/90). "He's having some" (ibid.). Lancaster's transfer on 12/13/90 (Matt Lait, *Los Angeles Times,* 12/15/90). "in fine spirits" (*Hollywood Reporter,* 3/15/91). "He's doing as" (AP, *Hollywood Reporter,* 6/4/91). "Burt's very strong" (Robert Osborne, *Hollywood Reporter,* 9/20/91). "It is absorbing" (*Variety,* 4/8/91, Tone.). The New York reviews of *Separate but Equal* are dated 4/5/91. "the most valiant" (anonymous/AI). "Of all the" (Fowler/AI). "It came as" (Lewis Beale, New York *Daily News,* 10/22/94).

EPILOGUE

"The Lancaster career" (Canby). "It's like this" (Redelings). "He loved his" (McLaglen/AI). "I sometimes think" (Windeler). "Well, you know" (Crist). "Burt Lancaster is" (unknown publication).

Bibliography

BOOKS

Adamson, Joe (interviewer). *A Directors Guild of America Oral History: Byron Haskin.* Metuchen, N.J.: Directors Guild of America and Scarecrow Press, 1984.

Arnold, Edwin T., and Eugene L. Miller. *The Films and Career of Robert Aldrich.* Knoxville: University of Tennessee Press, 1986.

Astor, Mary. *A Life on Film.* New York: Delacorte, 1971.

Balio, Tino. *United Artists: The Company That Changed the Film Industry.* Madison: University of Wisconsin Press, 1987.

Bertolucci, Bernardo, with Donald Ranvaud, translated from the Italian by Ranvaud. *Bertolucci by Bertolucci.* London: Plexus, 1982.

Bishop, Jim. *The Mark Hellinger Story.* New York: Appleton-Century-Crofts, 1952.

Bosworth, Patricia. *Montgomery Clift.* New York: Harcourt Brace Jovanovich, 1978.

Burgess, Anthony. *You've Had Your Time: The Second Part of the Confessions.* New York: Grove Weidenfeld, 1991.

Calvet, Corinne. *Has Corinne Been a Good Girl? The Intimate Memoirs of a French Actress in Hollywood.* New York: St. Martin's Press, 1983.

Carney, Raymond. *American Dreaming: The Films of John Cassavetes and the American Experience.* Berkeley: University of California Press, 1985.

Chase, Josephine. *New York at School.* New York: Public Education Association of the City of New York, 1927.

Clinch, Minty. *Burt Lancaster.* New York: Stein & Day, 1984.

Considine, Shaun. *Mad as Hell: The Life and Work of Paddy Chayefsky.* New York: Random House, 1994.

Cottrell, John. *Laurence Olivier.* New York: Prentice Hall, 1975.

Crist, Judith. *Take 22: Moviemakers on Moviemaking.* New York: Viking Press, 1984.

Curtis, Tony, and Barry Paris. *Tony Curtis: The Autobiography.* New York: William Morrow and Co., 1993.

De Carlo, Yvonne, with Doug Warren. *Yvonne: An Autobiography.* New York: St. Martin's Press, Thomas Dunne, 1987.

Diorio, Al. *Barbara Stanwyck: A Biography.* New York: Coward-McCann, 1983.

Douglas, Kirk. *The Ragman's Son.* New York: Simon and Schuster, 1988.

Edwards, Anne. *Judy Garland: A Biography.* New York: Simon and Schuster, 1974, 1975.

Emery, Fred. *Watergate: The Corruption of American Politics and the Fall of Richard Nixon.* New York: Times Books, 1994.

Fine, Marshall. *Bloody Sam: The Life and Films of Sam Peckinpah.* New York: Donald I. Fine, 1991.

Flannigan, Hallie. *Arena.* New York: Duell, Sloan, and Pearce, 1940.

Fontaine, Joan. *No Bed of Roses.* New York: William Morrow and Co., 1978.

French, Philip, ed. *Malle on Malle.* London: Faber and Faber, 1993.

Fury, David. *The Cinema History of Burt Lancaster.* Minneapolis: Artists Press, 1989.

Gansberg, Alan L. *Little Caesar: A Biography of Edward G. Robinson.* London: New English Library, 1983.

Gardner, Ava. *Ava: My Story.* New York: Bantam Books, 1990.

Goldman, William. *Adventures in the Screen Trade.* New York: Warner Books, 1983.

Goodman, Ezra. *The Fifty Year Decline and Fall of Hollywood.* New York: Simon and Schuster, 1961.

Grade, Lew. *Still Dancing: My Story.* New York: HarperCollins, 1987.

Graham, Don. *No Name on the Bullet: A Biography of Audie Murphy.* New York: Viking Press, 1989.

Graham, Sheilah. *Confessions of a Hollywood Columnist.* William Morrow and Co., 1969.

Green, Abel, and Joe Laurie Jr. *Show Biz: From Vaude to Video.* New York: Henry Holt & Co., 1951.

Grobel, Lawrence. *The Hustons.* New York: Charles Scribner's Sons, 1989.

Harding, Bill. *The Films of Michael Winner.* London: Frederick Muller, 1978.

Henreid, Paul, with Julius Fast. *Ladies' Man: An Autobiography.* New York: St. Martin's Press, 1984.

Higham, Charles. *Ava: A Life Story.* New York: Delacorte Press, 1974.

———. *Kate.* New York: W. W. Norton, 1975.

———. *Audrey: The Life of Audrey Hepburn.* New York: Macmillan, 1984.

———. *Merchant of Dreams: Louis B. Mayer, M.G.M. and the Secret Hollywood.* New York: Donald I. Fine, 1993.

Hirschhorn, Clive. *The Columbia Story.* London: Octopus Group, 1989.

Holden, Anthony. *Olivier.* London: Weidenfeld and Nicolson, 1988.

Hunter, Allan. *Burt Lancaster: The Man and His Movies.* New York: St. Martin's Press, 1984.

Huston, John. *An Open Book.* New York: Alfred A. Knopf, 1980.

Kaminsky, Stuart M. *John Huston: Maker of Magic.* Boston: Houghton Mifflin, 1978.

———. *Coop: The Life and Legend of Gary Cooper.* New York: St. Martin's Press, 1980.

Katz, Ephraim. *The Film Encyclopedia.* New York: Thomas Y. Crowell, 1979.

Kelley, Kitty. *His Way: The Unauthorized Biography of Frank Sinatra.* New York: Bantam Books, 1986.

Kemp, Philip. *Lethal Innocence: The Cinema of Alexander Mackendrick.* London: Methuen, n.d.

Keysar, Helene. *Robert Altman's America.* Oxford: Oxford University Press, 1991.

Kiernan, Thomas. *Sir Larry: The Life of Laurence Olivier.* New York: Times Books, 1981.

Kisselhoff, Jess. *You Must Remember This: An Oral History of Manhattan from the 1890s to World War II.* San Diego: Harcourt Brace Jovanovich, 1989.

Kolker, Robert Philip. *Bernardo Bertolucci.* London: British Film Institute Publishing, 1984.

LaGuardia, Robert. *Monty: A Biography.* New York: Arbor House, 1977.

Leigh, Janet. *There Really Was a Hollywood.* New York: Doubleday, 1984.

MacShane, Frank. *Into Eternity: The Life of James Jones, American Writer.* Boston: Houghton Mifflin, 1985.

Madsen, Axel. *John Huston.* New York: Doubleday, 1978.

Manchester, William. *The Glory and the Dream: A Narrative History of America, 1932–1972.* Boston: Little, Brown, 1973.

Marx, Arthur. *Red Skelton.* New York: Dutton Books, 1979.

McGilligan, Patrick. *Robert Altman: Jumping off the Cliff.* New York: St. Martin's Press, 1989.

Morley, Sheridan. *Gladys Cooper: A Biography.* New York: McGraw-Hill, 1979.

————. *The Other Side of the Moon: A Biography of David Niven.* New York: Harper and Row, 1985.

Moss, Robert F. *The Films of Carol Reed.* New York: Columbia University Press, 1987.

Navasky, Victor. *Naming Names.* New York: Viking Press, 1980.

Nesbitt, Cathleen. *A Little Love and Good Company.* Owings Mills, Md.: Stemmer House, 1977.

O'Connor, John, and Lorraine Brown, eds. *Free, Adult, Uncensored: The Living History of the Federal Theatre Project.* Washington, D.C.: New Republic Books, n.d.

Orsi, Robert Anthony. *The Madonna of 115th Street: Faith and Community in Italian Harlem, 1880–1950.* New Haven, Conn.: Yale University Press, 1985.

Peret, Geoffrey. *There's a War to Be Won: The United States Army in World War II.* New York: Random House, 1991.

Phillips, Gene D. *The Films of Tennessee Williams.* London: Philadelphia Art Alliance Press, Associated University Presses, 1980.

Plecki, Gerard. *Robert Atlman.* Boston: Twayne Publishers, 1985.

Pratley, Gerald. *The Cinema of John Frankenheimer: The International Film Guide Series.* London: A. Zwemmer Ltd., 1969.

Reed, Oliver. *Reed All About Me: The Autobiography of Oliver Reed.* London: W. H. Allen, 1979.

Reed, Rex. *Travolta to Keaton.* William Morrow and Co., 1979.

Rivers, Joan, with Richard Meryman. *Still Talking.* New York: Turtle Bay, 1991.

Robinson, Edward G., with Leonard Spigelgass. *All My Yesterdays.* New York: Hawthorn Books, 1973.

Rosenzweig, Sidney. *Casablanca and Other Major Films of Michael Curtiz.* Ann Arbor, Mich.: UMI Research Press, 1982.

Schary, Dore. *Heyday.* Boston: Little, Brown, 1979.

Schifano, Laurence, translated from the French by William S. Byron. *Luchino Visconti: The Flames of Passion.* London: Collins, 1990.

Schorer, Mark. *Sinclair Lewis: An American Life.* New York: McGraw-Hill, 1961.

Selznick, Irene Mayer. *A Private View.* New York: Alfred A. Knopf, 1983.

Servadio, Gaia. *Luchino Visconti: A Biography.* New York: Franklin Watts, 1983.

Shipman, David. *Judy Garland: The Secret Life of an American Legend.* New York: Hyperion, 1993.

Smith, Lorna. *Judy—With Love.* London: Robert Hale & Company, 1975.

Spoto, Donald. *Stanley Kramer: Film Maker.* New York: G. P. Putnam's Sons, 1978.

Tavernier, Bernard (translated for the author by Kent Jones). *Amis Américains, Entretiens avec les grands auteurs d'Hollywood.* Paris: Institut Lumière/Actes Sud, 1993.

Thomas, Bob. *King Cohn.* New York: G. P. Putnam's Sons, 1967.

———. *Joan Crawford: A Biography.* New York: Simon and Schuster, 1978.

———. *Golden Boy: The Untold Story of William Holden.* New York: St. Martin's Press, 1983.

Wallis, Hal, and Charles Higham. *Starmaker: The Autobiography of Hal Wallis.* New York: Macmillan, 1980.

Wapshott, Nicholas. *The Man Between: A Biography of Carol Reed.* London: Chatto & Windus, 1990.

Weales, Gerald. *Clifford Odets, Playwright.* New York: Pegasus, 1971.

Wiley, Mason, and Damien Bona. *Inside Oscar: The Unofficial History of the Academy Awards, Fourth Updated Edition.* New York: Ballantine Books, 1993.

Windeler, Robert. *Burt Lancaster.* London: W. H. Allen, 1984.

Winters, Shelley. *Shelley, Also Known as Shirley.* William Morrow and Co., 1980.

———. *Shelly II: The Middle of My Century.* New York: Simon and Schuster, 1989.

Woodward, Ian. *Audrey Hepburn.* London: W. H. Allen, 1984.

Yule, Andrew. *Fast Fade: David Puttnam, Columbia Pictures and the Battle for Hollywood.* New York: Delacorte, 1989.

Zinnemann, Fred. *A Life in the Movies: An Autobiography.* New York: Charles Scribner's Sons, 1992.

MAJOR ARTICLES

Alexander, Shana. "Will the Real Burt Please Stand Up?" *Life,* September 6, 1963.

Christy, George. "*Architectural Digest* Visits Burt Lancaster." *Architectural Digest,* October 1982.

Demaris, Ovid. "He'd Rather Take a Chance." *Parade,* November 6, 1988.

Gow, Gordon. "Energy." *Films and Filming,* January 1973.

Hoffman, Alice. "Act of Love!" *Photoplay,* c. 1954–55.

Itria, Helen. "Story of a Heart Man" *Look,* October 20, 1953.

Lancaster, James. "I'll Bet on Burt." *Photoplay,* January 1953.

Martin, Pete. "Hollywood Hard Guy." *Saturday Evening Post,* September 11, 1948.

———. "I Drop In on Burt Lancaster." *Saturday Evening Post,* June 24, 1961.

Mitchell, John G. "The Amazing World of Burt Lancaster." Los Angeles *Herald Examiner,* August 6, 13, 20, 1961.

Mitgang, Herbert. "On Lancaster's Road to 'Success.' " *The New York Times,* June 30, 1957.

Oppenheimer, Peer J. "Burt Lancaster: The Star Nobody Knows." *Family Weekly,* March 18, 1962.

Shipp, Cameron. "Burt Lancaster." *Cosmopolitan,* August 1955.

Train, Sylvia. "Between Takes." *Toronto Sun,* February 20, 1977.

Waterbury, Ruth. "Burt's Bouncing Brood." *Photoplay,* c. 1956–57.

———. "Rich Rebel." *American Weekly,* April 9, 1961.

OTHER ARTICLES CITED IN NOTES

Adams, Val. New York *Daily News,* March 3, 1976.

Alpert, Don. *Los Angeles Times,* April 10, 1960.

Austin, John. *Hollywood Reporter,* January 10, 1979.

Blowen, Michael. *The Boston Globe,* September 28, 1988.

Bradbury, Joseph T. *White Tops,* May–June 1972.

———. *Bandwagon,* March–April 1992.

Brady, Thomas F. *The New York Times,* March 18, 1949.

———. *The New York Times,* December 24, 1950.

Brownell Jr., William H. *The New York Times,* January 18, 1953.

———. *The New York Times,* December 27, 1953.

Buckley, Tom. *The New York Times,* December 7, 1979.

Byrne, Bridget. Los Angeles *Herald Examiner,* February 1, 1970.

Canby, Vincent. *The New York Times,* May 24, 1981.

Carroll, Harrison. *Los Angeles Evening Herald & Express,* May 27, 1950.

———. Los Angeles *Herald Examiner,* May 9, 1952.

———. Los Angeles *Herald Examiner,* January 31, 1953.

———. Los Angeles *Herald Examiner,* January 9, 1966.

Champlin, Charles. *Los Angeles Times,* September 10, 1988.

———. *TV Times, Los Angeles Times,* March 18–24, 1990.

Chase, Chris. *The New York Times,* September 2, 1983.

Couderc, Pierre. *White Tops,* March–April 1965.

Cravat, Nick. *Movie Stars Parade,* November 30, 1949.

Crawly, Tony. *Game,* August 1975.

Douglas, Cathleen McGuigan. *Newsweek,* September 14, 1981.

Drama-Logue, April 2–8, 1981.

Eyles, Allen, and Barrie Pattison. *Films and Filming,* February 1967.

Falk, Quentin. *Sight and Sound,* Autumn 1992.

Farber, Stephen. *The New York Times,* November 2, 1986.

Gamorekian, Barbara. *The New York Times,* April 7, 1991.

Gardella, Kay. *New York Sunday News,* June 8, 1975.

Gelmis, Joseph. *Newsday,* July 18, 1966.

Glenn, Larry. *The New York Times,* February 18, 1962.

Gross, Larry. *Millimeter,* May 1975.

Hale, Wanda. New York *Daily News,* February 15, 1965.

Hall, William. *Los Angeles Times,* February 20, 1977.

Hall, William, and Tony Crawly. *Game,* February 1975.

Harmetz, Aljean. *The New York Times,* March 25, 1982.

———. *The New York Times,* June 24, 1987.

Harris, John. Los Angeles *Herald Examiner,* December 25, 1973.

Hartford, Margaret. *Los Angeles Times,* June 27, 1971.

Harvey, Duston. *Chicago Sun-Times,* July 11, 1971.

Harvey, Evelyn. *Colliers,* August 6, 1954.

Hecht, Harold. *Hollywood Reporter,* November 14, 1955.

Hobart, John. *San Francisco Chronicle,* c. October 1947.

Hopper, Hedda. *Los Angeles Times,* June 11, 1948.

———. *Los Angeles Times,* August 12, 1951.

———. *Chicago Tribune Magazine,* May 22, 1955.

Husock, Howard. *The Public Interest,* Fall 1992.

Hyams, Joe. New York *Herald Tribune,* January 1956.

Jamison, Barbara Berch. *The New York Times Magazine,* August 23, 1953.

Johnson, Erskine. *Los Angeles Daily News,* January 30, 1954.

Johnson, Grady. *The New York Times,* December 5, 1954.

Kahn, R. T. *Chicago Tribune,* July 1976.

Kamm, Herbert. *New York World-Telegram,* January 27, 1962.

Kilday, Gregg. *Los Angeles Times,* November 4, 1973.

Kirkley, Donald. *Baltimore Sun,* July 30, 1950.

Knebel, Fletcher. *Look,* November 19, 1963.

Kocian, Billy. *Variety,* August 16, 1978.

Lancaster, Burt. *The Saturday Evening Post,* c. 1947–48.

———. Ringling Bros. and Barnum & Bailey program, 1951.

———. *Hollywood Reporter,* November 12, 1951.

———. New York *Herald Tribune,* January 31, 1954.

————. *New York World-Telegram,* August 21, 1955.

————. *Hollywood Reporter,* November 14, 1955.

————. *Salesman's Opportunity,* February 1957.

Lantos, Jeffrey. *American Film,* October 1986.

Leogrande, Ernest. New York *Daily News,* September 2, 1983.

Lichtman, Herb A. *American Cinematographer,* June 1962.

Loynd, Ray. Los Angeles *Herald Examiner,* February 13, 1977.

————. Los Angeles *Herald Examiner,* March 6, 1977.

Lukk, Tiu. *American Cinematographer,* February 1979.

Mann, Roderick. *Los Angeles Times,* December 6, 1987.

Marsh, Paul. *Screenland,* September 1946.

Meyer, Frank. *Variety,* June 25, 1975.

Mindlin Jr., Michael. *The New York Times,* November 27, 1955.

Mishkin, Leo. New York *Herald Tribune,* June 9, 1964.

Mitgang, Herbert. *The New York Times,* June 14, 1953.

Park, Jeanie. *The New York Times,* September 4, 1988.

Pendleton, Randolph. *Newark Evening News,* August 12, 1969.

Pomeroy, Linda. *Modern Screen,* October 1969.

Prouse, Derek. *The Christian Science Monitor,* July 8, 1962.

Pryor, Thomas M. *The New York Times,* October 17, 1948.

Rainer, Peter. Los Angeles *Herald Examiner,* June 21, 1981.

Redelings, Lowell E. *Beverly Hills Citizen-News,* January 14, 1947.

Richard, Julie. *Los Angeles Times,* December 2, 1983.

Sarris, Andrew. *Village Voice,* October 13, 1975.

————. *Village Voice,* July 5, 1976.

Schallert, Edwin. *Los Angeles Times,* July 14, 1953.

————. *Los Angeles Times,* March 3, 1955.

Scheuer, Philip K. *Los Angeles Times,* November 5, 1952.

————. *Los Angeles Times,* 1954.

————. *Los Angeles Times,* January 11, 1959.

————. *Los Angeles Times,* January 23, 1966.

Schumach, Murray. *The New York Times,* April 30, 1961.

Scott, John L. *Los Angeles Times,* c. 1949–50.

Smith, Cecil. *TV Times, Los Angeles Times,* June 22–28, 1975.

Smith, Darr. *Los Angeles Daily News,* January 18, 1950.

————. *Los Angeles Daily News,* July 6, 1950.

————. *Los Angeles Daily News,* October 4, 1950.

Stang, Joanne. *The New York Times,* August 14, 1966.

Strassberg, Phil. *Arizona Republic,* February 27, 1972.

Sutherland, Alex. *Screen International,* March 12, 1983.

Tuber, Keith. *Orange Coast Magazine,* January 1987.

Unger, Arthur. *Christian Science Monitor,* June 20, 1975.

Verrill, Addison. *Variety,* October 1, 1975.

Watts, Stephen. *The New York Times,* August 19, 1951.

Waugh, John C. *The Christian Science Monitor,* January 10, 1961.

Webb Jr., James H. *Bandwagon,* May–June 1981.

Weiller, A. H. *The New York Times,* April 10, 1955.

Whitcomb, Jon. *Cosmopolitan,* February 1959.

Williams, Bob. *New York Post,* June 19, 1975.

———. *New York Post,* December 13, 1976.

Williams, Dick. *Los Angeles Mirror,* January 15, 1961.

Wilson, Earl. New York *Daily News,* December 31, 1948.

Wilson, Elizabeth. *Liberty,* January 1949.

Wilson, Liza. *American Weekly Magazine,* July 4, 1954.

Wood, Thomas. New York *Herald Tribune,* February 24, 1952.

———. New York *Herald Tribune,* May 13, 1956.

Index